Northwest Vista Coll
Learning Resource Center
3535 North Ellison Drive
San Antonio, Texas 78251

Y0-DVQ-618

PROPERTY, WELFARE, AND FREEDOM IN THE THOUGHT OF THOMAS PAINE

PROPERTY, WELFARE, AND FREEDOM IN THE THOUGHT OF THOMAS PAINE
A Critical Edition

Edited by
Karen M. Ford

Mellen Critical Editions and Translations
Volume 7

The Edwin Mellen Press
Lewiston•Queenston•Lampeter

Library of Congress Cataloging-in-Publication Data

Ford, Karen M.
    Property, welfare, and freedom in the thought of Thomas Paine : a critical edition /
Karen M. Ford.
      p. cm. -- (Mellen critical editions and translations ; v.7)
    Includes bibliographical references and index.
    ISBN 0-7734-7481-1
    1. Paine, Thomas, 1737-1809--Views on economics. 2. Free enterprise--History. I.
Paine, Thomas, 1737-1809. II. Title. III. Series.

    HB119.P26 F67 2001
    330.12'2--dc21

                                       00-069109

This is volume 7 in the continuing series
Mellen Critical Editions and Translations
Volume 7 ISBN 0-7734-7481-1
MCET Series ISBN 0-7734-8292-X

A CIP catalog record for this book is available from the British Library.

The Edwin Mellen Press
Box 450
Lewiston, New York
USA 14092-0450

The Edwin Mellen Press
Box 67
Queenston, Ontario
CANADA L0S 1L0

The Edwin Mellen Press, Ltd.
Lampeter, Ceredigion, Wales
UNITED KINGDOM SA48 8LT

Printed in the United States of America

This book is dedicated to the memory of

Barbara Grammel

1961-1998

MELLEN CRITICAL EDITIONS AND TRANSLATIONS

EDITORIAL DIRECTOR
Maurice Hindle

Mellen Critical Editions and Translations
is a new series which makes historically significant but neglected texts
available to the research community in a fully annotated scholarly form.
Each work, which will have originated usually before
1900, is prepared and presented by
scholarly specialists.

EDITORIAL POLICY
Proposals for volumes in this series, which are invited from
scholars working in any field of the humanities and human
sciences, should be submitted for consideration to:
Dr Maurice Hindle c/o The Edwin Mellen Press, Mellen House,
Unit 17 Llambed Ind. Est., Lampeter, Ceredigion,
Wales, United Kingdom SA48 8LT.

Contents

Contents

List of Illustrations[*]

---

[*] (Between pages 242 and 243.)

Preface

Tom Paine roused, and still arouses, strong emotions. In reviewing the impact of the French Revolution, John Adams vented his spleen at the man he saw as epitomising all that he found hardest to stomach about the age in which he had lived:

> I am willing you should call this the Age of Frivolity as you do, and would not object if you had named it the Age of Folly, Vice, Frenzy, Brutality, Daemons, Buonaparte, Tom Paine, or the Age of the Burning Brand from the Bottomless Pit, or anything but the Age of Reason. I know not whether any man in the world has had more influence on its inhabitants or affairs for the last thirty years than Tom Paine. There can be no severer Satyr on the age. For such a mongrel between pig and puppy, begotten by a wild boar on a bitch wolf, never before in any age of the world was suffered the poltroonery of mankind, to run such a career of mischief. Call it then the Age of Paine.[1]

More than any other political theorist, Paine was deeply and practically involved in the politics of his day - and involved in a way which brought him into dramatic confrontation with the governments of France, England and America. Robespierre sought to have him guillotined; Pitt had him outlawed and would doubtless have been pleased to see him hang; and he aroused fierce emotions in America both during the Revolution and subsequently when he returned as the infamous author of the *Age of Reason* in 1802. Paine's intensely political life, the part he played in fundamentally democratising and re-shaping the popular politics of his day, and the lasting enmity which many of his political and especially his religious writings generated, have tended to obscure his real intellectual gifts and his substantive intellectual contribution to the political theory of democratic politics in the late eighteenth and early nineteenth centuries. Even among his still extensive supporters, there is a tendency to accept that Paine's principal qualities

---

[1] Cited in D. Hawke, *Paine* (London: W.W. Norton, 1974: repr.1993), p.7.

are his powerful prose style, his antipathy to systematic inequality, and his hatred of the superstition, force and fraud which attended both government and established religion alike. But, what is missing in this excess of antagonism and enthusiasm is a clear sense of Paine's real intellectual contribution to the development of modern liberalism and political radicalism. Scholars of the history of political thought have rather frequently written him off as unoriginal, derivative and as primarily a stylist. As a result his contribution to political theory, and especially to economic thought and to the inter-relations between these domains, have not had the serious scholarly attention which they deserve. Yet, doing justice to Paine is not easy. His intellectual position is complex, and is sometimes obscured in his writing by pressing political needs or rhetorical flourishes. And the challenge of determining what can be regarded as Paine's basic commitments, and what can be taken as symptomatic of more fleeting pressures, is not easily met.

Karen Ford's collection of Paine's writings, and the extensive Introduction she has contributed, bring the full weight of modern scholarship to bear on Paine's economic and political thought. She opens a line of enquiry on Paine which encourages us to address a range of familiar texts from a new angle, while also bringing forward neglected texts, and her reading of Paine's political and economic thought lays the groundwork for a revision and revaluation of his standing within the canon of the history of political thought. The Paine whom Adams despised will never be entirely eclipsed by revisionary interpretation, but we are coming increasingly to understand that Adams and others raged against Paine in large part because his writings posed a fundamental challenge to their understanding of their political and economic context. As this collection demonstrates, a full understanding of the real character of his contribution to political economy is indispensable in grasping just how deeply his work engaged with and sought to transform his contemporaries' world.

Mark Philp   Oriel College, Oxford.

Acknowledgements

In putting together this collection of Paine's texts, I have drawn on many years of my research on Paine over which I incurred innumerable debts of gratitude. In particular I would like to thank Prof. Fred Rosen at University College London who first sparked my interest in Paine and Prof. Hillel Steiner and Dr. Ursula Vogel at the University of Manchester for their supervision of my PhD research, funded by the E.S.R.C. from 1991 to 1994. I would also like to thank Dr. Gregory Claeys, Prof. John Keane and Prof. Bernard Vincent for their comments on my presentation at the international symposium: Thomas Paine and the Horizons of Democracy, organised by the Thomas Paine Society in 1994.

I am grateful also to the staff at the British Library, in the Rare Books reading room in Bloomsbury and in the Newspaper Library in Colindale, the Bodleian Library in Oxford, the John Rylands University Library in Manchester, the Widner Library at Harvard University and the Van Pelt Library at the University of Pennsylvania. Special thanks go to the very helpful staff at the Working Class Movements Library in Salford, which houses a superb collection of Paine's texts and to Xiaowei Waldron in Philadelphia, who braved a heat-wave to obtain copies of several of the texts collected here.

I must also thank Douglas Mudd of the National Numismatic Collection at the National Museum of American History in Washington, DC, John Keyworth, curator of the Museum of the Bank of England and Ray Walker and Ruth Frow at the Working Class Movements Library in Salford, for their help in assembling and obtaining permission to use the illustrations. I am also grateful to the staff at the Media Centre Staff Workshop at Manchester University and to Mark Maynard, Computer Officer at Leicester University, for their assistance.

Finally, having thoroughly underestimated the work and time involved in editing such a collection, I would like to express my thanks to Maurice Hindle for his patience and advice and to Dr. Mark Philp for his preface. Professor Hillel

Acknowledgements

Steiner and Professor Nicholas Cull were also of great assistance in proof reading. I am also grateful to Nick and my friends, family and colleagues at Leicester and Manchester University, for their sympathy and support during the completion of this project.

Note on the Texts

In reproducing these various pamphlets and letters, my aim has been to provide a historically accurate text with clear explanatory notes and a critical evaluation of its importance. I have therefore followed the policy of keeping as far as possible Paine's spellings and grammatical (and, in some cases, ungrammatical) structures. Many of Paine's editors have altered the text in the name of consistency or in the style or spelling of their day, using either British or American conventions. The style of my own day requires that as far as possible original spellings should be maintained. However, the original texts were set by different printers in different parts of the world and so there is little consistency in spelling, often even in the same text. Cheaper editions were hastily set and included many printing errors, which perhaps do not merit this reverence for the original. I have decided to maintain this lack of consistency, and have deviated from this principle only when an alternative original suggests a misprint. Paine's grammar may seem clumsy to the modern reader, especially his overuse of the semicolon. It is an easy target for those who wish to belittle or disparage Paine, but this merely serves to disclose their suspicion of his radical democratic ideas. For Paine's fame stems from his genius for rhetoric, but this is not the rhetoric of the great statesman or humanist man of letters, but the hasty and overexcited rhetoric of the eighteenth century tavern, the source of the revolutionary tide that was to change his world. I suggest that any reader who fails to find inspiring passion in his words read these texts aloud, as if to rouse a rabble. His clumsy grammar and misspelled ideals are very much part of this atmosphere.

There are so many editions of *Common Sense*, including editions in different languages, that the work merits a bibliography of its own. The extracts given here are taken from Robert Bell's edition despite Paine's dispute with the printer.[1] I have used both the first edition, which was sanctioned by Paine, and Bell's third edition in combination to allow for printing errors in the first. Both these editions can be found in the Early American Imprints series of microprints, produced by the American Antiquarian Society, which are ordered according to Charles Evans' catalogue of American publications.[2] The first edition, printed in Philadelphia from Bell's shop in Third Street, priced two shillings, appeared on 10 January 1776. I have included only several short extracts of this text, which runs to seventy-nine pages. Bell's 'complete' third edition, priced three shillings is considerably longer and includes several other pieces, including Paine's additions and appendix. These were pirated from Bradford's 'second' edition published on 14 February and sold at one shilling.[3] It also includes a *Dialogue between Montgomery and an American Delegate* signed by T. P. esq. although it is not clear that this piece was in fact written by Paine.[4]

The Crisis No. VII. To the People of England is taken from the *Pennsylvania Packet*, 12 November 1778. It is part of a series, known as *The Crisis Papers* or *American Crisis*, published together by Paine's editors.[5] The

---

[1] Both Aldridge and Gimbel give a thorough account of this dispute. See Alfred Owen Aldridge, *Thomas Paine's American Ideology* (London: Associated University Presses, 1984), pp. 40-45; Richard Gimbel, *Thomas Paine: A Bibliographical Checklist of 'Common Sense' with an Account of its Publication* (New Haven: Yale University Press, 1956).

[2] *Early American Imprints 1639-1800*, ed. by C. K. Shipton (Worcester, Mass: American Antiquarian Society, Readex Microprint); *Charles Evans' American Bibliography 1639-1820, A Chronological Dictionary of all Books, Pamphlets and Periodical publications printed in the United States of America*, 14 vols (Chicago: Hollister, 1909). Where appropriate, I have given the Evans catalogue numbers for the Shipton Microprints.

[3] Paine was in dispute with Bell over the terms of the contract for the publication of the first edition. Bell produced a second edition not authorised by Paine, who then instructed William Bradford to publish a new edition, with appendices, which was announced as the second edition. Shortly after Bell published his pirated 'third' edition, which included other pieces that Paine clearly distanced himself from. See Gimbel, *Bibliographical Checklist*, p. 21. See *Early American Imprints*, Ev. 14966.

[4] The *Dialogue* had previously appeared in the *Pennsylvania Packet* on 19 February 1776. It is 'not believed to have been written by Paine, although attributed to him by many writers' including Conway. See Gimbel, *Bibliographical Checklist*, p. 54 & 'Dialogue Between the Ghost of General Montgomery just arrived from the Elysian Fields; and an American Delegate, in a Wood near Philadelphia' (19 February 1776), *Writings*, I, 163-4.

[5] Eric Foner finds that Carey was the first to put *The Crisis* together in an unauthorised collected works in 1797 [see *Thomas Paine: Collected Writings*, ed. by Eric Foner (New York: The Library of America, 1995), p. 857] although Sherwin's edition is perhaps the most influential

Crisis papers were published in newspapers and as pamphlets throughout the War of Independence, designed to boost support for the war. They cover a number of different issues and can be read completely independently of each other. Also included in this collection are *The Crisis No. IX* and *The Crisis Extraordinary*. The former is taken from the corrected copy in *Pennsylvania Packet and General Advertiser*, 13 June 1780 but was also published as a pamphlet on 9 June 1780 by John Dunlap in Philadelphia.[6] *The Crisis Extraordinary* was published in Philadelphia on 4 October 1780 by William Harris at his store in Second Street at 4 dollars. I have omitted from this piece a postscript on the subject of Benedict Arnold's treachery. Also included here is the second part of what has become known as *Crisis X*. Evans catalogues this as a pamphlet published by John Dunlap in Philadelphia on 5 March 1782.[7] The main body of the text entitled 'On the King of England's Speech' is omitted here. I have included only the latter part entitled 'On the Expences, Arrangements and Disbursements for carrying on the War, and finishing it with Honour and Advantage' printed in the *Pennsylvania Gazette*, 6 March 1782.[8] 'To the People of America' is taken from the *Pennsylvania Packet*, 4 April 1782.[9] It has not usually been listed as a part of the Crisis series but relates to many of the issues dealt with in the series.

The extract given here from *Public Good* is taken from a pamphlet printed in Philadelphia by John Dunlap in Market Street, 30 December 1780. Evans does

---

[*Thomas Paine: The American Crisis*, ed. by W. T. Sherwin (London: Sherwin, 1817)]. Later editors, such as Conway and P. S. Foner, include different pieces in *The Crisis* and ascribe different numbers to the collection so that *Crisis No. VII* is called 'American Crisis No. VIII'.

[6] Sherwin numbers this 'American Crisis No. X'. See *Early American Imprints*, Ev. 15985 & Ev. 16917.

[7] *Early American Imprints*, Ev. 16918 & Ev. 17648

[8] Eric Foner suggests that *Crisis X* never existed but was included by Carey. See E. Foner, *Collected Writings*, p. 857. Sherwin numbers this 'American Crisis No. XI'. *The Pennsylvania Gazette* was published by David Hall (1714-1772) & John Sellers (1749-1804) in Philadelphia from 1779-1815 [*Pennsylvania Gazette and Weekly Advertiser* until 1782].

[9] The piece also appeared in the *Pennsylvania Gazette* and the *Pennsylvania Journal* (3 April). *The Pennsylvania Packet and Daily Advertiser* was published in Philadelphia by John Dunlap and David C. Claypoole on Market Street sold at four pence, from 1771-1790 and at this time issued tri-weekly. The *Pennsylvania Journal; or, Weekly Advertiser* was published by William Bradford in Philadelphia from 1742-1793.

not list other editions of *Public Good*.[10] I have omitted the bulk of the thirty-eight-page pamphlet, which examines in detail Virginia's historical claim to the western territories. Two letters are also included in this collection out of six letters on the subject of taxation, published in the *Providence Gazette* in Rhode Island. These were first reprinted by Harry H. Clark in 1939.[11] All six letters might easily have been included as a chapter entirely devoted to Paine's campaign to promote the five-percent duty in Rhode Island, but the two reproduced are the most interesting and many of the arguments are repeated. I have taken the text from the *Providence Gazette*: 'In Answer to the Citizens of Rhode Island on the Five Percent Duty' on 28 December 1782 and 'On the Five Percent Duty' on 1 February 1783.[12]

Dissertations on Government; the Affairs of the Bank; and Paper Money was published as a pamphlet in Philadelphia in February 1786, printed by Charles Cist on Fourth Street for Hall & Sellers & Prichard. Paine also wrote ten letters on the subject of the bank crisis that were published in Philadelphia newspapers between 1785 and 1787. These have never before been reproduced together. The first is found in the *Pennsylvania Gazette*, 21 December 1785, including a letter to Fitzsimmons dated 19 April 1785.[13] The second was printed in the *Pennsylvania Packet*, 25 March 1786, followed by letters in the same newspaper on 28 March, 4 April, and 7 April 1786. The latter was also published in the *Pennsylvania Gazette* on 12 April 1786. Confusingly a letter entitled 'Number III' appeared in the *Pennsylvania Packet*, 20 April 1786. 'On the Advantages of a Public Bank' appears in the *Packet*, 20 June 1786 and the next day in *Freeman's*

---

[10] *Early American Imprints*, Ev. 16920

[11] *Six New Letters of Thomas Paine, Being Pieces on the five per cent duty addressed to the Citizens of Rhode Island*, ed. by Harry H. Clark (Madison: University of Wisconsin Press, 1939).

[12] *The Providence Gazette and Country Journal* was published weekly in Providence, Rhode Island from 1766-1825. The first of these letters also appeared in the *Pennsylvania Journal* and the *Gazette* on 4 December 1782 and the *Packet* on 5 December.

[13] This letter was first reproduced by A. O. Aldridge in 'Why Did Thomas Paine Write on the Bank?' *Proceedings of the American Philosophical Society*, 93: 4 (1949), 310-315. See also *Early American Imprints*, Ev. 19880.

Journal.[14] I used the text from the *Packet*. The two most neglected letters appeared in the *Gazette*, No. V titled 'On the Affairs of the State' on 20 September 1786 and 'No. VI' on 8 November 1786.[15] The final letter headed 'Addressed to the Opposers of the Bank.' appeared in the *Gazette*, 7 March 1787.

Prospects on the Rubicon was written in London in September 1787 and printed by J. Debrett of Piccadilly and appeared shortly before the opening of Parliament. This pamphlet is not found in many collections and does not appear to have been particularly influential as the crisis to which it is addressed was successfully averted. It was also published in Amsterdam (in French) and in Dublin by P. Byrne of Grafton Street in 1788. The version I have used was printed by James Ridgeway of York Street, London in 1793, and re-titled *Prospects on the War and Paper Currency*. It is similar to the first American edition published by Fisher and Cole of Baltimore in 1794. I have noted where these versions deviate. *The Decline and Fall of the English System of Finance* on the other hand was a considerable success, reaching several editions in 1796. I have used the fourteenth edition published in Paris by Hartley, Adland & Son of Rue Neuve de Berry and in London by D. I. Eaton of Newgate Street. I have also included a short extract from a letter written by Paine to George Danton (1759-94), then a prominent member of the Committee of Public Safety, dated 6 May 1793. This letter was found by Taine in French archives and reproduced in full by John Durand in *Documents on the American Revolution* in 1889.[16]

I have also reproduced here an extract from *Rights of Man Part the Second Combining Principle and Practice*. As with *Common Sense*, many editions exist from different publishers. I have used the ninth edition printed for

---

[14] *Freeman's Journal* was published by Francis Baily in Philadelphia, 1781-92.
[15] Some of the bank crisis letters were reproduced in *The Complete Writings of Thomas Paine*, ed. by P. S. Foner, 2 vols (New York: Citadel, 1945; repr. 1974), II, 277-302, but this collection did not include these two or the first letter found by Aldridge. This neglect was addressed by Eric Foner in 1995, although his collection includes *only* these two missing letters out of the ten. E. Foner, *Collected Writings*, pp. 359-367.
[16] *Documents on the American Revolution: Translated from Documents in the French Archive*, ed. by John Durand (New York: Henry Holt, 1889), p. 257.

J. S. Jordan of Fleet Street in 1792, priced at three shillings. This was checked against the eighth edition by the same publisher and cheaper editions of both parts such as P. Byrne's third edition published in Dublin in 1792, and the sixpenny edition printed by H. D. Symonds of Paternoster Row in London. The text given here does not take account of later changes published by Eaton.[17] The complete edition of both parts of the *Rights of Man* is readily available in a number of modern paperback editions. *Agrarian Justice opposed to Agrarian Law, and to Agrarian Monopoly* first appeared in Paris in 1797, published by W. Adlard. I have used the London edition of the same year published by T. Williams, of Little Turn-stile, Holborn and priced at 3 pence.

Within the texts Paine's notes are denoted by their original symbols and my own notes by arabic numerals. An asterism (***) denotes an omission from the text. A biographical glossary provides information on individuals mentioned in the text.

---

[17] See E. Foner, *Collected Writings*, p. 860.

Chronology

1737   29 January: Thomas Paine born in Thetford, Norfolk.

1757   January: Serves on privateer the *King of Prussia* for six months. Attended public lectures on science given by Benjamin Martin and James Ferguson in London.

1762   December: Joined Excise Service, posted to Grantham, Lincolnshire.

1768   February: Posted to Lewes, Sussex.

1771   Marries Elizabeth Ollive.

1774   April: Dismissed from Excise Service and Ollive's tobacco business sold. September: Meets with Benjamin Franklin, American Agent in London. 5 September: First Continental Congress meets in Philadelphia. 30 November: Paine arrives in Philadelphia, near death with 'ship fever'.

1775   January: Begins work as journalist and editor for Robert Aitkin's *The Pennsylvania Magazine*. 19 April: British troops attack colonial militiamen at Lexington and Concord, Massachusetts. 10 May: Second Continental Congress meets in Philadelphia. June: Congress issues first bills of Continental Currency payable in Spanish milled dollars.

1776   10 January: *Common Sense* is published, selling 120,000 copies by April. 4 July: Congress adopts the Declaration of Independence. Paine serves with the Pennsylvania militia's 'Flying Camp', later as aide to General Nathaniel Greene before joining General Washington at Trenton. 19 December: Starts publishing *The Crisis Papers* to rally morale.

1777   17 April: Appointed secretary to Congress's new Committee of Foreign Affairs. 17 October: British defeated at Saratoga, marking a turning point of the war.

1778   9 July: Articles of Confederation signed creating the United States. December: Paine publicly attacks Silas Deane for improperly profiting from loan negotiated between France and America.

1779   8 January: Forced to resign his post having disclosed secret negotiations thus embarrassing the French government.

1779   2 November: Appointed Clerk to Pennsylvania State Assembly.

1780   Privately initiates a subscription to fund Congressional troops, later to become the Bank of Pennsylvania. November 1780: Resigns as Clerk to the Assembly. Possibly paid by the Indiana Company, Paine writes *Public Good* in support of Congress's claim to western territories.

1781   March: Travels with Colonel John Laurens to France to obtain loans and supplies for war effort, returning in August. 19 October: Lord Cornwallis surrenders at Yorktown, Virginia, ending the British struggle to keep the American colonies. 31 December: Continental Congress grants a charter to the Bank of North America, followed by a state charter granted by the Pennsylvania Assembly in April 1782.

1782   February: Robert Livingston and Robert Morris agree to pay Paine $800 a year from secret Congressional funds to write in support of taxes for the Union government. March: Lord North resigns as British Prime Minister. November: Paine travels to Rhode Island to begin campaign for five-percent duty.

1783   September: The Peace of Paris formally ends the War of Independence. December: William Pitt, the Younger, becomes Prime Minister.

1784   In compensation for services to the revolution, the New York State Assembly gives Paine a small farm at New Rochelle.

1785   14 April: Bill to repeal Bank of North America's state charter is passed by Pennsylvania Assembly on second reading.

1785   13 September: The Bank of North America's Pennsylvania charter is repealed.

1786   21 February: Delaware Assembly grants the Bank of North America a charter. 3 May: Paine is accused in *Freeman's Journal* of prostituting his pen and of being a drunkard, due to his support for the bank. Franklin is elected president of Supreme Executive Council and a new assembly is returned in Pennsylvania.

1787   17 March: The Bank of North America's charter is restored by the Pennsylvania Assembly limited to 14 years. 26 April: Paine sets sail for France to sell his iron bridge design. May: The Constitutional Convention meets in Philadelphia to negotiate a Federal Constitution. 21 July: Paine presents his bridge design to French Academy of Sciences but fails to find backers. September: Paine returns to England and visits his mother in Thetford.

1788   26 August: Paine patents bridge in London and work begins on construction in Sheffield.

1789   April: The United States ratify the Federal Constitution. The new Congress meets and elects George Washington president. 17 June: The third estate of the French Estates General meets in the Tennis Court at Versailles and declares itself a National Convention. 14 July: The Bastille is attacked by a Paris mob and the prisoners set free. 26 August: The Declaration of the Rights of Man is announced.

1790   1 November: Burke's *Reflections on the Revolution* is published, condemning the French Revolution, and is later met with replies from Wollstonecraft, Mackintosh and others, setting off a fierce political controversy in Britain.

1791   22 February: Paine joins the controversy with his reply to Burke, *Rights of Man*. 21 June: King Louis XVI and Marie-Antoinette are captured after attempted flight.

1792   16 February: Second part of the *Rights of Man* is published. Over 200,000 copies are sold by the year's end. 25 May: A Royal proclamation bans *Rights of Man, Part Second*, launching a government campaign to repress the radical reform movement. 6 September: Paine elected deputy for Calais to French National Convention. 10 August: An attack on the Tuileries signals the end of the monarchy. 2-7 September: 1300 prisoners are massacred by the mob - the 'Terror' begins. 21 September: The Convention votes to abolish the monarchy. October: Paine is appointed with Condorcet to a committee to write new French constitution. 18 December: Paine is tried in London for seditious libel.

1793   21 January: Louis XVI is executed. France declares war on Britain. 2 June: The Girondins are arrested and the Convention purged by the Jacobin faction. 10 October: Robespierre and the Committee of Public Safety consolidate their power. December: Denounced by the Convention for his Girondin associations, Paine is arrested and imprisoned in the Palais de Luxembourg, Paris.

1794   Jan: The first part of *The Age of Reason* is published, setting out Paine's Deist faith and condemning Christianity. The American minister in Paris, Gouverneur Morris, refuses to help Paine. July: Robespierre is executed. Thirty thousand people had been killed under his regime. November: Paine is released from prison and recuperates in the house of the new American minister, James Monroe.

1796   April: Paine publishes the *Decline and Fall of the English System of Finance* predicting the collapse of the Bank of England.

1797   *Agrarian Justice* is published in reaction to Babeuf's land reform campaign.

1800   Thomas Jefferson is elected president of United States

1802   30 October: Paine returns to United States.

1809   8 June: Paine dies in poverty aged 72.

Introduction

Tom Paine was an international revolutionary. His writings influenced the events of the American and French revolution and sparked popular unrest and political debate in Britain. Paine still inspires people today. His fans include an extraordinary range of people with a variety of political interests. His writings inspire grass roots political activists engaged in local campaigns as well as national leaders.[1] Paine's readers today are attracted to the same qualities in his writing as his eighteenth century readers: the accessible simplicity of his style; his rhetoric of ridicule; the inspiration of his political principles. His polemical pamphlets, written to encourage and legitimate eighteenth century revolution against powers now long dead or apparently dormant, are still capable of rousing twenty-first century readers in their own political struggles. The passions raised by the mere mention of his name reflect the power of his writing, the relevance of his ideas and the genius of his rhetoric.

---

[1] While Michael Foot and Tony Benn are more representative of his followers, both Presidents Reagan and Bush quoted Paine in speeches. See Michael Foot, 'Eternal Defender of Revolution', *The Observer*, 17 March 1991 & Tony Benn, 'Heroes & Villains: Thomas Paine', *Independent Magazine*, 18 August 1990, p. 46. Ronald Reagan makes a number of references to Paine in his presidential speeches. See *Public Papers of the Presidents of the United States*, Ronald Reagan, 1982-88 (Washington DC: Government Printing Office, 1982-91), 1982: I, 689; 390; II, 1178; 1983: I, 364; 1984: I, 803 & 894-5; 1984: II, 1361 & 1461: 1988-89: II, 1081. George Bush made two references, including the 16 January 1991, 'Address to the Nation announcing allied military action in the Persian Gulf'. See *Public Papers of the Presidents of the United States*, George Bush, 1989-91 (Washington DC: Government Printing Office, 1990-2), 1989: I, 504; 1991: I, 44.

Paine is not, however, regarded by the establishment, academic or political, as one of the great political thinkers, in the same league as Thomas Hobbes or John Locke. Students of history are encouraged to read his major works to enhance their understanding of the events they inspired, but he is frequently neglected in the history of political thought. Indeed, it is often claimed that Paine did not add anything original to the canon of political theory, but merely expounded in powerful language the established political theory of the time.[2] This opinion is encapsulated in Anthony Burgess's claim that:

> Most of us find it hard to think of him as anything other than Tom Paine, the Christian name both contemptuous and affectionate. Like Jack Wilkes, he lives on as a tribune of the people, though nobody now reads him [...] The trouble with Tom Paine is that he has no philosophical arguments: his task is to inflame, and we are now past being inflamed against his particular enemies - the monarchy, the British constitution, the Christian church.[3]

Even those writers who have sought to analyse Paine's ideas critically have questioned his status as a political philosopher. A. J. Ayer, whose judgement on philosophers must be respected, claims Paine was only 'a brilliant journalist', who 'did not, [...] make any original contribution to political philosophy.[4]

A closer look at Paine demonstrates the paucity of this view. Paine's political theory is radical and original in his time and ours. This originality is most apparent in his approach to the developing capitalist economy. It is found in his welfare proposals, which first appear in *Rights of Man Part Second* in 1792. Paine justifies these redistributive policies in a unique theory of property set out in *Agrarian Justice*; unique because redistribution is justified by a theory of natural rights and individualism which has become the brand logo of the

---

[2] See Aldridge, *American Ideology*, p. 136; A. J. Ayer, *Thomas Paine* (London: Faber & Faber, 1988), pp. 14-34.

[3] Anthony Burgess, 'A Man More of Eloquence than Erudition', *The Observer*, 30 May 1993, p. 62.

[4] Ayer, *Paine,* pp. 12-13. See also Mark Philp, *Paine* (Oxford: Oxford University Press, 1989), p. ix & 64; Gregory Claeys, *Thomas Paine: Social and Political Thought* (London: Unwin

libertarian assault on the socialist welfare state. Further Paine's recognition of a conflict between the requirements of economic freedom and a commitment to representative democracy distinguishes him from his contemporaries, and many of ours.

The purpose of this volume is to collect together some often neglected texts in which Paine discusses a variety of economic issues. The point is not to present Paine as an economist, for he is not. Rather it is my contention that Paine's views on these economic issues are vital to a proper understanding of his politics: a politics that is still enlightening to our present political concerns. It is not possible to include every obscure pamphlet or letter to a newspaper in which Paine refers to economic or financial matters.[5] In Paine's time, as in our own, economic issues were pervasive political concerns and thus economic arguments are often used in his political writings. Taxation is a good example. Before he took up writing Paine worked as an Excise man collecting taxes. Later he was hired by Robert Morris (1734-1806) to write in support of raising taxes for Congress. But no special interest is required for taxes to be a perennial issue. Taxation was a root cause of both the American and the French revolution. It would simply not be possible to write about politics in these times without discussing taxes.

The focus of my critical interpretation of Paine's political thought is on three problems in which politics and economics are inextricably bound together. The first is the consistency of Paine's apparent free-market liberalism with his proposals for a system of welfare benefits. Paine did not, as is sometimes claimed, metamorphose from being an early champion of the ideas of Adam Smith to suddenly developing a proto-type welfare socialism in 1792. On the

---

Hyman, 1989), p. 2; A. Williamson, *Thomas Paine, His Life, Work and Times* (London: Allen & Unwin, 1973).

[5] Where I have referred in the introductory material to Paine's writings not included here, I have for the most part referred to Conway's easily accessible collection: *The Writings of Thomas Paine*, ed. by Moncure D. Conway, 4 vols (New York: Burt Franklin, 1908; repr. 1969) [hereafter

contrary, the most original aspect of his welfare plan is its consistency with a natural rights defence of economic freedom. If there was a change in his political thought it occurred in 1785 when he defended the bank he had helped to create against the democratic assembly trying to destroy it. It is in the context of this bank crisis in Philadelphia that we can best assess the relationship between Paine's radical politics and the new economic institutions of emergent capitalism. Paine's writings on the bank crisis, here published together for the first time, are crucial to our understanding of his political and economic thought.

The bank crisis raises the second problematic issue in interpreting Paine's thought: the possible conflict between liberty and democracy. There appears to be a central tension in Paine's work between freedom expressed in terms of democratic institutions and the right of the majority, and freedom guaranteed by a written constitution that incorporates individual natural and civil rights. This tension is at the heart of liberal democracy and it would be remarkable indeed if Paine had succeeded in solving it.[6] This crisis between individual liberty and democracy could well have emerged in an area quite unrelated to economics. Yet it is more than historical accident that he fought for *economic* freedom against the tyranny of the majority. The protection of the right to property is a pervasive issue throughout his writings. Until the Pennsylvania Assembly launched its attack on the security of the Bank of North America, Paine had been an unqualified believer in unchecked representative democracy. But when challenged, it is democracy that must yield. It is Paine's theory of democracy that is modified, but not compromised, by this conflict, rather than his support for the free market.[7]

Writings]. Pieces not included in that collection will be cited from P. S. Foner, *Complete Writings* or E. Foner, *Collected Writings*.

[6] For a detailed exploration of this problem, see Karen M. Ford, 'The Political Theory of Thomas Paine (1737-1809): Is There a Conflict between Liberty and Democracy?' (unpublished doctoral thesis, University of Manchester, 1995).

[7] For an alternative view see John Keane, 'Tom Paine and 'The People': The Dangers of Popular Sovereignty,' *Times Literary Supplement*, 31 March 1995, pp. 13-14. Keane argues that after the bank crisis, Paine rejected the pure doctrine of popular sovereignty, which Keane terms

This reassessment of the relationship between individual liberty and democracy brought Paine to a solution that can only be described as republican. This brings us to the third problem which I will address in interpreting Paine's thought. Paine was drawn to a conception of freedom that consisted in a constitutional government in which sovereignty was always limited, but without repudiating his solid commitment to democracy. I will argue that the bank crisis brought Paine to a new kind of republicanism, which rejected the traditional balanced constitution of monarchy, aristocracy and democracy, prioritised individual rights against government and was not afraid to extend a property based franchise to all. Today the most pertinent issue in the study of Paine's political thought is whether this is indeed republicanism or whether Paine's solution represents the advent of liberalism.[8] Perhaps it does not matter much what we call it, except that, as a liberal, Paine's commitment to democracy is diminished by economic freedom and individual rights. Only within a republican conception of freedom can Paine's commitment to democracy be taken seriously.

The writings included here provide the evidence needed for a proper understanding of these three interpretative problems. Paine's early free trade arguments in favour of American independence can be contrasted, and compared, with his welfare proposals. Paine's arguments in favour of taxes to fight the War of Independence can be assessed in the light of his libertarian arguments against taxation by oppressive and corrupt governments. His defence of the rights of the shareholders of the Bank of North America to issue bank notes is placed next to his denunciation of the issue of paper money by state legislatures and the accumulation of national debt in England. In many respects, looking at these issues presents a liberal account of Paine's thought: protecting free trade and private property, taxation only for a minimal state, against extensive public debt

---

'republican fundamentalism', in favour of judicially enforced constitutional limits, so moving closer to the thought of John Adams.

[8] See for example Mark Philp, 'English Republicanism in the 1790's,' *The Journal of Political Philosophy*, 6:3 (1998), 235-262.

and in favour of monetary restraint. On the other hand, republicanism was also opposed to public indebtedness and paper money, not so much because of economic fears but because such new financial institutions were thought to corrupt the political system and deprave its virtuous citizens.

After a brief account of Paine's life, I will set out some of the problems in interpreting Paine's political thought, presenting an outline of his political theory founded on a principle of equality, most importantly on the equality of rights. Before tracing Paine's economic thought, I will offer a brief résumé of the background of economic ideas in the late eighteenth century and the development of paper money, national debt and public banking. This will provide the tools necessary to address the three interpretative issues outlined above.

The texts presented here are not grouped in chronological order but according to five core themes, each of which deserves its own short introduction. Chapter 1 sets out Paine's initial interest in free trade as a key argument in favour of American independence. The texts in this chapter also demonstrate that the core elements of Paine's free-market economics were already in place before his exposure to Smith's *Wealth of Nations* and form a basic ground of his rejection of monarchy and support for representative democracy. Chapter 2 collects together various pieces in which Paine explores means of raising public funds for fighting the War of Independence. These texts demonstrate Paine's support for legitimate taxation, fairly distributed, and touch upon a number of other issues such as public debt and paper money. Chapter 3 focuses on the bank crisis, presenting together for the first time all Paine's writings on this matter. My focus is on the effect of the crisis on Paine's political thought. Chapter 4 draws together a number of other pieces in which Paine addresses the subject of public debt and paper money, particularly in the quite different economic environment of contemporary Europe. Lastly, Chapter 5 considers Paine's two quite distinct proposals for a system of welfare benefits and the theory of property and redistributive justice implied within these two original plans.

I

A Revolutionary Life

In 1792, Thomas Paine was the British Government's public enemy number one. Effigies of Tom Paine were burnt in Cambridge, Leeds and Manchester. Popular poems and songs denounced him. Medals depicted him hanging from a gibbet. A royal proclamation banned his book and five Scotsmen were sent to the penal colony in Australia for disseminating his ideas. The Pitt government orchestrated this repression in response to huge popular support for Paine's ideas. *Rights of Man* was the best selling book ever: 50,000 copies were sold in the first three months alone, perhaps 200,000 in the first year to a population of only 10 million. Public readings of *Rights of Man* were common in the popular political societies that flourished, bringing perhaps 40,000 working-class people into political debate for the first time. Numerous towns and cities planted 'Liberty Trees' and rioters in the streets of Edinburgh cried out 'Tom Paine and no King!' And yet, remarkably, until the age of 38, Paine made no mark in history.

Born in Thetford, Norfolk, the son of a Quaker corset (or stay) maker, Paine attended Thetford Grammar School up to the age of 12. Shortly before his 20th birthday, seeking adventure on the high seas, he joined the privateer, *King of Prussia*. After a spell in London as a journeyman stay-maker, he opened a shop in Sandwich in Kent where he married Mary Lambert in 1759. When Mary died in childbirth within only a year of marriage, Paine followed her father into the unpopular but supposedly secure profession of Excise Officer. He was posted to Grantham, Lincolnshire, collecting customs duties and patrolling the coast for smugglers. He was unfairly dismissed from the Excise, accused of stamping unexamined goods. Paine then worked in London as a teacher until reinstated in

the Excise in Lewes, Sussex in 1768. There he married Elizabeth Ollive, taking
over her late father's tobacco shop.

In Lewes he became involved in politics, serving as a local official and
star of the Headstrong Club, a debating society meeting in the White Hart tavern.
He became involved in his first political campaign: to raise the salaries of Excise
Officers, for which he wrote a short pamphlet. Despite valiant scholarly effort, no
other evidence has been found of Paine engaging in writing at this time. His part
in the campaign resulted in dismissal from the Excise service. He left for London
in 1774; his tobacco business and his second marriage both failed. Though his
early years are characterised by bankruptcy and personal failure, Paine's one real
success was, as one biographer has termed it, to be well informed.[1] Having
received only a basic education at Thetford Grammar (Latin and Greek excluded
due to his father's religion), he educated himself, attending Benjamin Martin and
James Ferguson's (1710-1776) public lectures in natural philosophy. His early
interest in Newtonian science later brought him into contact with Benjamin
Franklin (1706-90), then the American colonial representative in London. With a
letter of introduction from the famous colonial, Paine embarked for America.

By 1774, the dispute between the American colonists and the British
government had reached crisis point. Since 1766, the colonies had been in a
political wrangle with Parliament over jurisdiction and taxes. Shortly before
Paine's arrival, delegates of a Continental Congress gathered in Philadelphia and
voted to boycott British goods until their rights were recognised. The political
atmosphere was passionate but not yet revolutionary. Paine found the American's
'attachment to Britain [...] obstinate, and it was at that time a kind of treason to
speak against it'. They disliked only the present government. Their object was
reconciliation.[2] In April 1775, acting on information that arms were being stored

---

[1] Jack Fructman Jr., *Thomas Paine: Apostle of Freedom* (New York: Four Walls Eight
Windows, 1994) p. 16. For intriguing new research on the fate of Elizabeth Paine, see Christopher
Rumsey, 'The Wife of a Revolutionary' *Thomas Paine Society Bulletin*, 2:4, 1999, 14-21.
[2] See below p. 136.

in Concord, near Boston, British troops shot local militiamen and burned properties in Lexington. Despite his recent arrival, Paine felt 'it was time for every man to stir'.[3] The first shots of the American Revolution had been fired and yet in all the debates in the assemblies and conventions, in numerous pamphlets and newspapers, no one dared mention the inevitable - independence from Britain - no one except Tom Paine.

In January 1776, Paine published an anonymous pamphlet called *Common Sense* arguing for separation from the motherland and for a republican constitution to replace British rule. Americans had been killed by the King's forces, and there was no going back. *Common Sense* demonstrated that the colonial economy could survive and even thrive without the trade system of the British Empire. There would always be a market for American products 'while eating is the custom of Europe.'[4] Paine gave detailed figures showing that American resources were sufficient to build a navy and suggested colonial assemblies could be transformed into republican state governments under a Continental Congress. Whilst many Americans remained loyal to George III, believing his ministers and advisers were at fault, Paine denounced the King as a brutal despot and denied the legitimacy of all monarchy, the world's predominant form of government.

Paine's claim that the revolution made him an author is misleading.[5] He began working as a journalist as early as January 1775, editing and contributing to Robert Aitken's *The Pennsylvania Magazine; or, American Monthly Museum.* As these articles are published under pseudonyms, it is not always clear which were written by Paine but we can certainly include many literary pieces, in prose and verse, on subjects ranging from the beauty of nature to the death of General Wolfe.[6] But since Aitken was opposed to the *Magazine*'s use as a political forum,

---

[3] See below p. 137.
[4] See below p. 118.
[5] See below p. 137
[6] Aldridge, *American Ideology*, pp. 286-291.

Paine's entry into the revolutionary debate was delayed. Encouraged by new
friends such as Benjamin Rush (1745-1813), Paine published *Common Sense* as a
pamphlet, which became the most widely read political argument of its time.[7]
The pamphlet undoubtedly helped transform colonial resistance into a revolution
aimed at independence and set out the bare bones of the future system of
American government.

In July, whilst fighting against the British, Congress declared America
independent and began the long process of establishing a new form of
government. Paine served as aide to Generals Washington and Greene on the
battlefield but his greatest contribution to the war effort was maintaining morale.
He wrote the *Crisis* papers to rally support for a war that the colonists appeared to
be losing. 'These are the times that try men's souls', Paine wrote:

> The summer soldier and the sunshine patriot will, in this crisis,
> shrink from the service of their country; but he that stands it *now*,
> deserves the love and thanks of man and woman. Tyranny, like
> hell, is not easily conquered; yet we have this consolation with us,
> that the harder the conflict, the more glorious the triumph.[8]

Washington ordered these powerful words to be read to the starving, freezing
volunteer troops on Christmas Eve before launching the successful attack on
Trenton. The astonishing achievement of the triumph of the ragtag colonist army
over the mighty British Empire flowed from this pivotal moment.

Paine served as secretary to the Foreign Affairs committee in the
Continental Congress until his resignation over the Silas Deane affair in 1779.
Deane (1737-1789), a businessman hired by Congress to negotiate aid from
France, was publicly accused by Paine of profiting from the deal. Paine revealed
the secret negotiations and embarrassed the French government. He was later
vindicated but the affair showed he had many powerful enemies in Philadelphia.
Although the political and business elite in Philadelphia found his political

---

[7] John Keane, *Tom Paine: A Political Life* (London: Bloomsbury, 1995), p. 111; Aldridge, *American Ideology*, p. 45; Gimbel, *Bibliographical Checklist*, p. 57.
[8] 'The Crisis I' (*Pennsylvania Journal* 19 December 1776), *Writings*, I, 170.

propaganda useful in keeping up war-time morale, many influential men regarded him as an uneducated upstart and his ideas as dangerously democratic. In 1776, Paine was allied with the radical faction in Philadelphia, serving on their price control committees and supporting the new constitution and a wide electoral franchise.[9] This faction displaced the state legislature and held a constitutional convention, instituting the most democratic constitution ever known. Almost all adult males could vote for representatives in a single chamber assembly and one of the first acts of the Assembly was to abolish slavery.[10] However, Paine also worked with conservatives like Robert Morris, writing in favour of taxes to support the war effort and helping to establish the Bank of North America to finance the army.

Increasingly Paine withdrew from politics, living now in Bordentown, New Jersey, working on a variety of scientific inventions. In 1787, he decided to return to Europe, to visit his mother in England and to find backing for his radical design for an iron bridge.[11] For the second time in Paine's life, revolutionary events surrounded him, this time in France. The Bastille, symbol of autocratic despotism, was stormed and burned to the ground. Paine and the radical circle he mixed with in London supported the revolution and celebrated its successes publicly as part of their campaign for parliamentary reform in Britain. Edmund Burke MP (1729-97), once a part of this radical circle and a supporter the

---

[9] John Adams was wrong to claim that Paine co-wrote the Pennsylvania Constitution of 1776 [See J. P. Selsam, *The Pennsylvania Constitution of 1776: A Study in Revolutionary Democracy* (New York: Da Capo Press, 1936; repr. 1971), p. 186], as Paine was away from Philadelphia on military service at the time of the convention ['To the People' (*Pennsylvania Packet*, 18 March 1777), in P. S. Foner *Complete Writings*, II, 270]. Aldridge suggests that Paine's pamphlet *Four Letters on Interesting Subjects* had a considerable effect on the outcome, however. See Aldridge, *American Ideology*, pp. 238-9 & pp. 256-7. For Paine's involvement in the Philadelphia price control committees, see Eric Foner, *Tom Paine and Revolutionary America* (Oxford: Oxford University Press, 1976), p. 146 and below pp. 52 & 441.

[10] On 29 February 29, 1780, the Assembly legislated that no child born in Pennsylvania would be a slave after the age of 28. Conway exaggerates Paine's involvement in the passage of this act. See *Writings*, I, 4-9.

[11] The design was considered by the French Academy of Sciences but not built in France. A prototype was eventually built near Paddington in London and a similar construction used over the Wear at Sunderland. See Keane, *Paine*, pp. 271-282.

American Revolution, was concerned that events in France would go too far and end in despotism. The same revolutionary extremism might also spread to Britain. In *Reflections on the Revolution in France*, Burke set out his seminal philosophy of conservatism. He condemned the French revolutionaries' attempt to rebuild society and government from scratch on rational principles. Most importantly, Burke condemned the English radicals' interpretation of the British constitution. Dr. Richard Price (1723-91), a dissenting minister had compared the events in France to the events of the Glorious Revolution in 1688. That settlement, upon which British government is based had, Price claimed, established the principle that the people had a right to choose their own form of government. On the contrary, Burke claimed that the English people, through the Parliament of 1689, had given that right away, having sworn to obey William and Mary and their heirs forever.

Paine's reply, *Rights of Man*, challenged Burke's claims and ridiculed his rhetoric.[12] In *Part Second*, he set out the case for a republican government, denouncing monarchy and aristocracy and, most dangerously, proposing that constitutional reform could be achieved only through a national convention. This proposal challenged the sole legitimacy of Parliament over the law and the constitution. It was a proposal for a popular revolution in Britain. The great success of *Rights of Man* led Burke to suggest prosecuting Paine for libel on the British Constitution. The Pitt government launched a massive campaign attacking Paine. Government agents provoked or paid for riots and effigy burnings against him. Paine left for France, having been elected as a delegate to the National Convention by Calais, and was tried in his absence and outlawed from England.

In France, Paine was appointed to a committee to draft a constitution. He established a republican society arguing for the abolition of the monarchy. However, pleading that it was the system of monarchy and not the man who was

---

[12] Many of the other numerous replies to Burke's *Reflections* are collected in *Radicalism and Reform: Responses to Burke 1790-1792*, Political Writings of the 1790's, ed. by Gregory Claeys, 2 vols (London: Pickering and Chatto, 1995).

at fault, he appealed to the convention to save the life of Louis XVI. This lost him favour with Robespierre and the Jacobin party and, now identified with the moderate Girondin faction in the assembly, he was arrested in December 1793. Whilst Paine was in jail, his friends published his new work: *The Age of Reason*. Here Paine set out his religious faith: Deism. Paine believed that his faith in God saved his life when Robespierre signed a warrant for his execution. The story goes that because he was sick with fever, Paine's door was open when the executioner's mark was placed. As the mark was written on the inside of the door, Paine was not taken the following morning. His appeals to the American Ambassador, Gouverneur Morris (1752-1816), were ignored. Whether due to personal animosity or because of instructions from President Washington, nothing was done to secure Paine's release until after Robespierre's fall and the arrival of a new ambassador, James Monroe (1758-1831). Paine remained in Paris, working in the convention and writing, most notably a pamphlet on property rights entitled *Agrarian Justice*.

In 1802, Paine returned to America, spending most of his time in New York and at his farm in New Rochelle. *Age of Reason*, misinterpreted as atheism, made him unpopular, to the extent that a stage coach driver refused him passage for fear he might be struck by lightning. As he lay dying, virtually penniless in Greenwich Village, religious zealots broke into his room to force him to confess the divinity of Christ. He was buried on his farm in New Rochelle but this is not the end of Paine's story. In 1819, William Cobbett (1763-1835) dug up his bones, intending to return them to England for use as an icon in his political campaign.

Nothing is known of the fate of his bones, but Paine's ideas continue to be dug up generation after generation in the fight against oppressive government.[13]

---

[13] For claims that Paine's skull has re-appeared in Australia, see M. Speigelman, 'Can DNA Analysis Reveal Whether Skull is Paine's' at http://www.thomas-paine.com/tpnha/track.html (1999).

II

Problems in Interpreting Paine's Political Theory

Paine, it is often claimed, is not a political theorist but a 'mere polemicist' reacting to political events without any consistent or systematic political theory. His major writings are written in direct reference to historical events, supporting a particular interpretation of these events with the intention of gaining popular support for a cause. This, in itself, cannot deny Paine's work the status of political theory. Most significant works of political theory relate in some way to a particular cause in a historical conflict. It is also claimed that Paine's political philosophy is not original, that it is based on popular perceptions of Locke's ideas combined with a hotchpotch of ideas from other traditions.[1] All political thinkers build on previous traditions and take as their starting point the prevailing ideology of their time. Yet despite these reservations, in several areas, notably property theory, Paine's thought was certainly original, if not seminal.

Paine is not a philosopher. The epistemological and metaphysical grounding of his claims on rights or equality is left unexplored. He makes little or no attempt to define key concepts such as liberty, natural rights and justice. Paine was writing for a mass audience with very little education. Yet, in the canon of Western political thought there are many writers who would fail this same test. Burke in particular is often inconsistent and fails to define key terms. Perhaps it would be wrong to describe either of these two polemicists as philosophers. Hobbes, Locke, Rousseau and Marx are all much better philosophers but even

---

[1] See Aldridge, *American Ideology*, p. 136; Ayer, *Paine*, pp. 14-34.

they, in their political works, occasionally ignore some of the philosophical problems at the root of their polemic.[2]

Even admitting that Paine was not writing philosophy, there is a political theory in his writings that can be systematically presented and shown to be internally consistent. There is textual evidence that Paine believes himself to be designing a new political system and to be discovering and declaring political principles in the same way that Newton had discovered the principles of gravity. He describes his preferred polity as a system and refers to the 'science of government' in which he believes himself to be engaged. He believes that the political issues he addresses are universal, that the causes he espouses are the causes of all mankind. He also claims to reason from principles that are eternal.[3] This is implicit in his rejection of antiquity and precedent. Existing for a long time does not make an institution legitimate, if it was founded on wrong principles, such as Monarchy founded on conquest, or religion founded on mystery and deceit. He asserts that 'Time with respect to principles is an eternal NOW: it has no operation on them; it changes nothing of their nature and qualities.'[4] This implies that the principles that Paine thought were right and wrong, true and false, in his time, he thought would still be so in the future, although our understanding and knowledge of scientific principles and their application may change.[5]

There is some inconsistency in Paine's thought. On certain subjects, Paine changed his mind. He did not support universal male suffrage until after 1778 and probably did not develop his theory of voting as a universal right until much

---

[2] Claeys and Philp also assert that Paine deserves a place (perhaps minor) in the canon of political thought. Philp, *Paine*, p. 115, Claeys, *Thomas Paine*, pp. 2-3.

[3] See p. 116 below and 'The Crisis II: To Lord Howe' (January, 1777); 'Rights of Man Part Second, Combining Principle and Practice' (February 1792); 'Letter Addressed to the Addressers on the Late Proclamation' (1792); 'Dissertation on First Principles of Government' (July 1795), *Writings*, I, 179; II, 428; III, 61; 260.

[4] 'First Principles' (1795), *Writings*, III, 260.

[5] See 'The Crisis V: To Gen. Sir William Howe' (March 1778); 'Answer to Four Questions on the Legislative and Executive Powers' (May 1791); 'Rights of Man, Being an Answer to Mr.

later in France. His theory of natural and civil rights is not found in detail in early works, such as *Common Sense,* and was probably developed around the time of his letter to Thomas Jefferson (1743-1826) on the subject in 1789. His initial support for a unicameral legislature wavered during the bank crisis in 1785-7. Whilst Aldridge suggests that he may have been considering a fund to aid young and old poor as early as 1775, Paine did alter his initial view that poverty was caused by too much government alone.[6] In addition to developing his political views, Paine's tone and style also changes over time. The use of biblical language and reference in his American writings is replaced in his European works by the language of science and experience. Living in a time of revolutionary change, Paine learnt from his political experience. Paine intended to write political theory, although his writings tend to stress the application of these principles to particular political circumstances rather than searching for their validity. In some cases, such as natural equality, Paine leaves these principles unjustified as though self-evident. However, if certain key assumptions are taken as given, such as natural equality and a basic universal level of reason, it is possible to describe the key conceptual elements of Paine's political theory relatively systematically.

A Political Theory Founded on Equality

The principle of equality is the foundation of Paine's moral and political thought. It forms the basis of his critique of monarchy, his defence of democracy, his conception of liberty, his welfare plans and his natural rights theory. When one considers equality as his basic principle, his system of thought is understood at its most original and unique. None of his contemporaries, and few political thinkers

Burke's Attack on the French Revolution' (February 1791); 'The Age of Reason' (January 1794) & 'The Existence of God' (1797), *Writings,* I, 245-248, II, 244 & 281, IV, 52, 242-5.

[6] See Aldridge, *American Ideology,* pp. 29-30; Ayer, *Paine,* p. 8; Williamson, *Thomas Paine,* p. 37, suggests Paine might have been interested in such schemes before leaving England.

since, have placed so much authority on the principle of natural equality, nor supported without question its implications.

Paine's principle of equality can be simply stated in the form: all *men* are *morally* equal by virtue of their humanity. It is not clear that Paine included women in this human equality.[7] The principal human characteristics which all men share are a basic level of reason sufficient for moral agency, self-ownership and the natural rights which are derived from these features. The importance of human dignity to Paine's conception of freedom suggests that his idea of natural equality may be similar to the liberal conception of 'equality of worth' or 'equality of respect and concern'. This is not to say that Paine did not accept that some men were more intelligent or more talented than others, only that they share a basic rationality sufficient for moral agency. Paine offers no proof of man's natural equality. He offers this as a basic article of faith, his first foundational principle.[8]

---

[7] It is surprising that Paine so consistently ignores the position of women in his writings. Aldridge shows that it is unlikely that two early *Pennsylvania Magazine* articles on women, ascribed to Paine by Conway and P. S. Foner, were written by him, particularly 'An Occasional Letter on the Female Sex', which appears to be a copy of a pamphlet previously published in London. In any case, these articles contain virtually nothing on the subject of political rights. See Aldridge, *American Ideology*, p. 287-288 & *Writings*, I, 59-64. Paine was concerned for the native inhabitants of British colonies in India, Native Americans and African slaves. He advocated the extension of full citizenship to all men by virtue of their humanity. That he did not express the logical conclusion of this argument to women cannot be excused by the novelty of this idea in his time. See Philp, *Paine*, pp. 74-5. Condorcet, his close friend and collaborator had earlier put the case for women having equal natural rights very capably in 1790, and it seems almost inconceivable that they had not discussed the issue. See *Condorcet: Selected Writings*, ed. by K. Baker (Indianapolis: Bobbs-Merrill, 1976), pp. 97-104. Paine socialised in London with Mary Wollstonecraft and must have been aware of her *A Vindication of the Rights of Woman*, although she did not demand immediate political rights for women. See Mary Wollstonecraft, *A Vindication of the Rights of Women*, ed. by Miriam Brody (London: Penguin, 1975 repr. 1992), p. 265. It is possible that Paine's omission of reference to women's rights may be conscious, although there is insufficient evidence in his writings for a proper consideration of his attitude to women. From the point of view of presenting an interpretation of Paine's political theory, it poses some language problems. Where I am describing Paine's thought, I have used his sexist language, because I have no evidence that he intended women to be included in his ascription of rights to humans, however illogical that may seem.

[8] See 'Age of Reason' (1794), *Writings*, IV, 21-2. Note that Paine only expresses a belief here and does not claim demonstrated knowledge of these moral precepts.

Paine's Theology

The most important task for this rationality is knowledge of God's existence and intentions. Paine's Deist theology, as much as his political thought, is founded on equality. In *Age of Reason,* he rejects organised religion based on revelatory texts because it cannot satisfy the principle of equality.[9] Any text supposed to be the word of God needs to be comprehensible to mankind as a whole. Thus it cannot be exclusive to one language or system of writing, nor can it require an intermediary priest to interpret and explain it. God's will can only be learned by examining His creation, the natural world. Only this form of revelation is unquestionably of divine origin and is available equally to all men with a basic level of reason.[10] In addition to the physical laws of the universe, such as those discovered by Isaac Newton, Paine believes there are also natural laws governing human behaviour that can be discovered through reason and experience. Paine's deism encompasses not only a claim to a rational belief in God's existence and His rationality but also in His benevolence which, he claims, can be inferred from the provision of the 'wealth of creation'; the earth and its products, for mankind.

Equality of Natural Rights.

The most obvious expression of Paine's principle of human equality is his claim for equal natural and civil rights. The assumption of political equality is at the root of his political theory: his concept of consent, his constitutionalism and his support for democracy. Any form of government that violates the equality of rights is illegitimate and unjust. Natural rights are, for Paine, inalienable and imprescriptible. We have these rights *because* we are born free and equal. Paine claims our rights cannot be granted by government, but are divinely given by birth

---

[9] 'Age of Reason' (1794), *Writings,* IV, 45-46; See also Ian Harris, 'Paine and Burke: God, Nature and Politics' in *Public and Private Doctrine: Essays in British History presented to Maurice Cowling,* ed. by M. Bentley (Cambridge: Cambridge University Press, 1993), pp. 34-62.

[10] See Harris, 'Paine and Burke', pp. 34-62.

as part of our existence. For the origin of our rights, we must look to our maker. This is the central claim in Paine's political writings and as such his theory stands or falls upon our acceptance of his belief in natural rights. Some might see this as the fatal flaw, particularly when a belief in natural rights is now often treated in much the same way as a belief in alchemy. For this reason, any attempt to interpret Paine's political theory for a contemporary intellectual audience must find an adequate explanation of this central claim.

Claeys suggests that Paine's natural rights can be understood as psychological properties, as he claims they are 'mechanically contained within ourselves as individuals.'[11] Mark Philp postulates that, in the absence of a theological or philosophical justification for belief in natural rights, Paine's basic claims could be grounded in an alternative structure, taking a lead from Jürgen Habermas's theory of communicative rationality.[12] Philp's use of Habermas's Discourse Ethics is a helpful step in this difficult task, but by concentrating on the ethics of democracy, it cannot cover all the natural rights that Paine suggests, such as the natural right to the earth.

Natural rights are for Paine inherent in and deducible from natural equality. Men are equal in their membership of mankind and as such there is no one man who naturally has a right to power over the other, since, if there was, he would be a different species of creature. Natural rights can thus be seen as badges of this equality of freedom. If X attempts to exercise power over Y, a claim that this is a violation of Y's natural right, is simply a claim that in virtue of their moral equality, X is wrong to do so because Y ought to be free from X's

---

[11] See Claeys, *Thomas Paine*, p. 91; Paine's letter to Thomas Jefferson is published in P. S. Foner, *Complete Writings*, II, 1298-1299.

[12] Philp, *Paine*, p. 115. In considering Philp's assertion, it is worth remarking on Paine's use of the concept of reason. Throughout his works, this concept is his most powerful argumentative tool. This brief survey has focused on the principle of equality as the pervasive idea in Paine's writings, but the concept of rationality is just as important to our understanding of Paine's thought. Along with equality, rationality is used to attack biblical revelation, to denounce monarchy and aristocracy and to legitimise democracy. It is extremely difficult to analyse this concept of reason because Paine uses it uncritically, assuming that it is clear to his readers what he means by the

domination.   If rights as badges represent our natural equality, they must necessarily be distributed equally.[13]   It has sometimes been thought that because Paine derives natural rights from the objective fact of an individual's existence, his conception of rights could be likened to Hobbes's descriptive rights to do what one has the power to do.[14]   However, a deeper consideration of Paine's theory of rights elicits a normative view of rights, particularly when we consider his quite original distinction between natural and civil rights.   Civil rights are required to enforce the normative natural rights that we do not have the power to exercise individually.

In a letter to Jefferson in 1789, he describes an original position in which men contract to create a society together:

> As all their rights in the first case are natural rights, and the exercise of those rights supported only by their own natural individual power, they would begin by distinguishing between those rights they could individually exercise and those rights they could not. Of the first kind are the rights of thinking, speaking, forming and giving opinions [...] Of the second kind are those of personal protection, of acquiring and possessing property, in the exercise of which the individual natural power is less than the natural right.[15]

As Paine explains in *Rights of Man,* the second kind of natural right becomes a civil right under government.   Natural rights are all those which appertain to man in right of his existence.   They include what Paine terms 'intellectual rights, or rights of the mind' such as liberty of conscience and 'those rights of acting as an individual for his own comfort and happiness, which are not injurious to the natural rights of others.'   Although we have natural rights before the formation of

---

terms reason, rational and irrational. He often treats reason as a value in itself, even as a disembodied, reified force, akin to Providence.

[13] 'First Principles' (1795), *Writings*, III, 271.

[14] See Philp, *Paine*, p. 114. In an article in the *Pennsylvania Journal* in 1777, Paine does suggest such a conception of natural rights: 'A *natural* right is an animal right; and the power to act it, is supposed, either fully or in part, to be mechanically contained within ourselves as individuals.' 'Candid and Critical Remarks on a Letter Signed Ludlow' (*Pennsylvania Journal*, 4 June 1777) in P. S. Foner, *Complete Writings*, II, 274.

[15] 'Letter to Jefferson', P. S. Foner, *Complete Writings*, II, 1298.

a government, many of these rights are only secure under the protection of government. Paine's distinction between natural and civil rights depends on his distinction between those rights that are fully exercisable in the state of nature and those which are not. When men enter into a political society they keep the rights which were perfect in nature and agree on new civil rights to guarantee those rights which were threatened. Of these civil rights, Paine explains 'although the right is perfect in the individual, the power to execute them is defective.' These imperfect natural rights require replication by civil rights but are not given up, rather they 'are the foundation of all his civil rights.'[16] The perfect rights, such as freedom of conscience, are not dependent on society and remain natural rights. Though not threatened in the state of nature, these rights are now at risk from the creation of a civil power. Thus even these intellectual and inoffensive rights need protection against government.

As an example, Paine gives the right to judge in one's own cause, a natural right. The right of judgement in the mind is never given up, but the right of redress, useless without the power to accompany it, is deposited in the common stock of society.[17] The individual has not alienated this right wholly, however, as Paine claims he is part proprietor of this common stock, and can draw on the capital as a matter of right. The natural right is suppressed in exchange for a more powerful civil right but not given up. No rights are lost by this process: 'Man did not enter society to become *worse* than he was before, nor to have fewer rights than he had before, but to have those rights better secured.'[18] Unlike Rousseau's citizen, the holders of Paine's civil rights do not give up their normative natural rights, only the right to enforce them unilaterally. This suppression of individual action holds only while the equivalent civil rights are enforced and respected by

---

[16] 'Rights of Man' (1791), *Writings*, II, 306-7.
[17] 'Candid and Critical Remarks' (1777), P. S. Foner, *Complete Writings*, II, 274.
[18] 'Rights of Man' (1791), *Writings*, II, 306.

the government. However, our civil rights are subject to collective interpretation. Only natural rights are unalterable.[19]

This creation of civil rights is symbolised by the social contract, which Paine sees, not as a pre-historic event, as this would no longer have any authority, but as a constitution created by a constitutional convention for that purpose and periodically updated. Only a contract, which provides a government capable of, and with the principal aim of, the enforcement of these rights could be given the rational consent of the people. Only a government founded on this rational consent is legitimate.

The Right of Each Generation

The natural equality and rights that Paine asserts are God-given to all men. They are not passed down from father to son. Each man is born with a full stock of rights. This implies that the contractual agreement that legitimises government must be renegotiated with each newborn boy.[20] This implication of his foundational principle of equality is at the heart of one of the most pervasive and original of Paine's derived principles. This principle, which I have termed the 'right of each generation principle' for shorthand, asserts that each generation has the right to choose its form of government and that no generation has the right to give up or exchange the rights of their descendants or to bind future generations in a perpetual contract.[21]

The right of each generation principle forms the basis of Paine's attack on hereditary forms of government, monarchy and aristocracy. These traditional

---

[19] 'Candid and Critical Remarks' (1777), P. S. Foner, *Complete Writings*, II, 274. Paine seems to suggest here that a bill or declaration of rights should contain only natural rights, with civil rights being contained in a separate constitution representing the creation of a 'civil community for the mutual good and support of each other.'

[20] Paine does accept parental authority over children, although some of his contemporary detractors humorously suggested otherwise. Parents are the guardians, but not the owners of their children's rights.

[21] See below p. 302.

forms of government are rejected in favour of representative government. This satisfies his principle of equality by giving all men a part in their government. However, Paine recognises the possibility that majority rule can act despotically in denying the equal rights of a minority. The role of the constitution is to limit the power of government to prevent such infringements of rights. Any constitution or fictional social contract that fails to do so fails Paine's test of legitimacy. But, in binding all majorities to these civil and natural rights agreed upon at the time of the formation of government, the constitution would violate the principle of the right of each generation. This problem necessitates the constant review and possible revision of the social contract or constitution by each generation. This solution leaves natural rights, which are presented as immutable eternal truths, at the mercy of democratic acceptance and thus dependent on Paine's faith in rationality prevailing. Paine's adoption of Locke's test of legitimacy is thus taken to its full implication. Not only must government be based on rational consent, but also this consent must be expressed by each generation, at least negatively, by their conscious decision not to revise the constitution left by their fathers' generation.

Equality of Property

Paine also uses the principle of equality to attack the existing system of property rights. In *Agrarian Justice*, Paine argues that as the natural earth was given to men equally in common, the present situation, in which most resources were held by the few and many had nothing at all, could not be just. His principle of equality does not stretch, however, to advocating levelling. His solution is a programme of welfare transfers to compensate the poor for their dispossession. He rejects the possibility of an agrarian redistribution aiming at equal plots of land, and communistic attempts to hold resources in common, because such proposals fail to recognise the individual's right to that part of his wealth that is due to his labour and initiative. This distinctive theory of economic justice reflects Paine's attempt to combine the principle of basic equality with a strong concept of individuality.

It has been suggested by Gregory Claeys that Paine's argument from natural equality in *Agrarian Justice* is inconsistent with his earlier rejection of revelation in *Age of Reason*.[22] Claeys suggests that his claim in *Agrarian Justice*, that 'the earth in its natural uncultivated state was, and ever would have continued to be, *the common property of the human race,*'[23] can only be supported by the Old Testament, particularly Genesis which Paine earlier dismissed as unreliable fiction. Claeys suggests that the source for Paine's assertion of original common ownership is the natural law tradition, which in turn relies on Genesis. (Paine writes only that it is 'a position not to be controverted.') Claeys argues that Paine cannot ascribe the idea of common ownership to a Deist account of Divine intention. However, as we have seen above the principle of basic equality is intrinsic to his rejection of revelation. Paine's claim in *Agrarian Justice* that all men have a natural right to the earth is no different to the central claim of his entire political theory - that men hold certain equal natural rights - except that the natural right to earth concerns control over something outside of the individual, although at the same time essential to his existence.

Foundational Equality

At the heart of Paine's political theory is a concept of rights to which the value of equality is central. Paine is not interested in strict material equality but in equality of rights. This equality is natural and therefore divine. Paine's assertion of man's equality is the most important of the principles, which he views as the starting point of his political thinking. Throughout his writings Paine asserts that the equality of rights is found in the creation.[24] He claims that all religions agree

---

[22] Claeys, *Thomas Paine*, pp. 203-206. See also above p. 19.
[23] See below p. 518.
[24] The appeal to creation is limited by Paine's rejection of Genesis, which itself depends on a foundational belief in equality. See above p. 19 & Claeys, *Thomas Paine*, p. 204; Harris, 'Paine

on unity of man, by which he seems to mean the idea that men are equal at least in that they share a common feature of humanity. Perhaps we can find a justification for equality, which is consistent with Paine's scientific Deism in the claim 'Man was his high and only title, and a higher cannot be given.'[25] Is Paine suggesting as Locke claimed that equality can be derived from the classification of human beings as one species? This would seem to be the thrust of Paine's claim in *Rights of Man* that 'Through all the vocabulary of Adam there is not such an animal as a Duke or a Count.'[26]

Membership of the human species is then Paine's grounds for equality. This equality is natural but not physical. It is not that no man is stronger than another, but that they are equal in rights. These rights are in this way natural rights that belong to men by virtue of their existence as men, not from any recognition or artificial construction by other men or society. Such rights 'are not *gifts* from one man to another, nor from one class of men to another'

> A declaration of rights is not a creation of them, nor a donation of them. It is a manifest of the principle by which they exist, followed by a detail of what the rights are; for every civil right has a natural right for its foundation, and it includes the principle of a reciprocal guarantee of those rights from man to man. As, therefore, it is impossible to discover the origin of rights otherwise than in the origin of man, it consequently follows, that rights appertain to man in right of his existence only, and must therefore be equal to every man.[27]

The ambiguity of the principle of equality is at the heart of many of the conceptual conflicts in Paine's political theory. There is a central tension between two sorts of political equality. Firstly, there is a commitment to equal natural and

---

and Burke', pp. 34-62, 'Age of Reason' (1794), *Writings*, IV, 21-2. Paine does appeal to the Mosaic account of creation stating that only the distinction in sexes is implied. See 'Rights of Man' (1791), *Writings*, II, 303-305 and below p. 516.

[25] 'Rights of Man' (1791), *Writings*, II, 303.

[26] John Locke, *Two Treatises of Government*, ed. by Peter Laslett, Cambridge Texts in the History of Political Thought (Cambridge: Cambridge University Press, 1960; repr. 1991), p. 269; 'Rights of Man' (1791), *Writings*, II, 320.

[27] 'First Principles' (1795), *Writings*, III, 271.

civil rights, which embody an equality of negative liberty. Secondly, there is an equality of participation in collective power, the equality of democracy. These two egalitarian commitments both have the status of claims based on natural rights and neither is given priority. One distributes equally in individuals a power against government, the other a power to govern, and the potential conflict between them is one of the most problematic issues in the political theory of liberal democracy.

Two Traditions: Liberalism and Republicanism

The liberal tradition can be found in Paine's espousal of natural rights, his advocacy of minimal government and his theory of legitimacy founded on the consent of individuals. It is his adherence to this tradition that has resulted in the notion that Paine's writings contain merely a democratic version of Locke's political theory. However, Paine's liberalism is more modern than Locke's as can be seen in the similarity of his ideas to those of the Scottish Enlightenment economists and of later liberals in the nineteenth century. The republican tradition is also strongly in evidence in his writings, although for many reasons this is harder to identify.

Separating the republican tradition from the liberal tradition involves a comparison between incommensurable objects. Classical republicanism developed as a challenge to a political philosophy entirely different from liberalism. While we can trace elements of liberal thought before 1800, this term and these distinctions would not have been recognised by the writers and thinkers we might attribute them to. The major political disputes to which Paine responded were disputes between groups of men, who all claimed to admire the classical republican texts. Liberalism and other competing political traditions adopted ideas from the republican tradition, setting up new distinctions and problems not recognised by republican thinkers. Within these political traditions, there is a great variety of ideas and changes of emphasis over time. This is particularly true of classical republicanism, which has been traced by many historians, but particularly by Pocock, from the ancient Greek and Roman writers, Aristotle and Polybius and Cicero, to fifteenth century Italian republicans such as Machiavelli, and then to the seventeenth century English 'Country' opposition, represented by such as Harrington, Sidney, Trenchard and Gordon.[28] Although these writers have been shown to share key concepts and concerns and were undoubtedly influenced by their predecessors, they are all responding to unique historical events and represent in each case a body of special interests which they are using classical republican theory to defend.

The political ideology of the early eighteenth century centred on a Harringtonian adoption of Machiavellian republicanism. It has been asserted by Robbins, Pocock and Bailyn that this was still the dominant opposition ideology in Paine's time, in England and in the American colonies. These works are revisionist in that they reject the previous scholarly consensus that Lockean ideology dominated not only the principles of the 1688 revolution and the reform movements in the 18th century, but also the American Revolution. Isaac Kramnick writes that:

> The liberal individualist heritage preoccupied with private rights
> has to a great extent, been replaced by a republican tradition
> emphasising citizenship and public participation, a tradition with
> roots deep in the classical and renaissance worlds.[29]

However, Kramnick argues that, while 'the republican hypothesis' might be correctly applied to the early eighteenth century, the reform movements of the late eighteenth century in which Paine plays a part were more influenced by Locke and the natural law tradition than the classical republicanism of their Country predecessors. Further, Kramnick argues that the insistence on the paradigm of

---

[28] J. G. A. Pocock, *The Machiavellian Moment: Florentine Political Thought and the Atlantic Republican Tradition* (Princeton: Princeton University Press, 1975), pp. 382-384.

[29] I. Kramnick, *Republicanism & Bourgeois Radicalism: Political Ideology in Late Eighteenth Century England and America* (London: Cornell University Press, 1990), p. 629.

classical republicanism distorts our view of the late eighteenth century reformers, such as Paine, because this scholarship also insists on the irrelevance of class in political discourse at this time. The late eighteenth century reformers that Kramnick refers to - Burgh, Cartwright, Price, Priestly, Towers and Paine, and the reforming associations, the Society for Constitutional Information and the London Corresponding Society - all blended the language and concerns of classical republicanism with Lockean ideas as though there were no ideological conflict between them.[30]

Both classical republicanism and Lockean liberalism sought to restore the rights of Englishmen but there is a fundamental difference in their justification for such rights. For the republican these rights are due to a man because he is English - a vital component of his independence, his civic virtue and the balanced constitution. They are destroyed by corruption; by the influence of the crown over the commons through patronage, and must be restored by a return to the ancient constitution, a historical institution legitimised by tradition. For the natural law tradition, including Paine, these rights are due to a man because he is human. They are justified ahistorically and are pre-political. They do not depend on the common good or on maintaining the health of the republic.

Classical republicanism defines corruption in terms of credit and patronage, while Lockean liberalism accepts these new forms of wealth. The radicals of the late eighteenth century demanded the extension of the franchise to the new, urban and often dissenting middle class. They did not see real property as a prerequisite for political power nor identify new forms of mobile wealth with corruption and vice. Rather a new economic dichotomy developed between industriousness and idleness. The new urban middle classes are virtuous because they create wealth, while both the poor and the aristocracy are idle. Private selfishness can create public virtue, according to the new economics of

---

[30] Locke's work itself contains some republican ideas: the separation of powers, and a definition of freedom, which is being subject to law and not a slave. Locke's ideas cannot then be taken as a pure paradigm of liberal ideas but there are some notable differences.

Mandeville and Smith. Private interest is not a threat to the common good and is natural, while political authority, and the claim of the common good, must be legitimised by the consent of individuals. Without such authority, mutual benefits of exchange could maintain a temporarily stable society, naturally generated and guided by the natural laws of the market. To the Lockean liberal, it is the collective political force that is in danger of disrupting social harmony, while the republican fears that the private interests of the individual will disrupt a natural political society. Therefore, the liberal is concerned to promote liberty as the rights of individuals against the state, while the republican promotes the liberty of the collective whole from wayward individuals by promoting the duties of individuals to participate in the state. These duties are often expressed as rights, such as the right to bear arms in defence of the republic.

There has been considerable historiographical debate concerning the influence of classical republicanism on the American Revolution. Clinton Rossiter's work, *The Seedtime of the Republic* in 1953 was followed by works by Robbins, Bailyn, Wood and Pocock, among others, who argued that the dominant ideology driving the American Revolutionaries and British radicals was the same as, or at least derived from, the classical republican ideology adopted by the seventeenth century English 'country' opposition.[31] Further, Murrin, McCoy, Banning and McDonald argue that classical republican ideology continued to shape the Americans' political ideas in the building of their constitutions and in their first party conflict between Federalists and Jeffersonian Republicans.[32]

---

[31] See C. Rossiter, *The Seedtime of the Republic: the Origin of the American Tradition of Political Liberty* (New York: Harcourt, Brace, 1953); C. Robbins, *The Eighteenth Century Commonwealthman: Studies in the Transmission, Development and Circumstance of English Liberal Thought* (Cambridge, Mass: Harvard University Press, 1959); B. Bailyn, *The Ideological Origins of the American Revolution*, 2nd edn. (Cambridge, Mass: Belknap; 1967 repr. 1992); G. S. Wood, *The Creation of the American Republic 1776-1787* (Chapel Hill: University of North Carolina Press, 1969).

[32] See J. M. Murrin, 'Republican Ideology and the Triumph of the Constitution 1789-93,' *William and Mary Quarterly*, 3rd Series, 31 (1974), 167-188; D. R. McCoy, 'Republicanism and American Foreign Policy: James Madison and the Political Economy of Commercial Discrimination 1789-94,' *William and Mary Quarterly*, 3rd Series, 31 (1974), 633-646; L. Banning, *The Jeffersonian Persuasion: Evolution of a Party Ideology* (Ithaca, New York: Cornell

There is evidence to suggest that this tradition was in the process of dramatic upheaval at the very time Paine was writing, so much so that a world view that described itself as republican can be distinguished from classical republican thought and may even be part of the first liberal theories. Appleby has argued that although the American revolutionaries were dominated by republican ideology, the experience of revolutionary upheaval and new forms of wealth creation fundamentally changed the nature of their ideology so that a new, modern and liberal, republicanism emerged.[33] All the major 'republican hypothesis' historians agree that the creation of a new republic changed the form of republicanism, so that the first party system can be understood as a quarrel between the purist classical republicans and the new republicans, although this division can by no means be understood to reflect the simplicity of classical Federalists against democratic republicans.

Also, as Appleby and McDonald have pointed out, if classical republicanism was such a pervasive ideology as Pocock insists it would have to be in order to characterise action, then, republican language and forms would have to be used to justify any opposition to the established regime. If republicanism was the language of legitimacy, it must also be the language of political discourse in general. Appleby argues that new forms of wealth creation brought new economic ideas into the political realm, which were not easily assimilated in the classical tradition, and which saw economic matters as domestic as opposed to political. Appleby asserts that a liberal tradition emerged in the first party dispute in America through an attempt to express a liberal theory in republican language. Appleby cites Paine as one of the champions of 'new' liberal republicanism. In Paine's political circle, republicanism was understood to mean radical change, not nostalgia for a lost Spartan paradise.

University Press, 1978); F. McDonald, *The Presidency of Thomas Jefferson* (Lawrence: University Press of Kansas, 1976).
[33] See J. Appleby, 'Republicanism in Old and New Contexts', *William and Mary Quarterly*, 3rd Series, 43 (1986), 20-34.

Paine's conception of democracy and liberty reveals the extent of his adherence to the republican tradition.[34] The treatment of these concepts by the republican tradition differs greatly from the liberal tradition. Put simply, republicanism gives priority to the constitutional stability of the collective political body and often associates freedom with political participation, while liberalism gives priority to the freedom of the individual from the power of the collective political body. Paine's political theory represents a new form of republicanism that incorporates many elements of the liberal tradition. In doing so, Paine departs from many of the concerns of classical and English republicanism, but retains essential elements, which distinguish his thought from the pure liberalism of the nineteenth century. The terms of this marriage, and the role of Paine's concept of rationality in facilitating matrimonial harmony, are essential to our understanding of Paine's political theory.

---

[34] This is not to say that Paine was necessarily influenced by the writers I have identified with this tradition, only that his political theory can be interpreted as being similarly republican in character. For a useful account of Paine sources, see Caroline Robbins, 'The Life Long Education of Thomas Paine, 1737-1809' *Proceedings of the American Philosophical Society*, 127:3 (1983), 135-140.

III

Paine's Economics

It is misleading to call the subject matter of this collection Paine's economics, but while he has no economic theory, Paine's writings are riddled with his opinions on economic problems: the state regulation of trade, the justification and relative merits of different methods of taxation, public debt and new financial institutions, and the amelioration of poverty. One puzzle in interpreting Paine's thought is how these opinions fit into the economic theory of the late eighteenth century. The year 1776 saw a revolution not only in America but also an intellectual revolution in the field of political economy. The publication of Adam Smith's *Wealth of Nations* was recognised even in its own time as the key event in this revolution, although, like all great advances, its roots can be found in much earlier thought. Despite its favourable reception, the economic model that was the principle target of this new science of economics, mercantilism, continued to characterise the organisation of economic life in Britain well into the next century.

Economics, Politics and Ethics in the Eighteenth Century

Mercantilism dominated European economic thought from the sixteenth century. While today it seems easy to caricature, the enormous success of the British colonial system of trade can in part be attributed to its central tenets.[1] Mercantilists recognised the benefit of trade as the path to national prosperity and

---

[1] An account of the historiographical debate on mercantilism can be found in *Revisions in Mercantilism*, ed. by D. C. Coleman (London: Methuen, 1969); *Mercantilism*, ed. by Lars Magnusson, 4 vols (London: Routledge, 1995).

international power and they argued for its strict regulation by a powerful state with these ends in mind. The key to national prosperity was to keep wealth, in the form of gold and silver money, in the country, by maintaining a favourable balance of trade, that is, to ensure that imports of money exceed exports.

For this reason, mercantilists supported state control of foreign trade through protective tariffs and prohibitions on the export of bullion. In order to foster domestic industry the export of certain raw materials such as wool was prohibited, and the export of manufactured goods was encouraged by bounties, while imports of luxuries and finished textiles were discouraged by duties. The Navigation Acts kept trade in English ships, given privileged access to English and colonial ports. The internal economy was also regulated in the interests of national strength. Agricultural innovation in the production of food and raw materials for domestic industry such as flax was encouraged particularly by the Enclosure Acts. The importation of corn was strictly controlled to encourage domestic self-sufficiency. The control of prices and wages by the medieval guilds had been supplanted by the state, which readily extended its control to sumptuary laws that prohibited or limited the consumption of certain goods associated with immorality or luxury, such as alcohol, while encouraging others, such as the consumption of fish.[2]

The expansion of the British Empire afforded the prospect of keeping trade entirely internal. The colonies were viewed as a source of raw materials that could furnish the growing manufacturing sector in the motherland, while creating a market for finished goods. This bilateral trade would always be favourable to British interests. Colonial trade was protected by monopolies that outlawed competition from either foreign or colonial enterprise, such as the powerful East India Company. Foreigners were excluded by the use of Navigation Acts and customs duties. The system was not favourable to the economic development of

---

[2] Elizabethan 'fish days' supported the domestic fisheries and maintained a body of trained mariners for use by the navy. See P. W. Buck, *The Politics of Mercantilism* (New York: Octagon Books, 1974), pp. 1-53.

the colonies themselves, but mercantilism was grounded on a belief in furthering the prosperity, not of individuals, but of the nation, to which it was assumed the settlers, dependant on England for protection, would remain loyal.

The political significance of mercantilism is this priority given to the interests of the state. Buck suggests a connection between mercantilism and the doctrine of the divine right of Kings, but whatever their view of how the state should be organised it is their view of the relationship between the state and the economy that distinguishes them from later economic thinkers.

> Mercantilists saw government as a protector of domestic industry and as a promoter of economic improvements and internal trade. They emphasised the need for political intervention to guarantee the consonance of public and private interests [...]. For individual actors [...] this view of things required that the concerns of trade and profit seeking whenever appropriate, yield to the highest public policy. The merchant's ultimate guide [...] was...his identification with the power and prestige of his nation. In short, the individual subject's desires as tradesmen must remain must remain subordinate to his common responsibilities as patriotic citizen.[3]

The concern that private and public interests may not be consonant is a perennial theme found in the early modern republican tradition. Unlike the mercantilists, the republican solution is not the enforcement of public aims by a strong central state but a hostility to trade in general. Republicans such as Harrington place an emphasis on landed property as the source, not of wealth, but of political security. Citizenship requires the ownership of land to ensure the match between private and public interest. The idea of trade as destructive to the civic virtue that binds the republic can be traced from Machiavelli through to Rousseau, and was used in England as a justification for the social primacy of a land-owning elite over the merchant class.[4] Those engaged in trade are regarded

---

[3] R. T. Teichgraeber, *'Free Trade' and Moral Philosophy: Rethinking the Sources of Adam Smith's Wealth of Nations* (Durham: Duke University Press, 1986), p. 19.

[4] See J. G. A. Pocock, 'Virtue and Commerce in the Eighteenth Century.' *Journal of Interdisciplinary History,* 3: 1 (1972) 119-34. Machiavelli suggests in *The Prince* that German

as suspect citizens apt to pursue private interests and form alliances with foreigners. The republic must therefore be as far as possible self-sufficient, reinforcing their common interests. Luxury goods such as imported wines and fine clothing are unnecessary and have a tendency to corrupt civic virtue by highlighting the distinctions between citizens inimical to equality and social harmony. The republican tradition saw international commerce as a threat to social order and a strong state. In assuming that the state could benefit from a regulated international trade, the mercantilist tradition departed from the republican paradigm.

The English Whigs that had long used this republican paradigm as the language of legitimacy were also challenged by this hostility to trade. During the eighteenth century, the Whig attitude to commerce underwent a fundamental change; one which reflected a revolution in the English economy that needed no foundation in ideology. This revolution was the development of a new form of property, more productive than land and yet mobile. The new mobile property was paper: bills of credit representing a share in the national debt, bills of exchange used for foreign and colonial trade, bills issued by the Bank of England and Scotland representing private deposits, and shares in companies, often enjoying their monopoly status. The accumulation of wealth in the form of pieces of paper was as strange and unsettling to the eighteenth century Englishman as it is for us to reflect on our own wealth as existing primarily in the virtual reality of cyberspace.[5] Even more unsettling was the realisation that the value of this

---

cities have maintained their republican freedom better than Italian cities because they have less trade and contact with foreigners, but in the *Discourses* also criticises the landed nobility for pursuing private interests at the expense of the public interest. Machiavelli's hostility is not so much to trade as to the potential for private wealth to assume public power. See Niccolo Machiavelli, *The Prince and other Writings*, ed. by Bruce Penman (London: Dent, 1991), pp. 79-80 & p. 211. See also Rousseau 'Plan for Corsica' in J. J. Rousseau, *Political Writings*, ed. & trans. by F. Watkins (Wisconsin: The University of Wisconsin Press, 1986), pp. 277-330 and James Harrington, *The Commonwealth of Oceana: and a System of Politics*, ed. by J. G. A. Pocock (Cambridge: Cambridge University Press, 1992).

[5] On the revolutionary potential of electronic cash see 'Electronic money: so much for the cashless society', *Economist*, 26 November 1994, pp. 25-30; Glyn Davies, *A History of Money*

property depended ultimately on public confidence; a point well made when in 1720 the South Sea Bubble exploded, very nearly scuppering the financial revolution before it really began.[6]

The enormous profits made by colonial trade and financial speculation brought a new class of men into politics and brought the traditional political class, the land-owning aristocracy, into trade. Traditional 'Country' or anti-court attitudes opposed the new form of wealth and insisted on the primacy of land. Again, the Country concerns were with patronage and the standing army but the financial revolution brought a new form of corruption in the form of national debt. Public Credit and paper money were seen to diminish the independence necessary to each branch of government, by creating a monied interest that would support the court and high taxation on land. This concern was grounded on the thesis that real property, in the form of land, sustains civic virtue while mobile property, and commerce in general, encourages selfish private interests rather than concern for the common good. The new form of wealth was accused of corrupting the constitution, by creating a vested private interest in the accumulation of national debt, shared by the commercial classes and the government placemen.

Increasingly, the Country Opposition accepted trade as consistent with agrarian values of independence and virtue. Corruption now became politically defined; credit, stock jobbing and placemen corrupted the independence of the Commons from the Lords and the Crown. We can identify a new kind of Whig discourse, which accepts the new wealth and its association with trade as the cement that holds commercial society together. Pocock finds that this 'new

---

from Ancient Times to the Present Day (Cardiff: University of Wales Press, 1996), pp. 280 & 646-7.

[6] The South Sea Company was founded in 1711. Ostensibly a trading company, its main purpose was to speculate on Treasury Bills. Holders of government debt were able to trade their bills for company stock. The issue was heavily subscribed resulting in rapidly inflating market values and 'investment mania'. In 1720 the company colluded with the government to bring in the 'Bubble Act' forbidding the formation of new joint-stock companies. Though intended to counter rivals, the new restrictions lead to a sudden collapse in its stock value. Investors were left with worthless pieces of paper, until the government and the Bank of England stepped in. A similar scandal was experienced in France the same year due to the collapse of Law's banking scheme.

version of the classical theory of corruption was necessitated by an awareness of the growing relations between government, war, and finance' and further that 'mercantilist warfare caused a revival of interest in the external relationships of commonwealths with other commonwealths and with empires'. Some might call this 'Commercial Whiggism' a new kind of republicanism; others might see it as the beginning of the death of the republican hold over English politics and the birth of a new economic philosophy: free-market liberalism.[7]

The development of the free-market challenge to mercantilist orthodoxy came from two related groups both associated with the Enlightenment. In the 1750s the French Physiocrat economists developed a powerful critique of the mercantilist policies pursued by the *Ancien Regime*, particularly fiscalism, the attempt by the state to secure as much revenue as possible. Quesnay (1694-1774) and Mirabeau (1715-1789) drew from the new philosophy of reason and freedom a 'science of natural law' applied to economics. They argue, along with earlier proponents of free trade, that state intervention can never encourage trade as much as giving individuals a free reign in determining and pursuing their own interests. Therefore, they propose a policy of *laissez-faire*. The state should refrain from regulating trade, particularly in grain, release labour from feudal control and allow nature to regulate the economy through natural law. In part, the Physiocrat claim was economic: the mercantilist system fails because it mistakes wealth for money. The Physiocrats identify land and agriculture as the only true source of wealth. But in part their claim was also political: following Locke, the Physiocrats identified a natural right to the fruits of one's labour and therefore to property. The overburden of taxation was therefore an attack on human freedom. Taxation must instead be collected only on the surplus product, and only on the portion due to the state as the co-proprietor of the land.[8]

---

[7] See Pocock, *The Machiavellian Moment,* p. 460; Claeys, *Thomas Paine,* p. 45; Philp, 'English Republicanism', p. 247.

[8] See Buck, *Politics of Mercantilism*, pp. 63-72; E. Fox-Genovese, *The Origins of Physiocracy* (Ithaca: Cornell University Press, 1976) p. 54. Whilst the term *laissez-faire* was introduced by the French Physiocrats, the application of this term to English writers at this time may be

The other assault on mercantilism is most closely associated with Adam Smith (1723-90) and David Hume (1711-76), but can also be ascribed to a number of less well known figures of the Scottish Enlightenment such as Francis Hutcheson (1649-1746), Lord Kames (1696-1782) and Adam Ferguson (1723-1816). In many ways, Smith's 'system of natural liberty' is similar to Quesnay's but on a number of points they disagree. Rather than land and agriculture being the source of wealth, Smith identifies labour and the market value of the products of labour as the source of wealth, and thus the individual's natural right to the fruits of his labour is even more central to his idea of economic freedom. Smith describes a natural system of free trade that regulates value and production through supply and demand. The invisible hand of market forces is well known to us today, but was a staggering advance in the science of economics.

Paper Money and the Bank of North America

Paper money was not invented in America but certainly went through all the agonies of adolescence there. Its origin is found in the mercantilist policies of the British government, which kept English silver and gold in Britain, starving the colonies of a medium of exchange. In addition to commodities such as tobacco and wampum, a variety of foreign silver coins were used, predominantly the Spanish peso or dollar.[9] The value of silver and gold (specie) was artificially

anachronistic. The *Oxford English Dictionary*, 2nd edn, (Oxford: Clarendon, 1989) gives the first citation in English as 1825. The term does not seem to have gained common currency in English until the mid-nineteenth century. Given that Paine seems to have been aware of the work of the French Physiocrats, the application of the term to his ideas does not seem inappropriate although he did not use it himself.

[9] The peso was also known as a piece of eight because it was at one time worth eight Spanish reales. See John J. McCusker, *Money and Exchange in Europe and America 1600-1775: A Handbook* (Chapel Hill: University of North Carolina Press, 1978) pp. 5-7. Tobacco was used as currency, particularly in Virginia, and later as backing for paper bills of credit. See Joseph A. Ernst, *Money and Politics in America 1755-1775* (Chapel Hill: University of North Carolina Press, 1973) p. 21 & 140. Wampum was a Native American currency made from clamshells strung together. It was also used by colonists: for example in 1664 Stuyvesant arranged a loan in

increased by colonial legislation, to encourage its importation. Thus Pennsylvania merchants kept accounts in 'Pennsylvania Currency' which might be paid in a variety of coins and monetary devices, in notional pounds, shillings and pence, at a value greater than the English equivalent.[10] Such measures were restricted in 1704 by a royal proclamation, which limited colonial currencies to 133.3% of the English pound or six shillings to a Spanish dollar. From 1690 onwards, colonial legislatures followed the growing European practice of using paper representations of debt as a circulating medium.[11]

The colonial legislatures issued Bills of Credit, which were usually non-interest bearing and circulated as money. They were often backed only by tender laws that guaranteed their validity in payment of public, and sometimes private, debts.[12] Government expenditure in notes could be repaid by accepting the notes later against tax debt; thus the bills formed a public debt. Such issues were disliked particularly by British merchants because they were often discounted (they depreciated in value) especially in other colonies. The London merchants and Board of Trade fought to restrict both the emissions and the tender laws that forced them to accept the notes. Between 1720 and 1751 the British government increasingly restricted the power of colonial legislatures to issue paper. Issues were allowed only to pay for defence and market emergencies, requiring permission from London. Tender laws applied to private transactions were

---

wampum to pay construction workers. Steel drills allowed colonists to mass-produce wampum resulting in depreciation. See Davies, *History of Money*, p. 458.

[10] Pennsylvania currency was a money of account, or 'imaginary money' as was the English pound sterling, its value set by legislative act. 'Real' money was in guineas, shillings, and other silver coins. In 1700, the exchange value was £174 Pennsylvania currency to £100 sterling. After 1709, it remained at £133.33 per £100 sterling, known as Proclamation Money. See McCusker, *Money and Exchange,* p. 176 & Ernst, *Money and Politics*, p. 13.

[11] The first public paper money in America was issued by the Massachusetts Bay Colony in 1690 to pay military expenses. The first note in Europe was issued by a Bank in Stockholm in 1660 to represent a copper coin that weighed 43 pounds! See McCusker, *Money and Exchange*, p. 119 & Eric P. Newman, *The Early Paper Money of America* (Racine: Whitman, 1967), p. 7.

[12] Colonial legislatures also issued notes though loan offices backed by land mortgages and sometimes sinking funds. Private banks also issued notes on mortgaged land such as Colman's in Boston (1740). See Newman, *Early Paper Money*, p. 9; B. L Daniels, *Pennsylvania: Birth Place of Banking in America* (Philadelphia: Pennsylvania Bankers Association, 1976), pp. 4-8.

outlawed and contracts for debt permitted to specify payment in specie. The Currency Act of 1764 also banned paper money backed by public legal tender. The colonies continued print money by various means of circumventing these regulations whilst campaigning to repeal the Currency Act.[13] In 1773, an amendment restricted the act's application to tender laws for private transactions, allowing legislatures to promise to accept the notes at par for taxes and other public debts.[14]

The Currency Act and the monetary situation of the colonies directly contributed to the revolution and were cited in the Declaration of Rights and Grievances. Thus it seemed obvious to the colonists to print money in their defence. A number of factors contributed to the massive inflation in paper money experienced. Firstly, many people hoarded gold and silver, which was believed to have intrinsic value thus increasing the demand for a circulating medium. Secondly the states, acting independently and now free from English control, issued many notes in addition to the issues of Continental Currency approved by the First and Second Continental Congress and in increasingly small denominations. But as the war seemed to be going in British favour (Continental Currency was banned in British occupied areas), confidence in government issued paper money, even for the most loyal of patriots, collapsed.

By 1780, Congress redeemed Continental Currency at a rate of 40-1. Pennsylvania currency was worth less than half a percent of its pre-war value. Thus, what Paine called the 'American experiment' collapsed dramatically, leaving the war torn states with no circulating medium and thus no way to collect taxes to finance the War of Independence, except goods and services in kind. In 1780 it was Paine's task, as clerk to the Pennsylvania Assembly, to read in camera a letter from George Washington reporting the exhaustion of the army's human

---

[13] Franklin's mission to London in 1764 was to persuade the ministry to repeal the Currency Act, having written a pamphlet outlining the need for paper money in the colonies. It was whilst in London that Franklin met Paine in 1774.

[14] See Ernst, *Money and Politics*, pp. 18-89.

and material resources. Paine immediately withdrew his salary and donated $500

Pennsylvania currency to Blair McClenachan, a prominent Philadelphia

businessman, to start a fund to provide the government with credit. Robert Morris

and McClenachan added £200 each in hard currency.[15] On the 17 June, Morris

called a meeting at the City Tavern at which a syndicate was formed which a

month later became the Pennsylvania Bank to which ninety-two patriots

subscribed £300,000. Congress agreed that the bank could issue notes bearing an

interest of 6% and secured its capital with £50,000 (plus £260,000 later) in

exchange for the provision of the army with 3 million rations and 300 hogshead of

rum. The bank operated out of a store on Front Street and Walnut.

On 17 May 1781, Morris submitted a plan to Congress for 'establishing a

national bank for the United States of North America'. In spite of Madison's

opposition, the proposal was passed on 26 May.[16] This established the Bank of

North America as a subscription of $4000,000 in shares of $400 each payable in

specie. Congress appointed twelve directors to serve without compensation who

would elect a president.[17] Most of the participants in the Pennsylvania Bank

transferred their stock to the new bank, at a meeting at the City tavern on 1

November, which also attracted new shareholders. Four hundred and fifty

thousand dollars was furnished by the French government. Morris, Thomas

Fitzsimmons (1741-1811) and James Wilson (1742-98) were among the original

directors appointed and Thomas Willing, Morris's business partner, was the first

president.[18] The bank would support the Treasury by making loans on capital and

---

[15] See below p. 42.
[16] James Madison (1751-1836) thought Congress was exceeding its powers. He later established the 'Second Bank of the United States'.
[17] See W. F. Dunaway, *A History of Pennsylvania* (New York: Prentice-Hall, 1946), p. 306.
[18] See *Supplement to the Pennsylvania Gazette*, 7 September 1785, p. 6. Half of the silver brought back from France by Colonel John Laurens (1754-1782) and Paine, acting as his assistant was used in the initial establishment of the bank, amounting to $250,000. See David D. Wallace, *The Life of Henry Laurens* (New York: Russell & Russell, 1915), p. 485. Janet Wilson reports that although the bank's twelve directors were elected by the stockholders, the annual election soon became a formality due to the narrow class base of the stockholders; all were from merchant or professional families of Philadelphia, many of them related by marriage and often formerly Tory or loyalist but then conservative and Federalists. See Janet Wilson, 'The Bank of North

providing a much-needed circulating medium by issuing notes on the credit of the stock. Continental Congress granted the bank a charter on 31 December 1781. It was certainly the first genuine commercial bank in the United States and in some ways acted as a central bank. Hamilton's later attempt to establish a national central bank and common currency in 1791 has always been called 'the First Bank of the U. S' but Paine's bank also has a strong claim to this title:

> Considering its national purpose, its national charter, the national subscription to its initial capital stock, its services to the national treasury during 1782-3 and its temporary national monopoly, it would not be incorrect to designate it the first bank of the United States.[19]

The Bank of North America opened for business on 7 January 1782 from the backroom of Tench Francis's general store on Chestnut Street. By July, Congress had borrowed $400,000 and was requesting more. The Pennsylvania Assembly also borrowed from the bank on the future excise revenue and rewarded it with a state charter on 26 April. The bank advanced $80,000 for the state quota to Congress and lent the state $22,500 for a ship to protect the Delaware. Other states also recognised the bank. Massachusetts granted a charter in 1782, Connecticut guaranteed their notes for payment of taxes and Rhode Island passed a counterfeiting law. The bank thrived: by 1783 stockholders received 14½% dividends and new shares were issued at £500. The Philadelphia example was followed by other states, resulting in the Massachusetts Bank and the Bank of New York established in 1784.[20] Although a great success, in 1785 a campaign began in the Pennsylvania assembly to weaken the bank by removing its state

---

America and Pennsylvania Politics 1781-87,' *The Pennsylvania Magazine of History and Biography,* 46: 1, (1942), 3-28.

[19] Daniels, *Birth Place of Banking*, pp. 15-16.

[20] The Bank of North America continued to trade as a commercial bank, despite the suspension of its charter in 1785-7 and the loss of its federal charter in 1787. It merged with the Commercial Trust Co. in 1923, losing its name in a merger with an insurance company in 1929. See Daniels, *Birth Place of Banking*, pp. 19-21; Newman, *Early Paper Money*, p. 264; Wilson, 'The Bank of North America', 3-28.

charter. The details of this crisis and its effect on Paine's political thought are examined in Chapter 3.

The lack of a common currency and the huge variety of notes issued in America during this period created an economic and financial chaos that it is hard for us to imagine. Scarcity of a medium of exchange must be numbered among one of the causes of the American Revolution, although, despite the establishment of a unique federal and representative form of government, the United States did not establish a uniform common currency until 1863.[21] As the war caused considerable movement of population, one can imagine the difficulties presented by purchasing simple items with a variety of forms of money. The shortage of coin money occasioned small denominations of paper, as little as a sixth of a dollar. Often the notes continued to circulate in torn portions.

Great advances were made in printing notes by Paine's patron Benjamin Franklin, who developed a method of printing on both sides and of using natural leaf prints to foil forgers. His company Franklin & Hall, later Hall & Sellers, was responsible for printing notes for Congress, Pennsylvania, New Jersey and Delaware. John Dunlap (1742-1812), founder of the *Pennsylvania Packet*, also printed notes for Pennsylvania. As these printers were the publishers of newspapers and many pamphlets, it is worth noting that the printing trade had a vested interest in printed large of paper money.[22] The bills were printed on imported English paper until, during the revolution, it became common to use American-made paper.[23] Forgery was common and discouraged by a variety of means, including complexity of design and unevenly torn counterfoils. Newman reports that an engraver James Smither of Philadelphia was accused by Paine of forging Continental currency in 1778. The penalty was death, as was frequently alluded to on the notes themselves by the slogan 'to counterfeit is death'. Other

---

[21] *The National Bank Act*, 12 February 1863.
[22] See above p. xix.
[23] The very patriotic printer Paul Revere marked his notes 'American Paper'. See Newman, *Early Paper Money*, p. 17.

slogans appealed to the user's patriotism or even warned 'Time flies so Mind Your Business', no doubt reminding the holder of the note's rapidly depreciating value. Many emblems were used, increasingly patriotic devices, sometimes referring to the purpose of the public expenditure it represented. For example, the Pennsylvania issue of 10 April 1775 for the construction of workhouses and prisons depicts the workhouse on Walnut Street. The Bank of North America notes were engraved bearer notes, signed by Thomas Willing and Tench Francis, the cashier.[24]

National Debt and the Bank of England.

The constant wrangling between parliament and the Stuart Kings over finance, which characterised English politics of the seventeenth century, was solved in part by the development of a complex system of public borrowing. The government borrowed money by issuing interest-bearing stock, the profits of which gave the stock-holding class a vested interest in government spending. The Bank of England was founded in 1694 as a joint-stock company. Its charter initially of twenty-one years duration allowed it a capital of £1.2 million, most of which was loaned to the government. The bank made short term advances on deposits, paid military expenses abroad through its credit with foreign banks and issued bills to pay government debts. In 1708, it was granted a monopoly in joint stock banking which lasted until 1826. Private banks were allowed to issue bills of credit but limited to six partners, were restricted in their capital and thus drew on the credit of the Bank of England, which thus became the banker's banker. From 1715, the Bank funded the Government's annual supply, issued as transferable stock. Its permanency was assured by an agreement that it could not be dissolved until its government loans were repaid, an unlikely event. In 1720, Walpole called upon

---

[24] See illustrations between pp. 242-243 below. A useful guide to these paper notes is provided in Newman, *Early Paper Money*. In 1789, the bank issued change bills of one penny,

the bank to support private credit by saving the South Sea company from collapse.[25] Thus the Bank of England was effectively acting as a central bank: the government's banker and the lender of last resort.

A number of factors kept government spending high. Firstly, Britain was at war much of the time, in 1702-13, 1739-48, 1756-63 and 1775-83, mostly waged against France. Seventy-five percent of the funding for these wars was borrowed in interest-bearing Treasury notes. Walpole's sinking fund ensured confidence in these notes by providing for their redemption at a certain period of time. But the interest on this outstanding debt alone was huge and rapidly escalating. Secondly, political stability was maintained by a complex system of patronage. What the Stuarts failed to do by force, the Hanoverian Kings achieved through the greasy palm of personal profit. The Crown, often through the Prime Minister, employed its right of appointment to control the House of Commons. The 'places', awarded to those who supported the government, sometimes carried genuine responsibility but always provided opportunities for private profit.

An example is the position of paymaster general, used by a number of influential politicians to make their fortune.[26] The position required the holder to act as trustee over the funds to be used for military expenses and expend them when required. In the interim, the holder was able to invest the funds and privately profit from his investment. Other places were attached to further rights of patronage that allowed personal influence. The Crown also awarded pensions to its supporters. The political elite was thus divided into two groups, the court, men who currently supported the Crown and enjoyed their favour and the opposition, which did not. The House of Commons mirrored this division, consisting in those who enjoyed the patronage of the king or the current court members and the 'country' members, who were occasionally independent but

---

when circulating copper was temporarily refused, printed by Benjamin Franklin Bache.
[25] See above, p. 37.
[26] For example, William Pitt, the Elder, (1708-1778) was Paymaster General 1746-54.

often loyal to noble patrons of the opposition.[27] Thus frequently the Country Opposition complained that the influence of the crown over the commons was too strong and that the balanced constitution was being corrupted by allocating public finance to private individuals through places and pensions, although they usually changed their tune once included in the spoils.

By 1784, England appeared to be heading for bankruptcy. The shortfall, between revenue from taxes and the funds required for government expenses and the interest on the funded debt, amounted to more than £2 million. William Pitt, the Younger, (1759-1806) set out to secure public credit by introducing a sinking fund in 1786 to restructure the national debt. Further, he planned to reduce future spending by making peace with France. In 1786, William Eden (1744-1814) was called upon to negotiate a Commercial treaty with Vergennes (1717-87), the French minister, which would guarantee freedom of trade between the two nations and give each a stake in keeping the peace. Peace and commercial recovery restored the balances of gold in the Bank of England and increased confidence in government stocks. Most importantly, Pitt took measures to reduce the government's reliance on national debt by increasing revenue.[28]

The existing heavy tax burden gave Pitt little room for manoeuvre. The chief source of revenue was the land tax. Landowners had to pay ten percent of the value of their estate. The disproportionate representation of landowners in parliament, both in the House of Lords and through their younger brothers and cousins in the commons, ensured no increase in land taxes could be made. Further, the revenue was diminishing relative to inflation, as while real land prices rose there was no revaluation of taxable values on large estates. New taxes

---

[27] The crown was not the only source of patronage. For example the Duke of Newcastle, Thomas Pelham-Hollis (1693-1768) controlled vast resources, most notably control of a number of 'rotten boroughs' or parliamentary seats that he could sell for money or influence. When he or his family, the Pelhams, were included in the ministry, this patronage was added to the influence of the crown, but when in opposition was employed against it.

[28] See Jeremy Black, *British Foreign Policy in an Age of Revolutions* 1783-1793 (Cambridge: Cambridge University Press, 1994), pp. 135-136.

introduced tended to be indirect taxes, which fell most heavily on the new urban middle classes, underrepresented in parliament. Excise duties were introduced in 1733 on domestic liquor, salt, glass, soap, paper, candles, leather, starch, bricks and fabric. Beer was taxed several times over, on malt, hops and the finished product and provided a considerable portion of the revenue from indirect taxes. Special taxes were levied on items regarded as luxuries or emblems of moral depravity, such as hair powder and playing cards, but also on houses, windows, and servants. Newspapers and business documents carried a stamp duty of eight percent. Customs duties on imports also provided a significant proportion of revenue, on tobacco, wine, brandy, tea, sugar, iron, textiles and grain, although diminished by widespread smuggling, which Pitt sought to curtail. Local taxes, known as poor rates were also collected on buildings and land. Despite the reliance on national debt, the burden on the English tax payer was greater, and more regressive, than in its neighbours in Europe, including France, where the effects of unequal taxation would result in revolution and the overthrow of existing property rights.[29] Pitt succeeded in introducing an income tax, which came into effect in 1799, to fund the expenditure of the war of 1793-1815. Half of this considerable cost was paid from revenue rather than debt, although the war increased the national debt from £228,000,000 to £876,000,000.

The war with France put a considerable burden on the Bank of England. Expenses abroad between 1793-7 amounted to £33,000,000, most of which was lent by the bank in advance on expected revenue. This practice, commonly used since 1715, was formalised by Pitt's amendment to the Bank's charter in 1793, omitting the clause that forbade the bank to advance money not sanctioned by parliament.[30] The Commons' traditional power of the purse was thus weakened by the Prime Minister's ability to spend now and request later. The government's

---

[29] See Peter Mathias & Patrick O'Brien, 'Taxation in Britain and France 1715-1810: A Comparison of the Social and Economic Incidence of Taxes Collected for the Central Governments', *Journal of European Economic History*, 5: 3 (1976), 601-650.

[30] A practice dubbed 'ways and means' providing the title for Paine's final chapter to the *Rights of Man*. See below p. 463.

spending and their foreign loans to their allies exhausted the bank's gold supply, resulting in their inability to support provincial and city banks in crisis. Rumours of the failed French attempt to invade England in December 1796 caused a run on the bank, culminating in the announcement in 1797 of the suspension of cash payments. Effectively at this time, until the restoration of the Gold standard in 1816, the banknote became a state issue paper note, supported by confidence in government credit and in 1810 a tender law.[31]

France also had financial problems. By 1787, Louis XVI's government was bankrupt. Calonne and Brienne presented new tax proposals to the Assembly of Notables and the parlement of Paris, including a graduated land tax. The aristocracy refused to give up their exemption from tax resulting in the calling of the Estates General. In 1789, the third estate rejected the right of the aristocracy and clergy to an equal share in government and declared themselves to be a national convention. New taxes on land, property and income were introduced but the assembly had little power to enforce or collect revenue whilst the most wealthy citizens refused to acknowledge their legitimacy. In November 1789, the assembly nationalised church lands, assuming the church's responsibility for education, poor relief and clerical maintenance, and issued notes or *assignats* which were interest-bearing notes of credit, convertible into land. In 1793, unsupported *assignats* were issued to fund the war with Britain, resulting in runaway inflation. In 1796, the assembly introduced a new currency backed in specie and credit was restored.[32]

---

[31] See Arthur Redford, *The Economic History of England 1760-1860* (London: Longmans, 1931; repr. 1948), pp. 88-93.

[32] See D. G. Wright, *Revolution and Terror in France 1789-1795* (Harlow: London, 1974; repr. 1989), pp. 38 & 53.

The Consistency of Paine's Economic Ideas

It has sometimes been charged that Paine's economic ideas are inconsistent or change over his lifetime. He has been interpreted as a free-market liberal, a Physiocrat, a socialist and even a mercantilist.[33]   Three periods suggest inconsistency. Firstly, in the early days of the American Revolution, Paine was associated with the radical faction in Philadelphia, supported by the urban artisan class. This faction fought against the conservatism of the proprietor and business classes in favour of independence and created a radical and very democratic new constitution for Pennsylvania in 1776. But in 1784 Paine seemed to join the conservatives in their campaign against unsupported paper money and in favour of a strong United States central government with tax raising powers. Some members of the constitutionalist (later anti-federalist) faction accused Paine of betrayal and writing for hire.

Secondly, there appears to be a transition in Paine's work occasioned by his return to Europe. In America, Paine supported the Bank of North America as a central bank and indirect taxation and argued in favour of moderate public debt, while in Europe, Paine was extremely critical of the Bank of England, the burgeoning national debt and the heavy tax burden on the English people.[34] Thirdly, Paine's welfare proposals have been the focus of much of the academic debate on his works. Redistribution of wealth and income seems inconsistent with some very *laissez-faire* attitudes in his earlier works.[35]   I will argue that Paine's economic ideas are indeed liberal, and can be described as *laissez-faire*, but that his welfare proposals in both *Rights of Man Part Second* and in *Agrarian Justice*, are consistent with, and perhaps even implied by this liberal economic

---

[33] See A. O. Aldridge, *Man of Reason: The Life of Thomas Paine* (London: Cresset Press, 1960), p. 121.
[34] See below p. 124 & p. 434.
[35] This inconsistency was the focus of an American debate in the 1930-40's. See J. Dorfman, 'The Economic Philosophy of Thomas Paine,' *Political Science Quarterly,* 53 (1938), 372-86; H. Penniman, 'Thomas Paine: Democrat,' *American Political Science Review,* 37 (1943), 244-62.

theory. This view is supported by J. W. Seaman and also partially by Gregory Claeys, who argues that Paine's welfare rights can be seen as a secularisation of natural law thinking on the right to charity, and that this natural law tradition is also responsible for his views on free trade.[36]

In Paine's early works there are several references to free trade, particularly in the context of American independence and international trade, indicating that he is aware of the theory of the free market associated with the Scottish Enlightenment. In the same year as Adam Smith's *The Wealth of Nations* was published, Paine predicts that free trade at sea will produce 'immense additions to the wealth of America.'[37] Although his focus is on international free trade, his early writings suggest that he has already taken on board the major political components of free-market liberalism. By this I mean that Paine believes that only a minimal government is needed, that natural forces can regulate the market and that pursuit of individual interest will result in common good unless men are corrupted by oppressive governments.[38] These principles are found in his distinction between society and government in *Common Sense*.[39]

In *Rights of Man, Part Second,* we find Paine's most lucid expression of the ability of the market to regulate society and the minimal need for government. From the 'composition and constitution of man', and the diversity of men's

---

[36] J. W. Seaman, 'Thomas Paine: Ransom, Civil Peace and the Natural Right to Welfare,' *Political Theory*, 16: 1 (1988), 120-142; G. Claeys, 'Paine's *Agrarian Justice* and the Secularisation of Natural Jurisprudence', *Society for the Study of Labour History Bulletin,* 52: 3 (1987), 21-31 & Claeys, *Thomas Paine*, pp. 96-101.

[37] 'The Forester's Letters I: To Cato' (*Pennsylvania Journal*, 3 April 1776), *Writings*, I, 163-4.

[38] The use of the term 'minimal government' to describe Paine's idea that the necessary functions of government are, and ought to be limited, is anachronistic but valid, particularly when describing his view of society as a self regulating system of economic exchange. The term 'minimal government' is also applied to Paine's political theory by Claeys, *Thomas Paine*, p. 95, and Philp, *Paine*, p. 37.

[39] See below p. 113. The use of the term 'minimal government' to describe Paine's idea that the necessary functions of government are, and ought to be limited, is anachronistic but valid, particularly when describing his view of society as a self regulating system of economic exchange. It has been suggested that Paine's distinction in *Common Sense* between society and government represents the earliest attempt to defend civil society from an over powerful state. See John Keane, *Civil Society and the State* (London: Verso, 1988), p. 67, n. 6 & *Democracy and Civil*

talents for reciprocally accommodating their diverse wants, Paine claims we can discover 'a natural aptness in man', and a 'propensity to society, and consequently to preserve the advantages resulting from it', so that if formal government were abolished society will act as a 'general association,' ruled by common interest in security. Therefore, only minimal government is necessary or legitimate.[40] In his European writings, Paine seems so anti-government that it is hard to find a justification for government at all. His faith in human nature verges on Godwinian anarchism: 'It shews, that man, were he not corrupted by governments, is naturally the friend of man, and that human nature is not of itself vicious.'[41] Paine's faith in the ability of society to regulate itself, according to what he terms natural law or common interest, translates into a confidence in market forces.

Free-trade and the moral economy

This early free-market attitude is related to the colonial experience of the mercantile system in which Britain attempted to monopolise the trade of her colonies, and, after independence, to Paine's experience of popular attempts at price-fixing. He rejected the right or necessity of the British monopoly of American trade. It was of benefit to neither colony nor mother country and could only lead to resentment.

  Eric Foner has shown that Paine was involved in populist price-fixing committees in Philadelphia during the revolution. Paine's disgust with Silas Deane, Robert Morris and their associates as war profiteers led to his involvement in the price-fixing committees of Philadelphia, driven by this older view of the economy regulated by the state in the interest of consumer. The prevailing

---

Society (London: Verso, 1988), pp. 42-45. The term 'minimal government' is also applied to Paine's political theory by Claeys, *Thomas Paine*, p. 95, and Philp, *Paine*, p. 37.

 [40] 'Rights of Man II' (1792), *Writings*, II, 407.

 [41] 'Rights of Man II' (1792), *Writings*, II, 453, see also 'Letter to the Authors of *Le Républicain; ou le Defenseur du Gouvernement Réprésentatif*' (June 1791), *Writings*, III, 3.

economic theory among urban immigrants was not *laissez-faire* but a 'moral economy' view:

> The urban and rural poor, and many artisans as well, believed that the operations of the free market worked against their economic interest. They rejected the emerging doctrine of free trade [and] reaffirmed the traditional idea of a 'just price' for bread, which viewed millers and bakers as servants of the entire community, rather than normal entrepreneurs.[42]

This experience convinced Paine that prices could only be fixed by market forces. Foner argues that while Paine's involvement with the committees shows a tension between his *laissez-faire* attitudes and his concern for urban consumers in a period of cruel inflation, his subsequent collaboration with Robert Morris and other Philadelphia businessmen shows his conversion to the *laissez-faire* economics, though not their elitist politics. The failure of these methods to ensure the supply of goods to the market place convinced him that such 'moral economy' pressures are both unworkable and wrong in principle. It became clear to Paine, as well as to many artisan traders, that price-fixing merely served to drain the market, as farmers refused to bring their produce to a regulated market. Paine was later to warn Danton against price-fixing for this very reason.[43]

Throughout the inflation crisis Paine believed that the true cause of price rises was the increased issue of paper money. In *Crisis III*, he claims 'The quantity of money is too great, and [...] the prices of goods can only be effectually reduced by reducing the quantity of the money.'[44] The attack on paper money was in keeping with Robert Morris's doctrine of fiscal responsibility to which Paine had become committed in the 1780s. 'Paine's activities did not represent a complete break with his previous political and economic outlook', Foner claims.

> He had long been a proponent of strong central government, had been a strong critic of state-issue paper money, and had defended such new capitalist institutions as the Bank as essential props of

---

[42] Foner, *Revolutionary America*, p. 146.
[43] See Foner, *Revolutionary America*, pp. 183-4 and below p. 441.
[44] 'The Crisis III' (19 April 1777) *Writings*, I, 227.

American economic development. Paine had seen in 1779 that the
tradition of 'moral economy' was unable to regulate economic life
effectively, an experience which only strengthened his faith shared
by his new allies - in unregulated market relations.[45]

Paper Money, National Debt and Economic Freedom.

Paper money, and the public debt that it represents, is one of the most pervasive
economic themes in Paine's writings. Each of the pieces in this collection refers
to paper money in some degree, and for that reason, I have chosen to illustrate his
works with relevant notes of the period.[46]   Throughout his writings, Paine
consistently argues against the issue of paper not secured by specie, while
defending schemes like the Bank of North America.

Paine's persistent claim that only gold and silver are real money may seem
to some reminiscent of the mercantilist claim that wealth consists in the quantity
of specie. Aldridge claims 'Paine's economics are now outmoded. Virtually a
mercantilist, he considered gold and silver as the only form of capital'.[47] On the
other hand, Paine sometimes suggests that land is the only real wealth and often
recognised the value of labour and trade. But to say that gold and silver are the
only real money is not to say that wealth consists in specie. The importance Paine
placed on metallic money does not necessarily entail his believing that silver and
gold have intrinsic value in the way that land and commodities do. Money is
simply an object capable of storing of value in virtue of its recognition as a
medium of exchange. As Locke points out the value of money is entirely based
on a tacit agreement that it is valuable. Deflating paper currency was not an
efficient store of value, while the Spanish silver dollar maintained its value
according to the weight of silver it contained. A silver dollar might be valued
differently in England or Maryland but could nevertheless be exchanged for

---

[45] Foner, *Revolutionary America*, pp. 183-4.
[46] I am grateful for these images provided by the Smithsonian Institution, NNC, Douglas Mudd
and the Museum of the Bank of England.

goods in either place. To sell someone a piece of paper which can be exchanged for silver is vastly different from giving them a piece of paper with which they can pay taxes in a particular state that might soon no longer exist. This is not to accord silver coins intrinsic value, only to recognise its relative efficiency as money in the context of eighteenth century international trade and revolutionary upheaval.

Paine attacks paper money on the grounds of freedom, particularly unsupported notes and tender laws. Firstly, when backed by tender laws, paper money violated freedom of the individual and his right to property. The issue of Continental paper money was necessary for the war effort but Paine likens the devaluation of the currency to a tax on users of the money for the expense of the war.[48] Hence his distinction between Bank of North America notes convertible into specie and state-issue notes secured only by tender laws.[49] The depreciating value of government payments amounts to a form of unauthorised taxation.

Tender laws compelling traders to accept paper money at the same value as specie, forced them to sell goods at a lower value, giving part of their property to support the government. Such laws were, in his view, unconstitutional and arbitrary.[50] For Paine, freedom includes freedom from arbitrary taxation and thus also from the inflationary effects of irresponsible issues of paper money subject to tender laws. He is defending the right of an individual trader to make wise bargains on his own terms against the right of the government to raise funds in this way: 'A tender law [...] operates to take away a man's share of civil and natural freedom, and to render property insecure'.[51] Remarkably, considering his Quaker background, Paine goes so far as to suggest a death penalty for even

---

[47] Aldridge, *Man of Reason*, p. 121.
[48] 'Letter to the Abbé Raynal, on the Affairs of North America: in which the Mistakes in the Abbé's Account of the Revolution of America are Corrected and Cleared up' (August 1782), *Writings*, II, 89.
[49] See below p. 313.
[50] See below p. 316.
[51] See below p. 356.

proposing a tender law. His suggestion is no doubt intended ironically, reminding the reader of the equivalent harsh punishment for forgery, often printed on the notes themselves. Like forgery, tender laws force the seller to accept worthless money.[52]

The attack on paper money is continued in *Prospects on the Rubicon* in which he warns England that its reliance on paper money weakens the country in a potential war with France. In *The Decline and Fall of the English System of Finance* in 1796, Paine criticises the Bank of England and predicts the suspension of payments in gold in 1797. He describes two experiments in paper money; in America, continental money, and in France, the *assignats*, both of which resulted in devaluation. Paper money depends on tender laws for the confidence needed to support it; gold and silver rely on their natural scarcity for confidence. Not only will paper money crowd out specie, which will be used primarily for foreign commerce, but also by causing inflation it will devalue specie itself. The English financial system would work in the same way as paper money because the Bank of England issues notes secured not by gold and silver but on the National Debt.

Paine's position on public debt seems somewhat inconstant. In *Common Sense,* he sees the national debt as a vital part of the defence of America and the building of the new Republic. Even here, however, he thinks interest payments on the debt are an unnecessary burden upon taxpayers.[53] Certainly Paine is not opposed to public debt on the same grounds as the English Country party; namely, that it would strengthen the monied interest and weaken the influence of the landed interest that alone could maintain republican virtue and freedom. Paine recognises that the extension of the national debt in Britain in fact lessened the tax burden on the landed gentry, many of whom also dealt in government stocks. Paine was aware of Adam Smith's criticism of the English national debt and condemned the exponential increase due to constant war costs and unnecessary

---

[52] Paine has often been assumed to be against the death penalty on principle, and this is thought to influence his appeal against the execution of Louis XVI. See below p. 317 & above p. 44.

[53] See below p. 124.

placemen. The burden of the debt fell on poor or middle class taxpayers of the next generation who could not benefit from, or control, the mounting liability. Again Paine connects the debt to freedom of the individual. It was a violation of the freedom of English men and women to raise taxes to pay such an unnecessary debt.

The Ethical Basis of Paine's Laissez-Faire Economics

It has long been acknowledged that Paine shares many of the ideas of the Physiocrat *laissez-faire* and the Scottish philosophers' free-market systems.[54] Any consideration of Paine's sources is hampered by his own claim not to have used any but to have arrived at his ideas independently. Certainly Paine's later work exhibits a debt to Smith, who is extensively cited in the *Decline and Fall of the English System of Finance* and *Rights of Man*.[55] Paine's free-market ideas can be found in his writings as early as January 1776, as we shall see in Chapter One. *The Wealth of Nations* appeared in London on 9 March and could not have appeared in America until April. Harry Hayden Clark asserts that Paine's economic ideas correspond closely to the Physiocrats and it is certainly possible that he had been exposed to these ideas either by reading or by osmosis during political debate in the taverns and newspapers.[56]

Physiocracy would suggest an emphasis on land as the source of wealth, which Clark exaggerates in Paine's writings. Certainly, in his American writings, Paine does emphasise land as the source of *American* wealth, as it is the one good that America has in plentiful supply.[57] Paine often proposed government revenue

---

[54] See J. Appleby, *Capitalism and a New Social Order: The Republican Vision of the 1790's* (New York: New York University Press, 1984); Claeys, *Thomas Paine*, pp. 96-7; Foner, *Revolutionary America*, pp. 153-6; Harry H. Clark, 'Toward a Reinterpretation of Thomas Paine,' *American Literature*, V (May 1933), 133-45.

[55] Paine also refers to Quesnay and Turgot's 'moral maxims and systems of economy' in 'Rights of Man' (1791), *Writings*, II, 334-336.

[56] Aldridge also sees Paine as close to the Physiocrats, see Aldridge, *American Ideology*, p. 52; Clark, 'Toward a Reinterpretation', 133-45; Claeys, *Thomas Paine*, p. 97.

[57] See below p. 200.

through the sale of vacant land would be preferable to public debt or more taxes. But this dependence on land works only in America where it is plentiful and unoccupied. Paine's *Agrarian Justice* is notably anti-agrarian. It does not propose a redistribution of existing land holdings, but rather suggests that redistributed mobile capital may adequately substitute for the lost right to the land. Paine's apparent preoccupation with the needs of the farmers more often expresses the unity of interests between agriculture and trade. In the bank crisis letters we find Paine trying to convince the farmer that his prosperity depends on new financial institutions and the circulation of new forms of wealth, precisely because Paine recognises that land on its own will not increase wealth without a market for its products. In *Crisis III,* he claims that freedom of trade is 'an article of such importance, that the principal source of wealth depends upon it'[58]

It is possible that Paine was exposed to the ideas of the earlier Scottish enlightenment thinkers through his contact in London with natural scientists Benjamin Martin and James Ferguson and with the American philosophers, Franklin, Jefferson and Rush. The free-market critique of mercantilism can certainly be found in the writings of Hutcheson, Hume, Kames and Adam Ferguson.[59] As Richard F. Teichgraeber has shown, the economic ideas of Smith, Hume and Hutcheson are distinctively located in their naturalistic moral philosophy. For Hume and Smith, morality is founded in sentiment, rather than reason. This sentiment was in effect a natural sociability. In part then, the system of natural liberty is a moral system in which the mutual reciprocity of interests is satisfied by trade. Far from being inimical to virtue, trade for Smith and Hume is

---

[58] 'Crisis III' (1777) *Writings,* I, 204.
[59] Paine might also have drawn free-trade arguments from Joseph Priestley (1733-1804). See Claeys, *Thomas Paine,* p. 18 and G. Claeys, 'Virtuous Commerce and Free Theology: Political Economy and the Dissenting Academies 1750-1800', *History of Political Thought,* 20:1 (1999), 141-172. While it is certainly possible that Paine had come across Adam Ferguson's *Essay on Civil Society* (1767), Ferguson's association with the 'Common Sense' school of moral philosophy cannot be the origin of Paine's favourite pseudonym. For one thing, it was, by Rush's account, his suggestion that Paine adopt this title for his famous pamphlet, while Paine himself preferred 'Plain Truth', a pseudonym later adopted by one of his most virulent critics. See Aldridge, *American Ideology,* p. 37 & pp. 179-190.

one of the sources of morality.[60]   Paine's thought rarely touches upon moral philosophy, in fact he hardly mentions virtue at all, let alone discusses its origin. But it is remarkable that in his early writings his primary appeal is to sentiment rather than reason. The ethical justification for free trade provided by the Scottish thinkers provides a useful background for locating Paine's economic arguments within his political philosophy. Trade is for Paine, far from being a vice, a force that unites public and private interest between members of society and between countries and thus contributes to civilisation.

Paine's belief in society's ability to govern itself is based on his natural law ethics. Paine, like Adam Smith, envisaged society as an economic machine created by nature to satisfy man's wants through the medium of exchange. Paine's distinction between society and government is at the core of both his political and his economic ideas. Society can function for a short time without the monopoly of coercion in an established government. Paine's social contract precedes the establishment of government; no Leviathan enforcer is needed to establish the relationship of trust and obligation.   Morality, obligation and promise keeping exist prior to government; these are a product of society rather than government. Only the inevitable development of vice occasions the need for government: 'the badge of lost innocence.'[61]

Society is a natural organisation which stems from a 'natural aptness in man.' Mutual dependence and reciprocal interest hold the community together through a great chain of connection. This natural society arises from man's character, that of being unable to survive without the aid of society. It is governed by natural law created by these interests; thus the natural laws of society are the laws of the market based on self-interest. These natural laws arise not out of human convention but out of the natural characters of man himself. They are scientific laws which can be discovered by experience, working on objects in

---

[60] Teichgraeber, Free *Trade*, pp. 1-29.
[61] See 'Rights of Man II' (1792); 'Rights of Man' (1791), *Writings*, II, 406 & 309.

nature: man's needs and desires and the products that satisfy them. Thus Adam Smith's *The Wealth of Nations* describes the economic laws of society in the same way that Newton's *Principia* describes the physical laws of the universe.[62] That Paine saw society as an exchange mechanism based on interests, that is a free market, demonstrates that his economic theory was essentially a *laissez-faire* view. These natural laws also form the basis of government since Paine consistently claims 'that government is nothing more than a National Association acting on the principles of society.' [63] Government, whilst necessary, is best when it is limited to protecting the market.

Paine opposes price-fixing, unsupported paper money, increases in the English national debt, and supports the development of capitalist institutions that would aid the economic development of the new United States of America. The free market is not simply a matter of free trade between nations, but between men. Like Adam Smith, Paine believes the free market could work for the oppressed workers as well as the merchants and factory owners by allowing them to bargain for higher wages. He deplores the feudal practices of Europe; the guilds, the merchant monopolies, the Royal Charters, and he rejoices in the economic rights to be guaranteed by the new French Constitution to pursue any occupation in any place.[64]

Paine's emphasis on the sanctity of contract reveals the need for government in his conception of economic freedom. For it would seem that even if society has natural self-regulating forces, government, and therefore some taxation, is necessary. However, one of Paine's concerns is the stability necessary for bargains to be made. If a government can disrupt this stability arbitrarily, trust will evaporate and the self-regulating market becomes Hobbes's state of nature.

---

[62] Harry H. Clark links Paine's *laissez-faire* view to his 'Newtonian-Deist' religious belief shared by others in his circle such as Franklin, Jefferson and Barlow. See Clark, 'Toward a Reinterpretation', 133-45.
[63] 'Rights of Man II' (1792), *Writings*, II, 410-11.
[64] See below p. 503, 'Address and Declaration to our Fellow Citizens (20 August 1791), 'Rights of Man' (1791), *Writings*, II, 256 & 313.

Paine makes a clear connection between stable, predictable governments and capitalist development: 'A faithless arbitrary government cannot be trusted, and therefore in free countries only are Banks established'.[65] Freedom from cheats and from arbitrary, partial government is nevertheless situated within a market society with a limited republican government.

Welfare and the Right to Property

From this interpretation of Paine's economics, one might conclude that he holds a liberal, *laissez-faire* view. Certainly, he departs radically from the classical republican view that commerce and competition are a dangerous vice that could destroy the civic virtue upon which a republic depends. He appears to have taken on board the Lockean view of private property rights, entailing limited government and security of property, including freedom of acquisition, investment and exchange. Paine's desire for minimal government interference in the economy continues into his later works, even those which include welfare proposals. Much of 'Ways and Means' is taken up with reforms to reduce the tax and national debt burden on the middle class and poor. Paine argues that existing European hereditary governments are unnecessarily expensive, while the American republican government costs very little.[66] High levels of taxation in England were not only excessive but were not even being used to provide the necessary government services. Such iniquity lead to a revolution in France and might also in England if Parliament did not reform itself. The landowners and monied interest were using war and debt to fill their own pockets at the expense of the mass of citizens, who could do nothing while they were prevented from voting. This kind of *unnecessary* taxation is tyranny.

---

[65] See below p. 297.
[66] 'Rights of Man II' (1792), *Writings*, II, 427.

'Ways and Means' offers a detailed budget cutting programme designed to lessen the burden of taxation on the poor and the middle classes. He proposes spending cuts and the abolition of the commutation tax, duties on essentials such as candles and the poor rates. Instead, a new progressive tax on estates is levied for distribution to the poor. He suggests child benefit, a national education system, old-age pensions, one-off payments for births and marriages and workhouses in London. Paine's plan is not only to redistribute money but also to save it. It does, however, depend on some wild assumptions: that only the needy will claim benefits and that the expensive wars of the previous two centuries will cease under a reformed republican government. The progressive income tax is proposed to encourage large landowners to abandon primogeniture, so it will no longer be necessary for the younger sons to seek places salaried by taxes on the middle classes. These places are typical of the unnecessary level of government Paine is opposed to.

Rights of Man Part Second offers little justification for taking taxes from the rich to give to the poor. After all, the point he is making here is that just the reverse has been practised for centuries and reform would be cheaper and provide a freer, happier society. He does not imagine that there would be any objection to paying fewer taxes for a just welfare system rather than more taxes for unnecessary wars. His calculations are designed to show that the English could have a cheaper, less extensive government and still have tax money left over to give to the old and poor who suffer under the present regime. His aim remains limited, minimal government, allowing each man 'to pursue his occupation, and to enjoy the fruits of his labours and the produce of his property in peace and safety, and with the least possible expense.'[67]

Agrarian Justice proposes a simpler welfare system, designed not just for England but for any free country. A national fund is created from an inheritance tax to provide capital payments to every *person* at the age of twenty-one and an

---

[67] 'Rights of Man II' (1792), *Writings*, II, 443.

annual pension of ten pounds over fifty years of age. These welfare plans give rise to one of the most discussed problems in Paine's works. If Paine holds this theory of minimal government throughout his life, how can he, in the same works, suggest enforced redistribution of wealth from rich to poor? In the liberal defence of private property, taken from Locke, the natural right to property is derived from the right to the fruits of one's own labour, which, in turn, is derived from the natural right to one's own body. Surely, as Robert Nozick argues, any form of redistribution of resources from enforced taxation infringes upon the freedom of the individual to decide how his property is used, and if this property is generated by labour, this amounts to a form of slavery.[68] The libertarian view of minimal government restricts government spending only to the defensive and protective night-watchman functions that the state was instituted to perform. But what gives the night-watchman the right to force those individuals who benefit from protection and other community goods to pay for them if they did not consent to be protected? It is to this right that Paine is appealing in his welfare plans. Paine argues that these transfer payments are a form of compensation for past infringements on property and contract. In enforcing this compensation on those who benefit from the system of private property, the state is simply acting as a night-watchman.[69]

As the earth belonged originally to all men in common, the institution of private property without compensation to the dispossessed is a violation of that common property right. Nozick and Locke argue that the institution of capitalism is sufficient compensation for loss of the natural right to common property. Paine insists that if this were so he would not witness such misery around him. Further, he argues that the accumulation of capital would not be possible without the market which society supplies so that society is also due a cut in the profits for

---

[68] See Robert Nozick, *Anarchy State and Utopia* (Oxford: Blackwell, 1974; repr. 1986).

[69] The modernity of Paine's welfare proposals is emphasised by Philp's suggestion that Paine's theory of social justice in *Agrarian Justice* can be compared to John Rawls, *A Theory of Justice* (Oxford: Oxford University Press, 1972; repr. 1986). See Philp, *Paine*, p. 91 and below pp. 457-.

use of the market. These debts are to be paid with minimal interference to property holdings by way of an inheritance tax into a fund administered by a national bank. Paine argues that his welfare benefits are rights not gifts.[70] He derives this right from the natural right to the earth. These rights are consistent with the right to property upon which economic freedom is based. Paine is not asking the individual to give up the fruits of his labour or the improvement value of the land but only the rent he owes on the natural condition of the resources taken from the common stock plus a service charge for the use of the capitalist market economy. Therefore, the labour-based property rights of the individual, which Locke derives from the individual's ownership of his own body, are not infringed. Further, if a government were to enforce these compensation claims, it would simply be enforcing what would have been a fair contract at the institution of private property if it were ever possible to set up a voluntary contract between all people present and future.[71]

Agrarian Justice is anti-agrarianism: we cannot return to or forever remain in a society of equal land holdings. Private landed property allows great improvements in the quality and quantity of human life but, in order that it can be compatible with the common ownership of the natural earth, it requires compensation to be paid to future generations who arrive with no share in their

---

[70] Claeys argues that Paine's argument in *Agrarian Justice* shares much of the language and assumptions of the natural law theory of a social obligation to regulate property which is at the root of the moral economy attitude. In tracing Paine's welfare proposals back to earlier jurisprudential arguments for a right to subsistence and charity, Claeys tends to discount the originality of Paine's system of welfare payments from an enforced tax on private landed property and his insistence that these payments are due as a right, not as charity. However, Claeys does recognise that this represents 'a step of immense importance in the history of ideas of public welfare.' See Claeys, *Thomas Paine*, pp. 96-101 & 203-6. The effect of Paine's argument is not only to secularise the right to subsistence, as Claeys suggests, but also to politicise it. Although there is a moral element to Paine's argument, he is mainly contending for these rights on the political grounds of justice. That is, it is not only that the donors have a moral duty to provide, but also, more importantly, the recipients have a right to receive welfare. Where this right is violated, it is as much a violation of property rights as the non-payment of contractually binding debts. It is the purpose of government to enforce these rights legally, rather than the moral duty of an individual or society to provide charity to the poor.

[71] A thorough analysis of Paine's theory of property and distributive justice is given in Chapter 5 below.

natural inheritance. Government is necessary to protect these rights and thereby safeguard the freedom of all. This government intervention is therefore no different from the enforcement of fair bargains that Paine defended during the bank crisis, and it is not incompatible with minimal government. Paine's economic theory is thus a modified version of the natural liberty of Adam Smith. An individual should be free to buy and sell property at the market price and accumulate wealth through labour and capital investment as long as he/she is willing to pay the compensation due to society at the end of his/her life. Therefore Paine's list of economic rights would be longer than that of his *laissez-faire* contemporaries or 'right-libertarian' philosophers today and might include a right to education, an old age pension, some starting capital, but would also include the right to make unrestricted bargains and the right to property accumulated through labour, improvement and exchange.[72] The principal difference between Paine and Locke's theory of property is then only that Paine extends this protection further to include the compensation necessary to protect every one's natural right to the earth.

Socialism

Paine's contribution to socialist thought cannot be ignored. He was one of the first to offer concrete proposals for a welfare state. Arousing the political and economic consciousness of the working class, by directing his principle works at a much larger audience than his contemporaries, he can still be considered by socialists as a defender of the people. Michael Foot and Isaac Kramnick in their introduction to his major writings remind us that:

> Trapped as he was by the limitations of liberal social theory from seeing non-governmental threats to freedom, equality and democracy, confined as he was to seeing society only in terms of

---

[72] 'Left-libertarians', on the other hand, often embrace and extend Paine's conception of economic freedom. See below p. 460.

competitive individualism, it still bears repeating that there have
been precious few in the liberal camp who so passionately
assaulted privilege as Paine did. Few liberals were so fervently
committed to democracy and egalitarianism[73]

Paine's welfare society is very different from the socialist version. Socialists

typically advocate nationalisation of the means of production and government

regulation while Paine has faith in the market to perform most of the necessary

tasks of a centralised economy. Typically socialists hold an organic conception of

society, while Paine shares the individualist conception of the liberal tradition.

He does assume that there will be a shared conception of the public good but

certainly offers no talk of a universal class with universal interests.

It is not only modern socialists who criticise Paine's welfare state because

it does not go far enough. Thomas Spence (1750-1814) launched a scathing

attack on *Agrarian Justice* because it did not advocate land nationalisation.

Spence claims that Paine's *Agrarian Justice* involves the people selling their

birthright 'for a mess of porridge, by accepting of a paltry consideration in lieu of

their rights.'[74]   Spence, instead, offers a program in which all land is to be

controlled by parish councils who would rent out resources to citizens and use the

receipts to provide government services. He does not reject the market entirely,

but uses market forces in deciding the distribution of tenancies tendered to the

highest bidder. But Spence's economy is primarily rural; the principal resource

that the parish has is the land, not its population. Paine recognised that progress

in economic organisation through trade and manufacturing, cultivation and

technology increased the population. There was no hope of returning to the

agricultural economy of the feudal system with elected parish councillors as

landlords instead of aristocrats, which is essentially what Spence proposes.

---

[73] *Thomas Paine Reader*, ed. by M. Foot & I. Kramnick (London: Penguin, 1987) p. 28.

[74] Thomas Spence, *The Rights of Infants; in a dialogue between the Aristocracy and a Mother of children: to which are added, Strictures on Paine's Agrarian Justice*, (London: Spence, 1797) p. 11. A useful account of Spence's thought is given in Malcolm Chase, *The People's Farm: English Radical Agrarianism 1775-1840* (Oxford: Clarendon, 1988).

Instead, we have to enjoy the benefits of progress and minimise the disadvantages.

Paine's recognition of the benefits of *laissez-faire* was fostered by his experience in Philadelphia when many farmers and artisans still looked back to the days of the moral (feudal) economy. It was the paternalistic, communitarian ideas of this tradition that were adopted by early socialists such as Robert Owen, rather than the liberal, rights-based individualism which Paine and Spence shared. Paine avoided the threshold of socialism, providing us with a justification for welfare payments without subordinating the individual to an all-encompassing State. His welfare payments are characteristically capitalist; he never proposes nationalisation of the means of production, and he recognises that commerce is far better at satisfying men's wants than either a feudal or a centralised economy.

IV

Are Liberty and Democracy Consistent?

At the beginning of this introduction I set out three problems in interpreting Paine's political thought that depend on his views on such issues as paper money, public debt and welfare benefits. I have shown firstly that Paine held a *laissez-faire* view of political economy that is consistent with his attitude to money, public debt and taxation. It is also evident that we can draw from these texts a conception of economic freedom, based on the right of the individual to dispose of his property as he wishes and the sanctity of contract. Paine's welfare proposals, far from challenging this conception of freedom, are drawn from it. However, this concept of freedom does challenge Paine's undying support for representative democracy. Paine's economic ideas raise the second problem I have identified in interpreting Paine's political thought: whether individual freedom has priority over the will of the majority. This is of course a general problem for any believer in natural rights. Other natural rights, such as freedom of speech and freedom of religious practice present a similar challenge to democracy, but it was the defence of economic freedom that caused Paine to doubt his unlimited faith in representative government.

Representation and Democracy

Paine's support for democracy distinguishes his work from his contemporaries. Douglass shows that, while it was not unusual for a writer in the American Revolution to appeal to popular sovereignty, few continued to support democracy without qualification once independence was established.[1] In the decades following the Declaration of Independence, it was the idea of mixed government, in which representative government with only limited suffrage played a part, that won the day. This was not Paine's idea of the new age of democracy but John Adams's (1735-1826) more conservative model, set out in *Thoughts on Government* and incorporated into the state constitutions of Massachusetts, North Carolina, Virginia, New York and New Jersey.[2]

Paine opposes the adoption of the checks and balances in the British mixed constitution, both in the interest-based form of King, Lords and Commons and the American variant form, the balance of separated powers embodied in the bicameral legislature. Legitimate power does not need to be checked. Paine does not see democracy as a form of government that can be accepted only in a qualified form, and yet he does not abandon the concern for individual liberty in embracing democracy, and maintains a liberal Lockean concern for limited government. Paine's political theory is uncommon in that it fails to give priority to democracy or individual liberty in the event of a conflict such as the bank crisis. Given the status of the word at this time, it is perhaps not surprising that Paine rarely uses the term *democracy*, preferring to call his system *representative government*. Paine also uses the term *republican government* to describe representative government within a constitutional framework, which is itself subject to democratic control. This term is perhaps closer to the modern term *liberal democracy* in that it subjects the power of the majority to constitutional limits designed to protect liberty.

Paine values representative government instrumentally on the grounds of public interest or justice, as the most rational form of government and therefore the most efficient in protecting natural rights and individual liberty. If this was

---

[1] Elisha P. Douglass, *Rebels and Democrats: The Struggle for Equal Political Rights and Majority Rule during the American Revolution* (Chicago: Elephant Paperbacks, 1955; repr. 1989), p. 13.
[2] See Douglass, *Rebels and Democrats*, pp. 21-22.

the limit of his argument for democracy, then clearly, like most liberals, he would agree that whenever this was not so, that is, when individual liberty or natural rights were threatened by democracy itself, then liberty should prevail. But Paine also sees representative government as an intrinsic value, based on an inviolable natural right to govern oneself. Paine often suggests that the right to democracy is a collective right, using terms such as the right of a nation to choose, the will of a nation, the right of a generation or a people.[3] Paine also often suggests than individuals have a right to vote, which he describes as 'sacred', fundamental and owed to man in virtue of his existence. The status of this right is curious and will require a detailed examination.

Paine clearly rejected the classical republican link between property and citizen virtue, arguing against voting qualifications based on property ownership, on the grounds that wealth is ephemeral and often a matter of chance.[4] The

---

[3] A few examples include 'Address and Declaration' (1791); 'Rights of Man' (1791); 'Rights of Man II' (1792), *Writings*, II, 253-4, 361 & 442.

[4] See 'Rights of Man' (1791) & 'First Principles' (1795), *Writings*, II, 306, III, 265. Paine did however entertain the idea of exclusion on other grounds. Early works suggest that there were exceptions to the principle of equal suffrage on the grounds of dependence. In addition, during the War of Independence, Paine demands the exclusion of Tories from voting on the grounds that it would be 'unnatural and impolitic' to include those opposed to the nation's independent existence. It is not unusual to exclude parties who aim at revolution from the electoral process but it does suggest that the individual right to vote can be taken away. This would suggest that the right to vote was not a natural right but a right that is granted by society. After all, American Tories in 1777 are human. Tories were effectively excluded from the franchise in the Pennsylvania Constitution of 1776 by the Test Oath declaring non-allegiance to George III and a commitment to the establishment of a popular government. See 'Crisis III' (1777), *Writings*, I, 200-201 & Selsam, *The Pennsylvania Constitution*, pp. 138-9. In the following year, Paine also suggests the exclusion of criminals from voting and, more controversially, the exclusion of public and private servants from suffrage on the grounds that they cannot have sufficient independence. He argues that their ineligibility is by choice, and that as soon as 'they reassume their original independent character of a man and encounter the world in their own persons, they repossess the full share of freedom appertaining to the character.' The principle he is upholding is that 'no involuntary circumstance or situation in life can deprive a man of freedom'. This would seem to suggest that a man can give up his *civil* rights voluntarily, at least temporarily. See 'A Serious Address to the People of Pennsylvania on the Present Situation of their Affairs' (December 1778), in P. S. Foner, *Complete Writings*, II, 287. However, these exceptions are suggested within the context of an appeal for universal suffrage and a lifting of property qualifications in Pennsylvania. *A Serious Address* was intended to support the wide franchise provided in the Pennsylvania constitution against its critics who thought the constitution 'too free', that is, they thought the suffrage too extensive. Paine was merely trying to justify existing exclusions given the preceding argument for equality of rights. Private servants were excluded as they did not pay direct taxes independently

republican tradition argued that civic virtue, on which the survival of the republic depended, required that citizens were independent in that they already owned sufficient property to be immune to corruption. Paine rejects the link between wealth and virtuous independence and the idea that land needs special representation. Land as an interest 'enjoys the general protection of the world.'[5] At the same time, Paine appeals to the link between property and suffrage in his argument that all members of society have some property in their labour, their body and their equal share in the natural property of the undeveloped earth. In *Rights of Man*, Paine argues that everyone owns some property because they each own a share in the government itself. Everyone has a right to vote in the same way as shareholders have a right to vote at the annual general meeting of a company, the resources of which they jointly own. The right to vote becomes a species of property itself, just like a share certificate, so that to exclude some members amounts to robbery.[6]

Paine often suggests that suffrage ought to be linked to tax payments but claims that everyone should be included as all pay indirect taxation.[7] When voting rights in France were restricted to direct tax payers, Paine asks the Convention: 'What designation do you mean to give the rest of the people?'

---

of their masters, but there does not seem to have been an exclusion of public servants in the constitution of 1776. See 'A Serious Address' (1778), P. S. Foner, *Complete Writings*, II, 289.; 'Letter to the Addressers' (1792) & 'First Principles' (1795), *Writings*, III, 88 & 266-8.

[5] See below p. 473 and 'First Principles' (1795), *Writings*, III, 267.

[6] See 'Rights of Man II' (1792) & 'First Principles' (1795), *Writings*, II, 428, 501, III, 269, 265. See also 'A Serious Address' (1778), P. S. Foner, *Complete Writings*, II, 286-7. Unlike voters, shareholders can hold more than one vote according to their investment. Paine assumes that all hold equal shares in the government, but the investment each of us contributes in taxation is varied. Such a principle could lead Paine to a caricature of Mill's plural voting system where, rather than the intelligentsia enjoying extra votes, each voter could hold one vote for each pound they paid in tax. This could, I suppose, be used to justify plural voting systems, such as in nineteenth century Britain, lasting until 1906, where owners of business enjoyed voting rights, both in the constituency where they lived and in the location of their business premises. See M. Pearce & G. Stewart, *British Political History 1867-1990: Democracy and Decline* (London: Routledge, 1992), p. 188.

[7] 'Letter to the Addressers' (1792), *Writings*, III, 75.

suggesting that the denial of citizenship is a denial of their humanity.[8] Paine is asserting that suffrage is one of the rights owed to man by virtue of his humanity. What sense can we make of this claim? The right to vote cannot be a natural right, as voting and elections are dependent on the existence of a society to be governed.[9] Paine's fundamental right to vote is a civil right founded on a natural right to self-rule or self-ownership. Freedom from slavery is thus the basis for the civil right to participate in the decision-making processes. In any society, the right to self-rule is unenforceable and the necessary evil of government is required to arbitrate between men. The power to execute one's self-rule is lost and so the civil right of participation is required to fill this void.[10] Representative government is the only legitimate way of making collective decisions because it is the only way that recognises the equality of this right.[11] The right to vote creates in Paine's political theory an intrinsic relationship between liberty and

---

[8] 'The Constitution of 1795: Speech in the French National Convention' (7 July 1795), *Writings*, III, 280. The constitution of 1795 limited the franchise to citizens who paid any direct personal tax equivalent to three days work. By limiting the franchise of the 1792 constitution (and restoring the 1791 distinction between active citizens with political rights (direct tax-payers) and passive citizens with only civil rights) an estimated 1.5 million indirect tax-payers were disenfranchised. See I. Wolock, *The New Regime: Transformations of the French Civic Order 1789-1820's* (London: Norton, 1994) p. 81.

[9] See 'Rights of Man' (1791), 'First Principles' (1795), *Writings*, II, 306-7, III, 272.

[10] See 'First Principles' (1795), *Writings*, III, 272-3.

[11] See 'Letter to the Addressers' (1792), *Writings*, III, 91-2. This interpretation of Paine's justification for universal suffrage is useful as it opens some interesting questions concerning Paine's attitude to female suffrage. Paine's support for universal male suffrage through his religious belief in the natural equality of man may provide a clue to his attitude to the equality of the sexes. In several works, Paine claims that only distinctions between men and women are natural, while distinctions between economic classes are unnatural. See below p. 116 & p. 516; 'Rights of Man' (1791), *Writings*, II, 305. If only natural, divinely created difference can justify inequality, this might provide Paine with a reason for the exclusion of women from suffrage. Philp also suggests that Paine's willingness to deny women the vote may be linked to this claim of natural inequality, but he thinks 'it is inconceivable that he would accept the logic of his own argument which suggests that they are natural slaves!' See Philp, *Paine*, pp. 74-5. However, male and female are two types of one species - as distinct from other species of animals or things. Paine cannot deny that women are human. We could throw his question to the French Convention back at him - 'what designation do you mean to give the rest of the people?' In the Preface to *Agrarian Justice*, Paine follows his statement concerning the divine sexual distinction with the claim that 'he (God) gave them the earth for *their* inheritance.' (My emphasis.) Is it possible that we can detect a change in Paine's attitude to the equality of the sexes? His usually sexist use of the term 'man' is replaced by 'human' and 'person' in his statement of key principles. Further, women are

democracy. Exclusion from citizenship rights is equated with slavery: the absolute loss of personal freedom.[12] Self-ownership is removed without compensation in the form of civic participation. Paine derives these rights from what he believes to be the common features of humanity, (or at least adult maleness). A minimum level of rationality and an ability to understand the lessons of the Creation provide a moral status as a duty and rights bearer. Each of us belong to ourselves; we are not slaves, the property of other men.

The notion of natural rights, which supports Paine's justification for democracy, may not be as philosophically groundless as often suggested. Nevertheless, natural rights are universalist normative claims to truth and as such attract almost unanimous scepticism. Philp uses Habermas's theory of Discourse Ethics to show that Paine's natural rights, for example, to participation, free speech, association and freedom of conscience, can be understood as the procedural conditions of fairness in political discourse. Paine's political arguments are addressed to his readers as equals, conferring on them citizenship in the republic of political discourse. This citizenship carries with it all the essential elements of Paine's more abstract claims for natural rights. By attempting to persuade his readers of the truth of his claims, he recognises their natural right to judge for themselves and participate in a collective process, the outcome of which is determined by majority opinion.[13] To act rationally, a system of decision making must fit the conditions of communicative rationality. Discourse must be conducted fairly, according to the ideal speech situation that includes the condition of equality of participation. In Philp's view, the logic of these conditions is difficult to dispute: 'to do so would be to insist that force and fraud are essential to secure agreement on deliberative norms'.[14]

---

specifically included in his welfare proposals. They do after all pay indirect taxes from their labour. See below p. 518.
[12] 'First Principles' (1795), *Writings*, III, 267.
[13] Philp, *Paine*, pp. 115-117; Jürgen Habermas, 'Three Normative Models of Democracy', *Constellations* 1:1 (1994), 1-10.
[14] Philp, *Paine*, pp. 116-117.

Republican Government

Paine's idea of representative democracy was radical in its social inclusion and its rejection of the traditional republican principle that a balanced constitution was needed to check the dangerous tendencies of pure democracy. But it is wrong to say that Paine believed in pure unchecked democracy. He suggests two checks on the sovereignty of the majority. Firstly, representation itself is a device for ensuring that the most talented will be selected for government.[15] Secondly, Paine suggests that a *republican* government must be limited by a recognition of natural rights. Paine sets out his conception of republicanism in *Dissertation on Government* in reaction to the bank crisis, which directly challenged his faith in the rationality of democracy. Though the Pennsylvania Assembly was elected by a franchise that was remarkably broad for its time, it was capable of acting as arbitrarily and unjustly as a hereditary government. Democracy appeared to have borne out the warnings of those who favoured keeping elements of the mixed constitution to protect property against the tyranny of the majority.

In 1776, Paine contemplates a simple form of government consisting only of an assembly and a bill of rights, replacing the monarchs of Europe with the rule of law.[16] He is scathing of the concept of constitutional checks and balances, such as bicameralism.[17] Before 1786, Paine's constitutionalism is confused. Without checks and balances, the constitution lacks any institutional enforcement of its limits. The bank crisis forced Paine to set out his constitutional theory embodied

---

[15] See 'Rights of Man II' (1792), *Writings*, II, 420-21. Paine does not assume that the talented individuals who are chosen as representatives necessarily know more than their electors but they are forced by the electoral system to discuss issues with them: 'There is no doubt that discussion sheds light, and that a superior man may sometimes derive benefit from the ideas of a person less enlightened than himself.' See also 'Answer to Four Questions' (1791), *Writings*, II, 242.

[16] Paine was never in favour of wholly unlimited democracy. His early writings establish the need for constitutional limits on the power of the elected assembly. In *Common Sense*, he proposes a constitutional convention to frame a charter securing freedom, property, and religious freedom. See 'Common Sense: Addressed to the Inhabitants of America' (10 January 1776), *Writings*, I, 98.

[17] Paine's reconsideration of bicameralism is explored below p. 256.

in his earlier assertion that 'in America the law is king.'[18] In *Dissertation on Government*, Paine makes a distinction between representative government, the rule of the majority, and a republic. A republic is distinguished from a despotism by the location of sovereignty in the people rather than the despot but also by the principle on which the sovereign power is administered. Under despotism 'whatever the sovereign wills to do, [he has] the uncontrouled power of doing. He [...] makes the right and wrong himself and as he pleases.'[19] While this kind of power is, in Paine's view, suitable for armies that share a common purpose, nations are made up of individuals with a variety of mutual and conflicting interests and pursuits, the balance of which defines the common interest or public good.

The object of a republican administration is this public good: the collected good of individuals. This is the essence of republicanism for Paine, found in the origin of the word republic as 'the *public thing.*'[20] The foundation of public good is *justice* and its impartial administration, by which, Paine means the security of individual rights.[21] He defines a republic as a government in the interest of the public good rather than the interest of a single person, family or group. A republic is therefore not the same thing as a representative democracy; a republic is distinguished by a constitutional agreement to limit the power of government according to justice.[22] This distinction allows for the possibility of a democracy that is not a republic but elective despotism. Paine uses this argument to show that the assembly, in revoking the bank's charter, was exceeding its powers given in the Pennsylvania Constitution. This constitution represents an agreement by

---

[18] See 'Common Sense' (1776), *Writings*, I, 73. Compare to 'Answer to Four Questions' (1791), *Writings*, I, 99; II, 242-3.
[19] See below p. 273.
[20] 'Rights of Man II' (1792); 'Authors of *Le Républicain*' (1791), *Writings*, II, 421; III, 5.
[21] Paine seems to assume that the reader can understand the term justice uncontroversially. Injustice is described as a violation of a principle. That principle seems to apply to persons as individuals. The violation of this principle weakens the security of the individuals involved and therefore threatens the confidence of others that they will not be similarly violated. See below p. 276.
[22] See below p. 276.

the people to limit their collective power to the public good and the civil rights listed in that constitution embody these limits.

This principle of limited sovereignty seems to conflict with Paine's most useful tool in his quarrel with Burke: the right of each generation to govern itself.[23] A written constitution might well be thought of as one generation imposing a system of government on the next. Paine later insists that a successful constitution should be reviewed every seven years.[24] Rather than a hamstrung amendment procedure, Paine favours an alternative decision procedure, such as electing a special constitutional convention. This provides the stability required for good government without imposing a tyranny of the dead upon future generations. The 'rights of each generation' principle asserts that every new generation has the right to choose its own government. By this principle, Paine challenges the interpretation of Locke's theory of tacit consent which claims that the social contract of our ancestors can oblige us to obey. Paine's concept of consent is not capable of transfer by inheritance. As our natural rights belong to us by virtue of our existence rather than inheritance, our parents cannot give our rights up in a social contract. Paine not only rejects the terms of other conceptions of the social contract but also ridicules the idea that hereditary forms of government are based on consent at all, rather than on force and fraud.

As evidence for this, Paine employs his two weapons: right and reason. Firstly, no generation can have the right to establish a hereditary government by contract: the consent of their descendants is not theirs to give. Secondly, the irrationality of giving up one's rights to establish a contract that is binding for posterity suggests that agreement could only be achieved by deception. Paine's social contract is dynamic.[25] Every generation has the right to renew it and to

---

[23] See above p. 23 & below p. 302.

[24] This was included as an article in the Pennsylvania Constitution of 1776, so that whatever his involvement in the framework of that document, he would have been aware of the idea of including in a constitution a system for its revision.

[25] Paine does not himself use the expression 'social contract' but it is a useful shorthand for the general idea that a just or legitimate society must be grounded on principles which at least are

change it, and in doing so give their rational consent to be governed by it. The rationality of giving consent to government is dependent on the ability to change the form of government if it proves faulty. A written constitution created by a representative convention and containing amendment procedures allows each generation to exercise its right of consent to government, without recourse to revolution. The constitution can limit the collective power of the majority in a democracy, and yet, as long as it is not fixed in stone, it does not conflict with the right of each generation principle.[26]

Pieces of paper cannot hold the political ambitions of men in check, however powerful the rhetoric written upon them. Paine personifies the constitution, ignoring the fact it has to be interpreted and enforced by an institution such as the judiciary, which can then be said to be checking the power of the majority. Ultimately Paine believes that the people, being rational, will not allow the constitution to be corrupted by government interests and that the amendment procedure will satisfactorily protect against this by ensuring popular control of the constitution. The constitution belongs to the sovereign people. The government is subject to it and cannot change it.[27] The people are the only body that Paine trusts to uphold the constitution, by the pressure of public opinion, by voting out representatives who abuse their power, and in an emergency, by revolution against the usurpation of power.[28]

---

capable of being consented to by rational individuals. The social contract is some times described as an event, the origin of government, but also often described as being constantly renewed. See 'First Principles' (1795), *Writings*, III, 261. This conception of the conditions of legitimacy could be likened to the social discourse offered by Habermas, Ingram and others, where consent is developed through an on-going dialogue rather than a binding contractual agreement. See Attracta Ingram, *A Political Theory of Rights* (Oxford: Clarendon Press, 1994), pp. 119-120.

[26] See 'Rights of Man' (1791), *Writings*, II, 311. Paine describes the Pennsylvania constitution of 1776 as a perpetual constitution, because it includes the provision that a new convention be elected at the end of seven years to revise it. At this convention, this clause was itself revised and replaced by the right of the nation to alter the constitution whenever necessary - Paine preferred the former arrangement.

[27] 'Rights of Man II' (1792), *Writings*, II, 435.

[28] 'Anti-Monarchical Essay- For the Use of New Republicans' (October 1792), *Writings*, III, 108.

How then can he avoid the original problem of the tyranny of the majority? In order for the constitution to check the power of an elected assembly, it must be created and updated by a different assembly, mandated solely for this purpose, with no interest in government.[29] Democratic control over the constitution must be of a different character to that of the legislature, in the form of a constitutional convention. Although he must have been aware of the tendency in the American constitutional conventions for the same personalities to continue into government, Paine believes, because these representatives have no direct interest in the legislature, their decisions will be of a different character. The involvement of public opinion in the process is also crucial. All the proposed amendments were to be published and publicly debated before being either rejected or confirmed. Further, because their deliberations will be slow and public and because they will be addressing abstract and general rights, their decisions will be rational and based on principle rather than party interest.

The constitution must contain limits on public powers in the form of a list of civil rights.[30] Such a list of rights represents for Paine a set of principles agreed upon in the social contract, without which consent to government cannot be given. These principles distinguish a republic from despotism far more than representation.[31] The people when electing a constitutional convention must be thinking of these abstract principles and not ordinary acts of legislation and will therefore act rationally in universalising their needs as individuals into general principles which suit the public good. Paine does recognise the need to check democracy. This restraint of the majority, by the principles of justice outlined in the constitution, is what Paine means by republican government. Rather than being anti-democratic, the constitutional check on the majority is the expression of popular sovereignty in its original, constitutive capacity as an ongoing process of public debate. In this way, Paine ensures that each generation has the right to

---

[29] 'Rights of Man II' (1792), *Writings*, II, 445.
[30] 'Rights of Man' (1791), *Writings*, II, 310.
[31] 'Authors of *Le Républicain*' (1791), *Writings*, III, 9.

exercise its sovereignty without the need for revolution. Each generation can bind its own collective power, for a limited duration.[32]

This republican theory is Paine's response to the conflict between individual liberty and democracy. Paine is committed to democracy but nevertheless thinks the rule of the majority must be controlled by the constitution from whence they derived their power, in the name of sanctity of contract and other natural and civil rights that make up individual freedom. On the other hand, we cannot conclude from this that Paine gives priority to his conception of liberty over democracy. Paine avoids the problem of the undemocratic character of constitutional checks on the majority by putting the majority in charge of the constitution. Because he has an unbending faith in the universal light of reason, Paine ultimately gives priority to democracy over all other rights. He believes the rights he proposes are objective truths that will be perceived by all if the trouble is taken to consider the question deliberately and without bias and that if the majority consider the constitution in an open and free public debate they will defend their own liberty.

In so far as the constitution protects individual freedom, Paine's insistence on the right of a nation at any time to change its constitution again upsets the balance between liberty and democracy. Now it seems as though Paine gives priority to the rule of the majority over individual liberty, albeit in their

---

[32] Paine's view can be likened to John Rawls's *Theory of Justice* in which a hypothetical abstract original position is postulated where persons consider the principles of justice in complete ignorance of their actual particular circumstances. This veil of ignorance forces the participants to universalise the principles they consider without bias towards their particular situation. The conditions of the original position ensure that the principles of justice that are chosen are consistent with Kant's categorical imperative, that is, that they are universalised principles of morality. Paine often invokes this idea of universalising moral principles. For example, he warns the rich that property qualifications on suffrage may apply to them if they lose their money. See Rawls, *Theory of Justice* & 'A Serious Address' (1778), P. S. Foner, *Complete Writings*, II, 289. Similarly, the constitutional rights can be likened to the conditions of Habermas's ideal speech situation. The constitution thus sets up the conditions of democratic debate. The debate on the constitution is then a debate about the conditions of discourse. As the requirements of rational communication logically force the acceptance of certain norms of debate, the universalisation of individual rights is likely to achieve consensus, as Paine suggests. However, while it is clear how

constitutive capacity. What is to stop the majority changing the constitution to deny minority rights? Indeed nothing stopped the Constitutional Convention from excluding Negro slaves from equal civil rights in 1787. Paine's political theory is reduced to his belief in the progress of rationality. Democratic control of the constitution will secure individual freedom because it is rational to do so. As long as the process of constitution making and amending is based on equality of representation and reasoned public debate, when the majority consider the rights of man in abstract, the light of reason will prevail. If mistakes are made, they will be recognised and corrected by future generations. Paine denies the possibility that it is in the rational interest of the majority to deny the rights of the minority. Rather, when 'public matters are open to debate, and the public judgement free, it will not decide wrong, unless it decides too hastily.'[33] The balance between democracy and freedom in Paine's political theory depends on a theory of human nature that allows that voters, when presented with abstract questions of principle, will respond without the prejudice of particular interest. Any acceptance of Paine's political theory as consistent, in that he suggests that individual liberty and representative democracy are not only compatible, but also mutually conducive, depends therefore on our acceptance of the underlying claims about the capacity for abstract rational thought and the likelihood of its exercise.

National Sovereignty, Revolutionary War and Republican Freedom

So far, I have presented Paine's political theory as egalitarian and democratic. Paine saw his life's work as being dedicated to the cause of liberty.[34] There is, however, a great deal of difficulty in interpreting what Paine means by liberty. He uses the words liberty and freedom in a variety of ways and never sets out a

---

certain rights such as free speech and suffrage fit into this framework, the guarantee of fair contracts by the state is more difficult to explain. See above p. 73.

[33] 'Rights of Man II' (1792), *Writings*, II, 435.
[34] 'Appeal to the Convention' (August 1794), *Writings*, III, 147.

clear conception. As an interpreter, one has to admit that it may be that Paine never considered the question of what freedom actually means and, whilst using it to great rhetorical effect, he may also have used it inconsistently. We can group his references to liberty and freedom into three categories. Firstly, Paine often applies freedom to nationhood, particularly in the context of American independence. Secondly, he applies freedom to democracy, both collectively, in the nation and individually to the right to vote. Thirdly, he applies freedom to rights, sometimes applied to a nation governed by the rule of law and sometimes to the individual who enjoys freedom of speech, religion and property.

The conception of freedom as the attribute of a nation or polity is deeply rooted in the tradition of classical republican thought. Paine's idea of national independence can be described as freedom in two distinct ways. Firstly, Paine wanted freedom from colonial British rule. Secondly, he wanted freedom from George III and the flawed and corrupted English Constitution. In the first, the freedom is defined negatively by the absence of foreign rule; rule by an alien entity. In the second, the nation is free to govern itself without the imposition of a despot or an aristocratic class standing above and outside the community it rules. These two conceptions of national self-determination may be termed national sovereignty and popular sovereignty.

The combination in *Common Sense* of a call for independence with a call for representative democracy is fundamental to Paine's political theory. In Paine's republicanism, foreign conquerors and hereditary kings present the same evil. The artificial separation of the King from his people is a recurring theme in his attack on monarchy. Monarchs can have no understanding or shared interest with the people because the institution of monarchy depends on the myth of natural superiority to survive. The pomp and ceremony, the huge court expenses and aristocratic titles are designed to defraud the nation into believing that the ruling class are a different breed of men, separated from the nation, above the mass of people. A third conception of freedom also pervades Paine's writings. The freedom of the individual, embodied in his theory of natural and civil rights, is closer to the liberal tradition in which negative freedom is ascribed to individuals. In this conception of freedom, the community is presented not as the agent but as the obstacle to freedom (although often also the guarantor). Popular sovereignty may conflict with liberal individual freedom where the majority favours the infringement of the natural rights of a minority.

These three distinct conceptions of freedom combine to form Paine's unique blend of liberal republicanism. However, possible conflict between them suggests inconsistency. National sovereignty conflicts with both popular sovereignty and liberal individual freedom in cases where the invasion of one country is justified on the grounds of liberating the inhabitants from internal repression. Paine's anti-colonialism suggests a principle of national self-determination, albeit vaguely defined.[35] At the same time, Paine seeks to spread his revolutionary principles to other countries. Where the spread of revolutionary principles is coercive, that is achieved by military invasion, Paine could be accused of undermining this principle of national self-determination.[36] The most conspicuous example of Paine's readiness to abandon the idea of national sovereignty in favour of popular sovereignty is the advice he is supposed to have given to Napoleon Bonaparte on invading his native land. Dyck suggests that this plan in particular sullies Paine's claim to being a 'champion of the British people' or indeed a champion of freedom. This ignores the strength of Paine's critique of

---

[35] Even before his call for American independence in 1776, Paine's early magazine articles have a strong anti-colonialist theme. In 1775, he attacks the British role in the slave trade and Lord Clive's 'plunder' of India. In *A Serious Thought* he exposes the immorality of British Colonial rule; the cruelty in the East Indies, the use of American Indians as mercenaries and the taking of African Slaves. See 'African Slavery in America' (*Pennsylvania Journal*, 8 March 1775) & 'A Serious Thought' (*Pennsylvania Journal*, 18 October 1775), *Writings*, I, 4-9, 65-66. These early magazine articles are attributed to Paine by Conway and others, although there is insufficient evidence to be certain of their authorship. See Aldridge, *American Ideology*, pp. 286-291.

[36] Paine initially hoped the revolution would spread by the dissemination of ideas but supported and encouraged the invasion by French revolutionary armies of other countries as 'liberation'. See 'Letter to Raynal' (1782), 'Answer to Four Questions' (1791), 'Rights of Man' (1791), 'Rights of Man II' (1792), 'Address to the People of France' (September 1792), 'On the Propriety of Bringing Louis XVI to Trial' (Speech to the Convention, 21 November, 1792), 'The

monarchy as an oppressive regime.[37] Paine hoped that the revolution would spread to the whole of Europe because this would end the expensive and tragic wars by which the continent had been plagued since the development of the nation state. Republics would not go to war because the people would realise and express their common interest in peace and trade. Only monarchy requires perpetual wars to raise taxes, using the lives of their people as pawns in petty personal squabbles. Europe could eventually join together in a union like the United States and become one large republic ending all wars.[38] This would enhance the liberty of Europeans as a community but cannot be said to enhance national freedom, which would be subjugated to the will of the European majority. Dyck sees this project as anti-democratic, because he ignores the loftier aspirations of the federalist vision of both Paine and the contemporary pro-European left. Dyck claims that Paine 'would have mocked our insistence upon a

---

Eighteenth Fructidor: To the People of France and the French Armies' (September to November 1794), *Writings*, II, 124, 252, 278, 336, 393, III, 98, 115-117, 351 and below p. 151.

[37] On Paine's plans for invasion see Keane, *Paine*, pp. 440-444 & Ian Dyck, 'Local Attachments, National Identities and World Citizenship in the Thought of Thomas Paine', *History Workshop Journal*, 35 (1993), pp. 118, 121 & 130. Dyck suggests that Paine's encouragement of Napoleon was inconsistent with his claim that he never considered 'whether a thing is *popular* or *unpopular*, but whether it is *right* or *wrong*', as though Paine's motivation was to court the popularity of Napoleon. Making this judgement, Dyck can be criticised for the same error for which he faults Paine, that is, of not distinguishing between the government of a nation and the people. The popularity in question refers to the support of the majority, not of a personal patron, however powerful. Paine falsely believed that a revolution in Britain, even if sparked by a French invasion, would be popular, but more importantly he believed that it would be *right* for the people. In this context, in helping Napoleon plan the overthrow of the British government, Paine was championing the British people.

Paine defends his support for Napoleon's planned 'liberation' of England in two ways. Firstly, he believes that the English nation has no adequate voice to express its will and would rise up in revolution against the present government if the French invaded. Secondly, he argues that the conspiracy of European royal governments to destroy the French republic, and in particular the role of George III as Elector of Hanover in this conspiracy makes the government of Britain a matter of French interest. In Paine's opinion, 'that one nation has not a right to interfere in the internal government of another nation, is admitted...But whether an elector of the Germanic body shall be king of England is an external case, with which France has a right to interfere.' See 'Eighteenth Fructidor' (1794), *Writings*, 360.

[38] This idea of peace through democracy appears to be supported by recent scholarship. See Jack S. Levy, 'Domestic Politics and War', in *The Origin and Prevention of Major Wars*, ed. by R. Rothberg & T. Rabb (Cambridge: Cambridge University Press, 1989), pp. 79-100 & K. Doyle, 'Kant, Liberal Legacies, and Foreign Affairs', *Philosophy and Public Affairs* 12 (1983), 206-32.

democratic European Community' and would have seen our concerns about loss of sovereignty as 'a mere ruse to uphold and preserve British national identities'.[39]

National sovereignty was not Paine's primary purpose in the battle for self-determination. Rather he was fighting for national freedom defined by republican government. Freedom from British colonialism was only a means to the real American Revolution, a revolution in the form of government. Dyck argues that in his American writings, Paine places a greater importance on national sovereignty than on popular sovereignty, by defining citizenship in national terms, thus linking patriotism to the pursuit of independence and federalism, and only secondarily to democracy and republicanism. But Paine does not indicate which order of citizenship, of state or union, has priority. He argues that independence and republican freedom are inextricably linked because without freedom from foreign rule there is no possibility of democratic freedom.[40]

What then does Paine require for a nation to be free? He certainly means a nation being free from external rule but also suggests a wider conception of national freedom from despotism, foreign or domestic. In this sense, freedom is, for Paine, the right and the ability of a nation *as an association of individuals* to rule itself, implying popular sovereignty at least and perhaps also democracy. The liberal tradition of individual freedom presents further requirements on Paine's 'perfect and free' form of government. Individual freedom in the form of guarantees of natural and civil rights is balanced with the right of the majority to govern the whole through the constitution. Paine's distinct republicanism retains the pivotal role of the constitution in the republic whilst embracing democracy by giving the people control over the constitution itself. The free nation is thus free of foreign domination, and of internal despotism; a freedom ensured by a rational

---

For Paine's proposals for a 'European Congress' see Crisis X' (March 1782); 'Rights of Man' (1791), *Writings*, I, 340; II, 389.
[39] Dyck, 'Local Attachments', p. 118. Dyck's fears presuppose a limited vision of European union, which fails to recognise the possibility of a European democracy based on a constructed European people as opposed to a democracy between nations represented by their governments.
[40] See below p. 235.

and ethical, but democratically constructed, constitutional commitment to natural and civil rights.

The conflicts among these three ideas of liberty found in Paine's thought are still relevant to us today. The potential opposition between national sovereignty and democratic and individual freedom has a striking resonance with many international conflicts in which the principle of self-determination may prevent other nations from coming to the rescue of those who are oppressed by their own governments. This conflict is reflected in the intellectual struggle of the present age between universalist value systems and moral and political relativism. Paine's theory, unsurprisingly for a typical Enlightenment thinker, is unashamedly universalistic and supports arguments for increased international co-operation and recognition of the community of humanity.

Paine's conception of liberty can be understood on two distinct levels. On the one hand, he has a national or collective conception of liberty, which, far from being inconsistent with democracy, requires democratic and republican institutions. On the other hand, this republican liberty is dependent upon the guarantee of an individual conception of liberty in which *men* are guaranteed freedom from the imposed will of others, including the collective power. Both these conceptions of liberty are consistent with the concept of autonomy, acting according to rules of one's own making. The republic is free because it is limited by constitutional rules made by a democratic process in which all participate. The individual is free because constitutionally guaranteed rights allow him to pursue his own private interest autonomously and to participate in collective decisions which set the boundaries of his individual freedom. These two conceptions of freedom, national and individual, are not independent of each other. The perceived conflict between liberty and democracy is drawn from Rousseau's political theory in which the freedom of the individual is subsumed into the collective freedom of the republic. Paine, however, will not allow that citizens can be 'forced to be free'.[41] The freedom of the republic from the despotism of numbers is dependent on the recognition of individual freedom founded on objective natural rights. Paine thus gives priority to individual freedom over national freedom, although not over democracy as this is required by the individual right to vote.

The Terms of the Marriage: Paine's Republicanism Defended

Paine's political theory presents a third problematic issue for his interpreters. On the one hand Paine's free-market economics, his desire for minimal government and his natural rights foundation suggests that Paine is best interpreted as a classical liberal and thus is a remarkable precursor of the great liberal thinkers of the nineteenth century. On the other hand, Paine also exhibits a great debt to the republican tradition, particularly to the English commonwealth writers of the seventeenth century and to eighteenth century French republicans such as Montesquieu. Claeys interprets Paine's political theory as a combination of a commercial, natural rights tradition, which could be described as liberal, and democratic republicanism, which he dubs the 'American Marriage'.[42] Eric Foner also describes Paine's political theory as an inter-marriage of republican ideas of mass political participation and liberal ideas of the market economy.[43]

In a recent article Mark Philp argues that, rather than offering a radical form of republicanism, Paine's political thought 'shifts the debate about representation out of the republican paradigm and into a dramatically democratic and political egalitarian one.'[44] In part, Philp's argument is historical rather than interpretative. He argues that by couching his radical democratic ideals in the

---

[41] For Paine's view of Rousseau's conception of freedom see 'Rights of Man' (1791), *Writings*, II, 334-336.
[42] Claeys, *Thomas Paine*, p. 6.
[43] Foner, *Revolutionary America*, Ch. 5.
[44] Philp, 'English Republicanism', p. 252.

language of republicanism, Paine is partly responsible for the death of the latter tradition as the dominant paradigm in English thought and its replacement with the language of classical liberalism. Paine took the logic of republicanism, combined with the natural rights tradition, to its most egalitarian conclusion of equal rights and universal male suffrage. This conclusion proved too threatening to the vested interests of the ruling classes, who preferred instead the language of classical liberalism and its defence of property against the tyranny of the majority.

Philp also claims however that Paine's republicanism is limited to his support for representative democracy and anti-monarchism. He couples Paine with what he calls 'the popular or non-technical idiom' of republicanism as anti-monarchism, which can be dissociated from the classical republican tradition, which places its faith in the balanced constitution. It is certainly true that republicanism in England was associated with anti-monarchist ideas, and today in popular language is exclusively so. Republicanism survived through several centuries because of its adaptability to circumstance. Its primary concern is the accountability of power. In ancient democracies, republicans were concerned to limit the power of the majority. In Florence, Machiavelli was concerned to limit the power of the nobility and rich citizens. In England, the republicans' target was the Stuart monarchy that threatened to disrupt the balanced constitution and so in an English context republicanism became associated with anti-monarchy. Certainly this is suggested in Paine's writings until 1785 but, as we have seen above, the bank crisis forced Paine to concede the possibility of the 'despotism of numbers'. The new environment of democratic Philadelphia led Paine to develop his new brand of democratic republicanism, which he would later import to Europe.

Philp argues that Paine's concern to limit government and reduce taxation, and his welfare benefits, are expressly libertarian, and certainly that conclusion is borne out by an examination of the texts contained in this volume. Further he argues that Paine's distinction between society and government indicates a narrow view of politics, quite out of accordance with the classical republican concern for the *vivere civile*. Certainly there are good arguments for presenting Paine as a liberal rather than a republican. His use of the tradition of natural rights and his *laissez-faire* attitude to trade are documented above. Paine's attitude to paper money and public debt is quite out of character with republican concerns. He opposes paper money not because it is inimical to virtue but because it challenges individual freedom and private property. He specifically claims that limited national debt can be conducive to virtue.

On the other hand, we can also find evidence in his discussion of economic issues that his concerns are republican. Tax is a good example. The mercantilist tradition, in part responding to traditional English republican concerns, sought to use taxes to limit luxury, which was thought to threaten civic virtue. Luxuries encouraged citizens to put their private concerns ahead of the common good. Indeed Morris defended the Congress's five-percent duty partly on these grounds.[45] Paine does not employ this justification. Where he does suggest a duty on spirits, it is not on the grounds of morality but because he himself, famous for his enjoyment of brandy, wanted his enjoyment to support the Continental army.[46] Like other *laissez-faire* thinkers, Paine suggests that his own private vices, far from threatening the common good, can contribute to it through fiscal devices. On the other hand, Paine proposes taxes as a weapon against the imbalance of power. His libertarian arguments against taxes in *Rights of Man* defend legitimate private property, but his progressive tax on land is primarily aimed at reducing the inequality in holdings and the corruption of parliament engendered by primogeniture. This is a republican rather than a libertarian argument.

Paine's faith that public and private interests will be conjoined under representative government suggest that he can abandon the traditional republican concern that civic virtue, in the form of the sacrifice of private interest, is required

---

[45] See Continental Congress, *Journals*, XXII (1782), 429-43.
[46] See below p. 187.

to maintain the pursuit of the common good. His faith was challenged by corruption on numerous occasions. Paine's campaign against the war profiteering of Robert Morris and Silas Deane was pursued in spite of his personal interest. The pursuit of public good requires the watchful attentiveness of citizens willing to stand up to the vested interests of combined economic and political power. Paine often asserts his own independence, unfortunately not supported by historical evidence. In denying that he wrote for hire, we can discern a belief that financial dependence on others prevents an individual from expressing his opinions freely and thus impairs his right to participate in free political debate. Yet Paine rarely uses the language of republicanism. Virtue is mentioned in these texts only a handful of times. His republicanism is found not in his adoption of a paradigmatic discourse but in his concern for independence from all forms of domination.

My examination of the potential conflict between democracy and liberty in Paine's thought suggests that Paine can only be fully understood as a republican, although it is a very different republicanism from that of John Adams.[47] He argues for constitutional limits on democracy, which he specifically identifies as republican. This in itself does not prevent us from also interpreting his thought as liberal. Classical liberals, like Paine, were concerned to limit the possible tyranny of the majority in the name of natural rights and economic freedom. But Paine's solution is not a liberal one. Paine fails to give priority to freedom over democracy. Paine's republic is a representative democracy limited in its collective actions by a constitution that is created and adapted by the majority in a rational, discursive process. Its legitimacy is grounded on right: the right of each generation to choose its own form of government and its rulers, and the equal right of each individual to participate in this dialogue. It is also grounded on rationality: such a process will result in rational government because it is a rational process. Knowledge is collected from all participants and considered in a

---

[47] Compare to Keane, 'Tom Paine', pp. 13-14.

discursive process which results in an ever more rational outcome. The twin grounds of legitimacy, reason and right, both entail limits on the use of collective power, forbidding, for example, exclusion.

The most dramatic evidence of Paine's republicanism is found in his conception of freedom. As long as we consider his different ideas of freedom within a late twentieth century liberal paradigm in which freedom is understood as the absence of interference or the presence of self-mastery, Paine's use of liberty will appear inconsistent. For how can freedom refer both the collective will of the majority and to the individual's rights against that majority? Alternatively, if we consider Paine's use of freedom within the republican paradigm of his own time, it becomes clear that Paine's use of freedom is consistent with a conception of freedom as independence. Further, in combination with his inclusive conception of democracy, this provides a unique and very modern form of republicanism.

Three principal features of republican liberty can be identified in classical republican political theory. Firstly, a concern for the freedom of the republic - the polis or nation - from foreign rule by other states. The classical thinkers are primarily concerned with political stability in the form of freedom of a polis or empire from domination by others. Hobbes claims that the ancients' concern for liberty was *only* a concern for national freedom:

> The Athenians, and Romanes were free; that is, free Commonwealths: not that any particular men had the libertie to resist their own Representative; but that their Representative had the libertie to resist, or invade other people.[48]

The liberal tradition of freedom has rejected the republican tradition because it is concerned only with the freedom of the state, not of the individual.[49] Secondly, in

---

[48] Thomas Hobbes, *Leviathan,* ed. by Richard Tuck (Cambridge: Cambridge University Press, 1991), p. 149.

[49] Richard Mulgan argues that the modern liberal tradition is traceable to ancient Greece, particularly to Athens where individuality was encouraged at certain times. For example, he cites the Funeral Speech of Pericles by Thucydides. However freedom or eleutheria is a status concept such as freeman or citizen which while entailing legal, civil and political rights also entails the right of ownership of slaves so that; 'exercising power over others confirmed and enhanced one's

the classical republican tradition we find a strong link made between political participation by citizens and freedom. Pocock suggests that Machiavelli associates republican liberty with the experience of political participation or citizenship - a *vivere civile* and suggests that the liberty, which Machiavelli's citizens enjoy, is a communal freedom as opposed to individual liberty.[50] The concept of citizenship does carry some individual rights or liberties that are essential to the maintenance of civic virtue. These are rights of participation or the *vivere civile* and the carrying of arms and ownership of a limited amount of land. It is this ideal of the economically independent soldier citizen that suggests an element of individual freedom in the classical republican tradition.[51] Thirdly, the republican tradition identifies freedom with constitutional structures designed to balance various interests, classes or functions. The ancient originators of the tradition develop the idea of the mixed constitution or polity not as a guarantee of individual liberty but as a guarantee of internal stability and external strength. It is Montesquieu who identifies the balanced constitution with individual freedom which, through his influence, is incorporated into the American constitution.[52]

Paine's conception of liberty embodies many of the changes that Appleby identifies with nascent liberalism: the idea of progress, the importance of the

---

own freedom' R. Mulgan, 'Liberty in Ancient Greece,' in *Conceptions of Liberty in Political Philosophy*, ed. by Z. A. Pelczynski & J. Gray (London: Althone, 1984), pp. 7-23.

[50] Pocock, *The Machiavellian Moment*, p. 184.

[51] Quentin Skinner, 'The Paradoxes of Political Liberty' in *Liberty*, ed. by D. Miller, Oxford Readings in Politics and Government (Oxford: Oxford University Press, 1991), p. 203.

[52] Polybius (who was in fact Greek, but wrote in and about Rome) introduces into the mixed constitution the idea of balancing and checking power. Rather than balancing the power of economic classes in Aristotle's 'middle constitution', Polybius and Cicero are concerned to balance sources of political power: monarchy, aristocracy and democracy. It does not concern Polybius that this was an inaccurate picture of the sources of power in Rome. In this ancient source we can recognise the seeds of Montesquieu's transformed theory of the balanced constitution in which the functions of power, which Aristotle had defined but not made use of: the executive, legislative (or deliberative) and judicial, are balanced regardless of the source of legitimacy or economic interest represented by that power, in the interests of republican liberty. See Polybius, *The Rise of the Roman Empire*, ed. and trans. by I. S. Kilvert & F. W. Walbank (London: Penguin, 1979; repr. 1987), p. 312. Baron de Montesquieu, *The Spirit of the Laws*, trans. by T. Nugent (New York: Hafner Press, 1949), XI. 2, p. 149-151. See also F. McDonald, *Novos Ordo Seclorum: The Intellectual Origins of the Constitution* (Lawrence: University Press of Kansas, 1985), p. 67.

individual and a free trade economic policy. However, Paine's conception of liberty cannot be understood fully as liberal freedom. Liberal freedom can be understood as the absence of interference. Several of Paine's uses of freedom, particularly national independence, conflict with this ideal. Liberal freedom can make sense of national freedom only by analogy to the individual but Paine's conception requires more than the absence of interference from other nations. National freedom for Paine is also an internal condition: freedom from despotism.

Liberal freedom as the absence of interference specifically claims that freedom is not dependent on a form of government. The individual can be free from interference when ruled by a benevolent despot. Liberal freedom is freedom from government, including democracy. This might lead us to two possible conclusions. Firstly, we might find that Paine's political thought is marred by his inconsistent and underdeveloped use of the concept of freedom. Secondly, we might conclude that Paine holds a positive conception of freedom as self-mastery associated with Rousseau. Certainly, freedom as self-mastery would encompass the internal requirement of national freedom. But Paine's use of freedom to describe individual rights as a check on government fits ill with the positive conception of freedom. Paine specifically rejects the notion that an individual's interest might best be determined by the collective will and revels in the difference between individuals.

Paine's use of freedom can be made consistent only within the framework of a republican conception of freedom. The dominant idea of freedom in his time was that of freedom from arbitrary government defined by the rule of law. Freedom is the absence of domination. Its antonyms are slavery and dependence. Republican unfreedom can therefore occur when interference has not, where the individual is dependent on the arbitrary will of another. On the other hand, the republican citizen remains free when his actions are interfered with by the legitimate institutions of a just community. Republican freedom depends on self-ownership and the ownership of resources necessary to survival, but it does not depend on self-mastery. There is no idealist insistence on the substantive ethical goals of the free individual.[53]

Paine's conception of freedom is best understood as independence applied to both the nation and the individual. Collective independence is challenged by both external and internal domination. The despot violates freedom by claiming ownership over the nation. Individual independence is violated by arbitrary interference from others, including the government. It is guaranteed by the recognition of his natural rights in a written constitution and the exercise of civil rights of participation in public decision making. Equality of political power is required to ensure against the domination on one person or group. Independence is also violated by the inequality of private property that reduces men to servitude. Economic dependence on others prevents the individual from expressing his self-defined interest. Thus the republican conception of freedom incorporates and makes sense of all Paine's various uses of liberty and freedom.

This distinct conception of liberty as non-domination results in an interpretation of the tradition, which is in many ways hard to distinguish from modern liberalism that recognises the threat domination poses to freedom.[54] Philp

---

[53] Skinner has examined the role of this conception of freedom within the English commonwealth tradition. Pettit has also outlined this conception of freedom, which he terms anti-power. See Quentin Skinner, *Liberty before Liberalism* (Cambridge: Cambridge University Press, 1998) & Philip Pettit, *Republicanism: A Theory of Freedom and Government* (Oxford: Clarendon, 1997).

[54] Rawls himself acknowledges that his 'political liberalism' is consistent with some forms of republicanism which he distinguishes from 'civic humanism'. See John Rawls, *Political Liberalism* (New York: Columbia University Press, 1996), pp. 205-6. Brugger suggests that we can place modern republican positions on a triangular continuum between liberal-orientated, communitarian-orientated and pragmatic-orientated points. See Bill Brugger, *Republican Theory in Political Thought: Virtuous or Virtual* (London: Macmillan, 1999), p. 2. In part, the confusion arises from the emergence of two current conceptions of republicanism, a feature of its ongoing ability to adapt to the circumstances of the age. The modern revival of republican ideas emerged firstly in the 1970's at which time its concern was the alienation of citizens from the location of political power. Writers such as Arendt and Sandel argued for a republican emphasis on virtue as a communal ethic. In doing so, they described republicanism as a communitarian tradition devoted to the common good as a substantive ethical goal. At the same time historians such as Pocock and Skinner examined the republican tradition in the context of the Florentine republics, the English commonwealth tradition and the foundation of the American republic. Skinner, and recently Pettit, identified within the republican tradition a distinct conception of liberty that links

argues that non-domination as an ideal entails the acceptance of civic equality and a rejection of virtual representation and this further entails universal suffrage and equal electoral representation.[55] However, virtually no writer in the classical republican tradition argued for universal suffrage, and most refused even to accept actual voting for representatives as a form of political participation. Classical republican equality of participation was limited to those who could genuinely be described as independent, who owned their own body (thus eliminating slaves and women) and the means of production, usually land, eliminating the possibility of economic domination. Freedom as citizenship has always been a status concept, its value drawn from the existence of unfreedom. Only when republicanism is combined with a recognition of citizenship by virtue of humanity, as found in Paine's writings, does it imply universal suffrage. The natural rights foundation of Paine's thought is from the liberal side of the marriage. It is this which enables Paine to forge a new kind of republicanism which rejects property qualifications for voting except those that recognise each man's property in his own person.

Paine's new radical democratic and even libertarian republicanism may be responsible for the 'fatal paroxysm' that republicanism underwent between 1791 and 1801 and its disappearance as the dominant paradigm in English political thought.[56] However in its current revival, republicanism can draw much from Paine's works. One version of modern republicanism focuses on democratic participation but cannot take seriously the liberal espousal of rights as private defences against the public good. The other version of republicanism as anti-

---

the disparate branches of the tradition across time and space, but engenders a liberal interpretation focused on individual freedom.

[55] Philp, 'English Republicanism', p. 248. Philp also claims that the conception of freedom as non-domination cannot be necessary to the identification of a writer as a republican, as this excludes both Aristotle and Rousseau from the tradition. I for one am happy to exclude these two problem cases. Aristotle is to republicanism what Hobbes is to liberalism: a precursor, who while influential in developing the premises of the tradition fails to draw the necessary conclusions. Rousseau, at the other end of the spectrum, can be interpreted as a republican but the dominant interpretation of his works suggests rather that his marriage of republicanism with idealism departs too far towards romanticism to be included in the tradition.

[56] Philp, 'English Republicanism', p. 251.

power, like Paine, recognises individual rights as the foundation of the public good but, in doing so, fails to draw an adequate distinction between republicanism and modern liberalism. In focusing on dependence, particularly in the economic sphere, and on political accountability, contemporary republicanism might find in Paine's thought the distinction it seeks.

The writings collected here focus our attention on issues in Paine's thought that are often neglected but essential to the interpretation of his political thought as a unique blend of liberal republicanism. These texts highlight his consistent commitment to *laissez-faire* economic freedom even in his welfare proposals. Further, Paine's apparently ambiguous attitude to new economic institutions such as central banks, national debt and paper money, make sense only within the context of his championing of both freedom and democracy within this unique liberal-republican framework.

Note on Currencies and Exchange Values

The financial chaos of the revolutionary era is in part reflected in the variety of currencies that Paine uses in these texts. The best standard unit is the English pound sterling (£ or l), the value of which was fixed by law against a weight of silver. The Spanish silver dollar, which was remarkably stable during this period, was worth four shillings (s) and six pence (d) in English sterling. One pound in Pennsylvania currency was worth 7s. 6d. in sterling according to the proclamation of 1708. After independence, most states adopted the dollar as the unit of currency. In 1780 an English pound was worth $2.67 in Pennsylvania currency (One Spanish dollar was still valued at 7s 6d.) Maryland, Delaware and New Jersey shared this exchange rate but in 1780 a dollar was worth 8s in New York and Carolina and 6s in Virginia and New England. This accounts only for specie and even so the value of coins varied according to their age and issue.

Bills of credit and other paper money varied in value greatly, depending on their security. This was calculated according to official tables of depreciation. In May 1781, it took $225 in Pennsylvania paper money to buy $1 in hard currency. The French *livre* is also of interest given the dependence of the Continental Congress on French funds. A hundred pounds sterling was worth 2,345.28 *livre tournais* at 1775 exchange values.[1] Given this complexity of value it would be impossible to translate the amounts given by Paine in these texts into one currency, let alone into modern day equivalents. For a general guide it is

---

[1] See Newman, *Early Paper Money*, pp. 359-60; McCusker, *Money and Exchange*, p. 312.

common for historians to multiply amounts in English Pounds Sterling before 1793 by sixty and after that date by thirty.[2]

---

[2] For example, Christopher Hibbert, *George III: A Personal History* (London: Viking, 1998), p. 6. Recent research on the purchasing power of the English pound suggests £1 in 1778 is equivalent to £84.49 in 1998 and £1 in 1798 to £68.29 in 1998. See Robert Twigger, *Inflation: the Value of the Pound 1750-1998* (House of Commons Research Paper 99/20, 23 February 1999), p. 21.

THOMAS PAINE

ON THE BANK,

WELFARE,

AND

ECONOMIC FREEDOM

Chapter One

Free Trade and Independence

The first significant mark that Paine made upon the political world was his plea in 1776 for America to fight for independence as a sovereign union of states. His powerful and successful argument for independence is multi-pronged, incorporating practical appeals to America's ability to survive alone, an emotional appeal to freedom and justice and a thorough condemnation of monarchy and the British constitution. Within this argument, we can discern an economic argument for independence, against the mercantilist policy of British monopoly of American trade. Thus in 1776, Paine's original approach to economic questions is already apparent. I have included here two early pieces, an extract from *Common Sense* and one of his most interesting *Crisis* papers, which both illustrate the connection between Paine's campaign for American independence and his ideas on free trade.

Common Sense is, and was in Paine's own time, his most famous work and he continued to describe himself principally as its author to the end of his days. There are few books that can claim to have changed the world to the extent that this cheap pamphlet is recognised to have done. Even such a fierce critic as John Adams recognised its unique contribution to the achievement of American independence from the British Empire. It was the killing of eight Colonial militiamen at Lexington, Massachusetts that shifted Paine's view of the conflict from a 'dispute of law' to a war of between two nations, but for many other colonial rebels that shift was prompted by reading *Common Sense*.[1]

The pamphlet is constructed in four sections. The first details the origin of government, setting out an argument for representative government and a critical assessment of the British constitution. Paine's detailed denunciation of monarchy and the hereditary principle is fully explored in the second. The third section presents independence as the only acceptable solution to the struggle with Britain, particularly since the violence in Lexington. In the final section, Paine sets out to convince Americans that they can win a war against Britain. I have included here only brief extracts which include his economic arguments in favour of independence and the society-government distinction which provide a context for the other works included in this volume. This may result in the reader receiving a false impression of the complete document as focused on economic issues, but this is justified by the ready availability of paperback editions of *Common Sense*.

Paine's argument is set against the prevailing claim that the colonists were loyal to George III whilst waging war against the British Parliament's attempt to usurp their traditional rights. Paine set out a thorough critique of monarchy as an illegitimate, irrational and expensive form of government that only fools would accept. Further Paine argued that separation from Britain was inevitable given the geographical situation of the colonies. Against the common claim that Britain and America had a parent-child relationship, he argues that the parental relationship was breached by the use of force against the colonists. Not even savages make war upon their families. Paine's emotional appeal to the horror and

---

[1] In his *Autobiography* Adams tries to discredit the general opinion of *Common Sense's* importance in the revolution, even claiming that *Plain Truth's* argument against independence was more effective in converting men to the cause. He admits that 'it probably converted some to the Doctrine of Independence, and gave others an Excuse for declaring in favour of it.' *Diary and Autobiography of John Adams*, ed. by L. H. Butterfield, *The Adams Papers*, Series I (Cambridge, Mass.: Belknap, 1961) 3. 333-4.

injustice of the actions of the troops in Lexington and Concord is arguably what
turned the tide of American history: 'Have you lost a parent or a child by their
hands [...]? If you have [...] and still can shake hands with the murderers, then
you have the heart of a coward.[2]

Most importantly, *Common Sense* makes an economic argument for
independence: that the colonists would be materially better off as an independent
union of states. Their trade would prosper, and their industry thrive. Certainly
they could not be worse off, especially given the economic disruption of the
current events, with British goods boycotted by the colonists, and ports
blockaded.

> Emigrants of property will not choose to come to a country whose
> form of government hangs but by a thread, and who is every day
> tottering on the brink of commotion and disturbance: and numbers
> of the present inhabitants would lay hold of the interval to dispose
> of their effects, and quit the continent.[3]

Further, settlement with the British government would result in the imposition of
even more taxation to pay for their own repression.

Much of *Common Sense* is devoted to convincing the reader that America
can finance a war against the might of the British Empire. This is still today hard
to believe, given that the colonists were outnumbered in population, in military
force and in ships.[4] Britain could draw not only on its own trading wealth but also
on that of the rest of the Empire, particularly India. The American colonies were
little more than barely settled trading outposts dealing mostly in unfinished goods
and hugely dependant on British imports. Most importantly, Britain had the most
developed financial system in the world, so that military spending could be
financed by a public confidence in a market in national debt. Britain could fight

---

[2] 'Common Sense' (1776), *Writings*, I, 91. On Paine's appeal to sentiment, see Aldridge, *American Ideology*, p. 62.
[3] 'Common Sense' (1776), *Writings*, I, 95.
[4] The British army in America numbered 50,000 regular forces in addition to 30,000 Hessians and 30,000 American Loyalists. Although rebels outnumbered Loyalists two to one, Washington

now and pay later. Given the lack of either a consistent American currency or of financial institutions and given that the focus of the colonists' struggle was their objection to taxes, how could a continental convention raise money to build ships and arm, feed and clothe a militia army, let alone pay salaries? This would continue to be a theme of Paine's writings throughout the war and it is principally this problem which leads Paine into writing on themes such as taxation, national debt and paper money, as we shall see in Chapter 2.

What is most striking about *Common Sense* is the connection implied between freedom and trade or commerce. Free trade with Europe, or at least the end of British regulation of American trade, will protect America from invasion better than a colonial relationship with Britain, which Paine presents as Britain milking the colonies for its own economic interest. In this argument, there is an implicit rejection of the mercantilist economic logic. The same idea is more explicitly expressed in a pamphlet published a month later, designed to further boost the argument for independence whist Congress debated their impending declaration. In February 1776, in a pamphlet sometimes attributed to Paine, the ghost of the military hero of the British conquest of Canada, General Montgomery, predicts that freedom from British trade regulation will result in greater American wealth:

> A freedom from the restraints of the act of navigation I foresee will produce such immense additions to the wealth of this country that prosperity will wonder that you ever thought your present trade worth its protection.[5]

After the Declaration of Independence, Paine continued to remind his readers of the economic arguments in favour of their success. The promise of

---

never had more than 18,000 men to fight with. See Greg D. Feldmeth 'U.S. History Resources' http:/home.earthlink.net/~gfeldmeth/USHistory.html (31 March 1998).
    [5] 'Dialogue between Montgomery and an American Delegate' (1776), *Writings*, I, 163-4. This piece was attached to Bell's 'complete' addition of *Common Sense*. Richard Gimbel asserts that this is not written by Paine. Certainly, it seems unlikely given Paine's dispute with Bell at this time. Paine had sought to disclaim authorship from other additions to Bell's unauthorised editions. See above p. xviii & Gimbel, *Bibliographical Checklist*, p. 57.

future prosperity was used to bolster the morale of the struggling colonists impoverished by the disruption of trade and the destruction of property. In *Crisis III* he claimed

> The freedom of trade [...] is, to a trading country, an article of such importance, that the principal source of wealth depends upon it; and it is impossible that any country can flourish, as it otherwise might do, whose commerce is engrossed, cramped and fettered by the laws and mandates of another.[6]

Crisis VII contends that the economic advantages of independence were not limited to American interests but rather the British merchants and taxpayers will also benefit.[7] The version included here is found in the *Pennsylvania Packet* and so is surely intended primarily to boost American morale, despite being addressed to the people of England. Its publication coincides with the imminent departure of an unsuccessful mission to resolve the war in Britain's favour.[8] At this time, there must have been many waverers ready to surrender on the basis of a negotiated settlement, and thus the cause of independence was perhaps in need of a timely reminder of the arguments of 1776. But the text also suggests that Paine hoped to reach an English audience, at least the commissioners themselves and perhaps also the ministry.

It is important to note here that Paine is only arguing for freedom of international trade in the sense of no country regulating the trade of another. American merchants ought to be free to trade with merchants from all nations rather than being restricted to trade with Britain. These appeals to free trade cannot be interpreted as an argument for customs free competition between

---

[6] 'Crisis III' (1777), *Writings*, I, 204.

[7] See below p. 148.

[8] Parliament proposed a settlement based on the repeal of the offending legislation and a pledge not to tax the colonies. A Commission, headed by the Earl of Carlisle, and including William Eden and George Johnstone, was sent to negotiate with Congress in Philadelphia and appeal for popular support for peace in the newspapers. Although the Commission offered self-rule under monarchy, Congress resolved to treat any one seeking to negotiate as an enemy. The exposure of Johnstone's attempt to bribe Members of Congress, including Robert Morris, reaffirmed the popular resolve to accept only Britain's recognition of American independence. See Aldridge, *Man of Reason*, p. 59.

imported and domestically produced goods. Later Paine would argue in favour of taxes on imported goods, precisely to protect emerging American industry.[9] Taken on their own, these few quotations on international trade cannot be interpreted as suggesting Paine had a completely developed theory of a free market. They illustrate only Paine's rejection of the mercantilist principle that national wealth was generated by encouraging exports while restricting imports, in favour of a principle that 'trade flourishes best when it is free, and it is weak policy to attempt to fetter it.'[10]

Nevertheless, one can still find in *Common Sense* an indication of Paine's early adherence to key components of free-market liberalism. He distinguishes between society, which is natural and governed by natural laws of mutual satisfaction, and government, which is an association formed by men in society. Society is the intercourse between individuals whereby wants are mutually satisfied.[11] Government on the other hand is a coercive force, restraining our vices. It is a *necessary* evil. If men are to exchange goods and services, they must be assured that their bargains will be enforced and that the property they accumulate will be protected. However, because government is a necessary *evil* it must be restricted to a level where it performs only those functions for which it is instituted. It must never become an unnecessary evil. Paine believes that society can regulate itself for a while without government. He would later claim that such self-regulation was experienced during the American Revolution, although in 1776 he seems concerned at the prospect of anarchy.[12] In view of Paine's characterisation of society as a natural mechanism for the co-ordination of wants, I believe it is appropriate to identify his conception of society with 'the market'. What we have here, in that case, is an argument for *laissez-faire* government. Several writers have argued, however, that Paine's conception of society

---

[9] See below p. 213.
[10] See below p. 148.
[11] 'Common Sense' (1776), *Writings*, I, 69.
[12] See 'Rights of Man II' (1792), *Writings*, II, 407 and below p. 132.

encompasses more than the idea of an economic market, particularly John Keane who interprets these passages as the introduction into political thought of the seminal distinction between civil society and the state.[13]

The story Paine tells of a society of colonists forming themselves into a political society is reminiscent of the social contract device of earlier thinkers, particularly Locke. It is interesting that for his thought experiment, Paine does not remove the reader into an imaginary state of nature, but only across the ocean to a new world. As in Locke's state of nature, society and property rights are prior to the invention of government. Government is thus limited by the interests of natural society. Paine's use of this device is political: to establish representative democracy rather than monarchy as the most natural and rational form of government. But at the same time, it presents an argument for limited government. Thus as early as 1776, we find in Paine's thought a clear exposition of a Lockean liberal tradition of government limited by natural law and, if we interpret this natural law as market prominence, by property rights. We can also identify here an idea of freedom of the individual that is consistent with this Lockean liberal interpretation of his thought. Paine specifically ties American independence to freedom, not only the national freedom of the youthful America from its oppressive mother, but also the religious and economic freedom of individual Americans is at stake. Even a home-grown monarch will give them 'law at the point of the sword' and threaten their property and religious freedom.

Certainly, he departs radically from the classical republican view that commerce and competition are a dangerous vice that could destroy the civic virtue upon which the freedom of a republic depends. On the other hand, we also find evidence in *Common Sense* of a traditional republican fear of commerce as a corrupting force. Both Aldridge and Foner suggest that Paine's 'commercial republicanism' abandons this traditional link and, in doing so, combats traditional arguments against both new capitalist forms of wealth and equality of

---

[13] See Keane, *Civil Society*, p. 67, n. 6; Keane, *Democracy*, pp. 42-45; Keane, *Paine*, p. 190.

representation in the republic. In *Common Sense* Paine does in fact suggest such a link. England is not as prepared for war as the uncorrupted American colonists because of the effects of commerce in diminishing the 'spirit both of patriotism and military defence'. This one sentence challenges the claim that Paine sees no tension between civic virtue and unfettered commerce.[14] However, to draw the conclusion that Paine's republicanism remained closer to classical republicanism than the purely commercial Whiggism of Hume and Smith may go too far.[15] Elsewhere Paine always declares his support of free commerce and new capitalist institutions and denounces the connection between property and virtue. Philp argues that this decline of virtue through commerce in England was merely contingent and that Paine sees commerce as inimical to public spirit in monarchies only and not in republics where talent and ability, rather than sycophancy, are rewarded.[16]

In later works, Paine sees the diminished military spirit as a positive effect of commerce. In the *Rights of Man* he claims

> If commerce were permitted to act to the universal extent it is capable, it would extirpate the system of war, and produce a revolution in the uncivilized state of governments. The invention of commerce has arisen since those governments began, and is the greatest approach towards universal civilization, that has yet been made by any means not immediately flowing from moral principles.[17]

To attribute universal civilisation to free market forces is to be a true believer in *laissez-faire*. Paine believes that it is the exchange of goods which leads to a civil society in a nation and its occurrence between nations will similarly end the state of nature which exists between nations, resulting in international peace.[18] The

---

[14] See below p. 128.
[15] See Claeys, *Thomas Paine*, p. 47.
[16] See Philp, *Paine*, p. 46. Claeys makes a similar point on the different effects of commerce in monarchies and republics. See Claeys, *Thomas Paine*, p. 94.
[17] See below p. 465.
[18] The development of European Economic Community can be interpreted as just such an international society growing out of trade agreements.

idea that trade is conducive to peace is also used in *Crisis VII* where Paine suggests that war never in the interest of trade, counter to the Mercantilist idea of waging war to protect trading interests: 'to make war with those who trade with us, is like setting a bull-dog upon a customer at the shop door.'[19]

I have excluded from this extract most of Paine's critique of monarchy. Paine uses biblical references to demonstrate God's distaste for monarchy and argued that far from being established by divine right, 'Monarchy in every instance is the Popery of Government.'[20] The origin of monarchy, Paine argues, can only be in conquest, for even if the first monarch had been established by election, our ancestors cannot have given up our rights to his heirs. Paine would later develop this argument into his principle of the right of each generation to constitute their own government. Hereditary Monarchy is irrational, setting up minors and fools to govern and, far from being a force for peace as often claimed, it has resulted in numerous civil wars over the succession.

Paine presented monarchy as an expensive and inefficient method of government. Where there is a parliament to make laws and generals to fight battles, there is very little for Kings to do except 'sauntering away their lives without [...] advantage to the Nation'. At the end of his pamphlet, Paine offers an alternative form of government for the colonies. The opportunity has arisen to start a new nation with a legitimate constitutional form of government: 'to begin government at the right end.' He sets out a plan for a continental congress consisting of representatives of each state and a charter or constitution created by a continental conference elected for that purpose.[21] Paine's model of representative government is not well developed in 1776 and he offers few arguments in its defence. He does suggest however that it would be an

---

[19] See below p. 139.
[20] 'Common Sense' (1776), *Writings*, I, 79.
[21] 'Common Sense' (1776), *Writings*, I, 83-4 & 97.

inexpensive form, quoting Dragonetti.[22] In *Crisis VII*, Paine takes this critique of monarchy one step further. Not only can the American colonies be ruled better by representative government, but Britain too should rid itself of this expensive and useless practice and elect a congress in its stead.

This new form of government was explicitly republican in the popular sense of the absence of a King. Paine proposes an executive president to be elected by the congress. Further, in a phrase which is reminiscent of John Adam's later definition of a republic as 'a kingdom of laws, not men', Paine demands that 'in America the law is king. For as in absolute governments the King is Law, so in free Countries the Law *ought* to be King'. Certainly, in Paine's critique of monarchy, we find echoes of traditional English radical concerns that fit the tradition of republicanism. The Crown's use of patronage to maintain its power is denounces as expensive: 'In England a King hath little more to do than to make war and give away places; which in plain terms, is to impoverish the Nation' but also corrupting. Paine admires the elected commons as the 'republican part of the constitution' – it is this which English men glory in, 'the liberty of choosing an House of Commons from out of their own body' but it is corrupted and

> It is easy to see that when Republican virtue fails, slavery ensues.
> Why is the constitution of England sickly? but because monarchy
> hath poisoned the Republic; the Crown hath engrossed the
> commons?[23]

However, in identifying the commons as the only republican element, Paine explicitly rejects the doctrine of the balanced constitution, a point picked up by John Adams in his *Thoughts on Government*, a critique of *Common Sense*. Adams saw Paine's proposal for a unicameral congress and weak executive as dangerously democratic; a disagreement that apparently resulted in a hot-

---

[22] Marchese Giacinto Dragonetti (1738-1818) was an early Italian utilitarian. His *Treatise on Virtues and Rewards* was published in London in 1769. His work influenced Marchese de Cesare Beccaria (1738-94) an Italian jurist and philosopher best known for his work on punishment.
[23] See 'Common Sense' (1776) *Writings*, I, 97-100.

tempered personal dispute.[24] Paine's identification of republican government with representation *alone* has been seen as symptomatic of his rejection of the republican tradition.[25] This interpretation of Paine claims that his republicanism takes the form of anti-monarchy alone, replacing it with representative democracy limited only by natural rights and thus taking a significant step away from the republican tradition of a balanced constitution towards modern liberal democracy. This is consistent with the liberal *laissez-faire* economic attitudes we find in *Common Sense.*

The success of *Common Sense* was undoubtedly due to Paine's talent for rhetoric. Having ridiculed, monarchy and the English constitution, appealed to the colonists smarting wounds and addressed their practical concerns in a most practical manner, he created a fighting spirit that would eventually succeed against the odds. Whatever the economic advantage of independence, the focus of *Common Sense* is political. His central appeal is to freedom from arbitrary government. Not only did he appeal to the individual's religious and economic freedom but, remarkably Paine also persuaded settlers who previously saw their freedom as dependant on the rights of Englishmen to identify America as a nation: a nation defined by its unique love of freedom. This conception of freedom is personified and threatened in a passage reminiscent of later claims of an American destiny:

> O ye that love mankind! Ye that dare oppose not only the tyranny, but the tyrant, stand forth! Every spot of the old world is over-run with oppression. Freedom hath been hunted round the Globe. Asia, and Africa, have long expelled her.—Europe regards her like a stranger, and England hath given her warning to depart. O! receive the fugitive, and prepare in time an asylum for mankind.[26]

The same talent for rhetoric is found in *Crisis VII*. Paine's economic arguments for independence and his assertions that America can afford the war

---

[24] Aldridge notes that Adams's may have misinterpreted Paine's proposal for a congress as a plan for unicameral state constitutions. See Aldridge, *American Ideology*, pp. 198-205.

[25] See above p. 87 and Philp, 'English Republicanism', p. 252.

are developed and repeated. At the same time he insists that Britain will be bankrupted by the war, by the disruption to her trade and by the debt used to fund it. There is also a hint of his suspicion that, whilst not in the interest of the English people, it may well be in the financial interests of the court pensioners and placemen to expand the public debt. This connection between the willingness of the British government to go to war and the private financial interests of the ministry and their class would later be developed in Paine's thorough indictment of the English system of finance in 1797.[27]

---

[26] 'Common Sense' (1776), *Writings*, I, 100-101.
[27] See below p. 413.

COMMON SENSE

addressed to the

INHABITANTS OF AMERICA

***

Of the Origin and Design of GOVERNMENT *in general, with concise Remarks on
the English Constitution.*

SOME writers have so confounded society with government, as to leave little or no
distinction between them; whereas, they are not only different, but have different
origins. Society is produced by our wants, and government by our wickedness;
the former promotes our happiness *possitively* by uniting our affections, the latter
negatively by restraining our vices. The one encourages intercourse, the other
creates distinctions. The first is a patron, the last a punisher.

Society in every state is a blessing, but Government even in its best state is but
a necessary evil; in its worst state an intolerable one: for when we suffer, or are
exposed to the same miseries by a *Government*, which we might expect in a
country *without Government*, our calamity is heightened by reflecting that we
furnish the means by which we suffer. Government like dress is the badge of lost
innocence; the palaces of kings are built on the ruins of the bowers of paradise.
For were the impulses of conscience clear, uniform, and irresistibly obeyed, man
would need no other lawgiver; but that not being the case, he finds it necessary to
surrender up a part of his property to furnish means for the protection of the rest;
and this he is induced to do, by the same prudence which in every other case
advises him, out of two evils to choose the least. Wherefore, security being the
true design and end of government, it unanswerably follows, that whatever form
thereof appears most likely to ensure it to us, with the least expence and greatest
benefit, is preferable to all others.

In order to gain a clear and just idea of the design and end of government, let
us suppose a small number of persons settled in some sequestered part of the
earth, unconnected with the rest; they will then represent the first peopling of any

country; or of the world. In this state of natural liberty, society will be their first thought. A thousand motives will excite them thereto, the strength of one man is so unequal to his wants, and his mind so unfitted for perpetual solitude, that he is soon obliged to seek assistance and relief of another, who in his turn requires the same. Four or five united would be able to raise a tolerable dwelling in the midst of a wilderness, but one man might labour out the common period of life without accomplishing any thing; when he had felled his timber he could not remove it, nor erect it after it was removed; hunger in the mean time would urge him from his work, and every different want call him a different way. Disease, nay even misfortune would be death; for tho' neither might be mortal, yet either would disable him from living, and reduce him to a state in which he might rather be said to perish, than to die.

Thus necessity like a gravitating power would soon form our newly arrived emigrants into society, the reciprocal blessings of which, would supersede, and render the obligations of law and government unnecessary while they remained perfectly just to each other: but as nothing but Heaven is impregnable to vice, it will unavoidably happen, that in proportion as they surmount the first difficulties of emigration, which bound them together in a common cause, they will begin to relax in their duty and attachment to each other: and this remissness will point out the necessity of establishing some form of government to supply the defect of moral virtue.

Some convenient tree will afford them a State House, under the branches of which the whole Colony may assemble to deliberate on public matters. It is more than probable that their first laws will have the title only of REGULATIONS and be enforced by no other penalty than public disesteem. In this first parliament every man by natural right will have a seat.

But as the Colony encreases, the public concerns will encrease likewise, and the distance at which the members may be separated, will render it too inconvenient for all of them to meet on every occasion as at first, when their number was small, their habitations near, and the public concerns few and trifling.

This will point out the convenience of their consenting to leave the legislative part to be managed by a select number chosen from the whole body, who are supposed to have the same concerns at stake which those have who appointed them, and who will act in the same manner as the whole body would act were they present. If the colony continues encreasing, it will become necessary to augment the number of the representatives, and that the interest of every part of the colony may be attended to, it will be found best to divide the whole into convenient parts, each part sending its proper number: and that the *elected* might never form to themselves an interest separate from the *electors*, prudence will point out the propriety of having elections often: because as the elected might by that means return and mix again with the general body of the electors in a few months, their fidelity to the public will be secured by the prudent reflexion of not making a rod for themselves. And as this frequent interchange will establish a common interest with every part of the community, they will mutually and naturally support each other, and on this (not on the unmeaning name of king) depends the *strength of government; and the happiness of the governed.*

Here then is the origin and rise of government; namely, a mode rendered necessary by the inability of moral virtue to govern the world; here too is the design and end of government, viz. Freedom and security. And however our eyes may be dazzled with show, or our ears deceived by sound; however prejudice may warp our wills, or interest darken our understanding, the simple voice of nature and of reason will say, 'tis right.

I draw my idea of the form of government from a principle in nature which no art can overturn, viz. That the more simple any thing is, the less liable it is to be disordered, and the easier repaired when disordered; and with this maxim in view I offer a few remarks on the so much boasted constitution of England. That it was noble for the dark and slavish times in which it was erected, is granted. When the world was over-run with tyranny the least remove therefrom was a glorious rescue. But that it is imperfect, subject to convulsions, and incapable of producing what it seems to promise is easily demonstrated.

Absolute governments, (tho' the disgrace of human nature) hath this advantage with them, that they are simple; if the people suffer, they know the head from which their suffering springs; know likewise the remedy; and are not bewildered by a variety of causes and cures.   But the constitution of England is so exceedingly complex, that the nation may suffer for years together without being able to discover in which part the fault lies, some will say in one and some in another, and every political physician will advise a different medicine.

***

Of MONARCHY *and Hereditary Succession.*

MANKIND being originally equals in the order of creation, the equality could only be destroyed by some subsequent circumstance: the distinctions of rich and poor may in a great measure be accounted for, and that without having recourse to the harsh ill-sounding names of oppression and avarice.   Oppression is often the *consequence*, but seldom or never the *means* of riches: and tho' avarice will preserve a man from being necessitously poor, it generally makes him too timorous to be wealthy.

But there is another and greater distinction for which no truly natural or religious reason can be assigned, and that is, the distinction of Men into KINGS and SUBJECTS.   Male and female are the distinctions of nature, good and bad the distinctions of Heaven; but how a race of men came into the world so exalted above the rest, and distinguished like some new species, is worth enquiring into, and whether they are the means of happiness or of misery to mankind.[1]

***

THOUGHTS, *on the present* STATE *of* AMERICAN AFFAIRS.

IN the following pages I offer nothing more than simple facts, plain arguments, and common sense: and have no other preliminaries to settle with the reader, than

---

[1] Compare to a similar claim in *Agrarian Justice* below p. 516. See also p. 116 above.

that he will divest himself of prejudice and prepossession, and suffer his reason and his feelings to determine for themselves: that he will put *on* or rather that he will not put *off* the true character of a man, and generously enlarge his views beyond the present day.

Volumes have been written on the subject of the struggle between England and America. Men of all ranks have embarked in the controversy, from different motives, and with various designs; but all have been ineffectual, and the period of debate is closed. Arms as the last resource decide the contest; the appeal was the choice of the King, and the Continent has accepted the challenge.

It hath been reported of the late Mr. Pelham (who tho' an able minister was not without his faults) that on his being attacked in the House of Commons on the score that his measures were only of a temporary kind, replied, "*they will last my time.*"[2] Should a thought so fatal and unmanly possess the Colonies in the present contest, the name of ancestors will be remembered by future generations with detestation.

The Sun never shined on a cause of greater worth. 'Tis not the affair of a City, a Country, a Province, or a Kingdom; but of a Continent—of at least one eighth part of the habitable Globe. 'Tis not the concern of a day, a year, or an age; posterity are virtually involved in the contest, and will be more or less affected even to the end of time by the proceedings now. Now is the seed time of Continental union, faith and honour. The least fracture now, will be like a name engraved with the point of a pin on the tender rind of a young oak; the wound will enlarge with the tree, and posterity read it in full grown characters.

By referring the matter from argument to arms, a new æra for politics is struck—a new method of thinking hath arisen. All plans, proposals, &c. prior to the 19th of April, *i. e.* to the commencement of hostilities, are like the almanacks

---

[2] Henry Pelham (1695-1754) was Chancellor of Exchequer and effectively Prime Minister from 1743-1754. The measures referred to here are probably those Pelham introduced to balance the budget including renegotiating the national debt at a lower interest. Aldridge suggests that the comment cited by Paine was apocryphal. See Aldridge, *American Ideology*, p. 60.

of the last year; which, tho' proper then, are superceded and useless now.[3] Whatever was advanced by the advocates on either side of the question then, terminated in one and the same point, viz. a union with Great Britain; the only difference between the parties was the method of effecting it; the one proposing force, the other friendship; but it hath so far happened that the first hath failed, and the second hath withdrawn her influence.

As much hath been said of the advantages of reconciliation, which like an agreeable dream, hath passed away and left us as we were, it is but right, that we should examine the contrary side of the argument, and enquire into some of the many material injuries which these Colonies sustain, and always will sustain, by being connected with, and dependant on Great Britain.   To examine that connection and dependance on the principles of nature and common sense, to see what we have to trust to if separated, and what we are to expect if dependant.

I have heard it asserted by some, that as America hath flourished under her former connection with Great Britain, that the same connection is necessary towards her future happiness and will always have the same effect.—Nothing can be more fallacious than this kind of argument:— we may as well assert that because a child has thrived upon milk, that it is never to have meat, or that the first twenty years of our lives is to become a precedent for the next twenty.   But even this is admitting more than is true, for I answer, roundly, that America would have flourished as much, and probably much more had no European power taken any notice of her.   The commerce by which she hath enriched herself are the necessaries of life, and will always have a market while eating is the custom of Europe.

But she has protected us say some.   That she hath engrossed us is true, and defended the Continent at our expence as well as her own is admitted; and she

---

[3] On 19 April 1775 British troops searching for hidden arms fired on colonial militiamen in Lexington, killing eight, and later burnt houses in Concord.   The event signalled the escalation of hostilities beginning the War of Independence.

would have defended Turkey from the same motive, viz. the sake of trade and dominion.

Alas! we have been long led away by ancient prejudices and made large sacrifices to superstition. We have boasted the protection of Great Britain, without considering, that her motive was *interest* not *attachment*; that she did not protect us from *our enemies* on *our account*, but from *her enemies* on *her own account*, from those who had no quarrel with us on any *other account*, and who will always be our enemies on the *same account*. Let Britain wave her pretensions to the continent, or the continent throw off the dependance, and we should be at peace with France and Spain were they at war with Britain. The miseries of Hanover last war, ought to warn us against connections.[4]

It hath lately been asserted in parliament, that the colonies have no relation to each other but through the Parent Country, *i. e.* that Pennsylvania and the Jerseys and so on for the rest, are sister colonies by the way of England; this is certainly a very round-about way of proving relationship, but it is the nearest and only true way of proving enmity (or enemyship, if I may so call it.) France and Spain never were, nor perhaps ever will be our enemies as *Americans* but as our being the *subjects of Great Britain.*

***

Much hath been said of the united strength of Britain and the Colonies, that in conjunction they might bid defiance to the world: But this is mere presumption, the fate of war is uncertain, neither do the expressions mean any thing, for this Continent would never suffer itself to be drained of inhabitants, to support the British Arms in either Asia, Africa, or Europe.

Besides, what have we to do with setting the world at defiance? Our plan is commerce, and that, well attended to, will secure us the peace and friendship of

---

[4] The Electorate of Hanover was a personal possession of the Kings of England from 1714-1837. It was frequently threatened by Prussian and French interests, thus considerably effecting English foreign policy. In 1757, during the Seven Years War, George II's son the Duke of Cumberland (1721-1765) surrendered Hanover to the French at Klosterzeven, resulting in a yearlong occupation.

all Europe, because it is the interest of all Europe to have America a free port. Her trade will always be a protection, and her barrenness of gold and silver will secure her from invaders.

I challenge the warmest advocate for reconciliation, to shew, a single advantage that this Continent can reap, by being connected with Great Britain. I repeat the challenge, not a single advantage is derived. Our corn will fetch its price in any market in Europe, and our imported goods must be paid for buy them where we will.

But the injuries and disadvantages we sustain by that connection, are without number, and our duty to mankind at large, as well as to ourselves, instruct us to renounce the alliance: because, any submission to, or dependance on Great Britain, tends directly to involve this Continent in European wars and quarrels and sets us at variance with nations, who would otherwise seek our friendship, and against whom, we have neither anger nor complaint. As Europe is our market for trade, we ought to form no political connection with any part of it. 'Tis the true interest of America, to steer clear of European contentions, which she never can do, while by her dependance on Britain, she is made the make-weight in the scale on British politics.

Europe is too thickly planted with Kingdoms, to be long at peace, and whenever a war breaks out between England and any foreign power, the trade of America goes to ruin, *because, of her connection with Britain.* The next war may not turn out like the last, and should it not, the advocates for reconciliation now, will be wishing for separation then, because neutrality in that case, would be a safer convoy than a man of war. Every thing that is right or reasonable pleads for separation. The blood of the slain, the weeping voice of nature cries, 'TIS TIME TO PART. Even the distance at which the Almighty hath placed England and America, is a strong and natural proof, that the authority of the one over the other, was never the design of Heaven. The time likewise at which the Continent was discovered, adds weight to the argument, and the manner in which it was peopled encreases the force of it.——The Reformation was preceded by the discovery of

America; as if the Almighty graciously meant to open a sanctuary to the persecuted in future years, when home should afford neither friendship nor safety. The authority of Great Britain over this Continent is a form of government which sooner or later must have an end: And a serious mind can draw no true pleasure by looking forward, under the painful and positive conviction, that what he calls "the present constitution" is merely temporary. As parents, we can have no joy, knowing that *this government* is not sufficiently lasting to ensure any thing which we may bequeath to posterity: And by a plain method of argument, as we are running the next generation into debt, we ought to do the work of it, otherwise we use them meanly and pitifully. In order to discover the line of our duty rightly, we should take our children in our hand, and fix our station a few years farther into life; that eminence will present a prospect, which a few present fears and prejudices conceal from our sight.

***

I am not induced by motives of pride, party, or resentment to espouse the doctrine of separation and independance; I am clearly, positively, and conscientiously persuaded that 'tis the true interest of this Continent to be so; that every thing short of that is mere patchwork, that it can afford no lasting felicity,—that it is leaving the sword to our children, and shrinking back at a time, when a little more, a little farther, would have rendered this Continent the glory of the earth.

As Britain hath not manifested the least inclination towards a compromise, we may be assured that no terms can be obtained worthy the acceptance of the Continent, or any ways equal to the expence of blood and treasure we have been already put to.[5]

---

[5] The colonists' last attempt at reaching a compromise, the Olive Branch Petition, had been sent to England by the Second Continental Congress in July 1775. The King had refused to accept it and replied in his Speech to Parliament on 26 October 1775 that the colonists were protesting their loyalty 'whilst preparing for a general revolt'. The publication of *Common Sense* was timed to coincide with the arrival of the King's Speech and in fact its advertisement appeared in the

The object, contended for, ought always to bear some just proportion to the expence. The removal of North, or the whole detestable junto, is a matter unworthy the millions we have expended. A temporary stoppage of trade was an inconvenience, which would have sufficiently ballanced the repeal of all the acts complained of, had such repeals been obtained; but if the whole Continent must take up arms, if every man must be a soldier, 'tis scarcely worth our while to fight against a contemptible ministry only. Dearly, dearly, do we pay for the repeal of the acts, if that is all we fight for; for in a just estimation, 'tis as great a folly to pay a Bunker-hill price for law as for land.[6] As I have always considered the independancy of this Continent, as an event which sooner or later must arrive, so from the late rapid progress of the continent to maturity, the event could not be far off: Wherefore, on the breaking out of hostilities, it was not worth the while to have disputed a matter, which time would have finally redressed, unless we meant to be in earnest: otherwise, it is like wasting an estate on a suit at law, to regulate the trespasses of a tenant, whose lease is just expiring. No man was a warmer

---

same edition of the *Pennsylvania Evening Post*. Clearly Paine did not anticipate a favourable answer. See Gimbel, *Bibliographical Checklist*, p. 21.

[6] Lord North (1732-92) was Prime Minister from 1770-1782. Colonial resistance to British rule resulted from their opposition to a number of acts of legislation through which the British Parliament asserted their authority to tax the colonies. George Grenville (1712-70), Prime Minister from 1763-5, introduced the Sugar Act (1764) and the Stamp Act (1765) taxing newspapers, legal documents and business transactions, the Currency Act forbidding colonial issues of paper money and the Proclamation of 1763 limiting western expansion by settlers. The Sugar Act and Stamp Act were largely evaded and repealed in 1766, although Parliament's jurisdiction was maintained in the Declaratory Act 1766. Under Chatham's ministry, to the disapproval of many of his cabinet colleagues, Charles Townshend (1725-67) as Chancellor of the Exchequer imposed duties on lead, paint, glass and tea, which were largely repealed by Lord North's ministry in 1770. The Tea Act in 1773 exempted the British East India Company from duties on tea, resulting in the 'Boston Tea Party' demonstration. The Coercive Acts, or intolerable acts, closed Boston port and reduced Massachusetts to royal government. The Quebec Act, which gave French Roman Catholics in Canada religious freedom, was also enumerated among the Declaration of Rights and Grievances issued by the First Continental Congress in September 1774, which demanded the repeal of all legislation since 1763.

A Bunker-Hill price for land refers to the battle of Bunker Hill. After retreating from Lexington, the British Army lay low in Boston for several months, before attempting to seize and fortify the strategically placed but empty Charlestown peninsula in June 1775. The colonists established defended the point from Bunker's and Breed's Hill. General Howe (1729-1814) eventually captured the hills, forcing the colonists to retreat. British casualties were severe, losing

wisher for reconciliation than myself, before the fatal 19th of April 1775 (Massacre of Lexington), but the moment the event of that day was made known, I rejected the hardened, sullen tempered Pharaoh of England for ever; and disdain the wretch, that with the pretended title of FATHER OF HIS PEOPLE can unfeelingly hear of their slaughter, and composedly sleep with their blood upon his soul.

***

OF THE PRESENT ABILITY OF AMERICA, WITH SOME MISCELLANEOUS REFLECTIONS.

I Have never met with a man, either in England or America, who hath not confessed his opinion, that a separation between the countries, would take place one time or other: And there is no instance, in which we have shewn less judgment; than in endeavouring to describe what we call, the ripeness or fitness of the Continent for independance.

As all men allow the measure, and vary only in their opinion of the time, let us in order to remove mistakes, take a general survey of things, and endeavour if possible, to find out the *very* time.   But we need not go far, the enquiry ceases at once, for, the *time hath found us*.   The general concurrence, the glorious union of all things, prove the fact.

'Tis not in numbers, but in unity that our great strength lies: yet our present numbers are sufficient to repel the force of all the world.   The Continent hath at this time the largest disciplined army of any power under Heaven: and is just arrived at that pitch of strength, in which no single Colony is able to support itself, and the whole, when united, is able to do anything.   Our land force is more than sufficient, and as to Naval affairs, we cannot be insensible that Britain would never suffer an American Man of War to be built, while the Continent remained in her hands.[7]   Wherefore, we should be no forwarder an hundred years hence, in

1054 men, but the 411 American casualties highlighted the reality of fighting a war against such a mighty force.
    [7] See above p. 103.

that branch than we are now; but the truth is, we should be less so, because the timber of the Country is every day diminishing.

Were the Continent crowded with inhabitants, her sufferings under the present circumstances would be intolerable. The more sea port Towns we had, the more should we have both to defend and to lose. Our present numbers are so happily proportioned to our wants, that no man need be idle. The diminution of trade affords an army, and the necessities of an army creates a new trade.

Debts we have none: and whatever we may contract on this account will serve as a glorious memento of our virtue.[8] Can we but leave posterity with a settled form of government, an independant constitution of it's own, the purchase at any price will be cheap. But to expend millions for the sake of getting a few vile acts repealed, and routing the present ministry only, is unworthy the charge, and is using posterity with the utmost cruelty; because it is leaving them the great work to do and a debt upon their backs from which they derive no advantage. Such a thought is unworthy a man of honour, and is the true characteristic of a narrow heart and a pidling politician.

The debt we may contract doth not deserve our regard if the work be but accomplished. No nation ought to be without a debt. A national debt is a national bond: and when it bears no interest is in no case a grievance. Britain is oppressed with a debt of upwards of one hundred and forty millions sterling, for which she pays upwards of four millions interest. And as a compensation for her debt, she has a large navy; America is without a debt, and without a navy; but for the twentieth part of the English national debt, could have a navy as large again. The navy of England is not worth at this time more than three millions and an half sterling.

No country on the globe is so happily situated, or so internally capable of raising a fleet as America. Tar, timber, iron, and cordage are her natural produce. We need go abroad for nothing. Whereas the Dutch, who make large profits by hiring out their ships of war to the Spaniards and Portuguese, are obliged to import most of the materials they use. We ought to view the building a fleet as an article of commerce, it being the natural manufactory of this country. 'Tis the best money we can lay out. A navy when finished is worth more than it cost: And is that nice point in national policy, in which commerce and protection are united. Let us build; if we want them not, we can sell; and by that means replace our paper currency with ready gold and silver.

In point of manning a fleet, people in general run into great errors; it is not necessary that one fourth part should be sailors. The Terrible Privateer, Capt. Death, stood the hottest engagement of any ship last war, yet had not twenty sailors on board, though her complement of men was upwards of two hundred.[9] A few able and social sailors will soon instruct a sufficient number of active landmen in the common work of a ship. Wherefore, we never can be more capable to begin on maritime matters than now, while our timber is standing, our fisheries blocked up, and our sailors and shipwrights out of employ. Men of war, of seventy and eighty guns were built forty years ago in New England, and why not the same now? Ship building is America's greatest pride, and in which, she will in time excel the whole world. The great empires of the east are mostly inland, and consequently excluded from the possibility of rivalling her. Africa is in a state of barbarism; and no power in Europe, hath either such an extent of coast, or such an internal supply of materials. Where nature hath given the one, she has with-held the other; to America only hath she been liberal of both. The vast empire of Russia is almost shut out from the sea; wherefore, her boundless forests, her tar, iron, and cordage are only articles of commerce.

---

[8] Note that here Paine turns the traditional republican antipathy to public debt as inimical to virtue on its head and describes debt as virtuous!

[9] Paine's knowledge of the *Terrible's* crew is drawn from his experience as a youth. In November 1756, Paine joined the crew of this ship, but withdrew at the last minute at his father's insistence. Paine was lucky as the majority of the men were killed in battle shortly after. This news did not deter Paine from later joining the *King of Prussia*. See Keane, *Paine*, pp. 34-36 and above p. 7.

In point of safety, ought we to be without a fleet? We are not the little people now, which we were sixty years ago, at that time we might have trusted our property in the streets, or fields rather, and slept securely without locks or bolts to our doors or windows. The case now is altered, and our methods of defence, ought to improve with our increase of property. A common pirate, twelve months ago, might have come up the Delaware, and laid the city of Philadelphia under instant Contribution for what sum he pleased; and the same might have happened to other places. Nay, any daring fellow, in a brig of 14 or 16 guns, might have robbed the whole Continent, and carried off half a million of money. These are circumstances which demand our attention, and point out the necessity of naval protection.[10]

Some perhaps will say, that after we have made it up with Britain that she will protect us. Can we be so unwise as to mean that she shall keep a Navy in our Harbours for that purpose? Common sense will tell us, that the power which hath endeavoured to subdue us, is of all others, the most improper to defend us. Conquest may be effected under the pretence of friendship; and ourselves, after a long and brave resistance, be at last cheated into slavery. And if her ships are not to be admitted into our harbours, I would ask, how is she to protect us? A navy three or four thousand miles off can be of little use, and on sudden emergencies, none at all. Wherefore, if we must hereafter protect ourselves, why not do it for ourselves? why do it for another?

The English list of ships of war, is long and formidable, but not a tenth part of them are at any time fit for service, numbers of them not in being; yet their names are pompously continued in the list if only a plank is left of the ship: and not a fifth part, of such as are fit for service, can be spared on any one station at one time. The East and West Indies, Mediterranean, Africa, and other parts over which Britain extends her claim, make large demands upon her navy. From a

---

[10] On the 6 May 1776, two British warships in Delaware Bay were driven out by armed boats from Philadelphia. See Robert Secor, *Pennsylvania 1776* (Philadelphia: Pennsylvania State University, 1975) p. 330. Compare this passage with Paine's later confidence below p. 185.

mixture of prejudice and inattention, we have contracted a false notion respecting the navy of England, and have talked as if we should have the whole of it to encounter at once, and for that reason, supposed, that we must have one as large; which not being instantly practicable, have been made use of by a set of disguised tories to discourage our beginning thereon. Nothing can be farther from truth than this, for if America had only a twentieth part of the naval force of Britain, she would be by far an over match for her; because, as we neither have, nor claim any foreign dominion, our whole force would be employed on our own coast, where we should, in the long run, have two to one the advantage of those who had three or four thousand miles to sail over, before they could attack us, and the same distance to return in order to refit and recruit. And although Britain by her fleet hath a check over our trade to Europe, we have as large a one over her trade to the West Indies, which, by laying in the neighbourhood of the Continent lie entirely at its mercy.

Some method might be fallen on to keep up a naval force in time of peace, if we should not judge it necessary to support a constant navy. If premiums were to be given to merchants to build and employ in their service, ships mounted with 20, 30, 40 or 50 guns (the premiums to be in proportion to the loss of bulk to the merchant) fifty or sixty of those ships, with a few guard ships on constant duty would keep up a sufficient navy, and that without burdening ourselves with the evil so loudly complained of in England, of suffering their fleets in time of peace to lie rotting in the docks. To unite the sinews of commerce and defence is sound policy; for when our strength and our riches, play into each other's hand, we need fear no external enemy.

In almost every article of defence we abound. Hemp flourishes even to rankness, so that we need not want cordage. Our iron is superior to that of other countries. Our small arms equal to any in the world. Cannon we can cast at pleasure. Salt-petre and gun powder we are every day producing. Our knowledge is hourly improving. Resolution is our inherent character, and courage hath never yet forsaken us. Wherefore, what is it that we want? why is it that we hesitate?

From Britain we can expect nothing but ruin. If she is once admitted to the government of America again, this Continent will not be worth living in. Jealousies will be always arising; insurrections will be constantly happening; and who will go forth to quell them? who will venture his life to reduce his own countrymen to a foreign obedience? the difference between Pennsylvania and Connecticut, respecting some unlocated lands, shews the insignificance of a British government, and fully proves, that nothing but Continental authority can regulate Continental matters.

Another reason why the present time is preferable to all others, is, that the fewer our numbers are, the more land there is yet unoccupied, which instead of being lavished by the king on his worthless dependants, may be hereafter applied, not only to the discharge of the present debt, but to the constant support of government. No nation under Heaven hath such an advantage as this.

The infant state of the Colonies, as it is called, so far from being against, is an argument in favour of independance. We are sufficiently numerous, and were we more so, we might be less united. 'Tis a matter worthy of observation, that the more a country is peopled, the smaller their armies are. In military numbers the ancients far exceeded the moderns: and the reason is evident, for trade being the consequence of population, men become too much absorbed thereby to attend to any thing else. Commerce diminishes the spirit both of Patriotism and military defence. And history sufficiently informs us, that the bravest achievements were always accomplished in the non age of a Nation. With the encrease of commerce England hath lost its spirit. The city of London, notwithstanding its numbers, submits to continued insults with the patience of a coward. The more men have to lose, the less willing are they to venture. The rich are in general slaves to fear, and submit to courtly power with the trembling duplicity of a Spaniel.

Youth is the seed time of good habits as well in nations as in individuals. It might be difficult, if not impossible to form the Continent into one Government half a century hence. The vast variety of interests occasioned by an increase of trade and population would create confusion. Colony would be against Colony.

Each being able would scorn each other's assistance: and while the proud and foolish gloried in their little distinctions, the wise would lament that the union had not been formed before. Wherefore, the *present time* is the *true time* for establishing it. The intimacy which is contracted in infancy, and the friendship which is formed in misfortune, are of all others, the most lasting and unalterable. Our present union is marked with both these characters: we are young, and we have been distressed; but our concord hath withstood our troubles, and fixes a memorable Æra for posterity to glory in.

***

ADDITIONS AND APPENDIX

The first and second editions of this pamphlet were published without the following calculations, which are now given as a proof that the above estimation of the navy is a just one. See Entick's naval history, introd. page 56.

The charge of building a ship of each rate, and furnishing her with masts, yards, sails and rigging, together with a proportion of eight months boatswain's and carpenter's sea-stores, as calculated by Mr. Burchett, Secretary to the Navy.

For a ship of a	100 guns —	£ 35,553
	90 —	29,886
	80 —	23,638
	70 —	17,785
	60 —	14,197
	50 —	10,606
	40 —	7,558
	30 —	5,846
	20 —	3,710

And from hence it is easy to sum up the value, or cost rather, of the whole British navy, which in the year 1757, when it was as its greatest glory consisted of the following ships and guns:

Ships.		Guns.		Cost of one.		Cost of all.
6	—	100	—	35,553 *l.*	—	213,318 *l.*
12	—	90	—	29,886	—	358,632
12	—	80	—	23,638	—	283,656
43	—	70	—	17,785	—	746,755
35	—	60	—	14,197	—	496,895
40	—	50	—	10,606	—	424,240
45	—	40	—	7,558	—	340,110
58	—	20	—	3,710	—	215,180

85 Sloops, bombs, and fireships,
one with another, at   2,000   170,000

                                  Cost   3,266,786

           Remains for guns   233,214

                                                3,500,000

***

[That it is the interest of America to be separated from Britain.]

It is in reality a self-evident position: For no nation in a state of foreign dependance, limited in its commerce, and cramped and fettered in its legislative powers, can ever arrive at any material eminence. America doth not yet know what opulence is; and although the progress which she hath made stands unparalleled in the history of other nations, it is but childhood, compared with what she would be capable of arriving at, had she, as she ought to have, the legislative powers in her own hands. England is, at this time, proudly coveting what would do her no good, were she to accomplish it; and the Continent hesitating on a matter, which will be her final ruin if neglected. It is the commerce and not the conquest of America, by which England is to be benefited, and that would in a great measure continue, were the countries as independant of each other as France and Spain; because in many articles, neither can go to a better market.

***

Should affairs be patched up with Britain, and she to remain the governing and sovereign power of America, (which, as matters are now circumstanced, is giving up the point intirely) we shall deprive ourselves of the very means of sinking the debt we have, or may contract. The value of the back lands which some of the provinces are clandestinely deprived of, by the unjust extension of the limits of Canada, valued only at five pounds sterling per hundred acres, amount to upwards of twenty-five millions, Pennsylvania currency; and the quit-rents at one penny sterling per acre, to two millions yearly.[11]

It is by the sale of those lands that the debt may be sunk, without burthen to any, and the quit-rent reserved thereon, will always lessen, and in time, will wholly support the yearly expence of government. It matters not how long the debt is in paying, so that the lands when sold, be applied to the discharge of it, and for the execution of which, the Congress for the time being, will be the continental trustees.

***

The present state of America is truly alarming to every man who is capable of reflexion. Without law, without government, without any other mode of power than what is founded on, and granted by courtesy. Held together by an unexampled concurrence of sentiment, which, is nevertheless subject to change, and which, every secret enemy is endeavouring to dissolve. Our present condition, is, Legislation without law; wisdom without a plan; constitution without a name; and, what is strangely astonishing, perfect Independance contending for dependance. The instance is without a precedent; the case never existed before; and who can tell what may be the event? The property of no man

---

[11] English land laws required owners to pay the crown or proprietor a quit rent based on the number of acres. It stood at two shillings per hundred acre in Virginia. Failure to pay could result in repossession.

is secure in the present unbraced system of things. The mind of the multitude is left at random, and seeing no fixed object before them, they pursue such as fancy or opinion starts. Nothing is criminal; there is no such thing as treason; wherefore, every one thinks himself at liberty to act as he pleases. The Tories dared not have assembled offensively, had they known that their lives, by that act, were forfeited to the laws of the state. A line of distinction should be drawn, between, English soldiers taken in battle, and inhabitants of America taken in arms. The first are prisoners, but the latter traitors. The one forfeits his liberty, the other his head.

Notwithstanding our wisdom, there is a visible feebleness in some of our proceedings which gives encouragement to dissentions. The Continental Belt is too loosely buckled. And if something is not done in time, it will be too late to do any thing, and we shall fall into a state, in which, neither Reconciliation nor Independance will be practicable.

***

Put us, say some, on the footing we were on in sixty-three: To which I answer, the request is not now in the power of Britain to comply with, neither will she propose it; but if it were, and even should be granted, I ask, as a reasonable question, By what means is such a corrupt and faithless court to be kept to its engagements? Another parliament, nay, even the present, may hereafter repeal the obligation, on the pretence, of its being violently obtained, or unwisely granted; and in that case, Where is our redress?—No going to law with nations; cannon are the barristers of Crowns; and the sword, not of justice, but of war, decides the suit. To be on the footing of sixty-three, it is not sufficient, that the laws only be put on the same state, but, that our circumstances, likewise, be put on the same state; Our burnt and destroyed towns repaired or built up, our private losses made good, our public debts (contracted for defence) discharged; otherwise, we shall be millions worse than we were at that enviable period. Such a request, had it been complied with a year ago, would have won the heart and soul of the Continent—but now it is too late, "The Rubicon is passed."

The CRISIS No. VII.

To the PEOPLE of ENGLAND.

THERE are stages in the business of serious life in which to amuse is cruel, but to deceive is to destroy; and it is of little consequence, in the conclusion, whether men deceive themselves, or submit, by a kind of mutual consent, to the impositions of each other. That England has long been under the influence of delusion or mistake, needs no other proof than the unexpected and wretched situation that she is now involved in: And so powerful has been the influence, that no provision was ever made or thought of against the misfortune, because the possibility of its happening was never conceived.

The general and successful resistance of America, the conquest of Burgoyne, and a war with France, were treated in Parliament as the dreams of a discontented opposition, or a distempered imagination.[1] They were beheld as objects unworthy of a serious thought, and the bare intimation of them afforded the Ministry a triumph of laughter. Short triumph indeed! For every thing which has been predicted has happened, and all that was promised have failed. A long series of politics so remarkably distinguished by a succession of misfortunes, without one alleviating turn, must certainly have something in it systematically wrong. It is sufficient to awaken the most credulous into suspicion, and the most obstinate into thought. Either the means in your power are insufficient, or the measures ill planned; either the execution has been bad, or the thing attempted impracticable; or, to speak more emphatically, either you are not able, or Heaven is not willing. For, why is it that you have not conquered us? Who, or what has prevented you? You have had every opportunity that you could desire, and succeeded to your utmost wish in every preparatory means. Your fleets and armies have arrived in America without an accident. No uncommon misfortune hath intervened. No

---

[1] General John Burgoyne (1722-92) was forced to surrender to General Horatio Gates (1728-1806) at Saratoga on 17 October 1777, the first decisive British loss. Regarding the parallel war between Britain and France, see below p. 156.

foreign nation hath interfered until the time which you had allotted for victory was past. The opposition, either in or out of Parliament, neither disconcerted your measures, retarded or diminished your force. They only foretold your fate. Every ministerial scheme was carried with as high a hand as if the whole nation had been unanimous. Every thing wanted was asked for, and every thing asked for was granted. A greater force was not within the compass of your abilities to send, and the time you sent it was of all others the most favorable. You were then at rest with the whole world beside. You had the range of every court in Europe uncontradicted by us. You amused us with a tale of Commissioners of Peace, and under that disguise collected a numerous army and came almost unexpectedly upon us.[2] The force was much greater than we looked for; and that which we had to oppose it with, was unequal in numbers, badly armed, and poorly disciplined; beside which, it was embodied only for a short time, and expired within a few months after your arrival. We had governments to form; measures to concert; an army to raise and train, and every necessary article to import or to create. Our non-importation-scheme had exhausted our stores, and your command by sea intercepted our supplies. We were a people unknown, and unconnected with the political world, and strangers to the disposition of foreign powers. Could you possibly wish for a more favourable conjunction of circumstances? Yet all these have happened and passed away, and as it were left you with a laugh. They are likewise events of such an original nativity as can never happen again, unless a new world should arise from the ocean.

If any thing can be a lesson to presumption, surely the circumstances of this war will have their effect. Had Britain been defeated by any European power, her pride would have drawn consolation from the importance of her conquerors; but in the present case, she is excelled by those that she affected to despise, and her own opinions, retorting on herself, become an aggravation of her disgrace.

---

[2] The Carlisle Peace Commission was suspected of being planned as a distraction as the Commissioners arrived in Philadelphia in the summer of 1778, shortly before the British evacuation of the city.

Misfortune and experience are lost upon mankind, when they produce neither reflection nor reformation. Evils, like poisons, have their uses, and there are diseases which no other remedy can reach. It has been the crime and folly of England to suppose herself invincible, and *that*, without acknowledging or perceiving that a full third of her strength was drawn from the country she is now at war with. The arm of Britain has been spoken of as the arm of the Almighty, and she has lived of late as if she thought the whole world created for her diversion. Her politics, instead of civilizing, has tended to brutalize mankind, and under the vain unmeaning title of *"Defender of the Faith,"* she has made war like an Indian against the religion of humanity.[3] Her cruelties in the East-Indies will *never, never* be forgotten; and it is somewhat remarkable that the produce of that ruined country, transported to America, should there kindle up a war to punish the destroyer.[4] The chain is continued, though with a kind of mysterious uniformity, both in the crime and the punishment. The latter runs parallel with the former; and time and fate will give it a perfect illustration.

Where information is with-held, ignorance becomes a reasonable excuse; and one would charitably hope that the people of England do not encourage cruelty from choice but from mistake. Their recluse situation, surrounded by the sea, preserves them from the calamities of war, and keeps them in the dark as to the conduct of their own armies. They see not, therefore they feel not. They tell the tale that is told them and believe it and accustomed to no other news than their own, they receive it, stript of its horrors and prepared for the palate of the nation, through the channel of the London Gazette. They are made to believe that their Generals and armies differ from those of other nations, and have nothing of rudeness or barbarity in them. They suppose them what they wish them to be.

---

[3] 'Defender of the Faith' was a title given to Henry VIII by Pope Leo X in 1521, shortly before the schism of the Church of England from Rome. The title is maintained by his heirs and commonly paraded on English coins.

[4] The British atrocities in India were one of Paine's earliest concerns. See 'Reflections on the Life and Death of Lord Clive' (*Pennsylvania Magazine*, March 1775), *Writings*, I, 29-35. [Authorship in doubt. See Aldridge, *American Ideology*, p. 287.]

They feel a disgrace in thinking otherwise, and naturally encourage the belief from a partiality to themselves. There was a time when I felt the same prejudices and reasoned from the same errors; but experience, sad and painful experience has taught me better. What the conduct of former armies was I know not, but what the conduct of the present is I well know. It is low, cruel, indolent, and profligate; and had the people of America no other cause for separation than what the army has occasioned, *that alone* is cause enough.

The field of politics in England is far more extensive than that of news. Men have a right to reason for themselves, and though they cannot contradict the intelligence in the London Gazette, they may frame upon it what sentiments they please. But the misfortune is, that a general ignorance has prevailed over the whole nation respecting America. The Ministry and the Minority have both been wrong. The former was always so; the latter only lately so. Politics to be executively right, must have a unity of means and time, and a defect in either overthrows the whole. The Ministry rejected the plans of the Minority while they were practicable, and joined in them when they became impracticable. From wrong measures they got into wrong time, and have now completed the circle of absurdity by closing it upon themselves.

It was my fate to come to America a few months before the breaking out of hostilities. I found the disposition of the people such, that they might have been led by a thread and governed by a reed. Their suspicion was quick and penetrating, but their attachment to Britain was obstinate, and it was, at that time, a kind of treason to speak against it. They disliked the Ministry, but they esteemed the nation. Their ideas of grievance operated without resentment, and their single object was reconciliation. Bad as I believed the Ministry to be, I never conceived them capable of a measure so rash and wicked as the commencing of hostilities; much less did I imagine the nation would encourage it. I viewed the dispute as a kind of law-suit, in which I supposed the parties would find a way either to decide or settle it. I had no thoughts of independence or of arms. The world could not then have persuaded me that I should be either a soldier or an author. If I had any talents for either, they were buried in me, and might ever have continued so, had not the necessity of the times dragged and driven them into action. I had formed my plan of life, and conceiving myself happy, wished every body else so. But when the country, into which I had but just put my foot, was set on fire about my ears it was time to stir. It was time for every man to stir. Those who had been long settled had something to defend; those who were just come had something to pursue; and the call and the concern was equal and universal. For in a country where all men were once adventurers, the difference of a few years in their arrival could make none in their right.

The breaking out of hostilities opened a new suspicion in the politics of America, which though at that time very rare, has been since proved to be very right. What I allude to is, *a secret and fixt determination in the British Cabinet to annex America to the Crown of England as a conquered country.* If this be taken as the object, then the whole line of conduct pursued by the Ministry, though rash in its origin and ruinous in its consequences, is nevertheless uniform and consistent in its parts. It applies to every case and resolves every difficulty. But if taxation, or any thing else, be taken in its room, then is there no proportion between the object and the charge. Nothing but the whole soil and property of the country can be placed as a possible equivalent against the millions which the Ministry expended. No taxes raised in America could possibly repay it. A revenue of two millions sterling a year would not discharge the sum and interest accumulated thereon, in twenty years.

Reconciliation never appear[s] to have been the wish or the object of the administration, they looked on conquest as certain and infallible, and under that persuasion, sought to drive the Americans into what they might stile a general rebellion, and then crushing them with arms in their hands, reap the rich harvest of a general confiscation and silence them for ever. The dependants at Court were too numerous to be provided for in England. The market for plunder in the East-Indies was over; and the profligacy of government required that a new mine should be opened, and that mine could be no other than America conquered and forfeited. They had no where else to go. Every other channel was drained; and extravagance, with the thirst of a drunkard, was gaping for supplies.

If the Ministry deny this to have been their plan, it becomes them to explain what was their plan. For either they have abused us in coveting property they never laboured for, or they have abused you in expending an amazing sum upon an incompetent object. Taxation, as I mentioned before could never be worth the charge of obtaining it by arms, and any kind of formal obedience which America could have made, would have weighed with the lightness of a laugh against such a load of expence. It is therefore most probable, that the Ministry will at last justify their policy by their dishonesty, and openly declare that their original design was conquest: And in this case, it well becomes the people of England to consider how far the nation would have been benefited by the success.

In a general view there are few conquests that repay the charge of making them, and mankind are pretty well convinced that it can never be worth their while to go to war for profit sake. If they are made war upon, their country invaded, or their existence at stake, it is their duty to defend and preserve themselves, but in every other light and from every other cause is war inglorious and detestable. But to return to the case in question—

When conquests are made of foreign countries, it is supposed that the *commerce* and *dominion* of the country which made them are extended. But this could neither be the object nor the consequence of the present war. You enjoyed the whole commerce before. It could receive no possible addition by a conquest, but on the contrary, must diminish as the inhabitants were reduced in numbers and wealth. You had the same *dominion* over the country which you used to have, and had no complaint to make against her for breach of any part of the compact between you and her, or contending against any established custom, commercial, political or territorial. The country and the commerce were both your own when you *began* to conquer, in the same manner and form as they had been your own an hundred years before. Nations have sometimes been induced to make conquests for the sake of reducing the power of their enemies, or bringing it to a balance with their own. But this could be no part of your plan. No foreign authority was claimed here, neither was any such authority suspected by you, or acknowledged, or imagined by us. What then, in the name of Heaven, could you go to war for? or what chance could you possibly have in the event, but either to hold the same country which you held before, and that in a much worse condition, or to lose with an amazing expence what you might have retained without a farthing of charge?

War never can be the interest of a trading nation, any more than quarrelling can be profitable to a man in business. But to make war with those who trade with us, is like setting a bull-dog upon a customer at the shop door. The least degree of common sense shews the madness of the latter, and it will apply with the same force of conviction to the former. Piratical nations, having neither commerce or commodities of their own to lose, may make war upon all the world, and lucratively find their account in it. But it is quite otherwise with Britain. For, besides the stoppage of trade in time of war, she exposes more of her own property to be lost, than she has the chance of taking from others. Some ministerial gentlemen in Parliament have mentioned the greatness of her trade as an apology for the greatness of her loss. This is miserable politics indeed! because it ought to have been given as a reason for her not engaging in a war at first. The coast of America commands the West India trade almost as effectually as the coast of Africa does that of the Streights, and England can no more carry on the former without the consent of America, than she can the latter without a Mediterranean pass.

In whatever light the war with America is considered upon commercial principles, it is evidently the interest of the people of England not to support it; and why it has been supported so long against the clearest demonstrations of truth and national advantage, is to me, and must be to all the reasonable world, a matter of astonishment. Perhaps it may be said that I live in America, and write this from interest. To this I reply, that my principles are universal. My attachment is to all the world and not to any particular part, and if what I advance is right, no matter where or who it comes from. We have given the proclamation of your Commissioners a currency in our news-papers, and I have no doubt you will give this a place in yours. To oblige and be obliged is fair.

Before I dismiss this part of my address I shall mention one more circumstance in which I think the people of England have been equally mistaken; and then proceed to other matter.

There is such an idea existing in the world as that of *national honor,* and this, falsely understood, is oftentimes the cause of war. In a christian and philosophical sense mankind seem to have stood still at individual civilization, and to retain as nations all the original rudeness of nature. Peace, by treaty, is only a cessation of violence, for a reformation of sentiment. It is a substitute for a principle that is wanting, and ever will be wanting till the idea of *national honor* be rightly understood. As individuals we profess, ourselves christians, but as nations we are heathens, Romans, and what not. I remember the late Admiral Saunders declaring in the House of Commons, and that in the time of peace, "*that the city of Madrid laid in ashes was not a sufficient atonement for the Spaniards taking off the rudder of an English sloop of war.*" I do not ask whether this is christianity or morality, I ask whether it is decency? whether it is proper language for a nation to use? In private life we call it by the plain name of bullying, and the elevation of rank cannot alter its character. It is I think exceedingly easy to define what ought to be understood by *national honour,* for *that* which is the best character for an individual is the best character for a nation; and wherever the latter exceeds or falls beneath the former, there is a departure from the line of true greatness.

I have thrown out this observation with a design of applying it to Great Britain. Her idea of national honour seems devoid of that benevolence of heart, that universal expansion of philanthropy, and that triumph over the rage of vulgar prejudice, without which man is inferior to himself, and a companion of common animals. To know whom she shall regard or dislike, she asks what country they are of, what religion they profess, and what property they enjoy. Her idea of national honour seems to consist in national insult, and that to be a great people, is to be neither a christian, a philosopher, or a gentleman, but to threaten with the rudeness of a bear, and to devour with the ferocity of a lion. This perhaps may sound harsh and uncourtly, but it is too true, and the more is the pity.

I mention this only as her general character. But towards America she has observed no character at all; and destroyed by her conduct what she assumed in her title. She set out with the stile of *Parent*, or *Mother Country*. The association of ideas which naturally accompany this expression are filled with every thing that is fond, tender and forbearing. They have an energy particular to themselves and overlooking the accidental attachment of common affections, apply with peculiar softness to the first feelings of the heart. It is a political term which every mother can feel the force of, and every child can judge of. It needs no painting of mine to set it off, for nature only can do it justice.

But has any part of your conduct to America corresponded with the title you set up? If in your general national character you are unpolished and severe, in this you are inconsistent and unnatural; and you must have exceeding false notions of national honour, to suppose that the world can admire a want of humanity, or that national honour depends on the violence of resentment, the inflexibility of temper, or the vengeance of execution.

I would willingly convince you, and that with as much temper as the times will suffer me to do, that as you opposed your own interest by quarrelling with us, so likewise your national honour, rightly conceived and understood, was no ways called upon to enter into a war with America; had you studied true greatness of heart, the first and fairest ornament of mankind, you would have acted directly contrary to all that you have done, and the world would have ascribed it to a generous cause, besides which, you had (*though with the assistance of this country*) secured a powerful name by the last war.[5] You were known and dreaded

---

[5] Paine refers to the Seven Years War (1756-63) known in America as the French and Indian War. Britain and Prussia were allied against France, Austria, Russia, Sweden, Saxony, and Spain. Fighting took place in North America, the West Indies, West Africa, India, and Europe. France

abroad; and it would have been wise in you to have suffered the world to have slept undisturbed under that idea. It was to you, a force existing without expence. It produced to you all the advantages of real power; and you were stronger through the universality of *that charm*, than any future fleets and armies may probably make you. Your greatness was so secured and interwoven with your silence that you ought never to have awakened mankind, and had nothing to do but to be quiet. Had you been true politicians you would have seen all this, and continued to draw from the magic of a name, the force and authority of a nation.

Unwise as you were in breaking the charm, you were still more unwise in the manner of doing it. *Sampson* only *told the secret*, but *you* have *performed the operation*; you have shaven your own head, and wantonly thrown away the locks.[6] America was the hair from which the charm was drawn that infatuated the world. You ought to have quarrelled with *no* power; but with *her* upon *no* account. You had nothing to fear from any condescension you might make. You might have humoured her, even if there had been no justice in her claims, without any risk to your reputation; for Europe fascinated by your fame, would have ascribed it to your beneficence, and America, intoxicated by the grant, would have slumbered in her fetters.

But this method of studying the progress of the passions, in order to ascertain the probable conduct of mankind, is a philosophy in politics, which those who preside at St. James's have no conceptions of.[7] They know no other influence than corruption, and reckon all their probabilities from precedent. A new case is to them a new world, and while they are seeking for a parallel they get lost. The talents of Lord Mansfield can be estimated at best no higher than those of a

---

and Britain both allied with Native American peoples in their dispute over the Ohio Valley. Caused primarily by an unstable diplomatic situation left at the end of the war of the Austrian Succession, the war greatly enhanced Britain's international power, and reputation, although at a great cost. The national debt was increased by £130 million. Britain gained control of Florida and Canada but allowed France to retain her holdings in the West Indies.

[6] For the biblical account of Samson's hair see Judges, 13-16.

[7] The Palace of St. James was the location of the Royal Court.

Sophist.[8] He understands the subtleties but not the elegance of nature; and by continually viewing mankind through the cold medium of the law, never thinks of penetrating into the warmer region of the mind. As for Lord North, it is his happiness to have in him more philosophy than sentiment, for he bears flogging like a top and sleeps the better for it. His punishment becomes his support, for while he suffers the lash for his sins, he keeps himself up by twirling about. In politics, he is a good arithmetician, and in every thing else nothing at all.

There is one circumstance which comes so much within Lord North's province as a financier, that I am surprised it should escape him, which is, the different abilities of the two countries in supporting the expence; for, strange as it may seem, England is not a match for America in this particular. By a curious kind of revolution in accounts, the people of England seem to mistake their poverty for their riches; that is, they reckon their national debt as a part of their national wealth. They make the same kind of error which a man would do, who after mortgaging his estate, should add the money borrowed, to the full value of the estate in order to count up his worth, and in this case he would conceit that he got rich by running into debt. Just thus it is with England. The Government owed at the beginning of this war One Hundred and Thirty-five millions sterling, and though the individuals to whom it was due, had a right to reckon their shares as so much private property, yet to the nation collectively it was so much poverty. There is as effectual limits to public debts as to private ones, for when once the money borrowed is so great as to require the whole yearly revenue to discharge the interest thereon, there is an end to farther borrowing; in the same manner as when the interest of a man's debts amounts to the yearly income of his estate there is an end to his credit. This is nearly the case with England, the interest of her present debt being at least equal to one half of her yearly revenue, so that out of Ten Million annually collected by taxes, she has but Five she can call her own.

---

[8] Lord Mansfield (1705-93) was chief Justice in the King's bench from 1756. As a member of the ministry, he was unpopular due to his creative legal rulings, particularly in the field of trade law.

The very reverse of this was the case with America. She began the war without any debt upon her, and in order to carry it on, she neither raised money by taxes, nor borrowed it upon interest, but *created* it; and her situation at this time continues so much the reverse of yours that taxing would make her rich, whereas it would make you poor. When we shall have sunk the sum which we have created, we shall then be out of debt, be just as rich as when we began, and all the while we are doing it, shall feel no difference, because the value will rise as the quantity decreases.

There was not a country in the world so capable of bearing the expence of a war as America; not only because she was not in debt when she began, but because the country is young and capable of infinite improvement, and has an almost boundless tract of new lands in store, whereas England has got to her extent of age and growth, and has no unoccupied lands or property in reserve. The one is like a young heir coming to a large improvable estate; the other like an old man whose chances are over, and his estate mortgaged for half its worth.

In the second number of the Crisis, which I find has been re-published in England, I endeavoured to set forth the impracticability of conquering America.[9] I stated every case, that I conceived could possibly happen, and ventured to predict its consequences. As my conclusions were drawn not artfully but naturally, they have all proved to be true. I was upon the spot, knew the politics of America, her strength and resources, and by a train of services, the best in my power to render, was honoured with the friendship of the Congress, the army and the people. I considered the cause a just one. I know and feel it a just one, and under that confidence never made my own profit or loss an object. My endeavour was to have the matter well understood on both sides, and I conceived myself rendering a general service, by setting forth to the one the impossibility of being conquered, and to the other the impossibility of conquering. Most of the arguments made use of by the Ministry for supporting the war, are the very

---

[9] See 'Crisis II' (1777) *Writings*, I, 179-196.

arguments that ought to have been used against supporting it; and the plans, by which they thought to conquer, are the very plans in which they were sure to be defeated. They have taken every thing up at the wrong end. Their ignorance is astonishing, and were you in my situation you would see it. They may perhaps have your confidence, but I am persuaded that they would make very indifferent Members of Congress. I know what England is, and what America is, and from this compound of knowledge, am better enabled to judge of the issue, than what the King or any of his Ministers can be.

In this number I have endeavoured to shew the ill policy and disadvantages of the war. I believe many of my remarks are new. Those which are not so, I have studied to improve and place in a manner that may be clear and striking. Your failure is, I am persuaded, as certain as fate. America is above your reach. She is at least your equal in the world, and her Independence neither rests upon your consent, or can be prevented by your arms. In short, you spend your substance in vain, and impoverish yourselves without a hope.

But suppose you had conquered America, what advantage, collectively or individually, as merchants, manufacturers, or conquerors, could you have looked for. This is an object you never seem to have attended to. Listening for the sound of victory, and led away by the phrensy of arms, you neglected to reckon either the cost or the consequences. You must all pay towards the expence; the poorest among you must bear his share, and it is both your right and your duty to weigh seriously the matter. Had America been conquered, she might have been parcelled out in grants to the favourites at court, but no share of it would have fallen to you. Your taxes would not have been lessened, because she would have been in no condition to have paid any towards your relief. We are rich by contrivance of our own, which would have ceased as soon as you became masters. Our paper money will be of no use in England, and gold and silver we have none. In the last war you made many conquests, but were any of your taxes lessened thereby? On the contrary, were you not taxed to pay for the charge of making them, and has not the same been the case in every war?

To the Parliament I wish to address myself in a more particular manner. They appear to have supposed themselves partners in the chace, and to have hunted with the lion from an expectation of a right in the booty; but in this it is most probable they would, as legislators, have been disappointed. The case is quite a new one, and many unforeseen difficulties would have arisen thereon. The Parliament claimed a legislative right over America, and the war originated from that pretence. But the army is supposed to belong to the crown, and if America had been conquered through their means, the claim of the Legislature would have been suffocated in the conquest. Ceded or conquered countries are supposed to be out of the authority of Parliament. Taxation is exercised over them by prerogative and not by law. It was attempted to be done in the Granades a few years ago, and the only reason why it was not done, was because the crown had made a prior relinquishment of its claim. Therefore, Parliament have been all this while supporting measures for the establishment of their authority, in the issue of which, they would have been triumphed over by the prerogative. This might have opened a new and interesting opposition between the Parliament and the Crown. The Crown would have said that it conquered for itself, and that to conquer for Parliament was an unknown case. The Parliament might have replied, that America not being a *foreign* country, but a country in *rebellion*, could not be said to be *conquered*, but *reduced*; and thus continued their claim by disowning the term. The Crown might have rejoined, that however America might be considered at *first*, she became foreign at *last* by a declaration of Independence and a *treaty with France*; and that her case being, by *that treaty*, put within the law of nations, was out of the law of Parliament. The Parliament might have maintained, that as their claim over America had never been *surrendered*, so neither could it be *taken away*. The Crown might have insisted, that though the claim of Parliament could *not be taken away*, yet being an *inferior*, it might be *superceded*; and that, whether the claim was withdrawn from the object, or the object taken from the claim, the same separation ensued; and that America being subdued after a treaty with France, was to all intents and purposes a regal conquest, and of course the sole property of the King. The Parliament, as the legal delegates of the people, might have contended against the term *"inferior"* and rested the case upon the antiquity of power, and this would have brought on a set of interesting and rational questions.

First, What is the original fountain of power and honour in any country?

Secondly, Whether the prerogative does not belong to the people?

Thirdly, Whether there is any such thing as the English constitution?

Fourthly, Of what use is the Crown to the people?

Fifthly, Whether he who invented a crown was not an enemy to mankind?

Sixthly, Whether it is not a shame for a man to spend a million a year and do no good for it, and whether the money might not be better applied?

Seventhly, Whether such a man is not better dead than alive?

Eighthly, Whether a Congress, constituted like that of America, is not the most happy and consistent form of government in the world? —With a number of others of the same import.

In short, the contention about the dividend might have distracted the nation; for nothing is more common than to agree in the conquest and quarrel for the prize; therefore it is, perhaps, a happy circumstance, that our successes have prevented the dispute.

If the Parliament had been thrown out in *their* claim, which it is most probable they would, the nation, likewise would have been thrown out in *their* expectation; for as the taxes would have been laid on by the crown without the Parliament, the revenue arising therefrom, if any could have arose, would not have gone into the Exchequer, but into the privy purse, and so far from lessening their taxes, would not even have been added to them, but served only as pocket money to the Crown. The more I reflect on this matter the more am I astonished at the blindness and ill policy of my countrymen, whose wisdom seem[s] to operate without discernment, and their strength without an object.

To the great bulwark of the nation, I mean the mercantile and manufacturing part thereof, I likewise present my address. It is your interest to see America an independent country and *not* a conquered one. If conquered, she is ruined; and if ruined, poor; consequently the trade will be a trifle, and her credit doubtful. If independent, she flourishes, and from *her flourishing* must *your profits* arise. It matters nothing to you who governs America, if your manufactures find a consumption there. Some articles will consequently be obtained from other places, and it is right that they should, but the demand for others will encrease, by the great influx of inhabitants which a state of independence and peace will occasion, and in the final event you may be enriched. The commerce of America is perfectly free, and ever will be so. She will consign away no part of it to any nation. She has not to her friends, and certainly will not to her enemies, though it is probable that your narrow minded politicians, thinking to please you thereby, may some time or other make such an unnecessary proposal. Trade flourishes best when it is free, and it is weak policy to attempt to fetter it. Her treaty with France is on the most liberal and generous principles, and the French in their conduct towards her has [sic] proved themselves to be philosophers, politicians, and gentlemen.

To the Ministry I likewise address myself. You, gentlemen, have studied the ruin of your country, from which it is not within your abilities to rescue her. Your attempts to recover are as ridiculous as your plans which involved her are detestable. The Commissioners being about to depart, will probably bring you this and with it my sixth number to them; and in so doing they carry back more *Common Sense* than they brought, and you likewise will have more than when you sent them.

Having thus addressed you severally, I conclude by addressing you collectively. It is a long lane that has no turning. A period of sixteen years of misconduct and misfortune, is certainly long enough for any one nation to suffer under; and upon a supposition that war is not declared between France and you, I beg to place a line of conduct before you that will easily lead you out of all your troubles. It has been hinted before, and cannot be too much attended to.

Suppose America had remained unknown to Europe till the present year, and that Mr. Banks and Dr. Solander, in another voyage round the world, had made the first discovery of her, in the self same condition that she is now in, of arts, arms, numbers, and civilization.[10] What, I ask, in that case, would have been your conduct towards her, for *that* will point out what it ought to be now? The problems and their solutions are equal, and the right line of the one is the parallel of the other. The question takes in every circumstance that can possibly arise. It reduces politics to a simple thought, and is moreover a mode of investigation, in which, while you are studying your interest, the simplicity of the case will cheat you into good temper. You have nothing to do but to suppose that you have found America and she appears found to your hand, and while in the joy of your heart you stand still to admire her, the path of politics rises strait before you.

Were I disposed to paint a contrast, I could easily set off what you *have done* in the *present case*, against what you *would have done* in *that case*, and by justly opposing them, conclude a picture that would make you blush. But as when any of the prouder passions are hurt, it is much better philosophy to let a man slip into a good temper than to attack him in a bad one, for that reason therefore, I only state the case and leave yourselves to reflect upon it.

To go a little back into politics, it will be found, that the true interest of Britain lay in proposing and promoting the independence of America immediately after the last peace; for the expence which Britain had then incurred by defending America as HER OWN DOMINIONS, ought to have shewn her the policy and necessity of changing the *stile* of the country, as the *best* probable method of preventing future wars and expence, and the *only* method by which she could hold the commerce without the charge of sovereignty. Besides which, the title she assumed of *Parent Country* naturally led to, and pointed out, the propriety,

---

[10] Sir Joseph Banks (1743-1820) and Daniel Solander (1733-82) were botanists who accompanied Captain James Cook on his expedition around the world in 1768-71, collecting and cataloguing more than 2,600 new plant species, particularly in New South Wales. In 1772, Banks and Solander explored Iceland.

wisdom and advantage of a separation; for as in private life children grow into men, and by setting up for themselves extend and secure the interest of the whole family, so in the settlement of colonies large enough to admit of maturity, the same policy should be pursued and the same consequences would follow. Nothing hurts the affections both of parents and children so much as living too closely connected, and keeping up the distinction too long. Domineering will not do over those, who by a progress in life are become equal in rank to their parents, that is, when they have families of their own; and though they may conceive themselves the subjects of their advice, will not suppose themselves the objects of their government. I do not, by drawing this parallel, mean to admit the title of *Parent Country,* because, if due any where, it is due to Europe collectively and the first settlers from England were driven here by persecution. I mean only to introduce the term for the sake of the policy and to shew from your title, the line of your interest.

When you saw the state of strength and opulence, and that by her own industry, which America had arrived at, you ought to have advised her to set up for herself, and proposed an alliance of interest with her, and in so doing, you would have drawn, and that at her *own* expence, more real advantage, and more military supplies and assistance both of ships and men, than from any weak and wrangling government you could exercise over her. In short, had you studied only the domestic politics of a family, you would have learned how to govern the state; but, instead of this easy and natural line, you flew out into every thing which was wild and outrageous, till by following the passion and stupidity of the pilot you wrecked the vessel within sight of the shore.

Having shown what you *ought to have done,*— I now proceed to shew the reason why it was *not done.* The caterpillar circle of the Court had an interest to pursue, distinct from, and opposed to yours, for though by the Independence of America and an alliance therewith, the trade would have continued, if not encreased, as in many articles neither country can go to a better market, and though by defending and protecting herself, she would have been no expence to you, and consequently your national charges would have decreased and your taxes might have been proportionably lessened thereby, yet the striking off so many places from the Court Calendar was put in opposition to the interest of the nation. The loss of thirteen governmentships with their appendages, here and in England, is a shocking sound in the ear of a hungry courtier. Your present King and Ministry will be the ruin of you; and you had better risk a revolution and call a Congress, than be thus led on from madness to despair, and from despair to ruin. America has set you the example, and you may follow it and be free.

I now come to the last part, *a war with France.* This is what no man in his senses will advise you to, and all good men would wish to prevent. Whether France will declare war against you, is not for me in this place to mention or to hint even if I knew it, but it must be madness in you to do it first. The matter is come now to a *full crisis,* and peace is easy if willingly set about. Whatever you may think, France has behaved handsomely to you. She would have been unjust to herself to have acted otherwise than she did; and having accepted our offer of alliance, she gave you genteel notice of it. There was nothing in her conduct reserved or indelicate, and while she announced her determination to support her treaty she left you to give the first offence.[11] America, on her part, has exhibited a character of firmness to the world. Unprepared and unarmed, without form or government she singly opposed a nation that domineered over half the globe. The greatness of the deed demands respect; and though you may feel resentment, you are compelled both to WONDER and ADMIRE.

HERE I rest my arguments and finish my address. Such as it is, it is a gift and you are welcome. It was always my design to dedicate a *Crisis* to you, when the time should come that would properly *make it a Crisis;* and when, likewise, I should catch myself in a temper to write it, and suppose you in a condition to read it. *That* time has now arrived, and with it, the opportunity of conveyance. For the Commissioners—*poor Commissioners!*—having proclaimed, that *"yet forty days*

---

[11] See below p. 156.

and Nineveh shall be overthrown," have waited out the date, and, discontented with their God, are returning to their gourd. And all the harm I wish them is, that it may not *wither* about their ears, and that they may not make their exit in the belly of a Whale.[12]

 Philadelphia,   COMMON SENSE.
 November 11, 1778.

---

[12] After his brush with the whale, acting on Jehovah's instructions, Jonah warns the people of Ninevah of their imminent destruction. However, seeing the people's fear and sudden piety, Jehovah changes his mind and spares the city, whereupon Jonah sulks under a divinely provided gourd. Jehovah causes the gourd to wither to teach Jonah a lesson about mercy. See Jonah 3. 4.
 I have omitted here a postscript in which Paine warns the commissioners not to attempt to exceed the limited powers allotted to them by Parliament.

Chapter Two

Tax and Financing the War

Tax is one of Paine's favourite subjects; perhaps in part due to the years he spent trying to collect duties an Excise Officer. Popular English hatred for the Excise Service must have given him cause for thought on the merits of different methods of collecting government revenue. In *Common Sense* Paine argues that if the colonies reached a settlement with Britain, far from being released from the tax impositions at the root of their quarrel, they would be forced to pay more taxes to cover the cost of their own repression. Government is best when it is least expensive, a principle that continued to form the basis of his attack on the oppressive tax burden of the British government in the *Rights of Man*.

There is no inconsistency between Paine's dislike of taxes in some works and his writing in favour of measures to raise tax to fund the War of Independence in others. Taxes are evil when unnecessary and collected by a corrupt and irrational system of government. Throughout his works, Paine suggests that the British blend of monarchy and aristocracy serves to create unnecessary wars, providing the excuse to raise taxes and public debt, funding places and pensions for unnecessary jobs, to the private profit of the oligarchs. A representative government would share the same interests as its electors and would make every effort to minimise the tax burden and ensure that it was fairly distributed. The issues related to tax in Paine's writings are much the same as in our own time: what is the most just and efficient means of collecting tax and how should it be spent?

The War of Independence created a unique problem in public finance. The Continental Congress took on the considerable task of fighting the British Empire but, having not existed before, had no public resources to draw upon whatsoever. However patriotic, even a volunteer army needs to be fed and clothed, in addition to arms and medical supplies. Given the tradition of issuing paper money for defence purposes, their solution was logical. The Congress issued $241,552,780 of Continental Currency in eleven separate resolutions between May 1775 and January 1779. The notes represented money borrowed against future taxes to be levied by each individual state, and were to be payable in Spanish silver dollars.[1] But printing money is always a short-term solution, and the resulting inflation merely served to exacerbate the hoarding of hard currency. The taxes borrowed on failed to materialise, in part due to a shortage of currency to pay them in. Trade was restricted by port blockades and the boycott of British goods and many areas had been captured by the British, or devastated by the violence of the struggle, leaving little taxable trade or property.

The War of Independence was always going to be a difficult war to finance, caused as it was by a campaign against the imposition of taxes. Colonial resistance to British rule originated in their response to George Grenville's and Townshend's new taxes in the 1760's on sugar, newspapers, and imports of glass, lead, paint, paper and tea, and the government's attempts to counter tax evasion.[2] The measures were justified by the cost of defending the colonies against French and Indian attacks during Seven Years War and the quartering of troops in the colonies in case of further attacks. In part, the colonists' grievances were

---

[1] Newman, *Early Paper Money*, p. 13.
[2] See above p. 122, n. 6.

political: the British Parliament had no jurisdiction to impose taxes, which ought to be the free gift of colonial assemblies. In each case the taxes were accompanied by non-fiscal measures asserting Parliament's authority over colonial legislatures and the authority of government officials in disregarding traditional civil liberties, such as the Declaratory Act, the Quartering Act and the Coercive Acts. In part the issue was economic: the colonies had little gold or silver to pay taxes in, particularly after the restrictions imposed by the Currency Act of 1764.[3] The duties imposed unfairly privileged London based trade. The Tea Act in 1773 gave the British East India company exemption from taxes imposed on other tea importers, thus giving them a monopoly, out-pricing even the smugglers. Having gone to war to defend their freedom from taxes imposed by a distant and unrepresentative government, the colonists were loath to allow Congress the authority to raise taxes itself.

Paine's *Crisis* papers address the need for public finance, directly by appealing to American patriotism in support of taxes and indirectly by bolstering morale and thus confidence in public credit. On the one hand, Paine stresses the urgency of the situation and the need for resources, but on the other Paine reiterates the wealth of resources upon which they can draw, including their patriotism. Taxes in the colonies were often collected in kind; now Paine suggests that military service might be regarded as such. Rather than appealing for exemptions for tax, Paine asks those not touched personally by the ravages of war to supply the shortfall. He also announces the measures taken in Philadelphia to secure local currency in specie through private funds, now released from the constraints of the South Sea Bubble Act, and his own initiative to create a fund for Congress, which would later become the Bank of Pennsylvania.[4] Throughout,

---

[3] The Declaratory Act (1766) merely asserted the right of parliament to bind the colonies in all cases whatsoever. The Quartering Act (1765) imposed a duty on colonial legislatures to provide barracks for British troops and the Coercive Acts (1774), often known as the intolerable acts restricted the powers of local government in Massachusetts and closed the port of Boston. The Currency Act (1764) prohibited further issues of colonial paper money. See above p. 122.

[4] Paine seems unusually modest about his own contribution. See above p. 42.

Paine reminds his readers that, if the British win, their tax burden may be even greater.

The letters and pamphlets collected here suggest a number of alternative ways to finance the war. In Chapter 1 we saw that Paine had convincingly argued that America could afford to fight the British, and indeed could not afford not to. He enumerated her considerable resources and how these could be used as public finance. America had no debt, unlike her enemy and so could afford to borrow. However, public debt is based not on patriotism but on confidence. If the British won the war, certainly paper notes would be not 'worth a continental'.[5] Paine also suggested in *Common Sense* that having declared themselves a sovereign body, the United States could enter into treaty alliances with other nations and secure aid. This was the mission of Franklin, Arthur Lee (1740-92) and Silas Deane to France: to secure a secret treaty of commerce and alliance between Congress and King Louis XVI.[6] Vergennes, the French minister for foreign affairs was keen to aid the American rebels, but not at the risk of breaching treaty obligations drawing them into another expensive war with Britain. The King was also careful not to appear to support republican revolutionaries overthrowing a legitimate monarch. Deane was commissioned by Congress to purchase supplies, mostly arms, and allowed a five-percent commission on all purchases.

Meeting with Vergennes, Deane found plenty of help available. Beaumarchais (1732-99), Vergennes's secret agent established a shadow trading

---

[5] See Yasha Beresiner, *A Collectors Guide to Paper Money* (New York: Stein & Day, 1977) p. 31; Newman, *Early Paper Money*, p. 14.

[6] Benjamin Franklin, Silas Deane, and Arthur Lee were commissioned by Congress in September 1776 to negotiate with the French court. A Treaty of Amity and Commerce was signed in Paris on 6 February 1778 by Gérard de Rayneval (1729-1790), Franklin, Deane and Lee giving mutual 'most favoured nation status' and promising to protect shipping and fishing rights. This was accompanied by a Treaty of Alliance promising common cause if Britain declared war on France and a secret treaty brought Spain into the alliance. The treaties were ratified by Congress in May 1778 and Gérard was appointed French Minister Plenipotentiary to the United States in July. France openly supported America after April 1778. In addition to keeping British forces busy in the Mediterranean and the West Indies, France provided arms, naval support, 44,000 soldiers, and officers such as the Marquis de Lafayette (1757-1834). Holland joined the war in 1780 angered at British searches of neutral shipping. In 1781, the Baltic nations formed a League of Armed Neutrality to protect their trade with America.

company, Roderigue, Hortalez & Co. to ship arms and supplies to America. The company was secretly furnished with one million *livres* each from the French and Spanish governments and used arms from the French armoury, in addition to Beaumarchais's own funds. Deane presented this to Congress as a purchase to be repaid to the tune of 4.5 million *livres* including a commission for himself and Beaumarchais for its arrangement.[7] As secretary to the Congressional Foreign Affairs Committee, Paine had access to the secret documents relating to this negotiation and, acting on information from Arthur Lee, discovered that the sum was intended as a gift (for which Deane could expect no commission). In any case, the negotiations proved expensive for Paine as his exposure of Deane, and defence of his friend Lee, cost him his job and his reputation.[8] In fact, he turned out to be correct, but in the process Paine publicised diplomatic secrets, embarrassing the French Envoy Gérard (1729-1790), who needed to maintain the illusion of French neutrality. Paine was forced to resign his position in January 1779 and suffered much public animosity, particularly from Gouverneur Morris.

The scandal is indicative of Paine's attachment to truth and to his political integrity, at the expense of prudence. Both Eric Foner and John Keane argue that there was a deeper issue at stake in the scandal: war profiteering. Deane was not alone in being accused. Robert Morris also defended his allocation of

---

[7] One million *livres* was approximately £42,000 sterling at 1775 exchange values. See McCusker, *Money and Exchange*, p. 312. See also Keane, *Paine*, p. 173. Durand suggests that the debt was to be repaid in tobacco. See Durand, *Documents*, p. 88. There is evidence that Robert Morris and Willing had a plan to buy tobacco to trade in a syndicate with Rodriguez. See Thomas Perkins Abernethy, *Western Lands and the American Revolution* (New York: Russell & Russell, 1959), pp. 148-160. By a contract of July 1782, the United States recognised a debt of 18 million *livres* to the French crown, dating from 1778, to be repaid at 5% interest and negotiated terms for its repayment over 12 years. The contract also recognised a debt of 10 million *livres* paid secretly to the US though Holland in 1781, to be repaid to the King of France. In a further contract of February 1783, France advanced a loan of six million *livres* to the US. See *Treaties and Other International Acts of the United States of America*, ed. by Hunter Miller (Washington DC: Government Printing Office, 1931), 2, Doc. 1-40.

[8] Arthur Lee was appointed Minister Plenipotentiary to France by Congress in 1777 but fell out with Deane over the conduct of the Roderigue, Hortalez &co. Durand claims that Lee, a suspected anglophile, was a traitor, informing Lord Shelburne of the secret treaty arrangements, and lied to the Committee of Foreign Affairs. Lee was recalled in 1779 and led an enquiry into the affair in

government contracts to his own trading company and Thomas Mifflin (1744-1800) was accused of misusing public office for private gain. These scandals can be seen as a reflection of a shift from the classical republican ideal of virtuous citizens dedicated to the common good to a free-market liberal expectation of individual pursuit of private interest. Morris's defence was based on his inalienable right to dispose of his private property as he wished.[9] It is perhaps shocking to us that patriots such as Morris expected to personally profit from the arrangements they made for public finance during a war, but this merely reflects common practice in Britain, in which government places were farmed for profit. British politicians had long regarded places as personal property, and indeed we might be more surprised that anyone took Paine's complaints seriously.

Another means of financing the war suggested by Paine in *Common Sense* drew upon America's most plentiful asset: the vacant land. It was common for colonial governments to issue paper money secured by mortgages on vacant land through land offices.[10] Paine seems to have been thinking more in terms of selling rather than borrowing on the land, and was keen on populating the western territories. The Royal Proclamation of 1763 had restricted western expansion into Indian territory. During the War of Independence, settlers flooded into the area west of the Allegheny Mountains and the Ohio valley. However, the revolution posed a question of ownership. Did vacant western lands belong to each colony or to the crown, whose sovereignty was superseded by Continental Congress? Maryland argued for US ownership and New York ceded their western territory to Congress in 1780, but Virginia's claimed ownership over extensive western territory, later to become West Virginia and Kentucky.[11] In order to establish the right of the union over individual states, Paine presents in *Public Good* a very

---

1787. He was connected to Paine through his friendship with Arthur's brother, Richard Henry Lee (1732-94). See Durand, *Documents*, pp. 87-151; Keane, *Paine*, pp. 155, 165.

[9] See Keane, *Paine*, pp. 171-180; Foner, *Revolutionary America*, pp. 158-61.

[10] For example, the Pennsylvania Land Bank issued three series of notes on mortgaged land between 1723-29.

[11] See Abernethy, *Western Lands*, p. 148.

well researched argument, using documents supplied by the Indiana Company of land speculators. His dispatch of Virginia's claim is remarkable considering his lack of legal training. In view of his later theory of original common ownership in *Agrarian Justice*, it is interesting here that he does not claim that the land is unowned but inherited by the union from the crown. Despite his contact with Native American peoples in 1777, Paine ignores their right to this territory.[12]

I have not included his entire argument, which explores in great detail the history of Virginia as a colony and the Board of Trade's plans for its development. Paine examines the historical claim of the state of Virginia to the adjacent vacant territory, based on a series of royal charters. Using a variety of historical sources and geometrical arguments he demonstrates convincingly that Virginia's claim does not stand up to investigation. Rather the vacant territories belonged to the crown of England and therefore now belong to the United States collectively. Moreover, Paine argues that the sale of this land will be a greater common benefit, reducing the need to raise funds for Congress by other means and lays out a plan to create new states.

The question of the western territories was a sticking point in the negotiations over the Articles of Confederation begun in 1777, reaching agreement in June 1778, although not ratified by all states until 1781. The new agreement created the United States of America (a term Paine was one of the first to use) as a perpetual union. It was to be governed by Congress, to which each state could send up to seven delegates, although voting as one. The new Congress took on the debt contracted by the earlier Continental Congresses and created a US Treasury. This was to be supplied by the states according to quotas calculated on the value o f the land. Thus Virginia's claim over her western territory served only to increase her share.

---

[12] See Keane, *Paine*, pp. 148-150.

The Articles did not give Congress tax raising powers.[13]   A resolution by
Congress on 3 February 1781 asked each state to vest in Congress a power to
collect a five-percent duty on all imports, except arms, ammunition, clothing, salt
and some other essential items.[14]   Success of the measure depended on legislation
being passed in nine of the thirteen state legislatures.   Rhode Island assembly
voted to reject the duty and raise their quota by other means, sparking off a fierce
debate in the state newspapers.   Apparently at the behest of Robert Morris, now
Superintendent of Finances, and Robert Livingston (1746-1813), Secretary for
Foreign Affairs, Paine travelled to Providence, to convince Rhode Island of her
folly.   The six letters published in the *Providence Gazette* repeat Paine's familiar
arguments, against paper money and in favour of the uniform duty.[15]   Here Paine
presents a libertarian argument in favour of indirect taxation on the grounds that
individuals are free to refrain from purchasing foreign goods.   Against the
complaint that the tax fell peculiarly heavily on Rhode Island as a state which
primarily engaged in foreign trade, Paine argued that the tax could be passed on
and the resulting inflation would be minor compared to that caused by paper
money issues.

The failure of the states to meet their quota supplies for Congress, Rhode
Island's refusal to grant a five-percent duty and squabbles between the states over

---

[13] Suspicious of strong central government, the writers of the Articles planned to keep it weak.
Nine votes were necessary to pass legislation and each state had a veto on changes to the articles,
preventing the usurpation of increased powers from the states. The powers delegated by the states
were aimed at winning the war; control over the navy and army, declaring war, and making
treaties. It could borrow and issue money but its tax levying powers were limited to making
requisitions on the states. It could not draft troops or regulate trade, and had no independent
revenue. Executive functions were carried out by committees of Congress, rather than a single
authority. Rather akin to the European Community of the 1950's, it was intended as a 'firm
league of friendship...for their common defence' without threatening the sovereignty of the
individual states. See *Sources & Documents Illustrating the American Revolution 1764-1788 and
the Formation of the Federal Constitution*, ed. by S. E. Morison, 2nd edn (New York: Oxford
University Press, 1965; repr. 1972), p. 178.

[14] Continental Congress, *Journals of the Continental Congress, 1779-1781*, ed. by
Worthington Chauncey Ford, 34 vols (Washington DC: Government Printing Office, 1914) XXI,
103. Congress also asked for a land tax of $1 per 100 acres, a poll tax of $1, and a small excise
duty on spirits.

[15] Here I present only two of these letters. The others can be found in Clark, *Six New Letters*.

territorial rights and internal duties, all pointed out the need for a closer union between the states. In *Common Sense* Paine proposes a continental government organised on a federal basis with a constitution guaranteeing individual rights.[16] In *Public Good,* Paine again supports a strong union. By 1783, it was clear that the Articles of Confederation were insufficient. One of the most remarkable arguments contained in the second letter to Rhode Island (28 December 1782) is Paine's insistence on the need for a closer union.

This has sometimes been interpreted as an argument for strong *central* government, which would seem to clash with his plea throughout his writings for minimal, or limited, government. As Paine saw it, however, the national institutions created by the Articles of Confederation were too weak to effect any government functions at all. There is plenty of evidence in his writings that he favoured a federal system in which the individual states had considerable autonomy over domestic issues, although the federal government held tax raising and legislative powers independent of the state assemblies in order to secure national defence. The notion that federalism is necessarily inconsistent with minimal government is engendered by the twentieth century experience of the USA and other federal systems. The growth in the functions of government has been concurrent with and often occasioned by the strengthening of central government at the expense of state or local government. This is not a necessary connection if central government can carry out the necessary functions of minimal government more efficiently than local government and with less imposition on its citizens. This, of course, requires that increases in the powers of central government are balanced with a reduction in the power exercised by local government. An advocate of minimal government may still argue that the balance of power attributed to each level is wrong and that 'less' government, from the citizen's point of view may actually entail either a redistribution to existing higher levels or even more levels of government.

---

[16] See 'Common Sense' (1776), *Writings,* I, 97.

Paine's concept of minimal government is not an anarchist concept of an ideal of no government, but rather the idea that a government ought only impose on its citizens in order to perform the minimal range of functions for which government is created. The imposition of government can be unnecessary in two ways: firstly, if it is used to perform functions other than those 'for which it is created', such as taxation used to keep younger sons of the aristocracy in the manner to which they are accustomed, or, secondly, if the government is so ineffective as to fail to perform the functions on which its legitimacy depend, leaving its citizens subject to the inconveniences of both government and anarchy. Paine's concern over the Articles of Confederation was that the power of the confederation, particularly the power to raise taxes from the independent states, was insufficient to ensure the defence of American independence and trade, particularly against Britain. Later, in 1802, Paine explained that:

> During the tie of the old Congress, and prior to the establishment of the federal government, the continental belt was too loosely buckled. The several states were united in name but not in fact, and that nominal union had neither centre nor circle. The laws of one state frequently interfered with, and sometimes opposed, those of another. Commerce between state and state was without protection, and confidence without a point to rest on.[17]

He claimed that the proposal for forming a general government over the union came from him, in a Memorial written to Livingston, Robert Morris and Gouverneur Morris in 1783, due to Rhode Island's and Virginia's refusal to pay the 5% duty proposed by Congress. He apparently suggested that it was necessary 'to add a continental legislature to Congress to be elected by the several states'[18]

Paine was a federalist in two senses only. He was in favour of a federal system, that is the administration of a large nation by different levels of local and

---

[17] 'To the Citizens of the United States, and Particularly to the Leaders of the Federal Faction II' (November 1802), *Writings*, III, 386.
[18] 'To the Citizens of the US II' (1802), *Writings*, III, 386-387.

central government, each responsible for their own functionally defined jurisdiction.[19] He was also in favour of strengthening the existing central government against the power of the states to a necessary level to perform is function effectively. He was not a federalist in the later sense of supporting wholeheartedly either the new constitution of 1791, nor the philosophy behind it laid out in the *Federalist Papers*. On his return to the United States he was extremely critical of the new constitution, although not of its federal principle:

> It was only to the absolute necessity of establishing some federal authority, extending equally over all the States, that an instrument so inconsistent as the present federal Constitution is, obtained a suffrage. I would have voted for it myself, had I been in America, or even for a worse, rather than have none, provided it contained the means of remedying its defects by the same appeal to the people by which it was to be established.[20]

He was also critical of the Federalist administrations of Washington and Adams and allied with Jefferson's Republicans in the post-constitutional period. This use of the term federalism, of course, has little to do with the advocating of a federalist system of government. Most importantly, he can not be said to be a federalist in the sense of wanting the central government to take over the functions and sovereignty of state governments in its entirety.[21] He wanted only to redress the imbalance in the Articles of Confederation: 'The defect was not in the principle, but in the distribution of power.'[22]

Paine views the federal system as the cornerstone of the success of American experiment in government. It is therefore vital to his vision of democracy: 'The union of America is the foundation-stone of her independence'[23]

---

[19] His later proposals for a European Congress are too vague to suggest that this was also his vision of a European republic. See 'The Crisis X' (March 1782), *Writings*, I, 340; see also 'Rights of Man' (1791), *Writings*, II, 387.

[20] See 'Letter to Washington' (July 1796), *Writings*, III, 213.

[21] This, perhaps erroneous, sense of the term 'federalism' is often used pejoratively, for example in the present day discussions of the future of the European Union.

[22] 'Rights of Man II' (1792), *Writings*, II, 433.

[23] See below p. 213.

The states' own domestic jurisdiction is not a matter for contention, but they must nevertheless give up some of their sovereignty in order for the union to work: 'It is with confederated states as with individuals in society; something must be yielded up to make the whole secure.'[24] In *To the People of America* Paine appeals to individual states to abide by the decisions made by Congress. The states have sent representatives to Congress and have empowered that body to conduct the war, while their constituents deal with domestic affairs and internal legislation. He argues that given this delegation, the decisions of Congress must be obeyed by the states.[25]

The jurisdiction of Congress, in Paine's opinion covers 'those things which immediately concern the union, and for which the union was purposely established, and it is intended to secure.' The states are left with full control over internal legislation.[26] Although Paine always uses the term 'nation' to apply to America as a whole, some of his comments on the balance of powers between states and Congress suggest that he views the people of each state as possessing sovereignty over their own form of government.[27] It is impossible to infer from these remarks whether Paine would allow a right of secession or oppose the enforcement of civil rights by federal government. What is clear is that Paine views the Union as vital to the security and prosperity of the American people and that he does not think that strengthening the powers of central government over the states will infringe on the sovereignty of the people of that state. The power

---

[24] 'Crisis X' (1782), *Writings*, I, 375.

[25] See below p. 214.

[26] It is this distinction between the jurisdiction of different levels that is often at the root of support for and against federalism. Once a principle has been agreed upon (such as the 'principle of subsidiarity': that decisions should be made at the lowest possible level), interpretation of the principle is still a matter of negotiation. Paine's agitation for increased power for the Confederation did not depart from the principle that the Union was needed primarily to defend the states against the British, only that enforceable tax powers were necessary to this cause. See below p. 214.

[27] See below p. 215.

of individuals is strengthened by the duality of their citizenship: of their state and of the Union.[28]

The final piece in this chapter relates to Paine's own economic freedom and integrity. In the newspaper row over Rhode Island's duty, Paine was accused of writing for hire, a charge that he categorically denies in this letter. Throughout his life, similar charges would plague him, always met with denial.[29] Several biographers have unearthed evidence that Paine was indeed paid to write in a particular cause on several occasions. In 1782, Paine was paid a salary of $800 per annum by Morris, to write in support of Congress and taxation. The salary was drawn out of out of secret service funds with the agreement of Robert Livingston and George Washington. It is further alleged that the Indiana Company, speculating on land in Western Virginia, paid for *Public Good.* Durand reports that Gérard offered Paine £1000 to write on behalf of French interests in 1779, in part as compensation for his post in Congress, but later released Paine from this obligation owing to his unpopularity after the Deane affair.[30] Perhaps this amounts to evidence of lack of integrity, but more likely of his poverty. Paine frequently donated the proceeds of his writings to the causes they were written for and many of his pamphlets were produced at printer's cost to reach the widest audience.

Paine's primary incentive in writing was to spread his ideas, but this lack of interest in profits and royalties left him in poverty. At the end of the War of Independence, supported by a number of distinguished friends, Paine appealed for financial compensation for his services to the revolutionary cause in Congress and in several state assemblies. His letters of this period are uncomfortably reminiscent of ingratiating appeals for patronage, common in Georgian England.

---

[28] See below p. 235 and above p. 84.
[29] During the Bank Crisis, Paine was accused by Smiley of writing for hire and by pamphleteer Atticus of 'prostituting his pen'. See below p. 248.
[30] On Morris's salary see Foner, *Revolutionary America*, p. 189, Keane, *Paine*, pp. 217-218. Several writers have suggested Paine was paid for this defence of the land companies. See Keane,

New York awarded Paine a farm in New Rochelle and a considerable sum in honour of his achievements. Pennsylvania awarded him £500 for his wartime services.[31]   Despite his criticism of sinecure, he accepted these payments and clerkships in the national and Pennsylvanian legislatures, although these were hardly idle places. His disclaimer in the letter to Rhode Island included here, despite ample evidence that he was in fact being paid by Congress, demonstrates the importance to Paine of his independence as a writer. I suspect he would never have accepted payment to write for a cause he did not support in principle.[32] Certainly, it is evident from the writings collected in this chapter that Morris's secret fund did not substantially alter Paine's views on tax and paper money, nor on federalism and he would in any case have supported the five-percent duty.

Paine, pp. 220-222; Clark, *Six New Letters*, p. xi; cf. Abernethy, *Western Lands*, p. 214. See also Durand, *Documents*, p. 136. In contrast, see also Paine's note below p. 476.

[31] See Aldridge, 'Why did Paine Write on the Bank?', p. 313.

[32] See below p. 237 & Keane, *Paine*, p. 219.

The CRISIS, N° IX.

HAD America pursued her advantages with half the spirit that she resisted her misfortunes, she would, before now, have been a conquering and a peaceful people; but lulled in the lap of soft tranquillity she rested on her hopes, and adversity only has convulsed her into action. Whether subtilty or sincerity at the close of the last year induced the enemy to an appearance for peace, is a point not material to know; it is sufficient that we see the effects it has had on our politics, and that we sternly rise to resent the delusion.

The war, on the part of America, has been a war of natural feelings. Brave in distress; serene in conquest; drowsy when at rest; and in every situation generously disposed to peace. A dangerous calm, and the most heightened zeal, have, as circumstances varied, succeeded each other. Every passion, but that of despair, has been called to a tour of duty; and so mistaken has been the enemy of our abilities and disposition, that when she supposed us conquered, we rose the conquerors. The extensiveness of the United States and the variety of their resources; the universality of their cause, the quick operation of their feelings, and the similarity of their sentiments, have, in every trying situation, produced a *something,* which favoured by Providence, and pursued with ardour, has accomplished in an instant the business of a campaign. We have never deliberately sought victory, but snatched it; and bravely undone in an hour, the plotted operations of a season.

The reported fate of Charlestown, like the misfortunes of seventy-six, has at last called forth a spirit, and kindled up a flame, which perhaps no other event could have produced. If the enemy has circulated a falsehood, they have unwisely aggravated us into life, and if they have told us a truth, they have unintentionally done us a service. We were returning with folded arms from the fatigues of war and thinking, and sitting leiusurely [sic] down to enjoy repose. The dependence that has been put upon Charlestown threw a drowsiness over America. We looked on the business done—the conflict over—the matter settled—or that all which remained unfinished would follow of itself. In this state of dangerous relax, exposed to the poisonous infusions of the enemy, and having no common danger to attract our attention, we were extinguishing by stages the ardour we began with, and surrendering by peacemeals the virtue that defended us.[1]

Afflicting as the loss of Charlestown may be, yet if it universally rouse us from the slumber of a twelve months past, and renew in us the spirit of former days, it will produce an advantage more important than its loss. America ever *is* what she *thinks* herself to be. Governed by sentiment, and acting her own mind, she becomes as she pleases the victor or the victim.

It is not the conquest of towns, nor the accidental capture of garrisons, that can reduce a country so extensive as this. The sufferings of one part can ever be relieved by the exertions of another, and there is no situation the enemy can be placed in, that does not afford to us the same advantages she seeks herself. By dividing her force, she leaves every post attackable. It is a mode of war, that carries with it a confession of weakness, and goes on the principle of distress rather than conquest.

The decline of the enemy is visible not only in their operations but in their plans; Charlestown originally made but a secondary object in their system of attack, and it is now become their principal one, because they have not been able to succeed elsewhere. It would have carried a cowardly appearance in Europe, had they formed their grand expedition in seventy-six, against a part of the Continent, where there was no army, or not a sufficient one to oppose them; but failing year after year, in their impressions here, and to the eastward and northward, they deserted their first capital design, and prudently contenting themselves with what they can get, give a flourish of honor to conceal disgrace.

But this piece-meal work is not conquering the Continent. It is discredit in them to attempt it, and in us to suffer it. It is now full time to put an end to a war

---

[1] After a month of siege, Charleston had surrendered to the British on 12 May, resulting in the taking of 2500 prisoners of war.

of aggravations, which on one side, has no possible object, and on the other, has every inducement which honor, interest, safety and happiness, can inspire. If we suffer them much longer to remain among us, we shall become as bad as themselves. An association of vices will reduce us more than the sword. A nation hardened in the practice of iniquity, knows better how to profit by it, than a young country newly corrupted. We are not a match for them in the line of advantageous guile, nor they for us, on the principles we bravely set out with. Our first days were our days of honor. They have marked the character of America wherever the story of her wars are told; and convinced of this, we have nothing to do, but wisely and unitedly to tread the well known track.

The progress of a war, is often as ruinous to individuals, as the issue of it is to a nation; and it is not only necessary that our forces be such, that we be conquerors in the end, but that by timely exertions, we be secure in the interim. The present campaign will afford an opportunity which has never presented itself before, and the preparation for it, are equally necessary, whether Charlestown stand or fall. Suppose the first, it is in that case, only a failure of the enemy, not a defeat. All the conquest a besieged town can hope for, is not to be conquered; and compelling an enemy to raise the siege is to the besieged a victory. But there must be a probability amounting almost to a certainty, that would justify a garrison marching out to attack a retreat. Therefore should Charlestown *not* be taken, and the enemy abandon the siege, every other part of the Continent should prepare to meet them; and on the contrary, *should it be taken*, the same preparations are necessary, to balance the loss, and put ourselves in a position to co-operate with our allies, immediately on their arrival.

We are not now fighting our battles alone, as we were in seventy-six. England, from a malicious disposition to America, has *not* only not declared war against France and Spain, but the better to prosecute her passions here, has afforded those

Powers no military object, and avoids them to distress us.[2] She will suffer her West-India Islands to be over run by France, and her southern settlements to be taken by Spain, rather than quit the object that gratifies revenge. This conduct on the part of Britain, has pointed out the propriety of France sending a naval and land force to co-operate with America on the spot. Their arrival cannot be very distant, nor the ravages of the enemy long. In the mean time the part necessary to us, needs no illustration. The recruiting the army, and procuring the supplies, are the two things needful, and a capture of either of the enemy's divisions, will restore to America peace and plenty.

At a Crisis, big, like the present, with expectation and events, the whole country is called to unanimity and exertion. Not an ability ought now to sleep that can produce but a mite to the general good, nor even a whisper suffered to pass that militates against it. The necessity of the case, and the importance of the consequences, admit no delay from a friend, no apology from an enemy. To spare now, would be the height of extravagance, and to consult present ease, would be to sacrifice it, perhaps forever.

America, rich in patriotism and produce, can want neither men nor supplies, when a serious necessity calls them forth. The slow operation of taxes, owing to the extensiveness of collection, and their depreciated value before they arrived in the Treasury, have, in many instances, thrown a burthen upon Government, which has been artfully interpreted by the enemy into a general decline throughout the country. Yet this, inconvenient as it may at first appear, is not only remediable, but may be turned to an immediate advantage; for it makes no real difference, whether a certain number of men, or company of militia (and in this country every man is a militia-man), are directed by law, to send a recruit at their own expence, or whether a tax is laid on them for that purpose, and the man hired by government afterwards. The first, if there is any difference, is both cheapest and

---

[2] Britain declared war on France in response to the (no longer secret) Treaty of Alliance negotiated between the French court and the American ministers in Paris. British naval forces attacked the French coast on 17 June 1778 signalling the outbreak of war.

best, because it saves the expence which would attend collecting it as a tax, and brings the man sooner into the field than the modes of recruiting formerly used: And on this principle, a law has been passed in this State, for recruiting two men from each company of militia, which will add upwards to a thousand to the force of the country.

But the flame, which has broke forth in this city, since the report from New-York, of the loss of Charlestown, not only does honor to the place, but, like the blaze of seventy-six, will kindle into action, the scattered sparks throughout America.[3] The valour of a country may be learned by the bravery of its soldiery, and the general cast of its inhabitants, but confidence of success is best discovered by the active measures pursued by men of property; and when the spirit of enterprize becomes so universal, as to act at once on all ranks of men, a war may then, and not till then, be stiled truly popular.

In seventy-six the ardour of the enterprising part was considerably checked by the real revolt of some, and the coolness of others. But in the present case there is a firmness in the substance and property of the country to the public cause. An association has been entered into by the merchants, tradesmen, and principal inhabitants of the city, to receive and support the new State money at the value of gold and silver; a measure, which, while it does them honour, will likewise contribute to their interest, by rendering the operations of the campaign convenient and effectual.[4]

Neither has the spirit of exertion stopt here. A voluntary subscription is likewise began to raise a fund of hard money, to be given as bounties to fill up the full quota of the Pennsylvania line. It has been the remark of the enemy, that

---

[3] News of General Clinton's (1738-95) impending attack on Charleston would have reached Philadelphia first from New York from where Clinton's forces set sail south down the coast, taking thirty-eight days to reach Charleston on 1 February 1780. In Philadelphia, this may have seemed reminiscent of Howe's assault on the city in August 1777.

[4] This is the fund started by Blair McClenachan at Paine's instigation which a week after this publication would become the Bank of Pennsylvania, later the Bank of North America. See p. 42 above.

every thing in America has been done by the force of government; but when she sees individuals throwing in their voluntary aids, and facilitating the public measures in concert with the established powers of the country, it will convince her that the cause of America stands not on the will of a few but on the broad foundation of property and popularity.

Thus aided and thus supported, disaffection will decline, and the withered head of tyranny expire in America. The ravages of the enemy will be short and limited, and like all their former ones, will produce a victory over themselves.

COMMON SENSE.

Philadelphia, June 9, 1780.

At the time of writing this number of the Crisis, the loss of Charlestown, though believed by some, was more confidently disbelieved by others. But there ought to be no longer a doubt on the matter. Charlestown is gone, and I believe for the want of a sufficient supply of provisions. The man that does not now feel for the honor of the best and noblest cause that ever a country engaged in and exert himself accordingly, is no longer worthy of a peaceable residence among a people determined to be free.

C. S.

THE
CRISIS
EXTRAORDINARY.

ON THE SUBJECT OF TAXATION.

IT is impossible to sit down and think seriously on the affairs of America, but the original principles on which she resisted, and the glow and ardor they inspired, will occur like the undefaced remembrance of a lovely scene. To trace over in imagination the purity of the cause, the voluntary sacrifices made to support it, and all the various turnings of the war in its defence, is at once both paying and receiving respect. The principles deserve to be remembered, and to remember them rightly is repossessing them. In this indulgence of generous recollection we become gainers by what we seem to give, and the more we bestow the richer we become.

So extensively right was the ground on which America proceeded, that it not only took in every just and liberal sentiment which could impress the heart, but made it the direct interest of every class and order of men to defend the country. The war, on the part of Britain, was originally a war of covetousness. The sordid and not the splendid passions gave it being. The fertile fields and prosperous infancy of America appeared to her as mines for tributary wealth. She viewed the hive, and disregarding the industry that had enriched it, thirsted for the honey. But in the present stage of her affairs, the violence of temper is added to the rage of avarice; and therefore, that which, at our first setting out, proceeded from purity of principle and public interest, is now heightened by all the obligations of necessity; for it requires but little knowledge of human nature to discern what would be the consequence, were America again reduced to the subjection of Britain. Uncontrouled power, in the hands of an incensed, imperious, and rapacious conqueror, is an engine of dreadful execution; and woe be to that country over which it can be exercised. The names of Whig and Tory would then be sunk in the general term of Rebel, and the oppression, whatever it might be, would, with very few instances of exception, light equally on all.

Britain did not go to war with America for the sake of dominion, because she was then in possession; neither was it for the extension of trade and commerce, because she had monopolized the whole and the country had yielded to it; neither was it to extinguish what *she* might call rebellion, because before she began no resistance existed. It could then be from no other motive than avarice, or a design of establishing, in the first instance, the same taxes in America as are paid in England (which, as I shall presently show, are above eleven times heavier than the taxes we now pay for the present year 1780) or, in the second instance, to confiscate the whole property of America, in case of resistance and conquest, of the latter of which she had then no doubt.

I shall now proceed to show what the taxes in England are, and what the yearly expence of the present war is to her—What the taxes of this country amount to, and what the annual expence of defending it effectually will be to us; and shall endeavor concisely to point out the cause of our difficulties, and the advantages on one side, or the consequences on the other, in case we do, or do not, put ourselves in an effectual state of defence. I mean to be open, candid and sincere. I see a universal wish to expel the enemy from the country, a murmuring because the war is not carried on with more vigour, and my intention is to show as shortly as possible both the reason and the remedy.

The number of souls in England (exclusive of Scotland and Ireland) is seven millions*, and the number of souls in America is three millions.

The amount of the taxes in England (exclusive of Scotland and Ireland) was, before the present war commenced, eleven millions six hundred and forty two thousand six hundred and fifty three pounds sterling, which on an average is no less a sum than one pound thirteen shillings and threepence sterling per head per annum men, women, and children; besides county taxes, taxes for the support of

---

* This is taking the highest number that the people of England have been or can be rated at.

the poor, and a tenth of all the produce of the earth for the support of the bishops and clergy[†]. Nearly five millions of this sum went annually to pay the interest of the national debt contracted by former wars, and the remaining sum of six millions six hundred and forty two thousand six hundred pounds was applied to defray the yearly expence of government, the peace establishment of the army and navy, placemen, pensioners, &c. consequently the whole of the enormous taxes being thus appropriated, she had nothing to spare out of them towards defraying the expences of the present war or any other. Yet had she not been in debt at the beginning of the war as we were not, and, like us had only a land and not a naval war to carry on, her then revenue of eleven millions and a half pounds sterling would defray all her annual expences of war and government within each year.

But this not being the case with her, she is obliged to borrow about ten millions pounds sterling yearly, to prosecute the war she is now engaged in (this year she borrowed twelve) and lay on new taxes to discharge the interest; and allowing that the present war has cost her only fifty millions sterling, the interest thereon at five

---

[†] The following is taken from Dr. Price's state of the taxes of England, pages 96, 97, 98.
"An account of the money drawn from the public by taxes annually, being the medium of three years before the year 1776.

Amount of customs in England,	£	2,528,275.
Amount of the excise in England,		4,649,892
Land tax at 3s.		1,300,000
Land tax at 1s. in the pound,		450,000
Salt duties,		218,739
Duties on stamps, cards, dice, advertisements, bonds, leases, indentures, newspapers, almanacks, &c.		280,788
Duties on houses and windows,		385,369
Post office, seizures, wine licences, hackney coaches, &c.		250,000
Annual profit from lotteries,		150,000
Expence of collecting the excise in England,		297,887
Expence of collecting the customs in England,		468,703
Interest of loans an the land tax at 4s. expences of collection, militia, &c.		250,000
Perquisites, &c. to custom house officers, &c. supposed		250,000
Expence of collecting the salt duties in England, 10d. ½ per cent.		27,000
Bounties on fish exported,		18,000
Expence of collecting the duties on stamps, cards, advertisements, &c. 5 and ¼ per cent.		18,000
Total,	£. sp.	11,642,6531 out

per cent. will be two millions and an half, therefore the amount of her taxes now must be fourteen millions, which on an average is no less than forty shillings sterling per head, men, women and children throughout the nation. Now as this expence of fifty millions was borrowed on the hopes of conquering America, and as it was avarice which first induced her to commence the war, how truly wretched and deplorable would the condition of this country be, were she, by her own remissness, to suffer an enemy of such a disposition, and so circumstanced, to reduce her to subjection.

I now proceed to the revenues of America.

I have already stated the number of souls in America to be three millions, and by a calculation I have made, which I have every reason to believe is sufficiently right, the whole expence of the war, and the support of the several governments, may be defrayed for two million pounds sterling, annually; which, on an average, is thirteen shillings and four pence per head, men, women, and children, and the peace establishment at the end of the war will be but three quarters of a million, or five shillings sterling per head. Now throwing out of the question every thing of honor, principle, happiness, freedom, and reputation in the world, and taking it up on the simple ground of interest, I put the following case:

Suppose Britain was to conquer America, and, as conquerors was to lay her under no other conditions than to pay the same proportions toward her annual revenue which the people of England pay; our share, in that case, would be six million pounds sterling yearly; can it then be a question, whether it is best to raise two millions to defend the country, and govern it ourselves, and only three quarters of a million afterwards, or pay six millions to have it conquered, and let the enemy govern it.

Can it be supposed that conquerors would chuse to put themselves in a worse condition than what they granted to the conquered. In England, the tax on rum is five shillings and one penny sterling per gallon, which is one silver dollar and fourteen coppers. Now would it not be laughable to imagine, that after the expence they have been at, they would let either Whig or Tory in America drink it cheaper than themselves.   Coffee which is so considerable an article of consumption and support here is there loaded with a duty, which makes the price between five and six shillings sterling a pound, and a penalty of fifty pounds sterling on any person detected in roasting it in his own house. There is scarce an article of life you can eat, drink, wear, or enjoy that is not there loaded with a tax; even the light from heaven is only permitted to shine into their dwellings by paying eighteen pence sterling per window annually; and the humblest drink of life, small beer, cannot there be purchased without a tax of nearly two coppers a gallon, besides a heavy tax upon the malt, and another on the hops before it is brewed, exclusive of a land tax on the earth which produces them. In short, the condition of that country in point of taxation, is so oppressive, the number of her poor so great, and the extravagance and rapaciousness of the court so enormous, that were they to effect a conquest of America, it is then only that the distresses of America would begin. Neither would it signify any thing to a man whether he be what we call a Whig or a Tory. The people of England and the ministry of that country know us by no such distinctions. What they want is clear solid revenue, and the modes they would take to procure it, would operate alike on all. Their manner of reasoning would be short, because they would naturally infer that if we were able to carry on a war of five or six years against them, we are able to pay the same taxes which they do.

I have already stated that the expence of conducting the present war, and the government of the several states, may be done for two millions sterling, and the establishment in time of peace, for three quarters of a million.‡

As to navy matters, they flourish so well, and are so well attended to, in the hands of individuals, that I think it consistent on every principle of real use and economy, to turn the navy into hard money (keeping only three or four packets)

---

‡ I have made the calculations in sterling, because it is a rate generally known in all the states, and because likewise it admits of an easy comparison between our expences to support the war, and those of the enemy. Four silver dollars and an half is one pound sterling, and three pence over.

and apply it to promote the service of the army. We shall not have a ship the less; the use of them, and the benefit from them, will be greatly increased, and their expence saved. We are now allied with a formidable naval power, from whom we derive the assistance of a navy. And the line in which we can prosecute the war, so as to reduce the common enemy and benefit the alliance most effectually, will be by attending closely to the land service.

I estimate the charge of keeping up and maintaining an army, officering them, and all expences included, sufficient for the defence of the country, to be equal to the expence of forty thousand men at thirty pounds sterling per head, which is one million two hundred thousand pounds.

I likewise allow four hundred thousand pounds for Continental expences at home and abroad.

And four hundred thousand pounds for the support of the several state governments, the amount will then be,

For the army,	1,200,000
Continental expences at home and abroad,	400,000
Government of the several states,	400,000
Total	2,000,000

I take the proportion of this state, Pennsylvania, to be an eighth part of the Thirteen United States, the quota then for us to raise will be two hundred and fifty thousand pounds sterling; two hundred thousand of which will be our share for the support and pay of the army and Continental expences at home and abroad, and fifty thousand pounds for the support of state government.

In order to gain an idea of the proportion in which the raising such a sum will fall, I make the following calculation:

Pennsylvania contains three hundred and seventy five thousand inhabitants, men, women and children, which is likewise an eighth part of the whole inhabitants of the United States: therefore two hundred and fifty thousand pounds sterling to be raised among three hundred and seventy five thousand persons, is, on an average, thirteen shillings and fourpence per head per annum, or something more than one shilling sterling per month. And our proportion of three quarters of a million for the government of the country, in time of peace, will be ninety three thousand seven hundred and fifty pounds sterling, fifty thousand of which will be for the government expences of the state, and forty three thousand seven hundred and fifty pounds for Continental expences at home and abroad.

The peace establishment then will, on an average, be five shillings sterling per head. Whereas was England now to stop, and the war cease, her peace establishment would continue the same as it is now, viz. forty shillings per head; therefore was our taxes necessary for carrying on the war as much per head as hers now is, and the difference to be only whether we should, at the end of the war, pay at the rate of five shillings per head, or forty shillings per head, the case needs no thinking of. But as we can securely defend and keep the country for one third less than what our burthen would be if it was conquered, and support the governments afterward for an eighth of what Britain would levy on us, and could I find a miser whose heart never felt the emotion of a spark of principle, even that man, uninfluenced by every love but the love of money, and capable of no attachment but to his interest, would, and must, from the frugality which governs him contribute to the defence of the country, or he ceases to be a miser and becomes an ideot. But when we take in with it every thing that can ornament mankind; when the line of our interest becomes the line of our happiness; when all that can chear and animate the heart; when a sense of honor, fame, character, at home and abroad, are interwoven not only with the security but the increase of property, there exists not a man in America, unless he be a hired emissary, who does not see that his good is connected with keeping up a sufficient defence.

I do not imagine that an instance can be produced in the world, of a country putting herself to such an amazing charge to conquer and enslave another as Britain has done. The sum is too great for her to think of with any tolerable degree of temper; and when we consider the burthen she sustains as well as the disposition she has shewn, it would be the height of folly in us to suppose that she would not reimburse herself by the most rapid means, had she America once more within her power. With such an oppression of expence, what would an empty conquest be to her! what relief under such circumstances could she derive from a victory without a prize? It was money, it was revenue, she first went to war for, and nothing but *that* would satisfy her. It is not the nature of avarice to be satisfied with any thing else. Every passion that acts upon mankind has a peculiar mode of operation. Many of them are temporary and fluctuating; they admit of cessation and variety: But avarice is a fixed uniform passion. It neither abates of its vigour nor changes its object; and the reason why it does not is founded in the nature of things, for wealth has not a rival where avarice is a ruling passion. One beauty may excel another, and extinguish from the mind of man the pictured remembrance of a former one: But wealth is the phœnix of avarice, and therefore cannot seek a new object, because there is not another in the world.

I now pass on to shew the value of the present taxes, and compare them with the annual expence; but this I shall preface with a few explanatory remarks.

There are two distinct things which make the payment of taxes difficult; the one is the large and real value of the sum to be paid, and the other is the scarcity of the thing in which the payment is to be made; and although these appear to be one and the same, they are in several instances not only different, but the difficulty springs from different causes.

Suppose a tax to be laid equal to one half of what every man's yearly income is, such a tax could not be paid because the property could not be spared; and on the other hand, suppose a very trifling tax was laid to be collected in *pearls*, such a tax likewise could not be paid, because they could not be had. Now any person may see that these are distinct cases, and the latter of them is a representation of ours.

That the difficulty cannot proceed from the former, that is, from the real value or weight of the tax, is evident at the first view to any person who will consider it.

The amount of the quota of taxes for this state for the year, 1780 (and so in proportion for every other state) is twenty millions of dollar, which at seventy for one is but sixty four thousand two hundred and eighty pounds three shillings sterling, and on an average is no more than three shillings and five pence sterling per head per annum men, women and children, or fivepence per head per month. Now here is a clear positive fact, that cannot be contradicted, and which proves that the difficulty cannot be in the weight of the tax, for in itself it is a trifle and far from being adequate to our quota of the expence of the war. The quit rents of one penny sterling per acre on only one half the state, come to upwards of fifty thousand pounds, which is almost as much as all the taxes of the present year, and as those quit rents made no part of the taxes then paid, and are now discontinued, the quantity of money drawn for public service this year, exclusive of the militia fines, which I shall take notice of in the process of this work, is less than what was paid and payable in any year preceding the revolution, and since the last war; what I mean is that the quit rents and taxes taken together came to a larger sum then than the present taxes without the quit rents do now.[1]

My intention by these arguments and calculations is to place the difficulty to the right cause, and shew that it does not proceed from the weight or worth of the tax, but from the scarcity of the medium in which it is paid; and to illustrate this point still further, I shall now shew, that if the tax of twenty millions of dollars was of four times the real value it now is or nearly so, which would be about two hundred and fifty thousand pounds sterling, and would be our full quota, that this sum would have been raised with more ease, and less felt, than the present sum of only sixty four thousand two hundred and eighty pounds.

The convenience or inconvenience of paying a tax in money arises from the quantity of money that can be spared out of trade.

When the emissions stopt, the continent was left in possession of two hundred millions of dollars, perhaps as equally dispersed as it was possible for trade to do it. And as no more was to be issued, the rise or fall of prices could neither increase nor diminish the quantity. It therefore remained the same through all the fluctuations of trade and exchange.

---

[1] See above p. 131.

Now had the exchange stood at twenty for one, which was the rate congress calculated upon when they quoted the states the latter end of last year, trade would have been carried on for nearly four times less money than it is now, and consequently the twenty millions would have been spared with much greater ease, and when collected would have been of almost four times the value that they now are. And on the other hand, was the depreciation to be at ninety or one hundred for one, the quantity required for trade would be more than at sixty or seventy for one, and though the value of them would be less, the difficulty of sparing the money out of trade would be greater. And on these facts and arguments I rest the matter, to prove, that it is not the want of property, but the scarcity of the medium by which the proportion of property for taxation is to be measured out, that makes the embarrassment we lie under. There *is not* money enough, and what is equally as true, the people will not let there be money enough.

While I am on the subject of the currency, I shall offer one remark which will appear true to every body, and can be accounted for by nobody, which is, that the better the times were, the worse the money grew; and the worse the times were, the better the money stood. It never depreciated by any advantage obtained by the enemy. The troubles of seventy six, and the loss of Philadelphia in seventy seven, made no sensible impression on it, and every one knows that the surrender of Charlestown did not produce the least alteration in the rate of exchange, which for long before, and for more than three months after, stood at sixty for one. It seems as if the certainty of its being our own made us careless of its value, and that the most distant thoughts of losing it made us hug it the closer, like something we were loth to part with; or that we depreciate it for our pastime, which, when called to seriousness by the enemy, we leave off to renew again at our leisure. In short our good luck seem to break us, and our bad make us whole.

Passing on from this digression, I shall now endeavor to bring into one view the several parts I have already stated, and form thereon some propositions, and conclude.

I have placed before the reader, the average tax per head paid by the people of England; which is forty shillings sterling.

And I have shewn the rate on an average per head, which will defray all the expence of the war to us, and support the several governments without running the country into debt, which is thirteen shillings and fourpence.

I have shewn what the peace establishment may be conducted for, viz. an eighth part of what it would be, if under the government of Britain.

And I have likewise shewn what the average per head of the present taxes are, namely, three shillings and five pence sterling, or five pence per month; and that their whole yearly value in sterling is only sixty four thousand two hundred and eighty pounds. Whereas our quota to keep the payments equal with the expences, is two hundred and fifty thousand pounds. Consequently, there is a deficiency of one hundred and eighty five thousand seven hundred and twenty pounds, and the same proportion of defect, according to the several quotas, happens in every other state. And this defect is the cause why the army has been so indifferently fed, cloathed and paid. It is the cause, likewise, of the nerveless state of the campaign, and the insecurity of the country. Now if a tax equal to thirteen and fourpence per head will remove all these difficulties, make people secure in their homes, leave them to follow the business of their stores and farms unmolested, and not only keep out but drive out the enemy from the country; and if the neglect of raising this sum will let them in, and produce the evils which might be prevented, on which side, I ask, does the wisdom, interest and policy lie? Or rather would it not be an insult to reason to put the question. The sum when portioned out according to the several abilities of the people, can hurt no one, but an inroad from the enemy ruins hundreds of families.

Look at the destruction done in this city. The many houses totally destroyed, and others damaged; the waste of fences in the country round it, besides the plunder of furniture, forage and provision. I do not suppose that half a million sterling would reinstate the sufferers, and does this, I ask, bear any proportion to the expence that would make us secure. The damage on an average is at least ten pound sterling per head, which is as much as thirteen shillings and fourpence per head comes to for fifteen years. The same has happened on the frontiers, and in the Jersies, New York, and other places, where the enemy has been, Carolina and Georgia is likewise suffering the same fate.[2]

That the people generally do not understand the insufficiency of the taxes to carry on the war, is evident, not only from common observation, but from the construction of several petitions, which were presented to the assembly of this state, against the recommendation of congress of the 18th of March last, for taking up and funding the present currency at forty for one, and issuing new money in its stead. The prayer of the petition was, *That the currency might be appreciated by taxes* (meaning the present taxes) *and that part of the taxes be applied to the support of the army, if the army could not be otherwise supported.* Now it could not have been possible for such a petition to have been presented, had the petitioners known, that so far from *part* of the taxes being sufficient for the support of the army, the *whole* of them falls three fourths short of the year's expences.

Before I proceed to propose methods by which a sufficiency of money may be raised, I shall take a short view of the general state of the country.

Notwithstanding the weight of the war, the ravages of the enemy, and the obstructions she has thrown in the way of trade and commerce, so soon does a young country outgrow misfortune, that America has already surmounted many that heavily oppressed her. For the first year or two of the war, we were shut up within our ports, scarce venturing to look towards the ocean. Now our rivers are beautified with large and valuable vessels, our stores filled with merchandize, and the produce of the country has a ready market, and an advantageous price. Gold and silver, that for a while seemed to have retreated again within the bowels of the

---

[2] Arriving in Philadelphia to relieve Howe during the occupation from October 1777 to June 1778, Sir Henry Clinton was 'shocked to find the city deteriorated by occupation, houses destroyed, defaced, trees cut for firewood, streets lettered with rubbish.' Dunaway, *A History of Pennsylvania*, p. 183.

earth, is once more risen into circulation, and every day adds new strength to trade, commerce, and agriculture. In a pamphlet written by Sir John Dalrymple, and dispersed in America in the year 1775, he asserted, that, *two twenty gun ships, nay,* says he, *tenders of those ships, stationed between Albermarle sound and Chesapeak bay, would shut up the trade of America for 600 miles.* How little did Sir John Dalrymple know of the abilities of America![3]

While under the government of Britain, the trade of this country was loaded with restrictions. It was only a few foreign ports she was allowed to sail to.[4] Now it is otherwise; and allowing that the quantity of trade is but half what it was before the war, the case must shew the vast advantage of an open trade, because the present quantity under her restrictions could not support itself; from which I infer, that if half the quantity without the restrictions can bear itself up nearly, if not quite, as well as the whole when subject to them, how prosperous must the condition of America be when the whole shall return open with all the world. By trade I do not mean the employment of a merchant only, but the whole interest and business of the country taken collectively.

It is not so much my intention, by this publication, to propose particular plans for raising money, as it is to shew the necessity and the advantages to be derived from it. My principal design is to form the disposition of the people to such measures which I am fully persuaded is their interest and duty to adopt, and which needs no other force to accomplish them than the force of being felt. But as every hint may be useful, I shall throw out a sketch, and leave others to make such improvements upon it as to them may appear reasonable.

---

[3] Paine also cites Dalrymple's (1726-1810) pamphlet in the appendix to *Common Sense* where he calls it 'a whining Jesuitical piece'. See 'Common Sense' (1776), *Writings*, I, 113 and Sir John Dalrymple, *The Address of the People of Great-Britain to the Inhabitants of America* (London: T. Cadell, 1775).

[4] The Navigation and Trade Acts (1650-1696) enforced a British monopoly on intra-colonial trade. Two-thirds of American exports in 1760 was in enumerated goods, which by law had to be shipped to Britain and re-exported by British merchants.

The annual sum wanted is two millions, and the average rate in which it falls is thirteen shillings and fourpence per head.

Suppose, then, that we raise half the sum and sixty thousand pounds over. The average rate thereof will be seven shillings per head.

In this case we shall have half the supply that we want, and an annual fund of sixty thousand pounds whereon to borrow the other million; because sixty thousand pounds is the interest of a million at six per cent. and if at the end of another year we should be obliged, by the continuance of the war, to borrow another million, the taxes will be increased to seven shillings and sixpence; and thus for every million borrowed, an additional tax equal to sixpence per head must be levied.

The sum then to be raised next year will be one million and sixty thousand pounds: One half of which I would propose should be raised by duties on imported goods and prize goods, and the other half by a tax on landed property and houses, or such other means as each state may devise.[5]

But as the duties on imports and prize goods must be the same in all the states, therefore the rate per cent. or in what other form the duty shall be laid, must be ascertained and regulated by congress, and ingrafted in that form into the law of each state; and the monies arising therefrom carried into the treasury of each state. The duties to be paid in gold or silver.

There are many reasons why a duty on imports is the most convenient duty or tax that can be collected, one of which is, because the whole is payable in a few places in a country, and it likewise operates with the greatest ease and equality, because as every one pays in proportion to what he consumes, so people in general consume in proportion to what they can afford, and therefore the tax is regulated by the abilities which every man supposes himself to have, or in other words every man becomes his own assessor, and pays by a little at a time when it suits him to buy. Besides, it is a tax which people may pay or let alone by not consuming the articles; and though the alternative may have no influence on their conduct, the power of choosing is an agreeable thing to the mind. For my own part, it would be a satisfaction to me, was there a duty on all sorts of liquors during the war, as in my idea of things, it would be an addition to the pleasure of society, to know, that when the health of the army goes round, a few drops from every glass becomes theirs. How often have I heard an emphatical wish, almost accompanied by a tear, *"Oh, that our poor fellows in the field had some of this!"* Why then need we suffer under a fruitless sympathy, when there is a way to enjoy both the wish and the entertainment at once?

But the great national policy of putting a duty upon imports is, that it either keeps the foreign trade in our own hands or draws something for the defence of the country from every foreigner who participates it with us.

Thus much for the first half of the taxes, and as each state will best devise means to raise the other half, I shall confine my remarks to the resources of this state.

The quota then of this state of one million and sixty thousand pounds will be one hundred and thirty-three thousand two hundred and fifty pounds, the half of which is sixty-six thousand six hundred and twenty-five pounds; and supposing one fourth part of Pennsylvania inhabited, then a tax of one bushel of wheat on every twenty acres of land, one with another, would produce the sum, and all the present taxes to cease. Whereas the tythes of the bishops and clergy in England, exclusive of the taxes, are upwards of half a bushel of wheat on *every single* acre of land, good and bad, throughout the nation.[6]

In the former part of this paper, I mentioned the militia fines, but reserved speaking to the matter, which I shall now do: The ground I shall put it upon is,

---

[5] 'Prize goods' presumably refers to the luxury items upon which excise was traditionally levied such as coffee, tobacco, fine cloth, wines and spirits.

[6] Tithes were still collected in England by Anglican ministers who received ten percent of produce in kind from the local community. The practice had been a source of grievance since the 1650's, particularly in the Quaker community. Refusal to pay tithes could result in a prison

that two millions sterling a year will support a sufficient army, and all the expences of war, and government, without having recourse to the inconvenient method of continually calling men from their employments, which of all others is the most expensive and the least substantial. I consider the revenue created by taxes as the first and principal thing, and fines only as secondary and accidental things. It was not the intention of the militia law to apply the militia fines to any thing else but the support of the militia, neither do they produce any revenue to the state, yet these fines amount to more than all the taxes: for taking the muster roll to be sixty thousand men, the fine on forty thousand who may not attend, will be sixty thousand pounds sterling, and those who muster, will give up a portion of time equal to half that sum, and if the eight classes should be called within the year, and one third turn out, the fine on the remaining forty thousand would amount to seventy two millions of dollars, besides the fifteen shillings on every hundred pounds property, and the charge of seven and a half per cent for collecting in certain instances, which, on the whole would be upwards of two hundred and fifty thousand pounds sterling.

Now if those very fines disable the country from raising a sufficient revenue without producing an equivalent advantage, would it not be to the ease and interest of all parties to encrease the revenue, in the manner I have proposed, or any better, if a better can be devised, and cease the operation of the fines. I would still keep the militia as an organized body of men, and should there be a real necessity to call them forth, pay them out of the proper revenues of the state, and encrease the taxes a third or fourth per cent. on those who do not attend. My limits will not allow me to go farther into this matter, which I shall therefore close with this remark; that fines are, of all modes of revenue, the most unsuited to the minds of a free country. When a man pays a tax, he knows that the public necessity requires it, and therefore feels a pride in discharging his duty; but a fine

---

sentence. See Laura Brace, *The Idea of Property in Seventeenth Century England: Tithes and the Individual* (Manchester: Manchester University Press, 1998) p. 15 & p. 37.

seems an atonement for neglect of duty, and of consequence is paid with discredit, and frequently levied with severity.

I have now only one subject more to speak to, with which I shall conclude, which is, the resolve of congress on the 18th of March last, for taking up and funding the present currency at forty for one, and issuing new money in its stead.

Every one knows that I am not the flatterer of congress, but in this instance *they are right*; and if that measure is supported, the currency will acquire a value, which without it, it will not. But this is not all: It will give relief to the finances until such time as they can be properly arranged, and save the country from being immediately double taxed under the present mode. In short, support that measure, and it will support you.

I have now waded through a tedious course of difficult business, and over an untrodden path. The subject on every point in which it could be viewed was entangled with perplexities, and inveloped in obscurity, yet such are the resources of America, that she wants nothing but system to insure success.

COMMON SENSE.

PHILADELPHIA,
October 4, 1780.

PUBLIC GOOD,

BEING AN EXAMINATION into the Claim of Virginia to THE VACANT WESTERN TERRITORY, AND THE RIGHT OF the United States to the same to which is added Proposals for laying off a new State, to be applied as a Fund for carrying on the war or redeeming the national debt.

THE PREFACE

THE following pages are on a subject hitherto little understood, but highly interesting to the United States.

They contain an investigation of the claims of Virginia to the vacant western territory, and of the right of the United States to the same; with some outlines of a plan for laying out a new state, to be applied as a fund, for carrying on the war, or redeeming the national debt.

The reader, in the course of this publication, will find it studiously plain, and, as far as I can judge, perfectly candid. What materials I could get at I have endeavoured to place in a clear line, and deduce such arguments there from as the subject required. In the prosecution of it, I have considered myself as an advocate for the right of the states, and taken no other liberty with the subject than what a counsel would, and ought to do, in behalf of a client.

I freely confess that the respect I had conceived, and still preserve, for the character of Virginia, was a constant check upon those fallies [sic] of imagination, which are fairly and advantageously indulged against an enemy, but ungenerous when against a friend.

If there is any thing I have omitted or mistaken, to the injury of the intentions of Virginia or her claims, I shall gladly rectify it; or if there is any thing yet to add, should the subject require it, I shall as chearfully undertake it; being fully convinced, that to have matters fairly discussed, and properly understood, is a principal means of preserving harmony and perpetuating friendship.

THE AUTHOR

PUBLIC GOOD, &C.

WHEN we take into view the mutual happiness and united interests of the states of America, and consider the important consequences to arise from a strict attention of each, and of all, to every thing which is just, reasonable and honourable; or the evils that will follow from an inattention to those principles; there cannot, and ought not, to remain a doubt, but that the governing rule of *right* and of mutual good must in all public cases finally preside.

The hand of providence has cast us into one common lot, and accomplished the independence of America, by the unanimous consent of the several parts, concurring at once in time, manner and circumstances. No superiority of interest, at the expence of the rest, induced the one, more than the other, into the measure. Virginia and Maryland, it is true, might foresee, that their staple commodity, tobacco, by being no longer monopolized by Britain, would bring them a better price abroad: for as the tax on it in England was treble its first purchase from the planter, and they being now no longer compelled to send it under that obligation, and in the restricted manner they formerly were: it is easy to see, that the article, from the alteration of the circumstances of trade, will, and daily does, turn out to them with additional advantages.

But this being a natural consequence, produced by that common freedom and independence of which all are partakers, is therefore an advantage they are intitled to, and on which the rest of the states can congratulate them without feeling a wish to lessen, but rather to extend it. To contribute to the encreased prosperity of another, by the same means which occasion our own, is an agreeable reflection; and the more valuable any article of export becomes, the more riches will be introduced into and spread over the continent.

Yet this is an advantage which those two states derive from the independence of America superior to the local circumstances of the rest; and of the two it more particularly belongs to Virginia than Maryland, because the staple commodity of a considerable part of Maryland is flour, which, as it is an article that is the growth of Europe as well as of America, cannot obtain a foreign market but by under selling, or at least by limiting it to the current price abroad. But tobacco commands its own price. It is not a plant of almost universal growth, like wheat. There are but few soils and climes that produce it to advantage, and before the cultivation of it in Virginia and Maryland, the price was from four to sixteen shillings sterling a pound in England.*

But the condition of the vacant western territory of America makes a very different case to that of the circumstances of trade in any of the states. Those very lands, formed, in contemplation, the fund by which the debt of America would in the course of years be redeemed. They were considered as the common right of all; and it is only till lately that any pretension of claims has been made to the contrary.

That difficulties and differences will arise in communities ought always to be looked for. The opposition of interests, real or supposed; the variety of judgments; the contrariety of temper; and, in short, the whole composition of man, in his individual capacity, is tinctured with a disposition to contend; but in his social capacity there is either a right which, being proved, terminates the dispute, or a reasonableness in the measure, where no direct right can be made out, which decides or compromises the matter.

As I shall have frequent occasion to mention the word *right*, I wish to be clearly understood in my definition of it. There are various senses in which this term is used, and custom has, in many of them, afforded it an introduction contrary to its true meaning. We are so naturally inclined to give the utmost degree of force to our own case, that we call every pretension, however founded, *a right*; and by this means the term frequently stands opposed to justice and reason.

---

* See sir Dalby Thomas's historical account of the rise and growth of the West-India colonies. [(London 1690) It is interesting to note that here Paine cites uncritically a mercantilist writer - see Buck, *Politics of Mercantilism*, p. 58.]

After Theodore was elected king of Corsica, not many years ago, by the meer choice of the natives, for their own convenience in opposing the Genoese, he went over into England, run himself in debt, got himself into jail, and on his release therefrom by the benefit of an act of insolvency, he surrendered up, what he called, *his* kingdom of Corsica, as a part of his personal property, for the use of his creditors; some of whom may hereafter call this a charter, or by any other name more fashionable, and ground thereon what they may term a *right* to the sovereignty and property of Corsica. But does not justice abhor such an action, both in him and them, under the prostituted name of a *right*, and must not laughter be excited where ever it is told.[1]

A right, to be truly so, must be right within itself; yet many things have obtained the name of rights, which are originally founded in wrong. Of this kind are all rights by meer conquest, power or violence. In the cool moments of reflection we are obliged to allow, that the mode by which such a right is obtained, is not the best suited to that spirit of universal justice which ought to preside equally over all mankind. There is something in the establishment of such a right that we wish to slip over as easily as possible, and say as little about as can be. But in the case of a *right founded in right* the mind is carried chearfully into the subject, feels no compunction, suffers no distress, subjects its sensations to no violence, nor sees any thing in its way which requires an artificial smoothing.

From this introduction I proceed to examine into the claims of Virginia; first as to the right, secondly as to the reasonableness, and lastly as to the consequences.

***

When I first began this subject, my intention was to be extensive on the merits, and concise on the matter of the right; instead of which, I have been extensive on the matter of right, and concise on the merits of reasonableness: and this alteration in my design arose, consequentially, from the nature of the subject; for as a

---

[1] Theodore Baron von Neuhoff (1686-1756), a German adventurer, led the Corsican uprising against the Genoese in 1736 supported by the Turks and Tunisia. He was elected king and raised money selling knighthoods. He was well known in London (where he later settled) as a debtor.

reasonable thing the claim can be supported by no argument, and therefore needs none to refute it; but as there is a strange propensity in mankind to shelter themselves under the sanction of right, however unreasonable that supposed right may be, I found it most conducive to the interest of the case, to shew, that the right stands upon no better grounds than the reason. And shall therefore proceed to make some observations on,

The consequences of the claim.

T[he] claim being unreasonable in itself and standing on no ground of right, but such as, if true, must from the quarter it is drawn be offensive, has a tendency to create disgust and sour the minds of the rest of the states. Those lands are capable, under the management of the United States, of repaying the charges of the war, and some of them, as I shall hereafter shew, may, I presume, be made an immediate advantage of.

I distinguish three different descriptions of lands in America at the commencement of the revolution. Proprietary or chartered lands, as was the case in Pennsylvania. Crown lands, within the described limits of any of the crown governments; and crown residuary lands that were without, or beyond, the limits of any province; and those last were held in reserve whereon to erect new governments and lay out new provinces; as appears to have been the design by lord Hilsborough's letter and the president's answer, wherein he says "with respect to the establishment of a *new* colony on the *back* of Virginia, it is a subject of too great political importance for me to presume to give an opinion upon; however, permit me, my lord, to observe, that when that part of the country shall become populated, it may be a wise and prudent measure."[2]

---

[2] William Penn received a grant of land to set up a Quaker colony in Pennsylvania in 1681 in return for settling a debt owed by Charles II to Penn's father. Other proprietor colonies include Delaware, owned by the Penns, Maryland, and New Jersey. Colonies that had initially been founded by groups of proprietors or trustees, such as the Carolinas and Georgia, later became royal colonies. The Earl of Hillsborough (1718-1793) was Secretary of State for the American Department 1768-1772. The letter referred to here is quoted in detail in earlier (omitted) passages, and alludes to a plan to settle a new colony in present day Kentucky. The letter, written by

The [expression] is a *"new colony* on the *back* of Virginia" and referred to lands between the heads of the rivers and the Ohio. This is a proof that those lands were not considered within, but beyond, the limits of Virginia as a colony; and the other expression in the letter is equally descriptive, namely, *"We do not presume to say, to whom our gracious sovereign shall grant his vacant lands."* Certainly then, the same right, which, at that time, rested in the crown, rests now in the more supreme authority of the United States; and therefore, addressing the president's letter to the circumstances of the revolution it will run thus,

"We do not presume to say to whom the *sovereign United States* shall grant their vacant lands, and with respect to the settlement of a *new colony* on the *back* of Virginia, it is a matter of too much political importance for me to give an opinion upon; however, permit me to observe, that when that part of the country shall become populated it may be a wise and prudent measure."

It must occur to every person, on reflection, that those lands are too distant to be within the government of any of the present states; and, I may presume to suppose, that were a calculation justly made, Virginia has lost more by the decrease of taxables, than she has gained by what lands she has made sale of; therefore, she is not only doing the rest of the states wrong in point of equity, but herself and them an injury in point of strength, service and revenue.

It is only the United States, and not any single State, that can lay off new states and incorporate them in the union by representation; therefore, the situation which the settlers on those lands will be in, under the assumed right of Virginia, will be hazardous and distressing, and they will feel themselves at last like the aliens to the commonwealth of Israel, their habitations unsafe and their title precarious.

And when men reflect on that peace, harmony, quietude, and security, which are necessary to prosperity, especially in making new settlements, and think that when the war shall be ended, their happiness and safety will depend on a union

---

Hillsborough in 1770 to the governor of the Virginia colony and president of the council, is used by Paine as evidence against Virginia's claim to the vacant lands.

with the states, and not a scattered people, unconnected with, and politically unknown to, the rest, they will feel but little inclination to put themselves in a situation, which, however solitary and recluse, it may appear, at present, will then be uncertain and unsafe, and their troubles will have to begin where those of the United States shall end.

It is probable that some of the inhabitants of Virginia may be inclined to suppose, that the writer of this, by taking up the subject in the manner he has done, is arguing unfriendly against their interest. To which he wishes to reply:

That the most extraordinary part of the whole is, that Virginia should countenance such a claim. For it is worthy of observing, that, from the beginning of the contest with Britain, and long after, there was not a people in America who discovered, thro' all the variety and multiplicity of public business, a greater fund of true wisdom, fortitude, and disinterestedness, than the then colony of Virginia. They were loved—They were reverenced. Their investigation of the assumed rights of Britain had a sagacity which was uncommon. Their reasonings were piercing, difficult to be equalled and impossible to be refuted, and their public spirit was exceeded by none. But since this unfortunate land scheme has taken place, their powers seem to be absorbed. A Torpor has overshaded them, and every one asks what is become of Virginia?

It seldom happens that the romantic schemes of extensive dominion are of any service to a government, and never to a people. They assuredly end at last in loss, trouble, division, and disappointment. And was even the title of Virginia good, and the claim admissible, she would derive more lasting and real benefit by participating [in] it, than by attempting the management of an object so infinitely beyond her reach. Her share with the rest, under the supremacy of the United States, which is the only authority adequate to the purpose, would be worth more to her, than what the whole would produce under the management of herself alone, and that for several reasons.

First, because her claim not being admissible nor yet manageable, she cannot make a good title to the purchasers, and consequently can get but little for the lands.

Secondly, because the distance the settlers will be at from her, will immediately put them out of all government and protection, so far, at least, as relates to Virginia: and by this means she will render her frontiers a refuge to desperadoes, and a hiding place from justice; and the consequence will be perpetual unsafety to her own peace and that of the neighbouring states.

Thirdly, because her quota of expence for carrying on the war, admitting her to engross such an immensity of territory, would be greater than she can either support or supply, and could not be less, upon a reasonable rule of proportion, than nine-tenths of the whole. And

Lastly, because she must sooner or later relinquish them, therefore to see her own interest wisely at first, is preferable to the alternative of finding it out by misfortune at last.

I have now gone thro' my examination of the claim of Virginia in every case which I proposed; and for several reasons wish the lot had fallen to another person.

But as this is a most important matter, in which all are interested, and the substantial good of Virginia not injured but promoted, and as few men have leisure, and still fewer have inclination, to go into intricate investigation, I have at last ventured on the subject.

The succession of the United States to the vacant western territory is a right they originally set out upon, and in the pamphlet, *Common Sense*, I frequently mentioned those lands as a national fund for the benefit of all; therefore, resuming the subject where I then left off, I shall conclude with concisely reducing to system what I then only hinted.

In my last piece, the *Crisis Extraordinary*, I estimated the annual amount of the charge of war and the support of the several governments at two million pounds sterling, and the peace establishment at three quarters of a million, and by a comparison of the taxes of this country with those of England, proved that the whole yearly expence to us, to defend the country, is but a third of what Britain would have drawn from us by taxes, had she succeeded in her attempt to conquer; and our peace establishment only an eighth part; and likewise shewed, that it was within the ability of the states to carry on the whole of the war by taxation without having recourse to any other modes or funds.[3] To have a clear idea of taxation is necessary to every country, and the more funds we can discover and organize the less will be the hope of the enemy, and the readier their disposition to peace, which it is now *their* interest more than *ours* to promote.

I have already remarked that only the United States and not any particular state can lay off new states and incorporate them in the union by representation; keeping, therefore, this idea in view, I ask, might not a substantial fund be quickly created by laying off a new state, so as to contain between twenty and thirty million of acres, and opening a land office in all the countries in Europe for hard money, and in this country for supplies in kind at a certain price.

The tract of land that seems best adapted to answer this purpose is contained between the Allegany Mountain and the river Ohio, as far north as the Pennsylvania line, thence extending down the said river to the falls thereof, thence due south into the latitude of the North-Carolina line, and thence east to the Allegany Mountain aforesaid.— I, the more readily, mention this tract, because it is fighting the enemy at their own weapons, as it includes the same ground on which a new colony would have been erected, for the emolument of the crown of England, as appears by lord Hilsborough and Dartmouth's letters, had not the revolution prevented its being carried into execution.[4]

It is probable that there may be some spots of private property within this tract, but to incorporate them into some government will render them more profitable to

---

[3] See above p. 176.
[4] Lord Dartmouth (1731-1801) succeeded Lord Hillsborough as Secretary of State for the American Department (1772-5). In earlier (omitted) passages, Paine quotes both Ministers' correspondence with the Virginia colony as evidence against Virginia's claim.

the owners, and the condition of the scattered settlers more eligible and happy than at present.

If twenty millions of acres of this new state be patented and sold at twenty pounds sterling per hundred acres, they will produce four million pounds sterling, which, if applied to continental expences only, will support the war for three years, should Britain be so unwise as to prosecute it against her own direct interest and against the interest and policy of all Europe. The several states will then have to raise taxes for their internal government only, and the continental taxes as soon as the fund begins to operate, will lessen, and if sufficiently productive will cease.

Lands are the real riches of the habitable world, and the natural funds of America. The funds of other countries are, in general, artificially constructed; the creatures of necessity and contrivance; dependent upon credit, and always exposed to hazard and uncertainty. But lands can neither be annihilated nor lose their value; on the contrary, they universally rise with population, and rapidly so, when under the security of effectual government. But this it is impossible for Virginia to give, and, therefore, that which is capable of defraying the expences of the empire, will, under the management of any single state, produce only a fugitive support to wandring individuals.

I shall now enquire into the effects which the laying out a new state under the authority of the United States, will have upon Virginia.

It is the very circumstance she ought to, and must, wish for, when she examines the matter thro' all its case and consequences.

The present settlers being beyond her reach, and her supposed authority over them remaining in herself, they will appear to her as revolters, and she to them as oppressors; and this will produce such a spirit of mutual dislike, that in a little time a total disagreement will take place, to the disadvantage of both.

But under the authority of the United States the matter is manageable, and Virginia will be eased of a disagreeable consequence.

Besides this, a sale of the lands, continentally, for the purpose of supporting the expence of the war, will save her a greater share of taxes, than the small sale she could make herself, and the small price she could get for them, would produce.

She would likewise have two advantages which no other state in the union enjoys, first, a frontier state for her defence against the incursions of the Indians; and the second is, that the laying out and peopling a new state on the back of an old one, situated as she is, is doubling the quantity of its trade.

The new state, which is here proposed to be laid out, may send its exports down the Missisippi [sic], but its imports must come thro' Chesapeak Bay, and consequently Virginia will become the market for the new state; because, tho' there is a navigation from it, there is none into it, on account of the rapidity of the Missisippi.

There are certain circumstances that will produce certain events whether men think of them or not. The events do not depend upon thinking, but are the natural consequence of acting; and according to the system which Virginia has gone upon, the issue will be, that she will get involved with the back settlers in a contention about *rights* till they dispute with her her own claims, and, soured by the contention, will go to any other state for their commerce; both of which may be prevented, a perfect harmony established, the strength of the states encreased, and the expences of the war defrayed, by settling the matter now on the plan of a general right; and every day it is delayed, the difficulty will be encreased and the advantages lessened.

But if it should happen, as it possibly may that the war should end before the money which the new state may produce be expended, the remainder of the lands therein may be set apart to reimburse those, whose houses have been burnt by the enemy, as this is a species of suffering which it was impossible to prevent, because houses are not moveable property: and it ought not to be, that because we cannot do every thing, that we ought not to do what we can.

Having said this much on the subject, I think it necessary to remark that the prospect of a new fund, so far from abating our endeavours in making every immediate provision for the supply of the army, ought to quicken us therein; for should the states see it expedient to go upon the measure, it will be at least a year before it can be productive. I the more freely mention this, because there is a dangerous species of popularity, which, I fear, some men are seeking from their constituents by giving them grounds to believe, that if they are elected they will lighten the taxes; a measure, which, in the present state of things, cannot be done without exposing the country to the ravages of the enemy by disabling the army from defending it.

Where knowledge is a duty ignorance is a crime; and if any man whose duty it was to know better, has encouraged such an expectation, he has either deceived himself or them: besides, no country can be defended without expence, and let any man compare his portion of temporary inconveniences arising from taxations, with the real distresses of the army for the want of supplies, and the difference is not only sufficient to strike him dumb, but make him thankful that worse consequences have not followed.

In advancing this doctrine, I speak with an honest freedom to the country; for as it is their good to be defended, so it is their interest to provide that defence, at least, till other funds can be organized.

As the laying out new states will some time or other be the business of the country, and as it is yet a new business to us, and as the influence of the war has scarcely afforded leisure for reflecting on distant circumstances, I shall throw together a few hints for facilitating that measure, whenever it may be proper for adopting it.

The United States now standing on the line of sovereignty, the vacant territory is their property collectively, but the persons by whom it may hereafter be peopled will also have an equal right with ourselves; and therefore, as new states shall be laid off and incorporated with the present, they will become partakers of the remaining territory with us who are already in possession. And this consideration ought to heighten the value of lands to new emigrants; because, in making the purchases, they not only gain an immediate property, but become initiated into the right and heirship of the states to a property in reserve, which is an additional advantage to what any purchasers under the late government of England enjoyed.

The setting off the boundary of any new state will naturally be the first step, and as it must be supposed not to be peopled at the time it is laid off, a constitution must be formed, by the United States, as the rule of government in any new state, for a certain term of years (perhaps ten) or until the state becomes peopled to a certain number of inhabitants; after which, the whole and sole right of modelling their government to rest with themselves.

A question may arise, whether a new state should immediately possess an equal right with the present ones in all cases which may come before Congress.

This, experience will best determine; but at first view of the matter it appears thus; That it ought to be immediately incorporated into the union on the ground of a family right, such a state standing in the line of a younger child of the same stock; but as new emigrants will have something to learn when they first come to America, and a new state requiring aid rather than capable of giving it, it might be most convenient to admit its immediate representation into Congress, there to sit, hear and debate, on all questions and matters, but not to vote on any till after the expiration of seven years.[5]

I shall in this place take the opportunity of renewing a hint which I formerly threw out in the pamphlet *Common Sense*, and which the several states will, sooner or later, see the convenience, if not the necessity, of adopting; which is, that of electing a Continental Convention, for the purpose of forming a

---

[5] Jefferson's Land Ordinance of 1784 regulated the formation of new states, dividing up the vacant territories into ten districts which could be admitted as new states in three stages, depending on the number of inhabitants, rather than a period of time. Only when the population reached 60,000 could the territory draft a constitution and apply for statehood.

Continental Constitution, defining and describing the powers and authority of Congress.

Those of entering into treaties, and making peace, they naturally possess, in behalf of the states, for their separate as well as their united good, but the internal controul and dictatorial powers of Congress are not sufficiently defined, and appear to be too much in some cases, and too little in others; and therefore, to have them marked legally out will give additional energy to the whole, and a new confidence to the several parts.

To the PEOPLE of AMERICA.

On the Expences, Arrangements and Disbursements for carrying on the War, and finishing it with Honour and Advantage.

WHEN any necessity or occasion has pointed out the convenience of addressing the public, I have never made it a consideration whether the subject was popular or unpopular, but whether it was right or wrong; for that which is right will become popular, and that which is wrong, though by mistake it may obtain the cry or fashion of the day, will soon lose the power of delusion, and sink into disesteem.

A remarkable instance of this happened in the case of Silas Deane; and I mention this circumstance with the greater ease, because the poison of his hypocrisy spread over the whole country, and every man, almost without exception, thought me wrong in opposing him. The best friends I then had, except Mr. Laurens, stood at a distance, and this tribute, which is due to his constancy, I pay to him with respect, and that the readier, because he is not here to hear it. If it reaches him in his imprisonment, it will afford him an agreeable reflection.[1]

"As he rose like a rocket, he would fall like the stick," is a metaphor which I applied to Mr. Deane in the first piece which I published respecting him, and he has exactly fulfilled the description.[2] The credit he so unjustly obtained from the public, he lost in almost as short a time. The delusion perished as it fell, and he soon saw himself stripped of popular support. His more intimate acquaintance[s] began to doubt and to desert him long before he left America, and at his departure he saw himself the object of general suspicion. When arrived in France, he endeavoured to effect by treason what he had failed to accomplish by fraud. His

---

[1] Henry Laurens (1742-1792) was captured at sea by the British on 3 September 1780 and imprisoned in the tower as a traitor rather than being treated as a prisoner of war. He was harshly treated and forbidden any visitors or correspondence.

[2] Paine launched his attack on Deane in the *Pennsylvania Packet*, 15 December 1778. See also 'To the Public on Mr Deane's Affair.' (January 1779), *Writings*, I, 409-437.

plans, schemes and projects, together with his expectation of being sent to Holland to negociate a loan of money, had all miscarried. He then began traducing and accusing America of every crime, which could injure her reputation. "That she was a ruined country; that she only meant to make a tool of France, to get what money she could out of her, and then to leave her and accommodate with Britain." Of all which, and much more, Colonel Laurens and myself, when in France, informed Dr. Franklin, who had not before heard of it.[3] And to compleat the character of traitor, he has, by letters to his country since, some of which, in his own hand writing, are now in the possession of Congress, used every expression and argument in his power to injure the reputation of France, and to advise America to renounce her alliance, and surrender up her independence.* Thus in France he abuses America, and in his letters to America he abuses France; and is endeavouring to create disunion between the two countries, by the same arts of double-dealing by which he caused dissentions among the Commissioners in Paris, and distractions in America. But his life has been fraud, and his character has been that of a plodding, plotting, cringing mercenary, capable of any disguise that suited his purpose. His final detection has very happily cleared up those mistakes, and removed those uneasinesses, which his unprincipled conduct occasioned. Every one now sees him in the same light; for towards friends or enemies he acted with the same deception and injustice, and his name, like that of *Arnold,* ought now to be forgotten among us.[4] As this is the first time I have mentioned him since my return from France, it is

---

[3] Paine had accompanied John Laurens on his mission to secure aid from the French government in 1781.

* Mr. William Marshal, of this city, formerly a pilot, who had been taken at sea and carried to England, and got from thence to France, brought over letters from Mr. Deane to America, one of which was directed to "Robert Morris, Esq." Mr. Morris sent it unopened to Congress, and advised Mr. Marshall to deliver the others there, which he did. The letters were of the same purport with those which have been already published under the signature of S. Deane, to which they had frequent reference.

[4] The two traitors Deane and Benedict Arnold (1741-1801) later met in London. See James Coy Hilton, *Silas Deane: Patriot or Traitor?* (Lansing: Michigan State University Press, 1975) p. 96.

my intention that it shall be the last.---From this digression, which for several reasons I thought necessary to give, I now proceed to the purport of my address.

I consider the war of America against Britain as the country's war, the public's war, or the war of the people in their own behalf, for the security of their natural rights, and the protection of their own property. It is not the war of Congress, the war of the Assemblies, or the war of Government, in any line whatever. The country first, by mutual compact, resolved to defend their rights and maintain their independence, *at the hazard of their lives and fortunes.* They elected their Representatives, by whom they appointed their members to Congress, and said, *act you for us, and we will support you.* This is the true ground and principle of the war on the part of America, and, consequently, there remains nothing to do, but for every one to fulfil his obligation.

It was next to impossible that a new country, engaged in a new undertaking, could set off systematically right at first. She saw not the extent of the struggle that she was involved in, neither could she avoid the beginning. She supposed every step she took, and every resolution she formed, would bring her enemy to reason, and close the contest. Those failing, she was forced into new measures; and these, like the former, being fitted to her expectations, and failing in their turn, left her continually unprovided and without system. The enemy likewise was induced to prosecute the war, from the temporary expedients we adopted for carrying it on. We were continually expecting to see their credit exhausted, and they were looking to see our currency fail; and thus, between their watching us and we them, the hopes of both have been deceived, and the childishness of the expectation has served to encrease the expence.

Yet who, through this wilderness of error, has been to blame? where is the man who can say, the fault has not in part been his? They were the natural, unavoidable errors of the day. They were the errors of a whole country, which nothing but experience could detect, and time remove. Neither could the circumstances of America admit of system, till either the paper currency was fixed or laid aside. No calculation of finance could be made on a medium falling without reason, and fluctuating without rule.

But there is one error which might have been prevented, and was not; and as it is not my custom to flatter, but to serve mankind, I will speak it freely. It certainly was the duty of every assembly on the continent to have known, at all times, what was the condition of its treasury, and to have ascertained at every period of depreciation, how much the real worth of the taxes fell short of their nominal value. This knowledge, which might have been easily gained, would have enabled them to have kept their constituents well informed, which is one of the greatest duties of representation. They ought to have studied and calculated the expences of the war, the quota of each State, and the consequent proportion that would fall on each man's property for his defence; and this must have easily shewn to them, that a tax of an hundred pounds could not be paid by a bushel of apples or an hundred of flour, which was often the case two or three years ago. But instead of this, which would have been plain and upright dealing, the little line of temporary popularity, the feather of an hour's duration, was too much pursued; and in this involved condition of things, every State, for the want of a little thinking, or a little information, supposed that it supported the whole expences of the war, when in fact it fell, by the time the tax was levied and collected, above three fourths short of its own quota.

Impressed with a sense of the danger to which the country was exposed by this lax method of doing business, and the prevailing errors of the day, I published, last October was a twelvemonth, *The Crisis Extraordinary,* on the revenues of America, and the yearly expence of carrying on the war. My estimation of the latter, together with the civil list of Congress, and the civil list of the several States, was Two Million Pounds sterling, which is very nearly Nine Millions of Dollars.[5]

---

[5] See above p. 176.

Since that time, Congress have gone into a calculation, and have estimated the expences of the war department and the civil list of Congress (exclusive of the civil list of the several governments) at Eight Millions of Dollars; and as the remaining million will be fully sufficient for the civil list of the several States, the two calculations are exceedingly near each other.

This sum of Eight Millions of Dollars they have called upon the States to furnish, and their quotas are as follows, which I shall preface with the resolution itself.

By the United States in Congress assembled,

October 30, 1781.

RESOLVED,

THAT the respective States be called upon to furnish the Treasury of the United States with their quotas of eight millions of dollars, for the war department and civil list for the ensuing year, to be paid quarterly, in equal proportions, the first payment to be made on the first day of April next.

Resolved, That a Committee, consisting of a member from each State, be appointed to apportion to the several states the quota of the above sum.

November 2d.

The Committee, appointed to ascertain the proportions of the several States of the monies to be raised for the expences of the ensuing year, report the following resolutions:

That the sum of Eight Millions of Dollars, as required to be raised by the resolutions of the 30th of October last, be paid by the States in the following proportion.

New-Hampshire,	-	373,598
Massachusetts,	-	1,307,596
Rhode Island,	-	216,684
Connecticut,	-	747,196
New-York,	-	373,598

New-Jersey,	-	485,679
Pennsylvania,	-	1,120,794
Delaware,	-	112,085
Maryland,	-	933,996
Virginia,	-	1,307,594
North-Carolina,	-	622,677
South-Carolina,	-	373,598
Georgia,	-	24,905

8,000,000 Dollars.

Resolved,

That it be recommended to the several States, to lay taxes for raising their quotas of money for the United States, separate from those laid for their own particular use.

On these resolutions I shall offer several remarks.

First, On the sum itself, and the ability of the country.

Secondly, On the several quotas, and the nature of a union. And,

Thirdly, On the manner of collection and expenditure.

First. On the sum itself, and the ability of the country. As I know my own calculation is as low as possible, and as the sum called for by Congress, according to their calculation, agrees very nearly therewith, I am sensible it cannot possibly be lower. Neither can it be done for that, unless there is ready money to go to market with; and even in that case, it is only by the utmost management and œconomy that it can be made to do.

By the accounts which were laid before the British parliament last spring, it appeared that the charge of only subsisting, that is feeding, their army in America, cost annually Four Million Pounds sterling, which is very nearly Eighteen Millions of Dollars. Now if, for Eight Millions, we can feed, clothe, arm, provide for and pay an army sufficient for our defence, the very comparison shows that the money must be well laid out.

It may be of some use, either in debate or conversation, to attend to the progress of the expences of an army, because it will enable us to see on what part any deficiency will fall.

The first thing is, to feed them and provide for the sick.

Secondly, to clothe them.

Thirdly, to arm and furnish them.

Fourthly, to provide means for removing them from place to place. And,

Fifthly, to pay them.

The first and second are absolutely necessary to them as men. The third and fourth are equally as necessary to them as an army. And the fifth is their just due. Now if the sum which shall be raised should fall short, either by the several acts of the States for raising it, or by the manner of collecting it, the deficiency will fall on the fifth head, the soldiers pay, which would be defrauding them, and eternally disgracing ourselves. It would be a blot on the Councils, the country, and the revolution of America, and a man would hereafter be ashamed to own he had any hand in it.

But if the deficiency should be still shorter, it would next fall on the fourth head, *the means of removing the army from place to place*; and, in this case, the army must either stand still where it can be of no use, or seize on horses, carts, waggons, or any means of transportation which it can lay hold of; and in this instance the country suffers. In short, every attempt to do a thing for less than it can be done for, is sure to become at last both a loss and a dishonour.

But the country cannot bear it say some. This has been the most expensive doctrine that ever was held out, and cost America millions of money for nothing. Can the country bear to be over-run, ravaged, and ruined by an enemy which will immediately follow where defence is wanting, and defence will ever be wanting where sufficient revenues are not provided. But this is only one part of the folly. The second is, that when the danger comes, invited in part by our not preparing against it, we have been obliged, in a number of instances, to expend double the sums to do that which at first might have been done for half the money. But this is not all. A third mischief has been, that grain of all sorts, flour, beef, fodder, horses, carts, waggons, or whatever was absolutely or immediately wanted, have been taken without pay. Now, I ask, why was all this done, but from that extremely weak and expensive doctrine, *that the country could not bear it?* that is, that she could not bear, in the first instance, that which would have saved her twice as much at last; or, in proverbial language, that she could not bear to pay a penny to save a pound; the consequence of which has been, that she has paid a pound for a penny. Why are there so many unpaid certificates in almost every man's hands, but from the parsimony of not providing sufficient revenues? Besides, the doctrine contradicts itself; because, if the whole country cannot bear it, how is it possible that a part should; and yet this has been the case. For those things have been had; and they must be had; but the misfortune is, that they have been had in a very unequal manner and upon expensive credit, whereas, with ready money, they might have been purchased for half the price, and no body distressed.

But there is another thought which ought to strike us, which is,----How is the army to bear the want of food, cloathing and other necessaries? The man who is at home can turn himself a thousand ways, and find as many means of ease, convenience or relief: But a soldier's life admits of none of those: Their wants cannot be supplied from themselves: For an army, though it is the defence of a State, is at the same time the child of a country, or must be provided for in every thing.

And lastly, The doctrine is false. There are not three millions of people, in any part of the universe, who live so well, or have such a fund of ability, as in America. The income of a common labourer, who is industrious, is equal to that of the generality of tradesmen in England. In the mercantile line, I have not heard of one who could be said to be a bankrupt since the war began, and in England they have been without number. In America almost every farmer lives on his own lands, and in England not one in a hundred does. In short, it seems as if the poverty of that country had made them furious, and they were determined to risk all to recover all.

Yet, notwithstanding those advantages on the part of America, true it is, that had it not been for the operation of taxes for our necessary defence, we had sunk into a state of sloth and poverty: For there was more wealth lost by neglecting to till the earth in the years 1776, 77, and 78, than the quota of tax amounts to. That which is lost by neglect of this kind, is lost for ever; whereas that which is paid, and continues in the country, returns to us again; and at the same time that it provides us with defence, it operates not only as a spur but as a premium to our industry.

I shall now proceed to the second head, viz. ON THE SEVERAL QUOTAS, AND THE NATURE OF A UNION.

There was a time when America had no other bond of union, than that of common interest and affection. The whole country flew to the relief of Boston, and, making her cause their own, participated [in] her cares and administered to her wants. The fate of war, since that day, has carried the calamity in a ten-fold proportion to the southward; but in the mean time the union has been strengthened by a legal compact of the States, jointly and severally ratified, and that which before was choice, or the duty of affection, is now likewise the duty of legal obligation.

The union of America is the foundation-stone of her independence; the rock on which it is built; and is something so sacred in her constitution, that we ought to watch every word we speak, and every thought we think, that we injure it not, even by mistake. When a multitude, extended, or rather scattered, over a continent, in the manner we are, mutually agree to form one common centre whereon the whole shall move, to accomplish a particular purpose, all parts must act together and alike, or act not at all, and a stoppage in any one is a stoppage of the whole, at least for a time.

Thus the several States have sent Representatives to assemble together in Congress, and they have empowered that body, which thus becomes their centre, and are no other than themselves in representation, to conduct and manage the war, while their constituents at home attend to the domestic cares of the country, their internal legislation, their farms, professions or employments: For it is only by reducing complicated things to method and orderly connection that they can be understood with advantage, or pursued with success.----Congress, by virtue of this delegation, estimates the expence, and apportions it out to the several parts of the empire according to their several abilities; and here the debate must end, because each State has already had its voice, and the matter has undergone its whole portion of argument, and can no more be altered by any particular State, than a law of any State, after it has passed, can be altered by an individual. For with respect to those things which immediately concern the union, and for which the union was purposely established and is intended to secure, each State is to the United States what each individual is to the State he lives in. And it is on this grand point, this movement upon one centre, that our existence as a nation, our happiness as a people, and our safety as individuals, depend.

It may happen that some State or other may be somewhat over or under rated, but this cannot be much. The experience which has been had upon the matter has nearly ascertained their several abilities. But even in this case, it can only admit of an appeal to the United States, but cannot authorise any State to make the alteration itself, any more than our internal government can admit an individual to do so in the case of an act of assembly; for if one State can do it, then may another do the same, and the instant this is done the whole is undone.

Neither is it supposable that any single State can be a judge of all the comparative reasons which may influence the collective body in quotaing out the continent. The circumstances of the several States are frequently varying, occasioned by the accidents of war and commerce, and it will often fall upon some to help others, rather beyond what their exact proportion at another time might be; but even this assistance is as naturally and politically included in the idea of a union as that of any particular assigned proportion; because we know not whose turn it may be next to want assistance; for which reason, that is the wisest state which sets the best example.

Though in matters of bounden duty and reciprocal affection, it is rather a degeneracy from the honesty and ardour of the heart to admit any thing selfish to partake in the government of our conduct, yet in cases where our duty, our affections, and our interest all coincide, it may be of some use to observe their union. The United States will become heir to an extensive quantity of vacant land, and their several titles to shares and quotas thereof will naturally be adjusted according to their relative quotas during the war, exclusive of that inability which may unfortunately arise to any State by the enemy holding possession of a part; but as this is a cold matter of interest, I pass it by, and proceed to my third head, viz.

ON THE MANNER OF COLLECTION AND EXPENDITURE.

It hath been our error, as well as our misfortune, to blend the affairs of each State, especially in money matters, with those of the United States; whereas it is our ease, convenience and interest to keep them separate. The expences of the United States for carrying on the war, and the expences of each State for its own domestic government, are distinct things, and to involve them is a source of perplexity and a cloak for fraud. I love method, because I see and am convinced of its beauty and advantage. It is that which makes all business easy and understood, and without which everything becomes embarrassed and difficult.

There are certain powers which the people of each State have delegated to their legislative and executive bodies, and there are other powers which the people of every State have delegated to Congress, among which is that of conducting the war, and, consequently, of managing the expences attending it; for how else can that be managed, which concerns every State, but by a delegation from each? When a State has furnished its quota, it has an undoubted right to know how it has been applied, and it is as much the duty of Congress to inform the State of the one, as it is the duty of the State to provide the other.

In the resolution of Congress already recited, it is recommended to the several States *to lay taxes for raising their quotas of money for the United States, separate from those laid for their own particular use.*

This is a most necessary point to be observed, and the distinction should follow all the way through. They should be levied, paid and collected separately, and kept separate in every instance. Neither have the civil officers of any State, or the government of that State, the least right to touch that money which the people pay for the support of their army and the war, any more than Congress has to touch that which each State raises for its own use.

This distinction will naturally be followed by another. It will occasion every State to examine nicely into the expences of its civil list, and to regulate, reduce and bring it into better order than it has hitherto been; because the money for that purpose must be raised apart, and accounted for to the public separately. But while the monies of both were blended, the necessary nicety was not observed, and the poor soldier, who ought to have been the first, was the last who was thought of.

Another convenience will be, that the people, by paying the taxes separately, will know what they are for; and will likewise know that those which are for the defence of the country will cease with the war, or soon after. For although, as I have before observed, the war is their own, and for the support of their own rights and the protection of their own property, yet they have the same right to know that they have to pay, and it is the want of not knowing that is often the cause of dissatisfaction.

This regulation of keeping the taxes separate has given rise to a regulation in the office of finance, by which it is directed:

"That the receivers shall, at the end of every month, make out an exact account of the monies received by them respectively, during such month, specifying therein the names of the persons from whom the same shall have been received, the dates and the sums; which account they shall respectively cause to be published in one of the newspapers of the State; to the end that every citizen may know how much of the monies collected from him, in taxes, is transmitted to the treasury of the United States for the support of the war; and also, that it may be known what monies have been at the order of the Superintendent of Finance. It being proper and necessary, that in a free country the people should be as fully informed of the administration of their affairs as the nature of things will admit."

It is an agreeable thing to see a spirit of order and œconomy taking place, after such a series of errors and difficulties. A government or an administration, who means and acts honestly, has nothing to fear, and consequently has nothing to conceal; and it would be of use if a monthly or quarterly account was to be published, as well of the expenditures as of the receipts. Eight millions of dollars must be husbanded with an exceeding deal of care to make it do, and therefore, as the management must be reputable, the publication would be serviceable.

I have heard of petitions which have been presented to the Assembly of this State (and probably the same may have happened in other States) praying to have the taxes lowered. Now the only way to keep taxes low is, for the United States to have ready money to go to market with; and tho' the taxes to be raised for the present year will fall heavy and there will naturally be some difficulty in paying them, yet the difficulty, in proportion as money spreads about the country, will every day grow less, and in the end we shall save some millions of dollars by it. We see what a bitter, revengeful enemy we have to deal with, and any expence is cheap compared to their merciless paw. We have seen the unfortunate Carolineans hunted like partridges on the mountains and it is only by providing means for our defence, that we not be in the same condition. When we think or talk about taxes, we ought to recollect that we lie down in peace, and sleep in safety; that we can that follow our farms or stores, or other occupations, in prosperous tranquility; and that these inestimable blessings are procured to us by the taxes that we pay. In this view, our taxes are properly our insurance money; they are what we pay to be made safe, and in strict policy, are the best money we can lay out.

It was my intention to offer some remarks on the impost law of *five per cent.* recommended by Congress, and to be established as a fund for the payment of the loan-office certificates, and other debts of the United States; but I have already extended my piece beyond my intention. And as this fund will make our system of finance compleat, and is strictly just, and consequently requires nothing but honesty to do it, there needs but little to be said upon it.

Philad. March 5, 1782.   C. ;

To the People of America.

Casting my eye over a former publication (the Crisis, No. 9) on the loss of Charlestown, I was tempted to introduce this address by a quotation from the first paragraph of that number, as it appeared to me exceedingly applicable to the present circumstances of the country.

"Had America pursued her advantages with half the spirit she resisted her misfortunes, she would before now have been a conquering and peaceful people; but lulled in the lap of soft tranquility, she rested her hopes, and adversity only could convulse her into action."[1]

This hath been the character of America in every part, and in every state and stage of the contest. Warmed by a love of liberty, and provoked by a sense of injuries, she encountered danger without fear, and misfortune without despondency: But no sooner was the point accomplished, than she returned with folded arms to rest, and seemed to wait with patience for new disasters.---Yet there is one reflection to be drawn from this character and conduct that is worth attending to, which is, that it is the sign and the natural effect of right principles, but not of right policy. Misfortune ever separates men in a bad cause, and unites them in a good one. The former are industrious only while they are prosperous, the latter while they are distressed. The one acts from impulse, the other from contrivance; and the whole mode and progress of their conduct, and their times of rest and action, are the reverse of each other.

But as we have learned knowledge from misfortune, let us likewise learn it from mistake; and wisely add for once, if we never do it again, the ardour of adversity to the strength of victory. Let us combine the glowing powers of resolute resistance with the tranquil advantages which conquest bestows; and render the present year as superior in system, as the latter was splendid in success.

---

[1] See above p. 167.

The progress and revolution of our domestic circumstances are as extraordinary as the revolution itself. We began with paper, and we end with gold and silver. We sat out with parties, and we are approaching to unity. The strength, the property, and even the fashion of the country, are confederated in her support. Like robust and healthy youth, she hath shook off the agues of the winter, and steps forward with constitutional bloom and vigour. By suffering distresses, she hath learned both to bear and to prevent them; and the experience of every day, whether drawn from good fortune or from bad, whether from wisdom or mistake, hath added something to her cause, and much to her judgment.

From this general state of circumstances I shall proceed to more particular matters.

In my last publication I stated the yearly expence of the war, namely eight millions of dollars; the nature of the union by which the States are bound together; and the propriety of keeping taxes for the defence of the country separate from the expences of government; the right of the people to be regularly informed of the monies received and expended; and the duty of the country to provide its several quotas.---Government and the people do not in America constitute distinct bodies. They are one, and their interest the same. Members of Congress, members of Assembly, or Council, or by any other name they may be called, are only a selected part of the people. They are the representatives of majesty, but not majesty itself. That dignity exists inherently in the universal multitude, and, though it may be delegated, cannot be alienated. Their estates and property are subject to the same taxation with those they represent, and there is nothing they can do, that will not equally affect themselves as well as others. If they call for supplies, they call on themselves in common with the country. Their situation enables them to know the more secret circumstances of things, and that such or such revenues are necessary for the security and defence of their constituents, and the accomplishment of the great object for which they are chosen. And here the distinction ends.

The furnishing ourselves with right ideas, and the accustoming ourselves to right habits of thinking, have a powerful effect in strengthening and cementing the mind of the country and freeing it from the danger of partial or mistaken notions. It is not all the ardour which the love of liberty can inspire, nor the utmost fortitude which the most heroic virtue can create, that will of themselves make us successful conquerors. We must come down to order, system and method, and go through the cool and judicious, as well as the animating and elevating parts of patriotism. Method is to natural power, what slight is to human strength, without which a giant would lose his labour, and a country waste its force.

At the commencement of the war much political wisdom was not absolutely necessary. The high spirit of the country in a great measure supplied its place, and the printing-presses furnished the means. They became our Peru and Mexico, and as we wanted we drew them forth.[2] Any body of men might at that time have carried on the war, who had resolution enough to proceed; because the difficulties of finance were then unknown, and the money came created to their hands. But those times are changed, and there is now a call on the wisdom and judgment, as well as on the firmness and patriotism of the country. Our situation is such, that the more is understood the better it will appear; and with the means in our power, we want nothing but the united disposition to employ them.

When America resolved on independance, and determined to be free, she naturally included within that resolution all the means, whether of men or money, necessary to effect it. She had laid herself out for greater sufferings, and more expence and loss, than she had hitherto experienced, except in Carolina and Georgia. The idea of getting rich had not in those days an existance. All she expected was to live, and all she hoped for was to be free. She had resolved to abandon her habitations, to desert her towns, and to form new settlements in the wilderness, rather than submit. There was no condition to which her imagination could extend that was not preferable to the oppressions that threatened her; and

---

[2] Peru and Mexico were the source of Spanish silver and gold.

the experience of several years has shewn her opinion just, and proved her resolution firm.

Yet while the war was carried on by the mass of general opposition, the business of the country got deranged. Agriculture, trade and commerce became neglected, and something like poverty began to appear. Yet the resolution suffered no abatement, and their losses served to provoke them the higher. But experience has shewn that the way to enrich a country, and render it systematically formidable, is to give every possible rest to the inhabitants, that they may follow their various occupations undisturbed. A man who is harrassed about, either by the inroads of the enemy, or by marching to oppose them, soon suffers more by loss of time and neglect of his affairs, than what a portion of taxes sufficient for his defence would amount to. And therefore it is to the good of the whole, as well as to the interest of the individual, that every one, who can, sets himself down to his business, and contributes his quota of taxes as one of the first duties he owes to his family, to himself, and to his country. Every amusement ought to be dispenced with, every indulgence curtailed, and every possible œconomy practised, both public and private, until a revenue sufficient for the protection and good of the country is obtained, and the debt to public justice satisfied.

I have no idea of that kind of policy which ends in expence, disappointment and disgrace; and those have ever been and ever will be the consequence of deficient and unequal revenues. America has resolved to defend herself, and to support her independance at all hazards and events. Every man's portion of that charge becomes his debt of honour, interest and happiness; and to see any one indulging himself at home while that portion is unpaid, and the soldier who defends him suffering in the field, is the highest dishonour a man can undergo.

It is a pity but some other word beside taxation had been devised for so noble and extraordinary an occasion, as the protection of liberty and the establishment of an independant world. We have given to a popular subject an unpopular name, and injured the service by a wrong assemblage of ideas. A man would be ashamed to be told that he signed a petition, praying that he might pay *less* than his share of the public expence, or that those who had trusted the public might never receive their money; yet he does the same thing when he petitions against taxation, and the only difference is, that by taking shelter under the name, he seems to conceal the meanness he would otherwise blush at. Is it popular to pay our debts, to do justice, to defend an injured and insulted country, to protect the aged and the infant, and to give to Liberty a land to live in? then must taxation, as the means by which those things are to be done, be popular likewise.

But to take a more local view of matters. Why has the back country been ravaged by the repeated incursions of the enemy and the Indians, but from the inability of the revenue to provide means for their protection? And yet the inhabitants of those countries were among the first to petition against taxation. In so doing, they eventually prayed for their own destruction, and, unhappily for them, their prayer was answered. Their quota of taxes would have been trifling, compared with their losses, and, what is still worse, their domestic sorrows. Alas! how unwisely, how unfeelingly, does a man argue, when he puts the safety of his family in competition with his tax.

There is so much of the honour, interest and independance of America staked upon taxation, that the subject must to every reflective mind make a strong impression. As we are now circumstanced, it is the criterion of public spirit; the touchstone of our good affections; and he who pays it the instant it is called for, does more for his country's good than the loudest talker in America. In vain are all our huzzas for liberty, without accompanying them with solid support. They will neither fill the soldier's belly, nor cloathe his back, they will neither pay the public creditors, nor purchase our supplies. They are well enough in their places and though they are the effusion of our hearts, they are no part of our substance.

The Assembly of this State, Pennsylvania, have unanimously gone through the bill for raising the sum of 1,120,000 Dollars, being their quota for the year: And, as an example worthy both of notice and imitation, the oppressed and distressed State of South-Carolina, notwithstanding the severity of its fate, has already done the same. Those people know, by woeful experience, the value of defence, and that the inconvenience of struggling with a tax for the protection of the country is not to be named, in competition with the losses they have borne, and the sorrows and sufferings they have undergone.

However inconvenient the tax may be, we know it can last but for a time. Our expences will cease with the war, and our taxation in consequence. But while the war continues, and so great a part of every thing that is dear and valuable to a country depends upon her revenue, I shall consider and treat taxation as a popular good. When the war shall be over, the case will be totally altered and my language, if I then speak at all, will be entirely different. Besides, America is a new character in the universe. She started with a cause divinely right, and struck at an object vast and valuable. Her reputation for political integrity, perseverance, fortitude and all the manly excellencies, stands high in the world, and it would be a thousand pities that, those happy introductions into life, she suffered the least spot or blot to fall upon her *moral* fame. Never let it be said, that the country who could do what America has done, defrauded the widow and the orphan of their property, and the soldier of his pay.

The tax will be attended with some inconvenience; but what is inconvenience, when compared with distress and the ruin and plunderings of an enemy. How many things of far greater inconvenience has America already undergone, nay, even flourished in the midst of, which she once thought impossible to be borne. I hold taxation, which is to be applied to her own defence and her own good, one of the lightest of her difficulties, when considered with those which were occasioned by the want of it. We have several times been on the crisis of destruction by the insufficiency of our public revenues, and the heart of America would have ached with concern and sorrow, could she at all times have known what her exact situation has been. It is now the only point we have to attend to, nay it is the only one that is worth attending to; for let us accomplish this, and the rest will follow; and that consolation which every man's mind will feel, at knowing that the public Treasury is furnished with an ability of providing for the defence of the country, will amply recompence the difficulties he may go through, and the endeavours he may make, in paying his allotted share. We shall be freed from the just murmurs of the suffering soldier; our eyes and ears will be no longer shocked with tales of slighted faith and suspected credit; and the face [of] our public, and of consequence of our private affairs, will wear a new and satisfied countenance. The idea, *that the country cannot bear it*, is a reproach upon her honour and firmness. She has borne ten times as much. Her fortitude and principles have been tried in a thousand instances of severer fortune; and it is a paradox not to be explained, and which ought to be exploded, that the people whom no force or misfortune could conquer, no temptation seduce, should, at the summit of success, trepan themselves into destruction by an ignoble and impolitic covetousness.

Let us be, in every respect, such a nation as we ought to be, and shew to the enemy that it is no more in her power to conquer us by system than by arms. The purse of America, with œconomy, is longer than that of Britain, managed as it is by corruption and extravagance. The people of America are not a poor people, why should they appear so. We hurt our credit, our honour, our reputation in the world, by proclaiming ourselves what we are not, and give encouragement to the enemy to prolong the war, by holding out an idea of our want of money to carry it on. It is easy to see by the complexion of the New-York papers, that the present spirited exertions of the country to keep her public treasury supplied have wounded the last hopes of the enemy. It is a blow they never expected America to give, and their astonishment is as great as their despair.

It is a remark, worth making, that the people have always been a step forwarder than their representatives. There never was a backwardness in the country to do its part, when the part to be done became known and understood. National money matters are naturally attended with a degree of intricacy, which renders them not so easily comprehended as those which are more simple and obvious. Those of America have, from the fluctuating state of the former currency, been involved in new and original difficulties, and it required much judicious management to bring them right, and a vigorous exertion in the country afterwards to keep them so.

The present condition of our money matters, as concisely as they can be stated, is as follows:

There is a large sum due to persons who have lent their money to the Loan-Office, and to those who have otherwise trusted the public. Those debts are to be ascertained and proved, and the money arising from the impost duty of five per cent. on all imported goods is to be applied as a fund for payment of the interest and principal, until the whole of them shall be discharged. This is the provision made for our debts already contracted, and when once the interest on them shall be regularly drawn, and the principal put into a train for payment, they will become as valuable as bond debts.

The sum of eight millions of dollars, which is apportioned out to be raised by the United States, is for the maintenance and other expences of the army, and to defray the government charges of the continent. If this sum is compared with the immense expence which Britain is at, the difference will appear exceedingly stinking. She is obliged to raise upwards of ninety millions of dollars in taxes and loans every year, to do what we can accomplish, with ready money and frugality, for eight millions. So great is the contrast between a country sunk in corruption and extravagance, and one whose object is founded in just principles, and her plans regulated by good management.

But the difference may be carried still further. When the war shall cease with us, our taxes for that purpose will cease with it. We know they cannot now last for any long time; whereas the taxes in Britain being laid on only for the purpose of paying interest, and never the principal of her debts, must continue for ever.

The publishing the sums of money received from each State, and expended on their united account, will be attended with several good effects. It will give satisfaction, which is a necessary object in national concerns. It will create emulation, and detect delinquency. The opener and fairer public business is transacted, the better it succeeds. Where no fraud is intended, there can be no occasion for concealment, and it is not only necessary that measures should be just, but that every body should know them to be so.

A few days will now carry us to the period of seven years war, and so extraordinary is the case, that instead of the country becoming poor and exhausted, she is grown rich and plentiful. There has been a singular fate attended all our wants, for whenever we imagined we should be ruined, by not having something which could not be done without, it arrived, as if of itself, just time enough to prevent the mischief. The last remarkable instance was the influx of hard money, almost at the very moment when the paper currency failed, by which the circumstances of public and private business are so materially improved, that matters cannot go wrong, if we set heartily about what is right.

COMMON SENSE

Providence Gazette, Rhode Island, December 28, 1782.

LETTER II.

In ANSWER *to the* CITIZEN OF RHODE-ISLAND, *on the Five per Cent. Duty.*

IN my former letter I mentioned the purpose for which the five per cent. duty is levied; namely, as a fund for the payment of the interest and principal of such debts as are or may be contracted, abroad or at home, for the defence of the United States. I am now to shew the convenience and equality of the mode; which I shall preface with a few occasional observations.

In this country, where every State is interested alike in the event of the war, and almost every man in it stands in the same predicament, there ought to be no occasion for persuasion; and I might as well expect that the Citizen of Rhode-Island should undertake to persuade me to my duty as I shall endeavour to persuade him. In proportion to our different circumstances, whatever they may be, we must be proportionably affected by a five per cent. duty. I can assure him too, that I am no public creditor, and therefore can have no individual interest in what I am writing. But I have the honor, interest and happiness, of a new and infant world at heart. She had done great things, and it would be a thousand pities to diminish that greatness, by anything that is little.

In speaking on this part of the subject, I put our foreign debt totally out of the question; because that is what we are all agreed in, and makes no part of the argument. It was contracted in hard money, and the value of it permanent. But we have a species of internal debt among us, the value of which is unfixed and admits of injury either way, and therefore it is necessary to ascertain as precisely as possible, and settle it, lest the fair and real creditor should involve his fate with the rapacious claimant, and thereby be exposed to suffer on the one hand, or that the public should pay more than they have a right to pay on the other.

I am sensible that I look with an equal impartiality towards both, and as I do not wish to pay too little, so neither would I pay too much. If the creditor has his interest to take care of, the debtor has his honor to preserve, and the loss to the one is full as severe as to the other. The States might appoint a general committee of accounts, to meet, adjust and settle all sorts of claims, prior to the commencement of the present system of finance.

But in the mean time, let us make the necessary provision for discharging what is really due, and supporting our reputation, and not embarrass that which is right with that which is wrong. What I cannot blame the Citizen of Rhode-Island for, his stating the matter erroneously, and treating it both imprudently and unfairly. He has brought cases into question which are totally foreign to it, and avoided the points which he might have spoken upon.

Two things only arc necessary---the settlement of the public accounts and the means of paying them off; and the question before us affords no other points. We did not undertake the defence of the country against a vindictive and powerful enemy without knowing that it would be attended with many and unavoidable expences; and we have prospered in that defence equal to our utmost expectations, and far better than we many times had reason to hope for. It was by the united effort of all America, which, like a bundle of rods could not only not be broken, but were capable of chastising, that this happiness has been effected, and by which it is still secured; and as the case before us is of the nature of an united effort, we cannot too seriously impress ourselves with the idea and principle of union by which we rose into greatness, and are known by to the rest of the universe. It is our Magna Charta---our anchor in the world of empires.

Since then our condition and preservation require money, can there be a more equal and easier way of raising the sum required for the discharge of these accounts than a duty of five per cent. on foreign imported goods? If the duty produces an overplus, so much the better, for the soldier wants it; he likewise is a creditor. If it should not raise enough, pay it as far as it will go, by the best method that can be devised, and let both the public and the creditors know the sums reserved and paid, and to whom and for what.

The duty then, I say, of five per cent. lights equally on all the States according to their several abilities. For it is not what States import the most or the least, but which, from their degrees of opulence or populousness, consume the most or least, that ascertain the quantity they severally bring towards the fund. Rhode-Island will pay but a small share of the duty, because she will consume but little; and all that she imports more than she consumes, is eventually paid by some other neighbouring States, and not by her.

If in America we had but one port, still the inhabitants of the State where that port was would pay no more of the five per cent. duty than in the present case; that is, they would pay only for what they consumed; and the States which had no port might pay much more duty than that which had, because they might severally consume more. In this case, every man throughout the United States would be assessed his five per cent. duty at one place; because there could be but one place of collection; and, consequently, the monies so raised upon the whole cannot be carried to the cause of the State in which it is collected; and this single observation oversets one objection which I have heard Rhode-Island has made.

It is a great convenience to a State to be situated so near the water, as to be eased of the expence of land carriage for foreign goods. This alone is far more than the duty of five per cent. and persons so conveniently circumstanced should, of all people, be the last to object.

Rhode-Island, by her situation enjoys some superior benefits in the union. Closely connected with the sea, she derives advantages under its flag, its commissions and pass ports, which the inhabitants of more remote places do not; and many reasons will, upon reflection, occur to shew, that her objections are not only wrongly founded, but wrongly judged of.

The Citizen of Rhode-Island has said that the duty of five per cent. will fall unequally. It is easy to say any thing. But he has not advanced a single case or argument to prove it; which he certainly would, if he could have discovered any.

He has likewise said many other things; but he has only said them, and left them to shift for themselves. Now a man ought never to leave an assertion to shift for itself. It is like turning out a sickly infant to beg a home in other people's houses.

But there is one other thing which this gentleman has not said; for he has not attempted to shew another way of raising the money, and he knows, full well as I do, that the situation of a country at war requires money. But I can tell him the reason why he has been silent on this head; it is because he cannot devise an easier way, nor any that so well suits the circumstances of Rhode-Island; because, being considerably in the line of commerce, she can easier raise it through that medium, than through any other. And this brings me to shew the convenience and lightness of the five per cent. duty, so far as respects the individual in any or all the States.

As a tax, it will scarcely be felt. The utmost difference it can make will be a very little more than a half-penny in the shilling, and in the fluctation of trade, it will be insensibly lost; for there is scarcely a day that passes over our heads, but in which the rise or fall of prices is much greater; and it will so naturally and easily divide and circulate itself through the community, that its productiveness will arise from the universality of its operation.

It will likewise be found not only the lightest of all other modes of raising money but the most convenient; for it operates with the ease of a tax in kind, without any of its difficulties and incumbrances. The man who might be scarce of money, has still money's worth; he comes to market, and, by such means as are most convenient to himself, disposes of it, and procures, in the lieu thereof, such imported articles as he has occasion for, and in that exchange he pays his portion of duty, without any other trouble.

It is likewise that kind of a duty which a man may pay or not; because he may chuse whether he will wear or consume foreign articles. It is a duty too which the consumer is never *called upon* to pay; because whenever it suits him he goes to buy, and not before, and there ends the matter.

It is a duty which is the most easily collected, because it is collected but in few places, and in the lump, without rambling over the world for it, and requires but few persons, and may be done at a small expence; and I am persuaded that when the States find the convenience of this mode in preference to others they will be inclined to throw some of their present taxes into the same channel. I have observed that the last convinced is often the most effectually convinced; and notwithstanding what the gentleman, who stiles himself a Citizen of Rhode-Island, has said, the State will have other opinions.[1] Now as what this gentleman first advanced respecting a perpetual revenue in the hands of an executive power is, in our situation, as a true and pure republic, futile and perfectly unapplicable, for the reasons advanced in my former letter, and as the weight of the duty is scarcely to be mentioned, and as the method is easier than any other which can be devised, and falls equally on all the States, and on the individuals in each state according to their several abilities, I should be glad to know what objections he has to it, or can advance, for at present he has supported none. He contented himself with stating a question at first setting out, which all America was agreed to before he put it, and consequently could be no question at all.

I observe his pieces are interspersed whith [sic] confused notions on government. His meaning may be good, and I have no reason to believe it is not; but, for want of distinguishing one sort of government from another, he draws conclusions which suit neither.

He does not see the difference between a country like England, where scarcely one man in a hundred is an elector, and this country, where every man is an elector, and may likewise be elected. Nor yet between the parliament of England (one house of which, the Peers, is perpetual, and the vacancies filled up by the Crown, and the other removeable only in seven years) and our constitutional governments, the representatives under which, both legislative and executive, are

---

[1] Paine's protagonist published a piece in the *Providence Gazette* on September 21, 1782 signed 'A Countryman' rather than 'A Citizen'. Clark summarises a number of pieces that put the case against the impost. See Clark, *Six New Letters*, p. xviii.

annually chosen by ourselves in most instances. Nor yet between the executive power possessed by the Crown, not to be touched at all, be it in hands ever so vicious, extravagant or ignorant, and the Congress of America, which, as member, are removeable at pleasure, and must be chosen every year. In short, he does not see the difference between the one country wrapt up in the most absurd species of slavery, and the other possessing and enjoying all their natural and civil rights; and thus, by carrying the jealousies necessary in people under a monarchy into the constitutions of a republic, he degrades the virtue on which republics are founded.

But there is an observation which this gentleman throws out, and likewise a second observation under another signature, both of which have considerable weight, and on which I shall offer some remarks.

The one is a quotation from Montesquieu, which was introduced into a former declaration of Congress, and is in these words: "When the power of making of laws and the power of executing them are united in the *same person*, or the *same body* of Magistrates, there can be no liberty; because apprehensions may arise, lest the same monarch or senate should enact tyrannical laws, to execute them in a tyrannical manner."

I shall pay all the regard to this quotation, which the Citizen of Rhode-Island wishes to be paid. Though, by the bye, it is very easy to see that Montesquieu means a power perpetually *existing* in the *same person* or *persons*, and not a power *vested* in those who are removeable at pleasure. I wish those who quote Montesquieu would strictly regard his applications. It was very properly said by Congress to Britain, whose government over us was absolute, but cannot be said by us to ourselves.

The other observation which I allude to is in Mr. Bradford's paper, of November 16th, in these words: — "No two States," says the writer, "have agreed on the measure (meaning the five per cent. duty) without particular provisoes and limitations of their own, differing from the others; it is therefore impossible that a regular systematical collection of the duties should take place, unless those limitations and provisos are first removed."

Now these two observations, taken either separately or collectively may be of use to us. They naturally apply to something wanting, and something defective. We want some laws which Congress cannot make, and when the States attempt them they are imperfect. Certainly then the whole of our system is not yet compleat.

The United States are, as Mr. Burke very justly stiles them, "The greatest Commonwealth on the face of the earth*." But all Commonwealths must have some laws in common, which regulate, preserve, and protect the whole.

What would the sovereignty of any one individual State be, if left to itself, to contend with a foreign power? It is on our united sovereignty, that our greatness and safety, and the security of our foreign commerce, rest. This united sovereignty then must be something more than a name, and requires to be as compleatly organized for the line it is to act in as that of any individual State, and, if any thing, more so, because more depends on it.

Every man in America stands in a two-fold order of citizenship. He is a citizen of the State he lives in, and of the United States; and without justly and truly supporting his citizenship in the latter, he will inevitably sacrifice the former. By his rank in the one, he is made secure with his neighbours; by the other, with the world. The one protects his domestic safety and property from internal robbers and injustice; the other his foreign and remote property from piracy and invasion, and puts him on a rank with other nations. Certainly then the one, like the other, must not and cannot be trusted to pleasure and caprice, lest, in the display of local authority, we forget the great line that made us great, and must keep us so.

In introducing these remarks I have followed a thought naturally arising from the observations made by the Citizen of Rhode-Island, and I find that experience begins to suggest the idea of an inadequacy in our confederated system to several cases which must necessarily happen; what I mean is, that the confederation is not

---

* See Mr. Burke's speech in the case of Mr. Laurens, December 17, 1781, in the parliamentary debates, page 185.

adapted to fit all the cases which the empire of the United States in the course of her sovereignty may experience; and the case before us shews that it is not adequate to every purpose of internal benefit and commercial regulation.

Several new and important matters have arisen since the confederation was formed. The entering into foreign alliances and treaties of commerce; the borrowing of foreign loans; the cessation of the emissions of the paper currency; the raising of supplies by taxes, and several others which might be enumerated. But as nothing can happen to which we are not equal the thing necessary is to think wisely and deliberately of them and divide accordingly.

A FRIEND TO RHODE-ISLAND *AND THE UNION*

Providence Gazette, Rhode Island, 1 February 1783.

LETTER VI

On the FIVE *PER CENT.* DUTY.

He that has a turn for public business, and integrity to go through it, untempted by interest, and unawed by party, must likewise sit down with the calm determination of putting up with the mistakes, petulance, and prejudices of mankind.

As I am not cramped by self-interest in viewing a public measure, it naturally presents itself to me without fetters; and my judgment, such as it is, being left free makes its determination without partiality. The merchant and the farmer are persons alike to me, and all places in America nearly the same. It is the general good, the happiness of the whole, that has ever been my object. Neither is there any Delegate that now is, or ever was in Congress, from the State of Rhode-Island, or elsewhere, who can say that the author of these letters ever sought from any man, or body of men, any place, office, recompence or reward, on any occasion for himself—I have had the happiness of serving mankind, and the honor of doing it freely.

If, then, any of the intimations in the paper of last week, respecting "mercenary writers" had the least illusion to me, the author of them is most unfortunate in his application; neither is it necessary to disown them, because the voice of the country will do it for me; And as it is impossible to wounded by a wasp that never had the power of stinging, it would be folly indeed to be discomposed at the buzzing of a harmless insect.

When I mentioned the metaphor of the rocket and the stick, I left the application to be made by others; and if any gentleman has applied it to himself, it is a confession that the metaphor fits him.

But to return to the subject of the five per cent. duty:

I cannot help viewing the clamour that has been raised against this measure, as arising, in some instances, from selfishness, and, in others, from a false idea of patriotism.

The gentlemen who are at the head of the opposition in this State, are those who are in the mercantile line.—To give their opposition an air of patriotism, they say, "Why do not Congress call on us for a quota?—We are willing to raise it, but we will not consent to a five per cent duty."

All this sounds mighty fine. But do not those gentlemen know, that of the annual quota, called for last year, there has not been a quarter part of it paid in, perhaps not above a sixth or an eighth, even in this State. And yet those gentlemen are exceedingly generous in proposing to raise more money by the same mode of taxation, or any other mode, provided that their commerce goes duty-free.

We are certainly the most wise or the most foolish people in the world, not to take in commerce as one of the funds of taxation. We are now doing what no other country in the world does, and what no other country on earth can long afford to do, for we are, in the first place, giving encouragement to the commerce of foreign countries at the risk of our own; and, in the second place, we are raising all our taxes on the necessaries of life, and suffering the luxuries of it to go free.

I am strongly persuaded, that the gentlemen who are in opposition to the measure are themselves convinced that the measure is right, because in their arguments they are continually flying off from the point, like sparks from a rocket, and drawing the eye of the beholder from the ground he stands upon.

The proper point or question before the public is, whether commerce ought to be taken in as one of the national funds?

When this point or question is settled in the affirmative, the next will be, which is the most just and equitable way of doing it? And,

Thirdly, which will be the most effectual method of securing the application of the monies so raised to the purpose for which they are intended?

These are the proper, natural and political questions upon the measures, and the only ones into which it can be divided. But the opposers, instead of keeping to these points, and beginning, as they ought to have done, with the first of them, have filled the papers of this State with wild declamations, idle and frothy rhapsody, foreign to the subject, and calculated only to bewilder and perplex, and prevent the measure being understood.

A long piece in the providence gazette of last week, signed A. C. has not a single line in it to the purpose; but, like all the rest on the same side, is contrived to shun the debate, by fomenting an uproar.

I have now, by stating the several parts of the question, put, as I conceive, the whole matter into a clear and intelligent train of being understood; and until those points are adjusted, every other method of treating the subject is useless. To which I may justly add, that the manner in which the gentlemen of the opposition have hitherto conducted their publications, serves only to unhinge the public mind, even in their own State, from every obligation of civil and moral society, and from the necessary duties of good government; and to promote profligacy, that may in time think all property common, and fall, when too late to prevent it, on their own heads.—The transition from disobedience to disorder is easy and rapid; and as the richest men now in the State of Rhode-Island are making tools of the poorest, I cannot help thinking but that the avarice of the former is trying a dangerous experiment: For the man who will say that he will enrich himself by smuggling, cuts asunder the laws that are to protect him, and exposes himself to a second plunder.

As I intend this to be my last publication in the State of Rhode-Island, I shall conclude it with such circumstances as may be an answer to any present or future remarks on the part I have taken.

I am not only convinced that the conduct of Rhode-Island is wrong, in her opposition to the five per cent. duty, but I am likewise persuaded that it will precipitate her into difficulties she does not at present foresee.

My design in taking the matter up was as much out of kindness to her, as to promote the general good of America. There may be those, in other states, who are privately urging on her, and putting her, in this instance, on the forlorn hope of disgrace, to avoid the reproach themselves:—But the part I have acted towards her has been open, friendly, and sincere.

In my personal acquaintance, in this State, I have scarcely met with a man, who was in the opposition to the measure, that did not confess to me, in the course of the conversation, *that commerce ought to be taken in as one of the funds for defraying the expenses of the war*; and I have met with numbers who are strong advocates for it.

I have likewise heard a great deal of the angry dislike of a few men, whose niggardly souls, governed only by the hope of the high price which their next or present cargoes may bring, have been throwing out intimations that my publications on this subject ought to be stopped in Rhode-Island; but I have ever met with any of them, or with any other person in the State, who did not pay me respect when he met me. Why any man should say one thing, and act another, or why he should endeavour to throw a blot on my reputation in the Providence news-paper, and yet show every possible civility to my face, I leave to those who can act a double part to explain.

But to shew those persons that I am not, like themselves, governed by self-interest and narrow thinking, I shall, for once in my lifetime, make free with the correspondence of my friends—men whose characters the persons in opposition will never imitate, and who personally and intimately knew me in various and trying situations. Neither could I take this liberty with the dead, or with the living, or reconcile it to my feelings, were it not on a public question, wherein the interest of the country and not of myself is concerned.

The writers in the Providence paper of last week, with a view of keeping up the bubble, fraud and avarice, of the opposition, held out that I was a mercenary writer. They may call me so a thousand times over, if they please, and when they have done, they may sit down in shame and disgrace. Even Mr. Howell, who is now in Providence, must be a witness to my integrity. But I will now produce much higher authorities than Mr. Howell.[1]

For this purpose I have put into the Printer's hands two letters, the one from a dear and intimate friend of mine, and of mankind, whose greatness of soul has laid his person in the dust, COL. LAURENS, whom I accompanied to France, to procure money for America. The other from Major-General GREENE, to whom I was a volunteer aid-de-camp in the gloomy times of 1776, since which an uninterrupted friendship has subsisted between us.[2]

The letter of Col. Laurens is in these words:

"Carolina, April 18, 1782.

I received the letter wherein you mention my horse and trunk (the latter of which was left at Providence). The misery which the former has suffered at different times, by mismanagement, has greatly distressed me—he was wounded in service, and I am much attached to him—if he can be of any service to you, I entreat your acceptance of him, more especially if you will make use of him in bringing you to a country (Carolina) where you will be received with open arms, and all that affection and respect which our citizens are anxious to testify to the author of————.

Adieu.—I wish you to regard this part of America (Carolina) as your particular home—and every thing that I can command in it, to be in common between us."

The letter from General Greene, among many other declarations of esteem and friendship, contains the following:

"Ashley-River (Carolina) November 18, 1782

Many people wish to get you into this country——

---

[1] David Howel (1747 -1824) was the leader of the states' rights-agrarian opposition to the five-percent duty in Rhode Island. Howel's election to Congress in the spring of 1782, ousted General James M. Varnum, who argued strongly in favour of the impost.

[2] Paine accompanied Col. John Laurens to France in 1781 (see above p. 206, n. 3.) Laurens was well regarded in Rhode Island having served there during the War of Independence. General Nathanael Greene (1742-86), was a native of Rhode Island and a hero of the War of Independence. Paine served as his aide in 1776-1777.

I see you are determined to follow your genius, and not your fortune. I have always been in hopes that Congress would have made some handsome acknowledgement to you for your past services.—I must confess that I think you have been shamefully neglected; and that America is indebted to few characters more than to you. But as your passion leads so fame, and not to wealth, your mortification will be the less.—Your name, from your writings, will live immortal.

At present my expences are great; nevertheless, if you are not conveniently situated, I shall take a pride and pleasure in contributing all in my power to render your situation happy."

It is needless for me to make any other remarks on these letters, than to say, that while I enjoy the high esteem and opinion of good and great men, I am perfectly unconcerned at the mean and snarling ingratitude of little incendiaries.

I now refer the reader to my five letters already published in the Providence Gazette, on the five per cent. duty, and more particularly to the last number.

A FRIEND TO RHODE-ISLAND AND THE UNION.

Providence, January 31, 1783

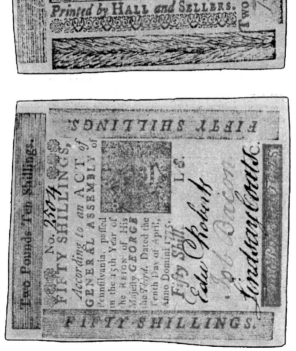

Fig. 1. Fifty Shillings Pennsylvania Currency note issued by the Pennsylvania Assembly on 10 April 1775. £25,000 of these notes and the £5 denomination were issued to fund the building of prisons and workhouses by an act of 18 March 1775. They were printed by Hall & Sellers, in two colours by depicting Walnut Street workhouse on the reverse. Signed by Edward Roberts. (The Smithsonian Institution, NNC, Douglas Mudd.)

Fig. 2. Half a Dollar Continental Currency note issued by Continental Congress, 17 February 1776. $4 million dollars of continental currency was issued by this resolution in twelve denominations. The sundail 'Fugio (time flies so) mind your business' emblem and the thirteen colonies linked together into one on the reverse were designed by Benjamin Franklin, the notes printed by Hall & Sellers. (The Smithsonian Institution, NNC, Douglas Mudd.)

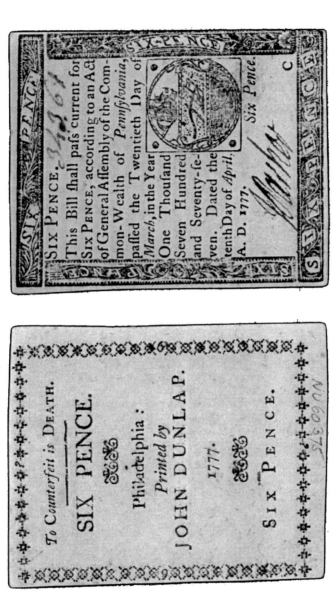

Fig. 3. Six Pence Pennsylvania Currency note issued by the Pennsylvania Assembly on 10 April 1777. £200,000 in Bills of credit was issued by an act of the assembly on 20 March 1777 to support the army. The notes are decorated with the arms of the Commonwealth of Pennsylvania depicting a ship, a plough and three wheat-sheaves. Printed by John Dunlap and signed by Joseph Parker. (The Smithsonian Institution, NNC, Douglas Mudd.)

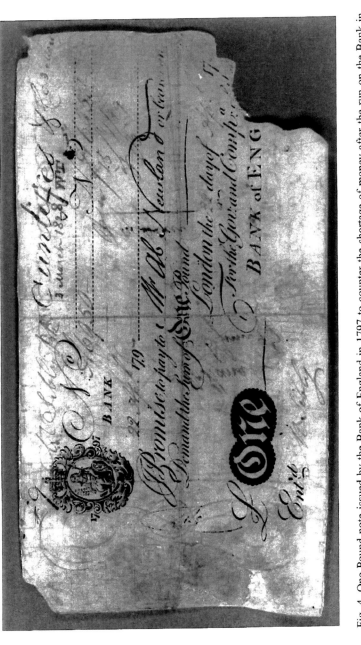

Fig. 4. One Pound note issued by the Bank of England in 1797 to counter the shortage of money after the run on the Bank in February and the subsequent suspension of payments in gold. (The Bank of England: John Keyworth)

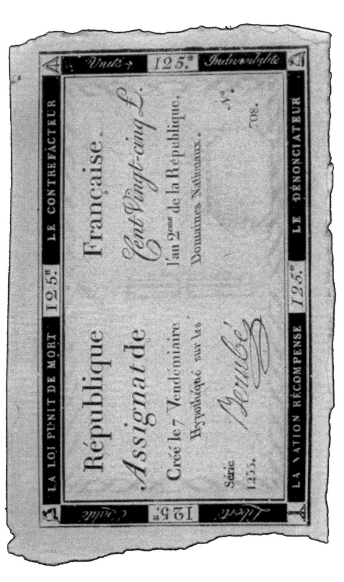

Fig. 5. A French Assignat issued, dated Vendémiaire 7, Second Year of the Republic (28 September 1793).[1] Originally issued as futures shares in the nationalisation of church lands, later notes used to fund the war were not secured and contributed rapid inflation. Note the slogan repeated 'The law punishes the counterfeiter with death.' (The Smithsonian Institution, NNC, Douglas Mudd.)

Chapter Three

The Bank Crisis - Philadelphia 1785-7

Following the achievement of American independence, Paine intended to retire from politics and settled in Bordentown, New Jersey to concentrate on scientific invention. However, he became embroiled in a political and economic controversy surrounding the state establishment of the Bank of North America in Pennsylvania. The bank crisis is fascinating in itself as arguably the world's first battle between representative democracy and capitalism. Paine's involvement is expressive of this struggle emerging in his thinking and for that reason the crisis has often been seen as crucial to understanding his political thought.

Paine had previously argued against the checks and balances that mirrored the British Constitution, which he thought undemocratic and corrupt. The crisis challenged Paine's assumption that a democratically elected assembly would act rationally and in the interests of the state as a whole, rather than according to party faction. For David Powell

The affair of the Bank was of small concern though, through the writer of 1785, it came to symbolise all the rest - the faith in man and reason on which Paine had built his creed.[1]

The crisis affected three key areas of Paine's political thought. Firstly, it led Paine to question his unicameralism. Secondly, in his bank crisis writings, he strongly associates the enforcement of contracts by the state with individual liberty. Thirdly, at this time, he develops his principle of the right of each generation. The democratic challenge to emerging capitalist institutions forced Paine to reassess his political ideas, but the bank crisis writings are also a fruitful source for exploring Paine's economic ideas; his defence of the independent bank, his attack on unsupported paper money and concern about the national debt.

The Causes and Events of the Crisis

Economic and political upheaval in Pennsylvania at the end of the war resulted in a popular campaign for the state issue of paper money. There was an acute lack of gold and silver coin in the colonies due to an unfavourable trade balance and such specie was now being used to pay off debts to British merchants and proprietors. Troops were sent home without financial compensation and land prices fell due to a plentiful supply in the west for settlers and confiscated Tory estates being sold off or given away. The general lack of circulating money left debts unpaid, exacerbating the economic crisis. 'Seizing upon the scarcity of money as the cause of their plight, the people of Pennsylvania in 1785 set up a cry for paper money.'[2]

---

[1] David Powell, *The Greatest Exile* (London: Hutchinson, 1989), p. 139.
[2] Wilson, 'The Bank of North America', pp. 6 & 5 n. 2. See also W. C. Plummer, 'Consumer Credit in Colonial Philadelphia', *The Pennsylvania Magazine of History and Biography*, 66:2 (1942), 389; J. T. Scharf & T. Westcott, *History of Philadelphia 1609-1884*, 3 vols (Philadelphia: L. H. Everts, 1884), I, p. 435. Scharf & Westcott estimate state debt at £548279, 10s, 8d, and in addition £183,232 owed to the late proprietors.

In 1785 there was support in both the Assembly and the newspapers for a proposal to open a state loan office to issue paper money in the form of bills of credit. Support was also evident from petitions from rural towns such as 'the People of the Northern Liberties' but was opposed by meetings in the townships of Philadelphia County, such as Germantown, fearing a fall in land prices and claiming that such an act would amount to a tax on land. A committee of merchants and traders, mostly bank directors or stockholders, meeting at the City Tavern on 23 February, petitioned the Assembly to refrain from issuing paper because of low public confidence. This was interpreted as a threat not to accept paper on the same terms as gold and silver coin, especially as the bank now started to call in loans to reassure investors but causing resentment among borrowers.[3] A bill was framed to issue £50,000 in bills and to enforce these as legal tender. The bank directors' threat to refuse to accept paper money as equivalent to specie enraged the paper money supporters who now called for the Assembly to repeal the bank's charter. Such an action threatened to destroy confidence in the bank. The bank's enemies believed that lack of specie was due to the bank's engrossing of coinage. The Assembly issued new bills of credit worth £150,000 and accepted a petition against the bank. A committee was established to investigate the public safety of the bank's affairs and 'the mischievous consequences of the institution to the fair trader'.[4]

The committee was made up of opponents of the bank, then in a majority in the Assembly, mostly western Scots-Irish farmers such as John Smiley (1741-1812) of Fayette County and Robert Whitehill (1738-1813) of Cumberland. Their report recommended repeal of the bank's charter on grounds of hoarding and export of specie through dividends to stockholders foreign and domestic and claimed that the bank's financial power gave it too much influence over the legislature.[5] On 14 April a bill to repeal the bank's state charter passed its second

[3] See Scharf & Westcott, *History of Philadelphia*, I, p. 438.
[4] See Wilson, 'The Bank of North America', p. 7.
[5] See below p. 293.

reading. When the Assembly determined to wait until after the summer adjournment to decide the fate of the bank, the directors attempted compromise by allowing paper deposit accounts that could not be transferred into specie accounts. Sixty-seven such accounts were opened but mostly by supporters of the bank - the paper money enthusiasts did not take advantage of the offer. James Wilson was commissioned by the president of the bank, Thomas Willing (1731-1821), to appeal to Continental Congress and was given £400 to write a pamphlet on the bank crisis.[6] The debate continued in the Pennsylvania newspapers but in the Assembly the bank party was outnumbered two to one. On 13 September 1785, the bank's charter was repealed, despite Willing and Wilson's appeal at the bar of the House. Stock fell to 6% below par and the bank's cash account also fell as foreign investors withdrew. The bank still had a Congressional Charter though its power was weak due to the low prestige of Congress at this time. The bank temporarily stopped discounting until it was clear there would not be a run.

On 21 December 1785, Paine published a letter in the *Pennsylvania Gazette* showing that he had been supporting the bank since 19 April 1785 but had not wanted to offend the Assembly publicly due to a recent gift of £500 bestowed on Paine by the Assembly for his services during the war. He claimed that he was forced to state his opinion as some pamphlets against the bank had been falsely attributed to him. In February 1786, Paine published a pamphlet entitled *Dissertations on Government; the Affairs of the Bank; and Paper Money*, stating his reasons for supporting the bank. He wrote eight other letters to Philadelphia newspapers on the subject of the bank, all reprinted here. On 21 February 1786, Delaware granted the bank a charter. Morris struggled to win back support in Pennsylvania. A petition to revive the charter attracted six hundred signatures and led to a renewal of debate in the Assembly. Paine reports

---

[6] See Wilson, 'The Bank of North America', p. 9. 'Considerations on the Bank of North America ' appeared as a supplement to the *Pennsylvania Gazette* in 17 September 1785. James Wilson (1742-98), a jurist and legal writer, was a director of the Bank of North America and acted as Morris's personal lawyer. Thomas Willing (1731-1821) was Robert Morris's business partner and president of the Bank of North America.

that 'No subject of debate that has been agitated before the legislature of Pennsylvania ever drew such crowded audiences as attended the house during the four days the debate lasted.'[7] The report recommending the repeal of the bill to repeal the charter was rejected 28-41, as was Morris's motion for suspension of the bill.

In the autumn elections the bank party fared slightly better than its opponents. The city of Philadelphia and Bucks and Chester County were now solidly conservative and Smiley lost his seat. Franklin was now president of Supreme Executive Council and able to put his weight behind a new charter with a limited capital and duration backed by a petition from citizens of Philadelphia. A new legislative committee was appointed and reported in favour of a modified charter. The anti-bank party was also backed by petitions but failed in their attempt to sabotage the bill by amendment. On 17 March 1787 the bank's charter was restored by *An Act to Revive the Incorporation of the Subscribers of the Bank of North America* although their capital was limited to $2 million and the duration of the charter was limited to 14 years.

Pennsylvania Politics 1776 -1790

The political tensions in Pennsylvania can be seen as a struggle between two factions, that can be traced back to the Penn charter that left artisan and agricultural interests disenfranchised.[8] The proprietorial oligarchy, which had been dominant in colonial Pennsylvania, was Tory and loyalist and those who did support independence (the Moderates) did so conservatively favouring property qualifications for voting and constitutions which mirrored the aristocratic 1689

---

[7] See below p. 330.
[8] See H. M. Tinkcom, *Republicans and Federalists in Pennsylvania 1790-1801: A Study in National Stimulus and Local Response* (Harrisburg: Pennsylvania Historical and Museum Commission, 1950), pp. 1-17. Aldridge suggests three factions: Tories, Moderate Whigs in favour of independence and radical Whig Independents. See Aldridge, *American Ideology*, p. 254.

settlement in England. They were opposed to the 1776 Pennsylvania Constitution and to the test laws that made loyalty to the constitution the only suffrage qualification. They campaigned for a federalist structure and a strong national executive. The conservatives were at first defeated by the democratic faction: a coalition of western rural interests and Philadelphia artisans who secured a radical constitution in 1776 providing a single assembly by universal suffrage with a plural executive and a council of censors to review the constitution periodically. The economic depression that followed the war drove a wedge between the agricultural and artisan interests in the democratic coalition. This allowed the anti-constitutionalists, later Federalists, to gain support from urban working classes and defeat the democratic interest, firstly over the federal constitution and then over a new Pennsylvanian Constitution in 1790. This was the counter-revolution to the 'revolution within a revolution'. The wedge that split the urban and rural democrats was the bank crisis of 1785-7.[9]

Paine's contribution to the debate on the bank has been seen as an indication of a temporary leaning towards conservatism. It was generally assumed at the time that Paine would support the anti-bank movement, as he had been allied with the democratic camp over the Pennsylvania constitution and the Silas Deane affair, and indeed Paine complained that some anti-bank literature had been falsely attributed to him. Paine was accused by a rural representative, John Smiley of Fayette County, of writing for hire and by pamphleteer Atticus of 'prostituting his pen.'[10] Paine's financial incentives are confusing. Aldridge has pointed out that though Paine had investments of £800 in the bank, he also had an interest with the majority party who had recently awarded him £500 for his wartime services.[11] Further, there is Paine's secret salary of $800 per annum from

---

[9] Tinkcom, *Republicans and Federalists*, pp. 1-17 and above p. 77.
[10] See Wilson, 'The Bank of North America', p. 22 and Aldridge, *Man of Reason*, p. 105. See above p. 165 and p. 10.
[11] Aldridge, 'Why did Paine Write on the Bank?', p. 313.

Morris.[12] Any profits made from *Dissertations on Government* were donated to the bank to set up a fund to ensure its political safety.[13]

It is not so odd that Paine should support the bank, having been partly responsible for its foundation. Phillip Foner asserts that claims that Paine was conservative over the bank do not 'take into account the fact that Paine's views were supported by the urban artisans for whom he was a spokesman.'[14] Certainly, the 1786 elections and petitions from the inhabitants indicate that there was substantial support for Paine's position in Philadelphia. Overall, Paine seems to have genuinely believed in the bank's worth as an institution and the injustice of the action of the Assembly.[15]

The Debate on the Bank in the Newspapers and the Assembly.

Among complaints against the bank, was the claim that it allowed merchants to fall into debt and that farmers could not borrow at high rates of interest nor come to Philadelphia every 45 days to renew notes. Further, it forbade paper money which was 'the medium of America' and which enabled settlers on the frontier to create wealth. The bank appeared to have a great potential influence over the legislature, especially in relation to foreign investors. Smiley and Whitehall feared America would be 'reduced once more into a state of subordination and dependence upon' a European power. Even John Adams, who was conservative in other respects, but also had rural interests, proclaimed that 'Banks have done more injury to the religion, morality, tranquillity, prosperity and [...] wealth of the nation than they can have done or ever will do good.'[16] Various letter writers joined the newspaper debate during the summer recess. 'A gazer on' suggested

---

[12] See above p. 165.
[13] See S. Edwards, *Rebel! A Biography of Thomas Paine* (London: New English Library, 1974), p. 123.
[14] P. S. Foner, *Complete Writings*, I, p. xxv, n. 12.
[15] See Aldridge, 'Why did Paine Write on the Bank?', p. 309.
[16] Wilson, 'The Bank of North America', p. 7.

that the democrat (anti-bank) party were hypocritical as they had recently tried to set up a rival bank.[17] 'A Philadelphia County Farmer' wrote that farmers should support the bank because the lack of money it was accused of causing raised prices for produce. 'Candid' maintained that the repeal of the charter was a violation of the social compact and therefore of morality.[18]

James Wilson's pamphlet, *Considerations on the Bank of North America* was written for Congress rather than for a popular readership (although it was printed as a supplement to the *Pennsylvania Gazette*) and was based on arguments taken from Burlamaqui and Blackstone. Wilson asserts that Congress's right to control the general interests of the states gives Congress sovereignty over the bank's charter, as repeal of the Charter would destroy financial confidence in all states and discourage foreign investors. In addition, Wilson argued that the Assembly had no right to revoke the charter as such an act would be particular rather than general. (This argument was also used against the charter.)[19]

The campaign to restore the charter provoked fierce debate in the Assembly. George Clymer (1739-1813), one of the bank's directors sitting in the house, accused the committee of 'precipitancy, prejudice and partiality' because they had not given the bank a fair hearing. Smiley accused Clymer of aristocracy because his claim that the bank's subscribers included 'the most respectable characters amongst us' implied that having more money rendered one more respectable. Robert Morris defended the bank claiming that it was the director's policy not to lend for exportation so that the bank discouraged the flood of specie abroad. The small amounts leaving the country in dividends were justified by the use of capital that foreign investment secured. Stockholders were not

---

[17] In 1784, a new Bank of Pennsylvania was proposed as a rival by a group of Quaker merchants and other businessmen, offering shares at £400. Some wanted easier credit but others were simply hostile to Morris as they felt excluded from holding Bank of North America stock. Morris feared that Philadelphia would be drained of capital but deflected the threat by merging the two banks. (See Foner, *Revolutionary America*, p. 193.)

[18] See Wilson, 'The Bank of North America', p. 9.

[19] See James Wilson, 'Considerations on the Bank of North-America', *Supplement to the Pennsylvania Gazette*, 7 September 1785, pp. 1-6.

accumulating vast wealth but enabling their capital to circulate rather than hoarding specie. Foreign investors would have an interest in the stability of the nation, rather than an opposing interest, so long as contracts were not broken. The bank increased the circulation of specie through profits paid and loans given. Morris argued that it was not a question of paper or not paper but who should issue it and on what security. He expressed surprise that farmers should be demanding paper money when many of them would not accept it in payment for produce.[20]

Findlay (1741-1821) asserted that the bank charter was inconsistent with the Pennsylvania Bill of Rights, which stated that government should not be for the emolument of one man, family or set of men, and unconstitutional because it was granted for perpetuity when even the constitution was subject to septennial review. He warned that Philadelphia would become like Hamburg and Dantzick (now Gdansk) controlled by monopolies. A Quaker farmer, George Logan (1753-1821), spoke for the bank, criticising the personalisation of the debate and pointing out that the bank provided loans for merchants to buy produce and for farmers to improve land. The debate tended towards personal attacks on both sides. Findlay accused Morris and Fitzsimmons of using their seats to gain personal privileges. In particular there were personal attacks on Paine. Paine responded to Smiley's insinuation and suggested that the anti-bank group was driven by a group of wealthy men trying to destroy the bank for their own commercial interest, such as George Emlen, one of directors of the 1784 Bank of Pennsylvania. 'Atticus', in the *Freeman's Journal*, accused Paine of prostituting his pen and of being a drunkard.[21]

---

[20] See Wilson, 'The Bank of North America', p. 19.
[21] The Pennsylvania Bill of Rights from the 1776 Constitution is included in a footnote to the *Dissertation on Government*, below p. 277. See also Wilson, 'The Bank of North America', p. 20 & p. 24-25; and below p. 335 & p. 338.

Paine's Writings on the Bank Crisis

Paine's first comment on the bank crisis is found in the *Pennsylvania Gazette* in December 1785. His letter appears immediately before the announcement of a bank stockholders meeting. Here he expresses concern over the precipitate action of the Assembly and the consequent threat to legislative stability and freedom. He includes a letter to Thomas Fitzsimmons, one of the founders and trustees of the bank, showing that he had supported the bank since April, despite his lack of comment. This was followed in February 1786 by a pamphlet, *Dissertations on Government*, in which he mounted a detailed defence of the bank. The pamphlet opens with a theoretical exposition arguing that under republican government the power of government is limited by mutually agreed rules in the constitution. Paine makes a distinction between legislative acts of the Assembly and agency acts of negotiated contracts between the state and individuals or corporations. The bank's charter is presented as a contract so that the power of the Assembly to revoke the charter is constitutionally limited. The pamphlet also presents some more practical arguments, including the debt of gratitude owed to the bank for the restoration of credit during the war. He argues for the usefulness of the bank for the economy and the danger of paper money and suggests that some of the opponents of the bank seek to destroy the bank for their private financial benefit.

Paine rebuts the committee report line by line, destroying the case against the bank. He argues that it was evidently not a dangerous influence on the Assembly, otherwise it would have been able to prevent the passage of the repeal of the charter. On the other hand, if the bank was constantly subject to the whim of the annual assembly, vested interests may lead to corruption of representatives. Finally he expresses great concern at the hastiness of the Assembly's action and considers the need for checks on a single legislature. In a letter in the *Pennsylvania Packet*, on 25 March, he again suggests that the anti-bank party is motivated by private financial gain, wanting to speculate on the issue of paper money. Another letter in the same paper, a few days later, addresses his own motives showing that supporting the bank is consistent with supporting the constitution against Morris's republicans, as the bank is so vital to the prosperity of all economic interests that it is supported by members of both parties.

Paine then begins a series of letters addressing the issues emanating from the bank crisis in the *Pennsylvania Packet* on 4 April. The first attacks Smiley for resorting to a personal attack on Paine's integrity, covered by member's privilege, rather than trying to refute the arguments of *Dissertation on Government*. The second again asserts Paine's own disinterested motives, and expresses concern at the activity of the single chamber legislature. Here Paine seems closest to Morris's republican view of the need for constitutional reform. He claims that all parts of Pennsylvania are hurt by the attack on the bank, apart from monied men like George Emlen, who stand to benefit from the lack of competitive capital. Number III, addressed *To The Public*, asserts the benefits of the bank to the true farmer's interest, as opposed to the interest of western frontiersmen who having only recently settled the land have as yet no need of to sell their produce. The longer established farming communities are fully in support of the bank, and have no use for unstable paper money. The next letter concerns the importance of a public bank to a thriving economy and links the existence of such an institution to semi-representative forms of government in England and Holland. Letter V appears to advocate strongly a constitutional change away from unicameralism and warns the public against electing men governed by party, rather than by the common interest. Letter VI denounces unsupported state issues of paper money and tender laws as an unconstitutional threat to freedom. Paine warns that the precedent of revoking the bank's charter also potentially destabilises any such issue, as the assembly can as easily revoke promises to redeem bills of credit made by a former assembly.[22] The final letter on the bank appears in the *Pennsylvania Gazette* in March 1787, ten days before the restoration of the charter. Addressed to the opponents the bank, it sums up the history of the bank

---

[22] See below p. 355.

and the motives of the anti-bank party, whom he accuses of being 'intoxicated with power'. Finally, he suggests restoring the charter as near as possible to the original.

Paine uses many practical and economic arguments supporting the bank's contribution to the public good, countering many of the opposing arguments. He sees the bank as a dynamic force in the young republic. He warns of the danger of paper money 'both the bubble and the iniquity of the day' which would lead, if uncontrolled, to depreciation of both money and morality. The bank was not monopolistic but rather a force against monopoly because it allowed small traders to exchange goods without cash flow problems. Although it has been asserted that Paine's support for the bank was conservative, the economic theory which lies at the root of his defence of the bank is in many ways radical, despite its adoption by wealthy men who were politically conservative in their fear of unchecked democracy. Paine's principal economic argument in support of the bank focuses on the principle that the prosperity of a nation is dependent not on the quantity of riches, but on the circulation of money. Against the committee's charge that the bank directors were hoarding scarce specie, Paine argues that the bank allowed savings to be used for investment rather than being locked out of circulation. As Pennsylvania could not produce 'real money' in the form of gold and silver, the economy was dependent on the sale of exports to generate income to purchase imports. Arguing that agriculture without markets would not generate increasing wealth, he thereby rejected the traditional 'moral economy' idea of a conflict of interest between land and trade. Paine frequently adopts this radical view of a shared economic interest in the active free market in his bank crisis writings. Further, Paine explicitly links the survival of the bank to freedom, condemning paper money and tender laws as unconstitutional assaults on the right to private property.

The Effect of the Bank Crisis on Paine's Political Theory.

In addition to Paine's economic defence of the bank, we find in these writings a number of constitutional arguments that illustrate the crisis in his democratic and constitutional theory precipitated by the affair of the bank. The arguments he employed in presenting the revoking of the bank's charter as unconstitutional are considered here in the context of the bank crisis and of his political thought as a whole.

Paine argued that his opponents in the Assembly had acted hastily and unconstitutionally, signalling his new concern for limits to majority rule. Paine recognised, for the first time, the possibility of 'the despotism of numbers' or the tyranny of the majority. The experiment in democracy in Pennsylvania had thrown Paine headfirst into the contradiction between his belief in popular sovereignty and his belief that 'nothing that is morally wrong can ever be politically right'. He had previously believed that reason, rather than party or factional interests, would triumph in democratic processes.[23] In order to establish that an act of a democratically elected assembly can be unconstitutional, Paine argues that, in a republic, popular sovereignty is limited from the outset by the principles of that republic. It is in reaction to the bank crisis, therefore, that Paine sets out his republican theory of government limited by constitutional rules.[24] The Assembly's rash action and failure to give the directors a hearing leads Paine to contemplate checks on the legislature such as a second house. He argues that it is the influence of parties that allows the unchecked assembly to act in with the same 'haste, rashness and passion' as aristocracy. Such instability of legislation would result in a lack of respect for the house and the law, endangering the rights and property of all men. It was a fatal precedent that would eventually be 'fatal to their power.'[25]

---

[23] See below p. 265.
[24] See above pp. 27- & 74-80.
[25] See below p. 267.

Paine was always suspicious of the view that a second chamber is necessary to check the power of faction in the legislature, as he associated this idea with the British theory of the mixed constitution. In works before the bank crisis, Paine rejects the idea of the need for a check on legitimate power as farcical or contradictory. His ridicule of the theory of the balanced constitution in *Common Sense* was the stimulus for John Adams's *Thoughts on Government*. Adams, who otherwise approved of Paine's call for independence, argues that a unicameral state government would be flighty, avaricious and lacked the unity necessary for effective executive action. Adams proposed a balanced system with long terms of office (eventually extending to life) for Senators and Governors with veto powers. Aldridge claims that Paine responded to Adams's bicameralism in the pamphlet *Four Letters on Interesting Subjects*, arguing that the reciprocal checking of two chambers would result in ill will and retard business. The idea of each house representing two different interests is rejected on the grounds that one house is needed to unify many different interests. Aldridge suggests that Paine's less rigid argument indicates that he was not completely committed to unicameralism at this time.[26]

The speed of the passage of the repeal of the bank's charter through the Assembly and the strength of party appeal against constituency interest shocked Paine and caused him to consider methods of checking this power, including bicameralism. However, he never let go of his belief in the ability of reasoned debate to prevent a unicameral legislature acting against the public interest. Nor did he abandon his distaste for attempts to democratise the theory of a mixed constitution that he saw as an unnecessary imitation of a corrupt old order. He

---

[26] See Aldridge, *American Ideology*, pp. 232-4. Adams's early disapproval of Paine's plan for a unicameral congress is recorded in a letter to his wife Abigail Adams in 19 March 1776. See *Adams Family Correspondence*, ed. by L. H. Butterfield, *The Adams Papers*, Series II (Cambridge, Mass.: Belknap, 1961), I. (1761-1776), p. 363. A heated discussion between the two on this point is also recorded in Adams's *Autobiography*. See Butterfield, *Diary and Autobiography*, 3:1, p. 333. See also B. Bailyn, *Ideological Origins*, pp. 288-91; Douglass, *Rebels and Democrats*, pp. 21-23; Aldridge, *American Ideology*, pp. 198-204. Adams's pamphlet had a significant effect on the Constitution of Virginia. See Morison, *Sources*, p. xxxix.

could never accept the Federalist idea of checks and balances and later he proposed methods of protecting liberty by slowing down the parliamentary process without creating undemocratic deadlocks.

In 1791, Paine is still adamant that a single chamber is preferable. He advises the French constitution builders to separate the assembly into two for debate only. As 'wherever the legislative body consists of one single chamber, it runs the risk of coming to rash decisions; whereas division offers one chance more for collected judgement.'[27] Nevertheless, he also warns against bicameralism, proposing that the two houses should vote as one, thus rejecting the central logic of bicameralism - of two houses checking each other's power. Such checking of power is undemocratic because it allows a minority, which happened to be a majority in the smaller house, to veto the majority in both houses. In fact, this problem could be solved by ensuring that both houses contained the same number, but Paine sees the only advantage of bicameralism as being the calming nature of listening to two separate debates.

Paine's faith in debate is rooted in his belief in a universal capacity for reason and his belief in the identity of individual and public interest. Of course, any experience that presents a choice between individual liberty and the power of the majority is likely to knock such faith. But even after his experience of the corruption of power and demagoguery in France, he still maintained his hostility to the mixed constitution. Both the gubernatorial veto and the veto of the smaller second chamber were imitations of the English system of government that he abhorred. 'Before we imitate anything, we ought to examine whether it be worth imitating.'[28]

Ironically, the 1790 bicameral Pennsylvania Constitution replaced the 1776 constitution, as a result of the loss of support the constitutionalists suffered through Paine's pen. The bank crisis divided the democratic faction that

---

[27] 'Answer to Four Questions' (1791), *Writings*, II, 242-243.
[28] 'Constitutional Reform: To the Citizens of Pennsylvania on the Proposal for calling a Convention' (August 1805), *Writings*, IV, 462.

supported the 1776 constitution into urban artisans who supported the bank (once Paine had shown where their interest lay) and western farmers who did not. This provided an excellent opportunity for the Federalists to gain support for their plan to bring the Pennsylvania Constitution more in line with the new Federal Constitution which imitated the English idea of a mixed constitution, tempering democratic fervour with checks and balances as well as property qualifications for voting. Paine recognised that the bank crisis had indicated a flaw in the constitution:

> The Pennsylvania Constitution of 1776 copied nothing from the English government [...] All the members of the Legislature established by that Constitution sat in one chamber, and debated in one body, and this subjected them to precipitancy.[29]

Such precipitance had been anticipated in the Constitution by the requirement that bills be published for public consideration. However, as no fixed time period had been given for this publicity, in practice the measure was ineffectual. In his last political pamphlet Paine still argues that this defect could be resolved without recourse to an imitation of the English system of government, but by a unicameral legislature divided in two for debates but united for voting. This would slow down the passions and encourage reason:

> The advantage would have been that one half, by not being entangled in the first debate, nor having committed itself by voting, would be silently possessed of the arguments [...] and be in a calm condition to review the whole.[30]

The bank crisis made Paine aware of the possible tyranny of the majority, but not sufficiently to outweigh his hostility to the mixed constitution. Checks and balances were not needed to control a trustworthy, and therefore legitimate, government and could slow the processes of government needlessly. Paine refers to Franklin's metaphor of tying two horses to opposite ends of a cart so that,

---

[29] 'Constitutional Reform' (1805), *Writings*, IV, 462.
[30] 'Constitutional Reform' (1805), *Writings*, IV, 462.

however strong the horses are, the wheels will not move until the cart is ripped apart. Torn over the need to prevent rashness without locking government into a struggle of opposing powers unable to act decisively, Paine suggests a compromise of two chambers voting as one.

Paine's primary constitutional argument in his bank crisis writings is that the charter is equivalent to a contract, binding upon the state and all present and future representatives of the state. In his first letter, Paine seems to be arguing that, because a legislature is a continuous body, it can bind itself in perpetuity. Aldridge points out that this is perhaps reminiscent of Burke's prescriptive argument that Paine would later rail against so effectively.[31] However, in *Dissertations on Government*, Paine develops his position arguing firstly that there is a distinction between laws and those acts of assembly that can be regarded as contracts and secondly that it is a presumption of power for one generation to bind its successors.

Paine distinguishes between acts of the assembly that are laws and those which are not laws but are contracts or agreements on the part of the state with individuals and therefore subject to the same general laws and principles of justice as all other contracts.[32] Laws are universal in operation and therefore fall on the legislators themselves. They include the distribution and administration of justice, the preservation of peace, the security of property and the raising of revenue. Agency transactions are matters of negotiation by the assembly on behalf of the people, such as contracts; sales, purchases and loans. These involve two parties bound to perform different parts for example, buying and selling, whereas under laws every man's part is the same, for example, refraining from a prohibited activity such as robbery. An agency act is not only an act of the assembly but of both parties. Such contracts are legally binding so that disputes should be dealt with in court in which case an individual has the same status as

---

[31] Aldridge, 'Why did Paine Write on the Bank?', p. 313.
[32] See below p. 282.

the state.[33] In agency transactions, the assembly is not a party of the contract but an agent on behalf of the state so that the performance of the contract devolves on succeeding assemblies as agents for the people. For the next assembly to dissolve the state of that obligation is an assumption of power, because the state is still the same state, only the agent has changed.

Paine contends that the bank's charter is a contract between the state and the directors with reciprocal obligations and that this is proved by the fact that the directors' consent was necessary for incorporation. Such contracts ought to be legally binding on both parties. Disputes should be litigable, rather than political: the state having the same status as an individual. In 1792, in Chisholm vs. Georgia, the U. S. Supreme Court ruled against the state of Georgia's right to revoke a charter, using Paine's words from *Dissertations on Government*. It is not so strange the bank's charter should be described as a contract. Atiyah points out that Royal Charters in England were often discussed and negotiated as if they were contracts between the state and the individual or company.[34] Paine agrees with the committee that the bank's charter is tyrannical in one respect: it's claim to perpetual existence. This violates the right of each generation principle.[35] Paine suggests that such contracts should be limited to thirty years and that this could also be done for laws to clear the statute books of outmoded legislation.

The bank crisis writings, particularly *Dissertation on Government*, disclose Paine's libertarian view that liberty is compromised if contracts are not legally binding even when a democratically elected assembly decides that a contract is contrary to the public interest. This demonstrates the tension in Paine's ideas between the new market-oriented view of the economy and his commitment to democracy, while the electorate still harboured many of the older

---

[33] See below p. 283.
[34] P. S. Atiyah, *The Rise and Fall of Freedom of Contract,* (Oxford: Clarendon Press, 1979), p. 94. On Chisholm vs. Georgia see Edwards, *Rebel!* p. 123,
[35] See below p. 302 & above p. 23.

traditions of the moral economy.[36]   Paine tries to combine democracy and 'economic freedom' by redefining their proper limits.   The bank's charter as a contract, binding upon the state and all present and future representatives of the state, cannot be perpetual but should be limited to thirty years.   Given this condition, the sanctity of contract is given priority over the power of the majority to exercise their will and thus presents a challenge to Paine's commitment to popular sovereignty.   Paine's opponent, Atticus, naturally asked 'Where is the benefit of annual election if the wisdom of one assembly may not be extended to correct the errors of the former?'   Paine's reply is found in his last political work, *Constitutions, Governments and Charters*.   Here he suggests the revision of the constitution so as to require that agency acts should be voted on by one assembly, then published and laid over till after the next election.[37]

   This commitment to democracy is not inconsistent with his commitment to economic freedom.   Legislatures could bind their successors for thirty years but must consult the electorate first.   Once committed, contracts must be enforced. This belief in the dependence of freedom on the sanctity of contract is symptomatic of Paine's free-market economic views.   How Paine viewed the nature of a contract makes little difference to this point.   The freedom he is defending is not so much the freedom of contract, that is, of the individual's freedom to determine the terms of the contracts into which he or she enters.[38] Rather Paine is concerned that the consistent enforcement of any contract by government enhances the freedom of the individual.

   Although Paine had already used the right of each generation principle against the institution of monarchy, the bank crisis forced him to develop this

---

[36] See Foner, *Revolutionary America*, pp. 146-209; Appleby, *Capitalism*; E. P. Thompson, 'The Moral Economy of the English Crowd in the Eighteenth Century,' *Past and Present*, 50 (1971), 76-136.

[37] See Foner, *Revolutionary America*, p. 199; 'Constitutions, Governments and Charters' (June 1805), *Writings*, IV, 468.

[38] Paine's conception of contract is a very modern one, in which the individual parties are free to decide specific terms, rather than giving consent to enter into traditionally defined status contracts (the terms of which are imposed by the state on individuals, such as marriage).

idea, by presenting a contradiction. Democracy requires that each successive assembly be free to overturn the acts of their predecessors, but individual liberty required that the assembly should be prevented from overturning agency acts to ensure the stability and predictability of contractual agreements, particularly in the developing financial system. As one of the principal aims of government was the expansion of individual freedom through the enforcement of contracts between individuals, agency acts of the previous legislature must be enforced in the name of liberty. This suggests that the legislature is a continuous body that can bind itself, as Burke would later claim for the English Parliament of 1688, but Paine reaches the conclusion that it is not the legislature that is a continuous body, but the sovereign population that elects it.[39] When the legislature is acting as an agent for the sovereign, the agent can bind the client even if the client subsequently hires a new agent. As long as such acts were limited to a certain number of years taken to represent a generation the problem was solved. David Wilson points out that this conclusion led Paine into further discussion of inter-generational rights with Jefferson, so that both suggested limits on legislation of nineteen (Jefferson) and twenty-one (Paine) years. Having already developed a theoretical basis for his argument against custom and precedent, Paine was better able to dismiss Burke's prescription, using the principle of the right of each generation.[40]

As already discussed in the general introduction above, Paine's constitutional defence against the tyranny of the majority depends on his optimistic view of human nature: if the majority consider the constitution on an open and free public debate they will defend their own liberty.[41] Freedom will eventually prevail. Is this what occurred in Philadelphia in the 1780s? The assembly acted rashly in repealing the bank's charter, but the electorate

---

[39] See Aldridge, 'Why did Paine Write on the Bank?', p. 313.
[40] See D. A. Wilson, *The Transatlantic Connection: Paine and Cobbett* (Montreal: McGill-Queen's University Press, 1988), p. 69; 'Rights of Man' (1791), *Writings*, II, 276-8.
[41] See above pp. 74-80.

considered the different opinions given in the newspapers and pamphlets and after two annual elections there was a majority in the house to renew the charter. In Paine's opinion the electorate voted in favour of their freedom. I suspect John Smiley did not see it that way.

Pennsylvania Gazette, 21 December 1785.

To the PRINTERS *of the* PENNSYLVANIA GAZETTE.

GENTLEMEN,

Please to insert the following in your next paper, and you will oblige yours, &c.

THOMAS PAINE

SEVERAL publications having at different times appeared in news-papers and in pamphlets, respecting the proceedings of the late House of Assembly against the *Charter of the Bank*, some of which I have been supposed to be the author of; I wish to have it known that I have never published any thing on that subject. As an individual, exercising my private opinion, I was concerned at the proceedings of the House on that business, because those proceedings appeared to me a breach of public faith, and hurtful to the general interest---and I constantly expressed this opinion, but published nothing on the subject.

The only sentiments of mine on this head (in writing) are in a letter to the Honorable Thomas Fitzsimons, Esq; so long ago as the 19th of April; and as several gentlemen have seen that letter, and remember it in part, I think it best to give the whole, which is as follows:

Brunswick, April 19, 1785

SIR,

I RECEIVED your favour of the 16th inst. by the stage-boat to Bordentown, which place I left yesterday for New-York, but the bad weather being likely to detain me to day, I shall dispose of it for the purposes of answering yours, and some other letters.

On the subject of the Bank, and the attack made on it by the Assembly, my sentiments and declaration have been free and open. It appears to me an ill-digested, precipitate, impolitic, faithless piece of business, in which party and prejudice is put for patriotism. I observe, by a remark in your letter, that the matter struck you as it did me; for if the people of Pennsylvania cannot exercise their judgment as men, and their privileges as citizens, without being threatened with the power and made to suffer under the lash of government, freedom is a mere name. I am the more confirmed in the rectitude of my opinion on this case, because it operates with me, not in conjunction, but in opposition to my interest, and to those for whom I had some degree of predilection.—The House is composed of men, with whom I have lived with more intimacy than with the generality of the citizens of Pennsylvania, and who have shewn more disposition to promote my interest than others have. The case between me and the Assembly stands thus: – They have advanced me five hundred pounds, and referred the matter to Congress, with an assurance of complying in such further measures as Congress shall adopt or recommend. But the House appears to me so exceedingly wrong in this business, both as to the matter and manner of it, that my private judgement on the case cannot go with them, and must go against them, disregarding consequences to myself.

As from a point of delicacy I absented myself from the company of the members while the matter respecting myself was depending.[1] I had little opportunity of knowing what was going on in the House, and none of what was intended to be brought on. When the affair of the Bank broke out, I met several of the members (accidentally) and they expressed themselves on the subject with a sort of triumph. It is a great deal of thinking a man may sometimes do in a little time; and tho' I am not hasty in altering an opinion, yet in this case it was otherwise. It immediately struck me in a very different light to what it did them, and appeared to me to extend to consequences they had not attended to. I mentioned to them what those consequences were, considering the matter in a *particular* view: That this quick rotation of doing and undoing, this facility of making and repealing laws, of granting charters and violating them, would eventually operate against themselves; because it has a tendency to strike at the constitution, which enabled the House, with so much ease, and often with too little deliberation, to exercise a power, that in the change and fluctuations of party

---

[1] See above p. 248 & p. 335.

might be dangerous to the rights and property of every man. That in a government where nothing was certain, the disposition to obedience would be so too-----that acts, when so easily and frequently changed, lost the force and dignity of laws, and ceased to command respect-----that their proceedings respecting the Bank was a dangerous precedent-----that it came under the description of *governing too much*-----and that, however gratifying it might be to their prejudice, it would, in my opinion, be fatal to their power.

It is not an agreeable thing for a man to stand in opposition to his friends, especially circumstanced with them as I was, for the matter respecting myself was then depending; but in this case I used the sincere freedom of a friend to them.

I found they put too much stress upon what they called the *dangerous influence of the Bank*. I replied, that the influence did not appear from it effects on any of the elections, and that the temper and complection of the House was an evidence that invalidated the assertion; to which I added, that I was apprehensive they had started a word that would change sides, and retort on themselves, for that it was probable a very general idea would arise, that the influence the House was assuming over the privileges of citizenship would be thought more dangerous than the influence of the Bank, which, admitting it to operate, could extend only to the city, and in the late election not even to that.

In conversation with a principal Member of the House on the subject, I mentioned to him that the House ought to hear the Bank previous to their publishing the bill for public consideration, which is after the second reading; for that as *considering* naturally included the idea of *judging*, the public ought to have the whole matter before them, and hear the Bank as well as its opposers; to which I added another reason, which was the reputation of the House; for that as the causes and reasons for a law are to be sat [sic] forth in the preamble, if the causes and reasons assigned in the preamble of the bill for taking away the Charter of the Bank should, when the House came afterwards to hear the Bank, be proved to be ill founded and groundless, it would put the House in a disagreeable situation. I was surprised when he told me that the bill had been read the second time that morning, and ordered to be published. From the manner in which the bill crept through the House on the second reading, I am apt to think its advocates are suspicious of more embarrassment than they at first conceived.

As to paper money, which makes a part of the politics of the house, and was one of the causes that led to the attack on the bank, it is a subject that will bear much investigation. There may be cases in which paper money may be generally serviceable; but it is an expedient, that should be used with the greatest caution, or we shall have all the evils of depreciation both of money and morals over again.[2]

There is but one way in which paper money can be secure and retain its value, and that the present system of the country does not provide for. If every house is to strike as much as it pleases, and exercise its discretion unlimited, where is the evil to end! I think the house misconceives its authority upon this case. It derives none from the Constitution, for that is silent on the subject, and only enables the house to make laws, not money, and provides no other means of revenue, than by taxation. Neither does the house copy practice from any custom in the English government, for where [sic] the government of that count[r]y, to create a revenue by paper, instead of raising it by taxes, it would be considered as an attempt at arbitrary power, erecting itself independent of the grants of the public. Neither is the present mode conformable to that practices before the war, for then there was a restraining power over the conduct of the house: as to the quantity to be struck, which prevented depreciation.

Perhaps it may be said, that while it is not a legal tender, in all cases, the evils may not be so extensive; but the house conceives it has this power; if so, there is no security for property, where such power can be exercised; and it is inconsistent with the nature and genius of the Constitution of Pennsylvania, to admit it: for the Constitution declares that the *acquiring, possessing and protecting property, are the certain natural inherent inalienable rights of the citizens*, and therefore, any

---

[2] Note here that Paine's antipathy to paper money is not solely economic but also ethical. Indebtedness is assumed to be inimical to virtue.

law of the Assembly which makes that a legal tender in payments, which is not equal in value to the property received, is a violation of the principle on which the Constitution is founded.

In writing you this letter, I have omitted all those matters which are familiar to the subject; such as the usefulness of the Bank in a commercial country; the conveniency it may be to government in certain cases, and sudden emergencies, and the services of the present Bank in the late war, and touched chiefly on such parts as are connected with it in its political consequences, and which it is probable do not occur to the generality of people.

I sincerely wish the affair had not arose. I have hitherto confined myself to such national matters only, as were connected with the independence of the country, and the issue of the contest. These having happily succeeded, I was in hopes every thing else would have gone well, and that the experience and discretion of the country and the government, would have been equal to its domestic concerns in all cases. I am much concerned to see it, otherwise, and sorry to find they want so much putting to rights.

In the progress of this affair, on the part of the Bank, one thing is necessary to attend to, which is, that of relying too much upon it as a law case; the House in their preamble have set out with a declaration that the Bank is injurious to the State, and in its consequences dangerous; unless this idea be removed as publicly as it is asserted, the merely considering the question of taking away the Charter as a law question, will not be effectual to all the circumstances to which the subject extends.—— But it is time to close my letter,

I am,

Your obedient humble servant,

THOMAS PAINE

Thomas Fitzsimons, Esq .

DISSERTATIONS

on

GOVERNMENT,

the

AFFAIRS of the BANK,

and

PAPER-MONEY.

PREFACE

I HERE *present the Public with a new performance. Some parts of it are more particularly adapted to the State of Pennsylvania, on the present state of its affairs: But there are others which are on a larger scale. The time bestowed on this work has not been long, the whole of it being written and printed during the short recess of the Assembly.*

As to parties, merely considered as such, I am attached to no particular one. There are such things as right and wrong in the world, and so far as these are parties against each other, the signature of COMMON SENSE *is properly employed.*

THOMAS PAINE.

Philadelphia, Feb. 18, 1786.

DISSERTATIONS ON GOVERNMENT, THE AFFAIRS OF THE BANK, AND
PAPER-MONEY.

EVERY Government, let its form be what it may, contains within itself a principle common to all, which is, that of a sovereign power, or a power over which there is no controul, and which controuls all others: And as it is impossible to construct a form of government in which this power does not exist, so there must of necessity be a place, if it may be so called, for it to exist in.

IN Despotic Monarchies this power is lodged in a single person, or sovereign. His Will is law; which he declares, alters, or revokes as he pleases, without being accountable to any power for so doing. Therefore, the only modes of redress, in countries so governed, are by petition or insurrection. And this is the reason we so frequently hear of insurrections in despotic governments; for as there are but two modes of redress, this is one of them.

PERHAPS it may be said that as the united ressistance of the people is able, by force, to controul the Will of the sovereign, that, therefore, the controuling power lodges in them: but it must be understood that I am speaking of such powers only as are constituent parts of the government, not of those powers which are externally applied to resist and overturn it.

IN Republics, such as those established in America, the sovereign power, or the power over which there is no controul and which controuls all others, remains where nature placed it; in the people; for the people in America are the fountain of power. It remains there as a matter of right, recognized in the constitutions of the country, and the exercise of it is constitutional and legal.——This sovereignty is exercised in electing and deputing a certain number of persons to represent and act for the whole, and who, if they do not act right, may be displaced by the same power that placed them there, and others elected and deputed in their stead, and the wrong measures of former representatives corrected and brought right by this means. Therefore the republican form and principle leaves no room for insurrection, because it provides and establishes a rightful means in its stead.

IN countries under a despotic form of government, the exercise of this power is an assumption of sovereignty; a wresting it from the person in whose hand their form of government has placed it, and the exercise of it there is stiled rebellion. Therefore the despotic form of government knows no intermediate space between being slaves and being rebels.

I shall in this place offer an observation which, though not immediately connected with my subject, is very naturally deduced from it, which is, That the nature, if I may so call it, of a government over any people may be ascertained from the modes which the people pursue to obtain redress; for like causes will produce like effects. And therefore the government which Britain attempted to erect over America could be no other than a despotism, because it left to the Americans no other modes of redress than those which are left to people under despotic governments, petition and resistance: and the Americans, without ever attending to a comparison on the case, went into the same steps which such people go into, because no other could be pursued: and this similarity of effects leads up to, and ascertains, the similarity of the causes or governments which produced them.

BUT to return. The repository where the sovereign power is placed is the first criterion of distinction between a country under a despotic form of government and a free country. In a country under a despotic government, the sovereign is the only free man in it.—— In a republic, the people retaining the sovereignty themselves, naturally and necessarily retain freedom with it: for wherever the sovereignty is, there must the freedom be; the one cannot be in one place and the other in another.

As the repository where the sovereign power is lodged is the first criterion of distinction; so the second is the principles on which it is administered.

A despotic government knows no principle but WILL. Whatever the sovereign wills to do, the government admits him the inherent right, and the uncontrouled power of doing. He is restrained by no fixed rule of right and wrong, for he makes the right and wrong himself and as he pleases.— If he happens (for a miracle may happen) to be a man of consummate wisdom, justice and moderation, of a mild affectionate disposition, disposed to business, and understanding and promoting the general good, all the beneficial purposes of government will be answered under his administration, and the people so governed may, while this is the case, be prosperous and easy. But as there can be no security that this disposition will last, and this administration continue, and still less security that his successor shall have the same qualities and pursue the same measures;

therefore no people exercising their reason and understanding their rights, would, of their own choice, invest any one man with such a power.

NEITHER is it consistent to suppose the knowledge of any one man competent to the exercise of such a power. A Sovereign of this sort, is brought up in such a distant line of life, and lives so remote from the people, and from a knowledge of every thing which relates to their local situations and interests, that he can know nothing from experience and observation, and all which he does know he must be told. Sovereign power without sovereign knowledge, that is, a full knowledge of all the matters over which that power is to be exercised, is a something which contradicts itself.

THERE is a species of sovereign power in a single person, which is very proper when applied to a commander in chief over an army, so far as relates to the military government of an army, and the condition and purpose of an army constitute the reason why it is so.

IN an army every man is of the same profession, that is, he is a soldier, and the commander in chief is a soldier too: therefore the knowledge necessary to the exercise of the power is within himself. By understanding what a soldier is, he comprehends the local situation, interest and duty of every man within, what may be called, the dominion of his command; and therefore the condition and circumstances of an army make a fitness for the exercise of the power.

THE purpose likewise, or object of an army, is another reason: for this power in a commander in chief, though exercised over the army, is not exercised against it; but is exercised thro' or over the army against the enemy. Therefore the enemy, and not the people, is the object it is directed to. Neither is it exercised over an army, for the purpose of raising a revenue from it, but to promote its combined interest, condense its powers, and give it capacity for action.

BUT all these reasons cease when sovereign power is transferred from the commander of an army to the commander of a nation, and entirely loses its fitness when applied to govern subjects following occupations, as it governs soldiers following arms. A nation is quite another element, and every thing in it differs not only from each other, but all of them differ from those of an army. A nation is composed of distinct, unconnected individuals, following various trades, employments and pursuits; continually meeting, crossing, uniting, opposing and separating from each other as accident, interest and circumstance shall direct.—An army has but one occupation and but one interest.

ANOTHER very material matter in which an army and a nation, differ is that of temper. An army may be said to have but one temper; for however the *natural* temper of the persons composing the army may differ from each other, there is a second temper takes place of the first: a temper formed by discipline, mutuality of habits, union of objects and pursuits, and the stile of military manners: but this can never be the case among all the individuals of a nation. Therefore the fitness, arising from those circumstances, which disposes an army to the command of a single person, and the fitness of a single person for that command, is not to be found either in one or the other, when we come to consider them as a sovereign and a nation.

HAVING already shewn what a despotic government is, and how it is administered, I now come to shew what the administration of a republic is.

THE administration of a republic is supposed to be directed by certain fundamental principles of right and justice, from which there cannot, because there ought not to, be any deviation; and whenever any deviation appears, there is a kind of stepping out of the republican principle, and an approach towards the despotic one. This administration is executed by a select number of persons, periodically chosen by the people, and act as representatives and in behalf of the whole, and who are supposed to enact the same laws, and pursue the same line of administration, as the people would do were they all assembled together.

THE PUBLIC GOOD is to be their object. It is therefore necessary to understand what Public Good is.

PUBLIC GOOD is not a term opposed to the good of individuals; on the contrary, it is the good of every individual collected. It is the good of all, because it is the good of every one: for as the public body is every individual collected, so the public good is the collected good of those individuals.

THE foundation-principle of Public Good is justice, and wherever justice is impartially administered the public good is promoted; for as it is to the good of every man that no injustice be done to him, so likewise it is to his good that the principle which secures him should not be violated in the person of another, because such a violation weakens *his* security, and leaves to chance what ought to be to him a rock to stand on.

BUT in order to understand more minutely, how the Public Good is to be promoted, and the manner in which the representatives are to act to promote it, we must have recourse to the original or first principles, on which the people formed themselves into a republic.

WHEN a people agree to form themselves into a republic (for the word REPUBLIC means the PUBLIC GOOD, or the good of the whole, in contradistinction to the despotic form, which makes the good of the sovereign, or of one man, the only object of the government) when, I say, they agree to do this, it is to be understood, that they mutually resolve and pledge themselves to each other, rich and poor alike, to support and maintain this rule of equal justice among them. They therefore renounce not only the despotic form, but the despotic principle, as well of governing as of being governed by mere Will and Power, and substitute in its place a government of justice.

BY this mutual compact the citizens of a republic put it out of their power, that is, they renounce, as detestable, the power of exercising, at any future time, any species of despotism over each other, or doing a thing, not right in itself, because a majority of them may have strength of numbers sufficient to accomplish it.

IN this pledge and compact* lies the foundation of the republic: and the security to the rich and the consolation to the poor is, that what each man has is his own;

---

*This pledge and compact is contained in the declaration of Rights prefixed to the constitution, and is as follows——

I. THAT all men are born equally free and independent, and have certain natural, inherent and unalienable rights, amongst which are the enjoying and defending life and liberty, acquiring, possessing and protecting property, and pursuing and obtaining happiness and safety.

II. THAT all men have a natural and unalienable right to worship Almighty God, according to the dictates of their own consciences and understanding: And that no man ought or of right can be compelled to attend any religious worship, or erect or support any place of worship, or maintain any ministry, contrary to, or against, his own free will and consent: Nor can any man, who acknowledges the being of a God, be justly deprived or abridged of any civil right as a citizen, on account of his religious sentiments or peculiar mode of religious worship: And that no authority can or ought to be vested in, or assumed by any power whatever, that shall in any case interfere with, or in any manner controul, the right of conscience in the free exercise of religious worship.

III. THAT the people of this state have the sole, exclusive and inherent right of governing and regulating the internal police of the same.

IV. THAT all power being originally inherent in, and consequently derived from, the people; therefore, all officers of government, whether legislative or executive, are their trustees and servants, and at all times accountable to them.

V. THAT government is, or ought to be, instituted for the common benefit, protection and security of the people, nation or community; and not for the particular emolument or advantage of any single man, family or set of men, who are a part only of that community: And that the community hath an indubitable, unalienable and indefeasible right to reform, alter or abolish government in such manner as shall be by that community judged most conducive to the public weal.

VI. THAT those who are employed in the legislative and executive business of the state may be restrained from oppression, the people have a right, at such periods as they may think proper, to reduce their public officers to a private station, and supply the vacancies by certain and regular elections.

VII. THAT all elections ought to be free; and that all free men having a sufficient evident common interest with, and attachment to the community, have a right to elect officers, or to be elected into office.

VIII. THAT every member of society hath a right to be protected in the enjoyment of life, liberty and property, and therefore is bound to contribute his proportion towards the expence of that protection, and yield his personal service when necessary, or an equivalent thereto: But no part of a man's property can be justly taken from him, or applied to public uses, without his own consent, or that of his legal representatives: Nor can any man who is conscientiously scrupulous of bearing arms, be justly compelled thereto, if he will pay such equivalent: Nor are the people bound by any laws, but such as they have in like manner assented to, for their common good.

I X. THAT in all prosecutions for criminal offences, a man hath a right to be heard by himself and his counsil, to demand the cause and nature of his accusation, to be confronted with the witnesses, to call for evidence in his favour, and a speedy public trial, by an impartial jury of the country, without the unanimous consent of which jury he cannot be found guilty: Nor can he be compelled to give evidence against himself; Nor can any man be justly deprived of his liberty, except by the laws of the land, or the judgment of his peers.

X. THAT the people have a right to hold themselves, their houses, papers, and possessions free from search or seizure; and therefore warrants without oaths or affirmations first made,

that no despotic sovereign can take it from him, and that the common cementing principle which holds all the parts of a republic together, secures him likewise from the despotism of numbers: For despotism may be more effectually acted by many over a few than by one man over all.

THEREFORE, in order to know how far the power of an Assembly, or a house of representatives can act in administering the affairs of a republic, we must examine how far the power of the people extends under the original compact they have made with each other; for the power of the representatives is in many cases less, but never can be greater than that of the people represented; and whatever the people in their mutual original compact have renounced the power of doing towards, or acting over each other, the representatives cannot assume the power to do, because, as I have already said, the power of the representatives cannot be greater than that of the people whom they represent.

IN this place it naturally presents itself that the people in their original compact of equal justice or first principles of a republic, renounced, as despotic, detestable and unjust, the assuming a right of breaking and violating their engagements,

---

affording a sufficient foundation for them, and whereby any officer or messenger may be commanded or required to search suspected places, or to seize any person or persons, his or their property, not particularly described, are contrary to that right, and ought not to be granted.

XI. THAT in controversies respecting property, and in suits between man and man, the parties have a right to trial by jury, which ought to be held sacred.

XII. THAT the people have a right to freedom of speech, and of writing, and publishing their sentiments; therefore the freedom of the press ought not to be restrained.

XIII. THAT the people have a right to bear arms for the defence of themselves and the state: and as standing armies in the time of peace, are dangerous to liberty, they ought not to be kept up: and that the military should be kept under strict subordination to, and governed by, the civil power.

XIV. THAT a frequent recurrence to fundamental principles, and a firm adherence to justice, moderation, temperance, industry and frugality are absolutely necessary to preserve the blessings of liberty and keep a government free; The people ought therefore to pay particular attention to these points in the choice of officers and representatives, and have a right to exact a due and constant regard to them, from their legislators and magistrates, in the making and executing such laws as are necessary for the good government of the state.

XV. THAT all men have a natural inherent right to emigrate from one state to another that will receive them, or to form a new state in vacant countries, or in such countries as they can purchase, whenever they think that thereby they may promote their own happiness.

XVI. THAT the people have a right to assemble together, to consult for their common good, to instruct their representatives, and to apply to the legislature for redress of grievances, by address, petition, or remonstrance.

contracts and compacts with, or defrauding, imposing or tyrannizing over, each other, and therefore the representatives cannot make an Act to do it for them, and any such an Act would be an attempt to depose, not the personal sovereign, but the sovereign principle of the republic, and to introduce despotism in its stead.

IT may in this place be proper to distinguish between that species of sovereignty which is claimed and exercised by despotic monarchs, and that sovereignty which the citizens of a republic inherit and retain.—— The sovereignty of a despotic monarch assumes the power of making wrong right, or right wrong, as he pleases or as it suits him. The sovereignty in a republic is exercised to keep right and wrong in their proper and distinct places, and never suffer the one to usurp the place of the other. A republic, properly understood, is a sovereignty of justice in contradistinction to a sovereignty of Will.

OUR experience in republicanism is yet so slender, that it is much to be doubted, whether all our public Laws and Acts are consistent with, or can be justified on, the principles of a republican government.

WE have been so much habited to act in committees at the commencement of the dispute, and during the interregnum of government, and in many cases since, and to adopt expedients warranted by necessity, and to permit to ourselves a discretionary use of power suited to the spur and exigency of the moment, that a man transferred from a committee to a seat in the Legislature imperceptibly takes with him the ideas and habits he has been accustomed to, and continues to think like a committee-man instead of a legislator, and to govern by spirit rather than by the rule of the constitution and the principles of the Republic.

HAVING already stated that the power of the representatives can never exceed the power of the people whom they represent, I now proceed to examine more particularly, what the power of the representatives is.

IT is, in the first place, the power of acting as legislators in making laws,—and in the second place, the power of acting in certain cases, as agents or negociators for the Commonwealth, for such purposes as the circumstances of the Commonwealth require.

A VERY strange confusion of ideas, dangerous to the credit, stability, and the good and honor of the Commonwealth has arisen by confounding those two distinct powers and things together, and blending every Act of the Assembly, of whatever kind it may be, under one general name of *"Laws of the Commonwealth,"* and thereby creating an opinion (which is truly of the despotic kind) that every succeeding Assembly has an equal power over every transaction, as well as law, done by a former Assembly.

ALL laws are Acts, but all Acts are not laws. Many of the Acts of the Assembly are Acts of agency or negociation, that is, they are Acts of contract and agreement, on the part of the State, with certain persons therein mentioned, and for certain purposes therein recited. An Act of this kind, after it has passed the House, is of the nature of a deed or contract, signed, sealed and delivered; and subject to the same general laws and principles of justice as all other deeds and contracts are: for in a transaction of this kind the State stands as an individual, and can be known in no other character in a court of justice.

By "LAWS" as distinct from the agency transactions, or matters of negociation, are to be comprehended all those public Acts of the Assembly or Commonwealth, which have a universal operation, or apply themselves to every individual of the Commonwealth. Of this kind are the Laws for the distribution and administration of justice, for the preservation of the peace, for the security of property, for raising the necessary revenue by just proportions, &c. &c.

ACTS of this kind are properly LAWS, and they may be altered and amended or repealed, or others substituted in their places, as experience shall direct, for the better effecting the purpose for which they were intended: and the right and power of the Assembly to do this, is derived from the right and power which the people, were they all assembled together, instead of being represented, would have to do the same thing: because, in Acts or laws of this kind, there is no other party than the public. The law, or the alteration, or the repeal, is for themselves;—and whatever the effects may be, it falls on themselves;—if for the better, they have the benefit of it—if for the worse, they suffer the inconvenience. No violence to any one is here offered——no breach of faith is here committed. It is therefore one of these rights and powers which is within the sense, meaning and limits of the original compact of justice which they formed with each other as the foundation principle of the Republic, and being one of those rights and powers, it devolves on their representatives by delegation.

As it is not my intention (neither is it within the limits assigned to this work) to define every species of what may be called LAWS (but rather to distinguish that part in which the representatives act as agents or negociators for the State, from the legislative part,) I shall pass on to distinguish and describe those Acts of the Assembly which are Acts of agency or negociation, and to shew that as they are different in their nature, construction and operation from legislative Acts, so likewise the power and authority of the Assembly over them, after they are passed, is different.

It must occur to every person on the first reflection, that the affairs and circumstances of a Commonwealth require other business to be done besides that of making laws, and consequently, that the different kinds of business cannot all be classed under one name, or be subject to one and the same rule of treatment.— —But to proceed——

By agency transactions, or matters of negociation, done by the Assembly, are to be comprehended as that kind of public business, which the Assembly, as representatives of the Republic, transact in its behalf, with certain person or persons, or part or parts of the Republic, for purposes mentioned in the Act, and which the Assembly confirm and ratify on the part of the Commonwealth, by affixing to it the seal of the State.

An Act of this kind, differs from a law of the before mentioned kind; because here are two parties and there but one, and the parties are bound to perform different and distinct parts: whereas, in the before mentioned law, every man's part was the same.

These Acts, therefore, though numbered among the laws, are evidently distinct therefrom, and are not of the legislative kind. The former are laws for the government of the Commonwealth; these are transactions of business, such as, selling and conveying an estate belonging to the public, or buying one; Acts for borrowing money, and fixing with the lender the terms and modes of payment; Acts of agreement and contract, with certain person or persons, for certain purposes; and, in short, every kind of Act in which two parties, the state being one, are particularly mentioned or described, and in which the form and nature of a bargain or contract is comprehended.——These, if for custom and uniformity sake we call them by the name of LAWS, are not laws for the government of the Commonwealth, but for the government of the contracting parties, as all deeds and contracts are; and are not, properly speaking, Acts of the Assembly, but joint Acts, or Acts of the Assembly in behalf of the Commonwealth on one part, and certain persons therein mentioned on the other part.

ACTS of this kind are distinguishable into two classes.——

FIRST, those wherein the matters inserted in the Act have already been settled and adjusted between the State on one part, and the persons therein mentioned on the other part. In this case the Act is the completion and ratification of the contract or matters therein recited. It is in fact a deed signed, sealed and delivered.

SECONDLY, those Acts wherein the matters have not been already agreed upon, and wherein the Act only holds forth certain propositions and terms to be accepted of and acceded to.

I SHALL give an instance of each of those Acts. First—the State wants the loan of a sum of money—certain persons make an offer to Government to lend that sum, and send in their proposals: the Government accept these proposals and all the matters of the loan and the payment are agreed on; and an Act is passed, according to the usual form of passing Acts, ratifying and confirming this agreement. This Act is final.

IN the second case,—The State, as in the preceding one, wants a loan of money—the Assembly passes an Act holding forth the terms on which it will borrow and pay: this Act has no force, until the propositions and terms are accepted of and acceded to by some person or persons, and when those terms are accepted of and complied with the Act is binding on the State.——But if at the meeting of the next Assembly, or any other, the whole sum intended to be borrowed, should not be borrowed, that Assembly may stop where they are, and discontinue proceeding with the loan, or make new propositions and terms for the remainder; but so far as the subscriptions have been filled up, and the terms complied with, it is, as in the first case, a signed deed: and in the same manner are all Acts, let the matters in them be what they may, wherein, as I have before mentioned, the State on one part, and certain individuals on the other part, are parties in the Act.

IF the State should become a bankrupt, the creditors, as in all cases of bankruptcy, will be sufferers; they will have but a dividend for the whole: but this is not a dissolution of the contract, but an accommodation of it, arising from necessity. And so in all cases of Acts of this kind, if an inability takes place on either side, the contract cannot be performed, and some accommodation must be gone into or the matter falls thro' of itself.

IT may likewise happen, tho' it ought not to happen, that in performing the matters, agreeably to the terms of the Act, inconveniences, unforeseen at the time of making the Act, may arise to either or both parties: in this case, those inconveniences may be removed by the mutual consent and agreement of the parties, and each finds its benefit in so doing: for in a Republic it is the harmony of its parts that constitutes their several and mutual Good.

BUT the Acts themselves are legally binding, as much as if they had been made between two private individuals. The greatness of one party cannot give it a superiority or advantage over the other. The State, or its representatives the Assembly, has no more power over an Act of this kind, after it has passed, than if the State was a private person. It is the glory of a Republic to have it so, because it secures the individual from becoming the prey of power, and prevents MIGHT from overcoming RIGHT.

IF any difference or dispute arise afterwards between the State and the individuals with whom the agreement is made, respecting the contract, or the meaning, or extent of any of the matters contained in the Act, which may affect the property or interest of either, such difference or dispute must be judged of, and decided upon, by the laws of the land, in a court of justice and trial by jury; that is, by the laws of the land already in being at the time such Act and contract was made.——No law made afterwards can apply to the case, either directly, or by construction or implication: For such a law would be a retrospective law, or a law made after the fact, and cannot even be produced in court as applying to the case before it for judgment.

THAT this is justice, that it is the true principle of republican government, no man will be so hardy as to deny:—If, therefore, a lawful contract or agreement, sealed and ratified, cannot be affected or altered by any Act made afterwards, cannot be affected how much more inconsistent and irrational, despotic and unjust would it be, to think of making an Act with the professed intention of breaking up a contract already signed and sealed.

THAT it is possible an Assembly, in the heat and indiscretion of party, and meditating on power rather than on the principle by which all power in a republican government is governed, that of equal justice, may fall into the error of passing such an Act, is admitted;—but it would be an actless Act, an Act that goes for nothing, an Act which the courts of justice, and the established laws of the land, could know nothing of.

BECAUSE such an Act would be an Act of one party only, not only without, but against the consent of the other; and, therefore, cannot be produced to affect a contract made between the two.——That the violation of a contract should be set up as a justification to the violator, would be the same thing as to say, that a man by breaking his promise is freed from the obligation of it, or that by transgressing the laws he exempts himself from the punishment of them.

BESIDES the constitutional and legal reasons why an Assembly cannot, of its own Act and authority, undo or make void a contract made between the State (by a former Assembly) and certain individuals, may be added what may be called, the natural reasons or those reasons which the plain rules of common sense point out to every man. Among which are the following.

THE Principals, or real parties, in the contract, are the State and the persons contracted with. The Assembly is not a party, but an Agent in behalf of the State, authorised and empowered to transact its affairs.

THEREFORE it is the State that is bound on one part and certain individuals on the other part, and the performance of the contract, according to the conditions of it, devolves on succeeding Assemblies, not as Principals, but as Agents.

THEREFORE, for the next or any other Assembly to undertake to dissolve the State from its obligation is an assumption of power of a novel and extraordinary kind.—It is the Servant attempting to free his Master.

THE election of new Assemblies following each other makes no difference in the nature of the thing. The State is still the same State.— The public is still the same body. These do not annually expire though the time of an Assembly does. These are not new-created every year, nor can they be displaced from their original standing; but are a perpetual, permanent body, always in being and still the same.

BUT if we adopt the vague inconsistent idea that every new Assembly has a full and complete authority over every Act done by the State in a former Assembly, and confound together laws, contracts, and every species of public business, it will lead us into a wilderness of endless confusion and insurmountable difficulties. It would be declaring an Assembly despotic for the time being.—— Instead of a government of established principles administered by established rules, the authority of Government by being strained so high, would, by the same rule, be reduced proportionably as low, and would be no other than that of a Committee of the State, acting with discretionary powers for one year. Every new election would be a new revolution, or it would suppose the public of the former year dead and a new public risen in its place.

HAVING now endeavoured to fix a precise idea to, and distinguish between, Legislative Acts and Acts of Negociation and Agency, I shall proceed to apply this distinction to the case now in dispute, respecting the charter of the Bank.

THE charter of the Bank, or what is the same thing, the Act for incorporating it, is to all intents and purposes an Act of Negociation and Contract, entered into, and confirmed between the state on one part, and certain persons mentioned therein on the other part. The purpose for which the Act was done on the part of the State is therein recited, viz. the support which the finances of the country would derive therefrom. The incorporating clause is the condition or obligation on the part of the State; and the obligation on the part of the Bank, is, "that nothing contained in that Act shall be construed to authorise the said Corporation to exercise any powers in this State repugnant to the laws or constitution thereof."

HERE are all the marks and evidences of a Contract. The parties—the Purport—and the reciprocal Obligations.

THAT this is a Contract, or a joint Act, is evident from its being in the power of either of the parties to have forbidden or prevented its being done. The State could not force the stockholders of the Bank to be a corporation, and therefore as their consent was necessary to the making the Act, their dissent would have prevented its being made; so on the other hand, as the Bank could not force the State to incorporate them, the consent or dissent of the State would have had the same effect to *do*, or to prevent its being done; and as neither of the parties could make the Act alone, for the same reason can neither of them dissolve it alone: But this is not the case with a law or Act of legislation, and therefore the difference proves it to be an Act of a different kind.

THE Bank may forfeit the charter by delinquency, but the delinquency must be proved and established by a legal process in a court of justice and trial by jury: for the State, or the Assembly, is not to be a judge in its own case, but must come to the laws of the land for judgment; for that which is law for the individual, is likewise law for the State.

BEFORE I enter further into this affair, I shall go back to the circumstances of the country and the condition the Government was in, for some time before, as well as at the time it entered into this engagement with the Bank, and this Act of incorporation was passed: for the Government of this State, and I suppose the same of the rest, were then in want of two of the most essential matters which governments could be destitute of——Money and Credit.——

IN looking back to those times, and bringing forward some of the circumstances attending them, I feel myself entering on unpleasant and disagreeable ground; because some of the matters which the attack on the Bank now make it necessary to state, in order to bring the affair fully before the Public, will not add honor to those who have promoted that measure and carried it through the late House of Assembly; and for whom, tho' my own judgment and opinion on the case oblige me to differ from, I retain my esteem, and the social remembrance of times past. But, I trust, those Gentlemen will do me the justice to recollect my exceeding earnestness with them, last spring, when the attack on the Bank first broke out; for it clearly appeared to me one of those overheated measures, which, neither the country at large, nor their own constituents, would justify them in when it came to be fully and clearly understood; for however high a party-measure may be carried in an Assembly, the people out of doors are all the while following their several occupations and employments, minding their farms and their business, and take their own time and leisure to judge of public measures; the consequence of which is that they often judge in a cooler spirit than their representatives act in.

IT may be easily recollected that the present Bank was preceded by, and rose out, of a former one, called the Pennsylvania Bank which began a few months before; the occasion of which I shall briefly state.

IN the spring of 1780, the Pennsylvania Assembly was composed of many of the same Members, and nearly all of the same connection, which composed the late House that began the attack on the Bank. I served as Clerk of the Assembly of 1780, which station I resigned at the end of the year and accompanied a much lamented friend the late Colonel John Laurens on an embassy to France.

THE spring of 1780 was marked with an accumulation of misfortunes. The reliance placed on the defence of Charlestown failed and exceedingly lowered or depressed the spirits of the country. The measures of Government, from the want of money, means and credit, dragged on like a heavy loaded carriage without wheels, and were nearly got to what a countryman would understand by a dead pull.[1]

THE Assembly of that year met, by adjournment at an unusual time, the tenth of May, and what particularly added to the affliction, was, that so many of the Members, instead of spiriting up their constituents to the most nervous exertions, came to the Assembly furnished with petitions to be exempt from paying taxes. How the public measures were to be carried on, the country defended, and the army recruited, clothed, fed, and paid, when the only resource, and that not half sufficient, that of taxes, should be relaxed to almost nothing, was a matter too gloomy to look at. A language very different from that of petitions ought to have been the language of every one. A declaration to have stood forth with their lives and fortunes, and a reprobation of every thought of partial indulgence would have sounded much better than petitions.

WHILE the Assembly was sitting a letter from the Commander in chief was received by the Executive Council and transmitted to the House. The doors were shut and it fell officially to me to read.

IN this letter the naked truth of things was unfolded. Among other informations the General said, that notwithstanding his confidence in the attachment of the army to the cause of the country, the distresses of it, from the want of every necessary which men could be destitute of, were arisen to such a

---

[1] See above p. 167. Paine's metaphor was likely designed to remind the reader of Laurens's triumphant arrival in Philadelphia on 6 November 1780 with a cartload of French silver brought overland from Rhode Island, evading British forces. Part of this cash had been used to boost the initial subscription of the bank. See above p. 206.

pitch, that the appearance of mutiny and discontent were so strongly marked on the countenance of the army that he dreaded the event of every hour.

WHEN the letter was read I observed a despairing silence in the House. No body spoke for a considerable time. At length a Member of whose fortitude to withstand misfortunes I had a high opinion, rose: "If," said he, "the account in that letter is a true state of things; and we are in the situation there represented, it appears to me in vain to contend the matter any longer. We may as well give up at first as at last."

THE Gentleman who spoke next, was (to the best of my recollection) a Member from Bucks county, who, in a cheerful note, endeavoured to dissipate the gloom of the House ——"Well, well" said he," don't let the House despair, if things are not so well as we wish, we must endeavour to make them better." And on a motion for adjournment, the conversation went no farther.

THERE was now no time to lose, and something absolutely necessary to be done, which was not within the immediate power of the House to do: for what with the depreciation of the Currency, and slow operation of taxes, and the petitions to be exempted therefrom, the treasury moneyless, and the Government creditless.

IF the Assembly could not give the assistance which the necessity of the case immediately required, it was very proper the matter should be known by those who either could or would endeavour to do it. To conceal the information within the House, and not provide the relief which that information required, was making no use of the knowledge and endangering the Public Cause. The only thing that now remained, and was capable of reaching the case, was private credit, and the voluntary aid of individuals; and under this impression, on my return from the House, I drew out the salary due to me as Clerk, enclosed five hundred dollars to a Gentleman in this City, in party of the whole, and wrote fully to him on the subject of our affairs.

THE gentleman to whom this letter was addressed is Mr. Blair M'Clenaghan. I mentioned to him, that notwithstanding the current opinion that the enemy were beaten from before Charlestown, there were too many reasons to believe the place was then taken and in the hands of the enemy; the consequence of which would be, that a great part of the British force would return, and join that at New-York. That our own army required to be augmented, ten thousand men, to be able to stand against the combined force of the enemy. I informed Mr. M'Clenaghan of General Washington's letter, the extreme distresses he was surrounded with, and the absolute occasion there was for the citizens to exert them selves at this time, which there was no doubt they would do, if the necessity was made known to them; for that the ability of Government was exhausted. I requested Mr. M'Clenaghan, to propose a voluntary subscription among his friends, and added, that I had enclosed five hundred dollars as my mite thereto, and that I would encrease it as far as the last ability would enable me to go.*

THE next day Mr. M'Clenaghan informed me, that he had communicated the contents of the letter at a meeting of Gentlemen at the Coffee-house, and that a subscription was immediately began—that Mr. Robert Morris and himself had subscribed two hundred pounds each, in hard money, and that the subscription was going very successfully on.—This subscription was intended as a donation, and to be given in bounties to promote the recruiting service. It is dated June 8th, 1780. The original subscription list is now in my possession—it amounts to four hundred pounds hard money, and one hundred and one thousand three hundred and sixty pounds continental.

WHILE this subscription was going forward, information of the loss of Charlestown arrived,† and on a communication from several Members of Congress to certain Gentlemen of this city, of the encreasing distresses and dangers then taking place, a meeting was held of the subscribers, and such other

---

* Mr. M'Clenaghan being now returned from Europe, has my consent to show this letter to any Gentleman who may be inclined to see it.
† Col. Tennant, Aid to General Lincoln, arrived the 14th of June, with despatches of the capitulation of Charlestown.

Gentlemen who chose to attend, at the City Tavern. This meeting was on the 17th of June, nine days after the subscriptions had began.

AT this meeting it was resolved to open a security subscription, to the amount of three hundred thousand pounds, Pennsylvania currency, in real money; the subscribers to execute bonds to the amount of their subscriptions, and to form a Bank thereon for supplying the army. This being resolved on and carried into execution the plan of the first subscriptions was discontinued, and this extended one established in its stead.

BY means of this Bank the army was supplied thro' the campaign, and being at the same time recruited, was enabled to maintain its ground: And on the appointment of Mr. Morris to be Superintendent of the finances the spring following, he arranged the system of the present Bank, stiled the Bank of North-America, and many of the subscribers of the former Bank transferred their subscriptions into this.

TOWARDS the establishment of this Bank, Congress passed an ordinance of incorporation December 21st 1781, which the Government of Pennsylvania recognized by sundry matters: And afterwards, on an application from the President and Directors of the Bank, thro' the mediation of the Executive Council, the Assembly agreed to, and passed the State Act of Incorporation April 1st 1782.

THUS arose the Bank——produced by the distresses of the times and the enterprising spirit of patriotic individuals.—— Those individuals furnished and risked the money, and the aid which the Government contributed was that of incorporating them.——It would have been well if the State had made all its bargains and contracts with as much true policy as it made this; for a greater service for so small a consideration, that only of an Act of incorporation, has not been obtained since the Government existed.

HAVING now shewn how the Bank originated, I shall proceed with my remarks.

THE sudden restoration of public and private credit which took place on the establishment of the Bank is an event as extraordinary in itself as any domestic occurrence during the progress of the Revolution.

HOW far a spirit of envy might operate to produce the attack on the Bank during the sitting of the late Assembly, is best known and felt by those who began or promoted that attack. The Bank had rendered services which the Assembly of 1780 could not, and acquired an honor which many of its Members might be unwilling to own, and wish to obscure.

BUT surely every wise Government acting on the principles of patriotism and Public Good would cherish an Institution capable of rendering such advantages to the Community. The establishment of the Bank in one of the most trying vicissitudes of the war, its zealous services in the public cause, its influence in restoring and supporting credit, and the punctuality with which all its business has been transacted, are matters, that so far from meriting the treatment it met with from the late Assembly, are an honor to the State, and what the body of her citizens may be proud to own.

BUT the attack on the Bank, as a Chartered Institution, under the protection of its violators, however criminal it may be as an error of Government, or impolitic as a measure of party, is not to be charged on the constituents of those who made the attack. It appears from every circumstance that has come to light to be a measure which that Assembly contrived of itself. The Members did not come charged with the affair from their constituents. There was no idea of such a thing when they were elected or when they met. The hasty and precipitate manner in which it was hurried through the House, and the refusal of the House to hear the Directors of the Bank in its defence, prior to the publication of the repealing Bill for public consideration, operated to prevent their constituents comprehending the subject: Therefore, whatever may be wrong in the proceedings lies not at the door of the Public. The house took the affair on its own shoulders, and whatever blame there is lies on them.

THE matter must have been prejudged and predetermined by a majority of the Members out of the House, before it was brought into it. The whole business appears to have been fixed at once, and all reasoning or debate on the case rendered useless.

PETITIONS from a very *inconsiderable* number of persons suddenly procured, and so privately done, as to be a secret among the few that signed them, were presented to the House and read twice in one day, and referred to a Committee of the House to *inquire* and report thereon. I here subjoin the Petition* and the

---

* Minutes of the Assembly, March 21, 1785.

Petitions from a considerable number of the inhabitants of *Chester* county were read, representing that the bank established at *Philadelphia* has fatal effects upon the Community; that whilst men are enabled, by means of the bank, to receive near three times the rate of common interest, and at the same time receive their money at very short warning, whenever they have occasion for it, it will be impossible for the husbandman or mechanic to borrow on the former terms of legal interest and distant payments of the principal; that the best security will not enable the person to borrow; that experience clearly demonstrates the mischievous consequences of this institution to the fair trader; that impostors have been enabled to support themselves in a fictitious credit, by means of a temporary punctuality at the bank, until they have drawn in their honest neighbours to trust them with their property, or to pledge their credit as sureties, and have been finally involved in ruin and distress; that they have repeatedly seen the stopping of discounts at the bank, operate on the trading part of the Community, with a degree of violence scarcely inferior to that of a stagnation of the blood in the human body, hurrying the wretched merchant who hath debts to pay into the hands of griping usurers; that the Directors of the bank may give such preference in trade, by advances of money, to their particular favorites, as to destroy that equality which ought to prevail in a commercial country; that paper-money has often proved beneficial to the state, but the bank forbids it, and the people must acquiesce: therefore, and in order to restore public confidence and private security, they pray that a bill may be brought in and passed into a law for repealing the law for incorporating the bank.

March 28.

The report of the committee, read March 25, on the petitions from the counties of *Chester* and *Berks,* and the city of *Philadelphia* and its vicinity, praying the act of Assembly, whereby the bank was established at *Philadelphia,* may be repealed, was read the second time as follows, viz.

The committee to whom was referred the petitions concerning the bank established at *Philadelphia,* and who were instructed to inquire whether the said bank be compatible with the public safety, and that equality which ought ever to prevail between the individuals of a republic, beg leave to report, That it is the opinion of this committee that the said bank, as at present established, is in every view incompatible with the public safety: that in the present state of our trade, the said bank has a direct tendency to banish a great part of the specie from the country, so as to produce a scarcity of money, and to collect into the hands of the stockholders of the said bank almost the whole of the money which remains amongst us. That the accumulation of enormous wealth in the hands of a society, who claim perpetual duration, will necessarily produce a degree of influence and power, which cannot be entrusted in the hands of any set of men whatsoever, without endangering the public safety. That the said bank, in its corporate capacity, is empowered to hold estates to the amount of ten millions of dollars, and by the tenor of the present charter, is to exist forever, without being obliged to yield any emolument to the government, or to

Report, and shall exercise the right and privilege of a citizen in examining their merits, not for the purpose of opposition, but with a design of making an intricate affair more generally and better understood.

SO far as my private judgment is capable of comprehending the subject, it appears to me, that the Committee were unacquainted with, and have totally mistaken, the nature and business of a Bank, as well as the matter committed to them, considered as a proceeding of Government.

THEY were instructed by the House to *inquire* whether the Bank established at Philadelphia was compatible with the public safety.

IT is scarcely possible to suppose the instructions meant no more than that they were to inquire of one another. It is certain they made no inquiry at the Bank, to inform themselves of the situation of its affairs, how they were conducted, what aids it had rendered the public cause, or whether any; nor do the Committee produce in their report a single fact or circumstance to shew they made any inquiry at all, or whether the rumors then circulated were true or false; but content

---

be at all dependent upon it. That the great profits of the bank, which will daily encrease as money grows scarcer, and which already far exceed the profits of European banks, have tempted foreigners to vest their money in this bank, and thus to draw from us large sums for interest.

That foreigners will doubtless be more and more induced to become stockholders, until the time may arrive when this enormous engine of power may become subject to foreign influence; this country may be agitated with the politics of European courts, and the good people of *America* reduced once more into a state of subordination, and dependence upon some one or other of the European powers. That at best, if it were even confined to the hands of Americans, it would be totally destructive of that equality which ought to prevail in a republic. We have nothing in our free and equal government capable of balancing the influence which this bank must create; and we see nothing, which in the course of a few years, can prevent the directors of the bank from governing Pennsylvania. Already we have felt its influence indirectly interfering in the measures of the legislature. Already the house of Assembly, the representatives of the people have been threatened, that the credit of our paper currency will be blasted by the bank; and if this growing evil continues, we fear the time is not very distant, when the bank will be able to dictate to the legislature, what laws to pass and what to forbear.

Your committee therefore beg leave further to report the following resolution to be adopted by the house, viz.

Resolved, that a committee be appointed to bring in a bill to repeal the act of Assembly, passed the first day of *April* 1782, entitled, "*An act to incorporate the subscribers to the bank of* North-America;" and also to repeal one other act of Assembly, passed the 18th of *March*, 1782, entitled, "*An act for preventing and punishing the counterfeiting of the common seal, bank bills and bank notes of the president, directors and company, of the bank of* North-America*, and for the other purposes therein mentioned.*"

themselves with modelling the insinuations of the petitions into a report and giving an opinion thereon.

It would appear from the report, that the Committee either conceived that the House had already determined how it would act without regard to the case, and that they were only a Committee for form sake, and to give a color of inquiry without making any, or that the case was referred to them, *as law-questions are sometimes referred to law-officers, for an opinion only.*

THIS method of doing public business serves exceedingly to mislead a country.——When the constituents of an Assembly hear that an enquiry into any matter is directed to be made, and a Committee appointed for that purpose, they naturally conclude that the inquiry *is made,* and that the future proceedings of the House are in consequence of the matters, facts, and information obtained by means of that inquiry.——But here is a Committee of inquiry making no inquiry at all, and giving an opinion on a case without inquiring into it. This proceeding of the Committee would justify an opinion that it was not their wish to *get,* but to *get over* information, and lest the enquiry should not suit their wishes, omitted to make any. The subsequent conduct of the House, in resolving not to hear the Directors of the Bank on their application for that purpose, prior to the publication of the Bill for the consideration of the people, strongly corroborates this opinion: For why should not the House hear them, unless it was apprehensive that the Bank, by such a public opportunity, would produce proofs of its services and usefulness, that would not suit the temper and views of its opposers?

BUT if the House did not wish or chuse to hear the defence of the Bank, it was no reason their constituents should not. The Constitution of this State, in lieu of having two branches of Legislature, has substituted, that, "To the end that laws before they are enacted may be more *maturely considered,* and the inconvenience of *hasty determinations* as much as possible prevented, all Bills of a public nature shall be printed for the consideration of the people˚."—The people, therefore,

---

˚ Constitution, section the 15th.

according to the Constitution, stand in the place of another House; or, more properly speaking, are a House in their own right.—But in this instance the Assembly arrogates the whole power to itself, and places itself as a bar to stop the necessary information spreading among the people.—— The application of the Bank to be heard before the Bill was published for public consideration had two objects.——First, to the House,—and secondly, thro' the House to the people, who are as another House. It was as a defence in the first instance, and as an appeal in the second. But the Assembly absorbs the right of the people to judge; because, by refusing to hear the defence, they barred the appeal.——Were there no other cause which the constituents of that Assembly had for censuring its conduct, than the exceeding unfairness, partiality, and arbitrariness with which its business was transacted, it would be cause sufficient.

LET the constituents of Assemblies differ, as they may, respecting certain peculiarities in the *form* of the Constitution, they will all agree in supporting its *principles*, and in reprobating unfair proceedings and despotic measures. Every constituent is a member of the Republic, which is a station of more consequence to him than being a member of a party, and tho' they may differ from each other in their choice of persons to transact the public business, it is of equal importance to all parties that the business be done on right principles: otherwise our laws and Acts, instead of being founded in justice, will be founded in party, and be laws and Acts of retaliation; and instead of being a Republic of free citizens, we shall be alternately tyrants and slaves.—But to return to the report.——

THE Report begins by stating that, "The Committee to whom was referred the petitions concerning the Bank established at Philadelphia, and who were instructed to *inquire* whether the said Bank be compatible with the public safety, and that equality which ought ever to prevail between the individuals of a Republic, beg leave to report "(not that they have made any *inquiry,* but) "That it is the *opinion* of this Committee that the said Bank as at present established, is, in every view, incompatible with the public safety."——But why is it so? Here is an opinion unfounded and unwarranted. The Committee have began their Report at the wrong end; for an opinion, when given as a matter of judgment, is an action of the mind which follows a fact, but here it is put in the room of one.

THE Report then says, "That in the present state of our trade the said Bank has a direct tendency to banish a great part of the specie from the country, and to collect into the hands of the stockholders of the Bank, almost the whole of the money which remains among us."

HERE is another mere assertion, just like the former, without a single fact or circumstance to shew why it is made or whereon it is founded.——Now the very reverse, of what the Committee asserts, is the natural consequence of a Bank. Specie may be called the stock in trade of the Bank, it is therefore its interest to prevent it from wandering out of the country, and to keep a constant standing supply to be ready for all domestic occasions and demands. Were it true that the Bank has a direct tendency to banish the specie from the country, there would soon be an end to the Bank; and, therefore, the Committee have so far mistaken the matter, as to put their fears in the place of their wishes: for if it is to happen as the Committee states, let the Bank alone and it will cease of itself, and the repealing Act need not have been passed.

IT is the interest of the Bank that people should keep their cash there, and all commercial countries find the exceeding great convenience of having a general depository for their cash.— But so far from banishing it, there are no two classes of people in America who are so much interested in preserving hard money in the country as the Bank and the Merchant. Neither of them can carry on their business without it. Their opposition to the paper-money of the late Assembly was because it has a direct effect, as far as it is able, to banish the specie and that without providing any means for bringing more in. The Committee must have been aware of this, and therefore chose to spread the first alarm, and groundless as it was to trust to the delusion.

AS the keeping the specie in the country is the interest of the Bank, so it has the best opportunities of preventing its being sent away, and the earliest knowledge of such a design. While the Bank is the general depository of cash no great sums can be obtained without getting it from thence, and as it is evidently prejudicial to its interest to advance money to be sent abroad, because in this case the money cannot by circulation return again, the Bank, therefore, is interested in preventing what the Committee would have it suspected of promoting.

IT is to prevent the exportation of cash, and to retain it in the country that the bank has on several occasions stopt the discounting notes till the danger has been passed.* The first part, therefore, of the assertion, that of banishing the specie, contains an apprehension as needless as it is groundless, and which, had the Committee understood, or been the least informed of the nature of a Bank, they could not have made. It is very probable that some of the opposers of the Bank are those persons who have been disappointed in their attempt to obtain specie for this purpose and now cloak their opposition under other pretences.

I NOW come to the second part of the assertion, which is, that when the Bank has banished a great part of the specie from the country, "it will collect into the hands of the stockholders almost the whole of the money which remains among

---

*The petitions say "That they have frequently seen the stopping of discounts at the bank, operate on the trading part of the Community, with a degree of violence scarcely inferior to that of a stagnation of the blood in the human body, hurrying the wretched merchant who hath debts to pay into the hands of griping usurers."

As the persons who say or signed this live somewhere in Chester county, they are not, from situation, certain of what they say. Those petitions have every appearance of being contrived for the purpose of bringing the matter on. The petitions and the report have strong evidence in them of being both drawn by the same person: for the report is as clearly the echo of the petitions as ever the address of the British Parliament was the echo of the King's speech.

Besides the reason I have already given for occasionally stopping discounting notes at the bank, there are other necessary reasons. It is for the purpose of settling accounts. Short reckonings make long friends. The bank lends its money for short periods, and by that means assists a great many different people and if it did not sometimes stop discounting as a means of settling with the persons it has already lent its money to, those persons would find a way to keep what they had borrowed longer than they ought, and prevent others being assisted. It is a fact, and some of the Committee know it to be so, that sundry of those persons who then opposed the Bank acted this part.

The stopping the discounts do not, and cannot, operate to call in the loans sooner than the time for which they were lent, and therefore the charge is false that "it hurries men into the hands of griping usurers":— and the truth is, that it operates to keep them from thence.

If petitions are to be contrived to cover the design of a house of Assembly and give a pretence for its conduct, or if a house is to be led by the nose by the idle tale of any fifty or sixty signers to a petition, it is time for the public to look a little closer into the conduct of its representatives.

us."—But how, or by what means, the Bank is to accomplish this wonderful feat the Committee have not informed us. Whether people are to give their money to the Bank for nothing, or whether the Bank is to charm it from them as a rattlesnake charms a squirrel from a tree, the Committee have left us as much in the dark about as they were themselves.

Is it possible the Committee should know so very little of the matter, as not to know that no part of the money which at any time may be in the Bank belongs to the stockholders; not even the original capital which they put in is any part of it their own, until every person who has a demand upon the Bank is paid, and if there is not a sufficiency for this purpose on the balance of loss and gain, the original money of the stockholders must make up the deficiency.

THE money, which at any time may be in the Bank, is the property of every man who holds a Bank note, or deposits cash there, or who has a just demand upon it from the city of Philadelphia up to fort Pitt, or to any part of the United States; and he can draw the money from it when he pleases. Its being in the Bank, does not in the least make it the property of the stockholders, any more than the money in the State Treasury is the property of the State Treasurer. They are only stewards over it for those who please to put it, or let it remain there: and, therefore, this second part of the assertion is somewhat ridiculous.

THE next paragraph in the Report is, "That the accumulation *of enormous wealth* in the hands of a *society* who claim perpetual duration will necessarily produce a degree of influence and power which cannot be entrusted in the hands of any set of men whatsoever" (the Committee I presume excepted) "without endangering the public safety."——There is an air of solemn fear in this paragraph which is something like introducing a ghost in a play to keep people from laughing at the players.

I HAVE already shewn that whatever wealth there may be, at any time, in the Bank, is the property of those who have demands upon the Bank, and not the property of the stockholders. As a Society they hold no property, and most probably never will, unless it should be a house to transact their business in, instead of hiring one. Every half year the Bank settles its accounts, and each individual stockholder takes his dividend of gain or loss to himself, and the Bank begins the next half year in the same manner it began the first, and so on. This being the nature of a Bank, there can be no accumulation of wealth among them as a society.

FOR what purpose the word "*society*" is introduced into the Report I do not know, unless it be to make a false impression upon people's minds. It has no connection with the subject, for the Bank is not a society, but a company, and denominated so in the Charter. There are several religious societies incorporated in this State, which hold property as the right of those societies, and to which no person can belong that is not of the same religious profession. But this is not the case with the Bank. The Bank is a company for the promotion and convenience of commerce, which is a matter in which all the State is interested, and holds no property in the manner which those societies do.

BUT there is a direct contradiction in this paragraph to that which goes before it. The committee, there, accuses the Bank of banishing the specie, and here, of accumulating enormous sums of it.——So here are two enormous sums of specie; one enormous sum going out, and another enormous sum remaining.——To reconcile this contradiction, the Committee should have added to their Report, *that they suspected the Bank had found out the Philosopher's stone, and kept it a secret.*

THE next paragraph is, "That the said Bank, in its corporate capacity, is empowered to hold estates to the amount of ten millions of dollars, and by the tenor of the present Charter is to exist for ever, without being obliged to yield any emolument to the Government, or be at least dependent on it."

THE committee have gone so vehemently into this business, and so completely shewn their want of knowledge in every point of it, as to make, in the first part of this paragraph, a fear of what, the greater fear is, will never happen. Had the committee known any thing of Banking, they must have known, that the objection against Banks has been (not that they held great estates, but) that they held none;

that they had no real, fixed, and visible property, and that it is the maxim and practice of Banks not to hold any.

THE Honorable Chancellor Livingston, late Secretary for foreign affairs, did me the honor of shewing, and discoursing with me on, a plan of a Bank he had drawn up for the State of New-York. In this plan it was made a condition or obligation, that whatever the capital of the Bank amounted to in specie, there should be added twice as much in real estates. But the mercantile interest rejected the proposition.

IT was a very good piece of policy in the Assembly which passed the Charter Act, to add the Clause to impower the Bank to purchase and hold real estates. It was as an inducement to the Bank to do it, because such estates being held as the property of the Bank would be so many mortgages to the Public in addition to the money capital of the Bank.

BUT the doubt is that the Bank will not be induced to accept the opportunity. The Bank has existed five years and has not purchased a shilling of real property: and as such property or estates cannot be purchased by the Bank but with the interest money which the stock produces, and as that is divided every half year among the stockholders, and each stockholder chuses to have the management of his own dividend, and if he lays it out in purchasing an estate to have that estate his own private property, and under his own immediate management, there is no expectation, so far from being any fear, that the Clause will be accepted.

WHERE knowledge is a duty, ignorance is a crime; and the Committee are criminal in not understanding this subject better. Had this Clause not been in the Charter, the Committee might have reported the want of it as a defect, in not empowering the Bank to hold estates as a real security to its creditors: but as the complaint now stands, the accusation of it is, that the Charter empowers the Bank to *give real security* to its creditors. A complaint never made, heard of, or thought of before.

THE second article in this paragraph is, "That the bank, according to the tenor of the present Charter is to exist for ever"——Here I agree with the Committee, and am glad to find that among such a list of errors and contradictions there is one idea which is not wrong, altho' the Committee have made a wrong use of it.

As we are not to live for ever ourselves, and other generations are to follow us, we have neither the power nor the right to govern them, or to say how they shall govern themselves. It is the summit of human vanity, and shews a covetousness of power beyond the grave, to be dictating to the world to come. It is sufficient that we do that which is right in our own day and leave them with the advantage of good examples.

As the generations of the world are every day both commencing and expiring, therefore, when any public Act of this sort is done it naturally supposes the age of that generation to be then beginning, and the time contained between coming of age, and the natural end of life, is the extent of time it has a right to go to, which may be about thirty years; for tho' many may die before, others will live beyond; and the mean time is equally fair for all generations.

If it was made an article in the Constitution, that all laws and Acts should cease of themselves in thirty years, and have no legal force beyond that time, it would prevent their becoming too numerous and voluminous, and serve to keep them within view in a compact compass. Such as were proper to be continued, would be enacted again, and those which were not, would go into oblivion. There is the same propriety that a nation should fix a time for a full settlement of its affairs, and begin again from a new date, as that an individual should, and to keep within the distance of thirty years would be a convenient period.

The British, from the want of some general regulation of this kind, have a great number of obsolete laws; which, tho' out of use and forgot, are not out of force, and are occasionally brought up for sharping purposes, and innocent unwary persons trepanned thereby.

To extend this idea still further,—it would probably be a considerable improvement in the political system of nations, to make all treaties of peace for a limited time. It is the nature of the mind to feel uneasy under the idea of a condition perpetually existing over it, and to excite in itself apprehensions that would not take place were it not from that cause.

WERE treaties of peace made for, and renewable every seven or ten years, the natural effect would be, to make peace continue longer than it does under the custom of making peace for ever. If the parties felt or apprehended any inconveniences under the terms already made, they would look forward to the time when they should be eventually relieved therefrom, and might renew the treaty on improved conditions. This opportunity periodically occurring, and the recollection of it always existing, would serve as a chimney to the political fabric, to carry off the smoke and fume of national fire. It would naturally abate, and honorably take off, the edge and occasion for fighting: and however the parties might determine to do it, when the time of the treaty should expire, it would then seem like fighting in cool blood: The fighting temper would be dissipated before the fighting time arrived, and negociation supply its place. To know how probable this may be, a man need do no more than observe the progress of his own mind on any private circumstance similar in its nature to a public one.———But to return to my subject———

To give Limitation is to give Duration: and tho' it is not a justifying reason, that because an Act or Contract is not to last for ever, that it shall be broken or violated to day, yet, where no time is mentioned, the omission affords an opportunity for the abuse. When we violate a contract on this pretence, we assume a right that belongs to the next generation; for tho' they, as a following generation, have the right of altering or setting it aside, as not being concerned in the making it, or not being done in their day, we, who made it, have not that right; and, therefore, the Committee, in this part of their report, have made a wrong use of a right principle; and as this Clause in the Charter might have been altered by the consent of the parties, it cannot be produced to justify the violation.———And were it not altered there would be no inconvenience from it. The term "for ever" is an absurdity that would have no effect. The next age will think for itself by the same rule of right that we have done, and not admit any assumed authority of ours to encroach upon the system of their day. Our *for ever* ends where their *for ever* begins.

THE third article in this paragraph is, that the Bank holds its Charter "without being obliged to yield any emolument to the Government."

INGRATITUDE has a short memory. It was on the failure of the Government, to support the Public Cause, that the Bank originated. It stept in as a support when some of the persons then in the Government, and who now oppose the Bank, were apparently on the point of abandoning the cause, not from disaffection, but from despair. While the expences of the war were carried on by emissions of continental money, any set of men, in Government, might carry it on. The means being provided to their hands, required no great exertions of fortitude or wisdom; but when this means failed, they would have failed with it, had not a public spirit awakened itself with energy out of doors. It was easy times to the Governments while continental money lasted. The dream of wealth supplied the reality of it; but when the dream vanished, the Government did not awake.

BUT what right has the Government to expect any emolument from the Bank? Does the Committee mean to set up Acts and Charters for sale, or what do they mean? Because it is the practice of the British Ministry to grind a toll out of every public institution they can get a power over, is the same practice to be followed here?

THE war being now ended, and the Bank having rendered the service expected, or rather hoped for, from it, the principal public use of it, at this time, is for the promotion and extension of commerce. The whole community derives benefit from the operation of the Bank. It facilitates the commerce of the country. It quickens the means of purchasing and paying for country produce, and hastens on the exportation of it. The emolument, therefore, being to the Community, it is the office and duty of Government to give protection to the Bank.

AMONG many of the principal conveniences arising from the Bank, one of them is, that it gives a kind of life to, what would otherwise be, dead money. Every merchant and person in trade, has always in his hands some quantity of cash, which constantly remains with him; that is, he is never entirely without: This remnant money, as it may be called, is of no use to him till more is collected to it. He can neither buy produce nor merchandize with it, and this being the case with every person in trade, there will be (tho' not all at the same) as many of those sums lying uselessly by, and scattered throughout the city, as there are persons in trade, besides many that are not in trade.

I SHOULD not suppose the estimation overrated, in conjecturing, that half the money in the city, at any one time, lies in this manner. By collecting those scattered sums together, which is done by means of the Bank, they become capable of being used, and the quantity of circulating cash is doubled, and by the depositors alternately lending them to each other, the commercial system is invigorated; and as it is the interest of the Bank to preserve this money in the country for domestic uses only, and as it has the best opportunity of doing so, the Bank serves as a sentinel over the specie.

IF a farmer, or a miller, comes to the city with produce, there are but few merchants that can individually purchase it with ready money of their own; and those few would command nearly the whole market for country produce: But, by means of the Bank, this monopoly is prevented, and the chance of the market enlarged. It is very extraordinary that the late Assembly should promote monopolizing; yet such would be the effect of suppressing the Bank; and it is much to the honor of those merchants, who are capable, by their fortunes, of becoming monopolizers, that they support the Bank. In this case, honor operates over interest. They were the persons who first set up the Bank, and their honor is now engaged to support what it is their interest to put down.

IF merchants, by this means, or farmers, by similar means, among themselves, can mutually aid and support each other, what has the Government to do with it? What right has it to expect emolument from associated industry, more than from individual industry? It would be a strange sort of Government, that should make it illegal for people to assist each other, or pay a tribute for doing so.

BUT the truth is, that the Government has already derived emoluments, and very extraordinary ones. It has already received its full share, by the services of the Bank during the war; and it is every day receiving benefits, because whatever promotes and facilitates commerce, serves likewise to promote and facilitate the revenue.

THE last article in this paragraph is "That the Bank is not the least dependent on the Government."

HAVE the Committee so soon forgot the principles of Republican Government and the Constitution, or are they so little acquainted with them, as not to know, that this article in their Report partakes of the nature of treason? Do they not know, that freedom is destroyed by dependance, and the safety of the State endangered thereby? Do they not see, that to hold any part of the citizens of the State, as yearly pensioners on the favor of an Assembly, is striking at the root of free elections? If other parts of their Report discover a want of knowledge on the subject of Banks, this shews a want of principle in the science of Government.

ONLY let us suppose this dangerous idea carried into practice, and then see what it leads to. If corporate Bodies are, after their incorporation, to be annually dependent on an Assembly for the continuance of their Charter, the citizens which compose those corporations, are not free. The Government holds an authority and influence over them, in a manner different from what it does over other citizens, and by this means destroys that equality of freedom, which is the bulwark of the Republic and the Constitution.

BY this scheme of Government any party, which happens to be uppermost in a State, will command all the corporations in it, and may create more for the purpose of extending that influence. The dependent Borough-Towns in England are the rotten part of their Government, and this idea of the Committee has a very near relation to it.

"IF you do not do so and so," expressing what was meant, "take care of your Charter," was a threat thrown out against the Bank. But as I do not wish to enlarge on a disagreeable circumstance, and hope that what is already said, is sufficient to shew the Anti-Constitutional conduct and principles of the Committee, I shall pass on to the next paragraph in the Report.——Which is——

"THAT the great profits of the Bank, which will daily encrease as money grows scarcer, and which already far exceed the profits of European Banks, have tempted foreigners to vest their money in this Bank, and thus to draw from us large sums for interest."

HAD the committee understood the subject, some dependance might be put on their opinion which now cannot. Whether money will grow scarcer, and whether the profits of the bank will increase, are more than the Committee know, or are judges sufficient to guess at. The Committee are not so capable of taking care of commerce, as commerce is capable of taking care of itself. The farmer understands farming, and the merchant understands commerce; and as riches are equally the object of both, there is no occasion that either should fear that the other will seek to be poor. The more money the merchant has, so much the better for the farmer, who has produce to sell: and the richer the farmer is, so much the better for the merchant, when he comes to his store.

As to the profits of the Bank, the stockholders must take their chance for it. It may some years be more and others less, and upon the whole may mot be so productive as many other ways that money may be employed. It is the convenience which the stockholders, as commercial men, derive from the establishment of the Bank, and not the mere interest they receive, that is the inducement to them. It is the ready opportunity of borrowing alternately of each other that forms the principal object: And as they pay as well as receive a great part of the interest among themselves, it is nearly the same thing, both cases considered at once, whether it is more or less.

THE stockholders are occasionally depositors and sometimes borrowers of the Bank. They pay interest for what they borrow, and receive none for what they deposit; and were a stockholder to keep a nice account of the interest he pays for the one and loses upon the other, he would find, at the year's end, that ten per cent upon his stock would probably not be more than common interest upon the whole, if so much.

As to the Committee complaining "that foreigners by vesting their money in the Bank will draw large sums from us for interest," it is like a miller complaining in a dry season, that so much water runs into his Dam that some of it runs over.

COULD those foreigners draw this interest without putting in any capital the complaint would be well founded; but as they must first put money in before they can draw any out, as they must draw many years before they can draw even the numerical sum they put in at first, the effect, for at least twenty years to come, will be directly contrary to what the Committee states: Because we draw *capitals* from them and they only *interest* from us, and as we shall have the use of the money all the while it remains with us, the advantage will always be in our favor.——In framing this part of the Report, the Committee must have forgot which side of the Atlantic they were on, for the case would be as they state it if we put money into their Bank instead of their putting it into ours.

I HAVE now gone thro', line by line, every objection against the Bank, contained in the first half of the Report; what follows may be called, *The Lamentations of the Committee,* and a lamentable pusillanimous degrading affair it is.—It is a public affront, a reflection upon the sense and spirit of the whole country. I shall give the remainder together as it stands in the Report, and then my remarks.

THE Lamentations are, "That foreigners will doubtless be more and more induced to become stockholders, until the time may arrive when this *enormous* engine of power may become subject to foreign influence, this country may be agitated by the politics of European Courts, and the good people of America reduced once more into a state of subordination and dependence upon some one or other of the European Powers. That at best, if it were even confined to the hands of Americans, it would be totally destructive of that equality which ought to prevail in a Republic. We have nothing in our free and equal Government capable of balancing the influence which this Bank must create; and we see nothing which in the course of a few years can prevent the Directors of the Bank from governing Pennsylvania. Already we have felt its influence indirectly interfering in the measures of the Legislature. Already the House of Assembly, the representatives of the people, have been threatened, that the credit of our paper currency will be blasted by the Bank; and if this growing evil continues, we fear the time is not very distant when the Bank will be able to dictate to the Legislature, what laws to pass and what to forbear."

WHEN the sky falls we shall all be killed. There is something so ridiculously grave, so wide of probability, and so wild, confused and inconsistent in the whole composition of this long paragraph, that I am at a loss how to begin upon it.——It is like a drowning man crying fire! fire!

THIS part of the Report is made up of two dreadful predictions. The first is, that if foreigners purchase Bank stock, we shall be all ruined:—The second is, that if the Americans keep the Bank to themselves we shall be also ruined.

A COMMITTEE of fortune-tellers is a novelty in Government; and the Gentlemen by giving this specimen of their art, have ingeniously saved their honor on one point, which is, that tho' the people may say they are not Bankers, nobody can say they are not Conjurors.—There is, however, one consolation left, which is, that the Committee do not know *exactly* how long it may be; so there is some hope that we may all be in heaven when this dreadful calamity happens upon earth.

BUT to be serious, if any seriousness is necessary on so laughable a subject.— If the state should think there is any thing improper in foreigners purchasing Bank stock, or any other kind of stock or funded property (for I see no reason why Bank stock should be particularly pointed at) the Legislature have authority to prohibit it. It is a mere political opinion that has nothing to do with the Charter or the Charter with that; and therefore the first dreadful prediction vanishes.

IT has always been a maxim in politics founded on, and drawn from, natural causes and consequences, that the more foreign countries which any nation can interest in the prosperity of its own so much the better. Where the treasure is there will the heart be also; and therefore when foreigners vest their money with us, they naturally invest their good wishes with it, and it is we that obtain an influence over them, not they over us.——But the Committee sat [sic] out so very wrong at first that the further they travelled the more they were out of their way; and now they have got to the end of their Report they are at the utmost distance from their business.

AS to the second dreadful part, that of the Bank overturning the Government, perhaps the Committee meant that at the next general election themselves might be turned out of it, which has partly been the case; not by the influence of the Bank, for it had none, not even enough to obtain the permission of a hearing from Government, but by the influence of reason and the choice of the people, who most probably resent the undue and unconstitutional influence which that House and Committee were assuming over the privileges of citizenship.

THE Committee might have been so modest as to have confined themselves to the Bank, and not thrown a general odium on the whole country. Before the events can happen which the Committee predict, the electors of Pennsylvania must become dupes, dunces and cowards, and therefore when the Committee predict the dominion of the Bank they predict the disgrace of the people.

THE Committee having finished their Report proceed to give their advice, which is,

"That a committee be appointed to bring in a bill to repeal the Act of Assembly passed the first day of April 1782, entitled, *"An Act to incorporate the subscribers to the Bank of North-America,"* and also to repeal one other Act of the Assembly passed the 18th of March 1782, entitled, *"An Act for preventing and punishing the counterfeiting of the common seal, Bank-bills, and Bank notes of the President, Directors and Company of the Bank of North-America, and for other purposes therein mentioned.""*

THERE is something in this sequel to the Report that is perplexed and obscure.

Here are two Acts to be repealed. One is, the incorporating Act.—The other, the Act for preventing and punishing the counterfeiting of the common seal, Bank bills, and Bank notes of the President, Directors and Company of the Bank of North-America.

IT would appear from the Committee's manner of arranging them, (were it not for the difference of their dates) that the Act for punishing the counterfeiting the common seal, &c. of the Bank, followed the Act of incorporation, and that the common seal there referred to is a common seal which the Bank held in consequence of the aforesaid incorporating Act.—But the case is quite otherwise. The Act for punishing the counterfeiting the common seal, &c. of the Bank, was passed prior to the incorporating Act, and refers to the common seal which the Bank held in consequence of the Charter of Congress, and the style which the Act expresses, of President, Directors and Company of the Bank of North-America, is the corporate stile which the Bank derives under the Congress Charter.

THE punishing act, therefore, hath two distinct legal points. The one is, an authoritative public recognition of the charter of congress. The second is, the punishment it inflicts on counterfeiting.

THE Legislature may repeal the punishing part but it cannot undo the recognition, because no repealing Act can say that the State *has not* recognized. The recognition is a mere matter of fact, and no law or Act can undo a fact or put it, if I may so express it, in the condition it was before it existed. The repealing Act therefore does not reach the full point the Committee had in view; for even admitting it to be a repeal of the State Charter, it still leaves another Charter recognized in its stead.—The Charter of Congress, standing merely on itself, would have a doubtful authority, but recognition of it by the State gives it legal ability. The repealing Act, it is true, sets aside the punishment but does not bar the operation of the Charter of Congress as a Charter recognized by the State, and therefore the Committee did their business but by halves.

I HAVE now gone entirely through the Report of the Committee, and a more irrational inconsistent contradictory Report will scarcely be found on the journals of any Legislature in America.

HOW the repealing Act is to be applied, or in what manner it is to operate, is a matter yet to be determined. For admitting a question of law to arise, whether the Charter, which that Act attempts to repeal, is a law of the land in the manner which laws of universal operation are, or of the nature of a contract made between the Public and the Bank (as I have already explained in this work) the repealing Act does not and cannot decide the question, because it is the repealing Act that makes the question, and its own fate is involved in the decision. It is a question of law and not a question of legislation, and must be decided on in a court of justice and not by a House of Assembly.

BUT the repealing Act, by being passed prior to the decision of this point assumes the power of deciding it, and the Assembly in so doing erects itself unconstitutionally into a tribunal of judicature, and absorbs the authority and right of the courts of justice into itself.

THEREFORE the operation of the repealing Act, in its very outset, requires injustice to be done. For it is impossible on the principles of a republican government and the Constitution, to pass an Act to forbid any of the citizens the right of appealing to the courts of justice on any matter in which his interest or property is affected; but the first operation of this Act goes to shut up the courts of justice, and holds them subservient to the Assembly. It either commands or influences them not to hear the case, or to give judgment on it on the mere will of one party only.

I WISH the citizens to awaken themselves on this subject.—Not because the Bank is concerned, but because their own constitutional rights and privileges are involved in the event. It is a question of exceeding great magnitude; for if an Assembly is to have this power the laws of the land and the courts of justice are but of little use.

HAVING now finished with the Report, I proceed to the third and last subject— that of Paper-Money.—

I REMEMBER a German farmer expressing as much in a few words as the whole subject requires: *"Money is Money and Paper is Paper."*——All the invention of man cannot make them otherwise. The alchymist may cease his labours, and the hunter after the philosopher's stone go to rest, if paper can be metamorphosed into gold and silver, or made to answer the same purpose in all cases.

GOLD and silver are the emissions of nature; paper is the emission of art. The value of gold and silver is ascertained by the quantity which nature has made in the earth. We cannot make that quantity more or less than it is, and therefore the value being dependent upon the quantity, depends not on man.——Man has no share in making gold or silver; all that his labours and ingenuity can accomplish is, to collect it from the mine, refine it for use and give it an impression, or stamp it into coin.

ITS being stamped into coin adds considerably to its convenience but nothing to its value. It has then no more value than it had before. Its value is not in the impression but in itself. Take away the impression and still the same value remains. Alter it as you will, or expose it to any misfortune that can happen, still the value is not diminished. It has a capacity to resist the accidents that destroy other things. It has, therefore, all the requisite qualities that money can have, and is a fit material to make money of; and nothing, which has not all those properties, can be fit for the purpose of money.

PAPER, considered as a material whereof to make money, has none of the requisite qualities in it. It is too plentiful, and too easily come at. It can be had any where, and for a trifle.

THERE are two ways in which I shall consider paper.

THE only proper use for paper, in the room of money, is to write promissory notes and obligations of payment in specie upon. A piece of paper, thus written and signed, is worth the sum it is given for, if the person who gives it is able to pay it; because, in this case, the law will oblige him. But if he is worth nothing, the paper-note is worth nothing. The value, therefore, of such a note, is not in the note itself, for that is but paper and promise, but in the man who is obliged to redeem it with gold or silver.

PAPER, circulating in this manner, and for this purpose, continually points to the place and person where, and of whom, the money is to be had, and at last finds its home; and, as it were, unlocks its master's chest and pays the bearer.

BUT when an Assembly undertake to issue paper *as* money, the whole system of safety and certainty is overturned, and property set afloat. Paper-notes given and taken between individuals as a promise of payment is one thing, but paper issued by an Assembly *as* money is another thing. It is like putting an apparition in the place of a man; it vanishes with looking at and nothing remains but the air.

MONEY, when considered as the fruit of many years industry, as the reward of labour, sweat and toil, as the widow's dowry and children's portion, and as the means of procuring the necessaries, and alleviating the afflictions of life, and making old age a scene of rest, has something in it sacred that is not to be sported with, or trusted to the airy bubble of paper-currency.

BY what power or authority an Assembly undertake to make paper-money is difficult to say. It derives none from the Constitution, for that is silent on the subject. It is one of those things which the people have not delegated, and which, were they at any time assembled together, they would not delegate. It is, therefore, an assumption of power which an assembly is not warranted in, and which may, one day or other, be the means of bringing some of them to punishment.

I SHALL enumerate some of the evils of paper-money, and conclude with offering means for preventing them.

ONE of the evils of paper-money is, that it turns the whole country into stock-jobbers. The precariousness of its value and the uncertainty of its fate continually operate, night and day, to produce this destructive effect. Having no real value in itself it depends for support upon accident, caprice and party, and as it is the interest of some to depreciate and of others to raise its value, there is a continual invention going on that destroys the morals of the country.

IT was horrid to see and hurtful to recollect how loose the principles of justice were let by means of the paper-emissions during the war. The experience then had should be a warning to any Assembly how they venture to open such a dangerous door again.

As to the romantic if not hypocritical tale, that a virtuous people need no gold and silver and that paper will do as well, [it] requires no other contradiction than the experience we have seen. Though some well-meaning people may be inclined to view it in this light, it is certain that the sharper always talks this language.

THERE are a set of men who go about making purchases upon credit, and buying estates they have not wherewithal to pay for; and having done this, their next step is to fill the news-papers with paragraphs of the scarcity of money and the necessity of a paper-emission, then to have it made a legal tender under the pretence of supporting its credit; and when out, to depreciate it as fast as they can, get a deal of it for a little price and cheat their creditors; and this is the concise history of Paper-money schemes.

BUT why, since the universal custom of the world has established money as the most convenient medium of traffic and commerce, should paper be set up in preference to gold and silver? The productions of nature are surely as innocent as those of art; and in the case of money, are abundantly, if not infinitely, more so. The love of gold and silver may produce covetousness, but covetousness, when not connected with dishonesty, is not properly a vice. It is frugality run to an extreme.

BUT the evils of paper-money have no end. Its uncertain and fluctuating value is continually awakening or creating new schemes of deceit. Every principle of justice is put to the rack and the bond of society dissolved: The suppression therefore of paper-money might very properly have been put into the Act for preventing Vice and Immorality.

THE pretence for paper-money has been, that there was not a sufficiency of gold and silver. This, so far from being a reason for paper-emissions, is a reason against them.

As gold and silver are not the productions of North-America, they are, therefore, articles of importation; and if we set up a paper-manufactory of money, it amounts, as far as it is able, to prevent the importation of Hard money, or to send it out again as fast as it comes in; and by following this practice we shall continually banish the specie, till we have none left, and be continually complaining of the grievance instead of remedying the cause.

CONSIDERING gold and silver as articles of importation, there will in time, unless we prevent it by paper-emissions, be as much in the country as the occasions of it require, for the same reasons there are as much of other imported articles. But as every yard of cloth manufactured in the country occasions a yard the less to be imported, so it is by money, with this difference, that in the one case we manufacture the thing itself and in the other we do not. We have cloth for cloth, but we have only paper-dollars for silver ones.

AS to the assumed authority of any Assembly in making paper-money, or paper of any kind, a legal tender, or in other language, a compulsive payment, it is a most presumptuous attempt at arbitrary power. There can be no such power in a Republican government: The people have no freedom, and property no security where this practice can be acted: And the Committee who shall bring in a report for this purpose, or the Member who moves for it, and he who seconds it merit impeachment, and sooner or later may expect it.

OF all the various sorts of base coin, paper-money is the basest. It has the least intrinsic value of any thing that can be put in the place of gold and silver. A hobnail or a piece of wampum far exceeds it. And there would be more propriety in making those articles a legal tender than to make paper so.

IT was the issuing base coin and establishing it as a tender, that was one of the principal means of finally overthrowing the power of the Stewart family in Ireland. The article is worth reciting as it bears such a resemblance to the process practised on paper money.

"Brass and copper of the basest kind, old cannon, broken bells, household utensils were assiduously collected; and from every pound weight of such vile materials, valued at four-pence, pieces were coined and circulated to the amount of five pounds nominal value. By the first proclamation they were made current in all payments to and from the King and the subjects of the realm, except in duties on the importation of foreign goods, money left in trust, or due by mortgage, bills or bonds; and *James* promised that when the money should be decried, he would receive it in all payments or make full satisfaction in gold and silver. The nominal value was afterwards raised by subsequent proclamations, the original restrictions removed, and this base money was ordered to be received in all kinds of payments. As brass and copper grew scarce it was made of still viler materials, of tin and pewter, and old debts of one thousand pounds were discharged by pieces of vile metal, amounting to thirty shillings in intrinsic value."‡ —Had King James thought of paper he needed not to have been at the trouble or expence of collecting brass and copper, broken bells and household utensils.[2]

THE laws of a country ought to be the standard of equity, and calculated to impress on the minds of the people the moral as well as the legal obligation of reciprocal justice. But tender-laws, of any kind, operate to destroy morality, and to dissolve by the pretence of law what ought to be the principle of law to support, reciprocal justice between man and man: And the punishment of a member who should move for such a law ought to be DEATH.

WHEN the recommendation of Congress in the year 1780 for repealing the tender-laws was before the Assembly of Pennsylvania, on casting up the votes, for and against bringing in a bill to repeal those laws, the numbers were equal, and

---

‡ Leland's history of Ireland, vol. iv. Page 265. [See Thomas Leland, *The History of Ireland from the Invasion of Henry II*, 3 vols (London: Nourse, Langman, Robinson, & Johnson, 1773).]
[2] Paine is here alluding to the mixed metal coinage struck in Ireland 1689-1691 by the former King James II to finance his abortive military campaign to regain the British throne from William III. The first issue included metal derived from melted cannons and was hence known as 'gun money'. When supplies of copper and brass ran out he used soft white metal. These latter issues were known in Irish as 'uim bog', meaning 'soft copper' or 'worthless coin' and gave the English language the term 'humbug'. The loss of Stuart power in Ireland is more usually attributed to the military success of William III and James's abandonment of Ireland after his defeat at the Battle of the Boyne in July 1690. See C. R. Jossett, *Money in Great Britain and Ireland*, (Newton Abbott, Devon: David & Charles, 1971), pp. 137-38. On Irish coinage see Peter Seaby, *Coins and Tokens of Ireland*, (London: Seaby, 1970) & S. J. Connolly, *The Oxford Companion to Irish History*, (Oxford: Oxford University Press, 1998), p. 589.

the casting vote rested on the Speaker, Colonel Bayard. "I give my vote" said he, "for the repeal, from a consciousness of justice; the tender-laws operate to establish iniquity by law."—But when the Bill was brought in, the House rejected it, and the tender-laws continued to be the means of fraud.

IF any thing had, or could have, a value equal to gold and silver it would require no tender-law: and if it had not that value it ought not to have such a law; and, therefore, all tender-laws are tyrannical and unjust, and calculated to support fraud and oppression.

MOST of the advocates for tender-laws are those who have debts to discharge, and who take refuge in such a law, to violate their contracts and cheat their creditors. But as no law can warrant the doing an unlawful act, therefore, the proper mode of proceeding, should any such laws be enacted in future, will be to impeach and execute the Members who moved for and seconded such a Bill, and put the debtor and the creditor in the same situation they were in, with respect to each other, before such a law was passed. Men ought to be made to tremble at the idea of such a barefaced act of injustice. It is in vain to talk of restoring credit, or complain that money cannot be borrowed at legal interest, until every idea of tender-laws is totally and publicly reprobated and extirpated from among us.

AS to paper-money, in any light it can be viewed, it is at best a bubble. Considered as property it is inconsistent to suppose that the breath of an Assembly, whose authority expires with the year, can give to paper the value and duration of gold. They cannot even engage that the next Assembly shall receive it in taxes. And by the precedent (for authority there is none) that one Assembly makes paper-money, another may do the same, until confidence and credit are totally expelled, and all the evils of depreciation acted over again. The amount, therefore, of Paper-Money is this, That it is the illegitimate offspring of Assemblies, and when their year expires they leave it a vagrant on the hands of the Public.

HAVING now gone thro' the three subjects proposed in the title to this work, I shall conclude with offering some thoughts on the present affairs of the State.

MY idea of a single Legislature was always founded on a hope, that whatever personal parties there might be in the State they would all unite and agree in the general principles of good government—that these party differences would be dropt at the threshold of the state-house, and that the Public Good or the good of the whole, would be the governing principle of the Legislature within it.

PARTY dispute, taken on this ground, would only be, who should have the honor of making the laws; not what the laws should be. But when party operates to produce party laws, a single House is a single person, and subject to the haste, rashness and passion of individual sovereignty. At least, it is an aristocracy.

THE form of the present Constitution is now made to trample on its principles, and the constitutional Members are anti-constitutional Legislators. They are fond of supporting the form for the sake of the power, and they dethrone the principle to display the sceptre.

THE attack of the late Assembly on the Bank discovers such a want of moderation and prudence, of impartiality and equity, of fair and candid enquiry and investigation, of deliberate and unbiassed judgment, and such a rashness of thinking and vengeance of power as is inconsistent with the safety of the Republic. It was judging without hearing and execution without trial.

BY such rash, injudicious and violent proceedings the interest of the State is weakened, its prosperity diminished and its commerce and its specie banished to other places.—Suppose the Bank had not been in an immediate condition to have stood such a sudden attack, what a scene of instant distress would the rashness of that Assembly have brought upon this city and State. The holders of Bank-notes, whoever they might be, would have been thrown into the utmost confusion and difficulties. It is no apology to say the House never thought of this, for it was their duty to have thought of every thing.

BUT by the prudent and provident management of the Bank, (tho' unsuspicious of the attack) it was enabled to stand the run upon it without stopping payment a moment, and to prevent the evils and mischiefs taking place which the rashness of the Assembly had a direct tendency to bring on; a trial that scarcely a Bank in Europe, under a similar circumstance, could have stood through.

I CANNOT see reason sufficient to believe that the hope of the House to put down the Bank was placed on the withdrawing the Charter, so much as on the expectation of producing a bankruptcy on the Bank, by starting a run upon it. If this was any part of their project it was a very wicked one, because hundreds might have been ruined to gratify a party-spleen.

BUT this not being the case, what has the attack amounted to, but to expose the weakness, and rashness, the want of judgment as well as justice, of those who made it, and to confirm the credit of the Bank more substantially than it was before.

THE attack, it is true, has had one effect, which is not in the power of the Assembly to remedy, it has banished many thousand hard dollars from the state.—By the means of the Bank, Pennsylvania had the use of a great deal of hard money belonging to citizens of other States, and that without any interest, for it laid here in the nature of deposit, the depositors taking Bank notes in its stead. But the alarm called those notes in and the owners drew out their cash.

THE banishing the specie served to make room for the paper-money of the Assembly, and we have now paper dollars where we might have had silver ones. So that the effect of the paper-money has been to make less money in the state than there was before. Paper-money is like dram-drinking, it relieves for a moment by deceitful sensation, but gradually diminishes the natural heat, and leaves the body worse than it found it. Were not this the case, and could money be made of paper at pleasure, every Sovereign in Europe would be as rich as he pleased. But the truth is, that it is a bubble and the attempt vanity. Nature has provided the proper materials for money, gold and silver, and any attempt of ours to rival her is ridiculous.

BUT to conclude——If the Public will permit the opinion of a friend who is attached to no party, and under obligation to none, nor at variance with any, and who through a long habit of acquaintance with them has never deceived them, that opinion shall be freely given.

THE Bank is an Institution capable of being made exceedingly beneficial to the State, not only as the means of extending and facilitating its commerce, but as a means of increasing the quantity of hard money in the State. The Assembly's paper-money serves directly to banish or croud out the hard, because it is issued *as* money and put in the place of hard money. But Bank-notes are of a very different kind, and produce a contrary effect. They are promissory notes payable on demand, and may be taken to the Bank and exchanged for gold or silver without the least ceremony or difficulty.

THE Bank, therefore, is obliged to keep a constant stock of hard money sufficient for this purpose; which is what the Assembly neither does, nor can do by their paper; because the quantity of hard money collected by taxes into the Treasury is trifling compared with the quantity that circulates in trade and through the Bank.

THE method, therefore, to increase the quantity of hard money would be to combine the security of the Government and the Bank into one. And instead of issuing paper-money that serves to banish the specie, to borrow the sum wanted of the Bank in Bank-notes on the condition of the Bank exchanging those notes at stated periods and quantities with hard money.

PAPER issued in this manner, and directed to this end, would, instead of banishing, work itself into, gold and silver; because it will then be both the advantage and duty of the Bank, and of all the mercantile interests connected with it, to procure and import gold and silver from any part of the world it can be got, to exchange the notes with. The English Bank is restricted to the dealing in no other articles of importation than gold and silver, and we may make the same use of our Bank if we proceed properly with it.

THOSE notes will then have a double security, that of the Government and that of the Bank; and they will not be issued *as* money, but as hostages to be exchanged for hard money, and will, therefore, work the contrary way to what the paper of the Assembly, uncombined with the security of the Bank, produces: And the interest allowed the Bank will be saved to Government by a saving of the expences and charges attending paper-emissions.

IT is, as I have already observed in the course of this work, the harmony of all the parts of a Republic, that constitutes their several and mutual good.   A Government, that is constructed only to govern, is not a Republican Government. It is combining authority with usefulness that in a great measure distinguishes the Republican system from others.

PAPER-MONEY appears, at first sight, to be a great saving, or rather that it costs nothing; but it is the dearest money there is. The ease with which it is emitted by an Assembly at first, serves as a trap to catch people in at last. It operates as an anticipation of the next year's taxes. If the money depreciates, after it is out, it then, as I have already remarked, has the effect of fluctuating stock, and the people become stock-jobbers to throw the loss on each other.—If it does not depreciate, it is then to be sunk by taxes at the price of *hard money;* because the same quantity of produce, or goods, that would procure a paper-dollar to pay taxes with would procure a silver one for the same purpose. Therefore in any case of paper-money it is dearer to the country than hard money by all the expence which the paper, printing, signing and other attendant charges come to, and at last goes into the fire.

SUPPOSE one hundred thousand dollars in paper-money to be emitted every year by the Assembly, and the same sum to be sunk every year by taxes, there will then be no more than one hundred thousand dollars out at any one time. If the expence of paper and printing, and of persons to attend the press while the sheets are striking off, signers, &c. be five per cent. it is evident that in the course of twenty years emissions, the one hundred thousand dollars will cost the country two hundred thousand dollars. Because the papermaker's and printer's bills, and the expence of supervisors and signers, and other attendant charges, will in that time amount to as much as the money amounts to; for the successive emissions are but a recoinage of the same sum.

BUT gold and silver require to be coined but once, and will last an hundred years, better than paper will one year, and at the end of that time be still gold and silver. Therefore the saving to Government, in combining its aid and security with that of the Bank in procuring hard money, will be an advantage to both, and to the whole community.

THE case to be provided against, after this, will be, that the Government do not borrow too much of the Bank, nor the Bank lend more notes than it can redeem; and, therefore, should any thing of this kind be undertaken, the best way will be to begin with a moderate sum, and observe the effect of it. The interest given the Bank operates as a bounty on the importation of hard money, and which may not be more than the money expended in making paper-emissions.

BUT nothing of this kind, nor any other public undertaking, that requires security and duration beyond the year, can be gone upon under the present mode of conducting Government. The late Assembly, by assuming a sovereign power over every Act and matter done by the State in former Assemblies, and thereby setting up a precedent of overhauling and overturning, as the accident of elections shall happen or party prevail, have rendered Government incompetent to all the great objects of the State. They have eventually reduced the Public to an annual body like themselves; whereas the Public are a standing permanent body, holding annual elections.

THERE are several great improvements and undertakings, such as inland navigation, building bridges, opening roads of communication thro' the state, and other matters of a public benefit, that might be gone upon, but which now cannot, until this governmental error or defect is remedied. The faith of Government, under the present mode of conducting it, cannot be relied on. Individuals will not venture their money, in undertakings of this kind, on an Act that may be made by one Assembly and broken by another. When a man can say that he cannot trust the Government, the importance and dignity of the Public is diminished, sapped and undermined; and, therefore, it becomes the Public to restore their own honor, by setting these matters to rights.

PERHAPS this cannot be effectually done until the time of the next Convention, when the principles, on which they are to be regulated and fixed, may be made a part of the Constitution.

IN the mean time the Public may keep their affairs in sufficient good order, by substituting prudence in the place of authority, and electing men into the Government, who will at once throw aside the narrow prejudices of party, and make the Good of the Whole the ruling object of their conduct.——And with this hope, and a sincere wish for their prosperity, I close my book.

Pennsylvania Packet, 25 March 1786.

For the PENNSYLVANIA PACKET and DAILY ADVERTISER

As I have always considered the bank as one of the best institutions that could be devised to promote the commerce and agriculture of the country, and recover it from the ruined condition in which the war had left both the farmer and the merchant, as well as the most effectual means to banish usury and establish credit among the citizens, I have always been a friend to it.

When the opposition to the bank first began last year, there were many people inclined to think that it arose from no other motives than those of party prejudice and ignorance of the business: But there were others who hesitated not to say that a large majority of the late assembly had formed their plan for carrying their funding bill, and were speculating on the purchase and sale of certificates, and determined to destroy every thing which they supposed might not unite with that scheme.

Which of these suppositions are best founded, or whether both of them are not too true, will be sufficiently known before the next election. One thing, however, is already proved, which is, that the late assembly have created one of the greatest fields of speculation ever known in Pennsylvania. The funding acts produce an interest, in many cases, of between twenty and thirty per cent. and the country is loaded with taxes to pay the speculations. In the mean time the opposition to the bank is kept up to amuse the people.

COMMON SENSE.

Pennsylvania Packet, 28 March 1786.

For the PENNSYLVANIA PACKET and DAILY ADVERTISER

THE bubble of Silas Deane and the bubble of the opposition to the bank have several circumstances in them that are alike. As an honest friend to the public I set myself to detect the one, and with the same motives of sincerity I shall pursue the other.

The leaders of this opposition having undertaken what they did not understand, are endeavouring to strengthen themselves by making it a party matter between the constitutionalists and the republicans. They find themselves losing ground and now seek to shelter their misconduct and mismanagement under this resource.

The bank as a national question has nothing to do with party.—As a means of encreasing the commerce and promoting the agriculture and prosperity of the country it is supported by numbers of the constitutionalists as well as republicans.

It would be a very poor excuse for a representative of Bucks or Berks, or any of the counties whose property depends on the ready sale and exportation of its produce, to tell their constituents, that though the attack on the bank last year had operated to reduce the market for their produce, and retard the exportation of it, yet the loss must be submitted to, for it was a party matter. A man in office may live by his party, or a man in power, and fond of displaying it, may make some sacrifices to preserve it.—But what is this to the farmer; he must live by his labour and the produce of his farm.

Nothing is more certain than that if the bank was destroyed, the market for country produce would be monopolized by a few monied men, who would command the price as they pleased. And it is a matter much to the honor of some merchants in the city, who by their fortunes could engross the trade to themselves that they support the bank as a public benefit to the commerce of the state.

Were there no other use of a bank than that of affording a safe convenient place where people who have spare cash by them which they do not immediately want, may lodge it until they had occasion for it; this alone, I say, were there no other use in a bank is a material advantage to the community, because it keeps the money in use and circulation that would otherwise be locked up.—There are in this city nearly six hundred people who constantly send their spare cash to the bank in this manner. They receive no interest for it, and in the mean time the country has the use of the money. Take away the bank and this money returns into the chests and coffers of its owners, where it lies locked up in death and darkness, and is, in the mean time, of no more use to the community than if it was in the mine.

If there are any who suppose that I have engaged myself in this business merely on account of the bank, I wish they would state their reasons. I am ready to satisfy any man either publicly or privately on this, or any other circumstance relating to my conduct therein. I know how and where the opposition began, and the manner it has been conducted, even to the writing of the report of the committee of the late house of assembly. And the persons concerned in this opposition have for ten years past known me too well even to believe that I am governed by self-interested motives.

COMMON SENSE

Pennsylvania Packet, 4 April 1786.

TO THE PRINTER

As the Press ought to be as sacred to liberty, as the privilege of Speech is to the Members of Assembly in debate, you will please to insert the following in your paper.

THOMAS PAINE.

IN the Pennsylvania Packet of last Tuesday is a publication signed *Common Sense* which begins in the following manner.

'The bubble of Silas Deane, and the bubble of the opposition against the bank, have several circumstances in them that are alike. As an honest friend to the public I set myself to detect the one, and with the same motives of sincerity I shall pursue the other.'

The concluding paragraph in that publication is, 'If there are any who suppose that I have engaged myself in this business merely on account of the bank, I wish them to state their reasons. I am ready to satisfy any man either publicly or privately on this or any other circumstance relating to my conduct therein. I know how and where the opposition began, and the manner it has been conducted, even to the writing the report of the committee of the late house of assembly. And the persons concerned in this opposition, have for ten years past known me too well to believe that I am governed by self-interested motives.'

Here is a fair and open opportunity given to any man either to charge me with it, or inform himself respecting it.

The pamphlet on the affair of the bank, under the signature of *Common Sense*, was published on the first day of the meeting of the present setting of the house, nearly six weeks ago. If the arguments used in that pamphlet in support of a public bank as beneficial to the state could have been refuted, or the facts or matters stated therein contradicted, it ought to have been done. It is a public question, a subject that concerns the interest of every man in the state, and any lights that could have been thrown thereon, either by those who were for, or those who were against such an institution, would have been acceptable to the public. No subject of debate that has been agitated before the legislature of Pennsylvania ever drew together such crouded audiences as attended the house during the four days the debate lasted. And it was very easy to discover from the countenance of the people that the debate has illuminated their minds, though it has been lost upon the opposing party in the house.

But instead of answering the pamphlet, or instead of making the charge I publicly invited, or obtaining the information I offered, the member from Fayette county, who can be at no loss to know my suspicions of his integrity on this business, which I shall in my subsequent publication lay before the public, gets up in his place, impertinently introduces the pamphlet to the house, and calls the writer of it "an unprincipled author whose pen is let out for hire."

Respect to the representative body of a free people, however wrong some of them, in my opinion, may be on this subject; the decency proper to be observed in such a place, and on such an occasion, and the manners due to a numerous and respectable audience, restrained me to silence, or I should have been justified in rising and contradicting him by the most plain and unequivocal word the English language can express.

I appeal to the honor, the feelings of any person, let his opinion respecting the institution of a bank be what it may, whether there can be a greater influence of meanness, and depravity, or a greater prostitution of legislative privilege, than, for a man, sheltered under the sanctioned authority of a representative, and speaking in his place, to make use of that opportunity to abuse private characters: for though the name was not mentioned, the person alluded to was sufficiently understood.

A perfect unlimited freedom of speech must be allowed in legislative debates; and that liberty includes every other the tongue is capable of, if a man is base enough to use it. Had he charged an individual with breaking open a house, or robbing on the highway, or had he declared that the circumstances of any private man were on the point of bankruptcy and thereby ruined his credit and his family, he might be called to order by the speaker or any of the members, but this is all. The privilege of the house protects him. There is no law can lay hold of him. This, then, being the situation of a member, restrained by no checks but the sense of honor and the force of principle, none who esteemed his own character would exceed the bounds.

From conduct like this the opposition to the bank can derive no reputation; and the suspicion will naturally spread, that where such methods are used something bad must be at the bottom. But if Mr. Smilie chose to make such an attack, why did he not do it in the first day's debate, I could then have answered him as I now do, the next day, or if he made it on the second day, I could have answered him on the third, or if on the third I could have answered him on the last day: but be reserved himself till just before the vote was taken, and when it could not be contradicted, for reasons too obvious to be mentioned.

In the debate of Friday evening a member from the city mentioned one of the causes of the opposition to the bank, and connected it with an allusion which, probably related to Mr. Smilie. As I am acquainted with the circumstance, I shall lay it before the public, and they will then judge of Mr. Smilie's political honesty in this business, and have a better insight into the opposition than they have yet had.

Last year the vote for taking away the charter of the bank was upwards of 50 to 12. The vote last Saturday for restoring it with an additional clause, was 30 to 39. Mr. Clymer, though strongly in support of the bank, voted against it in this question, because he was against the additional clause. If his vote had been for it, the numbers would have stood 31 to 38—consequently four more votes would have re-established the bank, and restored its full usefulness again to the country.

In the present house are twenty-four members who were members of the late house, and who voted for taking away the charter; yet with this number of clogged votes, the question for re-establishing had nearly been carried. On the question for restoring the charter, without the additional clause, the majority against it was thirteen.

By this state of the business in the house, and the great change of sentiment that is spreading through both the city and country, it is visible, that the people are recovering from the delusion and bubble of the last year.

COMMON SENSE.

Philadelphia, April 3.

Pennsylvania Packet, 7 April 1786.

To the PRINTERS.

As the Press ought to be as Sacred to Liberty, as the privilege of Speech is to the Members of Assembly in debate, you will please to insert the following in your paper.

THOMAS PAINE.

As I intend to begin and continue a series of publications on the usefulness of a public bank, to the trade, commerce and agriculture of the state, and as it is proper that a man's motives on public affairs should be known, I shall, in this publication endeavour, as concisely as I can, to bring into one view, such parts of my own conduct, as relates thereto. — In doing this, certain parts of Mr. Smilie's conduct will necessarily make their appearance.

As to the improper use which that member made of the privilege of speech in the house, of stiling me an unprincipled author, he is welcome to it, and I give him my consent to repeat it as often as he pleases and where ever he chuses. I shall make a few remarks on this part of the subject, and then proceed to more material matter.

While those members of the house who stile themselves constitutionalists, as well as those who act as the leaders of that party, appeared to me to pursue right measures and proceed on right principles, they had what assistance it was in my power to give them.

In the winter of 1778, a very strong opposition was made to the *form* of the constitution. As the constitution was then on an experiment, and the enemy in full force in the country, the opposition was injudicious. To this may be added another reason, which is, that the constitution, by having only a single house, was the best calculated form of civil government that could be devised for carrying on the war; because the simplicity of its structure admitted of dispatch, and dispensed with deliberation. But that which was then its blessing is now its curse. Things are done too rashly.

As the opposition was becoming formidable, the persons then in office and power, or those who hoped or expected to be so, became somewhat seriously alarmed, and they applied very solicitously to me to help them. I did so, and the service was gratis; and so has been every other which they have had from me, from that day to the present hour; and they might still have had it, and on the same terms, had they pursued just and wise measures of government, and an honest system of politics.—The service here alluded to is in a number of publications, entitled "A Serious Address to the People of Pennsylvania on the Present State of their Affairs." Before the appearance of those publications, the newspapers were filled with pieces in opposition to the constitution; none appeared afterwards, it is therefore reasonable to conclude they had some effect.— The constitutionalists got full possession of the government—they enjoyed their places and offices, and here the matter ended.

When the war ceased, there were those of all parties, as well of this state as of other states, who thought it unreasonable, as well as dishonorable to the country, to suffer the service of a man who had been a volunteer in its cause for so many years, to pass off unacknowledged. The principal mover in this business was the commander in chief. The state of New-York (being the place where the war ended) made the first step, and I mention it with a just sense of the generosity and gentility of their conduct.

The last time general Washington was in Philadelphia, he engaged the late president, Mr. Dickinson, to move the same matter in this state, which engagement that gentleman very honorably and friendly fulfilled, and the supreme executive council unanimously concurred with him in recommending it to the consideration of the assembly.[1]

---

[1] John Dickenson (1732-1808) was president of Pennsylvania from 1782 to 1785.

In this manner it came before the house, and at a time when those who *stile* themselves constitutionalists (for they are not so in principle) were by a turn of elections reinstated in the power they had lost for two or three years before. I mean the late house of assembly.

The matter respecting myself, on the recommendation of council, was before them at the very time they began their attack on the bank. It is therefore inconsistent, and even absurd, to suppose, that I could have any self-interested motives in opposing that attack, when they were on the point of deciding on a matter that immediately concerned my interest. Therefore my opposition to their politics at that critical time must be placed to other motives.

The recommendation of council respecting me was, in one of the stages of it, bro[ugh]t on in the house, a short time before the attack on the bank broke out. I shall place Mr. Smilie's declaration in the house at that time, against what he said in the same house a few days ago, and the event will probably be, that people will believe neither what he then said, nor what he now says.

Mr. Smilie then said, that "excepting general Washington, there was not a more disinterested patriot in America, than Mr. Paine," he now says, that "Mr. Paine is an unprincipled author, whose pen is let out for hire."—Thus you see my trumpeter can blow all sorts of tunes. And I am very sorry that such a high encomium as he has given me should stand upon such loose authority as himself. But the "balance" in this case is, that what I suffer by his praise, is made up to me by his censure.[†]

But to return to my point.—As it could not be interest that induced me to oppose their attack on the bank at the time here alluded to, it is proper I should declare what the motive was.

It was friendship to them. I saw very clearly they were going to destroy themselves by a rash, mad, unjust, tyrannical proceeding, and that they might not,

---

[†] Mr. Smilie, who loves to talk about what he does not understand, is always exposing his want of knowledge, in haranguing about the balance of trade.

I endeavoured in the most pressing and friendly manner to remonstrate with them, to point out the consequence, and caution them against it.

For this purpose, and with this design, I had repeated conversations with Mr. Smilie on the subject, as he appeared to make himself one of the most violent in the business. Not a soul belonging to the bank, or that had the least connection with it, or any other person, knew what I was then doing.—For as it was from motives of friendship that I then spoke, I kept it to myself, and it went no further that from me to them.

But Mr. Smilie is not the only one that I urged the same matters to. And I will here take the liberty (I hope I shall be pardoned in it) in mentioning the name of a gentlemen whose friendship and acquaintance I have always esteemed and wish to preserve—Colonel J. D. Smith.

As I knew he had a general acquaintance with the persons concerned in the opposition, there was scarcely a day passed, while the matter was before the house last year, that I did not go to him, and in the strongest and sincerest terms I could use, endeavour to impress him with the danger his friends were running into. That they would ruin the whole interest of the constitutional party by it. That the proceeding was so arbitrary and unjust, so despotic and tyrannical, that no body of men who went on such grounds, could support themselves or be supported in it. That the event would not only be the total overthrow of the constitutional party in the state, among whom were many that I sincerely esteemed, but that it would overset the constitution: because it could not fail to create an apprehension which would grow into a belief, that a single legislature, by having it in its power to act with such instant rashness, and without restrained, was a form of government that might be as dangerous to liberty, as a single person.

I expressed many of the same arguments to the then speaker, and it always appeared to me, from their manner of conversation on the subject, that there was something in the conduct and principles of the late house they did not approve, and strongly implied a wish that the matter had not been so rashly gone into.

But it is the fate of friendship, that where it is not accepted it is sure to offend. I do not apply this to the two last mentioned gentlemen; I should be unjust to them if I did. The matter, however, respecting myself in the house, went heavily on, after my sentiments on the attack on the bank were known. The acknowledgment the house made to me was not equal to the money I had relinquished to the state, exclusive of the service. The acknowledgment was connected with a proposition to renew the matter at a future day, and in this manner it now stands before the present house, there being at this time a committee on the business. Therefore I can have no interest in acting as I now do in opposition to a majority of the house, and it must be equally as clear that I am acting disinterestedly.

As the bill for abolishing the charter of the bank lay over till the last meeting of the late house, there was a probability the house would see its error, and reject what it had so rashly began. I therefore published nothing on the subject, during that time.

On my return to Philadelphia, in the winter, I found that experience had, in some measure, effected what reason and the right of things could not. Many who had been clamorous against the bank began to question the legality of the measure, and to apprehend ill effects from it.

The stockholders of the bank resolved to commence a suit; but the wound given to the faith of the state, together with the arbitrary principles on which the late house acted, were matters that concerned the people. They therefore brought *their* complaints before the present house from different parts of the state by memorial. Those memorials exhibit a charge of delinquency against the late house and call on the present house to redress the injury by undoing an unjust act. This is the ground the memorials go on. But it happens in this case that the matter of right is interwoven with a matter of interest. All the settled parts of Pennsylvania which carry on trade with the city and draw from thence returns of money by the sale of their produce, felt their interest hurt as well as their rights invaded. The attack on the bank operated as an attack on their pockets as well as on their principles. The city felt the same injury, and therefore they joined from a twofold motive in a demand of justice.

All this while the originating moving cause of the opposition to the bank remained a secret. Clamor filled the place of reason and argument. Influence, monopoly and danger, were held out to the people, and the mis-led multitude caught the bait.

But notwithstanding all this cry of influence, this clamour of monopoly, it is influence and monopoly that have produced the attack on the bank. There are certain men in Philadelphia, whether friends or otherwise to the revolution matters not, *they are monied men*. These men view a public bank as standing in the way of their private interest. Their wealth is not of so much value to them as it would be if the bank was demolished, and therefore they say *down with the bank*. To accomplish this point, so agreeable to their wishes, and advantageous to their wealth, they have been working through the ignorance of the late house in matters of commerce, and the nature of banks, and on the prejudices of others as leaders of that party, to demolish the bank. It might be error in the former, but it is wilful mischief in the latter; and as mischief is not lessened by the apology of error, nor encreased by the criminality of design, therefore those who sacrificed to duplicity, or those who sacrificed to prejudice, are, as to matters of public trust, alike the objects of public reprobation.

As one of the gentleman who oppose the bank, as standing in the way of his private interest, has not made any great secret of his reasons, there can be no impropriety in making him and his reasons public.

The gentleman I here mean is Mr. George Emlen.[2] However worthy or respectable a man may be in private life, yet when he from self-interested motives privately opposes a public institution, or get[s] others to do it, because it puts the credit of an honest, industrious tradesman, just and punctual in his dealings,

---

[2] See above p. 338.

though not so rich as himself, on a level with his wealth, it is but fair those reasons should be public.

The reasons Mr. Emlen has given for not signing the memorial lately presented to the house, and for his opposition to the bank, are, "that while the bank stands a monied man has no chance—that his money is not so valuable to him now as it would be then—that if the bank was demolished he could buy country produce for exportation cheaper."— If these are just reasons for demolishing the bank, let it be demolished—if they are popular reasons let them have their effect. But at any rate let them be known that they may be judged of.

These being Mr. Emlen's reasons for demolishing the bank, can any thing be more inconsistent and suspicious than that the members of assembly who have, all this while, been holding out to their country constituents that the bank is injurious to the former and the middling sort of people, can, I say, any thing be more inconsistent than to see men of such contrary declarations acting in concert to destroy the bank.

This is the age of negociation, compromise and coalition: but here is one that for wisdom or folly, exceeds them all. The coalition of lord North and Charles Fox is innocent childishness compared to this. How powerfully must Mr. Emlen's reason operate on the *worthy* loquacious member from Fayette county. How strong must be his conviction that the bank is injurious to the farmer, when Mr. Emlen assures him that were it not for the bank he could buy the farmer's produce for less money.

When I found that this coalition had taken place, and that Mr. Emlen was the friend of Mr. Smilie, and Mr. Smilie of Mr. Emlen, and that the entertainment of his table was open to the opposing members to the bank, I could not but be struck at the strangeness of the connection, and that Mr. Smilie might not be ignorant that he was made a dupe of, or subject himself to worse suspicions, I informed a friend of his, Dr. Hutchinson, of it, and desired him to communicate Mr. Emlen's reasons for opposing the bank to Mr. Smilie. This is at least three weeks ago.[3]

Having now stated to the public the circumstance I alluded to in my former piece, I shall reserve the continuation of the subject to a future paper.

Philadelphia, April 6.   COMMON SENS

---

[3] Dr. James Hutchinson (1752-93), a prominent physician and educator.

Pennsylvania Packet, 20 April 1786.

To the PUBLIC

NUMBER III

AS the debates and proceedings of the Assembly, on the report of the committee (to whom were referred the memorials of a very large and respectable number of freemen, in divers parts of the state, in behalf of the injured honor of the fame, and complaining of the improper, unconstitutional and faithless conduct of the late house, in their proceedings respecting the Bank of North-America) are advertized to be published in a pamphlet, by the person who usually attends the Assembly for the purpose of taking down debates, and as those debates, if correctly taken, will serve to set forth the unjust and arbitrary proceedings of the late house, and to shew the exceeding usefulness of a public Bank to the landed and commercial interest of the state, I shall, (after the present number) discontinue the remarks I have to offer on the subject, until those debates are in the hands of the public.

Having thus mentioned my intention, I shall confine my present remarks to such matters as more immediately relate to those debates.——Whoever will take a review of them, cannot but perceive that the speakers in opposition to the Bank are those, who from their remote situation feel themselves very little, if at all, interested in the prosperity of the more settled and improved parts of the state. Their ideas of government, agriculture and commerce, are drawn from and limited to their own frontier habitations; and their politics seem calculated to suit their particular situations, at the expence and detriment of the rest. By attempting this, they injure themselves and the event in this instance, as in all others of narrow and contracted politics, will turn out to their own disadvantage.

If those persons could not perceive that a Bank was beneficial to the landed interest, it must be—either because they have yet no produce to sell or export, or because they have no commercial intercourse with the market where the Bank is established at. But even in this case their policy is ill calculated, and badly applied.

The time will come, when they *will have* produce for sale and exportation, and consequently will then want a market and a ready means of turning it into cash; and whether that produce is brought to Philadelphia market or goes to Baltimore, the consequences to themselves will be nearly the same. The quick intercourse of commercial intelligence that passes between the two markets of Philadelphia and Baltimore, immediately operates to regulate the price of the one by the other; and whenever it falls here, from whatever cause it may be, it falls there.

There are two stages or degrees into which the landed interest in Pennsylvania progressively divides itself, viz. settlers and farmers. And as a man's ideas are generally produced in him by his present situation and condition, it will naturally follow, that if you investigate his situation you will get into the channel his thoughts run in, and find out their source, direction and extent.

The frontier parts of the state are called settlements, and the improved parts farms. A settler is not yet a farmer; he is only in the way of being so. In the stage of a settler, his thoughts are engrossed and taken up in making a settlement. If he can raise produce enough for the support of his family, it is the utmost of his present hopes. He has none to bring to market, or to sell, and therefore commerce appears nothing to him; and he cries out, that a Bank is of no use. But the case is, he is not yet in a condition to participate of its usefulness. When he is, he will think otherwise.

But the improved parts of the state, having undergone the hardship and labour attending the making new settlements, are now become farms, and the occupiers of them are farmers. The others, as I have before observed, are yet but settlements, and many of them only laid out to be such, and the occupiers of them are settlers. Therefore, when a back county member says that the Bank is of no use to the farmer, he means the settler, who has yet no produce to sell, and knows nothing about the matter. Of the twenty-eight who voted for restoring the Charter of the Bank, twenty-five are country members. Those gentlemen, by residing in the improved parts of the state, from whence the staple commodities of the country are brought, are certainly better judges of the usefulness of a public Bank, than those, who, from their distance, have no commercial intercourse with the market, and never visit it but when they are sent as representatives.

As to paper money, which so frequently occurs in the speeches of the back county members, I will, in a few words, explain their motive and meaning for it.

Not one of them will take it when it is made; but all of them will borrow it of the public, under the name of a Loan-Office, let the value of it be little or much, and trust the payment to the chance of depreciation, or other future events. According to the ideas which some of them threw out, they would continue striking an additional quantity every year, till the value of the first emissions was so reduced, that they would strike themselves out of debt, at the expence of all the settled and improved parts of the state.

But however paper money may suit a borrower, it is unprofitable, if not ruinous in the end, to every other person. The farmer will not take it for produce, and he is right in refusing it. The money he takes for his year's produce must last him the year round; and the experience he has had of the instability of paper money has sufficiently instructed him, that it is not worth a farmer's while to exchange the solid grain and produce of a farm for the paper of an Assembly, whose politics are changing with every new election, and who are here one year and gone another.

But the persons against whose immediate interest paper money operates the strongest, are the manufacturers and mechanics.

We all know there is no part of the continent where manufacturers and mechanics flourish so much as in the New-England states. They were famed for them before the war, and are so at this day.

But the circumstance which gave spring to those arts among them was, their banishing the use of paper money, which they effectually did many years before the war. The consequence was, that all the hard money that their export trade brought in remained among them; and as none of it could be spared to send abroad to purchase foreign manufactures, necessity obliged them to manufacture for themselves. It was by banishing paper money, that they established the arts, and retained among them a sufficiency of hard money.

I know some of the persons who put themselves at the head of the opposition against the Bank last year said, (for I was present), that they wished there was not a hard dollar in the country.

If this wish were, or could be, carried in practice, there could then be no other than paper money; the consequence of which would be, that all the hard money which the exports of the country brought in would be immediately sent out again, to purchase foreign manufactures and trinkets.

We are frequently passing acts to encourage manufactures, but the most effectual encouragement would be, to banish the practice of paper money. We have the experience of the New England states before us, which is preferable to all the reasoning that can be offered on the subject.

An independent country and paper money is a ridiculous connection. It is a weak, flimsy, idle system of government. We have as good a chance as other nations to share in the current coin of the world, gold and silver, did those who exercise the power of government understand it.

April 17th.   COMMON SENS

345

Pennsylvania Packet, 20 June 1786.

ON THE ADVANTAGES OF A Public Bank

IF the experience of other countries on the science of Banking be a matter worth attending to, there can be no hesitation in pronouncing in favour of a well-regulated public Bank. I shall therefore introduce this part of the subject by taking a concise view of the conduct of other nations on this subject.

In countries under a despotic government there are no public banks, because in such countries those who have wealth think it safer to conceal than to expose it. Public banks, therefore, are the offspring only of free countries, or of those which approach the nearest thereto; and in proportion as the people share in the government, in nearly that proportion do public banks prosper and are encouraged.

In Holland and in England, where the people, by their right of election and representation, participate in the government of the country, more than in any other of the same importance in Europe, that participation protects their wealth, and they trust it to a bank with safety: by this means all the money of the country is brought into use: whereas in countries where the people have no share in the government, and live under the continual apprehension of the power exercised over them, the rich secret their money, or keep it locked up for their own use only; and the bulk of the people, from the want of its free and confidential circulation, are kept poor.

It is not so much the quantity of wealth, as the quantity that circulates, that constitutes the monied riches of a country. If we may credit history and reports, there is more money in some countries, where the generality of the people are wretched and poor, than in some others that are esteemed rich; but in the one it is hoarded, and in the other it is dispersed by circulation and gives briskness and vigour to industry and improvement. One of the best methods to increase wealth in a country is to increase the circulation of it, by inducing every part of it to be brought forth, and constantly moving. A pound hoarded for a year, and then paid away, pays but one debt of twenty shillings in that time: but the same pound paid away every day, does the same service three hundred and sixty five times over.

Public banks, therefore, being the offspring of free countries, and of free countries only, or of such as approach the nearest thereto, and are not instituted in despotic governments, it is no reputation to the political principles of those persons, who endeavoured to suppress the institution of a public bank in this state.

The superior advantages of a public bank in a country to those of private ones are very evident. Private banks can only be set up by men of large fortune, and therefore they would be a monopoly in the hands of a very few: but in a public bank, divided into shares, the monopolizing system is destroyed, and the business thrown open, and any man in any part of the country may be a banker by being a stockholder.

In a private bank, the true condition of it can be known only to the proprietor. This being the case, he may extend his credit too much beyond his capital. He may trade, or speculate with the money deposited in his hands, and either by ill fortune in his projects, or fraudulent designs, may break. But in a public bank, there are too many people concerned to admit of secrecy; and the business is conducted by established rules, which cannot be dispensed with, or departed from. The directors are restrained from trading with the capital of the bank, or the money deposited there, and therefore the security of a public bank is greater than that of a private one. The proprietor likewise of a private bank, be he ever so substantial, will die: and when this happens, his affairs will be in the hands of executors, who are not always the best people to settle with: But in a public bank this never happens; its affairs never go into the hands of executors, because the directorship being filled up by election, never dies.

Had the persons who formed the scheme for opposing the bank been the institutors of it, it would then have been held out as one of the finest things imaginable. But such is the intoxicating spirit of party, and such the operation of envy, that where it cannot do the service that is wanted, it endeavours to prevent its being done. But in the instance of opposing the institution of the bank, the spirit of party carries something like a double face. Those who have been most clamorous against it, however they may conduct themselves in other places are nevertheless making use of its convenience.——If they are now convinced of the usefulness of such an institution, they ought to be candid enough to say it.——

One of the clamours against the bank was, that none but persons interested in the institution were its advocates and supporters. This is very true, if rightly understood, for every man is interested in supporting an institution that is of general utility. The stockholders are but a very small part of the numerous body of the citizens of the state, who are seeking to preserve and retain so useful an institution as a public bank. All the countries that are arrived at a degree of opulence sufficient to carry on any kind of trade by means of the produce of their lands, are as much if not more, interested in the matter than a stockholder. In short, every man who has any concern with money matters, and that every one has more or less, is in some degree benefited by an institution that serves, like the heart to the body, to give circulation through the state.

Another of the clamours was, that people could not borrow money as before. For this they may in a great measure thank their representatives, who by the instability of their political conduct, and the levity they have shewn in making and unmaking of laws, violating faith, and tampering with credit and paper-money, have made one man afraid to trust another; and this will ever be the case while such methods are practised.

But the most beneficial system of loaning, for the general interest of the country, is by means of a public bank. Loans for short periods serve to pay the farmer, the miller, the tradesman, the workman, &c. and hundreds are served in the course of a year to one that would be served by loans for a long period of time. The former system of loans was excellently adapted to the circumstances of the country at that time. It enabled people to make farms; but now that the farms are made, the best encouragement to the farmer is to provide means to buy and pay, in real money, for the produce he has to sell.

If the money that now compose the capital of the Bank could possibly be spared by the stockholders, which it cannot, and lent to individuals in different parts of the country for a number of years, only a very few persons could be served, compared with the numbers served now, and those only who had already considerable property to give in security; and the first borrowers would exclude all others from the chance of borrowing during the time for which they had borrowed themselves. He therefore who puts his money in the bank, lends it to a more general good, than if he were to trust it to the use of one person only for a number of years.

I shall conclude this paper with a declaration, that in this place may not be improper, which is, That from the first establishment of the bank, to the present hour, I have been its friend and advocate; yet I have never made the least use of it, or received the least personal service or favor from it, by borrowing or discounting notes, or in any other shape or manner whatever or of any person concerned with it directly or indirectly. I have kept cash at the bank, and the bank is at this time in account to me between eight and nine hundred pounds, for money which I brought from New-York, and deposited there ever since last September, and for which I do not receive a single farthing interest. This money the country has had the use of, and I think it safer under the care of the bank, until I have occasion to call for it, than in my own custody.

June 17th   COMMON SENSE

Pennsylvania Gazette, 20 September, 1786.

NUMBER V

On the Affairs of the STATE

At the commencement of the present constitution, it was strongly opposed, and as strongly contended for. This gave evidence to two parties, which have since maintained nearly an equal contest, sometimes the one, and sometimes the other, prevailing at elections.

Among those who at that time opposed the alteration of the constitution, I have my share, in a number of publications, entitled "A serious address to the people of Pennsylvania on the present state of their affairs."

Whether a single legislative Assembly, or a legislature composed of two branches, is best suited to support the just principles of equal liberty, is a point I never touched upon in any of those publications. My aim was to quiet the dispute, and prevent it from entangling the country, at a time when the utmost harmony of its powers was necessary to its safety. The constitution was upon experiment, and the manner in which a single House would use such an abundance of power would best determine whether it ought to be trusted with it.-- ---- Besides this the constitution very prudently held out, in the forty-seventh section, the probability of its own defects, by appointing the means (by a convention) at the period of every seven years, of adding new articles or amending defective ones. The words in the said section are:------

"The Council of Censors shall also have power to call a convention, to meet within two years after their sitting, if there appears to them an absolute necessity of amending any article of the constitution which may be defective, explaining such as may be thought not clearly expressed, and of adding such as are necessary for the preservation of the rights and happiness of the people." Therefore, any alteration which experience of circumstances shall prove necessary or proper is consistent with the constitution itself.

But the causes or reasons which then operated for not altering the constitution, could not be conclusively taken as causes or reasons for confirming it. With many people, those reasons went no further than to give the constitution a fair trial, or, rather, to give a single legislature a sufficient opportunity to shew with what degree of wisdom and prudence, impartiality and moderation, it would act. With others, the attempt to alter appeared to be ill-timed. And there were many who held an opinion, that has always prevailed among the political part of mankind, which is, that the form of government best calculated for preserving liberty in time of peace, is not the best form for conducting the operation of war; and that as the government of a single house had a considerable resemblance to the government of a single person, the present form, on account of the quickness of its execution, was preferable during the war to the proposed alterations.

There is, however, one fact very clearly deduced from the experience had, which is, that a single legislature, into the hands of whatever party it may fall, is capable of being made a compleat aristocracy for the time it exists: And that when the majority of a single house is made up on the ground of party prejudice, or fitted to be the dupes thereof, that its government, instead of comprehending the good of the whole dispassionately and impartially, will be that of party favor and oppression. To have established the present form as the best, it was absolutely necessary that the prejudices of party should have no operation within the walls of the legislature; for when it descends to this, a single legislature, on account of the superabundance of its power, and the uncontrouled rapidity of its execution, becomes as dangerous to the principles of liberty as that of a despotic monarchy. The present form was well intended, but the abuse of its power operates to its destruction. It withstood the opposition of its enemies, and will fall through the misconduct of its friends.

At the commencement of the revolution, it was supposed that what is called the executive part of a government was the only dangerous part; but we now see that quite as much mischief, if not more, may be done, and as much arbitrary conduct acted, by a legislature. In establishing the Executive Council, the constitution took care to prevent its being subject to inconsistent and contradictory conduct, and sudden convulsions. This is done by providing, that the periods after their elections shall not all expire at once. By this means, says the nineteenth section of the constitution, "there will in every subsequent year be found in the council a number of persons acquainted with the proceedings of the foregoing years whereby, the business will be more consistently conducted, and , moreover, the danger of establishing an inconvenient aristocracy be effectually prevented."

The council are as much the choice and representatives of the people as the assembly are, and have the same common interest in the community; and if it is necessary to guard against such events in the council, it is equally so in the legislature; and this would undoubtedly have been the case, could the convention have foreseen the capricious and inconsistent conduct of assemblies.

By the whole legislative power being entrusted to a single body of men, and that body expiring all at once, the state is subject to the perpetual convulsions of imperfect measures and rash proceedings; as by this means may happen (as it has happened already) that a number of men, suddenly collected, unexperienced in business, and unacquainted with the grounds, reasons and principles, which former assemblies proceeded on in passing certain acts, and without seeking to inform themselves thereof, may precipitate the state into disorder by a confused medley of doing and undoing, and make the grievances they pretend to remove.

Of this kind was the attack made by a late assembly on that most useful and beneficial institution, incorporated by a former assembly, *The Bank of North-America.* The proceedings on this business are a stain to the national reputation of the state. They exhibit a train of little and envious thinking, a scene of passion, of arbitrary principles and unconstitutional conduct; and the disgrace is filled up by assigning an untruth (which themselves have since acknowledged to) in the preamble of the act for annulling the charter of the Bank, as a cause for doing it. Such a disreputable circumstance in government could scarcely have happened, but from the cause I have already stated. For the Assembly which did it was newly formed, and elected on one of those sudden caprices which often happens in a free country, and there was not one man amongst them fully acquainted with the nature of the business they were going upon.

Public Banks are reckoned among the honors, privileges and advantages of a free people, and are never found among those under a despotic government. It is the confidence which people have in measures and principles of government, and the strict observance of faith and honor on the part of the government, which encourage people to put their money into circulation by means of a public Bank. A faithless or arbitrary government cannot be trusted, and therefore in free countries only are Banks established. In this state it has been the means of restoring that credit and confidence among individuals which for many years was lost, and without which, agriculture, commerce, and every species of business, must decline and languish.

As gold and silver are not the natural products of Pennsylvania, we have no other hard money that what the produce of the country exported to foreign parts brings in. This being the case, the interest of the farmers and the merchant, the one being employed to raise the produce, and the other to export it, are as naturally connected, as that of sowing the grain is connected with reaping the harvest; and any man must be held an enemy to the public prosperity, who endeavours to create a difference, or dissolve the mutual interest existing between them. The Plough and the Sail are the Arms of the state of Pennsylvania, and their connection should be held in remembrance by all good citizens.

As blood, tho' taken from the arm, is nevertheless taken from the whole body, so the attempt to destroy the Bank eventually operated to distress the farmer as well as the merchant; for if the one is prevented in the means of buying the produce of the country, the other, of consequence, is deprived of the opportunities of selling.

I shall conclude this paper with remarking, that so long as it shall be the choice of the people to continue the legislature in a single house, the circumstances of the country and the importance of the trust (being greater than that committed to any single body of men in any state of the union) evidently require, that the persons to be elected thereto be men freed from the bigotry and shackles of party, of liberal minds, and conversant in the means of increasing the riches of the state, and cultivating and extending the prosperity thereof.

COMMON SENSE

Philad. Sept. 15, 1786

Pennsylvania Gazette, 8 November 1786.

NUMBER VI

PAPER Money, Paper Money, and Paper Money! is now, in several of the states both the bubble and iniquity of the day. That there are some bad people concerned in schemes of this kind cannot be doubted, but the far greater part are misled. People are got so bewildered upon the subject that they put and mistake one thing for another. They say that Paper Money has improved the country—Paper Money carried on the war, and Paper Money did a great many other fine things.

Not one syllable of this is truth; it is all error from beginning to end. It was CREDIT which did these things, and that credit has failed, by non-performance, and by the country being involved in debt and the levity and instability of government measures.

We have so far mistaken the matter that we have even mistaken the name. The name is not Paper Money, but Bills of Credit: But it seems as if we were ashamed to use the name, knowing how much we have abused the thing. All emissions of paper for government purposes is not making of money, but making use of credit to run into debt by. It is anticipating or forestalling the revenue of future years and trusting the burden of redemption on future assemblies. It is like a man mortgaging his estate and leaving his successors to pay it off. But this is not the worst of it, it leaves us at best in the lurch by banishing hard money, diminishing the value of the revenue, and filling up its place with paper, that may be like something to day and to morrow nothing.

So far as regards Pennsylvania, she cannot emit bills of credit, because the assembly which makes such an emission cannot bind future assemblies either to redeem them or receive them in taxes. The precedent of revoking the charter of the bank, established by a former assembly, is a precedent for any assembly to undo what another has done. It circumscribes the power of any assembly in the year in which it sits that is, it cannot engage for the performance of any thing beyond that time. And as an assembly cannot issue bills of credit and redeem them within the year, and as it cannot by that precedent bind a future assembly so to do, it therefore cannot with the necessary security do it at all; because people will not put confidence in the paper promises or paper emissions of those who can neither perform the engagement within the time their own power exists nor compel the performance after that time is past. The politicians of the project for revoking the bank charter (as it was besides most wantonly done) to use a trite saying; aimed at the pidgeon and shot the crow—they fired at the bank and hit their own paper.

As to making these bills what is called legal tenders, we have no such thing in this state, which is one reason they have not depreciated more: But as it is a matter which engrosses the attention of some other states, I shall offer a few remarks on it.

The abuse of any power always operates to call the right of that power in question. To judge of the right or power of any assembly in America to make those bills a legal tender, we must have recourse to the principles on which civil government is founded; for if such an act is not compatible with those principles, the assembly which affirms such a power, assumes a power unknown in civil government, and commits treason against its principles.

The fundamental principles of civil government are security of our rights and persons as freemen, and the security of property. A tender law, therefore, cannot stand on the principles of civil government, because it operates to take away a man's share of civil and natural freedom, and to render property insecure.

If a man had a hundred silver dollars in his possession, as his own property, it would be a strange law that should oblige him to deliver them up to anyone who could discover that he possessed them, and take a hundred paper dollars in exchange. Now the case, in effect, is exactly the same, if he has lent a hundred hard dollars to his friend, and is compelled to take a hundred paper ones for them. The exchange is against his *consent*, and to his injury, and the principles of civil government provides for the protection, and not for the violation of his rights and property. The state, therefore, that is under the operation of such an act, is not in a state of civil government, and consequently the people cannot be bound to obey a law which abets and encourages treason against the best principles on which civil government is founded.

The principles of civil government extend in their operation to compel the exact performance of engagements entered into between man and man. The only kind of legal tenders that can exist in a country under a civil government is the particular thing expressed and specified in those engagements and contracts. That particular thing constitutes the legal tender. If a man engages to sell and deliver a quantity of wheat, he is not to deliver rye, any more than he who contracts to pay in hard money is at liberty to pay in paper or in any thing else. Such contracts or bargains have expressed the legal tender on both sides, and no assumed or presumptuous authority of any assembly can dissolve or alter them.

Another branch of this principle of civil government is, that it disowns the practice of retrospective laws. An assembly or legislature cannot punish a man by any new law made after the crime is committed; he can only be punished by the law which existed at the time he committed the crime. This principle of civil government extends to property as well as to life; for a law made after the time that any bargain or contract was entered into between individuals can no more become the law for serving that contract, than, in the other case, it can become the law for punishing the crime; both of those cased must be referred to the laws existing at the time the crime was done or the bargain made. Each party then knew the relative situation they stood in with each other, and on that law and on that knowledge they acted, and by no other can they be adjudged—Therefore all tender laws which apply to the alteration of past contracts, by making them dischargable on either side, different to what the law at the time they were made, is of the same nature as that law which inflicts a punishment different to what was the law at the time the crime was committed; For in all cases of civil government the law must be before the fact.

But was there no illegality in tender laws, they are naturally defective on another consideration. They cannot bind all and every interest in the state, because they cannot bind the state itself. They are, therefore, compulsive where they ought to be free; that is, between man and man, and they are actually free where, if at all, they ought to be compulsive: for in all cases where the state reserves to itself the right of freeing itself, it cannot bind the individual, because the right of the one stands on as good ground as that of the other.

COMMON SENSE

Philadelphia, Nov. 3, 1786

Pennsylvania Gazette, 7 March 1787

No. VII.

Addressed *TO THE* Opposers *OF THE* BANK

ERROR like guilt is unwilling to die. However strong the conviction, or clear the detection, it still disdains to yield, and though defeated struggles to survive. The opposers to the Bank, finding their cause as unpopular as it is unjust, are endeavouring to confound what they cannot confute, and to recover by contrivance what they lost by misconduct. Failing in the onset, they seek to embarrass the issue, and escape undefeated in the fog of perplexity.

New devices, as frivolous as they are unjust, are couched under new pretences, and held out to divide or to deceive. A small reinforcement, by any means obtained, might serve as a prop to their consequence, or an apology to their defeat.

When men have rashly plunged themselves into a measure, the right or wrong of it is soon forgotten. Party knows no impulse but spirit, no prize but victory. It is blind to truth, and hardened against conviction. It seeks to justify error by perseverance, and denies to its own mind the operation of its own judgement. A man under the tyranny of party spirit is the greatest slave upon earth, for none but himself can deprive him of the freedom of thought.

The obscure promoters of the opposition to the Bank imagined that their consequence would be lessened, and their influence circumscribed by the growing circumstances of the country. They hated the means that should raise it above themselves, and beheld the Bank as an instrument of public prosperity. The lower was the ebb, the easier they would ascend to the surface, and the more visible they would appear. Their sphere of importance was that of a general poverty, and their hopes depended on its duration. "Better to reign in hell than serve in heaven," was the language of Lucifer, and the same motives served to instigate the opposition.[1]

In this plan they were joined by a band of usurers, whose avarice of 50 and 60 per cent. was consequently opposed by the operation of the Bank, which discounted at the legal interest of six per cent. They were further supported by the speculators in the funding scheme, who were calculating to draw from the public an annual interest of 20 and 30 per cent, and encrease the value of the capital in their hands at least one hundred per cent. This is a caracatura which the public are truly interested in having explained. What but this could bring an assembly-man of the constitutional party and an usurer together.

Unjust measures must be supported by unjust means. No sooner was their scheme reprobated by men of integrity and independent principles, but invention was put to the rack, and truth to defiance, to weaken the credit of those who opposed the injustice of their proceedings. This man was bribed and that man was hired, and slander and falsehood, the ministering angels of malevolence, had full employment.

So far as any of their insinuations regard me, I put them to defiance. I challenge any man amongst them to come forth and made the assertion. I dare them to it; and with all the calm composure of integrity disdain their insinuations, and leave them to lick the file and bleed away their venom. An insinuation, which a man who makes it does not believe himself, is equal to lying. It is the cowardice of lying. It unites the barest part of that vice with the meanest of all others. An open liar is a highwayman in his profession, but an insinuating liar is a thief sculking in the night.

Could the opposition to the Bank succeed in effecting its downfall, the consequence would be their own destruction as a party in the state. The attempt

---

[1] Here Paine is quoting from Milton's *Paradise Lost*, first published in 1667. See John Milton, *Paradise Lost* (London: Penguin, 1996), p. 14, (I.263).

has already reduced their numbers and exasperated the country, and could they accomplish the end, it would be fatal to them. But they are happy in not having discernment enough to foresee the effects of their own measures. They persist because they have begun, and shun the prudence that would teach them to retreat.

Had the Bank closed its accounts as the opposition supposed it would at the passing of the repealing act, the confusion and distress in this city, and the effects that would have followed to the country, would have brought vengeance on the heads of the promoters of that measure. The quantity of cash that would have been taken away and for ever removed from this state, by the stockholders in distant parts, would have brought on a famine of money. I know one gentlemen who would have drawn out twenty-four thousand dollars, none of which would ever more have returned among us. Is there any man except a madman or an ideot, that will say we have too much money and want to have less. Can it be for the interest of this state to banish the wealth it possesses, at the very time it is complaining of the scarcity of cash?

The leaders of the opposition in this city are chiefly composed of those who live by posts and offices under the government, and if there are but taxes enough to pay their salaries, the distress would not reach their interest.

The opposition in the House of Assembly is chiefly supported by members from whom such an opposition has an indelicate appearance. It has the appearance of envy at the prosperity of all the old settled parts of the state. The commerce and traffic of the Back Country members and the parts they represent goes to Baltimore. From thence are their imports purchased and there do their exports go. They come here to legislate and go there to trade. In questions of commerce, and by commerce I mean the exports as well as the imports of a country, they are neither naturally nor politically interested with us, and the delicacy of the case when matters of this kind are agitated should have with them a greater weight.---What advantage persons thus situated can propose to themselves from a dissolution of the Bank at Philadelphia is not easy to perceive. The money drawn away by the stockholders in distant parts, though removed from this state, would not be deposited at Baltimore. It is very possible that a branch of the present Bank may extend there, and in this view they are defeating their own future interest:--- If one part of the State is thus to go on in opposing the other, no great good can arise to either. The principle is ungenerous and the policy injurious, and the more it is reflected upon the worse it will appear.

The cry and bubble, the falsehoods and insinuations that were raised against the Bank have sunk and wasted away as groundless clamours always will. The politics founded on such contrivances never succeed, and the event serves to involve the projectors in disgrace. A very little serious thinking was sufficient to convince any man, that the more money could be retained in the country the better, and that to break up the Bank and banish so large a capital from the state as the stockholders in distant parts have deposited with us, never more to return among us; could answer no man's purpose who had his living to work for, though it might not affect those who live by posts and offices. Would not that politician be considered as a madman in England, who should propose to break up the Bank in that nation, and send away to Holland and other countries the money which those foreigners have deposited with them: and he must be equally as vile a politician who proposes the same thing here.

So far as the part I have taken in the business has gone, it has been applied to preserve the money in the country, by supporting the Bank; and in this undertaking I am certain of the approbation of every serious thinking man who wishes to see the country in prosperous circumstances.

As for the crazy brained politicians who began and promoted the attack on the Bank, I have had experience enough of their abilities for several years past to know them sufficiently, and that a country under the management of their politics would be a perpetual scene of distraction and poverty.

I did not leave them when they were weak and distressed, but in the height of their prosperity, and in full possession of the government. I very explicitly and candidly stated to them my reasons for reprobating their conduct, and that at a time when themselves know it was against my interest to do it; and I very freely gave them my opinion (such as it was) that those unjust and despotic proceedings would work their downfall. But they were intoxicated with power, government-mad, too blind to foresee the consequence, and too confident to be advised. They trusted to the transitory popularity obtained by delusion, and supposed that a multitude deceived was never to be convinced.

But there are certain points in this business, which ought always to be kept in view.

The Bank originated on the inability of the government to carry on the war, and at a time when some of its present opposers were on the point of abandoning the cause. I speak this because I know it. But so unhappy is the spirit of envy, that it can be just to no merit but its own. The services which the Bank rendered have been a poison to those little minds, that at once receive and hate the good that others perform.

On the fall of the continental currency a band of usurers arose, and those who wanted to borrow paid from thirty to sixty per cent for their loans. These men are among the enemies of the Bank.

On the establishment of the Bank, nearly the whole of its abilities to lend were rendered to Congress, and so pressing and necessitous were the requisitions of that body, and so devoted was the Bank to the support of the public cause, that in more instances than one the Bank ran the risque of losing its whole capital. At this time the present opposers of the Bank lay snug with what hard money they had in their pockets, and contributed none of it to supply the public exigency.

On the termination of the war, all risk and danger being over, those same persons, so quiet then, and so noisy since, formed the scheme of setting up another Bank. Not from any public principle or for any public purpose; not to expel the enemy, for he was already expelled; but merely with a view to make money and profit. They had no hard money, God help them, not they, while there was danger of losing it; but when that danger was over, they could find hard money for a new bank. To carry this plan, and draw new associates to it, they proposed revising the Test-laws, which, as their scheme of a new Bank did not succeed, they afterwards voted against.

Disappointed in their plan of setting up another Bank, they immediately struck off on the contrary tack, propagated a report that Banks were injurious and dangerous, and brought in a bill to demolish that Bank they had attempted to rival. How they should ever expect that men who had reputations yet unlost should join or concur with them in such a contradictory and unprincipled round of projects, is a proof how little they regard reputation themselves. Their conduct is in itself a satire upon hypocrisy, and equalled only by the impudence of acting it.[2]

When the demands of Congress on the Bank ceased with the war, it was then enabled to employ its capital in promoting the domestic prosperity of the country; and it was fortunate for Pennsylvania that she possessed such a resource as the Bank, at the close of a war which had ruined her commerce, reduced her farmers, and impoverished her monied men; when she had, as it were, the world to begin anew, and when, had it not been for the intervention of the Bank, the usurers would have devoured the land.

The Bank went on, and no complaint was heard against it. Its impartial punctuality served to collect and restore the shattered remains of credit, and replace the confidence which the war and paper currencies had destroyed.

At this time, without provocation, without cause, and without any motive that was wise, just or honorable, the Assembly, unwarranted by their constituents, and unjustified by the pretence, commenced an attack upon its charter. They fabricated the tales they wished to have believed, and set them up for the voice of the people. A few runners out of doors kept up the alarm, and the public, unacquainted with the business, and unsuspicious of the deception, were trepanned into the lure.

That they had not the support of the people, is evident from the disapprobation which the two succeeding elections shew to their conduct. They dismissed from

---

[2] On the attempt in 1784 to set up a rival bank, see above p. 250.

their trust the promoters of that measure, and elected others, to redress the injustice their predecessors had committed.

If the inhabitants of the back western parts of the state are not benefited by the establishment of a Bank within the state; it is because their trade and commerce is carried out of it. They neither encrease its exports nor consume its imports, nor bear a proportionate share of the public burthens. Yet were the state of Maryland, to which place their commerce is carried, to emit a paper currency, there are none of those persons but would prefer a Pennsylvania bank note at Baltimore, that could at any time be changed into hard money, to the paper currency of a state of which they are not members. Therefore, instead of opposing the Bank on this narrow policy, they would have acted consistently with their interest to have supported it, and joined their endeavours to establish a branch of it in that state.

As to paper currencies, when we consider the fluctuating disposition of legislatures, the uncertainty of their movements, the probability of the division and separation of a state, disputes about the residence of government, and numerous other occurrences that may take place in a state, there can be no confidence placed in them. They stand on such a contingent foundation, on such a changeable connection of circumstances, and subject to such a multitude of events, not easy to foresee, and always liable to happen, that paper currencies can never be trusted to either as riches or as a medium of commerce; because a medium must in the nature of it be subject to the least possible fluctuation, or it is not a medium, and paper is subject to the greatest fluctuation of all other things, being capable of sinking to no value at all, of which this country has sufficient experience.

Pennsylvania being the centre of the thirteen states, her situation, with the assistance of a Bank, enabled her to carry on a trade upon the produce of other states. Through the medium of the Bank, for Bank notes had credit in all the states, she imported their productions, exported them again, became importers for those states, and gained a profit upon the trade. By this means the riches of

Pennsylvania were encreased, and many industrious people furnished with employment. Of this branch was the tobacco trade.

But matters of this kind form no part of the politics of the opposition. It is more agreeable to them to keep the country low and poor, that they may govern it the easier, than to see it prosperous, and beyond the reach of their influence.

These are some of the principal outlines in tracing the subject of the Bank. As to several little matters that have been started, as well in the assembly as out of it, they are not worth wasting the public time upon.

It is of very little consequence to the generality of people, and a matter which they do not trouble themselves about, because it does not affect them one way or the other, in what manner the stock-holders of the Bank conduct their private concerns, regulate their elections, and do many other domestic matters. Those who best know the business, best know how to manage it, and the object with the public is best answered, when that business is best performed. Those who place their money there, are the properest people to take care of it, and the better it is taken care of, the more security there is in the Bank.

The greater quantity of money which the credit of the Bank can bring into the state, the better for the people; for it is not the money collected within the state, but the monies drawn to it from distant parts, monies which would not be here were it not for the Bank, that forms the principal capital of the Bank.

As to the domestic matters of the Bank, even the opposition is obliged to be silent. The business of it has been conducted with unimpeached faithfulness and good management. Therefore the best, and only certain line to proceed on, in restoring its legal re-establishment, is to keep as near as possible to the line of its original charter. Of this we have had an experienced security, to which innovations may be dangerous and fatal.

Philad. March 5, 1787,   COMMON SENS

Chapter Four

National Debt and Paper Money

Most of the letters articles and pamphlets already presented in this collection touch upon the subject of public debt and paper money in America. On his return to Europe in 1787, Paine continued to write on these subjects in a European context. Two pamphlets were almost entirely devoted to discussing the runaway national debt in Britain and France and the financial devices that supported it. *Prospects on the Rubicon* was written in August 1787 and appeared in London shortly before the opening of Parliament in November.[1] Its target was Pitt's plan to refinance the national debt in order to raise money for rearmament faced with an international crisis in which it appeared Britain would be drawn into a war with France over the Dutch republic.

The crisis was sparked by the revolt of the Dutch Free Corps' against the Stadtholder, William V of Orange. The United Provinces of the Netherlands

---

[1] Parliament opened on 15 November 1787. Although *Prospects on the Rubicon* is dated as being written in London on 20 August 1787, Aldridge suggests that Paine left Paris only on August 30. According to Oldys, Paine arrived in London on 3 September. See Aldridge, *Man of Reason*, p. 121; Moncure D. Conway, *The Life of Thomas Paine: with a History of his Literary, Political and Religious Career in America, France and England*, ed. by Hypathia Bradlaugh Bonner, (London: Watts, 1892: repr. 1909) p. 94. Black suggests *Prospects* was published on 20 November. See Black, *British Foreign Policy*, p. 330.

faced a civil war between the bourgeois Patriots, inspired in part by their own republican traditions and in part by the success of the American revolutionaries, and the more conservative provincial governors loyal to the Orange family's hereditary role as military leader. In July 1786 the Free Corp Patriots removed control of the Hague garrison from William V, followed by his suspension as Captain-General in September. The revolt in Holland had several repercussions for international relations, not only in Europe but also in the colonial context of India and the Dutch East Indies. As in the American war, France supported financially the Dutch patriots, and was widely believed to be ready to intervene militarily. Britain's position was ambiguous in part due to divisions in Pitt's cabinet between those who favoured an inexpensive peace with France based on the commercial treaty negotiated by Eden and Vergennes in 1786, and those who feared French aggression. French support for the Patriots could be seen as an attempt to construct a united naval force along the English Channel, a threat epitomised by the development of a naval port at Cherbourg.[2]

Aldridge suggests that the pamphlet demonstrates that Paine was already pro-French in 1787 but was at this time working for peace, as was Pitt and the French ministry, with which Paine may have been corresponding. At this point, Aldridge argues 'Paine's fundamental principle, was that each nation, including England, should maintain adequate defence but not seek to dominate the military strength in Europe.' *Prospects* was not widely read, perhaps because it was too economic and too gloomy for his English fans.[3] Paine's aim was to show that despite the French financial crisis, it was as a nation more solvent than England and that French national bank was more credit worthy than the Bank of England.

France was widely believed to be close to national bankruptcy. In February 1787, Louis XVI called an Assembly of Notables, hoping to force through financial reform which would allow a land tax to be applied and

---

[2] For a full account of the crisis, see Black, *British Foreign Policy*, pp. 99-157.
[3] Aldridge, *Man of Reason*, pp. 119-22.

provincial assemblies to be introduced. Successive finance ministers, Calonne and Brienne failed to overcome the vested interests of the powerful aristocratic land-owning class. British finances on the other hand looked buoyant after their depletion in the American war. Black reports that 'whereas the bullion balance at the Bank of England had been only £590,000 in August 1783, by August 1785 it stood at £1,540,000 and by August 1791 £8,056,000.[4] Paine's argument in *Prospects* was unconvincing in view of Calonne's dissemination of the reality of French finances in Britain and Brienne's similar failure to secure reform. Many of Pitt's advisors feared however that French success in reform would enhance France's international and military power sufficiently to enable a French and Austrian invasion of the Netherlands.

The crisis came to a head in June 1787 when Wilhelmina of Orange, William V's wife, was roughly and disrespectfully treated by the Free Corps Patriots. The insult provided the pretext for her brother Fredrick William of Prussia to invade the Netherlands in support of his brother-in-law's position. Britain tentatively edged towards protecting her interest against a French counter attack, while securing Austrian compliance. In September, the Patriot rebellion collapsed and the loyalist forces recaptured The Hague reinstating William V as Stadtholder. The French forces retreated and the crisis was averted. France had been effectively hamstrung by her internal financial difficulties. With hindsight, Pitt correctly called the French bluff and Paine's predictions of financial disaster went unheeded. Rather than France being better financed than Britain, it was Brienne's inability to secure a restructuring of taxes in the Estates General which lead to the French retreat from the Rubicon in September 1787, followed by national bankruptcy and ultimately a revolution. Cheetham's early but unreliable biography of Paine charges that as 'the "Rubicon" [possessed] no merit it attracted no notice; it betrays, however his revolutionary design.'[5]

---

[4] Black, *British Foreign Policy*, p. 136.
[5] James Cheetham, *Life of Thomas Paine*, (London: Maxwell Bellard, 1817) p. 57.

The pamphlet was reprinted by James Ridgeway in 1793 under a new title, *Prospects on the War and Paper Currency.* At the end of the previous year, Paine, by now living in Paris, had been tried in his absence for seditious libel and his *Rights of Man* proscribed. Ridgeway's preface explains its re-publication.

> This pamphlet was written by Mr. Paine in the year 1787, on one of Mr. Pitt's armaments, namely, that against Holland. His object was to prevent the people of England from being seduced into a war, by stating clearly to them the consequences which would inevitably befall the credit of this country should such a calamity take place.—The minister has at length, however, succeeded in his grand project, after three expensive armaments in the space of seven years; and the event has proved how well founded were the predictions of Mr. Paine.—The person who has the authority to bring forward this pamphlet in its present shape, thinks his doing so a duty which he owes both to Mr. P—— and the people of England, in order that the latter may judge how far credit is to be given to the wild theories of Mr. Paine.

The skill of interpreting a historical text usually depends largely on intention: that of the author and that of the reader. Here we have an additional concern, the intention of the publisher. In the context of 1793, *Prospects on the War and Paper Currency* can been seen in a very different light. It could be intended to discredit Paine after the popularity of the *Rights of Man*, to show that credit ought not be given to such 'wild theories' and so perhaps this text should be treated as a hostile witness. However, Ridgeway's point is to show the consequences of a new war against France, not over Holland but over the legitimacy of Republican revolution. By republishing the text, he demonstrates Paine's prescience in predicting the French revolution and the escalating English national debt. Ridgeway's target appears to be Pitt's inability to reduce the national debt. *Prospects on the War* draws the essential link between the belligerent British foreign policy and the corrupt system of oligarchic rule. Paine asserts that placemen, pensioners and holders of government bonds have a vested interest in keeping Britain at war to justify increases in public borrowing and taxation. The relation between Britain's corrupt system of government and burgeoning public spending was a theme Paine would again highlight in the final chapter of his *Rights of Man Part Second* presented in Chapter 5.

This is also the theme of *The Decline and Fall of the English System of Finance* written in Paris in 1796. Here Paine presents, as a scientific discovery, a mathematical formula governing the escalation of national debt in each period of war. If this relation continues, he predicts, England will be bankrupt. His prediction struck a tone with common concerns over Britain's financial health, shared even by Pitt himself. Between 1783 and 1816, the national debt rose from 273 million to 816 million. In the same year as publication of *Decline and Fall* in London, the Bank of England was forced to suspend payments in specie. Bank notes would no longer be convertible into cash, until the establishment of the Gold Standard in 1816. To cope with the great demand for money, the Bank increased the volume of notes and for the first time issued one pound notes.[6] Whilst we might speculate that Paine's prediction was self-fulfilling, in that the publication of *Decline and Fall* must have dented financial confidence, his role in the crisis is perhaps even more significant than this. The trigger for the run on the Bank was a failed French invasion. The aborted landing in Pembrokeshire precedes Paine's campaign for an invasion of Ireland, but was no doubt encouraged by Paine's claims in Paris that England was ripe for revolution.[7]

Paine's principal target in this pamphlet is the Bank of England. He sets out the Banks' role as the lynchpin of the English financial system and as such the key instigator of potential instability. We have seen that Paine avidly supported the Bank of North America and strongly associated the existence of a strong and independent central bank with individual freedom. It may seem strange then that he attacks the Bank of England for performing similar functions. Paine's critique is based on his claim that the Bank of England is issuing notes beyond its

---

[6] See illustrations above between pp. 242-243.
[7] In 1798 Paine is thought to have advised Napoleon on his invasion plans, and suggested that the people of England, ready for revolution, would rise up to greet their French liberators. See Keane, *Paine*, pp. 440-444 and above p. 82.

capacity. The Bank accepts deposits in notes, and other paper, rather than gold and silver. The American experience warned against raising government funds by issuing notes insufficiently supported by reserves. Further, the Bank acts as banker to the government, but is not, as the Bank of North America was, limited in this capacity by its deposits. In 1715, the Bank of England was granted permission to issue transferable stock as a loan to government to cover the annual supply. The condition was the Bank's permanency; it could not be dissolved until the government loans were repaid, an extremely unlikely event. The Bank also acted as banker to the government and advanced money to other bankers by rediscounting bills of exchange, increasing the capacity of the rapidly multiplying local bank structure to loan money beyond their deposits. Paine argues that the connection between the Bank and the government threatens public ruin. The government's ability, through the Bank to increase spending indefinitely not only ensure public bankruptcy but also threatened the stability of the private funding system.

The pamphlet was popular, gaining fame and wide-scale circulation throughout Europe in six or seven weeks in several languages. The proceeds were as usual donated to a good cause, in this case, the relief of prisoners for debt in Newgate, London. As well as fitting the subject of the pamphlet, Paine may have had personal reasons for supporting the imprisoned debtors. Cheetham alleges that in 1789, Paine was arrested in London for debt, apparently owing £700 to Whiteside, a London merchant who was bankrupt. Paine had employed Whiteside to receive payments on his behalf from America and had borrowed against this account. Cheetham admits that Paine usually paid his debts and was regarded as financially honourable.[8] In view of his distaste for indebtedness demonstrated in these texts, Paine must have suffered great indignity by the experience.

---

[8] See Conway, *Life*, p. 251 and Cheetham, *Life*, p. 58.

Together with his letter to Citizen Danton, these pamphlets reiterate Paine's views on paper money. During the American Revolution, Paine witnessed the inflationary effects of attempts to raise government funds by issuing notes that were not backed up by reserves. The real exchange value of the notes fell, impoverishing savers at the mercy of speculators. In *Prospects on the Rubicon,* he warns England that its reliance on paper money weakens the country in a potential war with France because real money, gold and silver is not increased. France has benefited from the quantities of gold and silver imported into Europe through Spain and Portugal, while Britain's holdings of gold and silver have remained static.

Paine uses traditional arguments against the national debt such as the unnecessary burden of tax it produces but he does not link the borrowing and lending of money for gain with corruption and vice. This is reserved for tender laws, which he describes as tyrannical, unjust, and calculated to support fraud and oppression. Rather a national debt is a good thing provided it is based on proper securities and not continually increasing in scale. In *Common Sense,* Paine claims a national debt unites a country. 'No nation ought to be without a debt. A national debt is a national bond; and when it bears no interest, is in no case a grievance.'[9] Paine believed so strongly that Americans would recognise their interest in the common good that they would lend their money to the government for no interest. However, the English National Debt accrued since the Hanoverian succession is much larger than the capital to secure it, and increases in perpetuity due to the interest payments and incessant wars. Paine proposes taxing the interest on the national debt providing that the tax paid on interest was always less than other taxes on property.

Paine's attack on paper money and national debt may seem conservative in hindsight. The strength of the British economy in the nineteenth century may largely be attributed to the well-developed system of finance, but Paine is writing

---

[9] See above p. 124.

in the early days of such systems. Like other '*laissez-faire*' theorists, in our time and his, he warns that printing money without fiscal responsibility will lead to inflation, which hits hardest on the poor. It is a lesson which governments have been slow to learn. Adam Smith had also insisted that paper bank notes be based upon the solid ground of gold and silver and condemned legal tender paper money as unjust. Adam Smith's views on paper money and the national debt would have been known to Paine as they were widely circulated in Philadelphia by a defender of the Bank of North America, James Wilson. Indeed Paine refers to Smith's chapter on Public Debt in *Decline and Fall*.[10] Paine's assault on the spiralling national debt and paper money can be seen as part and parcel of his *laissez-faire* view rather than an conservative fear of emerging capitalism.

Paine's apparently changing view of national debt is in fact very consistent over his lifetime. Paine is in favour of bank paper and against unsupported paper. The Bank of England's reserves are not in his view sufficient to sustain the credit given to the British government. The system of finance is therefore unsustainable. In view of his earlier arguments, Paine might have added that unsupported paper money results in inflation and thus amounts to a tax on savings. As the Bank of England was able to lend money to the government without parliamentary authority, under the ways and means legislation, the system undermined the vital constitutional principle of the lower house's control of the purse. Paine's mathematical formula highlights the way in which the system allowed a government to fight wars which were to be paid by a future generation of taxpayers, and thus violating Paine's right of each generation principle. The present generation surely has a duty to prevent the imposition of even greater and nonviable debt on the next generation. Paine's opposition to the system of finance had revolutionary intent. His account of the spiralling national debt undermined the legitimacy of government by challenging the right to give consent on behalf of future taxpayers. But many of these arguments had already been

---

[10] See below p. 413.

made in *Rights of Man*. In the *Decline and Fall* it is sufficient to undermine international financial confidence in British funds, thus weakening his opponent with the stroke of a pen.

PROSPECTS ON THE WAR AND PAPER CURRENCY.

PREFACE.

AN expression in the British Parliament respecting the American war, alluding to Julius Cæsar having passed the Rubicon, has on several occasions introduced that river as the figurative river of war.

Fortunately for England, she is yet on the peaceable side of the Rubicon; but as the flames once kindled are not always easily extinguished, the hopes of peace are not so clear as before the late mysterious dispute began.

But while the calm lasts, it may answer a very good purpose to take a view of the prospects, consistent with the maxim, that he that goeth to war should first sit down and count the cost.

The nation has a young and ambitious Minister at its head, fond of himself, and deficient in experience; and instances have often shewn that judgment is a different thing to genius, and that the affairs of a nation are but unsafely trusted where the benefit of experience is wanting.

Illustrations have been drawn from the circumstances of the war before last to decorate the character of the present Minister, and, perhaps, they have been greatly over-drawn; for the management must have been bad to have done less than what was then done, when we impartially consider the means, the force, and the money employed.

It was then Great Britain and America against France singly, for Spain did not join till near the end of the war. The great number of troops which the American Colonies then raised and paid themselves, were sufficient to turn the scale, if all other parts had been equal. France had not at that time attended to Naval Affairs so much as she has done since, and the capture of French sailors before any declaration of war was made, which, however it may be justified upon policy, will always be ranked among the clandestine arts of war, assured a certain, but unfair advantage against her, because it was like a man administering a disabling dose over-night to the person whom he intends to challenge in the morning.

COMMON SENSE

20th August, 1787

London

HINTS ON WAR, &c.

RIGHT by chance and wrong by system, are things so frequently seen in the political world, that it becomes a proof of prudence neither to censure nor applaud too soon.

"The Rubicon is past," was once given as a reason for prosecuting the most expensive war that England ever knew. Sore with the event, and groaning beneath a galling yoke of taxes, she has again been led ministerially on to the shore of the same delusive and fatal river, without being permitted to know the object or the reason why.

Expensive preparations have been gone into; fears, alarms, dangers, apprehensions, have been mistically held forth, as if the existence of the nation was at stake, and at last the mountain has brought forth a French mouse.[1]

Whosoever will candidly review the present national characters of England and France, cannot but be struck with surprize at the change that is taking place. The people of France are beginning to think for themselves, and the people of England resigning up the privilege of thinking.

The affairs of Holland have been the bubble of the day; and a tax is to be laid on shoes and boots (so say the news-papers) for the service of the Stadtholder of Holland. This will undoubtedly do honour to the nation, by verifying the old English proverb, "Over shoes, over boots."

---

[1] While Ridgeway's edition agrees with the Baltimore edition that the mouse is French, both Byrne's edition printed in Dublin in 1788 and J. Debrett's edition (printed in London in 1787) of

But tho' Democritus could scarcely have forborne laughing at the folly, yet as serious argument and sound reasoning are preferable to ridicule, it will be best to quit the vein of unprofitable humour, and give the cause a fair investigation. But before we do this, it may not be improper to take a general review of sundry political matters that will naturally lead to a better understanding of the subject.[2]

What has been the event of all the wars of England, but an amazing accumulation of debt, and an unparalleled burthen of taxes. Sometimes the pretence has been to support one outlandish cause, and sometimes another. At one time Austria, at another time Prussia, another to oppose Russia and so on; but the consequence has always been TAXES. A few men have enriched themselves by jobs and contracts, and the groaning multitude bore the burthen. What has England gained by war since the year 1738, only fifty years ago, to recompence her for TWO HUNDRED MILLIONS sterling, incurred as a debt within that time, and under the annual interest of which, besides what was incurred before, she is now groaning? Nothing at all.

The glare of fancied glory has often been held up, and the shadowy recompence imposed itself upon the senses. Wars that might have been prevented have been madly gone into, and the end has been debt and discontent. A sort of something which man cannot account for is mixed in his composition, and renders him the subject of deception by the very means he takes not to be deceived.

That jealousy which the individuals of every nation feels [sic] at the supposed designs of foreign powers, fits them to be the prey of Ministers, and of those among themselves whose trade is war, or whose livelihood is jobs and contracts. "Confusion to the politics of Europe, and may every nation be at war in six months," was a toast given in my hearing not long since.—The man was in court

---

Prospects on the Rubicon has a Dutch mouse, while the Amsterdam edition in French simply has *un souris* without any nationality specified.
   [2] Paine rarely uses classical sources. Here he refers to Democritus, the Greek philosopher of 460-357 BCE.

to the Ministry for a job.—Ye gentle Graces, if any such there be, who preside over human actions, how must ye weep at the viciousness of man.

When we consider, for the feelings of Nature cannot be dismissed, the calamities of war and the miseries it inflicts upon the human species, the thousands and tens of thousands of every age and sex who are rendered wretched by the event, surely there is something in the heart of man that calls upon him to think! Surely there is some tender cord, tuned by the hand of its Creator, that still struggles to emit in the hearing of the soul a note of sorrowing sympathy. Let it then be heard, and let man learn to feel, that the true greatness of a nation is founded on the principles of humanity; and that to avoid a war when our own existence is not endangered, and wherein the happiness of man must be wantonly sacrificed, is a higher principle of true honour than madly to engage in it.

But independent of all civil and moral considerations, there is no possible event that a war could produce to England on the present occasion, that could in the most distant proportion recompence the expence she must be at.[3] War involves in its progress such a train of unforeseen and unsupposed circumstances, such a combination of foreign matters, that no human wisdom can calculate the end. It has but one thing certain, and that is increase of TAXES. The policy of European Courts is now so cast, and their interests so interwoven with each other, that however easy it may be to begin a war, the weight and influence of interfering nations compel even the conqueror to unprofitable conditions of peace.

Commerce and maritime strength are now becoming the fashion, or rather the rage of Europe, and this naturally excites in them a combined wish to prevent England encreasing its comparative strength by destroying, or even relatively weakening the other, and therefore, whatever views each may have at the

---

[3] Byrne edition has instead: 'there is no possible event that a war could produce benefits to England or France, on the present occasion, that could in the most distant proportion recompense to either, the expence she must be at.' This is similar to the Debrett edition and the Amsterdam edition in French.

commencement of a war, new enemies will arise as either gains the advantage, and continued obstacles ensue to embarrass success.[4]

The greatness of Lewis the Fourteenth made Europe his enemy, and the same cause will produce the same consequence to any other European Power. That nation, therefore, is only truly wise, who contenting herself with the means of defence, creates to herself no unnecessary enemies by seeking to be greater than the system of Europe admits. The Monarch or the Minister who exceeds this line, knows but little of his business. It is what the poet on another occasion calls—

"The point where sense and nonsense join."

Perhaps there is not a greater instance of the folly of calculating upon events, than are to be found in the treaties of alliance. As soon as they have answered the immediate purpose of either of the parties they are but little regarded. Pretences, afterwards are never wanting to explain them away, nor reasons to render them abortive. And if half the money which nations lavish on sp[e]culative alliances were reserved for their own immediate purpose, whenever the occasion shall arrive, it would be more productively and advantageously employed.

Monarchs and Ministers, from ambition or resentment, often contemplate to themselves schemes of future greatness, and set out with what appears to them the fairest prospect: In the mean while, the great wheel of time and fate revolves unobserved, and something, never dreamed of, turns up and blasts the whole. A few fancied or un-profitable laurels supply the absence of success, and the exhausted nation is HUZZA'D INTO NEW TAXES.

The politics and interests of European Courts are so frequently varying with regard to each other, that there is no fixing even the probability of their future conduct. But the great principle of alliancing seems to be but little understood, or

---

[4] This long sentence makes more sense in the earlier editions, such as Byrne's which reads 'a combined wish to prevent either England or France increasing its comparative strength'.

little cultivated in Courts, perhaps the least of all in that of England.—No alliance can be operative, that does not embrace within itself, not only the attachment of the Sovereigns, but the real interest of the nations.

The alliance between France and Spain, however it may be spoken of as a mere family compact, derives its greatest strength from national interest. The mines of Peru and Mexico are the soul of this alliance. Were those mines extinct, the family compact would most probably dissolve.

There exists not a doubt in the mind of Spain, what part England would act, respecting those mines, could she demolish the maritime power of France; and therefore the interest of Spain feels itself continually united with France. Spain has high ideas of honour, but they have not the same ideas of English honour. They consider England as wholly governed by principles of interest, and that whatever she thinks it her interest to do, and supposes she has the power of doing, she makes very little ceremony of attempting. But this is not all—There is not a nation in Europe but what is more satisfied that those mines should be in the possession of Spain, than in that of any other European nation, because the wealth of those mines, sufficient to ruin Europe in the hands of some of its powers is innocently employed with respect to Europe, and better and more peaceably distributed among them all, through the medium of Spain, than it would be through that of any other nation. This is one of the secret causes that combine so large a part of Europe in the interest of France, because they cannot but consider her as a standing barrier to secure to them the free and equal distribution of this wealth throughout all the dominions of Europe.

This alliance of interest is likewise one of the unseen cements that prevents Spain and Portugal, two nations not very friendly to each other, proceeding to hostilities. They are both in the same situation, and whatever their dislikes may be, they cannot fail to consider, that by giving way to resentment that would weaken and exhaust themselves, each would be exposed a prey to some stronger power.

In short, this alliance of national interest is the only one that can be trusted, and the only one that can be operative. All other alliances formed on the mere will and caprice of Sovereigns, of family connections, un-combined with national interests, are but the quagmire of politics, and never fail to become a loss to that nation who wastes its present substance on the expectancy of distant returns.

With regard to Holland, a man must know very little of the matter, not to know that there exists a stronger principle of rivalship between Holland and England in point of commerce, than prevails between England and France in point of power: and, therefore, whenever a Stadtholder of Holland shall see it his interest to unite with the principle of his country, and act in concert with the sentiments of the very people who pay him for his services, the means now taken by England to render him formidable, will operate contrary to the political expectations of the present day.

Circumstances will produce their own natural effects, and no other, let the hopes or expectations of man be what they may. It is not our doing a thing with the design that it shall answer such or such an end, that will cause it to produce that end; the means taken must have a natural ability and tendency within themselves to produce no other, for it is this, and not our wishes or policy, that governs the event.

The English Navigation Act was levelled against the interest of the Dutch as a whole nation, and therefore it is not to be supposed that the catching at the accidental circumstances of one man, as in the case of the present Stadtholder, can combine the interest of that country with this. A few years, perhaps a less time, may remove him to the place where all things are forgotten, and his successor, contemplating his father's troubles, will be naturally led to reprobate the means that produced them, and to repose himself on the interests of his country, in preference to the accidental and tumultuous assistance of exterior power.[5]

---

[5] The Navigation and Trade Acts of 1650-1696 enforced a British monopoly on intra-colonial trade and remained in effect until 1820. The restrictions imposed on foreign ships using British ports, given the scale of British possessions in the Caribbean and the East Indies, severely

England herself exhibits at this day, a species of this kind of policy. The present reign, by embracing the Scotch, has tranquilized and conciliated the spirit that disturbed the two former reigns. Accusations were not wanting at that time to reprobate the policy as tinctured with ingratitude towards those who were the immediate means of the Hanover succession. The brilliant pen of Junius was drawn forth, but in vain. It enraptured without convincing; and tho' in the plenitude of its rage it might be said to give elegance to bitterness, yet the policy survived the blast.[6]

What then will be the natural consequence of this expence, on account of the Stadtholder, or on a war entered into from that cause? Search the various windings and caverns of the human heart, and draw from thence the most probable conclusion, for this is more to be depended upon than the projects or declarations of Ministers.

It may do very well for a paragraph in a miserable common news-paper, or the wild effusions of romantic politicians, or the mercenary views of those who wish for war on any occasion, or on no occasion at all, but for the sake of jobs and contracts, to talk of French finesse or French intrigue; but the Dutch are not a people to be impressed by the finesse or intrigue of France or England, or any other nation. If there has been any finesse in the case, it has been between the Electorate of Hanover, the King of Prussia, and the Stadtholder, in which it is most probable the people of England will be finessed out of a sum of money.

The Dutch, as is already observed, are not a people open to the impression of finesse. It is lost upon them. They are impressed by their commercial interest. It

---

hampered Dutch shipping and were a source of Patriot grievance against the British. During the American War of Independence the bourgeois patriots supported free trade with America while their Stadtholder's ambivalence suggested pro-English sympathies contrary to Dutch commercial interests.

[6] Junius was the pseudonym adopted by the author of a famous series of satirical letters published in the *Public Advertiser* between 1769-72. The letters contributed to the downfall of the Grafton administration and increased the popularity of John Wilkes. W. H. Burr suggested that Paine himself might be Junius but this is unlikely. Boswell on the other hand thought it might be Burke. The true author was most likely Sir Philip Francis (1740-1818) a clerk in the war office

is the political soul of their country, the spring of their actions, and when this principle coincides with their ideas of freedom, it has all the impulse a Dutchman is capable of feeling.

The Opposition in Holland were the enemies of the Stadtholder, upon a conviction that he was not the friend of their national interests. They wanted no other impulse but this. Whether this defect in him proceeded from foreign attachment, from bribery or corruption, or from the well-known defects of his understanding, is not the point of enquiry. It was the effect rather than the cause that irritated the Hollanders.

If the Stadtholder made use of the power he held in the government to expose and endanger the interests and property of the very people who supported him, what other incentive does any man in any country require? If the Hollanders conceived the conduct of the Stadtholder injurious to their national interest, they had the same right to expel him which England had to expel the Stuarts; and the interference of England to re-establish him, serves only to confirm in the Hollanders the same hatred against England which the attempt of Lewis XIVth, to re-establish the Stuarts caused in England against France; therefore if the present policy is intended to attach Holland to England, it goes on a principle exceedingly erroneous.

Let us now consider the situation of the Stadtholder, as making another part of the question.

He must place the cause of his troubles to some secret influence which governed his conduct during the late war, or in other words, that he was suspected of being the tool of the then British Administration. Therefore, as every part of an argument ought to have its weight, instead of charging the French of intriguing with the Hollanders, the charge more consistently lies against the British Ministry, for intriguing with the Stadtholder, and endangering the nation in a war without a sufficient object. That which the Ministry are now doing confirms the suspicion,

---

from 1762-72. See Conway, *Life*, p. 20 & *Junius: including letters by the same writer under*

and explains to the Hollanders that collusion of the Stadtholder against their national interests, which he must wish to have concealed, and the explanation does him more hurt than the unnecessary parade of service has done him good.

Nothing but necessity should have operated with England to appear openly in a case that must put the Stadtholder on still worse terms with his countrymen. Had France made any disposition for war, had she armed, had she made any one hostile preparation, there might then have been some pretence for England taking a step, that cannot fail to expose to the world that the suspicions of the Hollanders against the Stadtholder were well founded, and that their cause was just, however unsuccessful has been the event.

As to the consequence of Holland in the scale of Europe, (the great stake, says some of the news-papers, for which England is contending) that is naturally pointed out by her condition: As merchants for other nations her interest dictates to her to be a neutral power, and this she always will be, unless she is made war upon, as was the case in the last war; and any expectation beyond what is the line of her interest, that is, beyond neutrality, either in England or France, will prove abortive. It therefore cannot be policy to go to war to effect that at a great expence, which will naturally happen of itself, and beyond which there is nothing to expect.

Let Holland be allied with England or with France, or with neither, or with both, her national conduct, consequently arising out of her circumstances, will be nearly the same, that is, she will be neutral. Alliances have such a natural tendency to sink into harmless unoperative things, that to make them a cause for going to war, either to prevent their being formed, or to break any already formed, is the silliest speculation that war can be made upon, or wealth wasted to accomplish. It would scarcely be worth the attempt, if war could be carried on without expence, because almost the whole that can be hoped at the risk and expence of a war, is effected by their natural tendency to inactivity.

---

other signatures, ed. by John Wade, 2 vols (London: Henry G. Bohn, 1850).

However pompous the declarations of an alliance may be, the object of many of them is no other than good-will, and reciprocally securing, as far as such security can go, that neither shall join the enemies of the other in any war that may happen. But the national circumstances of Holland, operate to ensure this tranquility on her part as effectually to the power she is not allied with, as the engagement itself does to the power with whom she is allied; therefore the security from circumstances is as good as the security from engagement.

As to a cordial union of interest between Holland and England, it is as unnatural to happen as between two individual rivals in the same trade: And if there is any step that England could take to put it at a still greater distance, it is the part she is now acting. She has increased the animosity of Holland on the speculative politics of interesting the Stadtholder, whose future repose depends upon uniting with the opposition in Holland, as the present reign did with the Scotch. How foolish then has been the policy, how needless the expence, of endangering a war on account of the affairs of Holland.

A cordiality between England and France is less improbable than between England and Holland. It is not how an Englishman feels but how a Dutchman feels, that decides this question. Between England and France there is no real rivalship of interest; it is more the effect of temper, disposition, and the jealousy of confiding in each other, than any substantial cause, that keeps up the animosity. But on the part of Holland towards England, there is over and above the spirit of animosity, the more powerful motives of interested commercial rivalship, and the galling remembrance of past injuries. The making war upon them under Lord North's administration, when they were taking no part in the hostilities, but merely acting the business of merchants, is a circumstance that will not easily be forgotten by them. On these reasons, therefore, which are naturally deduced from the operative feelings of mankind, any expectation of attaching Holland to England as a friendly power, is vague and futile. Nature has her own way of working in the heart, and all plans of politics not founded thereon will disappoint themselves.

Any one who will review the history of English politics for several years past, must perceive they have been directed without system. To establish this, it is only necessary to examine one circumstance fresh in the mind of every man.

The American war was prosecuted at a very great expence, on the publicly declared opinion, that the retaining America was necessary to the existence of England; but America being now separated from England, the present politics are, that she is better without her than with her. Both these cannot be true, and their contradiction to each other shews a want of system. If the latter is true, it amounts to an impeachment of the political judgment of government, because the discovery ought to have been made before the expence was gone into. This single circumstance, yet fresh in every man's mind, is sufficient to create a suspicion, whether the present measures are more wisely founded than the former ones; and whether experience may not prove, that going to war for the sake of the Stadtholder, or for the hope of retaining a partial interest in Holland, who, under any connection can, from circumstances, be no more than a neutral power, is not as weak policy as going to war to retain America.

If England is powerful enough to maintain her own ground and consequence in the world as an independent nation, she needs no foreign connection. If she is not, the fact contradicts the popular opinion that she is. Therefore, either her politics are wrong, or her true condition is not what she supposes it to be. Either she must give up her opinion to justify her politics, or renounce her politics to vindicate her opinion.

If some kind of connection with Holland is supposed to be an object worthy some expence to obtain, it may be asked why was that connection broken by making war upon her in the last war. If it was not then worth preserving without expence, is it now worth re-obtaining at a vast expence? If the Hollanders do not like the English, can they be made to like them against their wills? If it shall be said that under the former connection they were unfriendly, will they be more friendly under any other? They were then in as free a situation to chuse as any future circumstances can make them, and, therefore, the national governing sentiment of the country can be easily discovered, for it signifies not what or who a Stadtholder may be, that which governs Holland is, and always must be, a commercial principle, and it will follow this line in spite of politics. Interest is as predominant and as silent in its operations as love; it resists all the attempts of force, and countermines all the stratagem of controul.

The most able English Statesmen and Politicians have always held it as a principle, that foreign connections served only to embarrass and exhaust England. That, surrounded by the ocean, she could not be invaded as countries are on the Continent of Europe, and that her insular situation dictated to her a different system of politics to what those countries required, and that to be enleagued with them was sacrificing the advantages of situation to a capricious system of politics. That tho' she might serve them, they could not much serve her, and that as the service must at all times be paid for, it could always be procured when it was wanted; and that it would be better to take it up in this line than to embarrass herself with speculative alliances that served rather to draw her into a Continental war on their account, than extricate her from a war undertaken on her own account.

From this discussion of the affairs of Holland, and of the inadequacy of Holland as an object for war, we will proceed to shew that neither England nor France are in a condition to go to war, and that there is no present object to the one or the other to recompence the expence that each must be at, or atone to the subjects of either for the additional burthens that must be brought upon them. I defend the cause of the poor, of the manufactures [sic], of the tradesman, of the farmer, and of all those on whom the real burthen of taxes fall—but above all, I defend the cause of humanity.

It will always happen, that any rumour of war will be popular among a great number of people in London. There are thousands who live by it; it is their harvest; and the clamour which those people keep up in news-papers and conversations, passes unsuspiciously for the voice of the people, and it is not till after the mischief is done, that the deception is discovered.

Such people are continually holding up in very magnified terms the wealth of the nation, and the depressed condition of France, as reasons for commencing a war, without knowing any thing of either of these subjects.

But admitting them to be as true, as they are false, as will be hereafter shewn, it certainly indicates a vileness in the national disposition of any country, that will make the accidental internal difficulties to which all nations are subject, and sometimes encumbered with, a reason for making war upon them. The amazing encrease and magnitude of the paper currency now floating in all parts of England, exposes her to a shock as much more tremendous than the shock occasioned by the bankruptcy of the South Sea funds, as the quantity of credit and paper currency is now greater than they were at that time. Whenever such a circumstance shall happen, and the wisest men in the nation are, and cannot avoid being, impressed with the danger, it would be looked upon a baseness in France to make the distress and misfortune of England a cause and opportunity for making war upon her, yet this hideous infidelity is publicly avowed in England. The bankruptcy of 1719, was precipitated by the great credit which the funds then had, and the confidence which people placed in them. Is not credit making infinitely greater strides now than it made then? Is not confidence equally as blind now as at that day? The people then supposed themselves as wise as they do now, yet they were miserably deceived, and the deception that has once happened will happen again from the same causes.

Credit is not money, and therefore it is not pay, neither can it be put in the place of money in the end. It is only the means of getting into debt, not the means of getting out, otherwise the national debt could not accumulate; and the delusion which nations are under respecting the extention of credit is exactly like that which every man feels respecting life, the end is always nearer than was expected; and we become bankrupts in time by the same delusion that nations become bankrupts in property.

The little which nations know, or are some times willing to know, of each other, serves to precipitate them into wars which neither would have undertaken, had they fully known the extent of the power and circumstances of each other; it may therefore be of some use to place the circumstances of England and France in a comparative point of view.

In order to do this the accidental circumstances of a nation must be thrown out of the account. By accidental circumstances is meant, those temporary disjointings and derangements of its internal system which every nation in the world is subject to, and which, like accidental fits of sickness in the human body, prevent in the interim the full exertion and exercise of its natural powers.

The substantial basis of the power of a nation arises out of its population, its wealth and its revenues. To these may be added the disposition of the people. Each of these will be spoken to as we proceed.

Instances are not wanting to shew that a nation confiding too much on its natural strength, is less inclined to be active in its operations than one of less natural powers who is obliged to supply that deficiency by encreasing its exertions. This has often been the case between England and France. The activity of England arising from its fears, has sometimes exceeded the exertions of France reposing on its confidence.

But as this depends on the accidental disposition of a people, it will not always be the same. It is a matter well known to every man who has lately been in France, that a very extraordinary change is working itself in the minds of the people of that nation. A spirit that will render France exceedingly formidable whenever its government shall embrace the fortunate opportunity of doubling its strength by allying, if it may be so expressed, (for it is difficult to express a new idea by old terms) the Majesty of the Sovereign with the Majesty of the nation; for of all alliances this is infinitely the strongest and the safest to be trusted to, because the interest so formed, and operating against external enemies can never be divided.

It may be taken as a certain rule, that a subject of any country attached to the government on the principles above-mentioned is of twice the value he was before. Freedom in the subject is not a diminution, as was formerly believed, of the power of government, but an increase of it. Yet the progress by which changes of this kind are effected, requires to be nicely attended to.

Were governments to offer freedom to the people, or to shew an anxiety for that purpose, the offer most probably would be rejected. The purpose for which it was offered might be mistrusted. Therefore the desire must originate with, and proceed from the mass of the people, and when the impression becomes universal, and not before, is the important moment for the most effectual consolidation of national strength and greatness that can take place.

While this change is working, there will appear a kind of chaos in the nation; but the creation we enjoy arose out of a chaos, and our greatest blessings appear to have a confused beginning.

Therefore, we may take it for granted, that what has at this moment the appearance of disorder in France, is no more than one of the natural links in that great chain of circumstances by which nations acquire the summit of their greatness. The Provincial Assemblies already begun in France, are as full, or rather a fuller representation of the people than the Parliaments of England are.

The French, or, as they were formerly called, the Franks, (from whence came the English word Frank and Free) were once the freest people in Europe; and as nations appear to have their periodical revolutions, it is very probable they will be so again.[7] The change is already began. The people of France, as it was before observed, are beginning to think for themselves, and the people of England resigning up the prerogative of thinking.

We shall now proceed to compare the present condition of England and France as to population, revenues and wealth, and to shew that neither is in a condition of going to war, and that war can end in nothing but loss, and, most probably, a temporary ruin to both nations.

To establish this point so necessary for both nations to be impressed with, a

---

[7] This explanation of the words Frank and Free is not included in the French edition printed in Amsterdam.

free investigation of all the matters connected with it is indispensable: If, therefore, any thing herein advanced shall be disagreeable, it must be justified on the ground that it is better to be known in order to prevent ruin, than to be concealed, when such concealment serves only to hasten the ruin on.

OF POPULATION.

The population of France being upwards of twenty-four millions, is more than double that of Great Britain and Ireland; besides which France recruits more soldiers in Swisserland than England does in Scotland and Ireland. To this may likewise be added, that England and Ireland are not on the best terms. The suspicion that England governs Ireland for the purpose of keeping her low to prevent her becoming her rival in trade and manufactures, will always operate to hold Ireland in a state of sentimental hostilities with England.

REVENUES.

The Revenues of France are twenty-four millions sterling. The Revenues of England fifteen millions and an half. The taxes per head in France are twenty shillings sterling; the taxes per head in England are two pounds four shillings and two pence. The national debt in France including the life annuities (which are two-fifths of the whole debt, and are annually expiring) at eleven years purchase, is one hundred and forty-two millions sterling. The national debt of England, the whole of which is on perpetual interest, is two hundred and forty-five millions. The national debt of France contains a power of annihilating itself without any new taxes for that purpose; because it needs no more than to apply the life annuities as they expire to the purchase of the other three-fifths, which are on perpetual interest: But the national debt of England has not this advantage, and therefore the million a year that is to be applied towards the reducing it is so much additional tax upon the people, over and above the current service.

WEALTH.

This is an important investigation, it ought therefore to be heard with patience, and judged of without prejudice.

Nothing is more common than for people to mistake one thing for another. Do not those who are crying up the wealth of the nation, mistake a paper currency for riches? To ascertain this point may be one of the means of preventing that ruin which cannot fail to follow by persisting in the mistake.

The highest estimation that is made of the quantity of gold and silver in Britain at this present day is twenty millions: and those who are most conversant with money transactions, believe it to be considerably below that sum. Yet this is no more money than what the nation possessed twenty years ago, and therefore, whatever her trade may be, it has produced to her no profit. Certainly no man can be so unwise as to suppose that encreasing the quantity of bank notes, which is done with as little trouble as printing of news-papers, is national wealth.

The quantity of money in the nation was very well ascertained in the years 1773, 74, and 76, by calling in the light gold coin.

There were upwards of fifteen millions and a half of gold coin then called in, which, with upwards of two millions of heavy guineas that remained out, and the silver coin, made above twenty millions, which is more than there is at this day. There is an amazing increase in the circulation of Bank paper, which is no more national wealth than news-papers are; because an increase of promissary notes, the capital remaining unincreased, or not increasing in the same proportion, is no increase of wealth. It serves to raise false ideas which the judicious soon discover, and the ignorant experience to their cost.

Out of twenty millions sterling, the present quantity of real money in the nation, it would be too great an allowance to say that one fourth of that sum, which is five millions, was in London. But even admitting this to be the case, it would require no very uncommon powers to ascertain pretty nearly what proportion of that sum of five millions could be in the Bank. It would be ridiculous to suppose it could be less than half a million, and extravagant to suppose it could be two millions.

It likewise requires no very extraordinary discernment to ascertain how immense the quantity of Bank Notes, compared to its capital in the Bank must be, when it is considered, that the national taxes are paid in Bank Notes, that all great transactions are done in Bank Notes, and that were a loan for twenty millions to be opened at the meeting of Parliament, it would most probably be subscribed in a few days: Yet all men must know the loan could not be paid in money, because it is at least four times greater than all the money in London, including the Bankers and the Bank amount too. In short, every thing shews, that the rage that over-run America, for paper money or paper currency, has reached to England under another name. There it was called Continental Money, and here it is called Bank Notes. But it signifies not what name it bears, if the capital is not equal to the redemption.

There is likewise another circumstance that cannot fail to strike with some force when it is mentioned, because every man that has any thing to do with money transactions, will feel the truth of it, tho' he may not before have reflected upon it. It is the embarrassed condition into which the gold coin is thrown by the necessity of weighing it, and by refusing guineas that are even standing weight, and there appears to be but few heavy ones. Whether this is intended to force the Paper Currency into circulation, is not here attempted to be asserted, but it certainly has that effect to a very great degree, because people, rather than submit to the trouble and hazard of weighing, will take paper in preference to money. This was once the case in America.

The natural effect of encreasing and continuing to increase paper currencies is that of banishing the real money. The shadow takes place of the substance till the country is left with only shadows in its hands.

A trade that does not increase the quantity of real money in a country, cannot be styled a profitable trade; yet this is certainly the case with England: and as to credit, of which so much has been said, it may be founded on ignorance or a false belief, as well as on real ability.

In Amsterdam, the money deposited in the Bank is never taken out again. The depositors, when they have debts to pay, transfer their right to the persons to whom they are indebted, and those again proceed by the same practice, and the transfer of the right goes for payment; now could all the money deposited in the Bank of Amsterdam be privately removed away, and the matter be kept a secret, the ignorance, or the belief that the money was still there, would give the same credit as if it had not been removed. In short, credit is often no more than an opinion, and the difference between credit and money is that money requires no opinion to support it.

All the countries in Europe annually increase in their quantity of gold and silver except England. By the registers kept at Lisbon and Cadiz, the two ports into which the gold and silver from South America are imported, it appears that above eighty millions sterling have been imported within twenty years*. This has spread itself over Europe, and increased the quantity in all the countries on the Continent, yet twenty years ago there was as much gold and silver in England as there is at this time.

The value of the silver imported into Europe exceeds that of the gold, yet every one can see there is no increase of silver coin in England; very little silver coin appearing except what are called Birmingham shillings, which have a faint impression of King William on one side, and are smooth on the other.

In what is the profits of trade to shew itself but by increasing the quantity of that which is the object of trade, money. An increase of paper is not an increase of national profit any more than it is an increase of national money, and the

---

*From 1763 to 1777, a period of fifteen years of peace, the registered importations of gold and silver into Lisbon and Cadiz, was seventy millions sterling, besides what was privately landed.

confounding paper and money together, or not attending to the distinction, is a rock that the nation will one day split upon.

Whether the payment of interest to foreigners, or the trade to the East-Indies, or the nation embroling itself in foreign wars, or whether the amount of all the trade which England carries on with different parts of the world, collectively taken, balances itself without profit; whether one or all of these is the cause, why the quantity of money does not encrease in England is not, in this place, the object of enquiry. It is the fact and not the cause that is the matter here treated of.

Men immersed in trade and the concerns of a counting-house, are not the most speculative in national affairs, or always the best judges of them. Accustomed to run risks in trade, they are habitually prepared to run risks with Government, and though they are the first to suffer, they are often the last to foresee an evil.

Let us now cast a look towards the manufactures. A great deal has been said of their flourishing condition, and perhaps a great deal too much, for it may again be asked, where is the profit if there is no encrease of money in the nation?

The woollen manufacture is the staple manufacture of England, and this is evidently on the decline, in some, if not in all, its branches. The city of Norwich, one of the most populous cities in England, and wholly dependent on the woollen manufacture, is, at this day, in a very impoverished condition, owing to the decline of its trade.[8]

But not to rest the matter on a general assertion, or embarrass it with numerous statements, we will produce a circumstance by which the whole progress of the trade may be ascertained.

So long as thirty years ago the price paid to the spinners of wool was one shilling for twenty-four skains, each skain containing five hundred and sixty

---

[8] This is perhaps information that Paine had picked up when visiting his mother in Thetford on his arrival from France in September 1787. The causes of the crisis in 1788, particularly in the textile industry are examined in J. Hoppit, 'Financial Crises in Eighteenth Century England', *Economic History Review*, 2nd series, 39, 1986, 45 & 51.

yards. This, according to the term of the trade, was called giving a shilling for a shilling. A good hand would spin twelve skains, which was sixpence a day.

According to the increase of taxes, and the increased price of all the articles of life, they certainly ought now to get at least fifteen pence, for what thirty years ago they got a shilling for. But such is the decline of the trade, that the case is directly the contrary. They now get but ninepence for the shilling, that is, they get but ninepence for what thirty years ago they got a shilling for. Can these people cry out for war, when they are already half ruined by the decline of trade, and half devoured by the encrease of taxes?

But this is not the whole of the misfortunes which that part of the country suffers, and which will extend to others. The Norfolk farmers were the first who went into the practice of manuring their land with marle: but time has shewn, that though it gave a vigour to the land for some years, it operated in the end to exhaust its stamina; that the lands in many parts are worse than before they began to marle, and that it will not answer to marle a second time.

The manufactures of Manchester, Birmingham and Sheffield have had of late a considerable spring, but this appears to be rather on speculation than certainty. The speculations on the American market have failed, and that on Russia is becoming very precarious. Experience likewise was wanting to ascertain the quantity which the treaty of commerce with France would give sale to, and it is most probable the estimations have been too high, more especially as English goods will now become unpopular in France, which was not the case before the present injudicious rupture.

But in the best state which manufactures can be in, they are very unstable sources of national wealth. The reasons are, that they seldom continue long in one stay. The market for them depends upon the caprice of fashions, and sometimes of politics in foreign countries, and they are at all times exposed to rivalship as well as to change. The Americans have already several manufactures among them, which they prefer to the English, such as axes, scythes, sickles, houghs, planes, nails, &c. Window glass, which was once a considerable article of export from England to America, the Americans now procure from other countries, nearly as good as the English Crown Glass, and but little dearer than the common green window glass.

It is somewhat remarkable that so many pens have been displayed to shew what is called the increase of the commerce of England, and yet all of them have stopt short of the grand point, that is, they have gone no farther than to shew that a larger number of shipping, and a greater quantity of tonnage have been employed of late years than formerly: But this is no more than what is happening in other parts of Europe. The present fashion of the world is commerce, and the quantity encreases in France as well as in England.

But the object of all trade is profit, and profit shews itself, not by an increase of paper currency, for that may be nationally had without the trouble of trade, but by an increase of real money: therefore the estimation should have ended, not in the comparative quantity of shipping and tonnage, but in the comparative quantity of gold and silver.

Had the quantity of gold and silver increased in England, the ministerial writers would not have stopt short at shipping and tonnage; but if they know any thing of the matter, they must know that it does not increase, and that the deception is occasioned by the increase of paper instead of money, and that as paper continues to increase, gold and silver will diminish. Poorer in wealth, and richer in delusion.

Something is radically wrong, and time will discover it to be putting paper in the room of money.

Out of one hundred millions sterling of gold and silver, which must have been imported into Europe from South America since the commencement of the peace before last, it does not appear that England has derived or retains any portion of it.

Mr. Neckar states the annual increase of gold and silver in France, that is, the proportion which France draws of the annual importation into Europe, to be of upwards of one million sterling. But England, in the space of twenty years, does not appear to have encreased in any thing but paper currency.

Credulity is wealth while credulity lasts, and credit is, in a thousand instances, the child of credulity. It requires no more faith to believe paper to be money, than to believe a man could go into a quart bottle; and the nation whose credulity can be imposed upon by bottle conjuring, can, for a time, be imposed upon by paper conjuring.

From these matters we pass on to make some observations on the national debt, which is another species of paper currency.

In short to whatever point the eye is directed, whether to the money, the paper, the manufactures, the taxes, or the debt, the inability of supporting a war is evident, unless it is intended to carry it on by fleecing the skin over people[']s ears by taxes; and therefore the endangering the nation in a war for the sake of the Stadtholder of Holland, or the King of Prussia, or any other foreign affairs, from which England can derive no possible advantage, is an absurd and ruinous system of politics.

France, perhaps, is not in a better situation, and, therefore, a war where both must lose, and wherein they could only act the part of seconds, must historically have been denominated a boyish, foolish, unnecessary quarrel.

But before we enter on the subject of the national debt, it will be proper to make a general review of the different manner of carrying on war since the revolution to what was the practice before.

Before the Revolution the intervals of peace and war always found means to pay off the expence, and leave the nation clear of incumbrance at the commencement of any succeeding war; and even for some years after the Revolution this practice was continued.

From the year 1688, (the æra of the Revolution) to the year 1702, a period of fourteen years, the sums borrowed by Government at different times, amounted to forty-four millions; yet this sum was paid off almost as fast as it was borrowed; thirty-four millions being paid off, at the commencement of the year 1702. This was a greater exertion than the nation has ever made since, for exertion is not in borrowing but in paying.

From that time wars have been carried on by borrowing and funding the capital on a perpetual interest, instead of paying it off, and thereby continually carrying forward and accumulating the weight and expence of every war into the next. By this means that which was light at first, becomes immensely heavy at last. The nation has now on its shoulders the weight of all the wars from the time of Queen Anne. This practice is exactly like that of loading a horse with a feather at a time till you break his back.

The national debt exhibits at this day a striking novelty. It has travelled on in a circular progression till the amount of the annual interest has exactly overtaken, or become equal to, the first capital of the national debt, NINE MILLIONS. Here begins the evidence of the predictions so long foretold by the ablest calculators in the nation. The interest will in succession overtake all the succeeding capitals, and that with the proportioned rapidity with which those capitals accumulated; because by continuing the practice, not only higher and higher premiums must be given for loans, but the money, or rather the paper, will not go so far as it formerly did, and therefore the debt will encrease with a continually encreasing velocity.

The expence of every war, since the national debt began, has, upon an average, been double the expence of the war preceding it; the expence therefore of the next war will be at least two hundred millions, which will encrease the annual interest to at least seventeen millions, and consequently the taxes in the same proportion; the following war will encrease the interest to thirty-three millions, and a third war will mount up the interest to sixty-five millions. This is not going on in the spirit of prediction, but taking what has already been as a rule for what will yet be, and therefore the nation has but a miserable prospect to look at. The weight of accumulating interest is not much felt till after many years have passed over; but when it begins to be heavy, as it does now, the burthen encreases like that of purchasing a horse with a farthing for the first nail of the shoe and doubling it.

As to Mr. Pitt's scheme of reducing the national debt by a million a year, applied to the purchase of stock, it will turn out, to say no worse of it, a ridiculous and frivolous project: For if a minister has not experience enough to distinguish a feather in the air, and such there always will be, from the God of War, nor the clamours and interest of those who are seeking for jobs and contracts, from the voice and interest of the people, he will soon precipitate the nation into some unnecessary war: and therefore, any scheme of redemption of the debt, founded on the supposed continuance of peace, will, with such conduct, be no more than a balloon.

That the funding system contains within itself the seeds of its own destruction, is as certain as that the human body contains within itself the seeds of death. The event is as fixed as fate, unless it can be taken as a proof that because we are not dead we are not to die.

The consequence of the funding scheme, even if no other event takes place, will be to create two violent parties in the nation. The one goaded by taxes continually encreasing to pay the interest, the other reaping a benefit from the taxes by receiving the interest. This is very strongly shadowed forth, like the hand-writing on the wall, by the ingenious author of the Commercial Atlas, in his observations on the national debt.[9]

The slumber that for several years has over-shadowed the nation in all matters of public finance, cannot be supposed to last for ever. The people have not yet awakened to the subject, and this is taken for granted they never will. But, if a supposed unnecessary expenditure of between five and six millions sterling in the finances of France (for the writer undertakes not to judge of the fact) has awakened that whole nation, a people supposed to be perfectly docile in all national matters, surely the people of England will not be less attentive to their rights and properties. If this should not be the case, the inference will be fairly drawn, that England is losing the spirit that France is taking up, and that it is an

---

[9] This probably refers to William Playfair, *The Commercial and Political Atlas; representing by means of stained copperplate charts, the exports, imports, and general trade of England* (London: Playfair, 1786).

ingenious device in the Ministry to compose the nation to unpopular and unnecessary taxes, by shamming a victory when there was no enemy at hand.

In short, every war serves to encrease every kind of paper currency in the nation, and to diminish the quantity of gold and silver, by sending it to Prussia and other foreign countries.

It will not be denied, that credulity is a strong trait in the English character; and this has in no instance shewn itself more than in mistaking paper for money, except it be in the unaccountable ignorance of mistaking the debt of the nation for riches. But the suspicion is beginning to awake.

We will close this article with observing, that a new kind of paper currency has arose [sic] within a few years, which is that of country Bank Notes; almost every town now has its Bank, its Paper Mint, and the coinage of paper is become universal. In the mean time the melting down the light guineas, and recoining them, passes with those who know no better for an encrease of money; because every new guinea they see, and which is but seldom, they naturally suppose to be a guinea more, when it is really nothing else than an old guinea new cast.

From this account of the money, paper, and national debt of England, we proceed to compare it with the money, paper, and national debt of France.

It is very well known that paper has not the credit in France which it has in England, and that, consequently, there is much less of it. This has naturally operated to encrease the quantity of gold and silver in France, and prevent the encrease of paper.

The highest estimation of the quantity of gold and silver in England, as already stated, is twenty millions sterling, and the quantity of paper grafted thereon immense.

The quantity of gold and silver in France, is upwards of ninety millions sterling, and the quantity of paper grafted thereon trifling. France, therefore, has a long run of credit yet in reserve, which England has already expended; and it will naturally follow that when the Government of France and the nation shall adjust their differences by an amicable embrace of each other, that this reserved credit will be brought forth, and the power of France will be doubly encreased. The adjustment of these differences is but the business of a day, whenever its Government shall see the proper moment for doing it; and nothing would precipitate this event more than a war. The cry of war, from the injudicious provocations given by the British Ministry, and the disadvantageous effect of the Commercial Treaty, is becoming popular in France.

The near situation of France to Spain and Portugal, the two countries which import gold and silver, and her manufactures being better adapted to the warm climate of those countries than the manufactures of England, give her superior opportunities of drawing money into the nation; and as she has but little trade to the East Indies, the money so drawn in is not drawn out again, as in England. Another advantage is, that from the greatness of her dominions, she has no occasion to waste her wealth in hiring foreign troops, as is the practice with England; and a third advantage is, that the money which England squanders in Prussia and other countries on the Continent serves to encrease the wealth of France because a considerable part of it centres there through the medium of her commerce.

Admitting Great Britain and Ireland to contain ten millions of inhabitants, the quantity of money per head is forty shillings; the money per head in France is three pounds fifteen shillings, which is nearly double.

The national debt of England, compared to the whole amount of money in the nation, is as twelve is to one, that is, the debt is twelve times greater than all the money amounts to.

The national debt of France, compared to the whole amount of her money, is considerably less than as two is to one, that is, her debt is not so much as twice the amount of her money. France, therefore, as already stated, has an immense credit in reserve whenever the settlement of her present internal differences shall furnish her with the means of employing it; and that period, so much to be dreaded by England, is hastening on.

The annual interest of the national debt of England and France are nearly equal, being NINE MILLIONS sterling; but with this difference, that above three millions and a half of the annual interest of France are only life annuities. The interest, therefore, of her debt lessens every year, and she will have a surplus up to the amount of three millions and a half, to apply to the purchase of that part of the debt which is on perpetual interest; therefore, without any new taxes for that purpose, she can discharge her whole debt in less than a third of the time in which it can be done in England, according to Mr. Pitt's plan, with his additional tax of a million a year.

But let the event of Mr. Pitt's plan be what it may, as to reducing the debt, there is one circumstance that cannot fail to accompany it, which is, that of making it the interest of Government, in executing this plan, to undermine the interest of its creditors, or the value of the funds, for the purpose of purchasing at a cheaper rate.

The plan is founded on the presumption of a long uninterrupted peace, and that future loans would not be wanted, which cannot now be expected, for France in her turn is getting into a temper for war. The plan naturally strikes at the credit of Government, in contracting further debts; for were a loan to be opened to-morrow, the subscribers, naturally perceiving that it was the interest of Government to undermine them as soon as they became creditors, would consequently seek to secure themselves, by demanding higher premiums at first. It is a question whether a premium of thirty per cent is now as good as ten was before; and therefore the plan, in case of a war, instead of lessening the debt, serves to push it more rapidly on.

The Minister certainly never understood the natural operation of his plan, or he would not have acted as he has done. The plan has two edges, while he has supposed it to have only one. It strikes at the debt in peace, and at the credit in war.

The gentleman who originally furnished the Minister with this plan, now gives it totally up. He knew its operation both in peace and war, but the Minister appears not to have comprehended it: But if he has made a mistake, his youth and inexperience must be his apology.

The plan, unless it should be altered, that is given out for providing for the expence of the late armaments, is in reality no other than the American plan of paper money, and it is very probable that the Minister has received it from some American refugee.

The plan given out is, that the Minister is to borrow the MONEY of the Bank. Here is the delusion. The name of MONEY covers the deception. For the case is, that the Bank does not lend the real money, but it issues out an emission of Bank-paper, and the presumption is, that there will be no run upon the Bank in consequence of such an extraordinary emission; but if there should, no man can be at a loss in foreseeing the issue.

There are those who remember that on a former run, the Bank was obliged to prolong the time by paying shillings and sixpences, and it is universally credited, that a quantity of silver is now preserved in the Bank for the same purpose; but the device, to every person of reflection, shews that the capital is not equal to the demands, and that the Chapter of Accidents is part of the Bible of Bank.

It may be asked why do not the Government issue the paper instead of the Bank? The answer is, that it is exactly the same thing in the end, only with this difference in the mode, that were the Government to do it, it would be too visible a system of paper currency, and that a disguise is necessary.

Having recourse to the Bank, is a kind of playing the Bank off against the Funds. Fighting one kind of paper against another, and in the combat both will be sufferers.

In short, the delusion of paper riches is working as rapidly in England as it did in America. A young and inexperienced Minister, like a young and inexperienced Congress, may suppose that he sees mines of wealth in a printing-press, and that a nation cannot be exhausted while there is paper and ink enough to print paper money. Every new emission, until the delusion bursts, will appear to the nation an increase of wealth. Every merchant's coffers will appear a treasury, and he will swell with paper riches till he becomes a bankrupt.

When a Bank makes too free with its paper, it exposes itself in much the same manner which a Government does that makes too free with its power; too much credit is as bad as too little; and there is such a thing as governing too much, as well in a Bank as in a Government. But nothing exposes a Bank more than being under the influence, instead of the protection of Government, and whenever either the property or the credit of a Bank can be commanded or influenced by a Government, or a Minister, its destruction is not far off.

We have now stated the comparative condition of England and France as to money matters. But there yet remain some things necessary to be touched upon.

It is an error very frequently committed in the world to mistake disposition for condition.

France, with a much better permanent condition for war than England, is in a less disposition to enter into one, and this want of disposition in her is mistaken in England for want of condition; and on the other hand, the apparent disposition in England for war is mistaken by her for a condition to undertake and carry one on.

There appears a uniformity in all the works of Nature, from individual animals up to nations. The smaller animals are always the most fretful, passionate, and insulting. They mistake temper for strength, and often fall a sacrifice to vexatious impetuosity, while larger ones go calmly on, and require repeated provocations to incense them. France may yet be aggravated into war, and very probably will. Where the condition exists, the disposition may at any time take place. We may create temper, but we cannot create strength.

While the literature of England preserves an honourable rank among the nations of Europe, her national character is most miserably suffering in the world through her new[s]-papers. The most barefaced perfidiousness, the most abandoned principles are daily propagated. A total disregard to all the obligations of national faith and honour are publicly professed. Instead of that true greatness of heart, that calm grandeur of sentiment, that generous disdain of vulgar littleness that ought always to accompany the disputes of nations, scarcely any thing is to be seen but mean abuse and low scurrility. This is not the case in any other country in the world but England.

We will now proceed to conclude with a few additional observations on the state of politics.

For several weeks the nation was amused with the daily rumours of some great Cabinet secret, and admiring how profoundly the secret was kept, when the only secret was, that there was no secret to divulge.

But this opinion of a secret very well shews that the opinion of the nation was opposed to the opinion of the Minister, or the supposition of some great secret would not have taken place, as the affairs of the Stadtholder were then publicly known. It shews that the nation did not think the Stadtholder of Holland a sufficient reason for laying new taxes on England, and running into the risk and expence of a war, and great was the surprise when the declaration and counter declaration like twin mice peeped from the Cabinet.

But there is one secret that requires to be investigated, which is, whether the Minister did not know that France would not engage in a war, and whether the preparations were not an idle parade, founded on that knowledge.

Whether it was not meanly putting England under the banners of Prussia, and taking thereby a dishonourable advantage of the internal perplexity which France was then in, and which in its turn may happen to England, to assume the air of a challenge, which it must be known would not be accepted, because there was nothing to make the acceptance necessary.

Whether this conduct in the Minister does not mischievously operate to destroy the harmony that appeared to be growing up between the two nations; to lessen, if not totally destroy, the advantages of the Commercial Treaty, and to lay the seeds of future wars, when there was a prospect of a long and uninterrupted peace.

When there are two ways of accomplishing the same object, it almost always happens that the one is better than the other; and whether the Minister has not chosen the worst, a few observations will elucidate this point.

It signifies not what airy schemes, projects, or even treaties may be formed, especially if done under the point of the bayonet, for all that can be expected from Holland is neutrality. Her trade is with all nations, and it is from her neutrality that this trade has arisen. Destroy this neutrality and Holland is destroyed. Therefore it matters not what party sentiments men may be of in Holland as to the Stadtholdership, because there is still a superior banner under which all will unite.

Holland will not expose her trade to the devastations of England, by joining France in a war, neither will she expose it to France by joining England. It may very well be asked, what are England or France to Holland, that she should join with either in a war, unless she is compelled to it by one or the other making war upon her, as was the case in the last war.

Events may soon happen in Europe to make all the force that Prussia can raise necessary to her own defence, and Holland must be wise enough to see, that by joining England she not only exposes her trade to France, but likewise her dominions, because France can invade her in a quarter in which England cannot defend her, provided her Generals prove true, for Holland lies open to France by land. It is, therefore, more immediately the interest of Holland to keep on good terms with France; neither can England give her any equivalent to balance this circumstance. How foolish then are the politics which are directed to unnatural and impossible objects. Surely the experience of a century past is sufficient to shew to any man, except one of yesterday, what the conduct of Holland in all cases must be.

But there is another circumstance that does not fail to impress foreigners, and especially Holland; which is, that the immensity of the national debt of England, the prospect of its still encreasing, and the exorbitancy of her paper currencies, render her too insecure in herself to be much confided in by foreign nations for any length of time. Because that which must happen may soon happen.

Concerning the rescript delivered by the French Minister, there is one certain explanation to be put upon it, which is, that if France had been disposed for war, she would not have made that communication. The very making it goes to a full explanation of the parts; and as soon as Mr. Pitt obtained this knowledge, it appeared to him a safe moment to gird on his sword and when he found that France was as well weaponed as himself to propose to take it off again. This is in a few words the whole history of the campaign. A war Minister in peace, and a peace Minister in war. Brave where there is no danger, and prudent when there is.

The rescript could be nothing else than an explanation, on the part of France, of the situation she conceived herself to be subject to, and the probable consequences that might follow from it. This she was not obliged to make, and therefore her making it was a matter of civil communication towards a power she was at peace with, and which in return entitled her to a similar communication on the part of the British Cabinet. All this might have been done without either the expence, the tumult, the provocations, or the ill blood that has been created.

The alliance between France and the Dutch, was formed while the Stadtholder was a part of the Government, therefore France could not from that alliance take a part either for or against him. She could only act when the whole interest of the Republic was exposed to a foreign enemy, and it was not certain that this might not be the case.

The rescript, therefore, instead of being taken as a ground for war, was in itself a ground for peace, because it tended to bring on a discussion of all the circumstances of France and England relative to Holland, which would not have failed to place Holland in a state of neutrality, and that only will be the final event now; because, independent of all parties, no other is consistent with the whole national interest of that Republic.

But this is not being done, it is now left to the Dutch to do it for themselves.

An alliance with England, at the same time there is one existing with France, will secure this neutrality, so necessary to the Dutch Republic. By this stroke of politics she will be free from all obligations to join with either in a war, and be guaranteed by both. Her alliance with England will debar England from molesting her trade by sea, and that with France will debar France from the same thing, and likewise from invading her by land in all future cases. There are so many probable circumstances to arise on the Continent of Europe, that the situation of Holland requires this safeguard, more especially from France, on account of her land connection.

The rising greatness of the Russian Empire, the probable union of the interest of this Empire with that of Germany and France, and consequently with Spain, whose interests cannot be separated, and the probability of a rupture between the Emperor and the King of Prussia, are matters that cannot fail to impress the Dutch with the necessity of securing themselves by land as well as by sea, and to prevent their being drawn into the quarrels either of England or France.

Upon the whole, as there was a civil as well as an uncivil line of politics to be pursued, every man of humane and generous sentiments must lament it was not chosen.

A disposition for peace was growing up in every part of France, and there appeared at the same time a mutual one rising in England. A silent wish on both sides was universally expanding itself, that wars, so fatal to the true interest, and burthensome by taxes to the subjects of both countries might exist no more, and that a long and lasting peace might take place.

But instead of cultivating this happy opportunity, the pettish vanity of a young and unexperienced Minister, who balanced himself between peace and war to take his choice of circumstances, instead of principles, and who went into an expensive armament when there was none to contend with, and not till after the affairs of Holland might be said to be terminated, has destroyed those seeds of harmony that might have been rendered of more value to both nations than their fleets and armies.

He has permitted the nation to run mad under the universal influence of a groundless belief of vast hostile armaments in the East and West Indies, and the supposition of a secret that never existed. By this means the sparks of ill-will are afresh kindled up between the nations, the fair prospects of lasting peace are vanished, and a train of future evils fills up the scene; and that at a time when the internal affairs of France, however confused they at present appear, are naturally approaching to a great and harmonious encrease of its power.

THOMAS PAINE

York Street, St. James's Square,
20th August, 1787.

THE

DECLINE AND FALL

OF THE

ENGLISH SYSTEM OF FINANCE.

"On the verge, nay even in the gulph of bankruptcy"

Debates in Parliament

NOTHING, they say, is more certain than death, and nothing more uncertain than the time of dying; yet we can always fix a period beyond which man cannot live, and within some moment of which he will die. We are enabled to do this, not by any spirit of prophecy, or foresight into the event, but by observation of what has happened in all cases of human or animal existence. If then any other subject, such, for instance, as a system of finance, exhibits in its progress a series of symptoms indicating decay, its final dissolution is certain, and the period of it can be calculated from the symptoms it exhibits.

Those who have hitherto written on the English system of finance (the funding system) have been uniformly impressed with the idea of its downfall happening *some time or other*. They took, however, no data for that opinion, but expressed it predictively, or merely as opinion, from a conviction that the perpetual duration of such a system was a natural impossibility. It is in this manner that Dr. Price has spoken of it; and Smith, in his Wealth of Nations, has spoken in the same manner; that is, merely as opinion without data. "The progress," says Smith, "of the enormous debts, which at present oppress, and will in the long-run *most probably ruin*, all the great nations of Europe, (he should have said *governments*) has been pretty uniform." But this general manner of speaking, though it might make some impression, carried with it no conviction.[1]

---

[1] Note that Price's objection to national debt was founded on a republican and agrarian anti-luxury discourse. See Claeys, 'Virtuous Commerce', p. 164.

It is not my intention to predict any thing; but I will shew from data already known, from symptoms and facts which the English funding system has already exhibited publicly, that it will not continue to the end of Mr. Pitt's life, supposing him to live the usual age of a man. How much sooner it may fall, I leave to others to predict.

Let financiers diversify systems of credit as they will, it is nevertheless true, that every system of credit is a system of paper money. Two experiments have already been had upon paper money; the one in America, the other in France. In both those cases the whole capital was emitted, and that whole capital, which in America was called continental money, and in France assignats, appeared in circulation; the consequence of which was, that the quantity became so enormous, and so disproportioned to the quantity of population, and to the quantity of objects upon which it could be employed, that the market, if I may so express it, was glutted with it, and the value of it fell. Between five and six years determined the fate of those experiments. The same fate would have happened to gold and silver, could gold and silver have been issued in the same abundant manner as paper had been, and confined within the country as paper money always is, by having no circulation out of it; or to speak on a larger scale, the same thing would happen in the world, could the world be glutted with gold and silver, as America and France have been with paper.

The English system differs from that of America and France in this one particular, that its capital is kept out of sight; that is, it does not appear in circulation. Were the whole capital of the national debt, which at the time I write this is almost four hundred million pounds sterling, to be emitted in assignats or bills, and that whole quantity put into circulation, as was done in America and in France, those English assignats, or bills, would sink in value as those of America and France have done; and that in a greater degree, because the quantity of them would be more disproportioned to the quantity of population in England, than was the case in either of the other two countries. A nominal pound sterling in such bills would not be worth one penny.

But though the English system, by thus keeping the capital out of sight, is preserved from hasty destruction, as in the case of America and France, it nevertheless approaches the same fate, and will arrive at it with the same certainty, though by a slower progress. The difference is altogether in the degree of speed by which the two systems approach their fate, which, to speak in round numbers, is as twenty is to one; that is, the English system, that of funding the capital instead of issuing it, contained within itself a capacity of enduring twenty times longer than the systems adopted by America and France; and at the end of that time it would arrive at the same common grave, the Potter's field, of paper money.

The datum, I take for this proportion of twenty to one, is the difference between a capital and the interest at five per cent. Twenty times the interest is equal to the capital. The accumulation of paper money in England is in proportion to the accumulation of the interest upon every new loan; and therefore the progress to the dissolution is twenty times slower than if the capital were to be emitted and put into circulation immediately. Every twenty years in the English system is equal to one year in the French and American systems.

Having thus stated the duration of the two systems, that of funding upon interest, and that of emitting the whole capital without funding, to be as twenty to one, I come to examine the symptoms of decay, approaching to dissolution, that the English system has already exhibited, and to compare them with similar symptoms in the French and American systems.

The English funding system began one hundred years ago; in which time there have been six wars including the war that ended in 1697.

1. The war that ended, as I have just said, in 1697.
2. The war that began in 1702.
3. The war that began in 1739
4. The war that began in 1756.
5. The American war, that began in 1775.
6. The present war, that began in 1793.

The national debt, at the conclusion of the war which ended in 1697, was twenty-one millions and an half. (See Smith's Wealth of Nations, chapter on Public Debts). We now see it approaching fast to four hundred millions. If between these two extremes of twenty-one millions and four hundred millions, embracing the several expences of all the including wars, there exists some common ratio that will ascertain arithmetically the amount of the debt at the end of each war, as certainly as the fact is now known to be, that ratio will in like manner determine what the amount of the debt will be in all future wars, and will ascertain the period within which the funding system will expire in a bankruptcy of the government; for the ratio I allude to is the ratio which the nature of the thing has established for itself.

Hitherto no idea has been entertained that any such ratio existed, or could exist, that could determine a problem of this kind, that is, that could ascertain, without having any knowledge of the fact, what the expence of any former war had been, or what the expence of any future war would be; but it is nevertheless true that such a ratio does exist, as I shall shew, and also the mode of applying it.

The ratio I allude to is not in arithmetical progression, like the numbers

2, 3, 4, 5, 6, 7, 8, 9;

nor yet in geometrical progression, like the numbers

2, 4, 8, 16, 32, 64, 128, 256;

but it is in the series of one half upon each preceding number; like the numbers

8, 12, 18, 27, 40, 60, 90, 135.

Any person can perceive that the second number, 12, is produced by the preceding number, 8, and half 8; and that the third number, 18, is in like manner produced by the preceding number, 12, and half 12; and so on for the rest. They can also see how rapidly the sums increase as the ratio proceeds. The difference between the two first numbers is but four; but the difference between the two last is forty-five; and from thence they may see with what immense rapidity the national debt has increased, and will continue to increase, till it exceeds the ordinary powers of calculation, and loses itself in ciphers.

I come now to apply the ratio as a rule to determine in all the cases.

I begin with the war that ended in 1697, which was the war in which the funding system began. The expence of that war was twenty-one millions and an half. In order to ascertain the expence of the next war, I add to twenty-one millions and an half, the half thereof (ten millions and three quarters), which makes thirty-two millions and a quarter for the expence of that war. This thirty-two millions and a quarter, added to the former debt of twenty-one millions and an half, carries the national debt to fifty-three millions and three quarters. Smith, in his chapter on Public Debts, says, The national debt was at this time fifty-three millions.

I proceed to ascertain the expence of the next war, that of 1739, by adding, as in the former case, one half to the expence of the preceding war. The expence of the preceding war was thirty-two millions and a quarter; for the sake of even numbers, say, thirty-two millions; the half of which (16) makes forty-eight millions for the expence of that war.

I proceed to ascertain the expence of the war of 1756, by adding, according to the ratio, one half to the expence of the preceding war. The expence of the preceding war was taken at 48 millions, the half of which (24) makes 72 millions for the expence of that war. Smith, (chapter on Public Debts,) says, the expence of the war of 1756, was 72 millions and a quarter.

I proceed to ascertain the expence of the American war, of 1775, by adding, as in the former cases, one half to the expence of the preceding war. The expence of the preceding war was 72 millions, the half of which (36) makes 108 millions for the expence of that war. In the last edition of Smith (chapter on Public Debts,) he says, the expence of the American war was *more than an hundred millions.*

I come now to ascertain the expence of the present war, supposing it to continue as long as former wars have done, and the funding system not to break up before that period. The expence of the preceding war was 108 millions, the half of which (54) makes 162 millions for the expence of the present war. It gives symptoms of going beyond this sum, supposing the funding system not to break up; for the loans of the last year and of the present year are twenty-two millions each, which exceeds the ratio compared with the loans of the preceding war. It will not be from the inability of procuring loans that the system will break up. On the contrary, it is the facility with which loans can be procured that hastens that event. The loans are altogether paper transactions; and it is the excess of them that brings on, with accelerating speed, that progressive depreciation of funded paper money that will dissolve the funding system.

I proceed to ascertain the expence of future wars, and I do this merely to shew the impossibility of the continuance of the funding system, and the certainty of its dissolution.

The expence of the next war after the present war, according to the ratio that has ascertained the preceding cases, will be   243 millions.

Expence of the second war	364
—————— third war	546
—————— fourth war	819
—————— fifth war	1228
	3200 millions;

which, at only four per cent, will require taxes to the nominal amount of one hundred twenty-eight millions to pay the annual interest, besides the interest of the present debt, and the expences of government, which are not included in this account.   Is there a man so mad, so stupid, as to suppose this system can continue?

When I first conceived the idea of seeking for some common ratio that should apply as a rule of measurement to all the cases of the funding system, so far as to ascertain the several stages of its approach to dissolution, I had no expectation that any ratio could be found that would apply with so much exactness as this does. I was led to the idea merely by observing that the funding system was a thing in continual progression, and that whatever was in a state of progression might be supposed to admit of, at least, some general ratio of measurement, that would apply without any very great variation. But who could have supposed that falling systems, or falling opinions, admitted of a ratio apparently as true as the descent of falling bodies? I have not *made* the ratio, any more than Newton made the ratio of gravitation. I have only discovered it, and explained the mode of applying it.

To shew at one view the rapid progression of the funding system to destruction, and to expose the folly of those who blindly believe in its continuance, or who artfully endeavor to impose that belief upon others, I exhibit in the annexed table, the expence of each of the six wars since the funding system began, as ascertained by the ratio, and the expence of the six wars yet to come, ascertained by the same ratio.

FIRST SIX WARS.	1 — — 21 millions	SECOND SIX WARS.	1 — — 243 millions
	2 — — 33 millions		2 — — 364 millions
	3 — — 48 millions		3 — — 546 millions
	4 — — 72 millions*		4 — — 819 millions
	5 — — 108 millions		5 — — 1228 millions
	6 — — 162 millions		6 — — 1842 millions
	Total 444 millions		Total 5042 millions

Those who are acquainted with the power with which even a small ratio, acting in progression, multiplies in a long series, will see nothing to wonder at in this

---

* The actual expence of the war of 1739 did not come up to the sum ascertained by the ratio. But as that which is the natural disposition of a thing, as it is the natural disposition of a stream of water to descend, will, if impeded in its course, overcome by a new effort what it had lost by that impediment, so it was with respect to this war and the next (1756) taken collectively; for the expence of the war of 1756 restored the equilibrium of the ratio, as fully as if it had not been impeded. A circumstance that serves to prove the truth of the ratio more fully than if the interruption had not taken place. The war of 1739 was languid: the efforts were below the value of money at that time: for the ratio is the measure of the depreciation of money in consequence of the funding system; or what comes to the same end, it is the measure of the increase of paper. Every additional quantity of it, whether in bank-notes or otherwise, diminishes the *real,* though not the *nominal,* value of the former quantity.

table. Those who are not acquainted with that subject, and not knowing what else to say, may be inclined to deny it. But it is not their opinion one way, nor mine the other, that can influence the event. The table exhibits the natural march of the funding system to its irredeemable dissolution.—Supposing the present government of England to continue, and to go on as it has gone on since the funding system began, I would not give twenty shillings for one hundred pounds in the funds to be paid twenty years hence. I do not speak this predictively; I produce the data upon which that belief is founded: and which data it is every body's interest to know, who have any thing to do with the funds, or who are going to bequeath property to their descendants to be paid at a future day.

Perhaps it may be asked, that as governments or ministers proceeded by no ratio in making loans or incurring debts, and nobody intended any ratio, or thought of any, how does it happen that there is one? I answer, that the ratio is founded in necessity; and I now go to explain what that necessity is.

It will always happen, that the price of labor, or of the produce of labor, be that produce what it may, will be in proportion to the quantity of money in a country, admitting things to take their natural course. Before the invention of the funding system, there was no other money than gold and silver; and as nature gives out those metals with a sparing hand, and in regular annual quantities from the mines, the several prices of things were proportioned to the quantity of money at that time, and so nearly stationary as to vary but little in any fifty or sixty years of that period.

When the funding system began, a substitute for gold and silver began also. That substitute was paper; and the quantity increased as the quantity of interest increased upon accumulated loans. This appearance of a new and additional species of money in the nation soon began to break the relative value which money and the things it will purchase bore to each other before. Every thing rose in price; but the rise at first was little and slow, like the difference in units between two first numbers, 8 and 12, compared with the two last numbers 90 and 135, in the table. It was however sufficient to make itself considerably felt in a large transaction. When therefore government, by engaging in a new war, required a new loan, it was obliged to make a higher loan than the former loan, to balance the increased price to which things had risen; and as that new loan increased the quantity of paper in proportion to the new quantity of interest, it carried the price of things still higher than before. The next loan was again higher, to balance that further increased price; and all this in the same manner, though not in the same degree, that every new emission of continental money in America, or of assignats in France, were greater than the preceding emission, to make head against the advance of prices, till the combat could be maintained no longer. Herein is founded the necessity of which I have just spoken. That necessity proceeds with accelerating velocity, and the ratio I have laid down is the measure of that acceleration; or, to speak the technical language of the subject, it is the measure of the increasing depreciation of funded paper money, which it is impossible to prevent, while the quantity of that money and of bank notes continues to multiply. What else but this can account for the difference between one war costing 21 millions, and another war costing 160 millions?

The difference cannot be accounted for on the score of extraordinary efforts or extraordinary achievements. The war that cost 21 millions was the war of the confederates, historically called the grand alliance, consisting of England, Austria, and Holland, in the time of William the Third, against Louis the Fourteenth, and in which the confederates were victorious. The present is a war of a much greater confederacy—a confederacy of England, Austria, Prussia, the German Empire, Spain, Holland, Naples, and Sardinia, eight powers, against the French Republic singly, and the Republic has beaten the whole confederacy.—But to return to my subject.—

It is said in England, that the value of paper keeps equal with the value of gold and silver. But the case is not rightly stated; for the fact is, that the paper has *pulled down* the value of gold and silver to a level with itself. Gold and silver will not purchase so much of any purchasable article at this day as if no paper had appeared, nor so much as it will in any country in Europe where there is no paper.

How long this hanging together of money and paper will continue, makes a new case; because it daily exposes the system to sudden death, independent of the natural death it would otherwise suffer.

I consider the funding system as being now advanced into the last twenty years of its existence. The single circumstance, were there no other, that a war should now cost *nominally* one hundred and sixty millions, which when the system began cost but twenty-one millions, or that the loan for one year only (including the loan to the Emperor) should now be *nominally* greater than the whole expence of that war, shews the state of depreciation to which the funding system has arrived. Its depreciation is in the proportion of eight for one, compared with the value of its money when the system began; which is the state the French assignats stood a year ago (March, 1795) compared with gold and silver. It is therefore that I say, that the English funding system, has entered into the last twenty years of its existence, comparing each twenty years of the English system with every single year of the American and French systems, as before stated.

Again, supposing the present war to close as former wars have done, and without producing either revolution or reform in England, another war at least must be looked for in the space of the twenty years I allude to; for it has never yet happened that twenty years have passed off without a war, and that more especially since the English government has dabbled in German politics, and shewn a disposition to insult the world, and the world of commerce, with her navy. That next war will carry the national debt to very nearly seven hundred millions, the interest of which, at four per cent, will be twenty-eight millions, besides the taxes for the (then) expences of government, which will increase in the same proportion, and which will carry the taxes to at least forty millions; and if another war only begins, it will quickly carry them to above fifty; for it is in the last twenty years of the funding system, as in the last year of the American and French systems without funding, that all the great shocks begin to operate.

I have just mentioned that paper, in England, has *pulled down* the value of gold and silver to a level with itself; and that this *pulling down* of gold and silver money has created the appearance of paper money keeping up. The same thing, and the same mistake, took place in America and in France, and continued for a considerable time after the commencement of their system of paper; and the actual depreciation of money was hidden under that mistake.

It was said in America, at that time, that everything was becoming *dear*; but gold and silver could then buy those dear articles no cheaper than paper could; and therefore it was not called depreciation. The idea of *dearness* established itself for the idea of depreciation. The same was the case in France. Though every thing rose in price soon after assignats appeared, yet those dear articles could be purchased no cheaper with gold and silver, than with paper, and it was only said that things were *dear*. The same is still the language in England. They call it *dearness*. But they will soon find that it is an actual depreciation, and that this depreciation is the effect of the funding system; which, by crowding such a continually-increasing mass of paper into circulation, carries down the value of gold and silver with it. But gold and silver, will, in the long run, revolt against depreciation, and separate from the value of paper; for the progress of all such systems appears to be, that the paper will take the command in the beginning, and gold and silver in the end.

But this succession in the command of gold and silver over paper, makes a crisis far more eventful to the funding system than to any other system upon which paper can be issued; for, strictly speaking, it is not a crisis of danger, but a symptom of death. It is a death stroke to the funding system. It is a revolution in the whole of its affairs.

If paper be issued without being funded upon interest, emissions of it can be continued after the value of it separates from gold and silver, as we have seen in the two cases of America and France. But the funding system rests altogether upon the value of paper being equal to gold and silver; which will be as long as the paper can continue carrying down the value of gold and silver to the same level to which itself descends, and no longer. But even in this state, that of descending equally together, the minister, whoever he may be, will find himself beset with accumulating difficulties; because the loans and taxes voted for the service of each ensuing year will wither in his hands before the year expires, or before they can be applied. This will force him to have recourse to emissions of what are called exchequer and navy bills, which, by still increasing the mass of paper in circulation, will drive on the depreciation still more rapidly.

It ought to be known that taxes in England are not paid in gold and silver, but in paper (bank notes). Every person who pays any considerable quantity of taxes, such as maltsters, brewers, distillers, (I appeal for the truth of it, to any of the collectors of excise in England, or to Mr. Whitbread), knows this to be the case.[2] There is not gold and silver enough in the nation to pay the taxes in coin, as I shall shew; and consequently there is not money enough in the bank to pay the notes. The interest of the national funded debt is paid at the bank in the same kind of paper in which the taxes are collected. When people find, as they will find, a reservedness among each other in giving gold and silver for bank notes, or the least preference for the former over the latter, they will go for payment to the bank, where they have a right to go. They will do this as a measure of prudence, each one for himself, and the truth or delusion of the funding system will then be proved.

I have said in the foregoing paragraph that there is not gold and silver enough in the nation to pay the taxes in coin, and consequently that there cannot be enough in the bank to pay the notes. As I do not chuse to rest any thing upon assertion, I appeal for the truth of this to the publications of Mr. Eden (now called Lord Auckland), and George Chalmers, Secretary to the Board of Trade and Plantation, of which Jenkinson (now Lord Hawkesbury) is president.[3] [These sort of folks change their names so often that it is as difficult to know them as it is to

---

[2] Samuel Whitbread (1720-1796) was a prominent dissenter. In 1796, the family brewery set a new record, producing 100,000 barrels of porter in one season. His son, Samuel Whitbread (1758-1815) entered politics as a Whig reformer.

[3] See William Eden, *Some Remarks on the Apparent Circumstances of the War, in the fourth week of October 1795*, 2nd edn, (London: J. Walter, 1795); George Chalmers, *An Estimate of the*

know a thief.] Chalmers gives the quantity of gold and silver coin from the returns of coinage at the mint; and, after deducting for the light gold recoined, says, that the amount of gold and silver coin is *about twenty millions.* He had better not have proved this, especially if he had reflected, that *public credit is suspicion asleep.* The quantity is much too little.

Of this twenty millions (which is not a fourth part of the quantity of gold and silver there is in France, as is shewn in Mr. Neckar's Treatise on the Administration of the Finances) three millions at least must be supposed to be in Ireland, some in Scotland, and in the West Indies, Newfoundland, &c.[4] The quantity therefore in England cannot be more than sixteen millions, which is four millions less than the amount of the taxes. But admitting there to be sixteen millions, not more than a fourth part thereof (four millions) can be in London, when it is considered that every city, town, village, and farm-house in the nation must have a part of it, and that all the great manufactories, which most require cash, are out of London. Of this four millions in London, every banker, merchant, tradesman, in short every individual, must have some. He must be a poor shop-keeper indeed, who has not a few guineas in his till. The quantity of cash therefore in the bank can never, on the evidence of circumstances, be so much as two millions; most probably not more than one million; and on this slender twig, always liable to be broken, hangs the whole funding system of four hundred millions, besides many millions in bank notes. The sum in the bank is not sufficient to pay one-fourth of only one year's interest of the national debt, were the creditors to demand payment in cash, or demand cash for the bank-notes in which the interest is paid. A circumstance always liable to happen.

One of the amusements that has kept up the farce of the funding system is, that the interest is regularly paid. But as the interest is always paid in bank notes, and

---

Comparative Strength of Britain during the present and four preceding reigns; and of the losses of her trade from every war since the revolution, (London: C. Dilly and J. Bowen, 1782).
[4] Jacques Necker, (1732-1804) served as Director General of Finance for Louis XVI. See Jacques Necker, *A Treatise on the Administration of the Finances of France,* trans. by Thomas Mortimer (London: J. Walter, 1785; repr. from the French in 1784).

as bank notes can always be coined for the purpose, this mode of payment proves nothing. The point of proof is, can the bank give cash for the bank notes with which the interest is paid? If it cannot, and it is evident it cannot, some millions of bank notes must go without payment, and those holders of bank notes who apply last will be worst off. When the present quantity of cash in the bank be paid away, it is next to impossible to see how any new quantity is to arrive. None will arrive from taxes, for the taxes will all be paid in bank notes; and should the government refuse bank notes in payment of taxes, the credit of bank notes will be gone at once. No cash will arise from the business of discounting merchants bills; for every merchant will pay off those bills in bank notes, and not in cash. There is therefore no means left for the bank to obtain a new supply of cash, after the present quantity is paid away. But, besides the impossibility of paying the interest of the funded debt in cash, there are many thousand persons in London and in the country, who are holders of bank notes that came into their hands in the fair way of trade, and who are not stock-holders in the funds; and as such persons have had no hand in increasing the demand upon the bank, as those have had who for their own private interest, like Boyd and others, are contracting or pretending to contract, for new loans, they will conceive they have a just right that their bank notes should be paid first. Boyd has been very sly in France, in changing his paper into cash. He will be just as sly in doing the same thing in London, for he has learned to calculate; and then it is probable he will set off for America.

A stoppage of payment at the bank is not a new thing. Smith in his Wealth of Nations, book 2. chap. 2. says, that in the year 1696, exchequer bills fell forty, fifty, and sixty per cent, bank notes twenty per cent, and the bank stopt payment.—That which happened in 1696 may happen again in 1796. The period in which it happened was the last year of the war of king William. It necessarily put a stop to the further emissions of exchequer and navy Bills, and to the raising of new loans; and the peace which took place the next year was probably hurried on by this circumstance, and saved the bank from bankruptcy. Smith in speaking from the circumstances of the bank, upon another occasion, says (book 2. chap.

2.) — "This great company had been reduced to the necessity of paying in sixpences." When a bank adopts the expedient of paying in sixpences, it is a confession of insolvency.

It is worthy of observation, that every case of failure in finances, since the system of paper began, has produced a revolution in governments, either total or partial. A failure in the finances of France produced the French revolution. A failure in the finance of the assignats broke up the revolutionary government, and produced the present French Constitution. A failure in the finances of the old Congress of America, and the embarrassments it brought upon commerce, broke up the system of the old confederation, and produced the present federal constitution. If then, we admit of reasoning by comparison of causes and events, a failure of the English finances will produce some change in the government of that country.

As to Mr. Pitt's project of paying off the national debt by applying a million a year for that purpose, while he continues adding more than twenty millions a year to it, it is like setting a man with a wooden leg to run after a hare. The longer he runs the farther he is off.

When I said that the funding system had entered the last twenty years of its existence, I certainly did not mean that it would continue twenty years, and then expire as a lease would do. I meant to describe that age of decrepitude in which death is every day to be expected, and life cannot continue long. But the death of credit, or that state that is called bankruptcy, is not always marked by those progressive stages of visible decline, that marked the decline of natural life. In the progression of natural life, age cannot counterfeit youth, nor conceal the departure of juvenile abilities. But it is otherwise with respect to the death of credit; for though all the approaches to bankruptcy may actually exist in circumstances, they admit of being concealed by appearances. Nothing is more common than to see the bankrupt of to-day a man in credit but the day before; yet no sooner is the real state of his affairs known, than every body can see he had been insolvent long before. In London, the greatest theatre of bankruptcy in Europe, this part of the subject will be well and feelingly understood.

Mr. Pitt continually talks of credit, and the national resources. These are two of the feigned appearances by which the approaches to bankruptcy are concealed. That which he calls credit may exist, as I have just shewn, in a state of insolvency, and is always what I have before described it to be, *suspicion asleep.*

As to national resources, Mr. Pitt, like all English financiers that preceded him since the funding system began, has uniformly mistaken the nature of a resource; that is, they have mistaken it consistently with the delusion of the funding system; but time is explaining the delusion. That which he calls, and which they call, a resource, is not a resource, but is the *anticipation* of a resource. They have anticipated what *would have been* a resource in another generation, had not the use of it been so anticipated. The funding system is a system of anticipation. Those who established it an hundred years ago, anticipated the resources of those who were to live an hundred years after; for the people of the present day have to pay the interest of the debts contracted at that time, and all debts contracted since. But it is the last feather that breaks the horse's back. Had the system begun an hundred years before, the amount of taxes at this time to pay the annual interest at four per cent. (could we suppose such a system of insanity could have continued) would be two hundred and twenty millions annually; for the capital of the debt would be 5486 millions, according to the ratio that ascertains the expence of the wars for the hundred years that are past. But long before it could have reached this period, the value of bank notes, from the immense quantity of them, (for it is in paper only that such a nominal revenue could be collected,) would have been as low or lower than continental paper has been in America, or assignats in France; and as to the idea of exchanging them for gold and silver, it is too absurd to be contradicted.

Do we not see that nature, in all her operations, disowns the visionary basis upon which the funding system is built? She acts always by renewed successions, and never by accumulating additions perpetually progressing. Animals and vegetables, men and trees, have existed since the world began; but that existence has been carried on by successions of generations, and not by continuing the same men and the same trees in existence that existed first; and to make room for the new she removes the old. Every natural ideot can see this. It is the stock-jobbing ideot only that mistakes. He has conceived that art can do what nature cannot. He is teaching her a new system—that there is no occasion for man to die—That the scheme of creation can be carried on upon the plan of the funding system— That it can proceed by continual additions of new beings, like new loans, and all live together in eternal youth. Go, count the graves, thou ideot, and learn the folly of thy arithmetic.

But besides these things, there is something visibly farcical in the whole operation of loaning. It is scarcely more than four years ago that such a rot of bankruptcy spread itself over London, that the whole commercial fabric tottered; trade and credit were at a stand; and such was the state of things that, to prevent or suspend a general bankruptcy, the government lent the merchants six millions in *government* paper, and now the merchants lend the government twenty-two millions in *their* paper; and two parties, Boyd and Morgan, men but little known, contend who shall be the lenders. What a farce is this! It reduces the operation of loaning to accommodation paper, in which the competitors contend, not who shall lend, but who shall sign, because there is something to be got for signing.

Every English stock-jobber and minister boasts of the credit of England. Its credit, say they, is greater than that of any country in Europe. There is a good reason for this; for there is not another country in Europe that could be made the dupe of such a delusion. The English funding system will remain a monument of wonder, not so much on account of the extent to which it has been carried, as of the folly of believing in it.

Those who had formerly predicted that the funding system would break up when the debt should amount to one hundred or one hundred and fifty millions, erred only in not distinguishing between insolvency and actual bankruptcy; for the insolvency commenced as soon as the government became unable to pay the interest in cash, or to give cash for the bank notes in which the interest was paid, whether that inability was known or not, or whether it was suspected or not. Insolvency always takes place before bankruptcy; for bankruptcy is nothing more than the publication of* that insolvency. In the affairs of an individual, it often happens that insolvency exists several years before bankruptcy, and that the insolvency is concealed and carried on till the individual is not able to pay one shilling in the pound. A government can ward off bankruptcy longer than an individual; but insolvency will inevitably produce bankruptcy, whether in an individual or in a government. If then the quantity of bank notes payable on demand, which the bank has issued, are greater than the bank can pay off, the bank is insolvent; and when that insolvency is declared, it is bankruptcy.*

I come now to shew the several ways by which bank notes get into circulation: I shall afterwards offer an estimate on the total quantity or amount of bank notes existing at this moment.

---

*Among the delusions that have been imposed upon the nation by ministers to give a false coloring to its affairs, and by none more than by Mr. Pitt, is a motley, amphibious charactered thing called the *balance of trade*. This balance of trade, as it is called, is taken from the custom-house books, in which entries are made of all cargoes exported, and also of all cargoes imported, in each year; and when the value of the exports, according to the price set upon them by the exporter or by the custom-house, is greater than the value of the imports, estimated in the same manner, they say, the balance of trade is so much in their favour.

The custom-house books prove regularly enough that so many cargoes have been exported, and so many imported; but this is all that they prove, or were intended to prove. They have nothing to do with the balance of profit or loss; and it is ignorance to appeal to them upon that account: for the case is, that the greater the loss is in any one year, the higher will this thing called the balance of trade appear to be according to the custom-house books. For example, nearly the whole of the Mediterranean convoy has been taken by the French this year; consequently those cargoes will not appear as imports on the custom-house books, and therefore the balance of trade, by which they mean the profits of it, will appear to be so much the greater as the loss amounts to; and, on the other hand, had the loss not happened, the profits would have appeared to have been so much the less. All the losses happening at sea to returning cargoes, by accidents, by the elements, or by capture, make the balance appear the higher on the side of the exports; and were they all lost at sea, it would appear to be all profit on the custom-house books. Also every cargo of exports that is lost that occasions another to be sent, adds in like manner to the side of the exports, and appears as profit. This year the balance of trade will appear high, because the losses have been great by capture and by storms. The ignorance of the British Parliament, in listening to this hackneyed imposition of ministers about the balance of trade, is astonishing. It shews how little they know of national affairs; and Mr. Grey may as well talk Greek to them, as to make motions about the state of the nation. They understand only fox-hunting and the game-laws.

The bank acts in three capacities. As a bank of discount; as a bank of deposit; and as banker for the government.

First, as a bank of discount. The bank discounts merchants bills of exchange for two months. When a merchant has a bill that will become due at the end of two months, and wants payment before that time, the bank advances that payment to him, deducting therefrom at the rate of five per cent. per ann. The bill of exchange remains at the bank as a pledge or pawn, and at the end of two months it must be redeemed. This transaction is done altogether in paper; for the profits of the bank, as a bank of discount, arise entirely from its making use of paper as money. The bank gives bank notes to the merchant in discounting the bill of exchange, and the redeemer of the bill pays bank notes to the bank in redeeming it. It very seldom happens that any real money passes between them.[5]

If the profits of a bank be, for example, two hundred thousand pounds a year (a great sum to be made merely by exchanging one sort of paper for another, and which shews also that the merchants of that place are pressed for money for payments, instead of having money to spare to lend to government), it proves that the bank discounts to the amount of four millions annually, or 666,666l. every two months; and as there never remain in the bank more than two months pledges, of the value of 666,666l. at any one time, the amount of bank notes in circulation at any one time should not be more than to that amount. This is sufficient to shew that the present immense quantity of bank notes, which are distributed through every city, town, village, and farm-house in England, cannot be accounted for on the score of discounting.

---

[5] Bills of Exchange were the principal medium of international and imperial commerce. The Bills represented a debt to be paid by a merchant or agent in another country, limited to a short term (New York bills drawn on London had to be presented 30-40 days after 'sight'). The cost was calculated to take account of interest and shortness of available money. It allowed a Philadelphia merchant to pay a merchant in London without transporting specie across the ocean, an expensive and dangerous practice. For a detailed example, see McCusker, *Money and Exchange*, pp. 20-21.

Secondly, as a bank of deposit. To deposit money at the bank means to lodge it there for the sake of convenience, and to be drawn out at any moment the depositor pleases, or to be paid away to his order. When the business of discounting is great, that of depositing is necessarily small. No man deposits and applies for discounts at the same time; for it would be like paying interest for lending money, instead of for borrowing it. The deposits that are now made at the bank are almost entirely in bank notes, and consequently they add nothing to the ability of the bank to pay off the bank notes that may be presented for payment; and besides this, the deposits are no more the property of the bank than the cash or bank notes in a merchant's counting house are the property of his book-keeper. No great increase therefore of bank notes, beyond what the discounting business admits, can be accounted for on the score of deposits.

Thirdly. The bank acts as banker for the government. This is the connection that threatens ruin to every public bank. It is through this connection that the credit of a bank is forced far beyond what it ought to be, and still further beyond its ability to pay. It is through this connection that such an immense redundant quantity of bank notes have gotten into circulation; and which, instead of being issued because there was property in the bank, have been issued because there was none.

When the treasury is empty, which happens in almost every year of every war, its coffers at the bank are empty also. It is in this condition of emptiness that the minister has recourse to emissions of what are called exchequer and navy bills, which continually generates a new increase of bank notes, and which are sported upon the public without there being property in the bank to pay them.— These exchequer and navy bills (being, as I have said, emitted because the treasury and its coffers at the bank are empty, and cannot pay the demands that come in) are no other than an acknowledgment that the bearer is entitled to receive so much money. They may be compared to the settlement of an account, in which the debtor acknowledges the balance he owes, and for which he gives a note of hand; or to a note of hand given to raise money upon it.

Sometimes the bank discounts those bills as it would discount merchants bills of exchange; sometimes it purchases them of the holders at the current price; and sometimes it agrees with the minister to pay an interest upon them to the holders, and keep them in circulation. In every one of those cases an additional quantity of bank notes get into circulation, and are sported, as I have said, upon the public, without there being property in the bank, as banker for the government, to pay them: and besides this, the bank has now no money of its own; for the money that was originally subscribed to begin the credit of the bank with at its first establishment, has been lent to government, and wasted long ago.

"The bank" (says Smith, book 2. chap. 2,) "acts not only as an ordinary bank, but as a great engine of state; it receives and pays a greater part of the annuities which are due to the creditors of the *public.*" [It is worth observing, that the *public,* or the *nation,* is always put for the government in speaking of debts.] "It circulates" (says Smith) "exchequer bills, and it advances to government the annual amount of the land and malt taxes, which are frequently not paid till several years afterwards." [This advancement is also done in bank notes, for which there is not property in the bank.] "In those different operations" (says Smith) "*its duty to the public* may sometimes have obliged it, without any fault of its directors, *to overstock the circulation with paper money,*" —bank notes. How its *duty to the public* can induce it *to overstock that public* with promissory bank notes which it *cannot pay,* and thereby expose the individuals of that public to ruin, is too paradoxical to be explained; for it is on the credit which individuals *give to the bank,* by receiving and circulating its notes, and not upon its *own* credit or its *own* property, for it has none, that the bank sports. If however it be the duty of the bank to expose the public to this hazard, it is at least equally the duty of the individuals of that public to get their money and take care of themselves; and leave it to placemen, pensioners, government contractors, Reeves's association, and the members of both houses of Parliament, who have voted away the money at the nod of the minister, to continue the credit if they can, and for which their estates individually and collectively ought to answer, as far as they will go.

There has always existed, and still exists, a mysterious, suspicious connection, between the minister and the directors of the bank, and which explains itself no otherways than by a continual increase of bank notes. Without, therefore, entering into any further details of the various contrivances by which bank notes are issued, and thrown upon the public, I proceed, as I before mentioned, to offer an estimate on the total quantity of bank notes in circulation.

However disposed governments may be to wring money by taxes from the people, there is a limit to the practice established by the nature of things. That limit is the proportion between the quantity of money in a nation, be that quantity what it may, and the greatest quantity of taxes that can be raised upon it. People have other uses for money besides paying taxes; and it is only a proportional part of that money they can spare for taxes, as it is only a proportional part they can spare for house-rent, for clothing, or for any other particular use. These proportions find out and establish themselves; and that with such exactness, that if any one part exceeds its proportion, all the other parts feel it.

Before the invention of paper money (bank notes), there was no other money in the nation than gold and silver, and the greatest quantity of money that was ever raised in taxes during that period, never exceeded a fourth part of the quantity of money in the nation. It was high taxing when it came to this point. The taxes in the time of William the Third never reached to four millions before the invention of paper, and the quantity of money in the nation at that time was estimated to be about sixteen millions. The same proportions established themselves in France. There was no paper money in France before the present revolution, and the taxes were collected in gold and silver money. The highest quantity of taxes never exceeded twenty-two millions sterling; and the quantity of gold and silver money in the nation at the same time, as stated by Mr. Neckar, from returns of coinage at the mints, in his Treatise on the Administration of the Finances, was about ninety millions sterling. To go beyond this limit of a fourth part, in England, they were obliged to introduce paper money; and the attempt to go beyond it in France, where paper could not be introduced, broke up the government. This proportion therefore of a fourth part, is the limit which the thing establishes for itself, be the quantity of money in a nation more or less.

The amount of taxes in England at this time is full twenty millions; and therefore the quantity of gold and silver, and of bank notes, taken together, amounts to eighty millions. The quantity of gold and silver, as stated by Lord Hawkesbury's secretary (George Chalmers), as I have before shewn, is twenty millions, and therefore the total amount of bank notes in circulation, all made payable on demand, is sixty millions. This enormous sum will astonish the most stupid stock-jobber, and overpower the credulity of the most thoughtless Englishman; but were it only a third part of that sum, the bank cannot pay half-a-crown in the pound.

There is something curious in the movements of this modern complicated machine, the funding system; and it is only now that it is beginning to unfold the full extent of its movements. In the first part of its movements it gives great powers into the hands of government, and in the last part it takes them completely away.

The funding system set out with raising revenues under the name of loans, by means of which government became both prodigal and powerful. The loaners assumed the name of creditors, and though it was soon discovered that loaning was government jobbing, those pretended loaners, or the persons who purchased into the funds afterwards, conceived themselves not only to be creditors, but to be the *only* creditors.

But such has been the operation of this complicated machine, the funding system, that it has produced, unperceived, a second generation of creditors, more numerous and far more formidable, and withal more real than the first generation; for every holder of a bank note is a creditor, and a real creditor, and the debt due to him is made payable on demand. The debt therefore which the government owes to individuals is composed of two parts; the one about four hundred millions bearing interest, the other about sixty millions payable on demand. The one is called the funded debt, the other is the debt due in bank notes.

This second debt (that contained in the bank notes) has, in a great measure, been incurred to pay the interest of the first debt; so that in fact little or no real interest has been paid by government. The whole has been delusion and fraud. Government first contracted a debt in the form of loans with one class of people, and then run clandestinely into debt with another class, by means of bank notes, to pay the interest. Government acted of itself in contracting the first debt, and made a machine of the bank to contract the second.

It is this second debt that changes the seat of power and the order of things; for it puts it in the power of even a small part of the holders of bank-notes (had they no other motive than disgust at Pitt and Grenville's sedition bills) to controul any measure of government they found to be injurious to their interest; and that not by popular meetings, or popular societies, but by the simple and easy operation of with-holding their credit from that government; that is, by individually demanding payment at the bank for every bank note that comes into their hands. Why should Pitt and Grenville expect that the very men whom they insult and injure should at the same time continue to support the measures of Pitt and Grenville, by giving credit to their promissory notes of payment?[6] No new emissions of bank notes could go on while payment was demanding on the old, and the cash in the bank wasting daily away; nor any new advances be made to government or to the emperor to carry on the war; nor any new emission be made of exchequer bills.

"*The bank,*" says Smith, (book ii. ch. 2) "is *a great engine of state.*" And in the same paragraph he says, "*The stability of the bank is equal to that of the British government;*" which is the same as to say that the stability of the government is equal to that of the bank, and no more. If then the bank cannot pay, the *arch-treasurer of the holy Roman empire* (S.R.I.A.[*]) is a bankrupt. When Folly invented titles, she did not attend to their application; for ever since the government of England has been in the hands of *arch-treasurers*, it has been

---

[6] William Grenville, (1759-1834) was foreign minister 1791-1801.
[*] Part of the inscription on an English guinea.

running into bankruptcy; and as to the arch-treasurer *apparent*, he has been a bankrupt long ago. What a miserable prospect has England before its eyes!

Before the war of 1755 there were no bank notes lower than twenty pounds. During that war bank notes of fifteen pounds and of ten pounds were coined; and now, since the commencement of the present war, they are coined as low as five pounds. These five pounds notes will circulate chiefly among little shop keepers, butchers, bakers, market people, renters of small houses, lodgers, &c. All the high departments of commerce, and the affluent stations of life were already *overstocked,* as Smith expresses it, with the bank notes. No place remained open wherein to crowd an additional quantity of bank notes but among the class of people I have just mentioned, and the means of doing this could be best effected by coining five pound notes. This conduct has the appearance of that of an unprincipled insolvent who, when on the verge of bankruptcy to the amount of many thousands, will borrow as low as five pounds of the servants in his house, and break the next day.

But whatever momentary relief or aid the minister and his bank might expect from this low contrivance of five pound notes, it will increase the inability of the bank to pay the higher notes, and hasten the destruction of all; for even the small taxes that used to be paid in money will now be paid in those notes, and the bank will soon find itself with scarcely any other money than what the hair powder guinea tax brings in.

The bank notes make the most serious part of the business of finance: what is called the national funded debt is but a trifle when put in comparison with it; yet the case of the bank notes has never been touched upon. But it certainly ought to be known upon what authority, whether that of the minister or of the directors, and upon what foundation, such immense quantities are issued. I have stated the amount of them at sixty millions; I have produced data for that estimation; and besides this, the apparent quantity of them, far beyond that of gold and silver in the nation, corroborates therewith. But were there but a third part of sixty millions, the bank cannot pay half a crown in the pound; for no new supply of money, as before said, can arrive at the bank, as all the taxes will be paid in paper.

When the funding, system began, it was not doubted that the loans that had been borrowed would be repaid. Government not only propagated that belief, but it began paying them off. In time this profession came to be abandoned; and it is not difficult to see that bank notes will march the same way; for the amount of them is only another debt under another name; and the probability is, that Mr. Pitt will at last propose funding them. In that case bank notes will not be so valuable as French assignats. The assignats have a solid property in reserve in the national domains; bank notes have none; and besides this, the English revenue must then sink down to what the amount of it was before the funding system began; between three and four millions. One of which the *arch-treasurer* would require for himself, and the arch-treasurer *apparent* would require three quarters of a million more to pay his debts. *"In France,"* says Sterne, *"they order these things better."*[7]

I have now exposed the English system of finance to the eyes of all nations; for this work will be published in all languages. In doing this, I have done an act of justice to those numerous citizens of neutral nations who have been imposed upon by that fraudulent system, and who have property at stake upon the event.

As an individual citizen of America, and as far as an individual can go, I have revenged (if I may use the expression without any immoral meaning) the piratical depredations committed on the American commerce by the English government.— I have retaliated for France on the subject of finance; and I conclude with retorting on Mr. Pitt the expression he used against France, and

---

[7] Paine refers to the first line of the popular novel by Laurence Sterne (1713-1768). See Laurence Sterne, *A Sentimental Journey through France and Italy by Mr. Yorick* (London: P. Miller and J. White, 1774).

say, that the English system of finance "is on the verge, nay even in the gulph of bankruptcy."

THOMAS PAINE.

Paris, 19th Germinal,
4th year of the Republic,
April 8, 1796.

Paris, May 6, 2nd year of the Republic (1793).

CITOYEN DANTON:

As you read English I write this letter to you without passing it through the hands of a translator. I am exceedingly disturbed at the distractions, jealousies, discontents and uneasiness that reign among us and which, if they continue, will bring ruin and disgrace on the Republic.

***

I see also another embarrassing circumstance arising in Paris of which we have had full experience in America. I mean that of fixing the price of provisions. But if this measure is to be attempted it ought to be done by the Municipality. The Convention has nothing to do with regulations of this kind; neither can they be carried into practice. The People of Paris may say they will not give more than a certain price for provisions, but as they cannot compel the country people to bring provisions to market the consequence will be directly contrary to their expectations, and they will find dearness and famine instead of plenty and cheapness. They may force the price down upon the Stock in hand, but after that the market will be empty. I will give you an example—

In Philadelphia we undertook among other regulations of this kind to regulate the price of Salt; the consequence was that no Salt was brought to market, and the price rose to thirty-six shillings sterling per Bushel. The price before the war was only one shilling and six pence per Bushel; and we regulated the price of flour (*farine*) till there was none in the market and the people were glad to procure it at any price.

There is also a circumstance to be taken into the account which is not much attended to. The assignats are not of the same value they were a year ago and as the quantity encreases the value of them will diminish. This gives the appearance of things being dear when they are not so in fact, for in the same proportion that any kind of money falls in value articles rise in price. If it were not for this the quantity of assignats would be too great to be circulated. Paper money in

America fell so much in value from this excessive quantity of it that in the year 1781 I gave three hundred Paper dollars for one pair of worsted stockings. What I write you upon this subject is experience and not merely opinion.

I have no personal interest in any of these matters nor in any party disputes. I attend only to general principles.

As soon as a constitution shall be established I shall return to America; and be the future prosperity of France ever so great I shall enjoy no other part of it than the happiness of knowing it. In the mean time I am distressed to see matters so badly conducted and so little attention paid to moral principles. It is these things that injure the character of the Revolution and discourages the progress of liberty all over the world.

***

Votre Ami,

THOMAS PAINE.

CITOYEN DANTON.

Chapter Five

Welfare and the Property Rights of Man

The following two texts illustrate Paine's proposals for a system of welfare payments to ameliorate poverty. The first is an extract from the *Rights of Man*, a work almost as famous as *Common Sense*. Just as the earlier work was partially responsible for a Declaration of Independence and thus the birth of a new nation, *Rights of Man* unleashed a furore not only in Britain but throughout the world. Conway claims that Pitt went to war with France in 1793 not over the fate of Louis XVI but in order to thwart the spread of the ideas contained in the *Rights of Man*.[1] It was a war that would determine the fate of numerous European nations. Ironically 'Ways and Means', the final chapter of *Rights of Man Part Second*, is overwhelmingly an anti-war treatise that seeks to show that a republican Europe would be peaceful, prosperous and just. The chapter demonstrates the potential for cuts in government spending made possible by the end of pointless wars and the reform of the political and economic system. Paine himself remarks on the suspicious similarity between his plan for reducing taxes and Pitt's speech in

---

[1] Conway, *Life*, p. 160.

parliament on 31 January. Pitt's plan however only introduces tax cuts of £320,000 while Paine's reduction amounts to nearly six million.[2]

The welfare proposals might be thought to cast doubt on Paine's commitment to the rights of individuals when opposed to the interests of society and his *laissez-faire* belief in the free market. I will show that the theory of property presented here is a natural rights theory and is consistent with the liberal tenor of his general political theory. The proposals set out in these two works are very different. In 'Ways and Means' he proposes a progressive tax and a variety of welfare provisions as well as support for disbanded soldiers. In *Agrarian Justice*, he proposes only two benefits: a payment of fifteen pounds to everyone at the age of twenty-one and ten pounds per annum to the disabled and over-fifties. These are to be paid out of a national fund, the result of an inheritance tax of ten per cent, with an additional ten percent on property not inherited by close relatives of the deceased. The proposals in this work are intended not so much to alleviate poverty but to ensure that all have a chance to prosper. Therefore, Paine proposes that each adult should be given starting capital.[3]

Rights of Man is principally against war and the taxation it necessitates. Republican governments will no longer need to go to war because they will recognise that peace is in the common interest of all men. Paine argues that the

---

[2] In an appendix, Paine explains the suspicious circumstances of the delayed publication of the *Rights of Man Part Second*, which was to be published just before the new session of parliament and Pitt's announcement. It was given to the printer with sufficient time but with only two weeks to go the printer suddenly returned the copy, refusing to print it. Paine's story suggests it was the welfare plans, rather than 'the arguments on systems and principles of government' that caused the printer to stop. He also reports that the same printer had offered to buy the copyright for £1000, which Paine had refused, being wary of any attempt to prevent the book being published by selling the copyright to the government. The search for a new printer delayed the publication until after Pitt's announcement. Paine suspected that the original printer had been bribed or threatened. See *Writings*, II, 297-300. On the suppression of Joseph Johnson's edition of *Rights of Man* in 1791, see Richard Gimbel, *Thomas Paine Fights for Freedom in Three Worlds: the New, the Old and the Next* (New Haven: Yale University Library, 1959) p. 417.

[3] Fifteen pounds is so small amount that it can hardly be called capital. According to purchasing power calculations, it would be at today's prices a little over £1000, enough perhaps for an artisan to buy the tools of their trade, but insufficient to buy a subsistence farm. Starting a successful enterprise with such a small amount would require great business acumen. See Twigger, *Inflation*, p. 21.

heavy burden of taxation in Britain, and formerly in France, was due to financing perpetual and unnecessary wars and the resulting accumulation of the national debt. These wars are not waged in the interests of the tax-payers but of the monarchs and their surrounding court who use the excuse of war to raise taxes and the national debt in order to secure more personal benefits in the form of places and pensions. Peace will enable reformed governments to reduce taxation and the national debt considerably. Further a redistribution of the tax burden from the poor and middling classes to the rich will discourage large holdings and the undue influence they provide, and also discourage the immoral practice of primogeniture which leaves a mass of disinherited aristocrats scrambling for places. Paine's welfare transfers are proposed as a better use of taxation than fighting unnecessary wars and paying salaries to unnecessary placemen.

In 'Ways and Means', the use of taxes for benefits for the poor is justified on the grounds that firstly it is presently used for benefits for the rich, secondly it is in the interests of the greatest happiness of mankind. Paine believes the policy he is proposing is simply the obvious policy of a good government.[4] It is only in *Agrarian Justice* that Paine puts forward a 'theory of property'. The differences between the two works reflect the reasons for which they were written. *Rights of Man* was written to defend the French Constitution against Burke's assault. *Part Second* clarifies the positive political theory found in part one and presents it as part of a unified system. 'Ways and Means' demonstrates the practical and economic benefits of reformed government. *Agrarian Justice* was inspired by French events; Babeuf's (1760-97) attempt at a communist take-over of the revolution and proposals for the equal distribution of land. Paine also published the pamphlet in England in order to refute the Bishop of Llandaff's contention that God made both rich and poor.[5]

---

[4] See below p. 509.
[5] Richard Watson (1737-1816) was Bishop of Llandaff from 1782. See R. Watson, *An Apology for the Bible in a Series of Letters Addressed to Thomas Paine*, (London: Society for Promoting Christian Knowledge, 1796). François Babeuf (1760-97) was a French communist

A Theory of Property

Paine's theory of property in *Agrarian Justice* can be broken up into three separate lines of argument.[6] The first is that since the earth was given in common to all humanity, the owners of property owe 'ground-rent' to the rest of mankind, in compensation for the earth they have appropriated. The improvement of the land cannot be separated from the original state of the land but, as this is the result of an individual's labour, this part of the value of property does rightfully belong to the improver. However, this individual property is not exempt from Paine's second argument which is that, since personal property can only be accumulated in society, riches are a benefit of society. Therefore, the owner of the property owes interest to society for the benefits it provides. Paine estimates the rent due at 10% for land compensation and 10% for use of market. These are, of course, inevitably arbitrary figures as it is virtually impossible to estimate the original value of the land or the market.

Thirdly, Paine argues that unless the rich compensate the poor, the poor will not consider themselves to benefit from society. The rich minority faces the danger of being overthrown and dispossessed by the poor majority. This last argument is Paine's warning to the rich has been seen as an indication that Paine is trying to protect existing property rights in reaction to Babeuf's communist rising but can, I think, be understood to be not so much a separate argument from the previous two but rather it is their proof.[7] It is used to indicate the consequences of an unjust society. All three arguments are connected by the fundamental maxim that the situation of every person born into a state of civilisation with private property ought to be no worse than if the had never been invented.[8] Comparing the life of the American Indian with that of the European

---

who advocated a rigorous system of land reform. He adopted the title Gracchus referring to the Roman tradition of Agrarianism, the periodic equalization of land holdings.

[6] See below p. 519.

[7] Penniman, 'Paine: Democrat', 244-62.

[8] See below p. 517.

poor, he concludes that the masses would be better of in the state of nature than in their present society.

Paine's proposals are not an attempt to establish equality of property nor to abolish private property. It is enough for the rich to compensate the poor by redistributing a portion of their property in welfare entitlements available to all. Paine's view of private property is that of a social artefact which is justified by the progress it achieves. All social conventions are in his view the result of either agreement or conquest. They must be founded in a social contract or imposed upon a people by the illegitimate use of power. No rational man would agree to a society which would result in a mass of the people being worse off than they would have been in a state of nature. Unless a society is in the interests of all its citizens, it would be rational for those worse off to end this society and begin again. That there is a danger of the poor overthrowing the rich because of envy is an indication that society is not performing the function it was constituted to perform. An unjust society founded on conquest or theft rather than mutual interest must be illegitimate. Together these three lines of argument lead to Paine's proposals for the redistribution of property. No one would agree to a social contract giving a minority a monopoly control of the earth, which was given to all mankind in common, unless they were assured firstly that the dispossessed would be compensated for their loss. Secondly, the system would need to guarantee that all members would share some proportion of the benefits which private property can provide.

Comparing Paine's three arguments to Locke's theory of property in the second treatise demonstrates the distinctiveness of this theory of property and its relation to his overall political theory. In founding his theory of property in the common ownership of the earth, Paine was hardly original. On the contrary, Locke also begins from the same premise:

> Whether we consider natural reason, which tells us that men [...] have a right to their preservation, and consequently to meat and drink and such other things as nature affords to their subsistence,

or 'revelation', which gives us an account of those grants God made of the world to Adam, and to Noah and his sons, it is very clear that God, as King David says (Psalm CXV. 16), 'has given the earth to the children of men, given in to mankind in common.[9]

Locke's argument, however, justifies existing unequal property rights. As every man has a right to his own body (anything else would be slavery), he has a right to the fruits of his labour, his labour being a part of his body. As soon as an individual 'mixes' his labour with the natural earth, it becomes so inextricably linked with his labour and thus with his body that it becomes his property just as much as his own body is. Locke claims

> Though the earth and all inferior creatures be common to all men, yet every man has a 'property' in his own 'person'. This nobody has any right to but himself. The 'labour' of his body and the 'work' of his hands, we may say are properly his. Whatsoever, then he removes out of the state that nature hath provided and left it in, he hath mixed his labour with it, and joined to it something that is his own, and thereby makes it his property.[10]

It is this second step at which Paine's theory of property differs from Locke's. Paine argues that the labour and the natural earth can still be considered separately with regard to ownership. Though the labour of man might improve the natural earth, the natural earth still belongs to all mankind in common. Only the value of improvement belongs to the labourer. This leads Paine to the conclusion that compensation is due to the rest of mankind. Just as when land or any capital is lent by the owner or group owner they expect rent or interest to be paid from the profit made by the use of that land or capital, the use of the earth to create individual property should be expected to cost the user rent, paid to the owners of the natural earth. Proprietors of cultivated land therefore owe a ground-rent to the community.[11]

---

[9] Locke, *Two Treatises*, pp. 285-286.
[10] Locke, *Two Treatises*, pp. 287-288.
[11] See below p. 518.

Locke does not satisfactorily explain what gives an individual the right to mix his labour with the common property of all mankind, thus making it his and dispossessing the rest of that part. The appropriation of private property from the common ownership of mankind is justified by need. He asks 'was it a robbery thus to assume to himself what belonged to all in common? If such a consent as that was necessary, man would have starved notwithstanding the plenty God had given him.' He argues that the labour of the individual 'excludes the common right of other men', yet this will not hurt the rest since there is enough for everybody. This is because the earth is God-given and therefore cannot be spoiled - and so we can only take as much as we need. Plentiful provision ensures that 'there could then be little room for quarrels [...] about property so established'.[12] The invention of money provides the opportunity for exchange between men and for the accumulation of riches greater than need, resulting inequality. More property than needed can now be accumulated, so need can no longer justify this appropriation. Rather consent is now the justification offered:

> Since gold and silver, being little useful to the life of man in proportion to food, raiment and carriage, has its value only from the consent of men [...] it is plain that the consent of men have agreed to a disproportionate and unequal possession of the Earth - I mean out of the bounds of society and compact; for in governments the laws regulate it.[13]

So why is it then that Paine insists that the natural earth still remains in the proprietorship of mankind in common and only the improvement of value resultant of the individual's labour becomes his individual property? His argument rests on a contention that man does not possess the right to appropriate to his own use the common property of mankind. In Locke's first justification, that of need, it is assumed that man cannot enjoy his natural birthright without converting it into private property. If he is to eat acorns, they must become his at

---

[12] Locke, *Two Treatises*, p. 290.
[13] Locke, *Two Treatises*, pp. 286-7 & 301-2.

some point, by picking them, by bringing them home, or by digesting them. However when Paine talks of the natural earth he is not thinking of the fruits of the earth but of the capital stock which provides these fruits. This clearly remains in common ownership: the oak tree, the soil and the seed, which provided man with the opportunity to cultivate crops and satisfy his wants.

It is difficult to establish by textual evidence but it may be that Locke and Paine began with a very different view of what it means for property to be held in common. The century between the writing of *Second Treatises* and *Agrarian Justice* was the turning point of the long slow change between two different economic systems and so Locke and Paine's understanding of key economic terms such as common ownership are likely to be different. Locke was writing during the dying days of the feudal system, while Paine was writing at the accession to power of the capitalist system and at the birth of its first Prince, the Industrial Age. Locke therefore uses the example of common land, primarily a feudal institution, in his explanation of the appropriation of the natural earth into private ownership:

> We see in commons, which remain so by compact, that it is the taking any part of what is common, and removing it out of the state Nature leaves it in, which begins the property without which the common is of no use. And the taking of this or that part does not depend on the express consent of all the commoners. Thus the grass my horse has bit, the turfs my servant has cut and the ore I have digged in any place, where I have a right to them in common with others, become my property without the assignation or consent of anybody.[14]

It is curious that, after several hundred years of English commoners vainly petitioning Parliament to prevent the enclosure of common land by the aristocracy, Locke fails to recognise that the danger to the commoners lay not in the taking of the grass, or even the turf or the ore, but in the taking of the capital resource that provides it; the meadow, the moor and the mine.

---

[14] Locke, *Two Treatises*, p. 288-289.

Paine's choice of words indicate that he recognised the distinction between the capital and the product and was also aware of the distinct ownership of the two within the framework of sophisticated capitalist institutions that had not been fully developed in Locke's time. Thus when Paine refers to common ownership he naturally views the relationship between the owners and the users according to the primary mode of economic organisation of joint capital property in his time (and ours), the joint-stock company, rather than the feudal institution of common land. Paine describes his conception of common ownership thus: 'He would have been a joint life proprietor with the rest in the property of the soil, and in all its natural productions, vegetable and animal.'[15] Firstly, we see that the vegetables and animals are productions of the soil, which mankind owns as owner of the capital that produced them. We can also imagine unnatural productions such as cultivated crops which belong to the cultivator. Secondly, we might compare this joint life proprietorship with the ownership of stock in the Bank of North America. The stockholders cannot remove their portion of stock without selling it to another stockholder. Capital cannot be removed but stockholders receive dividends on the profits made by the bank. This stability of capital provides confidence in bank notes and in the economy as a whole. Of course, the analogy is incomplete because there is no provision for the natural proprietors of the earth to realise their asset by selling it. It would be irrational for a man to sell his stake in society but it would also be irrational not to demand the dividend due.

Locke's conception of common property is a negative concept: the right *not* to be excluded from the use of something, as opposed to private property, the right to exclude others. Common property understood as the absence of any right of exclusion is thus the absence of ownership – the earth is unowned. But Paine's conception is stronger as it involves the right of all not only to enjoy the fruits of their property but also to decide its use as capital. We might call this joint property. Such property cannot just be appropriated according to need in nature,

---

[15] See below p. 518.

only its natural products. But where it involves the appropriation of land for improvement necessary for civilisation, the land itself remains in a common ownership of mankind. Thus it would require their consent for its use. Paine could not accept that mankind would consent to such inequalities as Locke claimed they must have because it would never be rational to consent to such monopolisation without ensuring compensation for the owners of the natural earth. Further, it ignores the equal rights of future generations to their share. It is not enough that such civilisation will lead to improvements in the common stock unless all consenting parties would benefit in some degree from this increase. The rational and right thing to do would be to consent to such a system of private property rights on the condition that 'ground rent' be paid to the natural proprietors.

We can draw an analogy between the institution of a political system and of an economic system. While Locke uses the social contract or compact to justify any form of limited government; monarchy, aristocracy or democracy, Paine demands that the system chosen be the rational system for all the parties to choose. Rational consent could not legitimately be given to hereditary government. Similarly with consent to an economic system: while Locke uses consent to a system of private property to justify any distribution which might arise, Paine insists that it would be irrational for the majority to consent to their own poverty. Therefore, it is likely that such a system did not arise by consent but by conquest. Paine asserts in *First Principles of Government* that

> It is very well known in England (and the same will be found in other countries) the great landed estates now held in descent were plundered from the quiet inhabitants at the conquest. The possibility did not exist of acquiring such estates honestly. If it be asked how they could have been acquired, no answer but that of robbery can be given. That they were not acquired by trade, by commerce, by manufactures, by agriculture, or by any reputable employment is certain.[16]

---

[16] 'First Principles' (1795), *Writings*, III, 270.

Though Paine asserts that robbery has been committed where Locke denies it, Paine is not saying that 'property is theft'. Rather the existing property relations are theft because they dispossess the poor of their birthright, but the same property holdings with a system to compensate the poor would not be theft because this would mean that all benefited from the system of private property, not just those who held it. Property is not theft but a form of borrowing with interest.[17]

Rousseau also warns against the robbery of our common birthright, in *A Discourse in Inequality*, and blames on its invention all the dependence and immorality of social inequality. In the *Social Contract* however, Rousseau defends inequalities in wealth as necessary but warns against large divisions between rich and poor in a democracy. He does not propose, as Paine does, a system of state benefits to ensure that private property is mutually beneficial. He does however provide a justification for redistribution that Paine never asserts. Rousseau claims that the true right of property resides in the community because firstly only society can uphold the right of the first occupier against the right of the strongest and secondly property is one of the rights given up by individuals into a common pool on entering society.[18] Paine, in contrast, claims for the community only that part which was originally theirs and a tithe for the benefits of society to wealth production. The rest (he estimates at 80%) belongs to the individual. For Paine, rights are not given up by entering society; rather society is constituted for their better preservation.

Paine's second argument concerns the interest owed to society for the benefits it provides. This seems to be an afterthought for Paine in order to justify a general inheritance tax rather than a land tax. However it is important to Paine's

---

[17] Note that in *Agrarian Justice*, Paine does not blame the landholders for the crime of existing property holdings as he seems to in *First Principles of Government*, rather the fault is in the system. See below p. 520.
[18] See Jean Jacques Rousseau, *A Discourse on the Origins and Foundations of Inequality among Men*, trans. by M. Cranston (Harmondsworth: Penguin, 1984; repr. 1987), p. 109; Rousseau, *Social Contract*, I. 9, p. 65-68.

theory because it shows that he recognises that property involves more than just cultivated land but that great wealth could be acquired only by trade, that is, by the institution of the market, a product of society. As we have seen, Locke also recognises that exchange was the only means by which man could accumulate more than he needs. While Locke uses this argument to argue that inequality is founded on consent, Paine uses this argument to show that, while the opportunities society affords to the creation of wealth are great, a just society must share these benefits, otherwise those who do not benefit will have no interest in its preservation.

Natural society as a machine for satisfying wants led Paine, like other *'laissez-faire'* theorists, to demand that government, the necessary evil, be kept to a minimum: 'Government is no further necessary than to supply the few cases to which society and civilisation are not conveniently competent.'[19] Such cases he believes are few because of his faith in man's natural goodness which arises from his rationality: his ability to understand that his interest is linked to the common interest of society as a whole. Paine's welfare proposals do not disrupt this system of natural justice and liberty but enforces it by assuming that no one is excluded from their natural part in it. As we are all stockholders in the Earth, we should all benefit from the system which makes the best use of it, and certainly no one should be disadvantaged by social cooperation. This is as much part of our natural right as our personal freedom is. It is not so much a case of a government interfering with the economy as ensuring that all receive their due from it. The government's primary objective is to act as the fare inspector against free riders. The free market economy can only function when government protects the fair contract which is the basis of all exchange from the few cheats and frauds. This requires also that it ensures that property owners compensate the dispossessed. Paine's free market is that of Smith not Malthus - it is a natural system which

---

[19] 'Rights of Man II' (1792), *Writings*, II, 407.

benefits all mankind, not a mechanism for weeding out the weak from the strong by starvation.

The apparent inconsistency between economic freedom and the will of the majority found in the struggle to preserve the banks charter also poses some questions for Paine's theory of property rights. This was the subject of considerable scholarly debate in the 1930s and 1940s. J. Dorfman argues that Paine's defence the Bank of North America demonstrates his commitment to the sanctity of contracts over the will of the majority. Thus property rights are inalienable and constitute a limitation upon the sovereignty of the people.[20] Similarly Merriam and Parrington suggest that Paine firstly argues that the state should not interfere but later demands stringent state regulation.[21] Penniman argues in contrast that Paine's later works show he is fully committed to popular sovereignty, that in a democracy this could only be limited by inalienable natural rights, belonging to them by virtue of their existence. Penniman maintains that Paine's approval of the French Republic's sale of church lands to pay the national debt and his proposal for a progressive income tax indicate that he does not see property as an inalienable right. Indeed, in the *Crisis* papers, he suggests a special tax be levied on anyone who refuses to swear an oath denouncing George III.[22] While Dorfman asserts that Paine and Alexander Hamilton have the same economic objective of protecting property rights, Penniman claims that Paine wished property to serve all in society, while 'Hamilton wished the state to preserve property for those who owned it and certainly not to take it from them to help others.'[23] Thus popular sovereignty can determine limits on property according to social need.

---

[20] Dorfman, 'Economic Philosophy', 372-86.

[21] Penniman, 'Paine: Democrat', 244-62. See also V. L. Parrington, *Main Currents of American Thought*, 3 vols (New York: Harcourt Brace, 1927) 1. 334 and C. E. Merriam, 'Thomas Paine's Political Theories', *Political Science Quarterly* 14:3 (1899) 402.

[22] See below p. 478 & p. 498; 'Crisis III' (1777) *Writings*, I, 225-7.

[23] Penniman, 'Paine: Democrat', 246. Lause claims that Paine's legacy in America in the early nineteenth century centred on his redistributive justice. See Mark A. Lause 'The "Unwashed Infidelity": Thomas Paine and Early New York City', *Labour History* 27: 3 (1986) 385-409.

However, I think that popular sovereignty could be checked by property rights: the natural right of all men to the earth. In *Agrarian Justice*, Paine clearly does not think that a society, however democratic, could be just unless it compensates the majority for the monopoly of resources by the minority. By examining Paine's distinction between natural and civil rights, we see that the confusion lies in the distinct status of the right to natural earth and the right to private property. Paine distinguishes two classes of natural rights. Firstly there are 'those which appertain to man in right of his existence' which include 'all those rights of acting as an individual for his own comfort and happiness, which are not injurious to the natural rights of others'.[24] The right to the earth would seem to be such a right for how else can we satisfy our needs and wants except by enjoying the fruits of the earth.[25] Further, such enjoyment is not injurious to the natural rights of others, as long as the source of the fruits is not appropriated. As the natural earth cannot support a large population, there would be little competition for resources. Therefore, it seems that the right to earth is a natural right and so the requirement of compensation can limit popular sovereignty. Man did not enter into society to become worse off than he was before, but to have his rights secured.

The second class of natural rights are those which are due to man in nature but are impossible for the individual acting alone to enforce. These rights form the basis of the social contract in which civil rights are institution to protect these unguarded rights.   They include 'all those which relate to security and protection'.[26] The right to the fruits of one's labour, the improvement of the land, to individual property is this sort of right. We have a right to it based on our existence, that is self-ownership of the body but we cannot prevent it from being stolen by a gang of less industrious men. The first type of natural right man retains when he enters society, the second he throws into the common stock as a

---

[24] 'Rights of Man' (1791), *Writings*, II, 306.
[25] Compare to Locke's argument from need: Locke, *Two Treatises*, pp. 286-7.
[26] 'Rights of Man' (1791), *Writings*, II, 306.

member of society. He relies on society to protect such rights as civil rights. Individual private property is therefore subordinate to the sovereignty of justice and the will of the majority. Property rights of this kind will be protected only where they are compatible with the public good which seeks to balance competing interests. The natural right to earth is only consistent with the civil institution of private property when the members of that society can accept the requirement of compensation to the dispossessed.

Distributive Justice

Mark Philp has asserted that Paine's theory of the just distribution of property in *Agrarian Justice* can be likened to that of John Rawls in *A Theory of Justice*.[27] Certainly, Rawls's theory is useful to our understanding of Paine's theory but not only because of the similarities. One vital difference between Paine and Rawls will strengthen our view of Paine as a liberal, even libertarian. Rawls argues inequality can only be just in circumstances which benefit the least advantaged, thus generating his famous difference principle. Philp suggests that this could be understood in Paine's terms thus

> The appropriations of wealth is just when it simultaneously increases proportionally the fund which provides the starting capital of £15 to each person arriving at the age of 21 and a pension to all those over fifty or suffering from an incapacitating debility.

Philp admits that 'Paine's version [...] is less stringent, in that he falls short of Rawls's position by declaring that he cares not 'how affluent some may be, provided that none be miserable in consequence of it.'[28] This may suggest instead that a guaranteed minimum basic income would suffice, although Paine's welfare

---

[27] See Philp, *Paine*, pp. 90-97; Rawls, *Theory of Justice*.
[28] See below p. 521 & p. 525; Philp, *Paine*, p. 91.

payments are quite out of character with this approach.²⁹   Philp suggests that provision of starting capital for young adults can be likened to Rawls's condition of fair equality of opportunity.

Paine and Rawls also share the recognition that a well-ordered just society requires mutual understanding. Rawls suggests this is the 'fraternity' part of the theory which already encompasses liberty and equality. We find Paine's publicly shared conception of justice in *Dissertations* on *Government* in his claim that sovereignty in a republic is justice, where as in a despotism it is will.³⁰ Both Paine and Rawls insist that for society to be just it must at least have the potential to be the result of a mutually beneficial contract. Not only do both men base their theory of distributive justice on a hypothetical social contract but also both have a dynamic conception of that contract. Lastly, both Paine and Rawls give absolute priority to rights. For Paine, these are the ends for which civil society is created. Rawls insists that inequality in liberty or civil rights is never just, and 'cannot be justified by, or compensated for, by greater social and economic advantages.'³¹

---

²⁹ See for example, Stuart White, 'Liberal Equality, Exploitation, and the Case for an Unconditional Basic Income', *Political Studies*, 1997, 45:2, 312-326; P. Vanparijs, 'Why Surfers Should Be Fed: The Liberal Case for an Unconditional Basic Income', *Philosophy & Public Affairs*, 1991, 20:2, 101-131 & 'Reciprocity and the Justification of an Unconditional Basic Income: Reply to Stuart White' *Political Studies*, 1997, 45:2, 327-330; A. Williams, 'Resource Egalitarianism and the Limits to Basic Income', *Economics and Philosophy*, 1999, 15:1, 85-107; R. J. Van Der Veen, 'Real Freedom Versus Reciprocity: Competing Views on the Justice of Unconditional Basic Income', *Political Studies*, 1998, 46:1, 140-163; D. Purdy, 'Citizenship, Basic Income and the State' *New Left Review*, 1994, 208, 30-48. Also of interest is J. Sempere, 'An Efficiency Justification of Basic Income', *Trimestre Economico*, 1999, 66:262, 175-188. It is worth noting that Paine's justice can also be considered in the light of two other principles of just distribution, which Rawls rejects. The principle of average utility may loosely be described as requiring that social and economic inequalities be so arranged as to increase the average utility in that society. While Paine does sometimes seem to be approaching a utilitarian position, the average utility principle would not satisfy his criterion the condition of *every* person ought not to be worse than if he had been born before that the invention of property. See below p. 463. Similarly Paine considers efficiency in that he is cautious when it comes to making existing property holders worse off; advocating the right of the dispossessed while equally defending 'the right of the possessor to the part which is his.' See below p. 519. Further Paine proposes an inheritance or death tax rather than the progressive income tax because it will not disrupt the present possessors. But the difference principle comes closest to his argument that none should be worse off.
³⁰ See Philp, *Paine*, p. 90-92; see also above p. 276.
³¹ Rawls, *Theory of Justice*, p. 542ff.

However there is a fundamental difference between the two theories. While both give priority to civil rights, Rawls excludes welfare rights while Paine includes them. Rawls divides social goods into two groups, distinguishing between 'those aspects of the social system that define and secure the equal liberties of citizenship and those that specify and establish social and economic equalities'[32] Rawls's difference principle requires the provision of a social minimum but does not have the force of the guaranteed equal liberties. Paine however stresses that the transfers paid from the fund are rights and are grounded upon a natural right. Surely, if this is so, it must be equal to all the other natural rights which we entered society to protect. I believe we can distinguish between Paine and Rawls in this way: that for Paine we are entitled to the compensation for the loss of our natural property rights, while Rawls recognises no property rights prior to the original position. Therefore, Paine offers his universal redistributive payments to both rich and poor.[33]

While Paine's theory would not long survive the ravages of Rawls's foremost critic, Robert Nozick, it would at least stand up to one criticism that Rawls's cannot accommodate. Nozick proposes an 'Entitlement Theory of Distributive Justice', that is 'that a distribution is just if everyone is entitled to the holdings they possess under the distribution.'[34] He argues that only a minimal state, in which taxes were only appropriated from citizens by their express consent for use in public goods to which all had consented, can be considered just according to entitlement. Paine's redistributive rights are entitlements, at least in *Agrarian Justice*. Everyone is entitled to the holdings they possess if and only if they compensate for their loss those who were originally entitled to them by their existence as men, according to the principle of the fair bargain or rational contract. Thus Paine's theory is what Nozick calls a historical theory of justice in

---

[32] Rawls, *Theory of Justice*, p. 60.
[33] See below p. 529.
[34] Nozick, *Anarchy, State and Utopia*, p. 151.

distribution; that is whether a distribution is just depends on 'how it came about' as opposed to current-time slice principles such Rawls's difference principle.

The combination of an entitlement theory of justice with a conviction that the institution of private property in a free market does not in itself guarantee a benefit to all, suggests that Paine's *Agrarian Justice* can best be interpreted as a left libertarian position not to far distant from Hillel Steiner's in *An Essay on Rights*.[35] The comparison particularly draws out the emphasis both place on the inclusion of future generations, which most theories of justice ignore. However, in identifying Paine as a libertarian, I may well be accused of defeating my earlier argument for an interpretation of Paine as a republican. Surely one cannot be a libertarian republican? Paine's republicanism does however inhabit his left libertarian welfare proposals. Material inequality is not only unjust because it creates suffering but also because it engenders an imbalance of power. Paine's progressive tax is designed to prevent the accumulation of riches that warrants its own legislative chamber and the related practice of primogeniture which promotes political corruption. His proposed starting capital is intended to release the enterprising poor from their inevitable dependence on their employer. Left libertarianism recognises that the ownership of property is a necessary condition of freedom and that those excluded will experience such rights as a gross violation of their freedom. Republican freedom understood as the absence of dependence similarly requires both self-ownership and sufficient resources to preclude economic domination by others.

When I first began work on Paine ten years ago, it seemed that our established welfare system was still continually under threat from one version of *laissez-faire* economic theory. Though we rejoiced in the fall of totalitarian regimes, some of us also shuddered at the suggestion that finally capitalist *laissez-faire* ideology had triumphed throughout the world. I thought one might adopt a

---

[35] See Hillel Steiner, *An Essay on Rights*, (Oxford: Blackwell, 1994) & 'Liberty and Equality', *Political Studies*, xxix (1981), 555-569.

conception of property relations in a *laissez-faire* economy similar to Paine's, which would protect both our freedom and our comfort in equal measure. It does seem remarkable that these two principles do not seem as necessarily incompatible as they did in view of the narrowness of the political debate of 1989. It has often been noted that it is the central principles of Paine's thought, and not Burke's, that have become commonplace in our society. At the end of the twentieth century, we have a general respect for the principles of equality, human rights, representative government as well as economic freedom within the framework of a minimum standard of income. We are also well on the way to securing a European republic which guarantees peace and free trade. But Paine still has much to offer the twenty-first century, particularly in Britain, where the process of dismantling the last vestiges of hereditary principle in government has only recently begun. Paine's hope that free trade among republican governments might secure world peace is still hamstrung by the monopolising practices of certain rich nations. And of course there is still much progress needed in the actual recognition throughout the world of what we now call the Rights of Humans. It still cannot be said of any country in the world that the poor are happy and the taxes are not oppressive. 'When these things can be said, then may that country boast its constitution and its government'.[36]

---

[36] See below p. 509.

From *Rights of Man, Part Second, Combining Principle and Practice*

CHAP. V.

WAYS and MEANS OF IMPROVING THE CONDITION OF Europe,

INTERSPERSED WITH

Miscellaneous Observations

***

Whatever the form or constitution of government may be, it ought to have no other object than the *general* happiness. When, instead of this, it operates to create and encrease wretchedness in any of the parts of society, it is on a wrong system, and reformation is necessary.

Customary language has classed the condition of man under the two descriptions of civilized and uncivilized life. To the one it has ascribed felicity and affluence; to the other hardship and want. But however our imagination may be impressed by painting and comparison, it is nevertheless true, that a great portion of mankind, in what are called civilized countries, are in a state of poverty and wretchedness, far below the condition of an Indian. I speak not of one country, but of all. It is so in England, it is so all over Europe. Let us enquire into the cause.

It lies not in any natural defect in the principles of civilization, but in preventing those principles having a universal operation; the consequence of which is, a perpetual system of war and expence, that drains the country, and defeats the general felicity of which civilization is capable. All the European governments (France now excepted) are constructed not on the principle of universal civilization, but on the reverse of it. So far as those governments relate to each other, they are in the same condition as we conceive of savage uncivilized life; they put themselves beyond the law as well of GOD as of man, and are, with respect to principle and reciprocal conduct, like so many individuals in a state of nature.

The inhabitants of every country, under the civilization of laws, easily civilize together, but governments being yet in an uncivilized state, and almost continually at war, they pervert the abundance which civilized life produces to carry on the uncivilized part to a greater extent. By thus engrafting the barbarism of government upon the internal civilization of a country, it draws from the latter, and more especially from the poor, a great portion of those earnings, which should be applied to their own subsistence and comfort.—Apart from all reflections of morality and philosophy, it is a melancholy fact, that more than one-fourth of the labour of mankind is annually consumed by this barbarous system.

What has served to continue this evil, is the pecuniary advantage, which all the governments of Europe have found in keeping up this state of uncivilization. It affords to them pretences for power, and revenue, for which there would be neither occasion nor apology, if the circle of civilization were rendered compleat. Civil government alone, or the government of laws, is not productive of pretences for many taxes; it operates at home, directly under the eye of the country, and precludes the possibility of much imposition. But when the scene is laid in the uncivilized contention of governments, the field of pretences is enlarged, and the country, being no longer a judge, is open to every imposition, which governments please to act.

Not a thirtieth, scarcely a fortieth, part of the taxes which are raised in England are either occasioned by, or applied to, the purposes of civil government. It is not difficult to see, that the whole which the actual government does in this respect, is to enact laws, and that the country administers and executes them, at its own expence, by means of magistrates, juries, sessions, and assize, over and above the taxes which it pays.

In this view of the case, we have two distinct characters of government; the one the civil government, or the government of laws, which operates at home, the other the court or cabinet government, which operates abroad, on the rude plan of uncivilized life; the one attended with little charge, the other with boundless extravagance; and so distinct are the two, that if the latter were to sink, as it were by a sudden opening of the earth, and totally disappear, the former would not be deranged. It would still proceed, because it is the common interest of the nation that it should, and all the means are in practice.

Revolutions, then, have for their object, a change in the moral condition of governments, and with this change the burthen of public taxes will lessen, and civilization will be left to the enjoyment of that abundance, of which it is now deprived.

In contemplating the whole of this subject, I extend my views into the department of commerce. In all my publications, where the matter would admit, I have been an advocate for commerce, because I am a friend to its effects. It is a pacific system, operating to cordialize mankind, by rendering nations, as well as individuals, useful to each other. As to the mere theoretical reformation, I have never preached it up. The most effectual process is that of improving the condition of man by means of his interest; and it is on this ground that I take my stand.

If commerce were permitted to act to the universal extent it is capable, it would extirpate the system of war, and produce a revolution in the uncivilized state of governments. The invention of commerce has arisen since those governments began, and is the greatest approach towards universal civilization, that has yet been made by any means not immediately flowing from moral principles.

Whatever has a tendency to promote the civil intercourse of nations, by an exchange of benefits, is a subject as worthy of philosophy as of politics. Commerce is no other than the traffic of two individuals, multiplied on a scale of numbers; and by the same rule that nature intended for the intercourse of two, she intended that of all. For this purpose she has distributed the materials of manufactures and commerce, in various and distant parts of a nation and of the world; and as they cannot be procured by war so cheaply or so commodiously as by commerce, she has rendered the latter the means of extirpating the former.

As the two are nearly the opposite of each other, consequently, the uncivilized state of the European governments is injurious to commerce. Every kind of destruction or embarrassment serves to lessen the quantity, and it matters but little in what part of the commercial world the reduction begins. Like blood, it cannot be taken from any of the parts, without being taken from the whole mass in circulation, and all partake of the loss. When the ability in any nation to buy is destroyed, it equally involves the seller. Could the government of England destroy the commerce of all other nations, she would most effectually ruin her own.

It is possible that a nation may be the carrier for the world, but she cannot be the merchant. She cannot be the seller and buyer of her own merchandize. The ability to buy must reside out of herself; and, therefore, the prosperity of any commercial nation is regulated by the prosperity of the rest. If they are poor she cannot be rich, and her condition, be it what it may, is an index of the height of the commercial tide in other nations.

That the principles of commerce, and its universal operation may be understood, without understanding the practice, is a position that reason will not deny; and it is on this ground only that I argue the subject. It is one thing in the counting-house, in the world it is another. With respect to its operation it must necessarily be contemplated as a reciprocal thing; that only one half its powers resides within the nation, and that the whole is as effectually destroyed by destroying the half that resides without, as if the destruction had been committed on that which is within; for neither can act without the other.

When in the last, as well as in former wars, the commerce of England sunk, it was because the general quantity was lessened every where; and it now rises, because commerce is in a rising state in every nation. If England, at this day, imports and exports more than at any former period, the nations with which she trades must necessarily do the same; her imports are their exports, and *vice versa*.

There can be no such thing as a nation flourishing alone in commerce; she can only participate; and the destruction of it in any part must necessarily affect all.

When, therefore, governments are at war, the attack is made upon the common stock of commerce, and the consequence is the same as if each had attacked his own.

The present increase of commerce is not to be attributed to ministers, or to any political contrivances, but to its own natural operations in consequence of peace. The regular markets had been destroyed, the channels of trade broken up, the high road of the seas infested with robbers of every nation, and the attention of the world called to other objects. Those interruptions have ceased, and peace has restored the deranged condition of things to their proper order.*

It is worth remarking, that every nation reckons the balance of trade in its own favour; and therefore something must be irregular in the common ideas upon this subject.

The fact, however, is true, according to what is called a balance; and it is from this cause that commerce is universally supported. Every nation feels the advantage, or it would abandon the practice: but the deception lies in the mode of making up the accounts, and in attributing what are called profits to a wrong cause.

Mr. Pitt has sometimes amused himself, by shewing what he called a balance of trade from the custom-house books. This mode of calculating, not only affords no rule that is true, but one that is false.

In the first place, Every cargo that departs from the custom house, appears on the books as an export; and, according to the custom-house balance, the losses at sea, and by foreign failures, are all reckoned on the side of profit, because they appear as exports.

---

* In America the increase of commerce is greater in proportion than in England. It is, at this time, at least one half more than at any period prior to the revolution. The greatest number of vessels cleared out of the port of Philadelphia, before the commencement of the war, was between eight and nine hundred. In the year 1788, the number was upwards of twelve hundred. As the state of Pennsylvania is estimated as an eighth part of the United States in population, the whole number of vessels must now be nearly ten thousand.

Secondly, Because the importation by the smuggling trade does not appear on the custom-house books, to arrange against the exports.

No balance, therefore, as applying to superior advantages, can be drawn from those documents; and if we examine the natural operation of commerce, the idea is fallacious; and if true, would soon be injurious. The great support of commerce consists in the balance being a level of benefits among all nations.

Two merchants of different nations trading together, will both become rich, and each makes the balance in his own favour; consequently, they do not get rich out of each other; and it is the same with respect to the nations in which they reside. The case must be, that each nation must get rich out of its own means, and increases that riches by something which it procures from another in exchange.

If a merchant in England sends an article of English manufacture abroad, which costs him a shilling at home, and imports something which sells for two, he makes a balance of one shilling in his own favour; but this is not gained out of the foreign nation or the foreign merchant, for he also does the same by the articles he receives, and neither has a balance of advantage upon the other. The original value of the two articles in their proper countries were but two shillings; but by changing their places, they acquire a new idea of value, equal to double what they had first, and that increased value is equally divided.

There is no otherwise a balance on foreign than on domestic commerce. The merchants of London and Newcastle trade on the same principles, as if they resided in different nations, and make their balances in the same manner: yet London does not get rich out of Newcastle, any more than Newcastle out of London: but coals, the merchandize of Newcastle, have an additional value at London, and London merchandize has the same at Newcastle.

Though the principle of all commerce is the same, the domestic, in a national view, is the part most beneficial; because the whole of the advantages, an both sides, rests within the nation; whereas, in foreign commerce, it is only a participation of one half.

The most unprofitable of all commerce is that connected with foreign dominion. To a few individuals it may be beneficial, merely because it is commerce; but to the nation it is a loss. The expence of maintaining dominion more than absorbs the profits of any trade. It does not increase the general quantity in the world, but operates to lessen it; and as a greater mass would be afloat by relinquishing dominion, the participation without the expence would be more valuable than a greater quantity with it.

But it is impossible to engross commerce by dominion; and therefore it is still more fallacious. It cannot exist in confined channels, and necessarily breaks out by regular or irregular means, that defeat the attempt: and to succeed would be still worse. France, since the revolution, has been more indifferent as to foreign possessions; and other nations will become the same, when they investigate the subject with respect to commerce.

To the expence of dominion is to be added that of navies, and when the amount of the two are subtracted from the profits of commerce, it will appear, that what is called the balance of trade, even admitting it to exist, is not enjoyed by the nation, but absorbed by the government.

The idea of having navies for the protection of commerce is delusive. It is putting the means of destruction for the means of protection. Commerce needs no other protection than the reciprocal interest which every nation feels in supporting it—it is common stock—it exists by a balance of advantages to all; and the only interruption it meets, is from the present uncivilized state of governments, and which it is its common interest to reform.*

Quitting this subject, I now proceed to other matters.—As it is necessary to include England in the prospect of a general reformation, it is proper to enquire into the defects of its government.

---

* When I saw Mr. Pitt's mode of estimating the balance of trade, in one of his parliamentary speeches, he appeared to me to know nothing of the nature and interest of commerce; and no man has more wantonly tortured it than himself. During a period of peace, it has been havocked with the calamities of war. Three times has it been thrown into stagnation, and the vessels unmanned by impressing, within less than four years of peace.

***

I begin with charters and corporations.

It is a perversion of terms to say, that a charter gives rights. It operates by a contrary effect, that of taking rights away. Rights are inherently in all the inhabitants; but charters, by annulling those rights in the majority, leave the right by exclusion in the hands of a few. If charters were constructed so as to express in direct terms, "*that every inhabitant, who is not a member of a corporation, shall not exercise the right of voting,*" such charters would, in the face, be charters, not of rights, but of exclusion. The effect is the same under the form they now stand; and the only persons on whom they operate, are the persons whom they exclude. Those whose rights are guaranteed, by not being taken away, exercise no other rights than as members of the community they are entitled to without a charter; and, therefore, all charters have no other than an indirect negative operation. They do not give rights to A, but they make a difference in favour of A by taking away the right of B, and consequently are instruments of injustice.

But charters and corporations have a more extensive evil effect, than what relates merely to elections. They are sources of endless contentions in the places where they exist; and they lessen the common rights of national society. A native of England, under the operation of these charters and corporations, cannot be said to be an Englishman in the full sense of the word. He is not free of the nation, in the same manner that a Frenchman is free of France, and an American of America. His rights are circumscribed to the town, and, in some cases, to the parish of his birth; and all other parts, though in his native land, are to him as a foreign country. To acquire a residence in these, he must undergo a local naturalization by purchase, or he is forbidden or expelled the place. This species of feudality is kept up to aggrandize the corporations at the ruin of towns; and the effect is visible.

***

The persons most immediately interested in the abolition of corporations, are the inhabitants of the towns where corporations are established. The instances of Manchester, Birmingham, and Sheffield, shew, by contrast, the injury which those Gothic institutions are to property and commerce. A few examples may be found, such as that of London, whose natural and commercial advantage, owing to its situation on the Thames, is capable of bearing up against the political evils of a corporation; but in almost all other cases the fatality is too visible to be doubted or denied.

Though the whole nation is not so directly affected by the depression of property in corporation towns as the inhabitants themselves, it partakes of the consequence. By lessening the value of property, the quantity of national commerce is curtailed. Every man is a customer in proportion to his ability; and as all parts of a nation trade with each other, whatever affects any of the parts, must necessarily communicate to the whole.[1]

***

What is called the House of Peers, is constituted on a ground very similar to that, against which there is a law in other cases. It amounts to a combination of persons in one common interest. No better reason can be given, why a house of legislation should be composed entirely of men whose occupation consists in letting landed property, than why it should be composed of those who hire, or of brewers, or bakers, or any other separate class of men.

Mr. Burke calls this house, "*the great ground and pillar of security to the landed interest.*" Let us examine this idea.

What pillar of security does the landed interest require more than any other interest in the state, or what right has it to a distinct and separate representation from the general interest of a nation? The only use to be made of this power, (and

---

[1] Here Paine links the corruption in the House of Commons with election by unrepresentative corporations.

which it has always made,) is to ward off taxes from itself, and throw the burthen upon those articles of consumption by which itself would be least affected.

That this has been the consequence, (and will always be the consequence of constructing governments on combinations,) is evident with respect to England, from the history of its taxes.

Notwithstanding taxes have encreased and multiplied upon every article of common consumption, the land-tax, which more particularly affects this "pillar," has diminished. In 1778, the amount of the land-tax was £1,950,000 which is half a million less than it produced almost an hundred years ago,* notwithstanding the rentals are in many instances doubled since that period.

Before the coming of the Hanoverians, the taxes were divided in nearly equal proportions between the land and articles of consumption, the land bearing rather the largest share: but since that æra, nearly thirteen millions annually of new taxes have been thrown upon consumption. The consequence of which has been a constant encrease in the number and wretchedness of the poor, and in the amount of the poor-rates. Yet here again the burthen does not fall in equal proportions on the aristocracy with the rest of the community. Their residences, whether in town or country, are not mixed with the habitations of the poor. They live apart from distress, and the expence of relieving it. It is in manufacturing towns and labouring villages that those burthens press the heaviest; in many of which it is one class of poor supporting another.

Several of the most heavy and productive taxes are so contrived, as to give an exemption to this pillar, thus standing in its own defence. The tax upon beer brewed for sale does not affect the aristocracy, who brew their own beer free of this duty. It falls only on those who have not conveniency or ability to brew, and who must purchase it in small quantities. But what will mankind think of the justice of taxation, when they know, that this tax alone, from which the aristocracy are from circumstances exempt, is nearly equal to the whole of the

---

* See Sir John Sinclair's History of the Revenue. The land-tax in 1646 was £2,473,499.

land-tax, being in the year 1788, and it is not less now, £1,666,152 and with its proportion of the taxes on malt and hops, it exceeds it.—That a single article, thus partially consumed, and that chiefly by the working part, should be subject to a tax, equal to that on the whole rental of a nation, is, perhaps, a fact not to be paralleled in the histories of revenues.

This is one of the consequences resulting from an house of legislation, composed on the ground of a combination of common interest; for whatever their separate politics as to parties may be, in this they are united. Whether a combination acts to raise the price of any article for sale, or rate of wages; or whether it acts to throw taxes from itself upon another class of the community, the principle and the effect are the same; and if the one be illegal, it will be difficult to shew that the other ought to exist.

It is no use to say, that taxes are first proposed in the house of commons; for as the other house has always a negative, it can always defend itself; and it would be ridiculous to suppose that its acquiescence in the measures to be proposed were not understood before hand. Besides which, it has obtained so much influence by borough-traffic, and so many of its relations and connections are distributed on both sides the commons, as to give it, besides an absolute negative in one house, a preponderancy in the other, in all matters of common concern.

It is difficult to discover what is meant by the *landed interest*, if it does not mean a combination of aristocratical land-holders, opposing their own pecuniary interest to that of the farmer, and every branch of trade, commerce, and manufacture. In all other respects it is the only interest that needs no partial protection. It enjoys the general protection of the world. Every individual, high or low, is interested in the fruits of the earth; men, women, and children, of all ages and degrees, will turn out to assist the farmer, rather than a harvest should not be got in; and they will not act thus by any other property. It is the only one for which the common prayer of mankind is put up, and the only one that can never fail from the want of means. It is the interest, not of the policy, but of the existence of man, and when it ceases, he must cease to be.

No other interest in a nation stands on the same united support. Commerce, manufactures, arts, sciences, and every thing else, compared with this, are supported but in parts. Their prosperity or their decay has not the same universal influence. When the vallies laugh and sing, it is not the farmer only, but all creation that rejoice. It is a prosperity that excludes all envy; and this cannot be said of any thing else.

Why then, does Mr. Burke talk of his house of peers, as the pillar of the landed interest? Were that pillar to sink into the earth, the same landed property would continue, and the same ploughing, sowing, and reaping would go on. The aristocracy are not the farmers who work the land, and raise the produce, but are the mere consumers of the rent; and when compared with the active world are the drones, a seraglio of males, who neither collect the honey nor form the hive, but exist only for lazy enjoyment.

***

If a house of legislation is to be composed of men of one class, for the purpose of protecting a distinct interest, all the other interests should have the same. The inequality, as well as the burthen of taxation, arises from admitting it in one case, and not in all. Had there been a house of farmers, there had been no game laws; or a house of merchants and manufacturers, the taxes had neither been so unequal nor so excessive. It is from the power of taxation being in the hands of those who can throw so great a part of it from their own shoulders, that it has raged without a check.[2]

Men of small or moderate estates are more injured by the taxes being thrown on articles of consumption, than they are eased by warding it from landed property, for the following reasons:

---

[2] The game laws restricted hunting to those who owned or leased land worth over £100 per annum. The Black Act in 1723 and the Night Poaching Act in 1770 introduced harsh punishments for poaching and became a symbol of class conflict. See E. P. Thompson, *Whigs and Hunters: The Origin of the Black Act* (New York: Pantheon, 1975).

First, They consume more of the productive taxable articles, in proportion to their property, than those of large estates.

Secondly, Their residence is chiefly in towns, and their property in houses; and the encrease of the poor-rates, occasioned by taxes on consumption, is in much greater proportion than the land-tax has been favoured. In Birmingham, the poor-rates are not less than seven shillings in the pound. From this, as is already observed, the aristocracy are in a great measure exempt.

These are but a part of the mischiefs flowing from the wretched scheme of an house of peers.

As a combination, it can always throw a considerable portion of taxes from itself; and as an hereditary house, accountable to nobody, it resembles a rotten borough, whose consent is to be courted by interest. There are but few of its members, who are not in some mode or other participaters, or disposers of the public money. One turns a candle-holder, or a lord in waiting; another a lord of the bed-chamber, a groom of the stole, or any insignificant nominal office, to which a salary is annexed, paid out of the public taxes, and which avoids the direct appearance of corruption. Such situations are derogatory to the character of man; and where they can be submitted to, honour cannot reside.

To all these are to be added the numerous dependants, the long list of younger branches and distant relations, who are to be provided for at the public expence: in short, were an estimation to be made of the charge of aristocracy to a nation, it will be found nearly equal to that of supporting the poor. The Duke of Richmond alone (and there are cases similar to his) takes away as much for himself as would maintain two thousand poor and aged persons. Is it, then, any wonder, that under such a system of government, taxes and rates have multiplied to their present extent?

In stating these matters, I speak an open and disinterested language, dictated by no passion but that of humanity. To me, who have not only refused offers, because I thought them improper, but have declined rewards I might with reputation have accepted, it is no wonder that meanness and imposition appear disgustful. Independence is my happiness, and I view things as they are, without regard to place or person; my country is the world, and my religion is to do good.[3]

Mr. Burke, in speaking of the aristocratical law of primogeniture, says, "it is the standing law of our landed inheritance; and which, without question, has a tendency, and I think," continues he, "a happy tendency, to preserve a character of weight and consequence."

Mr. Burke may call this law what he pleases, but humanity and impartial reflection will denounce it as a law of brutal injustice. Were we not accustomed to the daily practice, and did we only hear of it as the law of some distant part of the world, we should conclude that the legislators of such countries had not arrived at a state of civilization.

As to its preserving a character of *weight and consequence,* the case appears to me directly the reverse. It is an attaint upon character; a sort of privateering on family property. It may have weight among dependent tenants, but it gives none on a scale of national, and much less of universal character. Speaking for myself,

---

[3] In an earlier (omitted) passage Paine adds the following note, which warrants inclusion as testament to this claim of personal independence:

'Politics and self-interest have been so uniformly connected, that the world, from being so often deceived, has a right to be suspicious of public characters: but with regard to myself, I am perfectly easy on this head. I did not, at my first setting out in public life, nearly seventeen years ago, turn my thoughts to subjects of government from motives of interest; and my conduct from that moment to this, proves the fact. I saw an opportunity, in which I thought I could do some good, and I followed exactly what my heart dictated. I neither read books, nor studied other people's opinion. I thought for myself. The case was this:

During the suspension of the old governments in America, both prior to, and at the breaking out of hostilities, I was struck with the order and decorum with which every thing was conducted: and impressed with the idea, that a little more than what society naturally performed, was all the government that was necessary; and that monarchy and aristocracy were frauds and impositions upon mankind. On these principles I published the pamphlet *Common Sense.* The success it met with was beyond any thing since the invention of printing. I gave the copy right to every state in the union, and the demand ran to not less than one hundred thousand copies. I continued the subject in the same manner, under the title of the *Crisis,* till the complete establishment of the revolution.

After the declaration of independence, Congress unanimously, and unknown to me, appointed me secretary in the foreign department. This was agreeable to me, because it gave me the opportunity of seeing into the abilities of foreign courts, and their manner of doing business. But a misunderstanding arising between congress and me, respecting one of their commissioners then in Europe, Mr. Silas Deane, I resigned the office, and declined, at the same time, the pecuniary offers made by the ministers of France and Spain, M. Gerard and Don Juan Mirralles.'

my parents were not able to give me a shilling, beyond what they gave me in education; and to do this they distressed themselves: yet, I possess more of what is called consequence, in the world, than any one in Mr. Burke's catalogue of aristocrats.

Having thus glanced at some of the defects of the two houses of parliament, I proceed to what is called the crown, upon which I shall be very concise.

It signifies a nominal office of a million sterling a year, the business of which consists in receiving the money. Whether the person be wise or foolish, sane or insane, a native or a foreigner, matters not. Every ministry acts upon the same idea that Mr. Burke writes, namely, that the people must be hood-winked, and held in superstitious ignorance by some bugbear or other; and what is called the crown answers this purpose, and therefore it answers all the purposes to be expected from it.[4]

***

With the revolution of 1688, and more so since the Hanover succession, came the destructive system of continental intrigues, and the rage for foreign wars and foreign dominion; systems of such secure mystery that the expences admit of no accounts; a single line stands for millions. To what excess taxation might have extended, had not the French revolution contributed to break up the system, and put an end to pretences, is impossible to say. Viewed, as that revolution ought to be, as the fortunate means of lessening the load of taxes of both countries, it is of as much importance to England as to France; and, if properly improved to all the advantages of which it is capable, and to which it leads, deserves as much celebration in one country as the other.

In pursuing this subject, I shall begin with the matter that first presents itself, that of lessening the burthen of taxes; and shall then add such matter and

---

[4] Here Paine reviews the historical level of taxation demonstrating that it is possible for the tax burden to fall, the annual amount of taxes levied in 1066 being £400,000 compared to £150,000 in 1266 and £100,000 in 1466. Taking his figures from Sir John Sinclair's *History of the Revenue*, he demonstrates that recent history has seen unprecedented increases in the tax burden from £500,000 in 1566 to 1,800,000 in 1666 and 17,000,000 in 1791.

propositions, respecting the three countries of England, France, and America, as the present prospect of things appears to justify: I mean, an alliance of the three, for the purposes that will be mentioned in their proper place.

***

The amount of taxes for the year, ending at Michaelmas 1788, was as follows:

Land-tax,	£ 1,950,000
Customs,	3,789,274
Excise, (including old and new malt,)	6,751,727
Stamps,	1,278,214
Miscellaneous taxes and incidents,	1,803,755
	£15,572,970

Since the year 1788, upwards of one million, new taxes have been laid on, besides the produce from the lotteries; and as the taxes have in general been more productive since than before, the amount may be taken, in round numbers, at £17,000,000.

N. B. The expence of collection and the drawbacks, which together amount to nearly two millions, are paid out of the gross amount; and the above is the nett sum paid into the exchequer.

This sum of seventeen millions is applied to two different purposes; the one to pay the interest of the national debt, the other to the current expences of each year. About nine millions are appropriated to the former; and the remainder, being nearly eight millions, to the latter. As to the million, said to be applied to the reduction of the debt, it is so much like paying with one hand and taking out with the other, as not to merit much notice.

It happened, fortunately for France, that she possessed national domains for paying off her debt, and thereby lessening her taxes: but as this is not the case with England, her reduction of taxes can only take place by reducing the current expences, which may now be done to the amount of four or five millions annually, as will hereafter appear. When this is accomplished, it will more than counterbalance the enormous charge of the American war; and the saving will be from the same source from whence the evil arose.

As to the national debt, however heavy the interest may be in taxes; yet, as it serves to keep alive a capital, useful to commerce, it balances by its effects a considerable part of its own weight; and as the quantity of gold and silver in England is, by some means or other, short of its proper proportion*, (being not more than twenty millions, whereas it should be sixty,) it would, besides the injustice, be bad policy to extinguish a capital that serves to supply that defect. But with respect to the current expence, whatever is saved therefrom is gain. The excess may serve to keep corruption alive, but it has no re-action on credit and commerce, like the interest of the debt.

It is now very probable that the English government (I do not mean the nation) is unfriendly to the French revolution. Whatever serves to expose the intrigue and lessen the influence of courts, by lessening taxation, will be unwelcome to those who feed upon the spoil. Whilst the clamour of French intrigue, arbitrary power, popery, and wooden shoes could be kept up, the nation was easily allured and alarmed into taxes. Those days are now past: deception, it is to be hoped, has reaped its last harvest, and better times are in prospect for both countries, and for the world.

Taking it for granted, that an alliance may be formed between England, France, and America for the purposes hereafter to be mentioned, the national expences of France and England may consequently be lessened. The same fleets and armies will no longer be necessary to either, and the reduction can be made ship for ship on each side. But to accomplish these objects, the governments must necessarily be fitted to a common and correspondent principle. Confidence can never take place, while an hostile disposition remains in either, or where

---

* Foreign intrigue, foreign wars, and foreign dominions, will in a great measure account for the deficiency.

mystery and secrecy on one side, is opposed to candour and openness on the other.

These matters admitted, the national expences might be put back, *for the sake of a precedent*, to what they were at some period when France and England were not enemies. This, consequently, must be prior to the Hanover succession, and also to the revolution of 1688.* The first instance that presents itself, antecedent to those dates, is in the very wasteful and profligate times of Charles the Second; at which time England and France acted as allies. If I have chosen a period of great extravagance, it will serve to shew modern extravagance in a still worse light; especially as the pay of the navy, the army, and the revenue officers has not encreased since that time.

The peace establishment was then as follows:—

See Sir John Sinclair's History of the Revenue.[5]

Navy, - - - - - - - - - - - - - - - -	£300,000
Army, - - - - - - - - - - - - - - - -	212,000
Ordnance, - - - - - - - - - - - - - -	40,000
Civil List, - - - - - - - - - - - - -	462,115
	£1,014,115

The parliament, however, settled the whole annual peace establishment at

---

* I happened to be in England at the celebration of the centenary of the revolution of 1688. The characters of William and Mary have always appeared to me detestable; the one seeking to destroy his uncle, and the other her father, to get possession of power themselves; yet, as the nation was disposed to think something of that event, I felt hurt at seeing it ascribe the whole reputation of it to a man who had undertaken it as a jobb, and who, besides what he otherwise got, charged six hundred thousand pounds for the expence of the fleet that brought him from Holland. George the First acted the same close-fisted part as William had done, and bought the Duchy of Bremen with the money he got from England, two hundred and fifty thousand pounds over and above his pay as king; and having thus purchased it at the expence of England, added it to his Hanoverian dominions for his own private profit. In fact, every nation that does not govern itself, is governed as a jobb. England has been the prey of jobbs ever since the revolution.

[5] John Sinclair (1754-1835), *The History of the Public Revenue of the British Empire*, 3rd edn, 3 vols (London: T. Cadell and W. Davies, 1803; repr. New York: A. M. Kelley, 1966).

1,200,000.* If we go back to the time of Elizabeth, the amount of all the taxes was but half a million, yet the nation sees nothing during that period, that reproaches it with want of consequence.

All circumstances then taken together, arising from the French revolution, from the approaching harmony and reciprocal interest of the two nations, the abolition of the court intrigue on both sides, and the progress of knowledge in the science of government, the annual expenditure might be put back to one million and a half, viz.

Navy - £500,000
Army - 500,000
Expenses of Government - - - - - - - - - - <u>500,000</u>
£1,500,000

Even this sum is six times greater than the expences of government are in America, yet the civil internal government in England, (I mean that administered by means of quarter sessions, juries, and assize, and which, in fact, is nearly the whole, and performed by the nation,) is less expence upon the revenue, than the same species and portion of government is in America.

It is time that nations should be rational, and not be governed like animals, for the pleasure of their riders. To read the history of kings, a man would be almost inclined to suppose that government consisted in stag-hunting, and that every nation paid a million a year to a huntsman. Man ought to have pride, or shame enough to blush at being thus imposed upon, and when he feel his proper character, he will.

***

---

* Charles, like his predecessors and successors, finding that war was the harvest of governments, engaged in a war with the Dutch, the expence of which encreased the annual expenditure to £1,800,000 as stated under the date of 1666; but the peace establishment was but £1,200,000.

As to the offices of which any civil government may be composed, it matters but little by what names they are described. In the routine of business, as before observed, whether a man be stiled a president, a king, an emperor, a senator, or any thing else, it is impossible that any service he can perform, can merit from a nation more than ten thousand pounds a year; and as no man should be paid beyond his services, so every man of a proper heart will not accept more. Public money ought to be touched with the most scrupulous consciousness of honour. It is not the produce of riches only, but of the hard earnings of labour and poverty. It is drawn even from the bitterness of want and misery. Not a beggar passes, or perishes in the streets, whose mite is not in that mass.

Were it possible that the Congress of America could be so lost to their duty, and to the interest of their constituents, as to offer General Washington, as president of America, a million a year, he would not, and he could not, accept it. His sense of honour is of another kind. It has cost England almost seventy millions sterling, to maintain a family imported from abroad, of very inferior capacity to thousands in the nation; and scarcely a year has passed that has not produced some new mercenary application. Even the physicians bills have been sent to the public to be paid. No wonder that jails are crowded, and taxes and poor-rates encreased. Under such systems, nothing is to be looked for but what has already happened; and as to reformation, whenever it come, it must be from the nation, and not from the government.

To shew that the sum of five hundred thousand pounds is more than sufficient to defray all the expences of the government, exclusive of navies and armies, the following estimate is added for any country, of the same extent as England.

In the first place, three hundred representatives, fairly elected, are sufficient for all the purposes to which legislation can apply, and preferable to a larger number. They may be divided into two or three houses, or meet in one, as in France, or in any manner a constitution shall direct.

As representation is always considered, in free countries, as the most honourable of all stations, the allowance made to it is merely to defray the expence which the representatives incur by that service, and not to it as an office.

If an allowance, at the rate of five hundred pounds *per ann.* be made to every representative, deducting for non-attendance, the expence, if the whole number attended for six months, each year, would be £ 75,000

The official departments cannot reasonably exceed the following number, with the salaries annexed:

Three offices,	at ten thousand pounds each,	30,000
Ten ditto,	at £5000 pounds each,	50,000
Twenty ditto,	at £2000 pounds each,	40,000
Forty ditto,	at £1000 pounds each,	40,000
Two hundred ditto,	at £500 pounds each,	100,000
Three hundred ditto,	at £200 pounds each,	60,000
Five hundred ditto,	at £100 pounds each,	50,000
Seven hundred ditto,	at £75 pounds each,	52,500
		£ 497,500

If a nation chuse, it can deduct four *per cent.* from all offices, and make one of twenty thousand *per ann.*

All revenue officers are paid out of the monies they collect, and therefore, are not in this estimation.

The foregoing is not offered as an exact detail of offices, but to shew the number of rate of salaries which five hundred thousand pounds will support; and it will, on experience, be found impracticable to find business sufficient to justify even this expence. As to the manner in which office business is now performed, the Chiefs, in several offices, such as the post office, and certain offices in the exchequer, &c. do little more than sign their names three or four times a year; and the whole duty is performed by under clerks.

Taking, therefore, one million and an half as a sufficient peace establishment for all the honest purposes of government, which is three hundred thousand pounds more than the peace establishment in the profligate and prodigal times of Charles the Second (notwithstanding, as has been already observed, the pay and salaries of the army, navy, and revenue officers, continue the same as at that period), there will remain a surplus of upwards of six millions out of the present current expences. The question then will be, how to dispose of this surplus.

Whoever has observed the manner in which trade and taxes twist themselves together, must be sensible of the impossibility of separating them suddenly.

First. Because the articles now on hand are already charged with the duty, and the reduction cannot take place on the present stock.

Secondly. Because, on all those articles on which the duty is charged in the gross, such as per barrel, hogshead, hundred weight, or tun, the abolition of the duty does not admit of being divided down so as fully to relieve the consumer, who purchases by the pint, or the pound. The last duty laid on strong beer and ale, was three shillings *per* barrel, which, if taken off, would lessen the purchase only half a farthing *per* pint, and consequently, would not reach to practical relief.

This being the condition of a great part of the taxes, it will be necessary to look for such others as are free from this embarrassment, and where the relief will be direct and visible, and capable of immediate operation.

In the first place, then, the poor-rates are a direct tax which every house-keeper feels, and who knows also, to a farthing, the sum which he pays. The national amount of the whole of the poor-rates is not positively known, but can be procured. Sir John Sinclair, in his History of the Revenue, has stated it at £2,100,587. A considerable part of which is expended in litigations, in which the poor, instead of being relieved, are tormented. The expence, however, is the same to the parish from whatever cause it arises.

In Birmingham, the amount of the poor-rates is fourteen thousand pounds a year. This, though a large sum, is moderate, compared with the population. Birmingham is said to contain seventy thousand souls, and on a proportion of seventy thousand to fourteen thousand pounds poor-rates, the national amount of poor-rates, taking the population of England at seven millions, would be but one million four hundred thousand pounds. It is, therefore, most probable, that the population of Birmingham is over-rated. Fourteen thousand pounds is the proportion upon fifty thousand souls, taking two millions of poor-rates as the national amount.

Be it, however, what it may, it is no other than the consequence of the excessive burthen of taxes, for, at the time when the taxes were very low, the poor were able to maintain themselves; and there were no poor-rates.* In the present state of things, a labouring man, with a wife and two or three children, does not pay less than between seven and eight pounds a year in taxes. He is not sensible of this, because it is disguised to him in the articles which he buys, and he thinks only of their dearness; but as the taxes take from him, at least, a fourth part of his yearly earnings, he is consequently disabled from providing for a family, especially, if himself, or any of them, are afflicted with sickness.

The first step, therefore, of practical relief, would be to abolish the poor-rates entirely, and in lieu thereof, to make a remission of taxes to the poor of double the amount of the present poor-rates, viz. four millions annually out of the surplus taxes. By this measure, the poor would be benefited two millions, and the house-keepers two millions. This alone would be equal to a reduction of one hundred and twenty millions of the national debt, and consequently equal to the whole expence of the American War.

It will then remain to be considered, which is the most effectual mode of distributing this remission of four millions.

---

* Poor-rates began about the time of Henry the Eighth, when the taxes began to encrease, and they have encreased as the taxes encreased ever since.

It is easily seen, that the poor are generally composed of large families of children, and old people past their labour. If these two classes are provided for, the remedy will so far reach to the full extent of the case, that what remains will be incidental, and, in a great measure, fall within the compass of benefit clubs, which, though of humble invention, merit to be ranked among the best of modern institutions.

Admitting England to contain seven millions of souls; if one-fifth thereof are of that class of poor which need support, the number will be one million four hundred thousand. Of this number, one hundred and forty thousand will be aged poor, as will be hereafter shewn, and for which a distinct provision will be proposed.

There will then remain one million two hundred and sixty thousand, which, at five souls to each family, amount to two hundred and fifty-two thousand families, rendered poor from the expence of children and the weight of taxes.

The number of children under fourteen years of age, in each of those families, will be found to be about five to every two families; some having two, and others three; some one, and others four: some none, and others five; but it rarely happens that more than five are under fourteen years of age, and after this age they are capable of service or of being apprenticed.

Allowing five children (under fourteen years) to every two families,

the number of children will be   630,000,

the number of parents, were they all living, would be   504,000

It is certain, that if the children are provided for, the parents are relieved of consequence, because it is from the expence of bringing up children that their poverty arises.

Having thus ascertained the greatest number that can be supposed to need support on account of young families, I proceed to the mode of relief or distribution, which is,

To pay as a remission of taxes to every poor family, out of the surplus taxes, and in room of poor-rates, four pounds a year for every child under fourteen years of age; enjoining the parents of such children to send them to school, to learn reading, writing, and common arithmetic; the ministers of every parish, of every denomination, to certify jointly to an office, for that purpose, that this duty is performed.

The amount of this expence will be,

For six hundred and thirty thousand children, at four pounds *per ann.* each,

£2,520,000

By adopting this method, not only the poverty of the parents will be relieved, but ignorance will be banished from the rising generation, and the number of poor will hereafter become less, because their abilities, by the aid of education, will be greater. Many a youth, with good natural genius, who is apprenticed to a mechanical trade, such as a carpenter, joiner, millwright, shipwright, blacksmith, &c. is prevented getting forward the whole of his life, from the want of a little common education when a boy.

I now proceed to the case of the aged.

I divide age into two classes. First, the approach of age, beginning at fifty. Secondly, old age commencing at sixty.

At fifty, though the mental faculties of man are in full vigour, and his judgment better than at any preceding date, the bodily powers for laborious life are on the decline. He cannot bear the same quantity of fatigue as at an earlier period. He begins to earn less, and is less capable of enduring wind and weather; and in those more retired employments where much sight is required, he fails apace, and sees himself, like an old horse, beginning to be turned adrift.

At sixty his labour ought to be over, at least from direct necessity. It is painful to see old age working itself to death, in what are called civilized countries, for daily bread.

To form some judgment of the number of those above fifty years of age, I have several times counted the persons I met in the streets of London, men, women, and children, and have generally found that the average is about one in sixteen or seventeen. If it be said that aged persons do not come much into the streets, so neither do infants; and a great proportion of grown children are in schools and in work-shops as apprentices. Taking, then, sixteen for a divisor, the whole number of persons in England, of fifty years and upwards of both sexes, rich and poor, will be four hundred and twenty thousand.

The persons to be provided for out of this gross number will be, husbandmen, common labourers, journeymen of every trade and their wives, sailors, and disbanded soldiers, worn out servants of both sexes, and poor widows.

There will be also a considerable number of middling tradesmen, who having lived decently in the former part of life, begin, as age approaches, to lose their business, and at last fall to decay.

Besides these, there will be constantly thrown off from the revolutions of that wheel, which no man can stop, nor regulate, a number from every class of life connected with commerce and adventure.

To provide for all those accidents, and whatever else may befal, I take the number of persons, who at one time or other of their lives, after fifty years of age, may feel it necessary or comfortable to be better supported, than they can support themselves, and that not as a matter of grace and favour, but of right, at one third of the whole number, which is one hundred and forty thousand, as stated in page 125 (p. 486), and for whom a distinct provision was proposed to be made. If there be more, society, notwithstanding the shew and pomposity of government, is in a deplorable condition in England.

Of this one hundred and forty thousand, I take one half, seventy thousand, to be of the age of fifty and under sixty, and the other half to be sixty years and upwards.—Having thus ascertained the probable proportion of the number of aged persons, I proceed to the mode of rendering their condition comfortable, which is,

To pay to every such person of the age of fifty years, and until he shall arrive at the age of sixty, the sum of six pounds *per ann.* out of the surplus taxes; and ten pounds *per ann.* during life after the age of sixty. The expence of which will be,

Seventy thousand persons, at £6 *per ann.*	420,000
Seventy thousand ditto, at £10 *per ann.*	700,000
	£1,120,000

This support, as already remarked, is not of the nature of a charity but of a right. Every person in England, male and female, pays on an average in taxes, two pounds eight shillings and sixpence *per ann.* from the day of his (or her) birth; and, if the expence of collection be added, he pays two pounds eleven shillings and sixpence; consequently, at the end of fifty years he has paid one hundred and twenty-eight pounds fifteen shillings; and at sixty, one hundred and fifty-four pounds ten shillings. Converting, therefore, his (or her) individual tax into a tontine, the money he shall receive after fifty years, is but little more than the legal interest of the nett money he has paid; the rest is made up from those whose circumstances do not require them to draw such support, and the capital in both cases defrays the expences of government. It is on this ground that I have extended the probable claims to one third of the number of aged persons in the nation.—Is it then better that the lives of one hundred and forty thousand aged persons be rendered comfortable, or that a million a year of public money be expended on any one individual, and him often of the most worthless or insignificant character? Let reason and justice, let honour and humanity, let even hypocrisy, sycophancy and Mr. Burke, let George, let Louis, Leopold, Frederic, Catherine, Cornwallis, or Tippoo Saib, answer the question.*

The sum thus remitted to the poor will be,

To two hundred and fifty-two thousand poor families,

containing six hundred and thirty-thousand children,   2,520,000

To one hundred and forty thousand aged persons,   <u>1,120,000</u>

£3,640,000

There will then remain three hundred and sixty thousand pounds out of the four millions, part of which may be applied as follows:

After all the above cases are provided for, there will still be a number of families who, though not properly of the class of poor, yet find it difficult to give education to their children; and such children, under such a case, would be in a worse condition than if their parents were actually poor. A nation under a well-regulated government should permit none to remain uninstructed. It is monarchical and aristocratical government only that requires ignorance for its support.

---

* Reckoning the taxes by families, five to a family, each family pays on an average, 12*l*. 7*s*. 6*d*. *per ann.* to this sum are to be added the poor-rates. Though all pay taxes in the articles they consume, all do not pay poor-rates. About two millions are exempted, some as not being house-keepers, others as not being able, and the poor themselves who receive the relief. The average, therefore, of poor-rates on the remaining number, is forty shillings for every family of five persons, which make the whole average amount of taxes and rates 14*l*. 17*s*. 6*d*. For six persons 17*l*. 17*s*. For seven persons 20*l*. 16*s*. 6*d*.

The average of taxes in America, under the new or representative system of government, including the interest of the debt contracted in the war, and taking the population at four millions of souls, which it now amounts to, and it is daily increasing, is five shillings per head, men, women, and children. The difference, therefore, between the two governments is as under:

	England			America		
	l.	*s.*	*d.*	*l.*	*s.*	*d.*
For a family of five persons	14	17	6	1	5	0
For a family of six persons	17	17	0	1	10	0
For a family of seven persons	20	16	6	1	15	0

Suppose then four hundred thousand children to be in this condition, which is a greater number than ought to be supposed, after the provisions already made, the method will be,

To allow for each of those children ten shillings a year for the expence of schooling, for six years each, which will give them six months schooling each year, and half a crown a year for paper and spelling books.

The expence of this will be annually*   £250,000.

There will then remain one hundred and ten thousand pounds.

Notwithstanding the great modes of relief which the best instituted and best principled government may devise, there will be a number of smaller cases, which it is good policy as well as beneficence in a nation to consider.

Were twenty shillings to be given immediately on the birth of a child, to every woman who should make the demand, and none will make it whose circumstances do not require it, it might relieve a great deal of instant distress.

There are about two hundred thousand births yearly in England; and if claimed, by one fourth,

The amount would be   —   £50,000

And twenty shillings to every new-married couple who should claim in like manner. This would not exceed the sum of   —   £20,000.

Also twenty thousand pounds to be appropriated to defray the funeral expences of persons, who, travelling for work, may die at a distance from their friends. By relieving parishes from this charge, the sick stranger will be better treated.

---

* Public schools do not answer the general purpose of the poor. They are chiefly in corporation towns from which the country towns and villages are excluded; or, if admitted, the distance occasions a great loss of time. Education, to be useful to the poor, should be on the spot; and the best method, I believe, to accomplish this, is to enable the parents to pay the expence themselves. There are always persons of both sexes to be found in every village, especially when growing into years, capable of such an undertaking. Twenty children, at ten shillings each, (and that not more than six months each year) would be as much as some livings amount to in the remote parts of England; and there are often distressed clergymen's widows to whom such an income would be acceptable. Whatever is given on this account to children answers two purposes, to them it is education, to those who educate them it is a livelihood.

I shall finish this part of the subject with a plan adapted to the particular condition of a metropolis, such as London.

Cases are continually occurring in a metropolis, different from those which occur in the country, and for which a different, or rather an additional mode of relief is necessary. In the country, even in large towns, people have a knowledge of each other, and distress never rises to that extreme height it sometimes does in a metropolis. There is no such thing in the country as persons, in the literal sense of the word, starved to death, or dying with cold from the want of a lodging. Yet such cases, and others equally as miserable, happen in London.

Many a youth comes up to London full of expectations, and with little or no money, and unless he get immediate employment he is already half undone; and boys bred up in London, without any means of a livelihood, and as it often happens of dissolute parents, are in a still worse condition; and servants long out of place are not much better off. In short, a world of little cases are continually arising, which busy or affluent life knows not of, to open the first door to distress. Hunger is not among the postponable wants, and a day, even a few hours, in such a condition, is often the crisis of a life of ruin.

These circumstances, which are the general cause of the little thefts and pilferings that lead to greater, may be prevented. There yet remain twenty thousand pounds out of the four millions of surplus taxes, which, with another fund hereafter to be mentioned, amounting to about twenty thousand pounds more, cannot be better applied than to this purpose. The plan will then be,

First, To erect two or more buildings, or take some already erected, capable of containing at least six thousand persons, and to have in each of these places as many kinds of employment as can be contrived, so that every person who shall come may find something which he or she can do.

Secondly, To receive all who shall come, without enquiring who or what they are. The only condition to be, that for so much, or so many hours work, each person shall receive so many meals of wholesome food, and a warm lodging, at least as good as a barrack. That a certain portion of what each person's work shall be worth shall be reserved, and given to him or her, on their going away; and that each person shall stay as long, or as short a time, or come as often as he chuse, on these conditions.

If each person stayed three months, it would assist by rotation twenty-four thousand persons annually, though the real number, at all times, would be but six thousand. By establishing an asylum of this kind, such persons to whom temporary distresses occur, would have an opportunity to recruit themselves, and be enabled to look out for better employment.

Allowing that their labour paid but one half the expence of supporting them, after reserving a portion of their earnings for themselves, the sum of forty thousand pounds additional would defray all other charges for even a greater number than six thousand.

The fund very properly convertible to this purpose, in addition to the twenty thousand pounds, remaining of the former fund, will be the produce of the tax upon coals, so iniquitously and wantonly applied to the support of the Duke of Richmond. It is horrid that any man, more especially at the price coals now are, should live on the distresses of a community; and any government permitting such an abuse, deserves to be dismissed. This fund is said to be about twenty thousand pounds *per annum*.

I shall now conclude this plan with enumerating the several particulars, and then proceed to other matters.

The enumeration is as follows:

First, Abolition of two million poor-rates.

Secondly, Provision for two hundred and fifty-two thousand poor families.

Thirdly, Education for one million and thirty thousand children.

Fourthly, Comfortable provision for one hundred and forty thousand aged persons.

Fifthly, Donation of twenty shillings each for fifty thousand births.

Sixthly, Donation of twenty shillings each for twenty thousand marriages.

Seventhly, Allowance of twenty thousand pounds for the funeral expences of persons travelling for work, and dying at a distance from their friends.

Eighthly, Employment, at all times, for the casual poor in the cities of London and Westminster.

By the operation of this plan, the poor laws, those instruments of civil torture, will be superceded, and the wasteful expence of litigation prevented. The hearts of the humane will not be shocked by ragged and hungry children, and persons of seventy and eighty years of age begging for bread. The dying poor will not be dragged from place to place to breathe their last, as a reprisal of parish upon parish.[6] Widows will have a maintenance for their children, and not be carted away, on the death of their husbands, like culprits and criminals; and children will no longer be considered as encreasing the distresses of their parents. The haunts of the wretched will be known, because it will be to their advantage; and the number of petty crimes, the offspring of distress and poverty, will be lessened. The poor, as well as the rich, will then be interested in the support of government, and the cause and apprehension of riots and tumults will cease.— Ye who sit in ease, and solace yourselves in plenty, and such there are in Turkey and Russia, as well as in England, and who say to yourselves, "Are we not well off", have ye thought of these things? When ye do, ye will cease to speak and feel for yourselves alone.

The plan is easy in practice. It does not embarrass trade by a sudden interruption in the order of taxes, but effects the relief by changing the application of them; and the money necessary for the purpose can be drawn from the excise collections, which are made eight times a year in every market town in England.

---

[6] The Poor Laws was the name given to the Elizabethan welfare legislation of 1597-1598, which provided systematic Parish relief for poor, funded by the poor rate, a local tax. The parish was mandated to apprentice pauper children, build houses for paupers but only for those born in the parish. Alien paupers and vagrants were ordered to return to their parishes and often moved on to the neighbouring parish. Those deemed 'idle' and beggars were jailed. Poor rates were also used to buy materials for work for the able-bodied and relief for the elderly, sick and insane but parish relief still mainly depended on charity.

Having now arranged and concluded this subject, I proceed to the next.

Taking the present current expences at seven millions and an half, which is the least amount they are now at, there will remain (after the sum of one million and an half be taken for the new current expences and four millions for the before-mentioned service) the sum of two millions; part of which to be applied as follows:

Though fleets and armies, by an alliance with France, will, in a great measure, become useless, yet the persons who have devoted themselves to those services, and have thereby unfitted themselves for other lines of life, are not to be sufferers by the means that make others happy. They are a different description of men to those who form or hang about a court.

A part of the army will remain at least for some years, and also of the navy, for which a provision is already made in the former part of this plan of one million, which is almost half a million more than the peace establishment of the army and navy in the prodigal times of Charles the Second.

Suppose then fifteen thousand soldiers to be disbanded, and that an allowance be made to each of three shillings a week during life, clear of all deductions, to be paid in the same manner as the Chelsea College pensioners are paid, and for them to return to their trades and their friends; and also that an addition of fifteen thousand sixpences per week be made to the pay of the soldiers who shall remain;

the annual expences will be:

To the pay of fifteen thousand disbanded soldiers,

at three shillings per week   —   —   £117,000

Additional pay to the remaining soldiers —   —   19,500

Suppose that the pay to the officers of the disbanded corps be the same amount

as sum allowed to the men   —   —   <u>117,000</u>

                                                            £253,500

To prevent bulky estimations, admit the same sum to the disbanded navy as

to the army, and the same increase of pay   —   —   <u>253,500</u>

                                        Total   £507,000

Every year some part of this sum of half a million (I omit the odd seven thousand pounds for the purpose of keeping the account unembarrassed) will fall in, and the whole of it in time, as it is on the ground of life annuities, except the encreased pay of twenty-nine thousand pounds. As it falls in, part of the taxes may be taken off; for instance, when thirty thousand pounds fall in, the duty on hops may be wholly taken off; and as other parts fall in, the duties on candles and soap may be lessened, till at last they will totally cease.

There now remains at least one million and a half of surplus taxes.

The tax on houses and windows is one of those direct taxes, which, like the poor-rates, is not confounded with trade; and, when taken off, the relief will be instantly felt. This tax falls heavy on the middling class of people.

The amount of this tax, by the returns of 1788, was,

		l.	*s.*	*d.*
Houses and windows: By the act of 1766,	—	385,459	11	7
Ditto By the act be 1779,	—	<u>130,739</u>	<u>14</u>	<u>5½</u>
	Total	516,199	6	0½

If this tax be struck off, there will then remain about one million of surplus taxes, and as it is always proper to keep a sum in reserve, for incidental matters, it may be best not to extend reductions further, in the first instance, but to consider what may be accomplished by other modes of reform.

Among the taxes most heavily felt is the commutation tax. I shall, therefore offer a plan for its abolition, by substituting another in its place, which will effect three objects at once:

First, That of removing the burthen to where it can best be borne.

Secondly, Restoring justice among families by a distribution of property.

Thirdly, Extirpating the overgrown influence arising from the unnatural law of primogeniture, which is one of the principal sources of corruption at elections.

The amount of commutation tax by the returns of 1788, was, £771,657   0   0

When taxes are proposed, the country is amused by the plausible language of taxing luxuries. One thing is called a luxury at one time, and something else at another; but the real luxury does not consist in the article, but in the means of procuring it, and this is always kept out of sight.

I know not why any plant or herb of the field should be a greater luxury in one country than another, but an overgrown estate in either is a luxury at all times, and as such is the proper object of taxation. It is, therefore, right to take those kind tax-making gentlemen up on their own word, and argue on the principle themselves have laid down, that of *taxing luxuries*. If they or their champion Mr. Burke, who, I fear, is growing out of date like the man in armour, can prove that an estate of twenty, thirty, or forty thousand pounds a year is not a luxury, I will give up the argument.

Admitting that any annual sum, say for instance, one thousand pounds, is necessary or sufficient for the support of a family, consequently the second thousand is of the nature of a luxury, the third still more so, and by proceeding on, we shall at last arrive at a sum that may not improperly be called a prohibitable luxury. It would be impolitic to set bounds to property acquired by industry, and therefore it is right to place the prohibition beyond the probable acquisition to which industry can extend; but there ought to be a limit to property, or the accumulation of it, by bequest. It should pass in some other line. The richest in every nation have poor relations, and those often very near in consanguinity.

The following table of progressive taxation is constructed on the above principles, and as a substitute for the commutation tax. It will reach the point of prohibition by a regular operation, and thereby supersede the aristocratical law of primogeniture.

TABLE I

A tax on all estates of the clear yearly value of fifty pounds, after deducting the land-tax, and up

	s.	d.
To £500	0	3 per pound
From 500 to 1000	0	6 per pound
On the second thousand	0	9 per pound
On the third ditto	1	0 per pound
On the fourth ditto	1	6 per pound
On the fifth ditto	2	0 per pound *** etc.
On the twenty-third ditto	20	0 per pound

The foregoing table shews the progression per pound on every progressive thousand. The following table shews the amount of the tax on every thousand separately, and in the last column, the total amount of all the separate sums collected.

TABLE II

				l.	*s.*	*d.*
An estate of	£50 *per ann.*	at	3d per pound pays	0	12	6
	100		3	1	5	0
	200		3	2	10	0
	300		3	3	15	0
	400		3	5	0	0
	500		3	7	5	0

After 500l.—the tax of sixpence per pound takes place on the second 500l—consequently an estate of 1000l. per ann. pays   21l. 15s. and so on.

	l.	s.	d.		l.	s.	l.	s.
For the 1st 500 at	0		3d per pound		7	5		
2d	500 at	0	6		14	10	21	15
2d	1000 at	0	9		37	11	59	5
3d	1000 at	1	0		50	0	109	5
4th	1000 at	1	6		75	0	184	5
5th	1000 at	2	0		100	0	284	5

***

At the twenty-third thousand the tax becomes twenty shillings in the pound, and consequently every thousand beyond that sum can produce no profit but by dividing the estate. Yet formidable as this tax appears, it will not, I believe, produce so much as the commutation tax; should it produce more, it ought to be lowered to that amount upon estates under two or three thousand a year.

On small and middling estates it is lighter (as it is intended to be) than the commutation tax. It is not till after seven or eight thousand a year that it begins to be heavy. The object is not so much the produce of the tax, as the justice of the measure. The aristocracy has screened itself too much, and this serves to restore a part of the lost equilibrium.

As an instance of its screening itself, it is only necessary to look back to the first establishment of the excise laws, at what is called the Restoration, or the coming of Charles the Second. The aristocratical interest then in power, commuted the feudal services itself was under by laying a tax on beer brewed for *sale*; that is, they compounded with Charles for an exemption from those services for themselves and their heirs, by a tax to be paid by other people. The aristocracy do not purchase beer brewed for sale, but brew their own beer free of the duty, and if any commutation at that time were necessary, it ought to have been at the expence of those for whom the exemptions from those services were intended*; instead of which, it was thrown on an entire different class of men.

But the chief object of this progressive tax (besides the justice of rendering taxes more equal than they are) is, as already stated, to extirpate the overgrown influence arising from the unnatural law of primogeniture, and which is one of the principal sources of corruption at elections.

It would be attended with no good consequences to enquire how such vast estates as thirty, forty, or fifty thousand a year could commence, and that at a time when commerce and manufactures were not in a state to admit of such acquisitions. Let it be sufficient to remedy the evil by putting them in a condition of descending again to the community, by the quiet means of apportioning them among all the heirs and heiresses of those families. This will be the more necessary, because hitherto the aristocracy have quartered their younger children and connections upon the public in useless posts, places, and offices, which when abolished will leave them destitute, unless the law of primogeniture be also abolished or superceded.

---

* The tax on beer brewed for sale, from which the aristocracy are exempt, is almost one million more than the present commutation tax, being by the returns of 1788, 1,666,152*l*. and, consequently, they ought to take on themselves the amount of the commutation tax, as they are already exempted from one which is almost one million greater.

A progressive tax will, in a great measure, effect this object, and that as a matter of interest to the parties most immediately concerned, as will be seen by the following table; which shews the nett produce upon every estate, after subtracting the tax. By this it will appear, that after an estate exceeds thirteen or fourteen thousand a year, the remainder produces but little profit to the holder, and consequently will pass either to the younger children, or to other kindred.

***

TABLE III

Shewing the nett produce of every estate from one thousand to twenty-three thousand pounds a year

No. of thousand per ann.	Total tax subtracted £	Nett produce £
1000	21	979
2000	59	1941
3000	109	2891
4000	184	3816
5000	284	4716
	***	
20,000	7780	12,220
21,000	8680	12,320
22,000	9630	12,370
23,000	10,630	12,370

N.B. The odd shillings are dropped in this table.

According to this table, an estate cannot produce more then [sic] 12,370*l.* clear of the land tax and the progressive tax, and therefore the dividing such estates will follow as a matter of family interest. An estate of 23,000*l.* a year, divided into five estates of four thousand each and one of three, will be charged only 1,129*l.* which is but five *per cent.* but if held by one possessor will be charged 10,630*l.*

Although an enquiry into the origin of those estates be unnecessary, the continuation of them in their present state is another subject. It is a matter of national concern. As hereditary estates, the law has created the evil, and it ought also to provide the remedy. Primogeniture ought to be abolished, not only because it is unnatural and unjust, but because the country suffers by its operation. By cutting off (as before observed) the younger children from their proper portion of inheritance, the public is loaded with the expence of maintaining them; and the freedom of elections violated by the overbearing influence which this unjust monopoly of family property produces. Nor is this all. It occasions a waste of national property. A considerable part of the land of the country is rendered unproductive by the great extent of parks and chases which this law serves to keep up, and this at a time when the annual production of grain is not equal to the national consumption*.—In short, the evils of the aristocratical system are so great and numerous, so inconsistent with every thing that is just, wise, natural, and beneficent, that when they are considered, there ought not to be a doubt that many, who are now classed under that description, will wish to see such a system abolished.

What pleasure can they derive from contemplating the exposed condition, and almost certain beggary of their younger offspring? Every aristocratical family has an appendage of family beggars hanging round it, which in a few ages, or a few generations, are shook off, and console themselves with telling their tale in alms-houses, work-houses, and prisons. This is the natural consequence of aristocracy. The peer and the beggar are often of the same family. One extreme produces the other: to make one rich many must be made poor; neither can the system be supported by other means.

---

* See the reports on the corn trade.

There are two classes of people to whom the laws of England are particularly hostile, and those the most helpless; younger children and the poor. Of the former I have just spoken; of the latter I shall mention one instance out of the many that might be produced, and with which I shall close this subject.

Several laws are in existence for regulating and limiting work men's wages. Why not leave them as free to make their own bargains, as the law-makers are to let their farms and houses? Personal labour is all the property they have. Why is that little, and the little freedom they enjoy to be infringed? But the injustice will appear stronger, if we consider the operation and effect of such laws. When wages are fixed by what is called a law, the legal wages remain stationary, while every thing else is in progression; and as those who make that law still continue to lay on new taxes by other laws, they encrease the expence of living by one law, and take away the means by another.

But if these gentlemen law-makers and tax-makers thought it right to limit the poor pittance which personal labour can produce, and on which a whole family is to be supported, they certainly must feel themselves happily indulged in a limitation on their own part, of not less than twelve thousand a year, and that of property they never acquired, (nor probably any of their ancestors), and of which they have made never acquire so ill a use.

Having now finished this subject, I shall bring the several particulars into one view, and then proceed to other matters.

The first EIGHT ARTICLES, are brought forward from page 136 [p. 493.]

1.   Abolition of two millions poor-rates.

2.   Provision for two hundred and fifty-two thousand poor families, at the rate of four pounds per head for each child under fourteen years of age; which, with the addition of two hundred and fifty thousand pounds, provides also education for one million and thirty thousand children.

3.   Annuity of six pounds (per annum) each for all poor persons, decayed tradesmen, and others (supposed seventy thousand) of the age of fifty years, and until sixty.

4. Annuity of ten pounds each for life for all poor persons, decayed tradesmen, and others (supposed seventy thousand) of the age of sixty years.

5. Donation of twenty shillings each for fifty thousand births.

6. Donation of twenty shillings each for twenty thousand marriages.

7. Allowance of twenty thousand pounds for the funeral expences of persons travelling for work, and dying at a distance from their friends.

8. Employment at all times for the casual poor in the cities of London and Westminster.

SECOND ENUMERATION

9. Abolition of the tax on houses and windows.

10. Allowance of three shillings per week for life to fifteen thousand disbanded soldiers, and a proportionate allowance to the officers of the disbanded corps.

11. Encrease of pay to the remaining soldiers of 19,500*l.* annually.

12. The same allowance to the disbanded navy, and the same encrease of pay, as to the army.

13. Abolition of the commutation tax.

14. Plan of a progressive tax, operating to extirpate the unjust and unnatural law of primogeniture, and the vicious influence of the aristocratical system.*

---

* When enquiries are made into the condition of the poor, various degrees of distress will most probably be found, to render a different arrangement preferable to that which is already proposed. Widows with families will be in greater want than where there are husbands living. There is also a difference in the expence of living in different counties; and more so in fuel.

Suppose then fifty thousand extraordinary cases,

at the rate of 10*l.* per family per ann.	£500,000
100,000 families, at 8*l.* per family per annum	800,000
100,000 families, at 7*l.* per family per annum	700,000
104,000 families, at 5*l.* per family per annum	520,000
And instead of ten shillings per head for the education of other children,	
to allow fifty shillings per family for that purpose to fifty thousand families	250,000
	£2,770,000
140,000 aged persons as before	1,120,000
	£3,890,000

This arrangement amounts to the same sum as stated in this work, page 131, including the L250, 000 for education; but it provides (including the aged people) for four hundred and four thousand families, which is almost one third of the families in England.

There yet remains, as already stated, one million of surplus taxes. Some part of this will be required for circumstances that do not immediately present themselves, and such part as shall not be wanted, will admit of a further reduction of taxes equal to that amount.

Among the claims that justice requires to be made, the condition of the inferior revenue-officers will merit attention. It is a reproach to any government to waste such an immensity of revenue in sinecures and nominal and unnecessary places and offices, and not allow even a decent livelihood to those on whom the labour falls. The salary of the inferior officers of the revenue has stood at the petty pittance of less than fifty pounds a year for upwards of one hundred years. It ought to be seventy. About one hundred and twenty thousand pounds applied to this purpose, will put all those salaries in a decent condition.

This was proposed to be done almost twenty years ago, but the treasury-board then in being startled at it, as it might lead to similar expectations from the army and navy; and the event was, that the King, or somebody for him, applied to parliament to have his own salary raised an hundred thousand a year, which being done, every thing else was laid aside.

With respect to another class of men, the inferior clergy, I forbear to enlarge on their condition; but all partialities and prejudices for, or against, different modes and forms of religion aside, common justice will determine, whether there ought to be an income of twenty or thirty pounds a year to one man, and of ten thousand to another. I speak on this subject with the more freedom, because I am known not to be a Presbyterian; and therefore the cant cry of court sycophants, about church and meeting, kept up to amuse and bewilder the nation, cannot be raised against me.

Ye simple men on both sides the question, do you not see through this courtly craft? If ye can be kept disputing and wrangling about church and meeting, ye just answer the purpose of every courtier, who lives the while on the spoil of the taxes, and laughs at your credulity. Every religion is good that teaches man to be good; and I know of none that instructs him to be bad.

All the before-mentioned calculations suppose, only sixteen millions and an half of taxes paid into the exchequer, after the expence of collection and drawbacks at the custom-house and excise-office are deducted; whereas the sum paid into the exchequer is very nearly, if not quite, seventeen millions. The taxes raised in Scotland and Ireland are expended in those countries, and therefore their savings will come out of their own taxes; but if any part be paid into the English exchequer, it might be remitted. This will not make one hundred thousand pounds a year difference.

There now remains only the national debt to be considered. In the year 1789, the interest, exclusive of the tontine, was 9,150,138*l*. How much the capital has been reduced since that time the minister best knows. But after paying the interest, abolishing the tax on houses and windows, the commutation tax, and the poor-rates; and making all the provisions for the poor, for the education of children, the support of the aged, the disbanded part of the army and navy, and encreasing the pay of the remainder, there will be a surplus of one million.

The present scheme of paying off the national debt appears to me, speaking as an indifferent person, to be an ill-concerted, if not a fallacious job. The burthen of the national debt consists not in its being so many millions, or so many hundred millions, but in the quantity of taxes collected every year to pay the interest. If this quantity continues the same, the burthen of the national debt is the same to all intents and purposes, be the capital more or less. The only knowledge which the public can have of the reduction of the debt, must be through the reduction of taxes for paying the interest. The debt, therefore, is not reduced one farthing to the public by all the millions that have been paid; and it would require more money now to purchase up the capital, than when the scheme began.

***

I return, as I promised, to the subject of the national debt, that offspring of the Dutch-Anglo revolution, and its handmaid the Hanover succession.

But it is now too late to enquire how it began. Those to whom it is due have advanced the money; and whether it was well or ill spent, or pocketed, is not their crime. It is, however, easy to see, that as the nation proceeds in contemplating the nature and principles of government, and to understand taxes, and make comparisons between those of America, France, and England, it will be next to impossible to keep it in the same torpid state it has hitherto been. Some reform must, from the necessity of the case, soon begin. It is not whether these principles press with little or much force in the present moment. They are out. They are abroad in the world, and no force can stop them. Like a secret told, they are beyond recall; and he must be blind indeed that does not see that a change is already beginning.

Nine millions of dead taxes is a serious thing; and this not only for bad, but in a great measure for foreign government. By putting the power of making war into the hands of the foreigners who came for what they could get, little else was to be expected than what has happened.

Reasons are already advanced in this work, shewing that whatever the reforms in the taxes may be, they ought to be made in the current expences of government, and not in the part applied to the interest of the national debt. By remitting the taxes of the poor, *they* will be totally relieved, and all discontent will be taken away; and by striking off such of the taxes as are already mentioned, the nation will more than recover the whole expence of the mad American war.

There will then remain only the national debt as a subject of discontent; and in order to remove, or rather to prevent this, it would be good policy in the stock-holders themselves to consider it as property, subject like all other property, to bear some portion of the taxes. It would give to it both popularity and security, and as a great part of its present inconvenience is balanced by the capital which it keeps alive, a measure of this kind would so far add to that balance as to silence objections.

This may be done by such gradual means as to accomplish all that is necessary with the greatest ease and convenience.

Instead of taxing the capital, the best method would be to tax the interest by some progressive ratio, and to lessen the public taxes in the same proportion as the interest diminished.

Suppose the interest was taxed one halfpenny in the pound the first year, a penny more the second, and to proceed by a certain ratio to be determined upon, always less than any other tax upon property. Such a tax would be subtracted from the interest at the time of payment, without any expence of collection.

One halfpenny in the pound would lessen the interest and consequently the taxes, twenty thousand pounds. The tax on waggons amounts to this sum, and this tax might be taken off the first year. The second year the tax on female servants, or some other of the like amount might also be taken off, and by proceeding in this manner, always applying the tax raised from the property of the debt toward its extinction, and not carry it to the current services, it would liberate itself.

The stockholders, notwithstanding this tax, would pay less taxes than they do now. What they would save by the extinction of the poor-rates, and the tax on houses and windows, and the commutation tax, would be considerably greater than what this tax, slow, but certain in its operation, amounts to.

It appears to me to be prudence to look out for measures that may apply under any circumstances that may approach. There is, at this moment, a crisis in the affairs of Europe that requires it. Preparation now is wisdom. If taxation be once let loose, it will be difficult to re-instate it; neither would the relief be so effectual, as to proceed by some certain and gradual reduction.

The fraud, hypocrisy, and imposition of governments, are now beginning to be too well understood to promise them any long career.

***

When it shall be said in any country in the world, my poor are happy; neither ignorance nor distress is to be found among them; my jails are empty of prisoners, my streets of beggars; the aged are not in want, the taxes are not oppressive; the rational world is my friend, because I am the friend of its happiness: when these things can be said, then may that country boast its constitution and its government.

Within the space of a few years we have seen two revolutions, those of America and France. In the former, the contest was long, and the conflict severe; in the latter, the nation acted with such a consolidated impulse, that having no foreign enemy to contend with, the revolution was complete in power the moment it appeared. From both those instances it is evident, that the greatest forces that can be brought into the field of revolutions, are reason and common interest. Where these can have the opportunity of acting, opposition dies with fear, or crumbles away by conviction. It is a great standing which they have now universally obtained; and we may hereafter hope to see revolutions, or changes in governments, produced with the same quiet operation by which any measure, determinable by reason and discussion, is accomplished.

When a nation changes its opinion and habits of thinking, it is no longer to be governed as before; but it would not only be wrong, but bad policy, to attempt by force what ought to be accomplished by reason. Rebellion consists in forcibly opposing the general will of a nation, whether by a party or by a government. There ought, therefore, to be in every nation a method of occasionally ascertaining the state of public opinion with respect to government. On this point the old government of France was superior to the present government of England, because, on extraordinary occasions, recourse could be had what was then called the States General. But in England there are no such occasional bodies; and as to those who are now called Representatives, a great part of them are mere machines of the court, placemen, and dependants.

I presume, that though all the people of England pay taxes, not an hundredth part of them are electors, and the members of one of the houses of parliament represent nobody but themselves. There is, therefore, no power but the voluntary will of the people that has a right to act in any matter respecting a general reform; and by the same right that two persons can confer on such a subject, a thousand may. The object, in all such preliminary proceedings, is to find out what the general sense of a nation is, and to be governed by it. If it prefer a bad or defective government to a reform, or chuse to pay ten times more taxes than there is occasion for, it has a right so to do; and so long as the majority do not impose conditions on the minority, different from what they impose upon themselves, though there may be much error, there is no injustice. Neither will the error continue long. Reason and discussion will soon bring things right, however wrong they may begin. By such a process no tumult is to be apprehended. The poor, in all countries, are naturally both peaceable and grateful in all reforms in which their interest and happiness is included. It is only by neglecting and rejecting them that they become tumultuous.

The objects that now press on the public attention are, the French revolution, and the prospect of a general revolution in governments. Of all nations in Europe there is none so much interested in the French revolution as England. Enemies for ages, and that at a vast expence, and without any national object, the opportunity now presents itself of amicably closing the scene, and joining their efforts to reform the rest of Europe. By doing this, they will not only prevent the further effusion of blood, and encrease of taxes, but be in a condition of getting rid of a considerable part of their present burthens, as has been already stated. Long experience however has shewn, that reforms of this kind are not those which old governments wish to promote, and therefore it is to nations, and not to such governments, that these matters present themselves.[7]

***

Never did so great an opportunity offer itself to England, and to all Europe, as is produced by the two Revolutions of America and France. By the former, freedom has a national champion in the western world; and by the latter, in

---

[7] Here Paine proposes an alliance between England, France, and America, enabling all three to dispense with the expence of keeping navies, a measure that would save France and England at least two million sterling per annum. Further the alliance would persuade Spain release her empire and allow free trade with independent countries in South America.

Europe. When another nation shall join France, despotism and bad government will scarcely dare to appear.

***

When all the governments of Europe shall be established on the representative system, nations will become acquainted, and the animosities and prejudices fomented by the intrigue and artifice of courts, will cease. The oppressed soldier will become a freeman; and the tortured sailor, no longer dragged through the streets like a felon, will pursue his mercantile voyage in safety.

***

In contemplating revolutions, it is easy to perceive that they may arise from two distinct causes; the one, to avoid or get rid of some great calamity; the other, to obtain some great and positive good; and the two may be distinguished by the names of active and passive revolutions. In those which proceed from the former cause, the temper becomes incensed and sowered; and the redress, obtained by danger, is too often sullied by revenge. But in those which proceed from the latter, the heart, rather animated than agitated, enters serenely upon the subject. Reason and discussion, persuasion and conviction, become the weapons in the contest, and it is only when those are attempted to be suppressed that recource is had to violence. When men unite in agreeing that a *thing is good*, could it be obtained, such for instance as relief from a burden of taxes and the extinction of corruption, the object is more than half accomplished. What they approve as the end, they will promote in the means.

Will any man say, in the present excess of taxation, falling so heavily on the poor, that a remission of five pounds annually of taxes to one hundred and four thousand poor families is not a *good thing?* Will he say, that a remission of seven pounds annually to one hundred thousand other poor families—of eight pounds annually to another hundred thousand poor families, and of ten pounds annually to fifty thousand poor and widowed families, are not *good things?* And to proceed a step further in this climax, will he say, that to provide against the misfortunes to which all human life is subject, by securing six pounds annually for all poor, distressed, and reduced persons of the age of fifty and until sixty, and of ten pounds annually after sixty, is not a *good thing*?

Will he say, that an abolition of two millions of poor-rates to the house-keepers, and of the whole of the house and window-light tax and of the commutation tax is not a *good thing*? Or will he say that to abolish corruption is a *bad thing*?

If, therefore, the good to be obtained be worthy of a passive, rational, and costless revolution, it would be bad policy to prefer waiting for a calamity that should force a violent one. I have no idea, considering the reforms which are now passing and spreading throughout Europe, that England will permit herself to be the last; and where the occasion and the opportunity quietly offer, it is better than to wait for a turbulent necessity. It may be considered as an honour to the animal faculties of man to obtain redress by courage and danger, but it is far greater honour to the rational faculties to accomplish the same object by reason, accommodation, and general consent.*

As reforms, or revolutions, call them which you please, extend themselves among nations, those nations will form connections and conventions, and when a few are thus confederated, the progress will be rapid, till despotism and corrupt government be totally expelled, at least out of two quarters of the world, Europe and America. The Algerine piracy may then be commanded to cease, for it is only by the malicious policy of old governments, against each other, that it exists.

---

* I know it is the opinion of many of the most enlightened characters in France (there always will be those who see further into events than others), not only among the general mass of citizens, but of many of the principal members of the former National Assembly, that the monarchical plan will not continue many years in that country. They have found out, that as wisdom cannot be made hereditary, power ought not; and that, for a man to merit a million sterling a year from a nation, he ought to have a mind capable of comprehending from an atom to a universe; which, if he had, he would be above receiving the pay. But they wished not to appear to lead the nation faster than its own reason and interest dictated. In all the conversations where I have been present upon this subject, the idea always was, that when such a time, from the general opinion of the nation, shall arrive, that the honourable and liberal method would be, to make a handsome present in fee simple to the person whoever he may be, that shall then be in the monarchical office, and for him to retire to the enjoyment of private life, possessing his share of general rights and privileges, and to be no more accountable to the public for his time and his conduct than any other citizen.

***

I have now gone through the whole of the subject, at least, as far as it appears to me at present. It has been my intention for the five years I have been in Europe, to offer an address to the people of England on the subject of government, if the opportunity presented itself before I returned to America. Mr. Burke has thrown it in my way, and I thank him. On a certain occasion three years ago, I pressed him to propose a national convention to be fairly elected for the purpose of taking the state of the nation into consideration; but I found, that however strongly the parliamentary current was then setting against the party he acted with, their policy was to keep every thing within that field of corruption, and trust to accidents. Long experience had shewn that parliaments would follow any change of ministers, and on this they rested their hopes and their expectations.

Formerly, when divisions arose respecting governments, recourse was had to the sword, and a civil war ensued. That savage custom is exploded by the new system, and reference is had to national conventions. Discussion and the general will arbitrates the question, and to this, private opinion yields with a good grace, and order is preserved uninterrupted.

Some gentlemen have affected to call the principles upon which this work and the former part of *Rights of Man* are founded, "a new-fangled doctrine." The question is not whether those principles are new or old, but whether they are right or wrong.

***

Thus wishing, as I sincerely do, freedom and happiness to all nations, I close the SECOND PART.

THOMAS PAINE

AGRARIAN JUSTICE

OPPOSED TO

AGRARIAN LAW,

AND TO

AGRARIAN MONOPOLY

BEING A PLAN FOR MELIORATING THE CONDITION OF MAN, BY CREATING IN EVERY NATION A NATIONAL FUND to pay to every Person, when arrived at the Age of *Twenty-One Years*, the Sum of *Fifteen Pounds* Sterling, to enable *him* or *her* to begin the World:

AND ALSO,

Ten Pounds Sterling per Annum during life to every person now living in the Age of *Fifty Years*, and to all others when they shall arrive at that Age, to enable them to live in Old Age without Wretchedness, and go decently out of the World.

PREFACE

THE following little Piece was written in the winter of 1795 and 96; and, as I had not determined whether to publish it during the present war, or to wait till the commencement of a peace, it has lain by me, without alteration or addition, from the time it was written.

What has determined me to publish it now is, a sermon, preached by WATSON, *Bishop of Llandaff.* Some of my readers will recollect, that this Bishop wrote a Book, entitled *An Apology for the Bible*, in answer to my S*econd Part of the Age of Reason.* I had procured a copy of his book, and he may depend upon hearing from me on that subject.[1]

At the end of the Bishop's Book is a List of the Works he has written, among which is the Sermon alluded to; it is entitled,

---

[1] See Watson, *Apology for the Bible.*

"THE WISDOM AND GOODNESS OF GOD, IN HAVING MADE BOTH RICH AND POOR; with an Appendix, containing REFLECTIONS ON THE PRESENT STATE OF ENGLAND AND FRANCE."

The error contained in this Sermon, determined me to publish my AGRARIAN JUSTICE. It is wrong to say that God made *Rich* and *Poor*; he made only *Male* and *Female*; and he gave them the earth for their inheritance.   *   *   *

   *   *   *   *

   *   *   *   *

   *   *   *   *

   *   *   *   *

   *   *   *   *

   *   *   *   *

Instead of preaching to encourage one part of Mankind in insolence

   *   *   *

   *   *   *   it would be better that Priests employed their time to render the general condition of man less miserable than it is. Practical religion consists in doing good; and the only way of serving God is, that of endeavouring to make his creation happy. All preaching that has not this for its object is nonsense and hypocrisy.[2]

AGRARIAN JUSTICE &c. &c.

To preserve the benefits of what is called civilized life, and to remedy at the same time the evils it has produced, ought to considered as one of the first objects of reformed legislation.

Whether that state that is proudly, perhaps erroneously, called civilization, has most promoted or most injured the general happiness of man, is a question that may be strongly contested.— On one side, the spectator is dazzled by splendid

---

[2] The stars seem to indicate missing words from the English edition.

appearances; on the other, he is shocked by extremes of wretchedness; both of which he has erected. The most affluent and the most miserable of the human race are to be found in the countries that are called civilized.

To understand what the state of society ought to be, it is necessary to have some idea of the natural and primitive state of man; such as it is at this day among the Indians of North America. There is not, in that state, any of those spectacles of human misery which poverty and want present to our eyes in all the towns and streets in Europe. Poverty, therefore, is a thing created by that which is called civilized life. It exists not in the natural state. On the other hand, the natural state is without those advantages which flow from Agriculture, Arts, Science, and Manufactures.

The life of an Indian is a continual holiday, compared with the poor of Europe; and, on the other hand, it appears to be abject when compared to the rich. Civilization, therefore, or that which is so called, has operated two ways, to make one part of society more affluent, and the other more wretched, than would have been the lot of either in a natural state.

It is always possible to go from the natural to the civilized state, but it is never possible to go from the civilized to the natural state. The reason is, that man, in a natural state, subsisting by hunting, requires ten times the quantity of land to range over, to procure himself sustenance, than would support him in a civilized state, where the earth is cultivated. When therefore a country becomes populous by the additional aids of cultivation, arts, and science, there is a necessity of preserving things in that state; because, without it, there cannot be sustenance for more, perhaps, than a tenth part of its inhabitants. The thing therefore now to be done, is, to remedy the evils, and preserve the benefits, that have arisen to society, by passing from the natural to that which is called the civilized state.

Taking then the matter up on this ground, the first principle of civilization ought to have been, and ought still to be, that the condition of every person born into the world, after a state of civilization commences, ought not to be worse than if he had been born before that period. But the fact is that the condition of millions, in every country in Europe, is far worse than if they had been born before civilization began, or had been born among the Indians of North America of the present day. I will shew how this fact has happened.

It is a position not to be controverted, that the earth, in its natural uncultivated state, was, and ever would have continued to be, the *common property of the human race*. In that state every man would have been born to property. He would have been a joint life-proprietor with the rest in the property of the soil, and in all its natural productions, vegetable and animal.

But the earth in its natural state, as before said, is capable of supporting but a small number of inhabitants compared with what it is capable of doing in a cultivated state. And as it is impossible to separate the improvement made by cultivation, from the earth itself, upon which that improvement is made, the idea of landed property arose from that inseparable connection; but it is nevertheless true, that it is the value of the improvement only, and not the earth itself, that is individual property. Every proprietor therefore of cultivated land, owes to the community a *ground-rent*; for I know no better term to express the idea by, for the land which he holds: and it is from this ground-rent that the fund proposed in this plan is to issue.

It is deducible as well from the nature of the thing as from all the histories transmitted to us, that the idea of landed property commenced with cultivation, and that there was no such thing as landed property before that time. It could not exist in the first state of man, that of hunters. It did not exist in the second state, that of shepherds: Neither Abraham, Isaac, Jacob, or Job, so far as the history of the Bible may be credited in probable things, were owners of land. Their property consisted, as is always enumerated, in flocks and herds, and they travelled with them from place to place. The frequent contentions at that time about the use of a well in the dry country of Arabia, where those people lived, shew also there was no landed property. It was not admitted that land could be located as property.

There could be no such thing as landed property originally. Man did not make the earth, and though he had a natural right to *occupy* it, he had no right to *locate* as *his property* in perpetuity any part of it: neither did the Creator of the earth open a land-office, from whence the first title-deeds should issue. From whence then arose the idea of landed property? I answer as before, that when cultivation began, the idea of landed property began with it, from the impossibility of separating the improvement made by cultivation from the earth itself upon which that improvement was made. The value of the improvement so far exceeded the value of the natural earth, at that time, as to absorb it; till, in the end, the common right of all became confounded into the cultivated right of the individual. But they are nevertheless distinct species of rights, and will continue to be so as long as the earth endures.

It is only by tracing things to their origin that we can gain rightful ideas of them, and it is by gaining such ideas that we discover the boundary that divides right from wrong, and which teaches every man to know his own. I have entitled this tract *Agrarian Justice*, to distinguish it from *Agrarian Law*. Nothing could be more unjust than Agrarian Law in a country improved by cultivation; for though every man, as an inhabitant of the earth, is a joint proprietor of it in its natural state, it does not follow that he is a joint proprietor of cultivated earth. The additional value made by cultivation, after the system was admitted, became the property of those who did it, or who inherited it from them, or who purchased it. It had originally an owner. Whilst therefore I advocate the right, and interest myself in the hard case of all those who have been thrown out of their natural inheritance by the introduction of the system of landed property, I equally defend the right of the possessor to the part which is his.

Cultivation is, at least, one of the greatest natural improvements ever made by human invention. It has given to created earth a ten-fold value. But the landed monopoly that began with it has produced the greatest evil. It has dispossessed more than half the inhabitants of every nation of their natural inheritance, without providing for them, as ought to have been done, as an indemnification for that loss, and has thereby created a species of poverty and wretchedness that did not exist before.

In advocating the case of the persons thus dispossessed, it is a right, and not a charity that I am pleading for. But it is that kind of right, which, being neglected at first, could not be brought forward afterwards, till heaven had opened the way by a revolution in the system of government. Let us then do honour to revolutions by justice, and give currency to their principles by blessings.

Having thus, in a few words, opened the merits of the case, I proceed to the plan I have to propose, which is,

To create a National Fund, out of which there shall be paid to every person, when arrived at the age of twenty-one years, the sum of Fifteen Pounds sterling, *as a compensation in part, for the loss of his or her natural inheritance by the introduction of the system of landed property.*

AND ALSO, *The sum of* Ten Pounds per annum, *during life, to every person now living of the age of fifty years, and to all others as they shall arrive at that age,*

MEANS BY WHICH THE FUND IS TO BE CREATED

I have already established the principle, namely, that the earth, in its natural uncultivated state, was, and ever would have continued to be, *the common property of the human race*— that in that state every person would have been born to property—and that the system of landed property, by its inseparable connection with cultivation, and with what is called civilized life, has absorbed the property of all those whom it dispossessed, without providing, as ought to have been done, an indemnification for that loss.

The fault, however, is not in the present possessors. No complaint is intended, or ought to be alleged against them, unless they adopt the crime by opposing justice. The fault is in the system, and it has stolen imperceptibly upon the world, aided afterwards by the Agrarian Law of the sword. But the fault can be made to reform itself by successive generations, and without diminishing or deranging the property of any of present possessors, and yet the operation of the fund can commence, and be in full activity the first year of its establishment, or soon after, as I shall shew.

It is proposed that the payments, as already stated, be made to every person, rich or poor. It is best to make it so, to prevent invidious distinctions. It is also right it should be so, because it is in lieu of the natural inheritance, which, as a right, belongs to every man, over and above the property he may have created, or inherited from those who did. Such persons as do not chuse to receive it, can throw it into the common fund.

Taking it then for granted that no person ought to be in a worse condition when born under what is called a state of civilization, than he would have been, had he been born in a state of nature, and that civilization ought to have made, and ought still to make, provision for that purpose, it can only be done by subtracting from property a portion equal in value to the natural inheritance it has absorbed.

Various methods may be proposed for this purpose, but that which appears to be the best, not only because it will operate without deranging any present possessors, or without interfering with the collection of taxes, or emprunts necessary for the purpose of government and the revolution, but because it will be the least troublesome and the most effectual, and also because the subtraction will be made at a time that best admits it, which is, at the moment that property is passing by the death of one person to the possession of another. In this case, the bequeather gives nothing: the receiver pays nothing. The only matter to him is, that the monopoly of natural inheritance, to which there never was a right, begins to cease in his person. A generous man would not wish it continue, and a just man will rejoice to see it abolished.

My state of health prevents my making sufficient enquiries with respect to the doctrine of probabilities, whereon to found calculations with such degrees of certainty as they are capable of. What therefore I offer on this head is more the result of observation and reflection than of received information; but, I believe it will be found to agree sufficiently enough with fact.

In the first place, taking twenty-one years as the epoch of maturity, all the property of a nation, real and personal, is always in the possession of persons above that age. It is then necessary to know, as a datum of calculation, the average of years which persons above that age will live; I take this average to be about thirty years; for, though many persons will live forty, fifty, or sixty years, after the age of twenty-one years, others will die much sooner, and some in every year of that time.

Taking then thirty years as the average of time, it will give, without any material variation one way or other, the average of time in which the whole property, or capital of a nation, or a sum equal thereto, will have passed through one entire revolution in descent, that is, will have gone by deaths to new possessors; for though, in many instances, some parts of this capital will remain forty, fifty, or sixty years in the possession of one person, other parts will have revolved two or three times before that thirty years expire, which will bring it to that average; for were one-half the capital of a nation to revolve twice in thirty years, it would produce the same fund as if the whole revolved once.

Taking then thirty years as the average of time in which the whole capital of a nation, or a -sum equal thereto, will revolve once, the thirtieth part thereof will be the sum that will revolve every year, that is, will go by deaths to new possessors; and this last sum being thus known, and the ratio per cent. to be subtracted from it being determined, it will give the annual amount or income of the proposed fund, to be applied as already mentioned.

In looking over the discourse of the English Minister, Pitt, in his opening of what is called in England the budget (the scheme of finance for the year 1796,) I find an estimate of the national capital of that country. As this estimate of a national capital is prepared ready to my hand, I take it as a datum to act upon. When a calculation is made upon the known capital of any nation, combined with its population, it will serve as a scale for any other nation, in proportion as its capital and population be more or less. I am the more disposed to take this estimate of Mr. Pitt, for the purpose of shewing to that Minister, upon his own calculation, how much better money may be employed, than in wasting it, as he has done, on the wild project of setting up Bourbon kings. What, in the name of

Heaven, are Bourbon kings to the people of England? It is better that the people have bread.

Mr. Pitt states the national capital of England, real and personal, to be one thousand three hundred millions sterling, which is about one-fourth part of the national capital of France, including Belgia. The event of the last harvest in each country proves that the soil of France is more productive than that of England, and that it can better support twenty-four or twenty-five millions of inhabitants than that of England can seven, or seven and a half.

The 30th part of this capital of £1,300,000,000 is £43,333,333, which is the part that will revolve every year by deaths in that country to new possessors; and the sum that will annually revolve in France in the proportion of four to one, will be about one hundred and seventy-three millions sterling. From this sum of £43,333,333 annually revolving, is to be subtracted the value of the natural inheritance absorbed in it, which perhaps, in fair justice, cannot be taken at less, and ought not to be taken at more, than a tenth part.

It will always happen, that of the property thus revolving by deaths every year, a part will descend in a direct line to sons and daughters, and other part collaterally, and the proportion will be found to be about three to one; that is, about 30 millions of the above sum will descend to direct heirs, and the remaining sum of £13,333,333 to more distant relations, and part to strangers.

Considering then that man is always related to society, that relationship will become comparatively greater in proportion as the next of kin is more distant. It is therefore consistent with civilization to say, that where there are no direct heirs, society shall be heir to a part over and above the tenth part *due* to society. If this additional part be from five to ten or twelve per cent. in proportion as the next of kin be nearer or more remote, so as to average with the escheats that may fall, which ought always to go to society and not to the government, an addition of ten per cent. more, the produce from the annual sum of £43,333,333 will be:

From £30,000,000 at ten per cent.	£3,000,000
From £13,333,333 at 10 per cent. with the Addition of ten per cent more.	£2,666,666
----------------- ---------------	
£ 43,333,333	£5,666,666

Having thus arrived at the annual amount of the proposed fund, I come, in the next place, to speak of the population proportioned to this fund, and to compare it with the uses to which the fund is to be applied.

The population (I mean that of England) does not exceed seven millions and a half, and the number of persons above the age of fifty will in that case be about four hundred thousand. There would not however be more than that number that would accept the proposed ten pounds sterling per annum, though they would be entitled to it. I have no idea it would be accepted by many persons who had a yearly income of two or three hundred pounds sterling. But as we often see instances of rich people falling into sudden poverty, even at the age of sixty, they would always have the right of drawing all the arrears due to them—Four millions, therefore, of the above annual sum of £ 5,666,666 will be required for four hundred thousand aged persons, at ten pounds sterling each.

I come now to speak of the persons annually arriving at 21 years of age. If all the persons who died were above the age of twenty-one years, the number of persons annually arriving at that age, must be equal to the annual number of deaths to keep the population stationary. But the greater part die under the age of twenty-one, and therefore the number of persons annually arriving at twenty-one, will be less than half the number of deaths. The whole number of deaths upon a population of seven millions and a half, will be about 220,000 annually. The number arriving at twenty-one years of age will be about 100,000. The whole number of these will not receive the proposed fifteen pounds, for the reasons already mentioned, though, as in the former case, they would be entitled to it.

Admitting then that a tenth part declined receiving it, the amount would stand thus:

Fund annually	£5,666,666
To 400,000 aged persons at £10 each ⎱	£4,000,000
To 90,000 persons of 21 years £15 sterling each ⎰	£1,350,000
	£5,350,000
remains	£. 316,666

There are, in every country a number of blind and lame persons, totally incapable of earning a livelihood. But as it will always happen that the greater number of blind persons will be among those who are above the age of fifty years, they will be provided for in that class. The remaining sum of £316,666 will provide for the lame and blind under that age, at the same rate of £10 annually for each person.

Having now gone through all the necessary calculations, and stated the particulars of the plan, I shall conclude with some observations.

It is not charity but a right—not bounty but justice, that I am pleading for. The present state of civilization, *   *   *   *   It is the reverse of what it ought to be, and   *   *   *   *[3]   The   contrast   of affluence and wretchedness continually meeting and offending the eye, is like dead and living bodies chained together. Though I care as little about riches as any man, I am a friend to riches because they are capable of good. I care not how affluent some may be, provided that none be miserable in consequence of it. But it is impossible to enjoy affluence with the felicity it is capable of being enjoyed, whilst so much misery is mingled in the scene. The sight of the misery, and the unpleasant sensations it suggests, which though they may be suffocated cannot be extinguished, are a greater drawback upon the felicity of affluence than the

---

[3] Other editions suggest: 'The present state of civilization is as odious as it is unjust. It is absolutely the opposite of what it should be, and it is necessary that a revolution should be made in it.'

proposed 10 per cent. upon property is worth. He that would not give the one to get rid of the other, has no charity, even for himself.

There are in every country some magnificent charities established by individuals. It is however but little that any individual can do when the whole extent of the misery to be relieved be considered. He may satisfy his conscience, but not his heart. He may give all that he has, and that will relieve but little. I[t] is only by organizing civilization upon such principles as to act like a system of pullies, that the whole weight of misery can be removed.

The plan here proposed will reach the whole. It will immediately relieve and take out of view three classes of wretchedness. The blind, the lame, and the aged poor; and it will furnish the rising generation with means to prevent their becoming poor; and it will do this, without deranging or interfering with any national measures. To shew that this will be the case, it is sufficient to observe, that the operation and effect of the plan will, in all cases, be the same, as if every individual were *voluntarily* to make his will, and dispose of his property, in the manner here proposed.

But it is justice and not charity, that is the principle of the plan. In all great cases it is necessary to have a principle more universally active than charity; and, with respect to justice, it ought not to be left to the choice of detached individuals, whether they will do justice or not. Considering then the plan on the ground of justice, it ought to be the act of the whole, growing spontaneously out of the principles of the revolution, and the reputation of it ought to be national and not individual.

A plan upon this principle would benefit the revolution by the energy that springs from the consciousness of justice. It would multiply also the national resources; for property, like vegetation, encreases by off-sets. When a young couple begins the world, the difference is exceedingly great whether they begin with nothing or with fifteen pounds a-piece. With this aid they could buy a cow, and implements to cultivate a few acres of land; and instead of becoming burthens upon society, which is always the case, where children are produced faster than they can be fed, would be put in the way of becoming useful and profitable citizens. The national domains also would sell the better, if pecuniary aids were provided to cultivate them in small lots.

It is the practice of what has unjustly obtained the name of civilization (and the practice merits not to be called either charity or policy) to make some provision for persons becoming poor and wretched, only at the time they become so.— Would it not, even as a matter of economy, be far better, to devise means to prevent their becoming poor. This can best be done by making every person, when arrived at the age of twenty-one years an inheritor of something to begin with. The rugged face of society, chequered with the extremes of affluence and of want, proves that some extraordinary violence has been committed upon it, and calls on justice for redress. The great mass of the poor, in countries, are become an hereditary race, and it is next to impossible for them to get out of that state of themselves. It ought also to be observed, that this mass increases in all countries that are called civilized. More persons fall annually into it, than can get out of it.

Though in a plan, of which justice and humanity are the foundation-principles, interest ought not to be admitted into the calculation, yet it is always of advantage to the establishment of any plan, to shew that it beneficial as a matter of interest. The success of any proposed plan, submitted to public consideration, must finally depend on the numbers interested in supporting it, united with the justice of its principles.

The plan here proposed will benefit all, without injuring any. It will consolidate the interest of the republic with that of the individual. To the numerous class dispossessed of their natural inheritance by the system of landed property, it will be an act of national justice. To persons dying possessed of moderate fortunes, it will operate as a tontine to their children, more beneficial than the sum of money paid into the fund: and it will give to the accumulation of riches a degree of security that none of old governments of Europe, now tottering on their foundation, can give.

I do not suppose that more than one family in ten, in any of the countries of Europe, has, when the head of the family dies, a clear property left of five hundred pounds sterling. To all such the plan is advantageous. That property would pay fifty pounds into the fund, and if there were only two children under age, they would receive fifteen pounds each (thirty pounds) on coming of age, and be entitled to ten pounds a year after fifty. It is from the overgrown acquisition of property that the fund will support itself; and I know that the possessors of such property in England, though they would eventually be benefited by the protection of nine-tenths of it, will exclaim against the plan. But, without entering into any enquiry how they came by that property, let them recollect, that they have been the advocates of this war, and that Mr. Pitt has already laid on more new taxes to be raised annually upon the people of England, and that for supporting the despotism of Austria and the Bourbons, against the liberties of France, than would annually pay all the sums proposed in this plan.

I have made the calculations, stated in this plan, upon what is called personal, as well as upon landed property. The reason for making it upon land is already explained; and the reason for taking personal property into the calculation, is equally well founded, though on a different principle. Land, as before said, is the free gift of the Creator in common to the human race. Personal property is the *effect of Society*; and it is as impossible for an individual to acquire personal property without the aid of society, as it is for him to make land originally. Separate an individual from society, and give him an island or a continent to possess, and he cannot acquire personal property. He cannot be rich. So inseparably are the means connected with the end, in all cases, that where the former do not exist, the latter cannot be obtained. All accumulation therefore of personal property, beyond what a man's own hands produce, is derived to him by living in society; and he owes, on every principle of justice, of gratitude, and of civilization, a part of that accumulation back again to society from whence the whole came. This is putting the matter on a general principle, and perhaps it is best to do so; for if we examine the case minutely, it will be found, that the accumulation of personal property is, in many instances, the effect of paying too little for the labour that produced it; the consequence of which is, that the working hand perishes in old age, and the employer abounds in affluence. It is perhaps impossible to proportion exactly the price of labour to the profits it produces; and it will also be said, as an apology for injustice, that were a workman to receive an increase of wages daily, he would not save it against old age nor be much the better for it in the interim. Make then Society the treasurer to guard it for him in a common fund, for it is no reason that because he might not make a good use of it for himself that another shall take it.

The state of civilization that has prevailed throughout Europe, is as unjust in its principle, as it is horrid in its effects; and it is the consciousness of this, and the apprehension that such a state cannot continue when once investigation begins in any country, that makes the possessors of property dread every idea of a revolution. It is the *hazard*, and not the principles of a revolution that retards their progress. This being the case, it is necessary as well for the protection of property as for the sake of justice and humanity, to form a system that whilst it preserves one part of society from wretchedness, shall secure the other from depredation.

The superstitious awe, the enslaving reverence, that formerly surrounded affluence, is passing away in all countries, and leaving the possessor of property to the convulsion of accidents. When wealth and splendour, instead of fascinating the multitude, excite emotions of disgust; when, instead of drawing forth admiration, it is beheld as an insult upon wretchedness: when the ostentatious appearance it makes serves call the right of it in question, the case of property becomes critical, and it is only in a system of justice that the possessor can contemplate security.

To remove the danger, it is necessary to remove the antipathies, and this can only be done by making property productive of a national blessing, extending to every individual. When the riches of one man above other shall increase the national fund in the same proportion; when it shall be seen that the prosperity of that fund depends on the prosperity of individuals; when the more riches a man acquires, the better it shall for the general mass; it is then that antipathies will cease, and property be placed on the permanent basis of national interest and protection.

I have no property in France to become subject to the plan I prose. What I have, which is not much, is in the United States of America. But I will pay one hundred pounds sterling toward this fund in France, the instant it shall be established; and I will pay the same sum England, whenever a similar establishment shall take place in that country.

A revolution in the state of civilization is the necessary companion of revolutions in the system of government. If a revolution in any country be from bad to good, or from good to bad, the state of what is called civilization in that country, must be made conformable thereto, to give that revolution effects. Despotic government supports itself by abject civilization, in which debasement of the human mind, and wretchedness in the mass of the people, are the chief criterians. Such governments consider man merely as an animal; that the exercise of intellectual faculty is not his privilege; *that he has nothing to do with the laws, but to obey them**; and they politically depend more upon breaking the spirit of the people by poverty, than they fear enraging it by desperation.

It is a revolution in the state of civilization, that will give perfection to the revolution of France. Already, the conviction that government, by representation, is the true system of government, is spreading itself fast in the world. The reasonableness of it can be seen by all. The justness of it makes itself felt even by its opposers. But when a system of civilization, growing out of that system of government, shall be so organized, that not a man or woman born in the republic, but shall inherit some means of beginning the world, and see before them the certainty of escaping the miseries, that under other governments accompany old age, the revolution of France will have an advocate and an ally in the heart of all nations.

---

* Expression of Horsley, an English Bishop, in the English parliament.

An army of principles will penetrate where an army of soldiers cannot—It will succeed where diplomatic management would fail—It is neither the Rhine, the Channel, nor the Ocean, that can arrest its progress—It will march on the horizon of the world, and it will conquer.

THOMAS PAINE

Means for carrying the proposed plan into execution, and to render it at the same time conducive to the public Interest

I.   Each canton shall elect in its primary assemblies, three persons as commissioners for that canton, who shall take cognizance, and keep a register of all matters happening in that canton, conformable to the charter that shall be established by law for carrying this plan into execution.

II.   The law shall fix the manner in which the property of deceased persons shall be ascertained.

III.   When the amount of the property of any deceased person shall be ascertained, the principal heir to that property, or the eldest of the co-heirs, if of lawful age, or if under age, the person authorized by the will of the deceased to represent him, or them, shall give bond to the commissioners of the canton, to pay the said tenth part thereof, within the space of one year, in four equal quarterly payments, or sooner, at the choice of the payers.   One half of the whole property shall remain as security until the bond be paid off.

IV.   The bonds shall be registered in the office of the commissioners of the canton, and the original bonds shall be deposited in the national bank at Paris. The bank shall publish every quarter of a year the amount of the bonds in its possession, and also the bonds that shall have been paid off, or what parts thereof, since the last quarterly publication.

V.   The national bank shall issue bank notes upon the security of the bonds in its possession.   The notes so issued, shall be applied to pay the pensions of aged persons, and the compensations to persons arriving at twenty-one years of age.—It is both reasonable and generous to suppose, that persons not under immediate necessity, will suspend their right of drawing on the fund, until it acquire, as it will do, a greater degree of ability. In this case, it is proposed that an honorary register be kept in each canton, of the names of the persons thus suspending that right, at least during the present war.

VI. As the inheritors of property must always take up their bonds in four quarterly payments, or sooner if they chuse, there will always be numeraire arriving at the bank after the expiration of the first quarter, to exchange for the bank notes that shall be brought in.

VII. The bank notes being thus got in circulation, upon the best of all possible security, that of actual property to more than four times the amount of the bonds upon which the notes are issued, and with numeraire continually arriving at the bank to exchange or pay them off whenever they shall be presented for that purpose, they will acquire a permanent value in all parts of the republic. They can therefore be received in payment of taxes or emprunts, equal to numeraire, because the government can always receive numeraire for them at the bank.

VIII. It will be necessary that the payments of the ten *per cent.* be made in numeraire for the first year, from the establishment of the plan. But after the expiration of the first year, the inheritors of property may pay ten *per cent.* either in bank notes issued upon the fund, or in numeraire. If the payments be in numeraire, it will lie as a deposit at the bank, to be exchanged for a quantity of notes equal to that amount; and if in notes issued upon the fund, it will cause a demand upon the fund equal thereto; and thus the operation of the plan will create means to carry itself into execution.

FINIS

Appendix:

Biographical Glossary

John Adams (1735-1826): a delegate to the Continental Congress and signatory of the Declaration of Independence, U. S. Minister to France 1777-1783 and to England 1785-88. He later became the second President of the U. S. 1796-1800. Although Adam's was initially impressed by *Common Sense* he was a virulent critic of Paine's plans for independent government in his *Thoughts on Government*. His son, John Quincy Adams, (1767-1848) also wrote *An Answer to Pain's Rights of Man* in 1793.

Major General Benedict Arnold (1741-1801): led a successful military career from 1775, culminating in his command in occupied Philadelphia in 1778. He was court marshalled for embezzlement but escaped with a reprimand. In 1780 he betrayed West Point and fled to the British line and accepted a command in the royal army. Arnold lived the remainder of his life in England.

François Babeuf (1760-97): a native of St. Quentin who led a popular campaign against private property. During the revolution, he founded the popular *Tribun du Peuple* in which he advocated a communist land reform under the pen of 'Gracchus Babeuf'. His conspiracy aimed to overthrow the Directorate to establish democratic communism but on discovery he met a common fate with the guillotine.

Sir Joseph Banks (1743-1820): a botanist who accompanied Captain James Cook on his expedition around the world in 1768-71, collecting and cataloguing more than 2,600 new plant species, particularly in New South Wales. In 1772, Banks explored Iceland with fellow botanist Daniel Solander (1733-82). Banks was elected president of the Royal Society in 1778 and, as the King's botanical adviser, set out the original plan for Kew Gardens. His plan to move breadfruit from Tahiti to the West Indies on Captain Bligh's *Bounty* resulted in the famous mutiny in 1789.

Pierre Augustin Caronde Beaumarchais (1732-99): an actor, musician, playwright, financial speculator, spy and a spy handler, and a master of disguise. His plays include *The Barber of Seville* and *The Marriage of Figaro*. He fled the French revolution, living in Holland and England from 1793.

General John Burgoyne (1722-92): a distinguished soldier, Member of Parliament, and playwright. He fought at Bunker Hill in 1775 and captured Ticonderoga. He was forced to surrender to Gates at Saratoga, the first decisive British loss.

Edmund Burke (1729-97): Member of Parliament, associated with the Rockingham Whigs. Famed for his philosophical writings and parliamentary speeches, Burke was tireless in his opposition to American policy and proposed 'economical reform' to reduce places and pensions. His prosecution of Warren Hastings of the East India Company irrevocably altered British rule in India. His most famous work, *Reflections on the Revolution in France*, was widely read and virulently debated. It served as a justification for Pitt's repression of the radical reform movement and the conservative counter-revolution throughout Europe.

Sir Henry Clinton (1738-95): British General, son of the Governor of New York. His gallantry in service was noted during the Seven Years War, resulting in his rapid rise to Major General. In 1775 he was posted to North America, and appointed Commander-in-Chief of the British forces in 1778. After the surrender of Yorktown, he resigned his command and returned to England. In 1794 he was appointed Governor of Gibraltar.

George Clymer (1739-1813): a Philadelphia businessman, sympathetic to the democratic faction. He was an officer in the Pennsylvania volunteers. In 1773 Clymer chaired a committee devoted to the boycott of tea and, in 1775, was a member of the Philadelphia Council of Safety. As a member of the Continental Congress, he signed the Declaration of Independence. His house was destroyed by the British army. He was a director of the Bank of North America. Elected again to Congress in 1780 and in 1784 to the Pennsylvania Assembly and later sat in the Constitutional Convention. Paine corresponded with Clymer frequently from Europe. In the 1790's he headed the Pennsylvania Excise department during the Whiskey Rebellion and negotiated a treaty with the Cherokee Indians in Georgia. He was president of the Philadelphia bank, and the Academy of Fine Arts, and vice president of the Philadelphia Agricultural Society in 1805.

Sir John Dalrymple (1726-1810): a Scottish historian and solicitor to the Board of Excise. His *Address of the People of Great-Britain to the Inhabitants of America* was published in 1775, detailing the illegitimacy and impossibility of colonial resistance to British rule.

William Legge, Earl of Dartmouth (1731-1801): Secretary of State for American Department from 1772-5. He was considered a friend to the colonies despite his support for parliamentary supremacy.

Silas Deane (1737-1789): born in Connecticut, he practised law in Wethersfield but made his fortune in trade with the West Indies. In 1768-1774 he was a prominent member of the Connecticut General Assembly. He was a delegate to Congress from

1774 and commissioned to seek supplies in France as early as March 1776. In April 1777 he became a Commissioner for Foreign Affairs until his recall due to Paine's public accusations of fraud. Although never fully exonerated, Deane was discharged from Congress to settle his accounts, and returned to France in July 1780, trading in plots of western lands for Morris, Livingston and Wilson. His accounts were finally settled in September 1781, although he was then accused of writing unpatriotic letters. He later lived in Ghent and London, where he met Benedict Arnold. In August 1789 on return to the US, he died on board the Boston Packet. In 1841 Congress awarded his heirs compensation $37,000 on the grounds that the audit was erroneous.

John Dickenson (1732-1808): famous as the author of the famous newspaper letters against the Townshend Acts 'Letters from a Pennsylvania Farmer' in 1767-68, He was a delegate to Continental Congress for Pennsylvania 1774-6 and later for Delaware. He opposed the Declaration of Independence, seeking moderation. Although an anti-constitutionalist, he served as President of Pennsylvania for three terms from 1782-85. He participated in drafting the Articles of Confederation, and was a member of Constitutional Convention in 1787, working in both Delaware and Pennsylvania to secure ratification.

William Eden, Baron Auckland (1744-1814): a court Member of Parliament from 1774, appointed Under Secretary of State for Southern Department in 1772, and to the Board of Trade and Plantations in 1776. His brother Robert Eden (1741-83) was the Royal Governor of Maryland 1767-76, fled in 1776. Eden organised Carlisle's peace commission to America in 1778. His writings on Irish politics were a great success, followed by his appointment as Carlisle's secretary when Viceroy to Ireland. He was elected to the Irish parliament and established the National Bank of Ireland. In 1783, under Portland's ministry, he was Vice Treasurer of Ireland but resigned in 1783 over the dismissal of the Fox-North coalition. Pitt appointed Eden as a Special Envoy to France to negotiate the Treaty of Commerce agreed in Sept. 1786. Further negotiations lead to France and England's agreement over Holland in Nov. 1787. He was appointed as Ambassador to Madrid, and was called upon to defend the French Commercial Treaty to the new revolutionary government in 1789. He later negotiated a commercial treaty with the US before his retirement from public life in 1793.

James Ferguson (1710-1776): a Scottish astronomer, who developed his interest in the stars while tending sheep. In London he collaborated with Benjamin Martin, a mathematician, optician and globe-maker. His lectures covered astronomy and mechanics, hydrostatics, pneumatics and optics.

William Findlay (1741-1821): a Western Pennsylvanian politician. Born in Ireland, Findlay served on the Council of Censors in 1783, and was a member of the Assembly in 1785-86, and the Supreme Executive Council 1789-90. Findlay was a delegate to the Pennsylvania Constitutional Convention 1790, which created the state senate of which he was a member 1799-1802. He was involved in the Whisky Rebellion in Western Pennsylvania in 1794 and represented his state in the US Congress in 1791 and 1803-17,

Thomas Fitzsimmons (1741-1811): born in Ireland, he was elected a member of Congress from 1782 and was a founder and director of the Bank of North America. He was a delegate to the Constitutional Convention in 1787 and served in the US House of Representatives 1789-95.

Charles James Fox (1749-1806): the youngest son of Lord Holland, he became a Member of Parliament at the age of nineteen and joined Lord North's ministry but resigned in 1775 in opposition to the American policy. A colourful and often scandalous character, and politically radical, he was disliked by the King but joined North in a coalition in 1783. He later became the leader of the opposition to Pitt, although his position was weakened by his fall out with Burke over the French Revolution. He was briefly recalled in 1806 after Pitt's death.

Benjamin Franklin (1706-90): Paine's most influential friend and patron, a statesman and a scientist, now famous for his early experiments with electricity. He established a successful printing house in Philadelphia and served in the colonial assembly. He was Postmaster General until his first mission to England in 1757 to present colonial grievances to Parliament. He returned to England on a similar mission 1764-75. He was a signatory of the Declaration of Independence, and secured a treaty of alliance with France as American Minister to Paris in 1776-1785. He was President of the Supreme Executive Council in Pennsylvania 1785-88 and a delegate to the Constitutional Convention in 1787.

Conrad Alexander Gérard de Rayneval (1729-1790): appointed French Minister Plenipotentiary to the United States in 1778-79 after the signing of the Treaty of Amity and Commerce.

Major General Nathanael Greene (1742-86): born in Rhode Island, he was a military hero of the War of Independence, noted for his action at Trenton in Dec. 1776 and Brandywine in September 1777, where Paine served as his aide. Appointed Commander of the Army of the South in 1780.

William Wyndham Grenville (1759-1834): followed his father, George Grenville (1712-70), into parliament in 1782, and became Paymaster-General in 1783 and Speaker in 1789. In 1791 he served as Pitt's foreign minister until resigning over Catholic emancipation in 1801.

William Hill, Earl of Hillsborough (1718-93): Secretary of State for American Department from 1768-1772. He favoured repressive measures toward the colonists.

General William Howe (1729-1814): joined the British army in 1746, serving under General Wolfe at Quebec in 1759. He was elected a Member of Parliament in 1758 on the strength of his military success and became Commander-in-Chief after his victory at Bunker Hill in 1775. He captured New York and White Plains and occupied Philadelphia. Failing to defeat the Washington in Valley Forge, he was superseded by General Clinton in 1778.

David Howel (1747-1824): born in Morristown, New Jersey but settled in Rhode Island. Howel represented the state's rights and agrarian opinion, ousting the federalist and commercial faction over the issue of the five per cent duty, by beating merchant General James M. Varnum in the congressional elections in 1782. He continued to serve as a delegate to Continental Congress until 1785. He founded the Rhode Island College and served on the Rhode Island Supreme Court 1786-7, and as Attorney General in 1784. He was appointed a US federal judge for Rhode Island in 1812.

Dr. James Hutchinson (1752-93): physician and educator. Having studied medicine in London, Hutchinson was Surgeon General of Pennsylvania 1778-84 and served on the Philadelphia Committee of Safety in 1788. He was a trustee of the University of Pennsylvania 1779-81, Professor of Chemistry 1791-93 and member of the American Philosophical Society.

Thomas Jefferson (1743-1826): elected to the Virginia House of Burgesses in 1769 and served as a delegate to the first Continental Congress. He is widely regarded to be responsible for drafting the Declaration of Independence. As a political radical and a Deist, he and Paine shared a great deal in common. In Virginia, as Governor, he campaigned for the abolition of primogeniture and the established church. In 1784 he was appointed Minister to France. He returned from Paris in 1789, when appointed Secretary of State. His opposition to Alexander Hamilton's Federalist Party resulted in a Democratic Republican faction developing around his leadership, a rift he tried to heal when elected the third President of the United States in 1800.

Henry Laurens (1742-1792): born in Charleston, South Carolina. An early opponent of British policy, he was elected president of the Congress of Carolina in June 1775. After the resignation of Hancock, he was appointed president of Continental Congress in November 1777. In 1780, on a mission to secure a loan and a treaty from Holland, he was captured by a British ship off Newfoundland. The capture of his papers brought the United Provinces into the war. He was committed to the Tower of London, on a charge of high-treason. His refusal to cooperate with or even recognise the sovereignty of the British crown was widely championed as a heroic act. Shelburne assisted his release after fourteen months, whereupon Congress appointed him minister to the peace negotiations in Paris. In 1782 he signed the Peace of Paris and then returned to retire in Carolina.

John Laurens (1754-1782): Henry Laurens's son, was educated in Geneva and studied law in London, where he was socially well-connected. In 1777 he visited Franklin in Paris on his way to join the Continental Army in Charleston, serving on Washington's staff where he became friends with Lafayette. His heroism at Germantown and his skilful handling of relations with the French fleet in Rhode Island resulted in his promotion to Lieutenant Colonel in 1778. In 1779 he raised a black regiment in South Carolina. In 1780 he was captured by the British while defending Charleston. After his release he travelled on an official mission to France, in the hope of securing further aid, taking Paine as his assistant. His successful negotiations with the French minister of finance, Necker, resulted in his arrival in Boston in August 1780 with 2,500 224 *livres* in cash and two cargoes of military supplies. His arrival in Philadelphia in with cartloads of silver was significant in restoring financial confidence. He returned to the army in the south where he died in a skirmish in 1782.

Arthur Lee (1740-92): born in Virginia, trained as a barrister in London, where he moved in opposition circles. His diplomatic career left him in the shadow of his more famous elder brothers, Richard Henry Lee (1732-94) and Francis Lightfoot Lee (1734-

1797) both of whom signed the Declaration of Independence. He was appointed Minister Plenipotentiary to France by Congress in 1777 but fell out with Silas Deane over the conduct of the Roderigue, Hortalez & Co. Lee was accused of passing news of the secret treaty to Lord Shelburne and was recalled in 1779. Lee himself led an enquiry into the Silas Deane affair in 1787.

Robert R. Livingston (1746-1813): born in New York and educated as a lawyer. He headed a successful business partnership with John Jay. He served as a delegate to Continental Congress in 1775-77, 1779-81 and 1784-5, arguing in 1776 for postponing the Declaration of Independence. He was appointed Secretary of Department of Foreign Affairs in January 1781 till June 1783. He served as Minister to France in 1801-1804, negotiating the Louisiana Purchase in 1803. He was also Chancellor of New York 1777-1801 and financed Robert Fulton's development of steamboats shipping.

George Logan (1753-1821): born in Germantown, Pennsylvania and educated in Edinburgh. He was elected to the Pennsylvania Assembly in 1785-88, and founded the Philadelphia Society for promotion of Agriculture. On an unofficial mission to France, Logan secured removal of French embargo on American fishing in 1798, an action which resulted in the Logan Act in 1799 which made it illegal for private citizens to intervene in dispute with foreign government. Nevertheless Logan went to England in 1810 to try to prevent war as a private citizen. He was a US Senator 1801-7.

Blair McClenachan (died 1812): born in Ireland and settled in Philadelphia, making his fortune in merchant banking and shipping. Founder of the first troop of Philadelphia cavalry during war, he raised money to aid forces and donated money and credit to Continental Congress in 1780. He was elected to the Pennsylvania House of Representatives in 1790-95 and the US House of Representatives 1797-99.

General Thomas Mifflin (1744-1800): from a prominent Philadelphia Quaker family, he served as a delegate to first Continental Congress and an officer in the Continental army. As Quartermaster General, he was accused of using army wagons to transport private goods for sale. He was a member of Constitutional Convention and later president of the supreme executive council in 1788-1790 and the first Governor of Pennsylvania in 1790-99, after the redrafting of the constitution in 1790, over which he presided.

James Monroe (1758-1831): served in the Virginia State Assembly, representing his state in Congress from 1783. He was elected to the US Senate in 1791 and appointed Minister to France, where he befriended and supported Paine. His opposition to the federalist faction resulted in his recall. From 1799 to 1802 he served as Governor of Virginia and took part in the Louisiana Purchase in 1803. In 1816 he was elected fifth President of the United States.

Gouverneur Morris (1752-1816): (not related to Robert Morris) a lawyer and a brilliant scholar, he was influential in drafting the New York state constitution in 1776. As a member of Congress from 1777, he served as Robert Morris's Assistant Superintendent of Finance from 1781 and later became his business partner. In 1785, he supported the bank in *An Address to the Assembly of Pennsylvania on the Abolition of the Bank of North America*. After participating in the Constitutional Convention in 1788, he pursued private business interests in Europe. He negotiated the commercial treaty between England and America in 1790 and from 1792-1794 served as Minister to France. He refused Paine the protection of the United States on the grounds that he had forfeited his citizenship by accepting honorary citizenship of the French republic. In 1798 Morris returned to the United States. He was elected to the Senate in 1800.

Robert Morris (1734-1806): emigrated from England to Philadelphia in 1747. Orphaned at the age of fifteen years, he was apprenticed to Charles Willing, a merchant and financier. His successful business partnership with Thomas Willing lasted from 1754-1793. He was a delegate to the Second Continental Congress and signatory of the Declaration of Independence. His is known as the 'Financier of the American Revolution' having been commissioned to procure supplies, negotiate bills of exchange, borrow money and manage the fiscal concerns of Congress. This he did with 'untiring zeal' and to great effect, often on his own private credit, averting the need for the army to seize goods. Morris personally subscribed £10,000 to the fund that he would later develop into the Bank of North America. Morris was appointed the first Superintendent of Finance, in 1781. His fortune was lost in a speculative shipping venture, and he ended his life bankrupt.

Jacques Necker (1732-1804): a native of Geneva, made his fortune in speculating in the French East India Company of which he became a director in 1765, in addition to founding a private bank. In 1777 he was appointed Director General of Finances to the court of Louis XVI. He succeeded in financing aid to the American cause without raising taxes but increased the public debt. His policy of reducing public expenditure by abolishing unnecessary places and reforming the inequitable and inefficient tax system failed to overcome the vested political interests, resulting in his dismissal in 1781. In 1788, he was recalled to court and successfully persuaded the King to call the Estates General and accept the legitimacy of the third estate.

Lord Frederick North (1732-92): Prime Minister from 1770 until his resignation in 1782, having failed to defeat the colonists. He later entered into a coalition with Charles Fox in 1783 and served in the Portland ministry.

Henry Pelham (1695-1754): his great political success is attributed to the patronage of Walpole and the political skill of his brother, Thomas Pelham-Hollis, the Duke of Newcastle. As Walpole's protege, he was appointed Secretary of War in 1724 and Paymaster of the Forces in 1730. In 1743 he was appointed Chancellor of the Exchequer, acting effectively as Prime Minister until his death. His ministry was noted for its stability, supported by both King and Commons. He successfully balanced the budget, restructured the national debt, reduced the land tax and introduced measures to stimulate trade.

William Pitt, the Elder, Lord Chatham (1708-1778): Member of Parliament for Old Sarum, a rotten borough, from 1735-47. He was Paymaster General in 1746-54, under the patronage of the Pelhams. His popularity in England was founded on his success as Prime Minister 1757-61 in winning the Seven Years War. Pitt resigned in 1761 in protest at the American policy and was elevated to the peerage in 1766. He continued to champion American liberties until his death.

William Pitt, the Younger (1759-1806): entered parliament in 1781 and was appointed Prime Minister at the age of 24, and dominated British politics until 1806. Initially a favourite amongst the radical opposition and campaign for parliamentary reform, Pitt's crackdown on radicalism in 1792 effectively wiped out the movement.

Charles Lennox, Duke of Richmond (1735-1806): served in the Seven Years War and then entered political life as a deputy to the Marquis of Rockingham 1770-1780. Richmond's radical proposals for constitutional reform offended many of his contemporaries. As an enthusiast for parliamentary reform, he joined the radical Shelburne faction but in 1782 refused to follow Charles Fox out of office, thus breaking with the radical Whigs.

Dr. Benjamin Rush (1745-1813): a physician and chemist. Born in Pennsylvania, he studied at Edinburgh and Paris. Rush was an influential mentor to Paine, encouraging him to publish *Common Sense*. He was a delegate to Continental Congress and a signatory of the Declaration of Independence. He served as Surgeon General to the Continental Army 1777-8. In 1799 he was appointed treasurer of the US Mint.

Sir John Sinclair of Ulbster (1754-1835): Member of Parliament from 1780-1811 and scientific agriculturalist. His *History of the Public Revenue of the British Empire* was published in 1785, although he is more famous for his *Statistical Account of Scotland* (1791-1799). He was responsible for the Enclosure Act of 1796, regarded as one of the causes of the highland clearances. He founded the Department of Agriculture of which he was president in 1793-8 and 1803-6.

John Smiley (1741-1812): born in Ireland and settled in western Pennsylvania in 1760. He served in the revolutionary war and was a member of the Pennsylvania Assembly 1784-86. He was a delegate to the Pennsylvania Constitutional Convention 1790, which created the Pennsylvania Senate of which he was a member 1790-93. He later represented his state in the US Congress 1793-95 and 1799-1812.

Thomas Spence (1750-1814): English teacher and radical bookseller. A member of the London Corresponding Society, he published a weekly journal *Pigs' Meat* from 1793-6, incorporating many radical pamphlets. His *Rights of Infants* in 1797 was critical of Paine's moderation in *Agrarian Justice*.

Theodore Baron von Neuhoff (1686-1756): German adventurer and adviser to the Emperor Charles VI. In 1736, supported by the Turks and Tunisia, he led the Corsican uprising against the Genoese. He was elected King and raised money selling knighthoods. Later he settled in London, where he was imprisoned for debt, and set free by subscription raised by Horace Walpole.

Charles Gravier, Comte de Vergennes (1717-87): following a distinguished diplomatic career, he was appointed foreign minister in 1774 under the ministry of Maurepas. Vergennes hoped to use the American rebellion to humble England and thereby restore the balance of power in Europe after France's losses in the Seven Years War, but without openly breaching treaty obligations. Paine thought he 'was not the friend of America' as 'with respect to principles Count Vergennes was a despot'.[1] He later negotiated the Peace of Paris in 1783, ending the War of American Independence, after which he pursued a policy of Anglo-French cooperation resulting in a commercial treaty with Pitt in 1786.

Richard Watson (1737-1816): Professor of Chemistry and Divinity and Bishop of Llandaff from 1782. He supported religious tolerance and parliamentary reform and criticised British policy in colonial America and slavery, but opposed the French revolution and responded to Paine's Deist critique of Christianity in 1796.

Robert Whitehill (1738-1813): born in Lancaster county, Pennsylvania. He became a spokesman for the western frontier communities and an outspoken advocate for independence. He was elected to the Pennsylvania convention that approved the Declaration of Independence and voted for the constitution of 1776. He was a member of the Assembly in 1776-78, 1784-87 and 1797-1801. He served on the Pennsylvania Council of Safety 1777 and Supreme Executive Council 1779-81. At the Pennsylvania Convention in 1787 to ratify the US constitution, he tried to delay voting on the grounds that the frontier regions needed more time to understand the new framework of government. He was a delegate to the Pennsylvania Constitutional Convention in 1790 which created the state senate in which he sat 1801-1805. Later a representative to the US Congress 1805-13.

Thomas Willing (1731-1821): born in Philadelphia, to a prominent merchant family. His successful business partnership with Robert Morris lasted from 1754-1793. Politically conservative, Willing voted against independence in the Pennsylvania assembly. He was President of Bank of North America, and later President of First Bank of the United States in 1791-1797. He was a delegate to the Continental Congress and Mayor of Philadelphia.

James Wilson (1742-98): a jurist and legal writer, emigrated to Philadelphia from Scotland in 1765. His *Considerations on the Nature and Extent of the Legislative Authority of the British Parliament* was influential in 1774. He was elected to the Pennsylvania legislature and as a member of Continental Congress signed of the Declaration of Independence. Wilson was unpopular in Philadelphia for his conservative views and his legal defence of loyalists. In 1779 his house was attacked by a mob. He was appointed a director of the Bank of North America and acted as Morris's personal lawyer. He was elected to Congress in 1782 and 1785. A member of the Constitutional Convention in 1787, he is though to have shared in drafting the constitution. He was appointed to the U. S. Supreme Court in 1789, but having fallen prey to a land speculation scheme, he fled Pennsylvania in 1797 to escape charges for non-payment of debt.

---

[1] 'Rights of Man' (1791), *Writings*, II, 335-336.

Bibliography

Abbreviations

WMQ   *William and Mary Quarterly*
PMHB   *The Pennsylvania Magazine of History and Biography*
PS   *Political Studies*
PSQ   *Political Science Quarterly*
PAPS   *Proceedings of the American Philosophical Society*

A.   Other Collections of Paine's Writings

Conway, Moncure D., ed., *The Writings of Thomas Paine*, 4 vols (New York: Burt Franklin, 1908; repr. 1969) [*Writings*]
Clark, Harry H., ed., *Six New Letters of Thomas Paine, Being Pieces on the five per cent duty addressed to the Citizens of Rhode Island*, (Madison: University of Wisconsin Press, 1939)
Foner, Eric, ed., *Thomas Paine: Collected Writings*, (New York: The Library of America, 1995)
Foner, P. S., ed., *The Complete Writings of Thomas Paine*, 2 vols (New York: Citadel, 1945; repr. 1974)
Foot, M. & Kramnick, I., eds, *Thomas Paine Reader* (London: Penguin, 1987)
Sherwin W. T., ed., *Thomas Paine: The American Crisis*, (London: Sherwin, 1817)

B.   Primary sources

1.   Newspapers

Pennsylvania Gazette and Weekly Advertiser (Philadelphia, Hall & Sellars, 1779-1782)
The Pennsylvania Gazette (Philadelphia, Hall & Sellars, 1782-1815)
The Pennsylvania Packet and Daily Advertiser (Philadelphia, Dunlap & Claypoole, 1771-1790)
Pennsylvania Journal; or, Weekly Advertiser (Philadelphia, Bradford, 1742-1793)
The Providence Gazette and Country Journal (Providence, R. I., 1766-1825)
Freeman's Journal (Philadelphia, Baily, 1781-92)

2.   Documents and Official Papers

Bush, George, *Public Papers of the Presidents of the United States, 1989-91*, 8 vols (Washington DC: Government Printing Office, 1990-2)
Continental Congress, *Journals of the Continental Congress, 1774-1789* ed. by Worthington Chauncey Ford, 34 vols (Washington DC: Government Printing Office, 1904-37)

Documents on the American Revolution: Translated from Documents in the French Archive, ed. by John Durand (New York: Henry Holt, 1889)
Reagan, Ronald, *Public Papers of the Presidents of the United States, 1982-88*, 14 vols (Washington DC: Government Printing Office, 1982-91)
Sources & Documents Illustrating the American Revolution 1764-1788 and the Formation of the Federal Constitution, ed. by S. E. Morison, 2nd edn (New York: Oxford University Press, 1965; repr. 1972)
Treaties and Other International Acts of the United States of America, ed. by Hunter Miller, 2 vols (Washington DC: Government Printing Office, 1931)
Twigger, Robert, *Inflation: the Value of the Pound 1750-1998* (House of Commons Research Paper 99/20, 23 February 1999)

3.   Collected Pamphlets

Claeys, Gregory, ed., *Radicalism and Reform: Responses to Burke 1790-1792*, Political Writings of the 1790's, 2 vols (London: Pickering and Chatto, 1995)
Early American Imprints 1639-1800, ed. by C. K. Shipton (Worcester, Mass: American Antiquarian Society, Readex Microprint)

4.   Books and Pamphlets

Adams, John, *The Adams Papers* ed. by L. H. Butterfield, Series I & II (Cambridge, Mass.: Belknap, 1961)
Adams, John Quincy, *An Answer to Pain's Rights of Man* (London, J. Stockdale, 1793)
Chalmers, George, *An Estimate of the Comparative Strength of Britain during the present and four preceding reigns; and of the losses of her trade from every war since the revolution*, (London, C. Dilly and J. Bowen, 1782)
Condorcet: Selected Writings, ed. by K. Baker (Indianapolis: Bobbs-Merrill, 1976)
Dalrymple, Sir John, *The Address of the People of Great-Britain to the Inhabitants of America* (London: T. Cadell, 1775)
Dragonetti, Marchese Giacinto, *Treatise on Virtues and Rewards* (London: 1769)
Eden, William, *Some Remarks on the Apparent Circumstances of the War, in the fourth week of October 1795*, 2nd edn (London: J. Walter, 1795)
Harrington, James, *The Commonwealth of Oceana: and a System of Politics*, ed. by J. G. A. Pocock (Cambridge: Cambridge University Press, 1992)
Hobbes, Thomas, *Leviathan*, ed. by Tuck, Richard, (Cambridge: Cambridge University Press, 1991)
Junius: including letters by the same writer under other signatures, ed. by John Wade, 2 vols (London: Henry G. Bohn, 1850)
Leland, Thomas, *The History of Ireland from the Invasion of Henry II*, 3 vols (London: Nourse, Langman, Robinson, & Johnson, 1773)
Locke, John, *Two Treatises of Government*, ed. by Peter Laslett, Cambridge Texts in the History of Political Thought (Cambridge: Cambridge University Press, 1960; repr. 1991)
Machiavelli, Niccolo, *The Prince and other Writings*, ed. by Bruce Penman (London: Dent, 1991)
Milton, John, *Paradise Lost* (London: Penguin, 1996)
Montesquieu, Baron de, *The Spirit of the Laws*, trans. by T. Nugent (New York: Hafner Press, 1949)

Necker, Jacques, *A Treatise on the Administration of the Finances of France*, trans. by Thomas Mortimer (London: J. Walter, 1785; repr. from the French in 1784)

Playfair, William, *The Commercial and Political Atlas; representing by means of stained copperplate charts, the exports, imports, and general trade of England* (London: Playfair, 1786)

Polybius, *The Rise of the Roman Empire*, ed. and trans. by I. S. Kilvert & F. W. Walbank (London: Penguin, 1979; repr. 1987)

Rousseau, Jean Jacques, *A Discourse on the Origins and Foundations of Inequality among Men*, trans. by M. Cranston (Harmondsworth: Penguin, 1984; repr. 1987)

Rousseau, Jean Jacques, *Political Writings*, ed. & trans. by F. Watkins (Wisconsin: The University of Wisconsin Press, 1986)

Sinclair, John, *The History of the Public Revenue of the British Empire*, 3rd edn, 3 vols (London: T. Cadell and W. Davies, 1803; repr. New York: A. M. Kelley, 1966)

Spence, Thomas, *The Rights of Infants; in a dialogue between the Aristocracy and a Mother of children: to which are added, Strictures on Paine's Agrarian Justice*, (London: Spence, 1797)

Sterne, Laurence, *A Sentimental Journey through France and Italy by Mr. Yorick* (London: Miller and White, 1774)

Watson, R. *An Apology for the Bible in a Series of Letters Addressed to Thomas Paine*, (London: Society for Promoting Christian Knowledge, 1796)

Wilson, James 'Considerations on the Bank of North-America', *Supplement to the Pennsylvania Gazette*, 7 September 1785, pp. 1-6.

Wollstonecraft, Mary, *A Vindication of the Rights of Women*, ed. by Miriam Brody (London: Penguin, 1975; repr. 1992)

C. Secondary Sources on Paine

1. Bibliography and Reference

Charles Evans' American Bibliography 1639-1820, A Chronological Dictionary of all Books, Pamphlets and Periodical publications printed in the United States of America, 14 vols (Chicago: Hollister, 1909)

Gimbel, Richard, *Thomas Paine Fights for Freedom in Three Worlds: the New, the Old and the Next* (Yale University Library, 1959) (Exhibition catalogue)

Gimbel, Richard, *Thomas Paine: A Bibliographical Checklist of 'Common Sense' with an Account of its Publication* (New Haven: Yale University Press, 1956)

Oxford English Dictionary 2nd edn, (Oxford: Clarendon, 1989)

Dupuy, Trevor N. & Hammerman, Gay M., *People and Events of the American Revolution* (New York: Bowker, 1974)

Marshall, James V., *The United States Manual of Biography and History*. (Philadelphia: James B. Smith, 1856)

Newman, Gerald, ed., *Britain in the Hanoverian Age 1714-1837: An Encyclopaedia* (New York: Garland, 1997)

2. Books

Aldridge, Alfred Owen, *Man of Reason: The Life of Thomas Paine* (London: Cresset, 1960)

Aldridge, Alfred Owen, *Thomas Paine's American Ideology* (London: Associated University Presses, 1984)

Ayer, A. J., *Thomas Paine* (London: Faber & Faber, 1988)

Cheetham, James, *Life of Thomas Paine*, (London: Maxwell Bellard 1817)

Claeys, Gregory, *Thomas Paine: Social and Political Thought* (London: Unwin Hyman, 1989)

Conway, Moncure D., *The Life of Thomas Paine: with a History of his Literary, Political and Religious career in America, France and England*, ed. by Hypathia Bradlaugh Bonner, (London: Watts, 1892; repr. 1909)

Edwards, S., *Rebel! A Biography of Thomas Paine* (London: New English Library, 1974)

Foner, Eric, *Tom Paine and Revolutionary America* (Oxford: Oxford University Press, 1976)

Fructman, Jack, Jr., *Thomas Paine: Apostle of Freedom* (New York: Four Walls Eight Windows, 1994)

Hawke, D., *Paine* (London: W. W. Norton, 1974: repr. 1993)

Keane, John, *Tom Paine: A Political Life* (London: Bloomsbury, 1995)

Philp, Mark, *Paine* (Oxford: Oxford University Press, 1989)

Powell, David, *The Greatest Exile* (London: Hutchinson, 1989)

Scoble, Jr. Thomas D., *Thomas Paine's Citizenship Record* (New Rochelle: Thomas Paine National Historical Association, 1946).

Williamson, A. *Thomas Paine, His Life, Work and Times* (London: Allen & Unwin, 1973)

Wilson, D. A., *The Transatlantic Connection: Paine and Cobbett* (Montreal: McGill-Queen's University Press, 1988)

3.   Articles

Aldridge, Alfred Owen, 'Why Did Thomas Paine Write on the Bank?', *PAPS,* 93: 4 (1949), 310-315

Claeys, Gregory, 'Paine's Agrarian Justice and the Secularisation of Natural Jurisprudence', *Society for the Study of Labour History Bulletin,* 52: 3 (1987), 21-31

Clark, Harry H., 'Toward a Reinterpretation of Thomas Paine', *American Literature,* 5 (1933), 133-45

Dorfman, J., 'The Economic Philosophy of Thomas Paine,' *PSQ,* 53 (1938), 372-86

Dyck, Ian, 'Local Attachments, National Identities and World Citizenship in the Thought of Thomas Paine', *History Workshop Journal,* 35 (1993), 117-135

Harris, Ian, 'Paine and Burke: God, Nature and Politics' in *Public and Private Doctrine: Essays in British History presented to Maurice Cowling*, ed. by M. Bentley (Cambridge: Cambridge University Press, 1993), pp. 34-62

Lause, Mark A., 'The "Unwashed Infidelity": Thomas Paine and Early New York City', *Labour History* 27: 3 (1986), 385-409

Merriam, C. E., 'Thomas Paine's Political Theories', *PSQ* 14:3 (1899), 389-403

Penniman, H., 'Thomas Paine: Democrat,' *American Political Science Review,* 37 (1943), 244-62

Philp, Mark, 'English Republicanism in the 1790's,' *The Journal of Political Philosophy,* 6:3 (1998), 235-262

Robbins, Caroline, 'The Life Long Education of Thomas Paine 1737-1809', *PAPS*, 127:3 (1983), 135-140
Rumsey, Christopher, 'The Wife of a Revolutionary', *Thomas Paine Society Bulletin*, 2:4, (1999), 14-21
Seaman, J. W. 'Thomas Paine: Ransom, Civil Peace and the Natural Right to Welfare,' *Political Theory*, 16: 1 (1988), 120-142

4.   Press and Electronic Articles

Benn, Tony, 'Heroes & Villains: Thomas Paine', *Independent Magazine*, 18 August 1990, p. 46.
Burgess, Anthony, 'A Man More of Eloquence than Erudition', *The Observer*, 30 May 1993, p. 62.
Foot, Michael, 'Eternal Defender of Revolution', *The Observer*, 17 March 1991, p. 49-50
Keane, John, 'Tom Paine and 'The People': The Dangers of Popular Sovereignty,' *Times Literary Supplement*, 31 March 1995, pp. 13-14.
Spiegelman, Martha, 'Can DNA Analysis Reveal Whether Skull is Thomas Paine's' at http://www.thomas-paine.com/tpnha/track.html (1999).
Feldmeth, Greg D., 'U.S. History Resources' at http:/home.earthlink.net/~gfeldmeth/ USHistory.html (31 March 1998)

5.   Unpublished Dissertation

Ford, Karen M., 'The Political Theory of Thomas Paine (1737-1809): Is There a Conflict between Liberty and Democracy?' (unpublished doctoral thesis, University of Manchester, 1995).

D.   Other Secondary Sources

1.   Books

Abernethy, Thomas Perkins, *Western Lands and the American Revolution* (New York: Russell & Russell, 1959)
Appleby, J. *Capitalism and a New Social Order: The Republican Vision of the 1790's* (New York: New York University Press, 1984)
Atiyah, P. S., *The Rise and Fall of Freedom of Contract,* (Oxford: Clarendon Press, 1979)
Bailyn, B., *The Ideological Origins of the American Revolution*, 2nd edn. (Cambridge, Mass: Belknap; 1967; repr. 1992)
Banning, L., *The Jeffersonian Persuasion: Evolution of a Party Ideology* (Ithaca, New York: Cornell University Press, 1978);
Beresiner, Yasha, *A Collectors Guide to Paper Money* (New York: Stein & Day, 1977)
Black, Jeremy, *British Foreign Policy in an Age of Revolutions* 1783-1793 (Cambridge: Cambridge University Press, 1994)
Brace, Laura, *The Idea of Property in Seventeenth Century England: Tithes and the Individual* (Manchester: Manchester University Press, 1998)
Brugger, Bill, *Republican Theory in Political Thought: Virtuous or Virtual* (London: Macmillan, 1999)

Bibliography

Buck, P. W., *The Politics of Mercantilism* (New York: Octagon Books, 1974)

Chase, Malcolm, *The People's Farm: English Radical Agrarianism 1775-1840* (Oxford: Clarendon, 1988)

Coleman, D. C., ed., *Revisions in Mercantilism*, ed. by (London: Methuen, 1969)

Connolly, S. J., *The Oxford Companion to Irish History*, (Oxford: Oxford University Press, 1998)

Daniels, B. L, *Pennsylvania: Birth Place of Banking in America* (Philadelphia: Pennsylvania Bankers Association, 1976)

Davies, Glyn, *A History of Money from Ancient Times to the Present Day* (Cardiff: University of Wales Press, 1996)

Douglass, Elisha P., *Rebels and Democrats: The Struggle for Equal Political Rights and Majority Rule during the American Revolution* (Chicago: Elephant Paperbacks, 1955; repr. 1989)

Dunaway, W. F., *A History of Pennsylvania* (New York: Prentice-Hall, 1946)

Ernst, Joseph A., *Money and Politics in America 1755-1775* (Chapel Hill: University of North Carolina Press, 1973)

Fox-Genovese, E., *The Origins of Physiocracy* (Ithaca: Cornell University Press, 1976)

Hibbert, Christopher, *George III: A Personal History* (London: Viking, 1998)

Hilton, James Coy, *Silas Deane: Patriot or Traitor?* (Lansing: Michigan State University Press, 1975)

Ingram, Attracta, *A Political Theory of Rights* (Oxford: Clarendon Press, 1994)

Jossett, C. R., *Money in Great Britain and Ireland*, (Newton Abbott, Devon: David & Charles, 1971)

Keane, John, *Civil Society and the State* (London: Verso, 1988)

Keane, John, *Democracy and Civil Society* (London: Verso, 1988)

Kramnick, I., *Republicanism & Bourgeois Radicalism: Political Ideology in Late Eighteenth Century England and America* (London: Cornell University Press, 1990)

Magnusson, Lars, ed. *Mercantilism*, 4 vols (London: Routledge, 1995)

McCusker, John J., *Money and Exchange in Europe and America 1600-1775: A Handbook* (Chapel Hill: University of North Carolina Press, 1978)

McDonald, F., *Novos Ordo Seclorum: The Intellectual Origins of the Constitution* (Lawrence: University Press of Kansas, 1985)

McDonald, F., *The Presidency of Thomas Jefferson* (Lawrence: University Press of Kansas, 1976)

Newman, Eric P., *The Early Paper Money of America* (Racine: Whitman, 1967)

Nozick, Robert, *Anarchy State and Utopia* (Oxford: Blackwell, 1974; repr. 1986)

Parrington, V. L., *Main Currents of American Thought*, 3 vols (New York: Harcourt Brace, 1927)

Pearce, M., & Stewart, G., *British Political History 1867-1990: Democracy and Decline* (London: Routledge, 1992)

Pettit, Philip, *Republicanism: A Theory of Freedom and Government* (Oxford, Clarendon, 1997).

Pocock, J. G. A., *The Machiavellian Moment: Florentine Political Thought and the Atlantic Republican Tradition* (Princeton: Princeton University Press, 1975)

Rawls, John, *A Theory of Justice* (Oxford: Oxford University Press, 1972; repr. 1986)

Rawls, John, *Political Liberalism* (New York: Columbia University Press, 1996)

Redford, Arthur, *The Economic History of England 1760-1860* (London: Longmans, 1931; repr. 1948)

Robbins, Caroline, *The Eighteenth Century Commonwealthman: Studies in the Transmission, Development and Circumstance of English Liberal Thought* (Cambridge. Mass: Harvard University Press, 1959)

Rossiter, Clinton, *The Seedtime of the Republic: the Origin of the American Tradition of Political Liberty* (New York: Harcourt, Brace, 1953)

Scharf, J. T. & Westcott, T., *History of Philadelphia 1609-1884*, 3 vols (Philadelphia: L. H. Everts, 1884)

Seaby, Peter, *Coins and Tokens of Ireland*, (London: Seaby, 1970)

Secor, Robert, *Pennsylvania 1776* (Philadelphia: Pennsylvania State University, 1975)

Selsam, J. P., *The Pennsylvania Constitution of 1776: A Study in Revolutionary Democracy* (New York: Da Capo Press, 1936; repr. 1971)

Skinner, Quentin, *Liberty before Liberalism* (Cambridge, Cambridge University Press, 1998)

Steiner, Hillel, *An Essay on Rights*, (Oxford: Blackwell, 1994)

Teichgraeber, R. T., *'Free Trade' and Moral Philosophy: Rethinking the Sources of Adam Smith's Wealth of Nations* (Durham: Duke University Press, 1986)

Thompson, E. P., *Whigs and Hunters: The Origin of the Black Act* (New York: Pantheon, 1975).

Tinkcom, H. M., *Republicans and Federalists in Pennsylvania 1790-1801: A Study in National Stimulus and Local Response* (Harrisburg: Pennsylvania Historical and Museum Commission, 1950)

Wallace, David D., *The Life of Henry Laurens* (New York: Russell & Russell, 1915)

Wolock, I., *The New Regime: Transformations of the French Civic Order 1789-1820's* (London: Norton, 1994)

Wood, G. S., *The Creation of the American Republic 1776-1787* (Chapel Hill: University of North Carolina Press, 1969)

Wright, D. G., *Revolution and Terror in France 1789-1795* (Harlow: London, 1974; repr. 1989)

2. Articles

'Electronic money: so much for the cashless society', *Economist*, 26 November 1994, pp. 25-30

Appleby, Joyce, 'Republicanism in Old and New Contexts', *WMQ,*, 3rd Series, 43 (1986), 20-34

Claeys, Gregory, 'Virtuous Commerce and Free Theology: Political Economy and the Dissenting Academies 1750-1800', *History of Political Thought*, 20:1 (1999), 141-172

Doyle, K., 'Kant, Liberal Legacies, and Foreign Affairs', *Philosophy and Public Affairs*, 12 (1983), 206-32

Hoppit, J. 'Financial Crises in Eighteenth Century England', *Economic History Review*, 2nd series, 39 (1986), 39-58.

Levy, Jack S, 'Domestic Politics and War', in *The Origin and Prevention of Major Wars*, ed. by R. Rothberg & T. Rabb (Cambridge: Cambridge University Press, 1989), pp. 79-100

Mathias, Peter & O'Brien, Patrick, 'Taxation in Britain and France 1715-1810: A Comparison of the Social and Economic Incidence of Taxes Collected for the Central Governments', *Journal of European Economic History*, 5: 3 (1976), 601-650

McCoy, D. R., 'Republicanism and American Foreign Policy: James Madison and the Political Economy of Commercial Discrimination 1789-94,' *WMQ,* 3rd Series, 31 (1974), 633-646

Mulgan, R., 'Liberty in Ancient Greece,' in *Conceptions of Liberty in Political Philosophy,* ed. by Z. A. Pelczynski, & J. Gray (London: Althone, 1984), pp. 7-23

Murrin, J. M., 'Republican Ideology and the Triumph of the Constitution 1789-93,' *WMQ,* 3rd Series, 31 (1974), 167-188

Plummer, W. C., 'Consumer Credit in Colonial Philadelphia', *PMHB,* 66:2 (1942), 385-409

Pocock, J. G. A., 'Virtue and Commerce in the Eighteenth Century.' *Journal of Interdisciplinary History,* 3:1 (1972) 119-34

Purdy, D., 'Citizenship, Basic Income and the State' *New Left Review,* 208 (1994), 30-48

Sempere, J. 'An Efficiency Justification of Basic Income', *Trimestre Economico,* 66:262 (1999), 175-188

Skinner, Quentin, 'The Paradoxes of Political Liberty' in *Liberty,* ed. by D. Miller, Oxford Readings in Politics and Government (Oxford: Oxford University Press, 1991), pp. 183-205

Steiner, Hillel, 'Liberty and Equality', *PS,* 29 (1981), 555-569

Thompson, E. P., 'The Moral Economy of the English Crowd in the Eighteenth Century', *Past and Present,* 50 (1971), 76-136

Van Der Veen, R. J., 'Real Freedom Versus Reciprocity: Competing Views on the Justice of Unconditional Basic Income', *PS,* 46:1 (1998), 140-163

Vanparijs, P., 'Why Surfers Should Be Fed: The Liberal Case for an Unconditional Basic Income', *Philosophy & Public Affairs,* 20:2 (1991), 101-131

Vanparijs, P., 'Reciprocity and the Justification of an Unconditional Basic Income: Reply to Stuart White' *PS,* 45:2 (1997), 327-330

White, Stuart, 'Liberal Equality, Exploitation, and the Case for an Unconditional Basic Income', *PS,* 45:2 (1997), 312-326

Williams, A., 'Resource Egalitarianism and the Limits to Basic Income', *Economics and Philosophy,* 15:1 (1999), 85-107

Wilson, Janet, 'The Bank of North America and Pennsylvania Politics 1781-87,' *PMHB,* 46:1 (1942), 3-28

Index

Index

MELLEN CRITICAL EDITIONS AND TRANSLATIONS